ROOM SERVICE

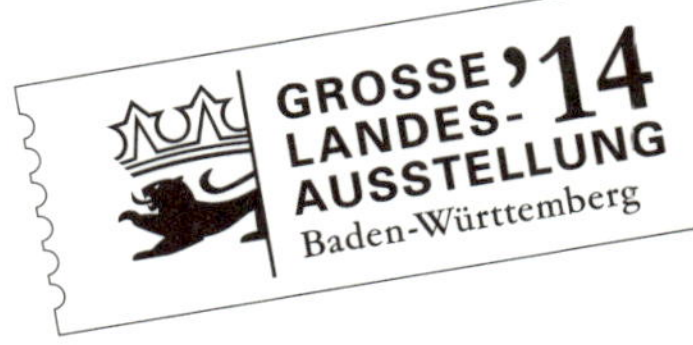

VERLAG DER BUCHHANDLUNG WALTHER KÖNIG

Titelbild / Cover picture: Andreas Gursky, TAIPEI, 1999

VOM HOTEL IN DER KUNST / ON THE HOTEL IN THE ARTS

UND KÜNSTLERN IM HOTEL / AND ARTISTS IN THE HOTEL

STAATLICHE KUNSTHALLE
BADEN-BADEN

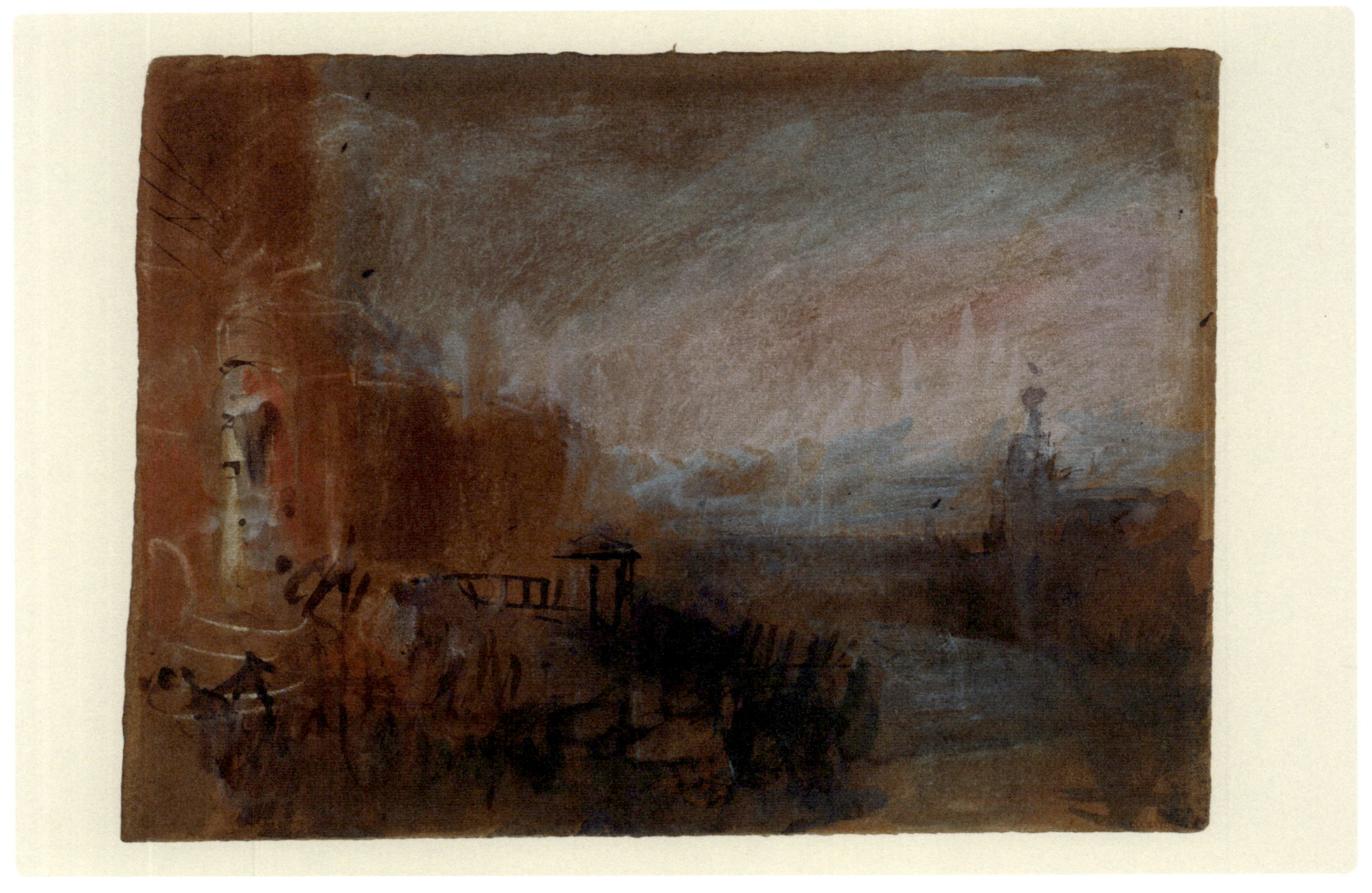

JOSEPH MALLORD WILLIAM TURNER

DIE DOGANA VON DEN TREPPENSTUFEN DES HOTELS EUROPA AUS

THE DOGANA FROM THE STEPS OF THE HOTEL EUROPA

1833, Kreide, Gouache und Wasserfarben auf Papier, 23 × 31 cm, Courtesy: Tate, London: Von der Nation als Teil des Turner Nachlasses akzeptiert 1856, © Tate, London, 2014 / 1833, chalk, gouache and watercolor on paper, 23 × 31 cm, courtesy: Tate, London, accepted by the nation as part of the Turner Bequest 1856, © Tate, London, 2014

VORWORT

JOHAN HOLTEN

Die Geschichte Baden-Badens ist unmittelbar mit der Geschichte seiner zahlreichen Gäste verbunden. Seit der Eröffnung des Hotels Badischer Hof im Jahre 1805 prägen die Grand Hotels entlang des Flusses Oos das Bild und Leben der Stadt. Die Große Landesausstellung der Staatlichen Kunsthalle Baden-Baden ROOM SERVICE – VOM HOTEL IN DER KUNST UND KÜNSTLERN IM HOTEL möchte nun im Jahre 2014 anhand dieses besonderen Erbes nachzeichnen, wie Künstler das Hotel als soziales Gebilde dargestellt, als Atelier genutzt und in eigener Weise in ihre Kunst mit einbezogen haben. Gleichzeitig möchte die Ausstellung selbst ein Kapitel in diese Geschichte einfügen, indem sie ganz neue Werke von beteiligten Künstlerinnen und Künstlern in zahlreichen Hotelzimmern, Foyers und einer Parkgarage präsentiert.

Die vor allem auf die letzten zweihundert Jahre zurückblickende Ausstellung beginnt ganz klassisch in der Kunsthalle: Joseph Mallord William Turner bereiste am Anfang des 19. Jahrhunderts den europäischen Kontinent und stieg oft in den damals modernsten Gasthäusern ab – den Grand Hotels. In der Ausstellung können wir einige der Aus- und Anblicke zeigen, die er dabei malerisch festgehalten hat. Auch die vermutlich erste Fotografie eines Hotels von William Henry Fox Talbot, dem Erfinder des *Zeichnens mit Licht,* kann in der Kunsthalle betrachtet werden. Daneben zeigen wir weitere Künstler und Fotografen des 19. Jahrhunderts, die sich mit der nun ganz neu ausgeprägten Gattung der bereits aus früheren Jahrhunderten bekannten Herbergen beschäftigt haben. An zwei besonderen Beispielen demonstriert die Ausstellung, wie sich seinerzeit auch Künstlerkolonien um und in Hotels eingerichtet haben: In Skagen etwa, einem Fischerdorf im nördlichen Dänemark, gelang es Peder Severin Krøyer, Kollegen und den Hotelbesitzer davon zu überzeugen, dass das dortige Brøndums Hotel ein ganz besonderes Flair bekäme, wenn man es zum Zentrum einer Künstlerkolonie machen würde. Das Experiment gelang. Auch aus Volendam in den Niederlanden, wo der Hotelbesitzer selbst den *Mehrwert* erkannt hatte und deshalb gezielt Künstler anwarb, zeigt die Ausstellung zahlreiche Beispiele dort entstandener Arbeiten, unter anderem von Paul Signac.

Lange galt das Interesse der Kunstschaffenden entweder der künstlerischen Gemeinschaft, der neuartigen und besonderen Architektur der Hotels oder dem immer wiederkehrenden Blick auf das Leben der jeweiligen fremden Stadt aus dem Hotelzimmer heraus. Seltsamerweise interessierten sich gerade die bildenden Künstler eher nicht für die Menschen im Hotelbetrieb selbst. Erst um 1900 wendet sich etwa der Maler Chaïm Soutine dem Personal zu. Seine Porträts von Zimmermädchen oder Hotelpagen zeigen die Kehrseite des Luxusphänomens. Auch Fotografen – allen voran August Sander – widmen sich nun verschiedenen Angestellten. Häufiger noch erscheinen allerdings in den Werken Hoteldirektoren repräsentativ vor dem Eingang ihrer Häuser oder am Schreibtisch beim Telefonieren.

Eine weitere Verschiebung des künstlerischen Interesses folgt ein halbes Jahrhundert später, als auch die

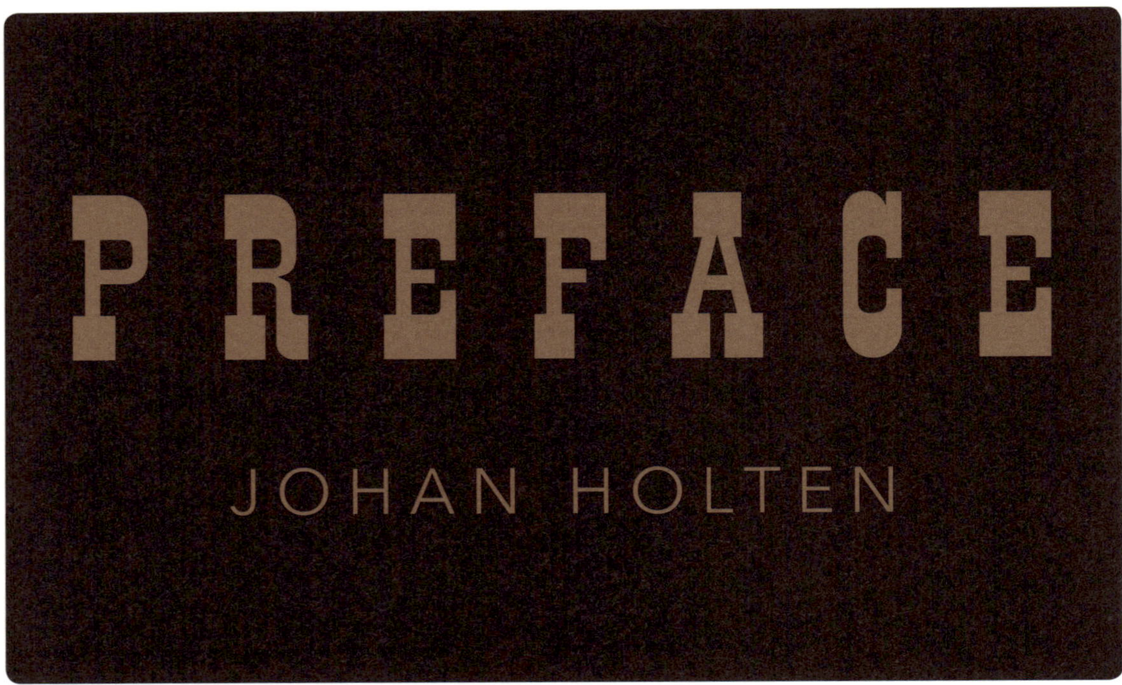

PREFACE

JOHAN HOLTEN

The history of Baden-Baden is intimately linked with the history of its numerous visitors. Since the opening of Hotel Badischer Hof in 1805, the grand hotels along the River Oos have shaped the image and life of the city. In 2014 the exhibition ROOM SERVICE—ON THE HOTEL IN THE ARTS AND ARTISTS IN THE HOTEL at the Staatliche Kunsthalle Baden-Baden draws on this special legacy to trace how artists have portrayed the hotel as a social structure, used the hotel as a studio, or incorporated it into their work in a unique manner. At the same time, the exhibition is intended as an additional chapter in this history; it presents utterly new works by participating artists in hotel rooms, lobbies, and a parking garage.

Looking back primarily over the past two hundred years, the exhibition begins in a classical manner at the Kunsthalle. In the early 18th century Joseph Mallord William Turner traveled the European continent, often alighting at the most modern guesthouses of the era, the grand hotels. In the exhibition we have been able to present a number of views from or of hotels that he captured in his paintings. The Kunsthalle also features what is probably the first photograph ever of a hotel, taken by William Henry Fox Talbot, the inventor of »drawing with light.« In addition, we show other artists and photographers from the 19th century, who took up the now newly defined genre of lodging houses, already a topic familiar from earlier centuries. Through two particular examples the exhibition demonstrates how also artist colonies established themselves in hotels of the period: In Skagen, for example, a fishing village in northern Denmark, Peder Severin Krøyer managed to convince artist colleagues as well as the hotel owner, that the local Brøndums Hotel would take on a very special flair if it were made the center of an artist colony. The exhibition also shows numerous example of works produced in Volendam in the Netherlands, including some by Paul Signac, where a hotel owner himself recognized the potential of such a situation and consciously tried to attract artists.

For a long time the attention of artists focused either on their artistic community, the new and unique architecture of the hotel, or the repeated view from a hotel room of life in a foreign city. Strangely, visual artists in particular were not interested the people working at the hotel. Not until around 1900 did hotel personnel become the subject matter of painter Chaïm Soutine's paintings. His portraits of chambermaids and messenger boys show a darker side of the phenomenon of luxury. Photographers—August Sander as a primary example—were also interested in different kinds of employees. However, a more common motif in their work was the image of the hotel director posing representatively at the entrance to his hotel or on the telephone at his desk.

A half a century later another shift in what interests artists occurs through reflections on decrepit, not so charming versions of the standardized hotel room. The modern »temporary home« outfitted to provide »mediocrity, mediocrity, and once again mediocrity,« as Volker Albus described in his essay, is one theme found in the exhibition, as is the strange charm that artists discover in New York's run-down

heruntergekommene, wenig charmante Ausformung von standardisierten Hotelzimmern reflektiert wird. Das moderne *Heim auf Zeit* mit seiner Ausrichtung auf »Durchschnitt, Durchschnitt und nochmals Durchschnitt«, wie Volker Albus in seinem Aufsatz beschreibt, wird ebenso ein Thema wie der skurrile Charme, den Künstler in dem *abgerockten* Chelsea Hotel in New York City entdecken. Martin Kippenberger wendet sich mit durchaus augenzwinkernder Geste dem Hotelbriefpapier als Grund und Bildbestandteil zu; Sophie Calle hingegen arbeitet einen Monat lang inkognito als Zimmermädchen und beginnt anhand ihrer Beobachtungen teils imaginäre Geschichten über die Bewohner des Hotels zu verfassen. Andere Künstler wie Andreas Gursky wenden sich wiederum den monumentalen Hotelatrien der Jetztzeit zu, die nun nicht mehr entlang der Reiserouten der *Grand Tour* wie zu Zeiten William Turners in Europa, sondern in Asien oder Amerika entstehen. In den 1990er-Jahren erfährt das Hotelzimmer eine neuerliche Umnutzung im künstlerischen Kontext, indem es nun nicht mehr nur als Atelier genutzt wird, wie etwa noch von Henri Matisse oder später Daniel Spoerri. Der 1993 noch blutjunge Kurator Hans Ulrich Obrist verwandelt ein Hotelzimmer in Paris in ein Museum auf Zeit und stellt Arbeiten von mehr als siebzig Künstlern auf den nur wenigen Quadratmetern seines Zimmers aus. Dieses Ereignis wird im historischen Teil der Ausstellung in der Kunsthalle bedacht und in einem eigenständigen Künstlerbuch dokumentiert, das anlässlich des Projektes ROOM SERVICE erscheint.

Gleichzeitig dient Obrists Ausstellungsidee von CHAMBRE 763 aus dem Carlton Palace in Paris als Blaupause für den Parcours durch die Räume der an ROOM SERVICE beteiligten Hotels in Baden-Baden. Die Besucher sind eingeladen, die noblen Herbergen als Kulturlandschaft zu erleben, indem sie Kunstwerke im Steigenberger Europäischer Hof, im Atlantic Parkhotel, im Rathausglöckel, im kleinen aber feinen Belle Epoque oder im legendären Brenners Park-Hotel & Spa entdecken, oder an der Theateraufführung teilzunehmen, die in Kooperation mit dem Theater Baden-Baden im Treppenhaus der historischen Gebäude des Radisson Blu Hotels Badischer Hof zu sehen sein wird.

IM zweiten Teil des Katalogs ist die Dokumentation der zahlreichen eigens für dieses Projekt sowie direkt für den jeweiligen Ort geschaffenen Installationen und weiteren auf dem Parcours zu sehenden Arbeiten und Performances zusammengefasst. Im Gegensatz zu der Ausstellung von Hans Ulrich Obrist in Paris 1993 werden die Künstler nicht in einem Zimmer mit ihren Werken präsentiert, sondern zahlreichen Künstlern wird die Möglichkeit gegeben, sich – auf sechs Hotels verteilt – auszubreiten. Im Europäischen Hof etwa wird den Besuchern eine *Hoteltherapie* der anderen Art geboten, indem sie sich auf die Kunstfigur Sherry der US-amerikanischen Performerin Ann Liv Young einlassen, oder sie folgen zur Geschichte des Hotels den Audiospuren der in Hamburg beheimateten Künstlergruppe LIGNA. Wer ein bisschen mehr Distanz zur Kunst wahren möchte, kann im gleichen Haus die Fotos von Florian Slotawa entdecken, die dokumentieren, wie er in zwölf unterschiedlichen Hotels das Mobiliar während nur einer Nacht verschoben und umgebaut hat, um es bei Tagesanbruch wieder zurück an den angestammten Platz zu stellen. Auch Teile der CHAMBRE-763-Ausstellung von Obrist werden in einem Zimmer dieses Hauses wieder zu erleben sein.

Im Atlantic Parkhotel wird es eine Zimmertür geben, hinter der ein Schauspieler im Bademantel bereitsteht, um im Auftrag des Künstlers Christian Andersson jedem der verblüfften Besucher einen Monolog vorzutragen, wenn dieser sich traut, an die Tür zu klopfen. Im Foyer des Hotels wird die sonst dort ausgestellte hauseigene Kollektion gegen die legendäre Kunstsammlung des Hotels Castell im schweizerischen Zouz ausgetauscht.

Im Rathausglöckel erwartet die Gäste ein besonderes Arrangement: Hier können sie zwei Hotelzimmer als Kunstwerk buchen, um darin zu wohnen. Zur Wahl stehen ein von Gabriela Oberkoffler gestaltetes Zimmer, das von der Geschichte der Hexen im Schwarzwald inspiriert ist, und ein Raum, der mit persönlichen Gegenständen, Vorhängen und sogar Bettwäsche aus dem winzigen Hong Konger Atelier von Lee Kit ausgestattet ist.

Im Hotel Belle Epoque dagegen kann man sich in einem der opulent ausgestatteten Zimmer ins Bett legen, um THE CHELSEA GIRLS von Andy Warhol anzuschauen, und beim Verlassen des Hotels sei dringend die Abkürzung durch die Parkgarage empfohlen. Inmitten der edlen Karossen ist dort eine weitere Arbeit platziert. In der Lobby des Brenners Park-Hotel & Spas dagegen starrt Cindy Sherman aus einem ihrer zahlreichen Frauenporträts die Besucher an. Eine Etage höher kann man zudem ein äußerst ungewöhnliches Zimmerinterieur entdecken – eine Installation von Christian Jankowski – oder sich im Rahmen eines Projekts von Naneci Yurdagül für nur eine Stunde den kompletten Luxus des legendären Hotels buchen, statt wie sonst üblich für einen ganzen Tag.

Die Große Landesausstellung ROOM SERVICE – VOM HOTEL IN DER KUNST UND KÜNSTLERN IM HOTEL greift ganz bewusst ein Thema auf, das fest verankert in den Traditionen des Kurortes Baden-Baden und damit auch in der Geschichte des Landes Baden-Württemberg ist. Sie zeichnet aber nicht nur seine Entwicklung in den letzten zweihundert Jahren nach und befragt das vielschichtige Phänomen aus verschiedensten Blickwinkeln,

Chelsea Hotel. With an ironic wink Martin Kippenberger uses hotel stationary as both a medium and compositional element. In contrast, Sophie Calle works incognito for a month as a chambermaid in a hotel and uses her observations to develop in part imaginary stories about the hotel inhabitants. Other artists such as Andreas Gursky examine the monumental hotel atria of the present, which one no longer finds along the routes of the *Grand Tour* in Europe, as during the time of William Turner, but in Asia and Europe. In the 1990s the hotel room undergoes a new kind of application in an artistic context, where it is no longer simply used as a studio, as in the case of Henri Matisse or later Daniel Spoerri. In 1993 the then fresh-faced curator Hans Ulrich Obrist transformed a hotel room in Paris into a temporary museum by presenting over seventy artists in the few square meters of his room. This event is also reflected upon and included in the exhibition at the Kunsthalle.

At the same time, Obrist's exhibition idea of CHAMBRE 763 in the Carlton Palace in Paris serves as a blueprint for the route that visitors can take through the buildings of the Baden-Baden hotels participating in ROOM SERVICE. Visitors are encouraged to experience these noble lodgings as part of the local cultural landscape by discovering works of art at the Steigenberger Europäischer Hof, the Atlantic Parkhotel, the Rathausglöckel, the small but exquisite Belle Epoque, and the legendary Brenners Park-Hotel & Spa. They can also take part in a theatrical performance that will be presented in cooperation with Theater Baden-Baden on the stairwell of the historical building of the Radisson Blu Hotel Badischer Hof.

THE second half of this catalogue includes the documentation of the numerous installations developed for this project and their given settings as well as the other works and performances on view along the route through the hotels. In contrast to the exhibition of Hans Ulrich Obrist in Paris in 1993, the artists are not all presented with their works in a single room, but many artists have been given the possibility to spread out, across six hotels. For example, at Europäischer Hof visitors are offered a different kind of »hotel therapy« by placing themselves in the hands of »Sherry,« a character played by the U.S. performance artist Ann Liv Young, or they can trace the history of the hotel through the audio clues left behind by the Hamburg artist group LIGNA. Anyone wishing to have a less immediate art experience can look at the photographs of Florian Slotawa, on view in the same hotel, which document how he shifted around and reconfigured the furnishings in twelve different hotel rooms over the course of a night, only then to put everything back at its place at the break of day. Also elements of the CHAMBRE 763 exhibition by Obrist can be experienced again in a room of this hotel.

At the Atlantic Parkhotel there is a door to a hotel room, behind which stands an actor in a bathrobe, who has been commissioned by artist Christian Andersson to perform a monologue to any surprised viewer daring to knock on the door. The hotel's own collection, which is usually presented in the lobby, has been exchanged with the legendary art collection of the Hotel Castell in Zouz, Switzerland.

A special constellation awaits guests at the Rathausglöckel. Here visitors can book two hotel rooms as live-in works of art. One is a room conceived by Gabriela Oberkoffler, which is inspired by the history of witches in the Black Forest, and another room is outfitted with the personal objects, curtains, and even sheets from the tiny Hong Kong studio of Lee Kit.

At the Hotel Belle Epoque one can lie down on the bed in an opulently furnished room to watch THE CHELSEA GIRLS by Andy Warhol, and when leaving the hotel it is definitely worth taking a short-cut through the parking garage. An additional work has been placed among the high-end vehicles. In the lobby of Brenners Park-Hotel & Spa, Cindy Sherman stares at guests from one of her numerous female portraits. One floor above, one also finds an unusual room interior, an installation by Christian Jankowski, or as part of a project by Naneci Yurdagül the full luxury experience of the legendary hotel can be booked for one hour, instead of the customary 24-hours.

ROOM SERVICE—ON THE HOTEL IN THE ARTS AND ARTISTS IN THE HOTEL is consciously dedicated to a theme that is deeply rooted in the tradition of Baden-Baden as a spa resort and thus also in the history of Baden-Württemberg. It not only traces its development over the past two hundred years and offers multiple perspectives on this complex phenomenon, but it carries the theme forward into the present and the recent past with numerous new works and installations. Perhaps it even points to the future to a certain extent. All of us who have worked for over two years on this publication and exhibition hope that you, dear readers and visitors, will join us on this journey.

I would like to thank the authors who contributed to this book and who have managed to describe the many, multi-faceted relationships between the hotel and the arts. Elena Korowin's contribution offers a starting point with a look at the European and American developmental history of the hotel as a cultural and social phenomenon. It is followed by a text by Volker Albus, who

sondern führt das Thema mit den zahlreichen neu entstandenen Werken und Installationen bis in die allerjüngste Vergangenheit und Gegenwart fort. Mithin deutet sie vielleicht sogar ein bisschen in die Zukunft. Wir alle, die an dieser Publikation und Ausstellung seit mehr als zwei Jahren gearbeitet haben, hoffen, dass Sie, liebe Leser und Besucher, sich mit uns auf die Reise begeben.

Mein Dank gilt den Autoren dieses Bandes, die es geschafft haben, die facettenreichen Verbindungen des Hotels mit der Kunst zu beschreiben. Elena Korowins Beitrag bildet den Auftakt mit einer europäisch-amerikanischen Entwicklungsgeschichte des Hotels als kultursoziologisches Phänomen, gefolgt von Volker Albus, der das Hotel im Speziellen wie Allgemeinen auf Fragen des Designs und dessen Auswirkungen auf den gemeinen Gast (mit zwinkernden wie tränenden Augen) untersucht.

Markus Miessen bietet in seinem Text konkrete Beispiele heutiger Hotels, die eine besondere Funktion als *Hideaways* haben, also als luxuriöse Refugien für viele Reisende dringlichen Bedürfnissen zu entsprechen scheinen. Bärbel Küster widmet sich hingegen den Künstlerreisen und ihrer Bedeutung von den Anfängen bis heute und Klaus Honnef vertieft in seinem Text ergänzend dazu das Thema der Fotografie und ihre spezifische Auseinandersetzung mit Hotels. Hendrik Bündge verzweigt den literarischen und den künstlerischen Umgang mit dem Gastgewerbe als beliebtes Sujet in der Moderne und Mette Bøgh Jensen beschreibt, warum die Hotels auch in Künstlerzirkeln dieser Zeit sehr gefragt waren. Dem Aneignen und Erfinden des Hotels in der Konzeptkunst der Nachkriegszeit widmet sich Luisa Heese, gefolgt von Sherill Tippins, die uns die eindrucksvolle und spannend-unterhaltsame Geschichte des Chelsea Hotels in New York City erzählt. Abschließend zeigt das beeindruckende Filmpanorama von Andreas Kilb, dass das Hotel – neben Künstlern und Literaten – besonders auch Drehbuchautoren und Kinoregisseure seit der Erfindung des bewegten Bildes gleichermaßen fasziniert und inspiriert hat.

Ich bedanke mich bei allen beteiligten Künstlern, die unser engagiertes Projekt mit Leihgaben und eigens für die Ausstellung produzierten Werken unterstützt und bereichert haben, sowie bei den zahlreichen Leihgebern aus dem In- und Ausland. Besonderer Dank gebührt dem internen und externen Team der Staatlichen Kunsthalle Baden-Baden für die aufwendige Realisierung der Ausstellung sowie des begleitenden Kataloges. Einen wichtigen Teil zum Gelingen von ROOM SERVICE haben nicht zuletzt die involvierten Hotels beigetragen sowie weitere Partner unseres Hauses in der Stadt Baden-Baden.

Die Staatliche Kunsthalle Baden-Baden bedankt sich für die großzügige finanzielle Unterstützung des Ministeriums für Wissenschaft, Forschung und Kunst Baden-Württemberg, welche das Zustandekommen dieser Großen Landesausstellung ermöglicht hat.

examines (with both a hint of irony and lament) the hotel in terms of general and specific aspects of design and its impact on the average guest.

In his text Markus Miessen offers concrete examples of contemporary hotels that have the special function of »hideaways,« of luxurious refuges that cater to the urgent needs of many travelers. In contrast, Bärbel Küster dedicates her contribution to artists' travels and their significance from the very beginning up through today. Klaus Honnef addresses the topic of photography and the particular relationship between the hotel and this medium. Hendrik Bündge follows the trajectories of literary and visual treatments of the hospitality business as a popular subject in the modern era, and Mette Bøgh Jensen describes why hotels are much in demand in contemporary artistic circles. Luisa Heese writes about the appropriations and inventions of the hotel in the conceptual art of the post-war era. Her text is followed by Sherill Tippins' contribution, which tells the memorable, exciting, and entertaining story of the Chelsea Hotel in New York City. Finally, Andreas Kilb's impressive film panorama demonstrates the extent to which the hotel has fascinated and inspired screenwriters and directors—as well as artists and writers—since the invention of the moving image.

My thanks go to all participating artists, who supported and enriched our ambitious project through loans and works produced specifically for the exhibition. I would also like to thank those who provided the many works on loan from Germany and abroad. Special thanks are owed to the internal and external team of the Staatliche Kunsthalle Baden-Baden for the demanding realization of the exhibition and the accompanying catalogue. Also the participating hotels and additional partners in the city of Baden-Baden have made an important contribution to the success of ROOM SERVICE.

The Staatliche Kunsthalle Baden-Baden wishes to express its thanks to the Ministry of Science, Research, and the Arts of Baden-Württemberg for its generous financial support, which has made this exhibition possible.

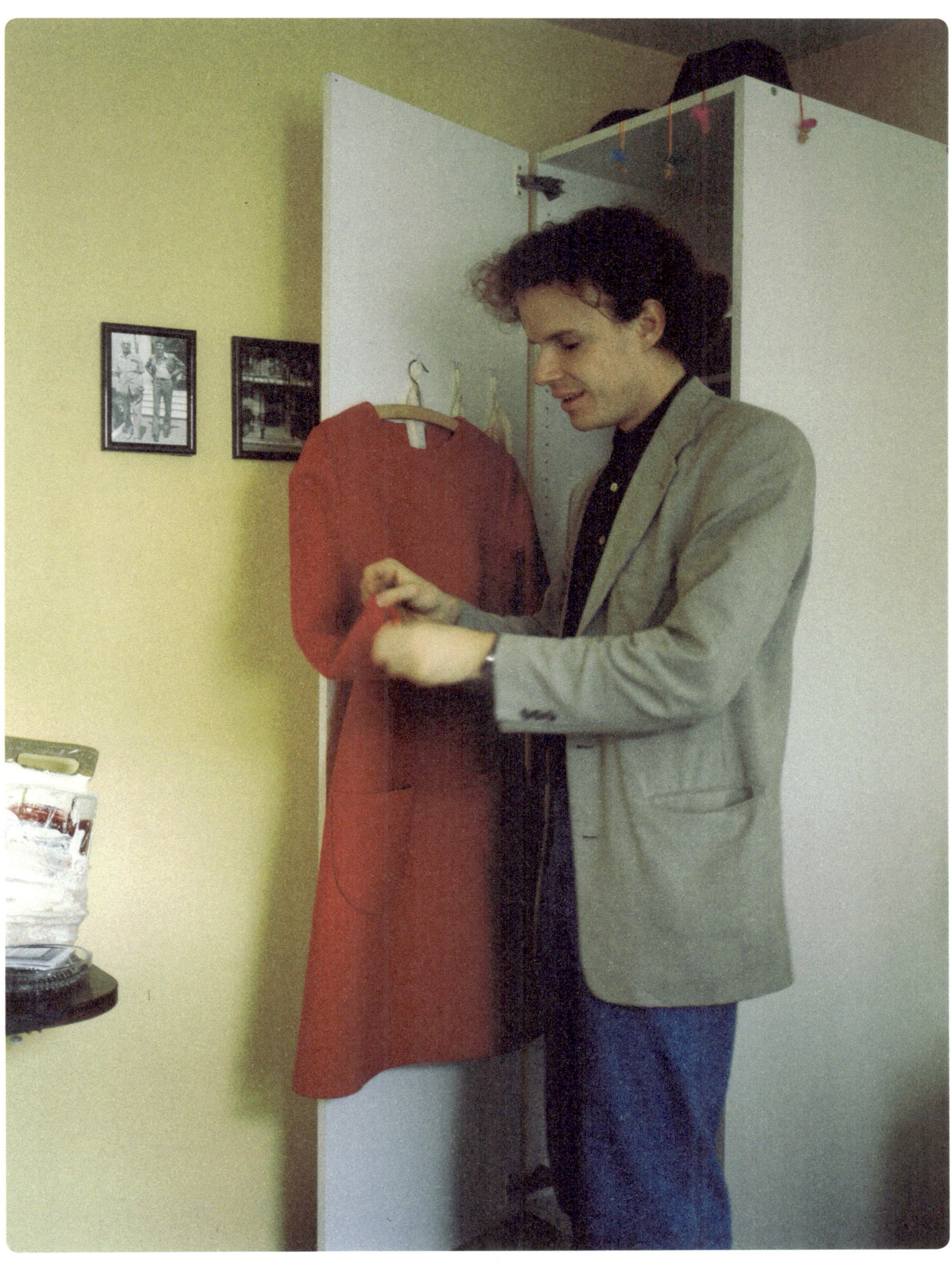

HANS ULRICH OBRIST IN DER VON IHM ORGANISIERTEN AUSSTELLUNG »HOTEL CARLTON PALACE: CHAMBRE 763« MIT EINER ARBEIT VON WIEBKE SIEM, 1993, FOTO: PIERRE LEGUILLON / HANS ULRICH OBRIST WITH A PIECE BY WIEBKE SIEM, INSTALLATION VIEW OF THE EXHIBITION »HOTEL CARLTON PALACE: CHAMBRE 763« WHICH HE ORGANIZED IN 1993, PHOTO: PIERRE LEGUILLON

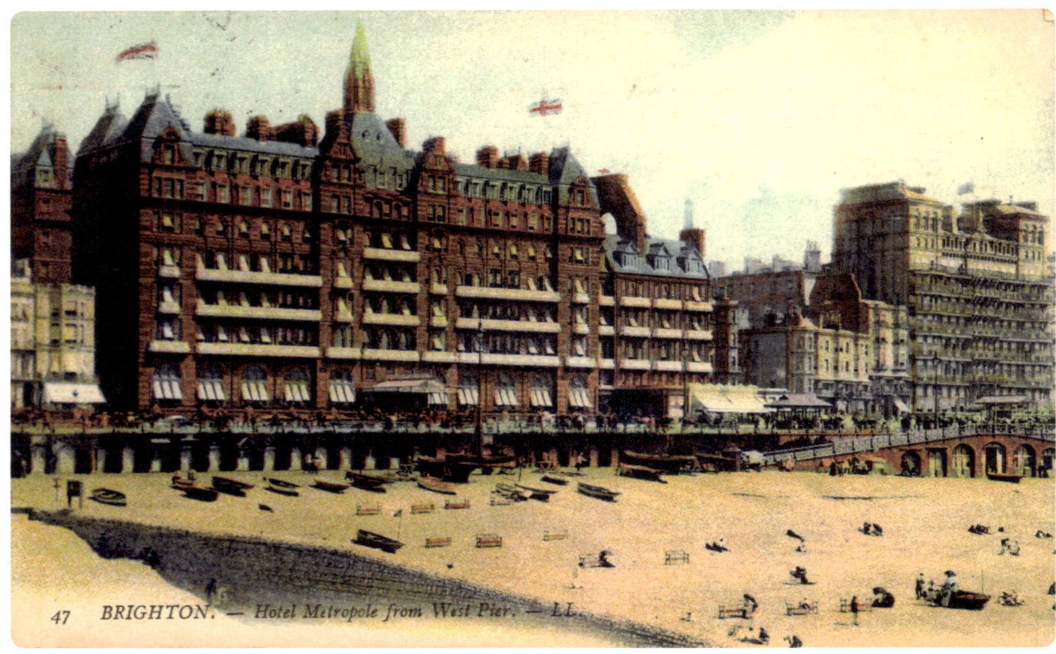

BRIGHTON, ENGLAND

Strand und Hotel Metropole, um 1900, kolorierte Postkarte
The Beach and Hotel Metropole, c. 1900, colored postcard

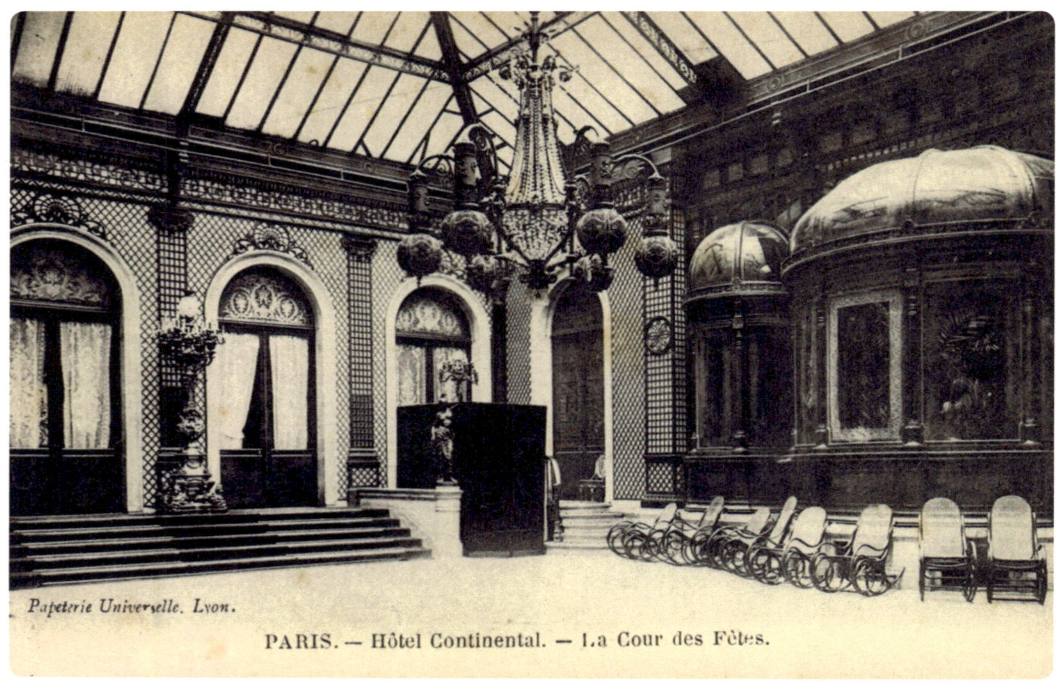

PARIS, FRANKREICH / FRANCE

Festsaal des Hôtels Continental, um 1900, Postkarte / Ballroom of the Hôtel Continental, c. 1900, postcard

DAS HOTEL

VON GASTLICHKEIT UND REPRÄSENTATION SEIT DER ANTIKE BIS HEUTE

ELENA KOROWIN

Ein Hotel ist viel mehr als nur eine praktische Übernachtungsmöglichkeit. – Es soll Zeitgenossen geben, die jahrelang finanziellen Verzicht üben, um eines Tages *einmal* in eines der weltbekannten Hotels fahren zu können. Solche Reisen versprechen außergewöhnliche Erlebnisse und atmosphärisches Neuland jenseits des häuslichen Umfelds. Kult und Reisealltag, Luxus und Misere: Jeder Mensch kann seine eigene Hotelgeschichte erzählen. – Allein das Wort, das aus dem Französischen (hôte = Gast / altfranz. ho(s)tel = Beherbergungsstätte) abgeleitet wurde und sich als Phänomen weltweit verbreitet hat, löst mannigfaltige Assoziationen aus. Berühmt geworden sind Hotels, die großen Künstlerlegenden als urbane Produktions- und Kultstätten dienten, etwa das Beat Hotel in Paris, das Chelsea Hotel in New York oder Hotelpaläste wie das Ritz Paris, deren noble Inneneinrichtung einst den Geist von Coco Chanel und diversen Hollywood-Diven atmete. Das Hotel, wie wir es heute kennen, unterscheidet sich von anderen Betrieben der Hotellerie, einem Überbegriff für jedwedes Gastgewerbe, primär durch Leistungsumfang und Charakter. Seit seiner Erfindung im ausgehenden 18. Jahrhundert hat das Hotel aber auch manche Veränderungen der Gesellschaft(en) begleitet und ist heute so weit verbreitet, dass seine Präsenz allerorten als selbstverständlich und selten hinterfragt hingenommen wird. Dabei ist es durchaus einer näheren Betrachtung würdig, denn als Sinnbild der Moderne schlechthin hat es sich parallel zu anderen wichtigen Veränderungen des Alltags im Verlauf des pulsierenden 19. Jahrhunderts etabliert. Essenzielle Aspekte des modernen Lebens wie etwa Mobilität, Anonymität und Vergänglichkeit bilden sich in der Institution Hotel ab, sind aber nur ein Teil jener Charakteristika, die es treffend beschreiben.[1] Als komplexes Phänomen spiegelt es Motive – soziale wie kulturelle –, die zeitlich weit hinter das 19. Jahrhundert zurückweisen.

GASTLICHKEIT

»Because in a modern world that is becoming ever more mobile and internationalized, we all, sooner or later, find ourselves in the position of the stranger.«[2]

Betrachtet man das Hotel als einen möglichen Ort, der Reisende auf bestimmte Art nicht privat beherbergt, sondern institutionell aufnimmt, so lässt sich seine Geschichte bis in die klassische Antike zurückverfolgen. Dieser Ursprung hat viele Wurzeln, darunter zählen Pilgerhäuser und Klöster, Poststellen und Tavernen. Zentrales und verbindendes Merkmal all dieser Einrichtungen war und ist: die Gastlichkeit. Auch als lateinisch *hospitalitas* bekannt, beruht dieses Prinzip auf Gegenseitigkeit und bedeutet, sich zu seinem Gegenüber so zu verhalten, wie man es für sich selbst in der gleichen Situation wünschen würde. Hospitalität steht somit für weit mehr als nur schlichte Herberge und Verpflegung – sie ist geprägt von religiösen Einflüssen, einer heiligen Verantwortung für den Gast, den unbehaust Reisenden. Dies war bereits in den polytheistischen Religionen eine wichtige Praxis und wurde in der Moderne schließlich zu einer ethischen Frage.[3] Ein Beispiel früh ausgebildeter Formen institutioneller

1 Andrew K. Sandoval-Strausz, *Hotel. An American History*, New Haven/London 2008, S. 3.

2 Ebd., S. 316.

3 Vgl. ebd., S. 1–4.

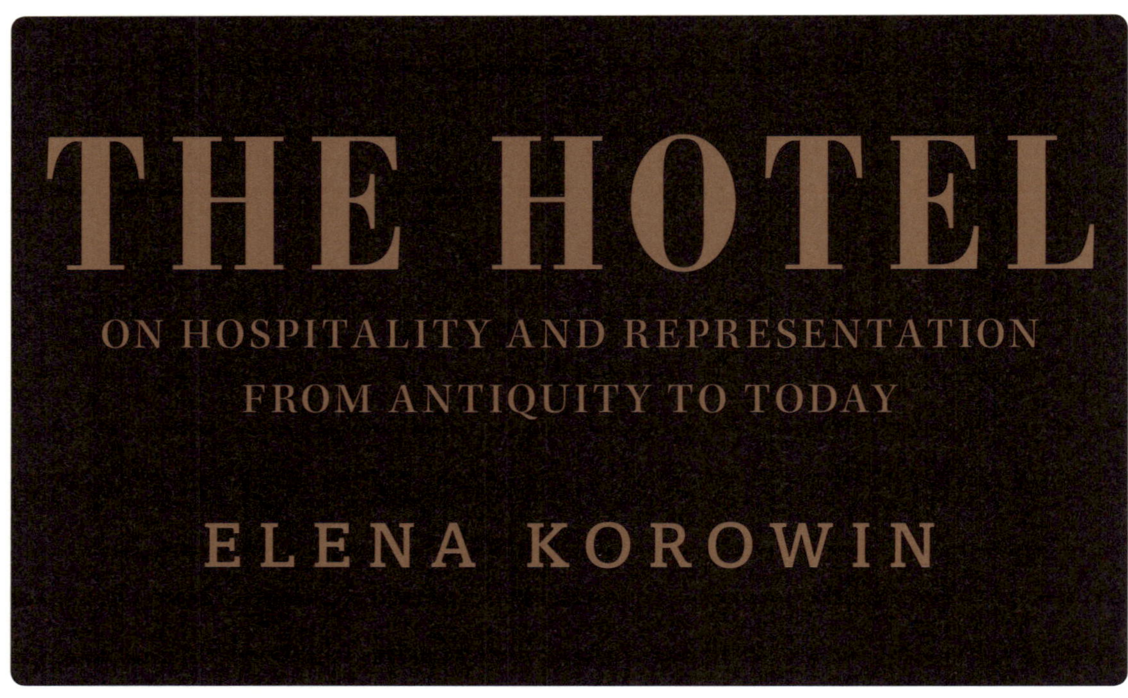

A hotel is more than simply a practical form of accommodation. Some people spend years saving their money to someday have the chance to stay in a world famous hotel. Such trips promise extraordinary experiences and an utterly new atmosphere beyond one's domestic environment. The cult of travel versus its everyday realities, luxury versus misery: everyone has a particular story to tell. Originally borrowed from the French (hôte = guest / Old French. ho(s)tel = lodging) and now a worldwide phenomenon, alone the word »hotel« gives rise to a host of associations. Some hotels have become famous for their cult status, as places where legendary artistic figures produced their works, such as the Beat Hotel in Paris, the Chelsea Hotel in New York, or hotel palaces like the Ritz Paris, whose elegant interior decor exuded the air of Coco Chanel and various Hollywood divas. The hotel of today differs from other establishments of the accommodations sector, and »hotel« is an overarching designation that indicates a certain typology and array of services. Since the invention of the hotel in the late 18th century, the institution has accompanied a number of transformations that society (or even various societies) has undergone, and today it is so prevalent that the presence of hotels has become a matter of course and is seldom called into question. The hotel is nevertheless worthy of closer examination; as an emblem of modernity par excellence, it emerged in parallel with other important changes in everyday life that took place over the course of the pulsing 19th century. Core aspects of modern life, such as mobility, anonymity, and transience are reflected in the institution of the hotel, but these are only some of the characteristics that describe it appropriately.[1] As a complex phenomenon, the hotel mirrors both cultural and social motifs whose origins substantially predate the 19th century.

HOSPITALITY

»Because in a modern world that is becoming ever more mobile and internationalized, we all, sooner or later, find ourselves in the position of the stranger.«[2]

If one considers the hotel as a potential place for housing travelers, not privately but within a receiving institution, then one can trace its history as far back as classical antiquity. This original function developed many later offshoots, including dormitories for pilgrims, monasteries, postal stations, and taverns. One of the main characteristics shared by these institutions was and is: hospitality. Familiar from the Latin word *hospitalitas,* this notion is based on a reciprocal relationship, and it means treating someone else in the same manner that one would wish to be treated, if in the same situation. Hospitality thus stands for much more than simply taking people in and feeding them; it is shaped by religious influences, a »holy« responsibility for the guest, the unsheltered traveler. This was already an important practice in polytheistic religions, and in the modern era it ultimately became a question of ethics.[3] One example of an early manifestation of institutional hospitality is the Greek *Leonidaion,* which served as lodgings appropriate for official visitors to Olympia on the occasion

1 Andrew K. Sandoval-Strausz, *Hotel: An American History* (New Haven, 2008), 3.

2 Ibid., 316.

3 Ibid., 1–4.

Gastlichkeit ist das griechische *Leonidaion,* das im 4. Jahrhundert v. Chr. in Olympia anlässlich der großen Festspiele als angemessene Unterkunft für offizielle Besucher diente. In ganz anderem Zusammenhang ließen die weiten Transportreisen entlang der Handelsrouten in China, Vorderasien und Afrika dort die sogenannte Karawanserei entstehen, eine umzäunte Zufluchts- und Lagerstätte für Menschen, Tiere und Waren.[4] In Europa wurden dagegen in der Frühzeit des Fernverkehrs häufig bestehende Wohnhäuser für die Reisenden hergerichtet. Sie standen damit in der Tradition der privaten Aufnahme von Gästen im eigenen Heim statt ihrer Unterbringung in einem zweckgebunden allein dafür errichteten Bauwerk. Wichtige Impulse, die schon eine mögliche Vorahnung des späteren Hotels geben, datiert Moritz Hoffmann auf die Zeit um 1500, als der vorhandene Wohlstand anfing auch den Fernverkehr zu nähren: Immer mehr Gasthöfe wurden in Städten und entlang der Landstraßen eröffnet. Ihr Publikum war heterogen: Kaufleute, Adelige, Pilger, Künstler, Kavaliere und Gelegenheitsreisende nutzten die Herbergen.[5] Doch bereits in dieser Zeit bildeten sich erste einschlägige Veränderungen der ursprünglichen Hospitalität heraus, denn die Ansprüche der *Gäste* nahmen mit der insgesamt steigenden Reisetätigkeit in Europa zu.[6] Eine allmähliche Ausweitung des Fernverkehrs ging einher mit der Erschließung neuer Transportwege durch den Ausbau von Straßen. Die größte Veränderung der vorindustriellen Reisekultur wurde im 16. Jahrhundert mit der Entdeckung Amerikas ausgelöst. Diese These wird von dem Historiker Andrew K. Sandoval-Strausz vertreten, der im frühen amerikanischen Kosmopolitismus und dem Wunsch, mehr Besucher auf den Kontinent zu locken, ausschlaggebende Prämissen für eine Weiterentwicklung der Gastwirtschaft insgesamt sieht. Für ihn ist das Hotel eine fraglos (US-)amerikanische Erfindung – er betont die enge Verflechtung der jungen Nation mit der kosmopolitischen Idee des Hotelgewerbes und datiert deren radikale Veränderung auf etwa 1790.[7] Im Nordamerika der hoffnungsfrohen Go-West-Manie sei demnach eine Steigerung der allgemeinen Mobilität besonders im 18. Jahrhundert als vielversprechender Fortschritt aufgefasst worden und man habe versucht, den Reisenden mit dem größtmöglichen Wohlwollen und Komfort zu begegnen. Eine nennenswerte intellektuelle Auseinandersetzung mit vergleichbaren Themen zeigte sich parallel dazu in Deutschland: Für Immanuel Kant etwa waren das Reisen und die internationale Kommunikation wesentliche Elemente für gegenseitiges Verständnis und eine friedliche kosmopolitische Konstitution der Welt.[8] In seinem philosophischen Entwurf *Zum ewigen Frieden* (1795) hat Kant das »Recht auf Hospitalität« als notwendigen Bestandteil eines anhaltenden Friedens definiert, womit man ihn ebenso als Vordenker heutiger Globalisierungstheorien betrachten könnte. Allerdings waren die Bedingungen des einfachen Reisens und der Gastlichkeit, die von Kant in seinem theoretischen Entwurf vorausgesetzt wurden, zu seinen Lebzeiten noch nicht erreicht.[9] Im nachweislich rasanten US-amerikanischen Fortschritt im Reisesektor ab etwa 1800 sieht Sandoval-Strausz die praktische Umsetzung von Kants theoretischen Überlegungen: »The creators of the American hotels were doing precisely this material work, and it makes sense to see Kant's theoretical efforts and hotel builders' architectural endeavors as manifestation of the same cosmopolitan impulse.«[10] Somit führte der Enthusiasmus der amerikanischen Gastlichkeit zum »materialistischen Kosmopolitismus«, der Kants »theoretischen Kosmopolitismus« ergänzte. Beide Konzepte beantworteten Fragen, die durch die Entwicklung der modernen und zunehmenden Mobilität aufgeworfen wurden.[11] In der (lebens-)praktischen Umsetzung gewann der »materialistische Kosmopolitismus« immer mehr Bedeutung: Die Vertreter des Hotelbetriebs orientierten sich weniger am religiösen oder ethischen Konzept der Hospitalität und hatten auch nicht »ewigen Frieden« im Sinn. Das Hotel hatte nicht zuletzt aus ökonomischen Gründen keinen idealistischen Überbau und diente schon bald einer aufsteigenden, durch bürgerliche Werte geprägten Gesellschaft als repräsentatives Modell von Öffentlichkeit.

REPRÄSENTATION UND FREIZEIT

»Der Bau sollte in die Ferne wirken und imponieren, denn ›die leblosen Formen überzeugen, die lebenden Psychen täuschen und zwar sich selbst und andere‹.«[12]

IM 17. und 18. Jahrhundert traf sich die feine Gesellschaft Europas noch im privaten Stadtpalais, dem *Hôtel particulier.* Die Räumlichkeiten dieser Bauten spiegelten die strenge gesellschaftliche Struktur dieser Epoche wider: Es gab private Wohnräume in einem Teil des Gebäudes und daneben, in einem anderen Bereich, Paradeapartments für gesellschaftliche Anlässe.[13] In den Zeiten des europäischen Ancien Régimes setzte sich die Gesellschaft der Paradeapartments lediglich aus Vertretern des Hofes zusammen. Nach den Revolutionen des 18. Jahrhunderts und im Zuge der Industrialisierung im 19. Jahrhundert veränderte der Aufstieg des Bürgertums die Gesellschaftsstruktur grundlegend und mit dieser auch die Ordnung des Stadtraums. Nachdem nun auch für Bürger mehr Rechte und Freiheiten gewährleistet waren, wollte diese neu aufgestiegene soziale Schicht ihre eigenen Paradeapartments bauen. Die Zahl der bürgerlichen Repräsentationsräume wuchs und so entstanden (unter anderem) große Hotelpaläste als Treffpunkte des neuen Geldadels.

4 Vgl. Moritz Hoffmann, *Geschichte des deutschen Hotels. Vom Mittelalter bis zur Gegenwart,* Heidelberg 1961, S. 11–12.

5 Vgl. ebd.

6 Vgl. ebd.

7 Sandoval-Strausz 2008 (wie Anm. 1), S. 314.

8 Immanuel Kant, *Zum ewigen Frieden. Ein philosophischer Entwurf* (1795), Digitale Bibliothek Sonderband, Kant-Werke, Bd. 11, S. 247–250.

9 Sandoval-Strausz 2008 (wie Anm. 1), S. 314.

10 Ebd.

11 Ebd., S. 315.

12 Über das Hotelrestaurant des Miramonte in Marienbad, zit. nach: Michael Schmitt, *Palast-Hotels. Architektur und Anspruch eines Bautyps 1870–1920,* Berlin 1982, S. 33.

13 Vgl. Norbert Elias, *Die höfische Gesellschaft. Untersuchungen zur Soziologie des Königtums und der höfischen Aristokratie,* Neuwied / Berlin 1969.

4 Moritz Hoffmann, *Geschichte des deutschen Hotels: Vom Mittelalter bis zur Gegenwart* (Heidelberg, 1961), 11–12.

5 Ibid.

6 See ibid.

7 Sandoval-Strausz 2008 (see note 1), 314.

8 Immanuel Kant, *Zum ewigen Frieden: Ein philosophischer Entwurf* [1795], Digitale Bibliothek Sonderband, Kant-Werke, vol. 11, 247–250.

9 Sandoval-Strausz 2008 (see note 1), 314.

10 Ibid.

11 Ibid., 315.

12 A description of the hotel restaurant in the *Miramonte* in Marienbad, quoted in: Michael Schmitt, *Palast-Hotels: Architektur und Anspruch eines Bautyps 1870–1920* (Berlin, 1982), 33.

13 Norbert Elias, *Die höfische Gesellschaft: Untersuchungen zur Soziologie des Königtums und der höfischen Aristokratie* (Neuwied, 1969).

14 Ibid.

of the festival games in the 4th century B.C. In a completely different context, the long transport journeys undertaken along trade routes in China, the Middle East, and Africa led to the development of the so-called »caravansary« in these regions, a fenced-in place of shelter and a storage site for people, animals, and goods.[4] In contrast, during the early phase of long-distance travel in Europe, existing residential buildings were often furnished to provide for travelers and were a continuation of the tradition of taking guests into one's private home instead of housing them in a building constructed exclusively for this purpose. Moritz Hoffmann dates important trends that possibly prefigured the later hotel to the period around 1500, when an existing degree of wealth began to foster long-distance travel. An increasing number of guesthouses opened in cities and along country roads. Their clientele was heterogeneous: merchants, nobles, pilgrims, artists, squires, and occasional travelers used these lodgings.[5] Already at this time, however, the first significant changes impacted the original notion of hospitality, since the expectations of the »guests« rose with the general increase in travel within Europe.[6] A gradual extension of long-distance travel was linked to the opening of new avenues of transport with the construction of streets. The greatest change in the pre-industrial culture of travel was spurred by the discovery of America in the 16th century; this theory is espoused by historian Andrew K. Sandoval-Strausz, who views early American cosmopolitanism and the desire to lure more visitors to the continent as key premises for new developments in lodgings as a whole. For him, the hotel is unquestionably a U.S. invention, and he emphasizes the cosmopolitan idea of the hotel business as enmeshed with the young nation, dating the country's investment in this idea to the radical changes that occurred around 1790.[7] In North America the high hopes that drove the go-West mania thus represented an increase in general mobility, particularly in the 18th century, and was viewed as a promising sign of progress. One therefore tried to provide travelers with the greatest possible sense of wellbeing and comfort. A notable intellectual study of comparable themes and topics was undertaken at the same time in Germany: Immanuel Kant, for example, considered travel and international communication to be key elements in fostering joint understanding and a peaceful, cosmopolitan constitution of the world.[8] In his philosophical essay PERPETUAL PEACE (1795) Kant defined the »right to hospitality« as a necessary component of lasting peace, an idea that would arguably allow him to be considered a prophet of contemporary globalizations theories. Nevertheless, the conditions that would permit easy travel and the kind of hospitality assumed by Kant in his theoretical writings did not develop within his lifetime.[9] Sandoval-Strausz views the demonstrably rapid development of the travel sector in the United States from 1800 onward as a practical application of Kant's theories: »The creators of the American hotels were doing precisely this material work, and it makes sense to see Kant's theoretical efforts and hotel builders' architectural endeavors as manifestation of the same cosmopolitan impulse.«[10] In other words, the enthusiastic hospitality found in America led to a »materialist cosmopolitanism« that complemented Kant's »theoretical cosmopolitanism.« Both concepts respond to questions raised by the increase in modern forms of mobility.[11] In its real-life, practical application, »materialist cosmopolitanism« took on more and more significance. Members of the hotel business became less oriented towards religious or ethical concepts of hospitality and were not concerned with »perpetual peace.« Economic factors were first and foremost in the hotel's lack of idealistic underpinnings, and the institution quickly came to serve as a representative model of public life for a burgeoning society defined by middle class values.

REPRESENTATION AND LEISURE

»The building is intended to unfold its effect and impress the viewer from a distance, for ›the lifeless forms are convincing, the living psyches are beguiled and beguile yet others‹.«[12]

IN the 17th and 18th century members of European »society« still gathered in the private city *palais*, or *hôtel particulier*. The rooms of these buildings mirrored the strict social order of this era. There were private apartments in one part of the building, and next to them in another section were the grand apartments used for social occasions.[13] In the period of the European *ancien régime*, the society populating these grand apartments only included members of the court. After the revolutions of the 18th century and in the wake of 19th-century industrialization, the rise of the middle class fundamentally altered the structure of society and also that of urban space. Once more rights and freedoms had been secured for ordinary citizens, this emerging class wished to construct its own grand apartments. The number of spaces serving a representative function to the middle class grew, and thus the large hotel palaces (among other structures) emerged as meeting points for this new moneyed nobility.

Hoffmann observes that particularly at this time an increasing number of simple cooking stands were turned into restaurants, and inns were replaced by hotels.[14] A representative ambiance and an imposing architecture became more important for the hotel (primarily in terms of the typology of the grand hotel) than merely serving the purpose of the overnight stay, as did may guesthouses. Hospitality

Hoffmann stellt fest, dass gerade in diesen Jahren immer mehr einfache Garküchen in Restaurants umgewandelt und Gasthöfe durch Hotels ersetzt wurden.[14] Ein repräsentatives Ambiente und eine imposante Architektur wurden für das Hotel (und primär den Typus des Grand Hotels) bedeutender als die bloße Funktion des Übernachtens, wie sie noch in vielen Gasthäusern gepflegt wurde. Die Gastlichkeit wurde nun mit Luxus und Glamour angereichert, was ihren Sinn nachhaltig veränderte.[15] In den neuen Palasthotels herrschten Privilegien und Exklusionen, die häufig vom Bürgertum und seinem Bedürfnis nach Selbstdarstellung diktiert wurden. Im fortschreitenden Alltag des Hotelgewerbes wurde nur der Gast zum König erklärt, der sich die Gastlichkeit standesgemäß oder finanziell leisten konnte, und auch hier etablierten sich rasch gewisse schichtenspezifische Verhaltensnormen: »Damals bildeten sich Regeln heraus, wie man mit dem Hotelbesitzer und seinem Personal verkehren soll. Man sollte nicht so protzig auftreten, damit man nicht gezwungen war, hohe Trinkgelder zu geben. Man sollte auch nicht zu bescheiden sein und sein Licht nicht unter den Scheffel stellen.«[16]

DIE HUMANISTISCHEN ÜBERLEGUNGEN KANTS HATTEN SCHLUSSENDLICH WOHL WENIGER WIRKUNG AUF DIE GESELLSCHAFT ALS DIE SICH STÄNDIG VERÄNDERNDE LEBENSART DIESER EPOCHE: Das Eisenbahnnetz wurde ausgebaut, die Reisetätigkeit gesteigert; zudem entwickelte sich ein neuer, bürgerlicher Begriff von Freizeit.

Freizeit war dem Adel einst unbekannt, doch nun sollte sie das alltägliche Leben bereichern: Nach getaner Arbeit verbrachte man seine Mußestunden bevorzugt in Gesellschaft oder die Ferien beispielsweise bei gesundheitsfördernden Prozeduren in den Kur- und Seebädern Mitteleuropas.[17] In jenen Zeiten des Pläsirs versuchten Neureiche, die fasziniert vom aristokratischen Lebensstil waren, sich diesem durch Nachahmung anzunähern und erreichten damit nicht selten eine Übersteigerung der klassenspezifischen Sitten und Gebräuche.

»Die Aristokratie begegnete also in diesen Hotels nicht nur der neuen Hochfinanz, sondern auch einer Personengruppe, die sich den Palast nur auf Zeit leisten konnte, für die das ›Mehr Scheinen‹ wichtig war. Dieses Streben ist bereits durch die Architektur vorgegeben.«[18] So besteht etwa die prunkvolle Hotelpromenade, die sich seit dem 19. Jahrhundert durch das tschechische Marienbad erstreckt, aus einer einzigen Aneinanderreihung von exquisiten Hotels, allesamt im klassizistischen Stil errichtet. Diese Ballung überdimensionierter, luxuriöser Bauwerke lässt auch an den heutigen Bauboom in den Vereinigten Arabischen Emiraten denken. Was im 19. Jahrhundert das Miramonte in Marienbad war, ist heute mit dem Burj Al Arab in Dubai vergleichbar. Im Sommer traf sich seinerzeit *tout le monde* in Kurstädten, deren architektonische Infrastruktur einer immer gleichen Dramaturgie folgte: Trinkhalle, Kasino, Konversationshaus. Im Zentrum des Treibens: das Grand Hotel, in dem rauschende Bälle veranstaltet wurden. Jetzt bewährte sich das Hotel auch als Bühne für die sogenannte feine Gesellschaft, die nach und nach ihre Stadtpaläste verließ. Adelige, Bürger, Künstler, Gauner, sie alle tummelten sich in der Lobby und im Ballsaal. Im beginnenden 20. Jahrhundert entstanden die ersten legendären Häuser, deren Namen schnell zu etablierten Statussymbolen der neuen Reisekultur wurden: Ritz in Paris, Waldorf-Astoria in New York, Adlon in Berlin – jede bedeutende Großstadt hatte ihre Hotelgiganten. Hier traf die *demi-monde* auf die *haut monde* und das neue Motto hieß: »Here you meet everybody and everybody meets you [...] Here you obtain the news, all the scandal, all the politics, and all the fun.«[19] Doch dieser unbeschwerte eskapistische Taumel in den neu erkorenen Paraderäumen hielt nicht lange an: Noch vor dem Trauma der beiden Weltkriege hatte das Grand Hotel seinen Höhepunkt überschritten. Und in der Folge wurden die Bauten vielfach zum Lazarett, Pflegeheim oder Wohnhaus umfunktioniert.[20] Seine Klientel wurde zusammen mit dem alten Europa nahezu ausgelöscht und hinterließ eine große Lücke, die erst in den 1950er-Jahren mit neuen Ideen aus der Neuen Welt gefüllt wurde.

MASSENTOURISMUS

»As tourism and travel have become an integral part of people's social and economic lifestyles, hotels have been transformed into crossroads of our nomadic society.«[21]

WIE Sandoval-Strausz schon für das 18. und 19. Jahrhundert feststellt, waren die USA stets eine innovative Ideenfabrik – auch für neue Hotelkonzepte. Im 20. Jahrhundert verstärkte sich diese Tendenz, basierend auf Faktoren wie dem Bau der Panamericana, der Aufnahme zahlreicher Immigranten und dem erstarkten Patriotismus nach dem aus US-amerikanischer Sicht siegreichen Ausgang beider Weltkriege. Bereits in den 1920er-Jahren entstanden entlang der Highways die Motels: Eine einfache, wenngleich signifikante Kombination der Worte Motor und Hotel, die bis heute ein Wahrzeichen des ambivalenten *American Way of Life* darstellen. Dieser Lebensstil hatte unterschiedliche Ausprägungen, verbreitete sich aber spätestens in der Nachkriegszeit über die ganze Welt. So gab es beispielsweise

14 Vgl. ebd.

15 Vgl. Jennifer M. Volland, Bruce Grenville, Stephanie Rebick (Hg.), *Grand Hotel. Redesigning Modern Life*, Ausst.-Kat. Vancouver Art Gallery, Ostfildern 2013.

16 Hoffmann 1961 (wie Anm. 4), S. 210.

17 Vgl. Schmitt 1982 (wie Anm. 12), S. 29.

18 Ebd., S. 30.

19 Der britische Schriftsteller Frederick Marryat, zit. nach: Donald Albrecht, *New Hotels for Global Nomads*, Ausst.-Kat. Cooper-Hewitt, National Design Museum, Smithsonian Institution, New York, London 2003, S. 21.

20 Vgl. Schmitt 1982 (wie Anm. 12), S. 169.

21 Albrecht 2003 (wie Anm. 19), S. 9.

15 See Jennifer M. Volland, Bruce Grenville, and Stephanie Rebick, eds., *Grand Hotel. Redesigning Modern Life,* exhibit. cat. Vancouver Art Gallery (Ostfildern, 2013).

16 Hoffmann 1961 (see note 4), 210.

17 See Schmitt 1982 (see note 12), 29.

18 Ibid., 30.

19 British author Frederick Marryat, quoted in: Donald Albrecht, *New Hotels for Global Nomads,* exhibit. cat. Cooper-Hewitt, National Design Museum, Smithsonian Institution, New York (London, 2003), 21.

20 See Schmitt (see note 12), 169.

21 Albrecht 2003 (see note 19), 9.

22 Stephanie Rebick, »Local Flavor, American Comfort: InterContinental Hotels in Latin America,« in *Grand Hotel* 2013 (see note 15), 52–57. For a criticism of post-war hotel architecture, see: Herbert Keck, »Profitable Raumverschwendung. Das Atriumhotel,« *Daidalos* 62 (1996), 42–51.

was enhanced by luxury and glamour, which had a lasting impact on its the meaning of the term.[15] Privilege and exclusiveness prevailed in the new palace hotels and were often dictated by the middle class and its need for self-representation. In the developing daily routine of the hotel business, only the customer able to afford such hospitality by nature of his pocketbook or social status was considered »king,« and even on this upper echelon certain class-specific behavioral norms quickly emerged: »At the time certain rules crystallized in terms of how one should behave towards a hotel owner and his personnel. One should not act overly pretentious, which would cause one to have to give higher tips. But one should neither be too modest and hide one's light under a bushel.«[16]

KANT'S HUMANISTIC DELIBERATIONS HAVE ULTIMATELY HAD LESS IMPACT ON SOCIETY THAN THE ONGOING TRANSFORMATIONS OF LIFESTYLE DURING THIS EPOCH. Rail lines were expanded; travel increased, and there emerged a new, bourgeois notion of freedom.

The nobility of the past had not known the concept of leisure time, and now this idea was viewed as enhancing everyday life. After completing one's work, one spent one's free time in the company of others or by taking vacations, for example by engaging in the health-promoting rituals of the spas and coastal resorts of Central Europe.[17] In such hours dedicated to *plaisir,* the nouveau riche tried by means of imitation to approximate the aristocratic lifestyle that fascinated them, and often they affected an over-exaggeration of class-specific rites and customs in the process.

»In these hotels the aristocracy not only encountered the new [world of] high finance but also a group of people able to afford a palace for a certain amount of time, for whom ›appearances‹ were important. This desire is present in the architecture.«[18] For example, along the magnificent hotel promenade extending through the Czech city of Marienbad since the 19th century is a unique series of exquisite hotels, all built in a classical style. This dense grouping of over-sized, luxurious buildings recalls today's building boom in the United Arab Emirates. The current equivalent to the Miramonte in 19th-century Marienbad is the Burj Al Arab in Dubai. In former times *tout le monde* gathered in spas in the summer, the architectural infrastructure of which always adhered to the same dramaturgy: a drinking hall, a casino, and a main building where people gathered and conversed. At the center of the action was the grand hotel, where glittering balls were held. The hotel subsequently also came to be favored as a platform for so-called »society,« which gradually left its city palaces. Aristocrats, members of the middle class, artists, and tricksters all cavorted about in the lobby and the ballroom. The first legendary hotels arose in the early 20th century, and their names soon became established status symbols in the new culture of travel: the Ritz in Paris, the Waldorf-Astoria in New York, and the Adlon in Berlin. Every important city possessed its own hotel giant. This is where the *demi-monde* encountered the *haut monde,* and the new motto became: »Here you meet everybody and everybody meets you . . . Here you obtain the news, all the scandal, all the politics, and all the fun.«[19] However, this careless, escapist delirium in these newly chosen representative spaces did not last long. The importance of the grand hotel began to wane even before the trauma of the two World Wars. Subsequently the buildings were turned into hospitals, sanatoriums, or apartment houses.[20] Its clientele was almost eliminated, along with old Europe, and this left a hole that was not filled until the 1950s—by new ideas from the New World.

MASS TOURISM

»As tourism and travel have become an integral part of people's social and economic lifestyles, hotels have been transformed into crossroads of our nomadic society.«[21]

AS Sandoval-Strausz argued for the 18th and 19th century, the U. S. has consistently served as an innovative idea factory—and this was true for new hotel concepts as well. This tendency became more pronounced in the 20th century and was based on factors such as the construction of the Panamericana, the influx of numerous immigrants, and heightened patriotism after what the Americans viewed as the victorious conclusion of both World Wars. Motels developed along the highways as early as the 1920s. The »motel,« a simple but significant combination of the words »motor« and »hotel,« is still an icon of the ambivalent *American Way of Life.* This lifestyle had various manifestations, but at least by the post-war era it had spread throughout the entire world. For example, in the 1950s Europe also witnessed a growth in these so-called motels. The *American Way of Life* was most clearly expressed in the uniform design of the dominant hotel chains that today are present on a global scale: Inter Continental, Hilton, and Marriott. Now travelers could experience American comfort everywhere. The standardized design was not a drawback but was instead considered contemporary and fashionable.[22] The numerous »all-inclusive« hotels throughout the globe could be seen as the consumption-oriented extension of this type of travel culture. The seemingly progressive transformation of the hotel in the 1950s had little impact on its basic functions—overnight

in den 1950er-Jahren einen Zuwachs von sogenannten Motels (dt. Autobahnraststätten) auch in Europa. Deutlich zeigte sich der *American Way of Life* im Einheitsdesign der einschlägigen, heute global agierenden Ketten InterContinental, Hilton oder Marriott. Überall konnten nun Reisende amerikanischen Komfort genießen. Man störte sich nicht am standardisierten Design, sondern empfand dieses im Gegenteil als zeitgemäß und schick.[22] Die konsumistische Fortführung dieser Form der Reisekultur kann man seit den letzten Jahrzehnten weltweit in den zahlreichen All-inclusive-Hotels betrachten. Die scheinbar progressiven Transformationen des Hotels in den 1950er-Jahren wirkten auf seine Grundfunktionen – Übernachtung und Verpflegung – nur wenig ein, schufen allerdings atmosphärische Änderungen, die das alte Grand Hotel nicht kannte. Als Theodor W. Adorno in seiner *Minima Moralia* über das Hotel schrieb, ignorierte er die Euphorie der Hotelbetreiber, Architekten und Designer. Er beschäftigte sich vielmehr mit jenen zeitgenössischen Nomaden, die in solchen Herbergen (sowie in ihrem Leben) auf sich selbst zurückgeworfen waren. Die neuen Dimensionen großer Hotelketten, in denen sich das Individuum verliert, und die Tristesse der Motels mit ihren gewissermaßen rastlosen Gästen beim Trinken und Fernsehen in selbst erzeugter (Un-)Ruhe und Ausweglosigkeit – sie sind ebenso charakteristisch für diese Zeit wie Adornos viel zitierte Texte über die »Entfremdung des Individuums noch in den feinsten Verästelungen des Alltagslebens«.[23] Und so kommt Adorno zu einem betrüblichen Resümee: »Daß das ›Restaurant‹ durch feindliche Abgründe vom Hotel, der leeren Hülse der Zimmer, geschieden ist, versteht sich von selbst, ebenso die Zeitbeschränkungen beim Essen und im unleidlichen ›room service‹, vor dem man in den Drugstore flüchtet, den offenbaren Laden, hinter dessen ungastlicher Theke ein Jongleur mit Spiegeleiern, knusprigem Speck und Eiskegeln als letzter Gastfreund sich bewährt. Im Hotel aber wird vom Portier selbst jede unvorhergesehene Frage mit dem mißmutigen Hinweis auf andere, meist geschlossene Schalter abgefertigt.«[24]

DIESE pessimistische Beschreibung eines amerikanischen Hotels von Adorno hat an Aktualität in der Jetztzeit wenig eingebüßt; und dennoch ist dies nur eine von enorm vielen Facetten der heutigen Hotelindustrie. Zahlreiche Trends haben sich in den letzten Jahrzehnten parallel entwickelt und rasant abgewechselt: Hotelketten und Konsumburgen der standardisierten Vollpension, Designhotels, Kapselhotels, Wellness- und Spa-Resorts, um nur einige zu nennen. Die Größe der Hotels wuchs zum Teil weiter an und längst sind Häuser wie diese zu autarken Konsumfestungen, zu intakten Städten innerhalb der Stadt geworden. Der zeitgenössische Verbraucher kennt sich in der vielfältigen Landschaft der Hotels aus, er weiß um seine Präferenzen und bedient sich bei der Wahl einschlägiger Reservierungs-Webseiten. Anders als im 19. Jahrhundert, wo Gäste in Palasthotels auch abgewiesen werden konnten, muss er nun nicht mehr um den Einlass bangen. Selbst unerschwingliche Herbergen sind nur noch selten gänzlich hermetische Festungen der High Society – für gewöhnlich kann der Neugierige eintreten und sich bei einem Drink zumindest Lobby und Bar aus der Nähe anschauen – oder diese in einem der zahlreichen *Coffee Table Books* zu Hause nachschlagen. Obwohl der Typus des Grand Hotels weiterhin seine Aura verteidigt, sind Bestrebungen, es in seiner alten Tradition wiederzubeleben, nicht selten zum Scheitern verurteilt. Im Zuge der Demokratisierung verblassen die Unterschiede, durch die sich die feine Gesellschaft einst separierte – also jene soziale Schicht, die den Charakter des Grand Hotels zum Fin de Siècle maßgeblich bestimmte. Der Pluralismus der heutigen Gesellschaften spiegelt sich in nahezu jeder größeren Stadt in den zahlreichen Übernachtungsangeboten, die auf jeden nur denkbaren speziellen Wunsch ausgerichtet sind. Die erwünschte Gastlichkeit seiner Herberge kann man sich nun in dem Maße aussuchen, wie es der finanzielle Rahmen erlaubt: von übersteigerter Aufmerksamkeit in einem Luxusresort bis hin zu dem durch Automaten ersetzten Personal eines Formule1-Hotels. Die ursprüngliche religiöse und ethische Praxis der Gastaufnahme beschränkt sich auf einzelne Ausnahmen wie Klöster und Pilgerhäuser, die sich durch die Jahrhunderte dieser Aufgabe verschrieben haben und heute vielerorts eine Renaissance beim gestressten und reizüberfluteten Menschen erleben. Der Großteil der Hotels dagegen bietet eine Hospitalität auf Knopfdruck. Als soziokulturelles Phänomen zeichnet somit das pluralistische Hotel von heute die zeitgenössischen gesellschaftlichen Strukturen und Veränderungen in gleicher Konsequenz nach, wie es durch sie bestimmt ist. Und wie das Hotel der Zukunft einmal aussehen könnte, ist bei der Dynamik aktueller und zudem vielgestaltigster Umwälzungen genauso unvorstellbar wie die Frage nach dem Hotelgast der Zukunft.

22 Vgl. dazu: Stephanie Rebick, »Local Flavour, American Comfort: InterContinental Hotels in Latin America«, in: *Grand Hotel*, 2013 (wie Anm. 15), S. 52–57. Eine Kritik der Hotelarchitektur der Nachkriegszeit bei: Herbert Keck, »Profitable Raumverschwendung. Das Atriumhotel«, in: *Daidalos 62*, 1996, S. 42–51.

23 Andreas Bernard, »Einleitung. Fünfzig Jahre ›Minima Moralia‹«, in: Andreas Bernard, Ulrich Raulff (Hg.): *Theodor W. Adorno ›Minima Moralia‹ neu gelesen*, Frankfurt am Main 2003, S. 8.

24 Theodor W. Adorno, *Minima Moralia. Reflexionen aus dem beschädigten Leben*, Gesammelte Schriften, Bd. 4, Frankfurt am Main 1971, S. 133.

23 Andreas Bernard, »Einleitung. Fünfzig Jahre ›Minima Moralia,‹« in *Theodor W. Adorno »Minima Moralia« neu gelesen,* ed. Andreas Bernard and Ulrich Raulff (Frankfurt am Main, 2003), 8.

24 Theodor W. Adorno, *Minima Moralia. Reflections on a Damaged Life,* transl. E. F. N. Jephcott (London, 2005), 117.

stay and refreshment—but it produced atmospheric transformations foreign to the grand hotel. When writing about the hotel in his *Minima Moralia,* Theodor W. Adorno ignores the euphoria of hotel operators, architects, and designers, instead examining the figure of the contemporary nomad who exists in isolation in such accommodations (as well as in daily life). The new dimensions of the large hotel chains, where people lose themselves, and the dreariness of motels where somehow restless guests drink and watch TV in self-created (nervous) calm and hopelessness—these are as characteristic of this era as Adorno's much-quoted texts about the »alienation of the individual even within the ramifications of everyday life.«[23] Adorno thus comes to the depressing conclusion: »That the ›Restaurant‹ is divided by gulfs of antagonism from the Hotel, an empty husk of rooms, is a matter of course, as are the time-limits on eating and on insufferable ›room service,‹ from which one flees to the drugstore, blatantly a shop, behind whose inhospitable counter a juggler with fried eggs, crispy bacon, and ice-cubes, proves himself the last solicitous host. But in the hotel every unforeseen question is disposed of by the porter with an irate nod to another counter, usually closed.«[24]

ADORNO'S pessimistic description of an American hotel is no less current today; but it is still only one of the very many facets of the contemporary hotel industry. Numerous trends have developed in parallel or in succession over the last few decades: hotel chains and the consumer palaces with standardized all-meals-included packages, design hotels, sleeping capsules, wellness and spa resorts, to name only a few. To a certain extent the size of the hotel has continued to grow, and such buildings, autonomous fortresses of consumption, have become intact cities within cities. Contemporary consumers are familiar with the varied hotel landscape. Knowing their preferences, they make avail to the appropriate booking websites. Unlike in the 19th century, when the palace hotels could turn down guests, today no one must worry about gaining access. Even exorbitant lodgings are seldom hermetic fortresses of high society. Usually the curious may enter and take a closer look at the lobby and bar while having a drink—or examine these interiors at home in one of the many »coffee table« books published on the subject. Although the typology of the grand hotel continues to staunchly maintain its aura, efforts to revive its old traditions are often doomed to failure. The differences that once defined elite society, that is the social class that largely characterized the grand hotels of the *fin de siècle,* are disappearing with increasing democratization. In almost every large city the pluralism of today's society is reflected in the numerous types of accommodations available and catering to any conceivable wish. Now one may select the desired degree of hospitality accompanying one's lodgings in accordance with one's budget—from the hyper-attentiveness experienced at a luxury resort to the machine replacements for personnel that populate the budget hotel. The originally religious and ethical practice of taking in guests now only exists in a few, limited exceptions, such as monasteries and pilgrims' hostels. Such institutions have remained dedicated to this purpose for centuries, and in many places they have been undergoing a revival among stressed and over-stimulated people. The majority of hotels, however, provide hospitality at the push of a button. As a socio-cultural phenomenon, today's pluralistic hotel is a reflection of contemporary social structures and shifts, which in turn define the institution. Given the dynamics of current and increasingly diverse transformations, the appearance of the future hotel is just as unimaginable as the nature of future hotel guest.

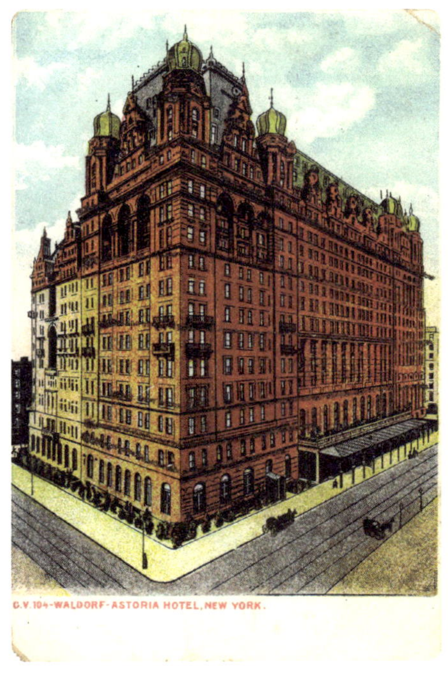

NEW YORK CITY, USA

Waldorf Astoria Hotel, kolorierte Postkarte
Waldorf Astoria Hotel, colored postcard

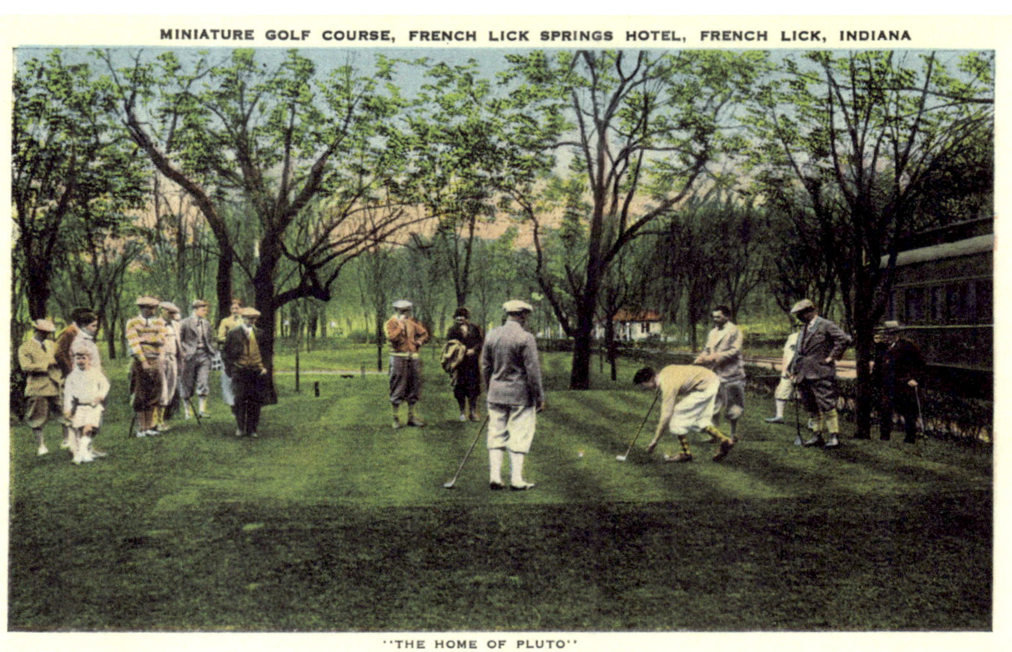

FRENCH LICK, INDIANA, USA

French Lick Springs Hotel, Minigolfkurs, kolorierte Postkarte
French Lick Springs Hotel, miniature golf course, colored postcard

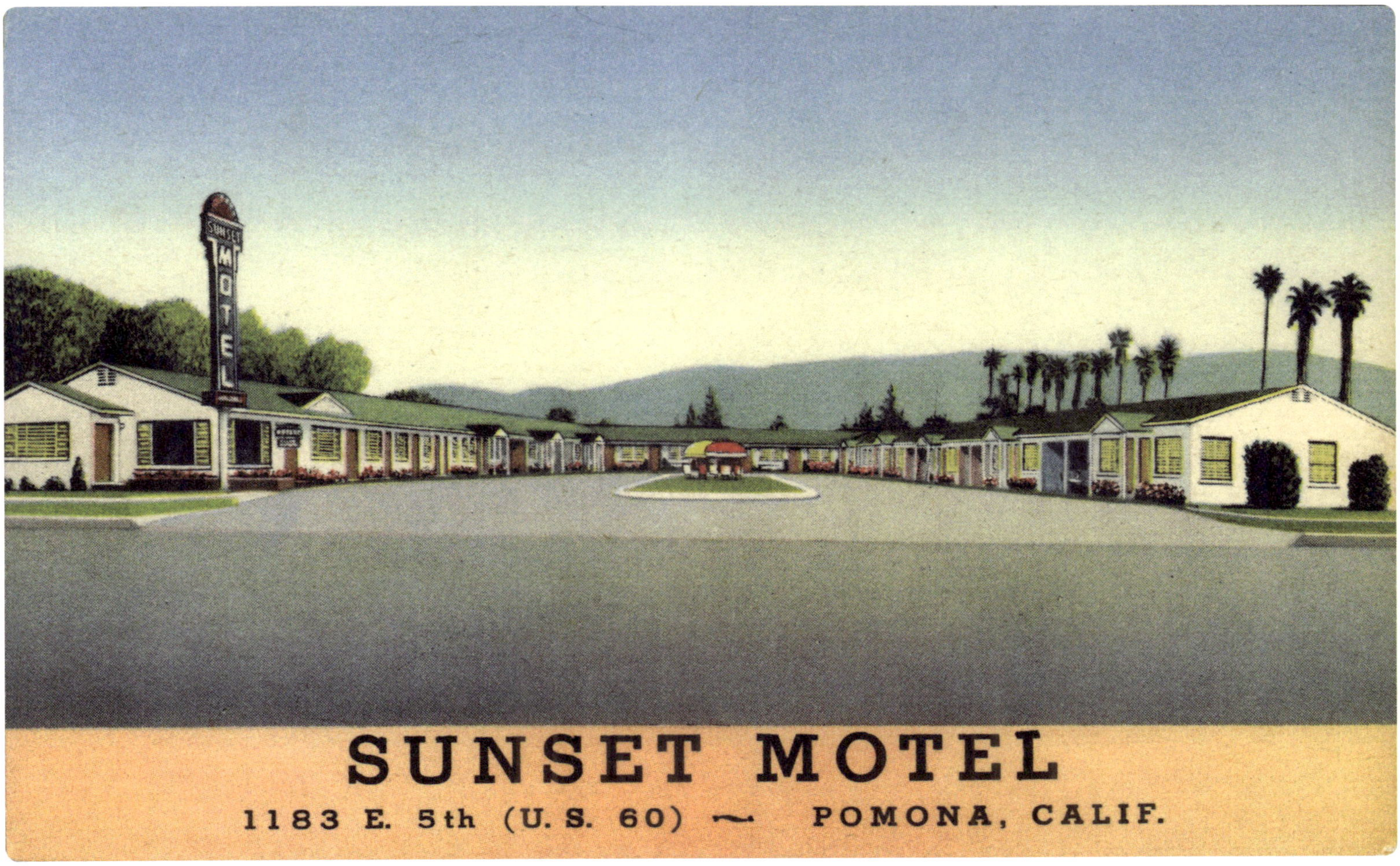

SUNSET MOTEL
1183 E. 5th (U. S. 60) — POMONA, CALIF.

POMONA, KALIFORNIEN, USA

Sunset Motel, kolorierte Postkarte / Sunset Motel, colored postcard

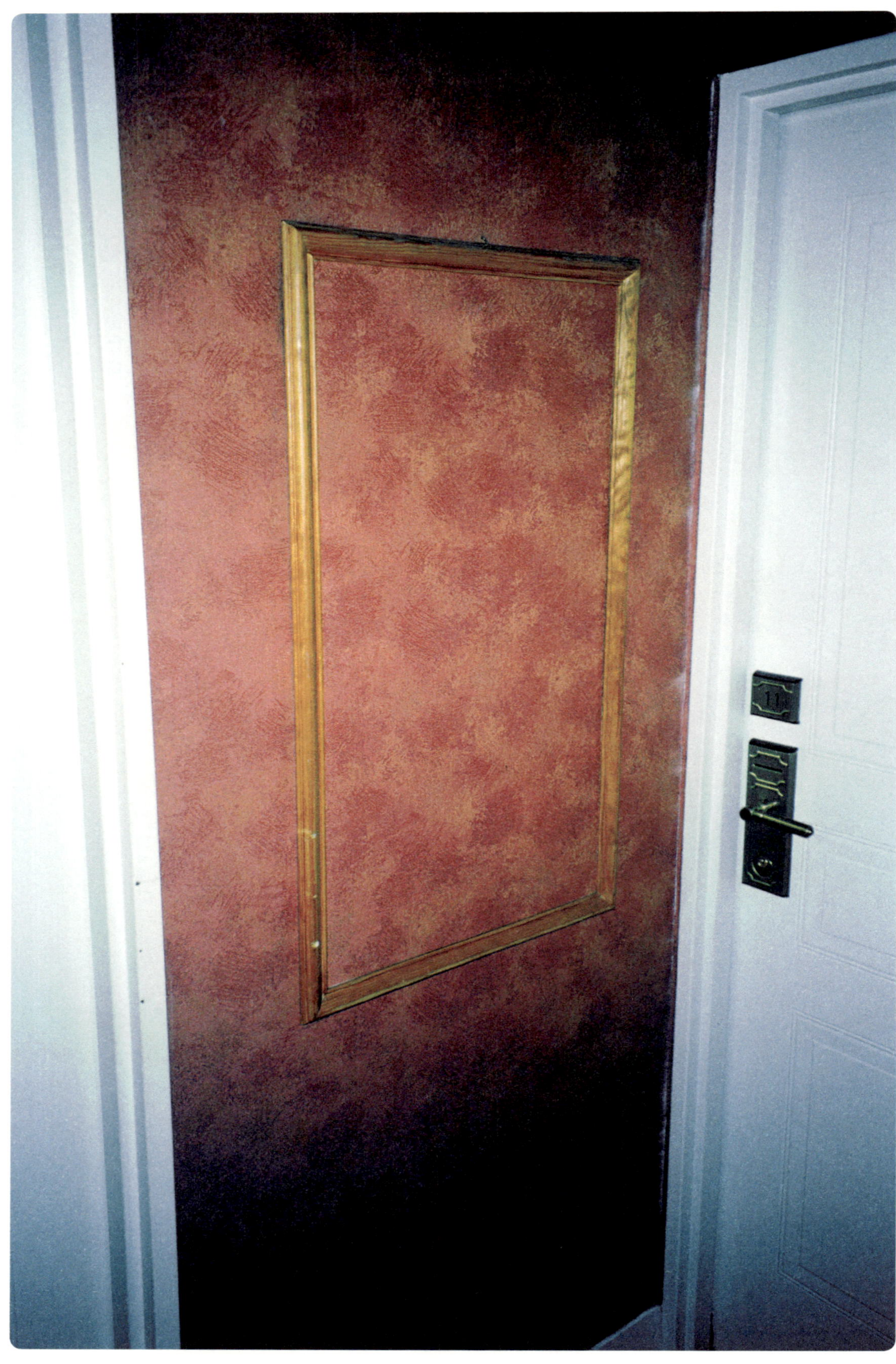

PARIS '03, FOTO / PHOTO: VOLKER ALBUS

HOTEL DADA

ÜBER DAS LEBEN UND LEIDEN IM HOTELZIMMER

VOLKER ALBUS

Als Viel- oder besser: Häufigreisender wird man immer wieder vom kreativen Potenzial des gemeinen Hotelzimmerarchitekten überrascht. Selbst nach gut 20-jähriger Ausstellungs-, Lehr- und Vortragstätigkeit im In- und Ausland und den damit verbundenen Übernachtungen in den unterschiedlichsten, mit einem bis fünf Sternen gekennzeichneten Unterkünften, sieht man sich immer wieder mit Einrichtungskonstellationen konfrontiert, die selbst dem erfahrensten Hotelgast bisweilen schmerzhafte Anpassungsfähigkeiten abfordern. Vor allem die durch technische Ausstattungselemente bestimmten Schnittstellen zwischen Raum und Gast mutieren nicht selten zu höchst ambitionierten Denksportaufgaben. Das beginnt schon mit dem per Chipkarte zu öffnenden Domizil (was häufig nicht reibungslos funktioniert und den erschlafften, im elften Stockwerk logierenden Gast zurück ins weit entfernte Foyer nötigt). Es setzt sich fort mit der zentralen, mittels der gleichen Karte einzuschaltenden Stromversorgung (an die selbstverständlich auch der Eisschrank und sämtliche Ladegeräte angeschlossen sind) und findet seinen kniffligen Höhepunkt in der Entschlüsselung der Bedienung von Lüftung, TV-Gerät und den sich über den gesamten Raum verteilenden Beleuchtungselementen. Insbesondere die subtile Ausdifferenzierung der diversen Lichtquellen, ihre oft wechselweise von Bett und Flur aus zu steuernde Einzel- oder Parallelschaltung und nicht zuletzt ihre obendrein variabel einstellbare Intensität, bedarf meist mehrerer, oft mit einem drei- bis viermaligen Hin und Her zwischen Bett, Bad und Flur verbundener Einstellungsproben.

Nun, irgendwann ist auch das Enigma der die Atmosphäre illuminierenden Schaltkreise durchschaut und der Gast kann sich ganz dem Komfort seines Heims auf Zeit hingeben. Und damit das auch tatsächlich halbwegs gelingt, müssen selbstverständlich auch die Rahmenbedingungen stimmen. Will sagen: Die innenarchitektonische *Hardware* vor Ort muss so gestaltet sein, dass sich tatsächlich *jeder* wohl fühlt, oder anders formuliert, dass kein Gast sich vom Design der Unterkunft in seinem ästhetischen oder moralischen Empfinden provoziert, womöglich gar verletzt fühlt.

KONKRET BEDEUTET DAS NICHTS ANDERES ALS: DURCHSCHNITT, DURCHSCHNITT UND NOCHMALS DURCHSCHNITT – UND DAS AUF INTERNATIONALEM NIVEAU. Egal, ob rustikal oder klassisch elegant, ob postmodern oder altfränkisch, im Hotelzimmer erreichen alle gängigen stilistischen Ausprägungen ein ultimatives Mittelformat. Hier verschmelzen die allgemein gültigen Vorstellungen und Vermutungen bezüglich bestimmter Stilrichtungen zu einem Extrakt populärster Klischees und Leitbilder. Nirgendwo sonst finden wir derartig gefällige Interpretationen von Philippe Starck oder Laura Ashley, Antonio Citterio oder Friedensreich Hundertwasser, Art déco oder Bauhaus wie in den Suiten und Kemenaten kommerzieller Gastlichkeit. Nur selten wird dabei das behauptete Designbekenntnis überbetont. Das heißt, selbst innerhalb bestimmter Motivlinien dominiert eine Art Muzak-Ästhetik[1], vergleichbar mit der allgegenwärtigen Musikberieselung in Kaufhäusern, Supermärkten und Verkehrsmitteln oder,

1 Als Muzak bezeichnet man den insbesondere aus Einkaufszentren und Hotelfoyers bekannten mehr oder weniger gleichförmigen Klangteppich, der permanent auf das Publikum herabrieselt; siehe hierzu auch: Joseph Lanza, *Elevator Music: A Surreal History of Muzak, Easy-Listening, and Other Moodsong*, London 1995.

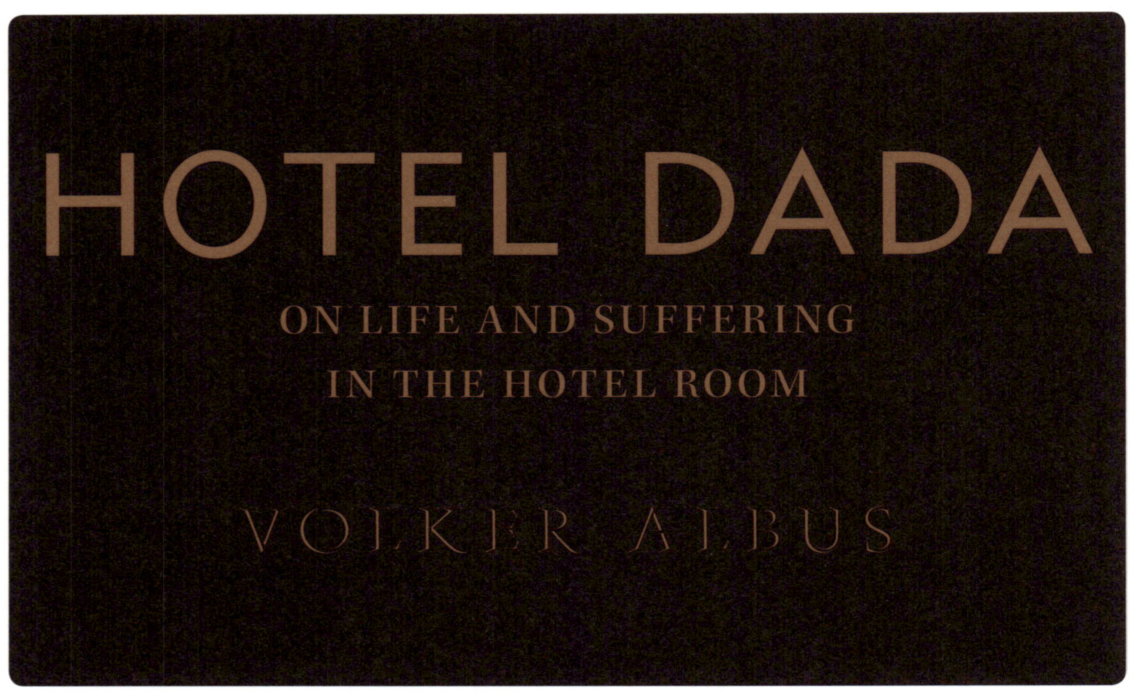

HOTEL DADA

ON LIFE AND SUFFERING IN THE HOTEL ROOM

VOLKER ALBUS

A frequent traveler, or better said someone who travels with regularity, I am repeatedly surprised by the creative potential demonstrated by the architects of everyday hotel rooms. Even after 20 years of exhibition, teaching, and lecturing experience at home and abroad and the associated stays at a most varied spectrum of hotels, from one-star to five-star accommodations, I consistently find myself confronted by rooms with design and furnishing constellations that demand a degree of adaptability painful even to the most experienced hotel guest. Above all, the technical devices that define the interface between the room and the guest often result in highly challenging mental exercises, in which one must be willing to engage. This starts with the domicile that needs to be opened with an electronic chip card (which frequently malfunctions, causing the exhausted guest to return from the 11th floor to the distant lobby). It continues with the centrally controlled electrical supply (which naturally also feeds the refrigerator and any potential charging devices) and climaxes with a devious twist in the challenge of decoding the operation of the central air, television, and lighting elements dispersed throughout the room. Particularly the subtle differences between various light sources, the individual or orchestrated switches situated either next to the bed or in the hall, and, not least, their varying and adjustable light intensity, often require three or four trips back and forth between the bed, bathroom, and hall in the attempt to make adjustments.

At some point the enigma of the atmospheric light circuitry has been penetrated, and the guest can concentrate on relaxing in the comfort of this temporary home. Of course, in order for this to work to even a limited extent, the surrounding conditions must be right. That is to say, the *hardware* of the interior architecture must be designed in such as manner that truly everyone feels comfortable, or to put it differently, that no guest is aesthetically or morally disturbed, let alone offended, by the design of the lodgings.

IN CONCRETE TERMS, THIS ESSENTIALLY MEANS MEDIOCRITY, MEDIOCRITY, AND ONCE AGAIN MEDIOCRITY, ON AN INTERNATIONAL LEVEL AS WELL. Regardless whether conceived as rustic or classically elegant, postmodern, or African, the typical stylistic renditions of the hotel room are realized in a supremely average manner. Here the generally applicable concepts and approximations of certain styles are distilled into the most popular clichés and visions. Nowhere else but in the suites and sleeping quarters of the commercial host do we find these kinds of watered-down interpretations of Philippe Starck and Laura Ashley, Antonio Citterio, and Friedensreich Hundertwasser, Art Deco, or Bauhaus. Only seldom is the ascribed mode of design carried to the point of exaggeration. This means that even within specific motifs a kind of muzak aesthetic[1] predominates, comparable to the omnipresent drizzle of music heard in department stores, supermarkets, and public transport systems.

Usually no less harmonious in its representative function is the structure of the rooms. If one adds together the individual components of a hotel room in correspon-

1 The term »muzak« is used to describe the more or less uniform background music that the public is continuously surrounded by, familiar in particular from shopping centers and hotel lobbies. See Joseph Lanza, *Elevator Music: A Surreal History of Muzak, Easy-Listening, and Other Moodsong* (London, 1995).

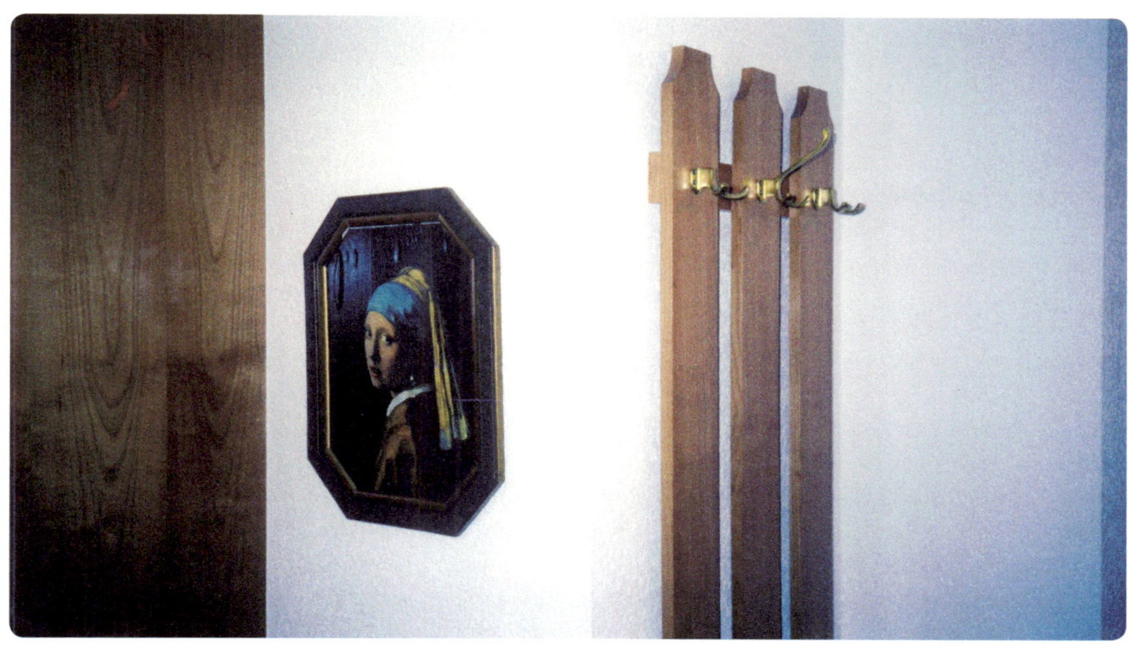

FREIBURG '03, FOTO / PHOTO: VOLKER ALBUS

übertragen auf ein Primetime-Format der deutschen Fernsehlandschaft, der durchgängigen Braun- und Beigetonigkeit einer Rosamunde-Pilcher-Verfilmung im ZDF.

Nicht minder repräsentativ ausbalanciert ist meist die Struktur der Zimmer. Denn addiert man die einzelnen Elemente eines Hotelzimmers entsprechend ihrer Gattungszugehörigkeit, ergibt sich daraus eine Art komprimierte Wohnung, ein Cross-over der ein *normales* Heim definierenden Funktionsbereiche. Sieht man einmal von der Küche ab, die sich allenfalls rudimentär in einem Eisschrank – Minibar – und einem besonders in angelsächsischen Bleiben beliebten Teekocher abbildet, zeichnet sich das durchschnittlich möblierte Hotelzimmer durch eine Zusammenlegung der charakteristischen Möbel des Schlaf-, des Wohn- und des Arbeitsbereichs aus.

Dominiert wird die Szenerie von *dem* Hotelmöbel schlechthin, dem Bett. Mit seiner Qualität steht und fällt das Wohlbefinden des Gastes. Das beginnt schon mit der Dimensionierung und der Positionierung im Raum. Zu schmale oder zu kurze Betten (oder gar Bettdecken!) machen die Übernachtung zur Tortur. Und Betten, die einseitig an eine Wand gerückt sind, wecken bestenfalls Kindheitserinnerungen oder führen zu eher klaustrophobischen Halluzinationsschüben während des Tiefschlafs. Glücklicherweise trifft man diese wandseitige Stellung der Schlafstatt in der Regel nur in Einzelzimmern der unteren Kategorie an und, das ist allerdings die Ausnahme, in den Hotelzimmern von Paris, wo das Bett in Etablissements der Ein-, Zwei-, Dreisternekategorie zumindest gefühlt größer als das Zimmer ist – was zu akrobatischen Turnübungen vornehmlich außerhalb des Bettes führt und man es dementsprechend vorzieht, erst gar nicht aufzustehen. Paris eben.

Im *klassisch* möblierten Hotelzimmer jenseits der französischen Capitale versucht man jedoch, den Gast nicht allzu direkt auf bettengebundene Aktivitäten festzulegen, sondern dem Ambiente den Anschein einer richtigen Wohnung zu geben. Das ist natürlich in erster Linie eine Frage des Platzes. Und der steht eigentlich nur in Häusern der absoluten *hors catégorie*[2] zur Verfügung. Ausladende Sitzgruppen mit Sofa, Sesseln und Couchtisch etwa finden sich ausschließlich hier. Und nicht nur das! Jedes noch so kleine, den großbürgerlichen Wohlstand demonstrierende Merkmal findet hier seine vordergründig rein dekorative Reminiszenz. Berge von Kissen, große und kleine Teppiche, mehrschichtige Vorhangdrapierungen, Vitrinen mit Vasen und Obstschalen, Blumenbouquets, Deckchen, Spiegel, Aschenbecher, Kerzenständer, Tisch- und Stehlampen, Zeitschriften, ja, ganze Bücherwände verleihen dem eigentlich nur temporär genutzten Ort den Anschein eines kontinuierlich über Generationen eingewohnten Stammsitzes. Nicht zu vergessen die Kunst, die diese Salons nicht selten wie die Gemächer eines kenntnisreichen Sammlers erscheinen lassen und ihr Panorama des luxuriösen Flitters in eine Aura des noblen Geschmacks erheben soll.

Dieses Bühnenbild erreicht bisweilen eine solche Perfektion, dass globetrottende und äußerst solvente Zeit-

2 Terminologie aus dem Radsport: Mit *hors catégorie* bezeichnet man dort die schwersten Berganstiege, z. B. während der Tour de France, die tatsächlich nur von den Besten der Besten gemeistert werden.

2 A term from bicycle racing: *hors catégorie* is used to describe the most difficult mountainous ascents, as found in the Tour de France, which truly only the best of the best can master.

dence with their respective functions, the result is a kind of condensed apartment, a crossover between the functional areas that would define a normal home. If one leaves out the kitchen, which always takes the rudimentary form of a refrigerator or mini-bar and an electric kettle (particularly popular in hotels in English-speaking countries), the averagely equipped hotel room is characterized by a compilation of the furnishings typical of sleeping, living, and working areas.

The setting is dominated by the ultimate piece of hotel furniture, the bed, the quality of which is crucial to a guest's wellbeing. This begins with its dimensions and positioning relative to the given space. Overly narrow or short beds (or even bedcovers!) can turn a night's sleep into a torture session. Beds that are pushed up against the wall on one side recall memories of childhood, at best, but tend to lead to waves of claustrophobic hallucinations during the deep sleep phase. Luckily one generally encounters this wall positioned piece of sleeping furniture in single rooms of the lowest category as well as in the exceptional situation of Paris hotel rooms, where in establishments with one, two, or three stars they seem to be even larger than the rooms themselves—which leads to acrobatics outside the bed, and so it's preferable to simply not get up. That's Paris.

Beyond the French capital, in hotel rooms with *classic* furnishings an attempt is made not to limit the guest to bed-related activities but to convey an ambiance simulating a real apartment. This is of course primarily a matter of space, a commodity that is really only available in establishments of the absolute *hors catégorie*.[2] Uncomfortable looking seating arrangements including a sofa, armchairs, and couch table are found exclusively in such hotels. And not only that! Every element of upper middle class luxury is suggested and manifested in purely decorative dimensions. Mountains of pillows, large and small rugs, multilayered swaths of curtains, glass cabinets with vases and bowls of fruit, bouquets of flowers, little blankets, mirrors, ashtrays, candlesticks, table lamps, standing lamps, newspapers, and, yes, even entire walls of books lend this only temporarily used place the appearance of a familial seat that has been in continuous use for generations. Not to be omitted is the art that is often used to make these salons seem like the private chambers of an expert collector by enhancing the interior panorama of a luxurious drop-in abode with an aura of elite taste.

This kind of theatrical scenario has meanwhile achieved such a level of perfection that our highly solvent, globetrotting contemporaries, such as Udo Lindenberg or the Karstadt Investor Nicolas Berggruen, now only live in hotels, thus having absolutely no private address in the traditional sense. (That social magnates of such caliber naturally have workplaces at their disposal, which are used exclusively by them or their company and that these individuals are in fact not as homeless as they pretend to be generally goes unmentioned.)

Nevertheless, these are ultimately the very kinds of legends that surround the people of the hotel, painted in the lurid tones of a society magazine, and that repeatedly give this form of temporary living its allure and overarching mystique. Regardless of the number of stars a lodging has acquired and the run-down corner of town in which it is situated, the very word »hotel« initially summons visions of good service, sleeping in, being far away, and stepping out of one's daily life. This is so rooted in the inherent self-understanding of this type of building that every last hotelier will attempt to maintain a fundamental typology of interior decor, even in institutions of the most basic category. This means that even a guest of the most economical price class should gain the impression not merely of renting a room to sleep in but accommodations for both living and working.

However, the actual furnishings diminish in quality with the decreasing number of stars. From two armchairs and a table—four stars—to an armchair and little side table in the three-star and then merely one seating option, including even the spartan stool in the hostel recommended by a faint, single star, the furnishings of the hotel room precisely replicate the gap between the villa and the single-room apartment of a 1960s slab cement building.

This also applies to the office. Whereas in the upper hotel categories this portion of the hotel room can look like the CEO command center of a mid-size company whose shares trade on the German Dax, the sober combination of desk, chair, and lamp in three- and two-star accommodations unmistakably conveys to the resident that he or she is by no means a beacon of success, at least not within the business world. Although not every guest is travelling in the service of some (global) company, those who are underway as »representatives of . . .« and who thus have their expenses covered by their supervising authority experience with every overnight stay in this kind of demonstrative averageness a form psychological demontage extraordinaire. No reprimand, no communiqué from the upper levels of management could be so demoralizing to the dependent employee as being housed in a hotel with only two or three stars. In this sense, it could be described as a most sophisticated form of intimidation, and if one can infer this kind of cheapo booking as a not-so-subtle hint, one would certainly be advised to quickly look for another job.

genossen wie Udo Lindenberg oder der Karstadt-Investor Nicolas Berggruen tatsächlich nur noch im Hotel wohnen, sie also gar keine Privatadresse im herkömmlichen Sinne mehr angeben. (Dass gesellschaftliche Größen dieses Kalibers selbstverständlich über ausschließlich von ihnen beziehungsweise ihrer Firma genutzte Arbeitsstätten verfügen, dass sie so *heimatlos,* wie sie vorgeben, nun auch wieder nicht sind, wird dabei allerdings nicht weiter thematisiert.)

Sei es drum, letztendlich sind es genau solche Legenden rund um die *Menschen im Hotel,* die, *Bunte*-mäßig aufgezogen, den Mythos dieser Form des Wohnens auf Zeit immer wieder neu befeuern und insgesamt sehnsuchtsvoll verklären. Egal, mit wie vielen Sternen eine Logis ausgezeichnet ist; egal, in welch' einer heruntergekommenen Ecke der Stadt ein Hotel angesiedelt ist, allein der Begriff *Hotel* assoziiert im ersten Moment durchweg Vorstellungen von gutem Service, von Ausschlafen, von Weit-weg-Sein, von Ausstieg aus dem Alltag. Somit begründet es sich im ureigenen Selbstverständnis dieser Gebäudegattung, dass auch noch der letzte Hotelier versuchen wird, die grundsätzliche Typologie des Interieurs selbst in der untersten Kategorien durchzuhalten. Das heißt: Auch dem Gast in den niederen Preisklassen soll der Eindruck vermittelt werden, dass er nicht nur ein Schlafzimmer mietet, sondern eine Unterkunft, in der er *auch* wohnen und *auch* arbeiten kann.

Allerdings nimmt die tatsächliche Ausstattung mit jedem Stern weniger deutlich ab. Von zwei Sesseln plus Tisch – vier Sterne – über einen Sessel plus kleinen Tisch in der Dreisterneklasse und nur noch einer Sitzgelegenheit bis zum spartanischen Hocker in der mit nur noch einem einzigen blassen Stern *ausgezeichneten* Herberge bildet die Einrichtung des Hotelzimmers exakt das Gefälle zwischen Villa und Einzimmerappartement in einer Plattenbausiedlung aus den 1960er-Jahren ab.

D**as gilt auch für das *Büro*.** Während dieses Segment der Einrichtung eines Hotelzimmers in den oberen Kategorien dem Kommandostand eines CEO eines mittleren Dax-Unternehmens gleichen kann, macht die nüchterne Kombination aus Schreibtisch, Stuhl und Lampe in den Zwei- und Dreisterneunterkünften jedem hier Einkehrenden unmissverständlich klar, was für ein kleines Licht er realiter darstellt – zumindest was seinen Status im Geschäftsleben anbelangt. Nun ist nicht jeder Gast in Diensten irgendeiner (global agierenden) Firma unterwegs, diejenigen aber, die *im Auftrag von* reisen, deren Rechnung also von einer über ihnen stehenden Instanz beglichen wird, erfahren mit jeder Übernachtung in einer derart offen demonstrierten Mittelmäßigkeit eine Psychobehandlung der Extraklasse. Keine Ermahnung, keine Empfehlung aus der Chefetage dürfte eine solche Tiefenwirkung auf das Gemüt des abhängig Beschäftigten entfalten wie die Einweisung in ein Drei- oder Zweisternehotel. Insofern könnte man auch von Mobbing auf höchstem Niveau sprechen, bedeutet doch eine solche Billigbuchung nichts anderes als einen ultimativer Wink mit dem Zaunpfahl, sich doch bitte schnellstens nach einer anderen Stelle umzusehen.

ES **ist jedoch nicht nur das *Design* eines solchen Büroverschlags, das sich bestens für ein derart infames Depressionsmartyrium eignet.** Auch die übrigen Insignien eines Hotelzimmers – Dusche, WC, Fernseher, Lüftung, Beleuchtung – addieren sich zu einer fast schon perfide zu nennenden Wohnkulisse. Denn dieses Sammelsurium von vertrauten Einrichtungselementen gibt in Wahrheit nur vor, genauso zu funktionieren, wie wir es von zu Hause gewohnt sind. In Wahrheit tut es das aber ganz und gar nicht. Duschen, die zu eng sind, Wasserströme, die man nicht regulieren kann, tropfende Toilettenspüler, ohrenbetäubende Lüftungen, schlecht positionierte Lampen, diffuses Licht, fleckige Bettwäsche, an der Decke oder auf Schränken montierte TV-Geräte, die, hat man sie endlich in Gang gesetzt, nur krisselige Fernsehbilder liefern, dünne Zwischenwände, elend schallintensive Bodenbeläge – all das summiert sich zu einer Collage des Schreckens, die mit dem eigentlichen Sinn und Zweck dieses Ortes, nämlich einem hier einkehrenden und obendrein zahlenden *Gast* ein erholsames Obdach zu gewähren, nicht mehr das Geringste zu tun hat. Wüsste man nicht, dass man sich in einem Hotelzimmer befindet, man könnte glatt auf die Idee kommen, sich in einer prototypischen Installation eines zeitgenössischen Künstlers à la John Bock, Manfred Pernice, Mike Kelley oder Sarah Lucas zu befinden. Und dann würde man vermutlich über die besonders gelungene ekelerregende Ästhetik der Oberflächen, das *dekonstruktivistische* Gegenüber einzelner Elemente und das einen aberwitzigen Dadaismus *kultivierende* Gesamtarrangement fabulieren.

Nun neigt man bisweilen schon allein aufgrund der Ausweglosigkeit, einer solchen Bleibe stante pede zu entkommen, dazu, diese Zufallsarchitektur in einem Anflug von Fatalismus genau so, also als so nie erlebte, völlig absurde Installation zu betrachten und dementsprechend distanziert zu goutieren; das Problem ist nur, dass einem angesichts des permanenten Terrors der im Zimmer nistenden Mikroorganismen wie Lüftung, TV-Gerät und Wasserspülung mit jeder ihrer Aktionen immer wieder bewusst wird, dass sich die Realität weitaus dadaistischer darstellt als das gelungenste Kunstwerk – zumindest was die Realitäten des Hotelzimmerdesigns anbelangt.

IT is not merely the *design* of this kind of minimal office unit that makes it a suitable medium for this kind of depressive martyrdom. Also the other insignia of the hotel room—the shower, toilet, television, air system, and lighting—create the aggregate image of a residential scenario that could almost be described as perfidious. This pieced-together collection of familiar furnishings and fittings actually only pretends to function in the way that we are accustomed to in our homes. In actuality it does not at all. Showers that are too small, streams of water that cannot be adjusted, running toilets, deafening ventilation, badly positioned lamps, diffuse lighting, stained sheets, televisions mounted onto the ceiling or shelving that, once finally brought into operation, only emit a picture of static, thin partitioning walls, horribly echoing flooring—together all these things produce a collage so horrifying that is has nothing more in common with the purpose and intention of the institution, that is to provide the visiting and paying guest a soothing place of refuge. If one were not certain of being in a hotel room, one might have the impression of being situated in an installation typical of a contemporary artist à la John Bock, Manfred Pernice, Mike Kelley, or Sarah Lucas. In that case, one would muse about the disgustingly alienating aesthetic of the surfaces, the deconstructive juxtaposition of individual components, and the crazy *cultivated* Dadaism of the entire ensemble.

If only due to the hopelessness of avoiding this kind of abode *stante pede,* one sometimes—in a moment of fatalism—tends to objectively savor this random architecture by viewing it as a yet unseen and absolutely absurd installation. However, the problem is that the permanent threat posed by the microorganisms nesting in the room, recalled by every activation of the ventilation, television, and water faucet, repeatedly makes one aware that reality is far more Dadaistic than the successful work of art, or at least so are the realities of hotel room design.

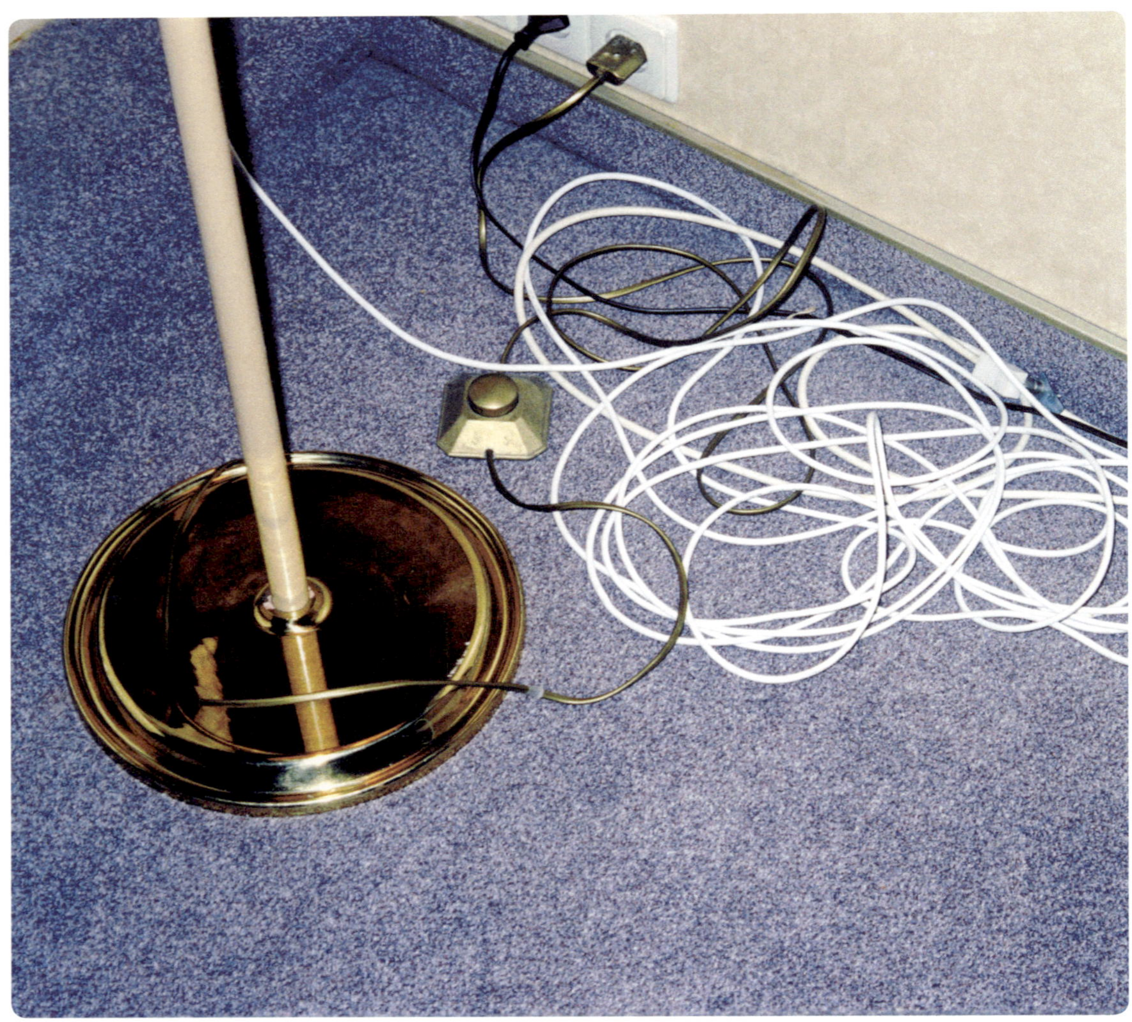

HARLEM '01 FOTO · PHOTO · VOLKER ALBUS

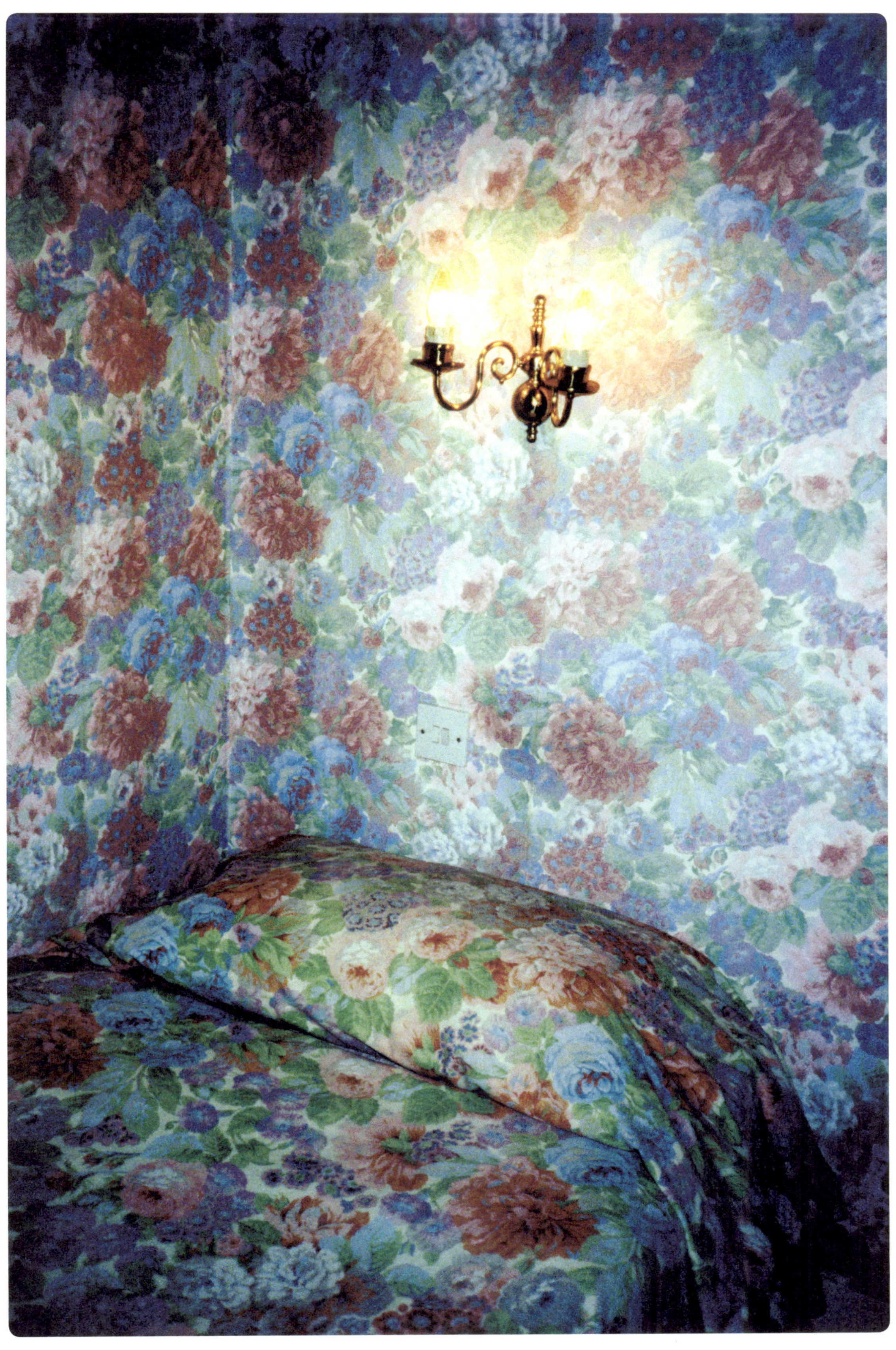

LONDON '95 FOTO · PHOTO · VOLKER ALBUS

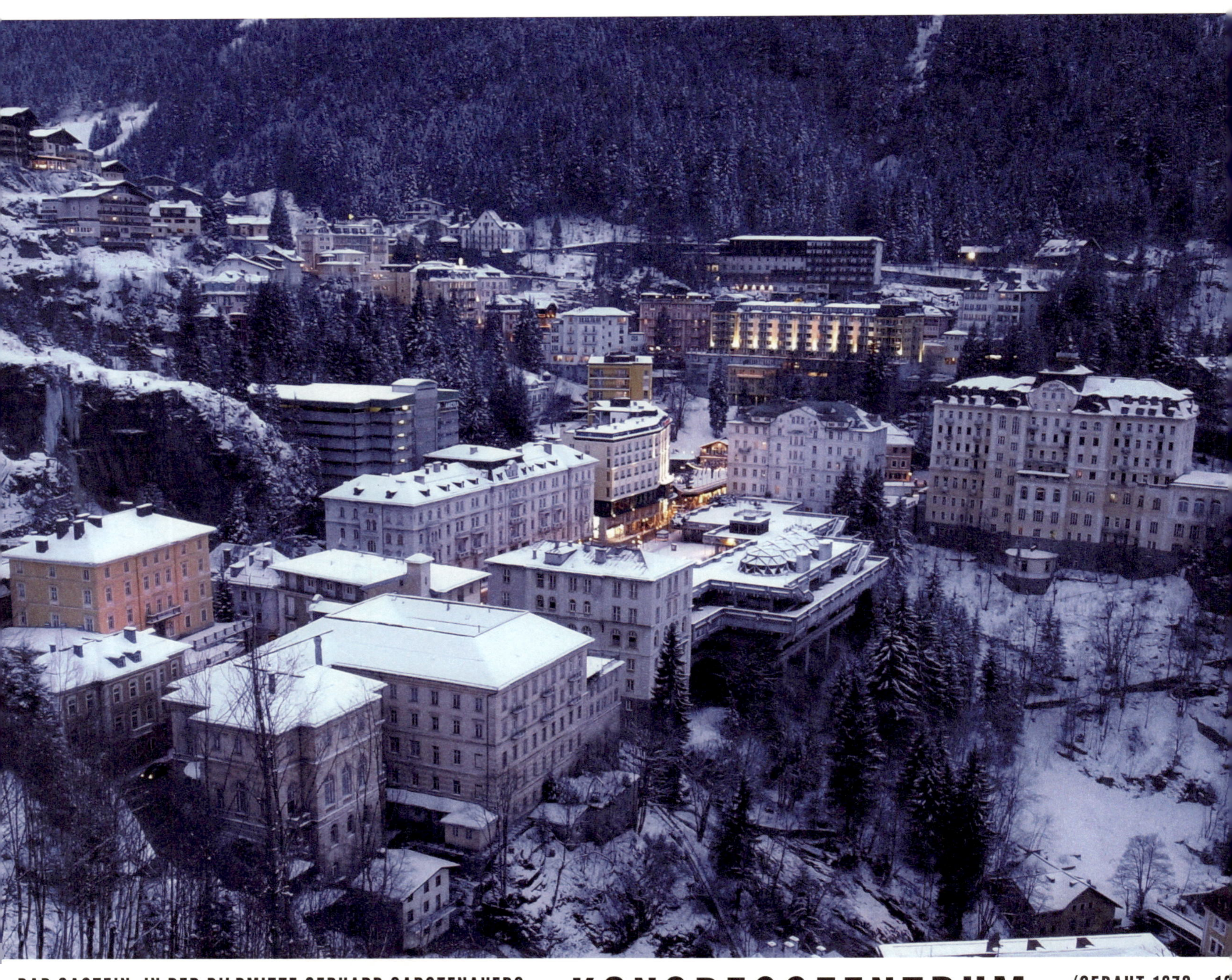

BAD GASTEIN, IN DER BILDMITTE GERHARD GARSTENAUERS »KONGRESSZENTRUM« (GEBAUT 1970 – 19
BAD GASTEIN, AT THE CENTER IS GERHARD GARSTENAUER'S (BUILT 1970 – 19

Foto / Photo: Markus Miessen

JENSEITS DES GENERISCHEN

DAS HOTEL ALS ORT DER TEMPORÄREN AUSNAHME

MARKUS MIESSEN

Was charakterisiert ein Hotel heutzutage? Und was zeichnet es in der Jetztzeit als einen Ort des temporären Wohnens aus? Wenn wir von Hotels sprechen, meinen wir entweder einzigartige, eher kleinere Familienunternehmen an einem Ende des Spektrums oder – am anderen Ende – große, zumeist global operierende Ketten, die versuchen, durch erhöhte wirtschaftliche Effizienz und große Buchungsvolumen über Onlineplattformen den Markt zu kontrollieren. Bei dieser Kluft zwischen dem einerseits Superlokalen und dem andererseits Superglobalen – zumindest hinsichtlich der organisatorischen Infrastrukturen hinter dem Physischen und Erfahrbaren – stellt sich die Frage, was es einem *Hotel* eigentlich ermöglicht, sowohl philosophisch als auch physisch einen irgendwie einzigartigen Raum und Ort zu konstruieren und zu produzieren. Aus der Perspektive eines Architekten darf man sich natürlich fragen, ob die Architektur selbst bei diesen Überlegungen eine Rolle spielen darf, kann oder sollte – sowohl hinsichtlich eines Terrains oder einer Geografie, die weiter zu fassen sind als allein das jeweilige Gebäude.

Hotels sollten Orte der persönlichen Erfahrung sein. Ein Hotel ist immer ein Schauplatz temporärer Mikrogesellschaften, ein Ort, der sich von der eigenen häuslichen Umgebung absetzt, an die man in der räumlichen und operativen Erfahrung gewöhnt ist. Hotels sollten nicht erproben generisch zu wirken, um Kunden anzuziehen, sondern sie sollten vielmehr versuchen, das Klientel, das sie ansprechen wollen, zu definieren. Dies gilt zumindest, wenn sie der Idee anhängen, dass ein Hotel ein Ort sein sollte, an den der Gast zurückkehrt, und es nicht nur eine einfache Dienstleistung für diejenigen erbringt, die allein einen Ort brauchen, wo sie nachts schlafen können. Gewiss gibt es viele unterschiedliche Hotelkonzepte oder wirtschaftliche Modelle für einen solchen Betrieb; einige von ihnen sind sogar extrem erfolgreich, wenn auch aus einer kulturellen Perspektive nicht alle unbedingt erstrebenswert sind. Historisch gesehen waren neue Technologien immer etwas, was Hoteliers aufgegriffen und umgesetzt haben. Heutzutage allerdings scheint das viel dringendere Anliegen zu sein, den Hotelraum zu *ent-technologisieren.*

In unserer zeitgenössischen Kultur, die geprägt ist von allerlei neuen Konzepten, Formaten und Typologien, ist es wichtiger denn je, Alleinstellungsmerkmale zu schaffen: Die Gründe dafür, dass ich als Kunde zu einem Domizil reisen und dort einchecken möchte, sind nicht selten, dass es ein spezifisches Versprechen gibt, was mich dort erwartet, das hoffentlich auch eingehalten wird. Und schon dieses Versprechen muss sich von den Verheißungen der anderen absetzen. Hotels werden immer mehr als grundsätzlich urbane Erlebnisse vermarktet und wahrgenommen, als Mikroutopien hinsichtlich des gesellschaftlichen Miteinanders in Bezug auf Nähe einerseits, aber – wenn nötig – auch Anonymität bietend, die für eine autonome Existenz mindestens ebenso notwendig ist.

Die meisten Hotels sind Räume der temporären menschlichen Aufbewahrung. Wenn man Glück hat, sind

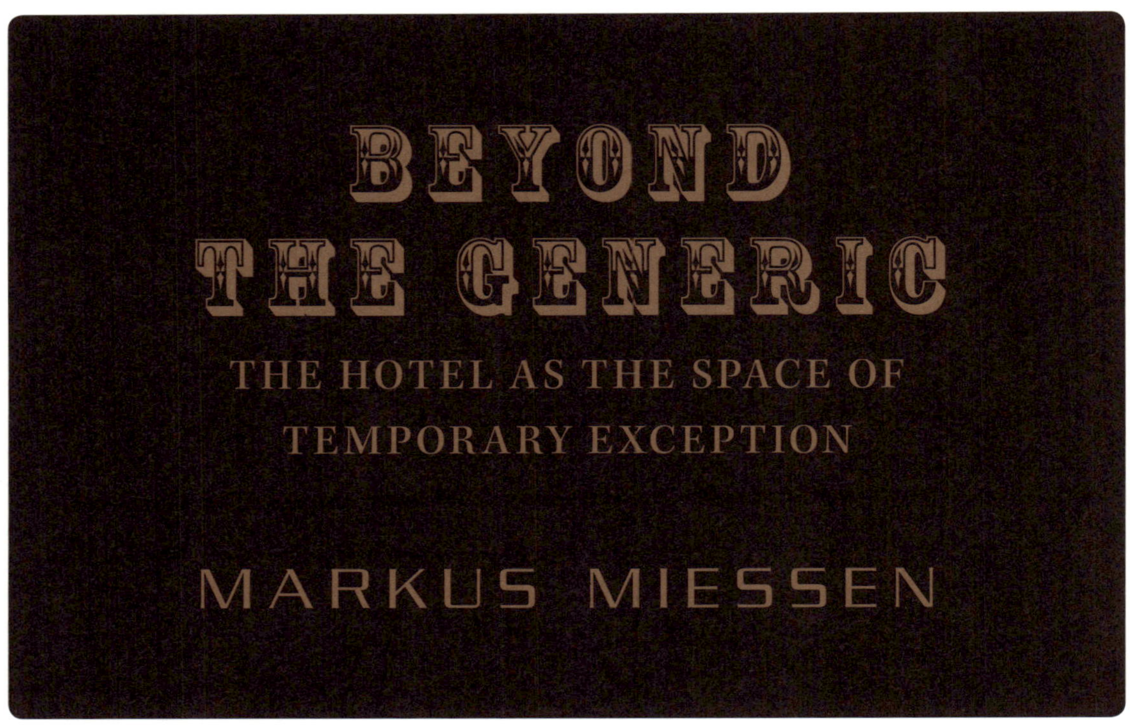

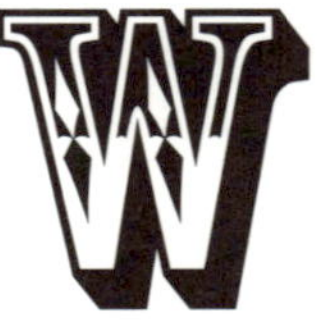

hat constitutes a hotel today? And what constitutes a hotel today as a space of temporary habitation? Usually when we refer to hotels, we mean either one-of-a-kind, small-scale, and often family-run businesses, at the one end of the spectrum, or large, mostly globally operated chains, which try to control the market by increasing economic efficiency and maintaining large-scale booking contracts with online platforms, at the other end. Within this divide between the superlocal and the superglobal—at least in terms of the organizational infrastructure behind the physical and experiencable—the question arises as to what allows a »hotel« to both philosophically and physically construct and produce a somewhat unique space and place. Speaking from the point of view of an architect, one wonders, of course, whether architecture may, can, or even should play a role in these considerations—maybe even in terms of a terrain and geography larger than simply the scale of an individual building.

Hotels should be spaces of and for personal experience. A hotel is always a space for temporary micro-societies, a space that sets itself apart from the domestic environment to which one is accustomed in one's everyday spatial and operational experience. Hotels should not pretend to be generic as a strategy for attracting customers but should to try to specify the clientele that they wish to attract—at least if they subscribe to the idea of the hotel as a place of return, rather than a simple service catering to those who merely need a good night's rest. Indeed, there are many different hotel concepts and economic models, some of them extremely successful, but not all are necessarily desirable from a cultural perspective. Historically, new technologies have always been something that hotel owners have attempted to implement. However, the most pressing need today seems to be a de-techologization of the hotel space.

Within our contemporary culture of novel concepts, formats, and typologies, it has become more important than ever to create unique selling points (USPs): reasons why I, as the customer, would wish to travel to and check into a residence, which represents and hopefully also delivers a certain and specific promise that sets itself apart from the promises of others. Hotels are increasingly being marketed and perceived as essentially urban experiences, as micro-utopias in terms of the social contract of proximity, which offers, if required, the anonymity that is necessary for an autonomous existence.

Most hotels are spaces of temporary human storage. If one is lucky, they are clean, looked after, and even serve an acceptable breakfast. As a guest, one often wishes for personal commitment on the part of the owners, who ideally still leave space for the individual. This points to the most important characteristic of a successful hotel. Even if part of a chain, each individual establishment should be managed as if it were one-of-a-kind and still in the hands of the founding family; its operations should be based on an understanding of trust, spatial generosity, and excellence in service. In a good hotel one will always remember rooms in

sie sauber, gepflegt und servieren sogar ein akzeptables Frühstück. Der Gast wünscht sich stets persönliches Engagement der Inhaber, das dem Individuum aber im Idealfall immer noch genügend Raum lässt. Dies verweist auf die wichtigste Eigenschaft eines erfolgreichen Hotels. Selbst wenn dieses Teil einer Kette ist, sollte jedes individuelle Haus so geführt werden, als wäre es einzigartig und immer noch in den Händen der Gründerfamilie; sein operatives Geschäft sollte auf Vertrauen, räumlicher Großzügigkeit und auf exzellentem Service basieren. In einem guten Hotel wird man sich stets an Zimmer erinnern, in dem man schon zuvor gute Nächte verbracht hat. Leider ist dies in den meisten Hotels einfach unmöglich. Gleichzeitig hat es einen gewissen Reiz, dass das Wesen vieler (vor allem auf Geschäftsleute ausgerichteter) Hotels generische Züge trägt, da sie gar nicht erst versuchen, Fragen der Individualität aufzugreifen, sondern einfach nur darauf angelegt sind, eine Umgebung zu schaffen, die vor allem rationalisiert und effizient funktioniert.

Ein gutes Hotel schafft nicht nur das Gefühl, in einem *Vakuum* zu sein, sondern es erlaubt uns, temporär unter anderen, hoffentlich weniger komplizierten Bedingungen agieren zu können. Vorübergehend *rebootet* es das System des Gastes, kommt quasi einem Neustart gleich. Dies bedeutet gleichzeitig, dass sich heutige Hotels auch mit der Frage des Arbeitsraumes auseinandersetzen müssen, selbst wenn dies nicht unbedingt das Bedürfnis nach einem richtigen Platz zum Arbeiten nach sich zieht. Angesichts der Rahmenbedingungen unserer Zeit, in denen die meisten Menschen heutzutage gewohnt sind zu agieren, ist es relativ unwahrscheinlich, dass die Gäste in einem Hotel vollkommen *unplugged,* also gänzlich losgelöst, sein wollen. Stattdessen bevorzugen sie vielmehr einen Szenenwechsel, eine Unterbrechung ihrer Routine(n), eine Atempause – quasi eine Parallelwirklichkeit. In einem Hotel, dessen Besuch sich lohnt, wird dem Gast vorsichtig – und idealerweise so, dass er es nicht merkt – geholfen, anders zu denken. Keinesfalls soll er auf eine stressige Art mental angeregt werden. Genau hier kommt das Konzept eines *Refugiums* ins Spiel: ein Ort, der abseits der ausgetretenen Pfade liegt und es dem Einzelnen ermöglicht, eine vorübergehende Distanz – sowohl körperlich als auch geistig – zwischen dem Alltäglichen und dem Außergewöhnlichen zu schaffen. Diese Erfahrung wird ermöglicht, wenn dem Gast multiple, also vielfältige Optionen angeboten werden und ihm persönliche wie programmatische Aktivitäten offen stehen, die Parallelwirklichkeiten schaffen.

Etliche Hotels kommen einem da in den Sinn: familiengeführte Alpenklassiker wie das Waldhaus Sils im schweizerischen Oberengadin, das Hotel Hochschober im österreichischen Kärnten oder außergewöhnliche Häuser wie das Grand Hotel Le Trois Rois in Basel, das ehemalige Railway Hotel in Hua Hin, Thailand (heute Centara Grand Beach Resort & Villas Hua Hin), und das Fasano in São Paolo. Jenseits dessen, was man herausragende Exzellenz nennen könnte, gibt es natürlich immer Sonderfälle, die sich durch ganz besondere Alleinstellungsmerkmale auszeichnen, indem sie sich auf spezifische Kulturangebote, besondere Programme oder gesundheitsbezogene Themen – wie beispielsweise im Lanserhof in der Nähe von Innsbruck – spezialisieren. Selbst kleine und preiswerte Einrichtungen können heutzutage in die internationale Karte der *places to be* aufgenommen werden, indem sie etwa unerwartete oder sogar künstlerische und bibliophile *Extras* anbieten, wie beispielsweise die Andreas-Züst-Bibliothek im Alpenhof in Oberegg. Andreas Züst war sowohl in der Schweiz als auch in der gesamten europäischen Kunstszene eine legendäre Figur. Er verkörperte das Ideal der Renaissance mit einem unersättlichen Appetit auf Wissen und war zudem ein Buchliebhaber. Seine Bibliothek spiegelt all diese Leidenschaften wider und enthält gut 12.000 Bände etwa über Meteorologie, Geologie, Astronomie, Physik, Botanik, Kunstgeschichte, Anthropologie, Polarexpeditionen, Fotografie, Malerei, Literatur, Musik, Kitsch, UFOs, die Hell's Angels und eine Vielzahl anderer Themen. Kurz gesagt, dies sind Bücher über fast alles, was die Essenz unserer Kultur ausmacht. Ein kulturbezogen ähnlich gewiefter Ansatz wird vom Hotel Castell in Zuoz verfolgt, dessen Renovierung der historischen Burg durch ein neues Gebäude ermöglicht wurde (entworfen vom niederländischen Architekturbüro UN Studio), das direkt neben den alten Mauern errichtet wurde und wesentlich zur Finanzierung des Hotelbetriebs beiträgt. Dieses Model setzt vor allem auf eine urbane Klientel, die sich für zeitgenössische kulturelle und künstlerische Diskurse interessiert und an ihnen auch selbst teilnimmt.

EINE VOLLKOMMEN ANDERE, ABER ZIEMLICH INTERESSANTE TYPOLOGIE WIRD IM DORF VNÀ IM SCHWEIZERISCHEN UNTERENGADIN ERPROBT, WO DAS HAUS PIZ TSCHÜTTA ALS EIN DEZENTRALISIERTES HOTEL BETRIEBEN WIRD. Es besteht aus einer Reihe von über das ganze Dorf verteilten individuellen Zimmern und Räumen. Auf diese Weise wird die Illusion geschaffen, dass der einzelne Gast ganz in die lokale Dorfkultur eintaucht. Gleichzeitig werden die einheimischen Bewohner so unterstützt, die der Anziehungskraft der Städte widerstanden haben. Ein solches Modell stellt mithin einen Gegenentwurf zur Typologie der zeitgenössischen Hotelkette dar, auch wenn sich selbst solche Unternehmen hier und da scheinbar authentisch an lokale Gegebenheiten anpassen. Diese Strategie wird etwa

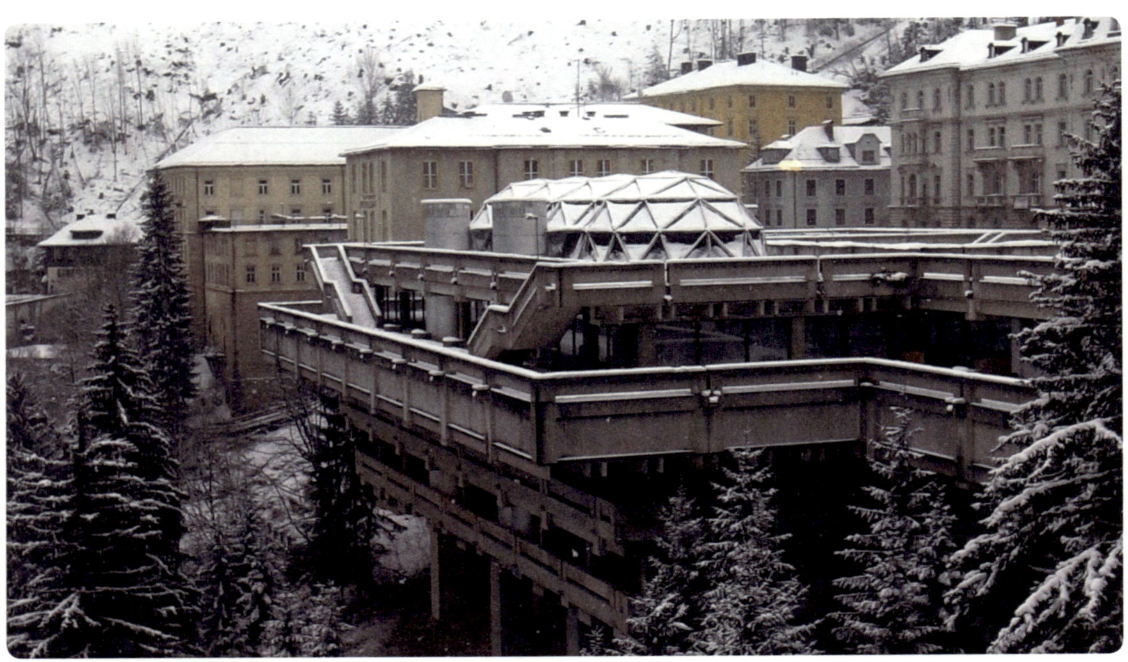

Gerhard Garstenauers
Gerhard Garstenauer's »Kongresszentrum«
Foto / Photo: Markus Miessen

which one has previous spent nights. Unfortunately, in most hotels this is simply impossible. At the same time, there is also something appealing about the generic nature of many (especially business-oriented) hotels, since they do not even attempt to address the question of individuality but simply try to create an environment that functions well in an operationally streamlined and efficient manner.

A good hotel does not only create the sense of being in a vacuum but allows one to temporarily operate under different, hopefully less complicated, circumstances. It temporarily reboots one's system. This also means that today's hotels must come to terms with the question of workspace, even if this does not necessarily entail the demand for a workspace proper. Given the new framework in which most people have become accustomed to operating today, it is now quite unlikely that guests want to be completely unplugged. Instead, they are looking for a change of scene, a break in routine(s), a momentary respite, and, hence, a parallel reality. In a hotel worth visiting, the guest is gently—and hopefully unnoticeably—being helped to think differently, to be mentally stimulated in a non-stressful manner. This is precisely where the concept of the »hideaway« comes into play: an off-route location that allows the individual to put a temporary distance—both physical and mental—between the everyday and the exceptional. This experience is founded on providing multi-optional possibilities and an ability to create personal, programmatic activities that create parallel realities.

A number of hotels come to mind: family-run alpine classics, such as the Waldhaus Sils in the Engadine or the Hochschober in Carinthia, and outstanding (grand) hotels, such as the Le Trois Rois in Basel, the Railway Hotel in Huahin, or the Fasano in São Paolo. Beyond what one might call outstanding excellence, there are of course special cases based on specific selling points, which focus on specific cultural offerings, special programs, or health-related topics, such as the Lanserhof near Innsbruck. Even small and inexpensive institutions can nowadays be included on the international map of places-to-be by offering somewhat unexpected or even artistic and bibliophile »extras,« such as the Andreas Züst library installed in the Alpenhof in St. Gallen. Andreas Züst was a legendary figure both within Switzerland and the European art world at large. He was a Renaissance man with an insatiable appetite for knowledge and also a booklover. His library reflected all of these passions and included some 12,000 volumes on topics such as the weather, geology, astronomy, physics, botany, the history of art, anthropology, polar expeditions, photography, painting, literature, music, kitsch, UFOs, Hell's Angels, and a myriad of other related subjects. In short, these were books on almost everything constituting the essence of our culture. A similar approach with equal cultural savvy is being explored by the Hotel Castell in Zuoz, whose historic

von der Ace-Gruppe (mit Häusern in Portland, New York, Los Angeles, Palm Springs, Seattle, London und Panama) verfolgt. Wieder andere Hotels treten als ein vermeintlich historisches Unternehmen auf, wie dies beim Chateau Marmont in Hollywood der Fall ist, einem Teil der André Balazs Properties (unter anderen auch Betreiber von The Standard Hotels, The Mercer, Sunset Beach), oder bei The Bowery Hotel in New York, das vom selben Team wie das Maritime Hotel und das Waverly Inn in der Stadt betrieben wird. Diese zweiten Zuhauses für Hipster lassen sich als eine schnell wachsende neue Spezies von Hotels bezeichnen, die eine neue, lokale Klientel kultivieren, die gar nicht unbedingt über Nacht bleibt. Stattdessen wird das Hotel als Treffpunkt und alternatives Wohnzimmer genutzt. In diesem Zusammenhang lässt sich ebenso die sowohl *trashy* als auch konservativ orientierte Verschmelzung von perfektem Professionalismus und Hipstertum nennen, wie man sie etwa in den Soho Houses (London, New York, Los Angeles, Berlin, Toronto, Miami und Somerset) findet.

EINIGE **der interessanten Fälle in der jüngeren Entwicklung alternativer Modelle temporären Wohnens und Homings sind jene Hoteliers, die erkannt haben, dass eine gewisse Sehnsucht nach Urbanität auch jenseits der Stadt existiert.** Mit anderen Worten: Sie haben es verstanden, ländliche Räume zu gestalten, die ihrer urbanen Klientel eine gewisse Komplexität bieten, allerdings ohne unnötig stressige Beziehungen – sie verschaffen Entspannung und soziales Potenzial ohne Verpflichtungen. Eine solche Herangehensweise benötigt spektakuläre ländliche Schauplätze, an denen die Hotels eine kreative Szenerie bereitstellen, deren Servicequalität zugleich das Angebot einer Plattform der Potenzialität beinhaltet. Ein solches Hotel geht auf die Bedürfnisse und Wünsche der Gäste ein (selbst, wenn diese gar nicht explizit formuliert werden oder jenen bewusst wären). Die *urbane* Komponente solcher Hotelräume liegt in der strategischen Vorausplanung einer verbindenden kreativen Ebene, eines salonartigen Gefüges, das eine intellektuelle Community generiert, selbst, wenn diese dann dort nicht unbedingt mit intellektuellen Fragen befasst ist. Betrachtet man dieses kulturelle Phänomen aus der Perspektive des Architekten, ist dieser Ansatz besonders interessant, weil er die Relevanz des Gestaltens unterstreicht. Dessen Bedeutung liegt hier weniger im Imaginieren und Produzieren einer anderen physischen, also räumlichen Wirklichkeit, sondern – viel wichtiger – im sorgfältigen und kontrollierten *Design* spezifischer Arten von Publikum. Dies gilt auch dann, wenn diese unterschiedlichen Publikumsgruppen möglicherweise gar nicht miteinander reden, wenn sie an den jeweiligen Orten sind. Es geht in diesem Zusammenhang von Architektur vor allem um das Generieren von Momenten, die sich in der unbewussten (Selbst-)Darstellung kontextualisierter Communities ausdrücken. Dieses Modell existiert ebenso innerhalb der urbanen Umgebung, wo an bestimmten Orten versucht wurde, (fast ländliche) Momente der Abgeschlossenheit zu schaffen, die temporär die Stadt ausblenden. Als Beispiel dafür sei etwa die interessante und demokratische Mischung von russischen und türkischen Badehäusern in der 10th Street in New York angeführt, die seit 1892 in gewisser Weise eine Rückzugsmöglichkeit bieten, obwohl sie sich, selbst total öffentlich und überfüllt, mitten in einer von brutaler und endloser Zurschaustellung definierten Stadt befinden.

Den Begriff des Hotels auf eine alternative Weise zu interpretieren bedeutet, sie nicht nur als Orte der Entspannung und des Rückzugs zu denken, sondern auch als produktive Rückzugsbereiche also, die Potenzial für kreative Arbeit bieten, selbst, wenn das *Produkt* eine verspätete Ankunft ist. Die kleine und zugleich grandiose österreichische Alpenstadt Bad Gastein etwa ist ein praktisches Ziel, wenn man verzweifelt das Zurückziehen *und* das Unerwartete braucht. Obwohl das Gasteiner Tal sein volles Potenzial noch nicht erreicht hat und auch immer noch unter sinkenden Besucherzahlen und den Folgen der seit dem späten 20. Jahrhundert schrumpfenden Bevölkerung leidet, birgt es ein interessantes Beispiel dafür, wie eine architektonische Szenerie als ein lokaler Anziehungspunkt für Communities funktionieren kann. Dieses Phänomen wurde bereits von dem österreichischen Architekten Gerhard Garstenauer (der letzte übrig gebliebene Brutalist Österreichs) untersucht, der in den 1960er- und 1970er-Jahren eine langfristig orientierte Strategie für das Gasteiner Tal entwickelte, und zwar sowohl hinsichtlich architektonischer Interventionen als auch mit Blick auf einen kulturellen Rahmen, der bestimmte Gemeinschaften in dieser abgelegenen Alpenregion verankern sollte.

Die zweieiigen Zwillingsbauten der örtlichen Hoteliers Evelyn und Thomas Ickrath, das Haus Hirt und das Miramonte, erlauben es dem Gast, zwei elegant nah zueinander gelegene, aber entgegengesetzte und dabei doch integrierte Konzepte dessen zu genießen, wie man temporär und dabei weg von zu Hause leben kann. Beide Gebäude repräsentieren Communities und Reiseziele im ständigen Wandel und Übergang, die sich fortwährend neu denken. Während die Philosophie des *zweiten Zuhauses* von Haus Hirth sich vor allem an diejenigen wendet, die vorübergehend aus ihrer täglichen, zumeist urbanen Umgebung aussteigen wollen, um sich verwöhnen zu lassen, ist das Miramote eine vollkommen andere Kategorie. Es erinnert an ein aufgemöbeltes Kreuzfahrtschiff für die Boheme, das flexibel genug ist, seine Richtung während der Fahrt zu ändern.

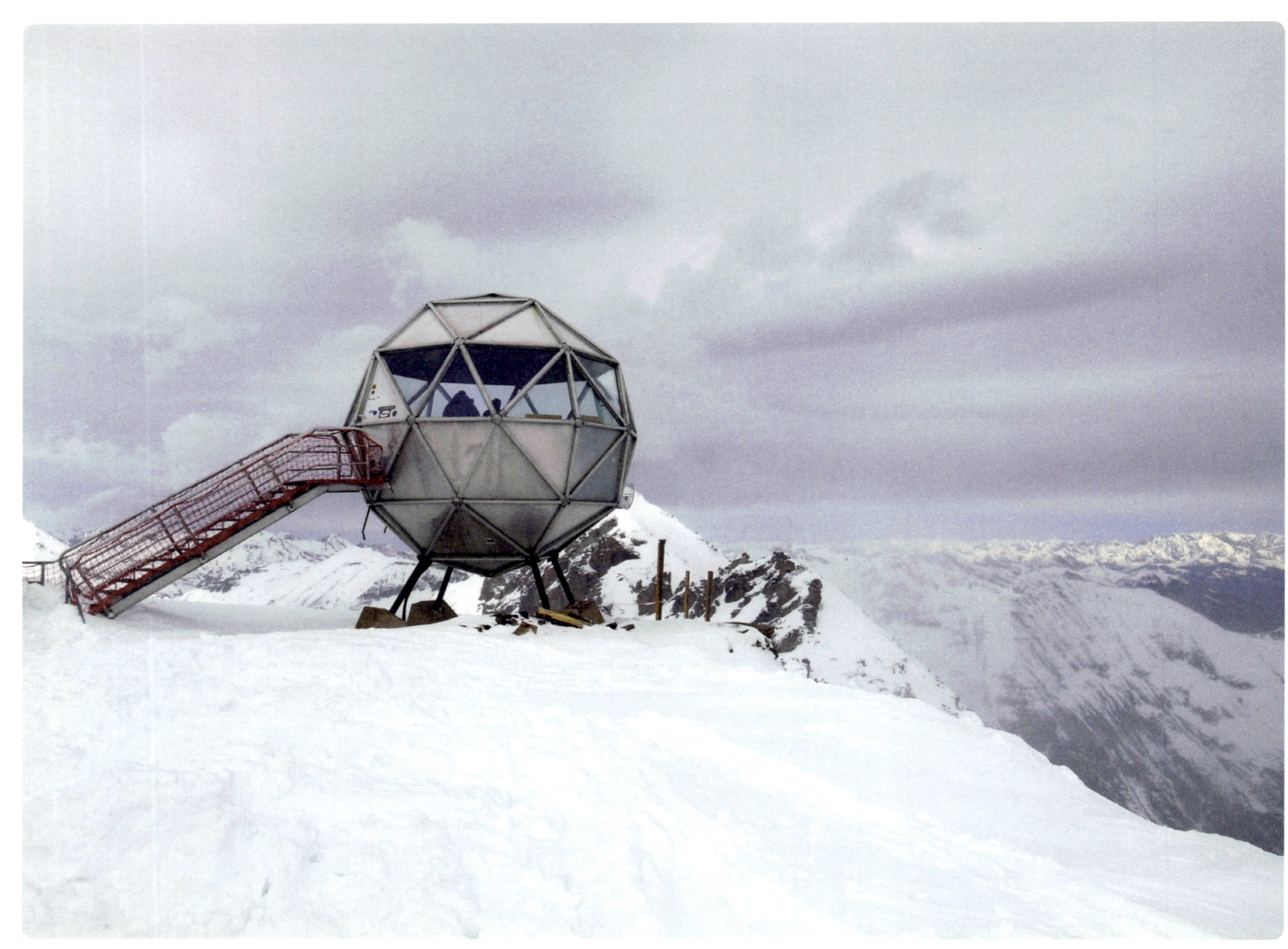

EINE VON GERHARD GARSTENAUERS GEODÄTISCHEN KUPPELN IN
ONE OF GERHARD GARSTENAUER'S GEODESIC DOMES AT SPORTGASTEIN,
HEUTE EIN TREFFPUNKT UND AUSSICHTSPLATTFORM / TODAY A MEETING POINT AND VIEWING PLATFORM
Foto / Photo: Markus Miessen

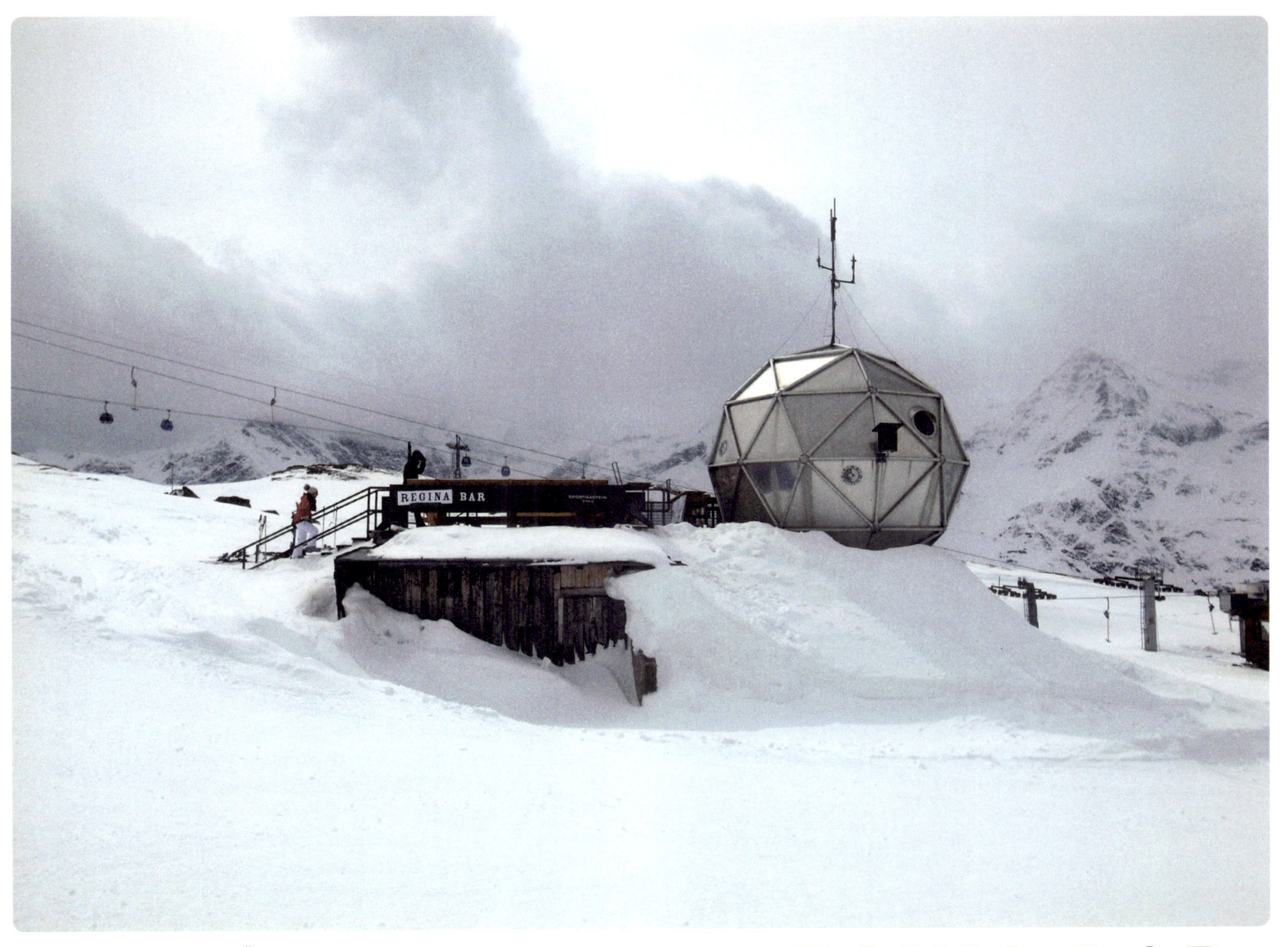

GARSTENAUERS GEODÄTISCHE KUPPEL IN SPORTGASTEIN, HEUTE
GARSTENAUER'S GEODESIC DOME IN SPORT GASTEIN, THE
»REGINA BAR«
DES HOTELS REGINA / OF THE HOTEL REGINA

Foto / Photo: Markus Miessen

castle renovation was made possible by a new building (designed by Dutch architects *UN Studio)* that was constructed next to the old and that cross-financed the hotel operation. This model heavily relies on an urban clientele, which is interested and involved in contemporary cultural and artistic discourses.

A COMPLETELY DIFFERENT BUT RATHER INTERESTING TYPOLOGY IS BEING EXPLORED IN THE SWISS LOWER-ENGADINE VILLAGE OF VNA, WHERE *PIZ TSCHÜTTA* OPERATES AS A DECENTRALIZED HOTEL, WHICH EXISTS AS A SERIES OF INDIVIDUAL ROOMS AND SPACES SPREAD OVER THE ENTIRE VILLAGE, thereby creating the illusion that the individual guest is fully immersed in the local village culture, while supporting the villagers who managed to withstand the draw of the cities. Such a model represents an antidote to the contemporary typology of the hotel chain, although such chains can be cloaked by seemingly authentic local customizations, a strategy pursued by the *Ace* group (Portland, New York, Los Angeles, Palm Springs, Seattle, London, and Panama), or by an apparently historic venture, as in the case of Chateau Marmont in Los Angeles, which is part of Andre Balazs Properties (The Standard Hotels, The Mercer, Sunset Beach et. al.), or New York City's The Bowery Hotel, which is run by the team behind the Maritime Hotel and the Waverly Inn. These hipster homes-away-from-home can be understood as a rapidly growing species of hotels, which cultivate a new, local type of clientele that does not necessarily stay overnight. Instead it uses the establishment as a local meeting ground and alternative living room. In this context one could also mention the both trashy and conservative amalgamation of full-on professionalism and hipsterism found at SoHo House (London, New York, Los Angeles, Berlin, Toronto, Miami, and Somerset).

SOME of the most interesting cases in the recent development of alternative models of temporary habitation and homing are the hoteliers who have understood that a certain craving for urbanity exists beyond the city. In other words, they have understood how to generate rural spaces, which maintain a certain complexity in terms of their urban clientele without creating unnecessary stressful relationships—offering relaxation as well as social potential without duties or obligations. Such an approach hinges on spectacular rural locations, while providing a creative setting in which service quality is equated with the delivery of a platform of potentiality. Such a hotel caters to ones needs and wishes (even if those have not been fully formulated or even realized by the guest). The »urban« component of such hotel spaces is instantiated by the strategic establishment of a creative common ground, a salon-like setting that generates an intellectual community, even if this community is not necessarily concerned with intellectual matters. When one observes this cultural phenomenon from the point of view of architecture, the approach is interesting precisely because it affirms the importance of design, not as lying in the imagination and production of a different physical reality, but—more importantly—in the careful and controlled »design« of specific audiences. Even if these audiences do not talk to one another while present at the respective venue. Hence, architecture in this context is about producing moments that are communicated by the subconscious rendering of contextualized communities. This model also exists in the urban environment, where certain venues have attempted to create (almost rural) moments of enclosure, which temporarily mask out the city. Examples include the interesting and democratic mix of the *Russian and Turkish bathhouses* on New York's 10th Street, which—since 1892—have offered a certain degree of refuge, although, super-public and crowded, they are situated in a city defined by brutal and endless public exposure.

Considering the notion of the hotel in an alternative fashion also means thinking of such spaces not only as venues of relaxation and refuge but also as spaces of production—retreats that offer potential for creative work, even if the »product« is a delayed arrival. The *petit* yet *grand* Austrian alpine town of Bad Gastein is a handy destination, when one is in desperate need of refuge and the unexpected. Although the Gasteiner Tal, the valley of Gastein, has not yet realized its full potential and is still suffering substantially from the difficulties of waning visitors and local population in the late 20th century, it serves as an interesting example of how an architectural setting can act as a localizer for communities. This phenomenon was already explored by Austrian architect Gerhard Garstenauer (Austria's last remaining Brutalist), who conceived and designed a long-term strategy for the Gasteiner Tal in the 1960s and 1970s, both in terms of architectural interventions and a cultural framework intended to anchor certain communities in this remote alpine region.

Local hoteliers Evelyn and Thomas Ickrath's non-identical twins, Haus Hirt and hotel Miramonte, allow the outsider to enjoy two opposing but integrated concepts, set in rather elegant physical proximity, of how to temporarily live abroad. Both Haus Hirt and Miramonte are buildings, communities, and destinations in flux and in transition, which never stop to rethink themselves. Whereas Haus Hirt's home-away-from-home philosophy caters to those who wish to temporarily zoom out of their daily, mostly

Ehrlich gesagt ist es gleichsam eine riesige Box, die alles enthält, was man brauchen könnte – also alles, was notwendig ist. Natürlich kann man hier wandern, Ski fahren, snowboarden und all die anderen Freuden, Aktivitäten und Möglichkeiten genießen, die man von einem schönen Alpenhotel erwartet. Nur kann man dies eben auch an vielen anderen Orten tun. Diese beiden Hotels jedoch – in Kombination mit der baulichen und geografischen Situation von Bad Gastein – unterscheiden sich grundlegend von vielen anderen.

Obwohl es durchaus Entspannung bietet, könnte das Miramonte auch ein Ort sein, an dem man, falls notwendig, über körperliche Aktivitäten hinaus produktiv sein kann; es ist eine Art alpiner Arbeitsrückzugsort. Neben dem Spa, den Yogakursen oder der urbanen Atmosphäre am Kamin bietet es auch eine Reihe von kürzeren und längeren Arrangements an, die das Hotel – fast automatisch – zu einem Anziehungspunkt für Gäste machen, denen es nichts ausmacht, ihren Arbeitsplatz temporär in die Berge zu verlegen – sei es, um einen Roman zu schreiben oder konzentriert ein Projekt voranzutreiben, während sie sich in einer angenehmen und stimulierenden Umgebung aufhalten.

Was heute wie ein Bastardnachkomme der Moderne auf einem Berggipfel aussieht, wurde ursprünglich 1911 entworfen und gebaut. In der Zwischenzeit ist es immer wieder umgestaltet und renoviert worden. Das Ergebnis ist jedoch viel mehr als nur ein Schluckauf von Ideen – die sorgfältig reflektierte Erprobung, wie man eine Identität konstruiert, hat hier eine Umgebung generiert, die auf zweierlei Art funktioniert: sowohl als ein stiller Rückzugsort als auch als anregender Arbeitsort, ein Artist-in-residence-Programm oder eine alpine Denkfabrik. Obwohl man zögert, Richard Florida anzuführen, ist hier eine Art kreative Klasse präsent, und man versteht diesen Fokus eher als Hilfe denn als Hürde. Ob sie nun aus Berlin, London, Amsterdam oder Buenos Aires kommen, sehen die meisten Stadtbewohner, die diesen Ort temporär bewohnen, ihn als die Umsetzung einer Vision: In den Bergen leben, während man sich mit den urbanen Menschen aus diversen bekannten oder auch fremden Milieus umgibt, die es alle auf die eine oder andere Art ermöglichen, über einen bestimmten kulturellen Code zu reflektieren, der eine kreative Atmosphäre schafft – und das, ohne dass der Einzelne zwingend daran teilnehmen, darüber kommunizieren oder ihn produzieren müsste.

DER (RÄUMLICHE) RAHMEN DES HOTELS LÄDT SOWOHL ZU ENTSPANNUNG ALS AUCH ZUR PRODUKTION VON INHALTEN EIN, REGT NEUE BEZIEHUNGEN UND FREUNDLICHE DEBATTEN AN, ERMÖGLICHT SOWOHL GRUPPENDYNAMIK ALS AUCH EINZELHAFT – FALLS NOTWENDIG. Kurz gesagt, es dient als Community-Generator, der behutsam einem Gefühl des Wohlbefindens den Weg bereitet. Auf diese Weise enden die Ferien nicht an der Stadtgrenze von Bad Gastein, sondern sie werden umsichtig in das eigene Zuhause transplantiert, wo die fernab von da erlebten Beziehungen weiterhin Ideen befördern können und – vereinfacht gesagt – so auch eine Art von mentalem und kulturellem Gleichgewicht herstellen.

Indem das Miramonte und das Haus Hirt sowohl ein äußeres als auch inneres Panorama miteinander verbinden, gelingt es hier, eine lokale Identität zu erzeugen, die mit der richtigen Menge urbaner Würze versehen ist und perfekt zu den Absurditäten von Bad Gastein als alpinem Raum der Ungewissheit passt. An einem verregneten, nebligen und grauen Tag – und diese Art von Tagen gehören hier zu den beliebtesten – ist die Szenerie tatsächlich nicht weit von einer Miniaturversion von *Gotham City* entfernt, allerdings in den Wasserfallauskerbungen des Nationalparks Hohe Tauern im Bundesland Salzburg in Österreich gelegen. Diese beiden Häuser sind keine Hotels im üblichen Sinn. Und sie gehören auch nicht in die allzu billige Typologie der *Designhotels.* Sie sind gemütliche Mikroumgebungen am oberen Ende eines tiefen Tals, mit einem frontalen Panorama der überwältigendsten architektonischen Erscheinungen der Alpenregion: ein Ort, wo Design und das Nachdenken über Design eine wesentliche Rolle im Alltagsleben spielt, dankenswerterweise ohne dass es *Design* genannt würde. Hier ermöglicht ein Raum dem Einzelnen Bedeutung zu produzieren und dabei den pragmatischen Belastungen des Alltagslebens zu entkommen.

urban, environments to enjoy being pampered for a good while, the Miramonte is a different species altogether. It resembles a revamped bohemian cruise liner, which is flexible enough to alter its direction as it moves along. Frankly, it is a huge box, which includes everything that one might need—meaning everything that is necessary. Needless to say, one can also go hiking, skiing, and snowboarding and experience all the other kind of treats, activities, and options that one would expect from a fine alpine lodging experience. Only, one can do that in many other places. However, the two hotels—in combination with the physical and geographic setting of Bad Gastein—are crucially different from those many other places.

Although offering a most relaxing experience, the *Miramonte* could also, if necessary, become a place where one could be productive beyond a physical activity; it is an alpine work-retreat of sorts. Apart from the spa, the yoga classes, or the urban bar atmosphere by the fireplace, it offers a selection of short- and long-term packages, which—almost by default—turn the hotel into a hot-house for guests who do not mind temporarily relocating their workspace to the mountains—whether to write a novel or develop a focused piece of work, while being in a pleasurable and stimulating physical and cultural environment.

What looks like a bastard-child of modernism on a hilltop was in fact originally designed and built in 1911. It has meanwhile gone through several iterations of refurbishment. More than a mere hick-up of ideas, careful retroactive exercises in how to construct an identity have generated an environment that works in two ways: as a silent retreat as well as a stimulating workspace, an artist-in-residence program or alpine think tank. Although one hesitates to cite Richard Florida, a kind of bastardized creative class is silently present here, and one understands this focus as a help more than a hindrance. Whether having arrived from Berlin, London, Amsterdam, or Buenos Aires, most of the urbanites inhabiting this place see it as a realization of a vision: living in the mountains while being able to surround oneself with the urban crowd from various familiar or alien milieus, which all, in one way or another, allow one to reflect on a certain cultural code that creates a productive turf—without having to necessarily engage, communicate, or produce.

THE (SPATIAL) FRAMEWORK OF THE HOTEL INVITES BOTH RELAXATION AND THE PRODUCTION OF CONTENT, STIMULATING NEW RELATIONSHIPS AND CORDIAL DEBATES, GROUP DYNAMIC AS WELL AS SOLITARY CONFINEMENT—IF NECESSARY. In short, it serves as a community generator that gently introduces a sense of well-being. In this manner one's time-off does not end at the gateway to Bad Gastein but is being carefully transplanted into one's own home, where the relationships experienced continue to trigger ideas and—simply put—some form of mental and cultural equilibrium.

Uniting an exterior and interior panorama, both Miramonte and Haus Hirt manage to induce a local identity that is tarnished by the right amount of urban flavor and perfectly fits into the absurdities of Bad Gastein as an alpine space of uncertainty. On a rainy, foggy, and grey day—which are among the favorite kinds of days there—this setting is actually not too far off a miniature version of *Gotham City,* albeit located in the waterfall recess of the *Hohe Tauern* national park in the Austrian state of Salzburg. These two venues are not hotels in the customary sense. Nor do belong to the all-too-cheap typology of »design hotels.« They are cozy micro-environments at the high end of a deep valley, with a frontal panorama of the Alps' most stunning architectural experience: a place where design and thinking about design play an integral role in everyday life, thankfully without being called »design.« It is a space where the individual produces meaning while escaping the pragmatic burdens of everyday life.

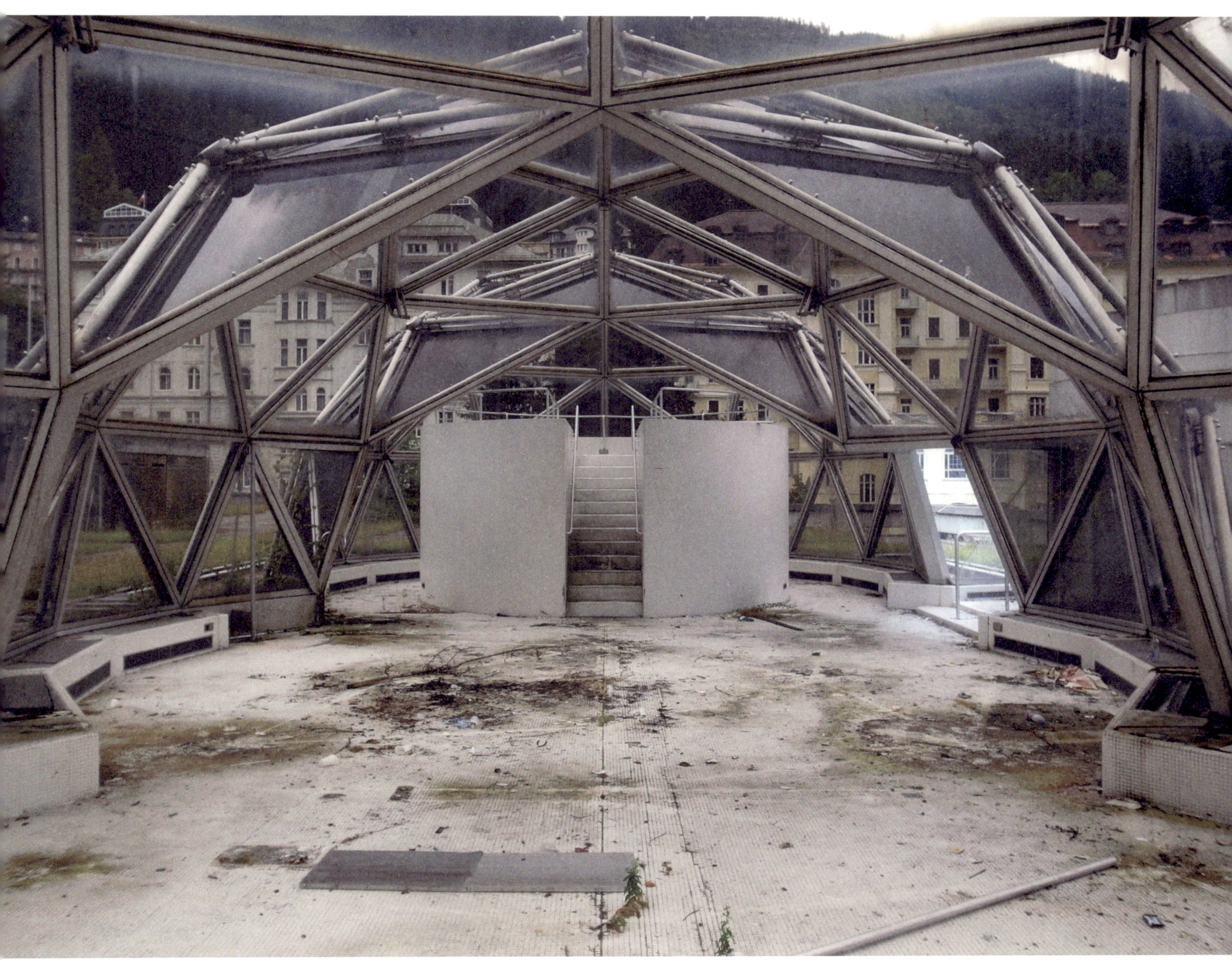

»KONGRESSZENTRUM«, BAD GASTEIN, BRACHLIEGENDES DACH MIT GEODÄTISCHER KUPPEL
ABANDONED ROOF AREA WITH A GEODESIC DOME

Foto / Photo: Markus Miessen

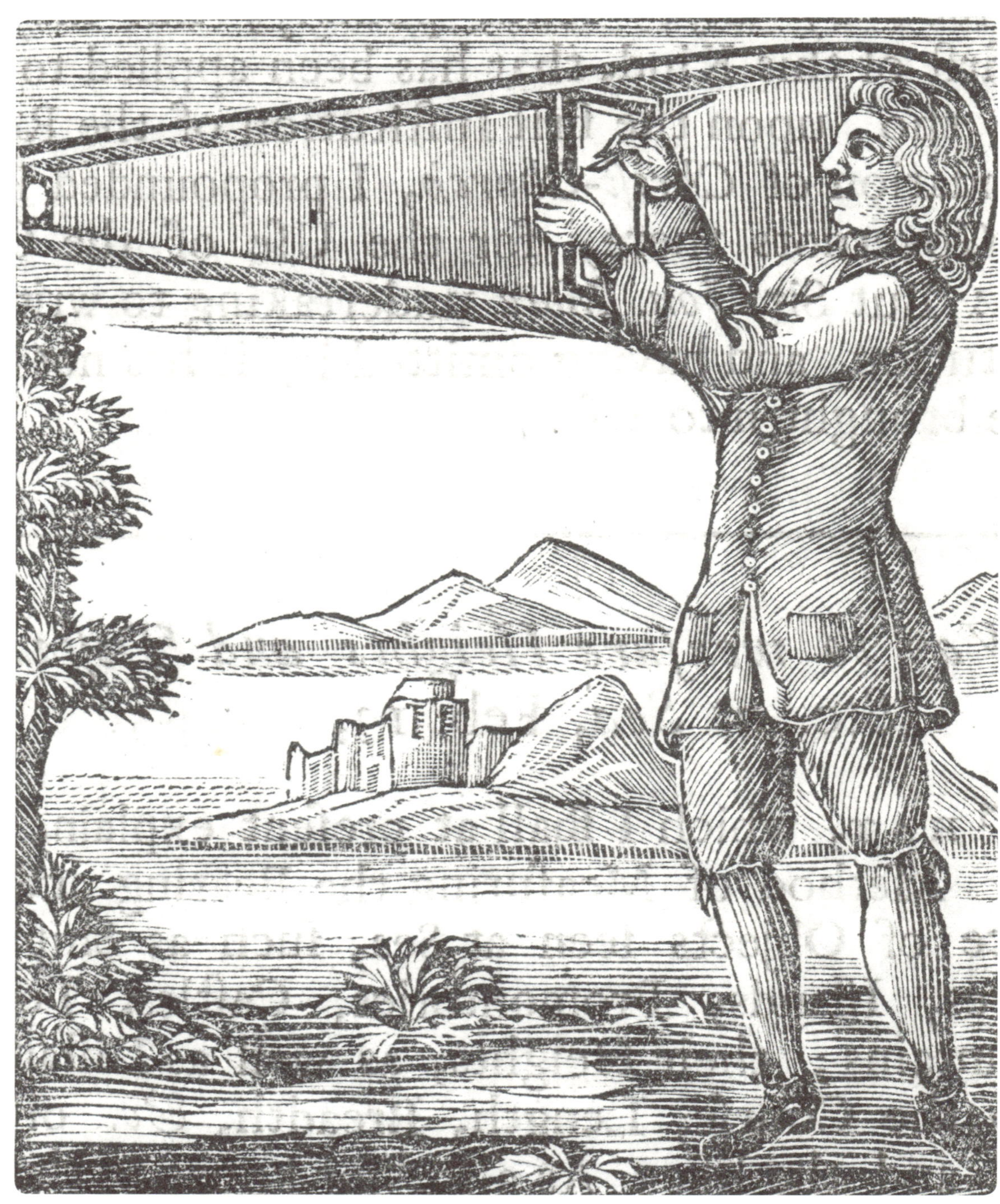

ABB. / FIG. 1 **RICHARD HOOKE**

TRAGBARE PORTABLE **CAMERA OBSCURA, 1694**

Holzschnitt aus: *Philosophical Experiments and Observations of the Late Eminent Dr. Robert Hooke,* hrsg. von W. & J. Innys, W. Derham, 1726, S. 295 / Woodcut-Illustration in: *Philosophical Experiments and Observations of the Late Eminent Dr. Robert Hooke,* ed. W. & J. Innys, W. Derham, 1726, p. 295

DAS REISENDE AUGE

ANMERKUNGEN ZUR KÜNSTLERREISE

BÄRBEL KÜSTER

Mobilität und Austausch sind Grundmotive der europäischen Kulturgeschichte. Künstler und Kunstwerke bewegen sich durch Zeit und Raum – allein den spezifischen Wahrnehmungsfokus für die Erfahrung fremder Länder und Objekte stellt jede Epoche neu ein. Man mag zwar die Erwähnung von Antonello da Messinas in den Niederlanden im 15. Jahrhundert in den Viten des Giorgio Vasari als eine Gründungsurkunde der Künstlerreise sehen – den Beginn des Reisens der Künstler markiert sie nicht.[1] Schon seit dem Mittelalter unternahmen Mitglieder der Zunft Gesellen- und Wanderreisen, um an fremden Orten oder bei dort heimischen Fürsten Anstellung zu finden. Die Höfe selbst zogen häufig zwischen verschiedenen Residenzen umher. Künstler reisten im Rahmen dynastischer Verbindungen der Fürstenhäuser und Staaten quer durch Europa bis nach Asien. So wurde Gentile Bellini mit einer künstlerischen Delegation 1479 nach Konstantinopel abgestellt, um dort die Mitglieder des Hofes zu porträtieren und venezianische Kunsttechniken verfügbar zu machen. An Albrecht Dürers Leben lässt sich die Vielfalt des künstlerischen Reisens ebenso ablesen, wie Peter Paul Rubens' Werk den Einsatz von Hofkünstlern zur Unterhaltung des jeweiligen Fürsten, aber auch in diplomatischen Missionen bezeugt.[2] Künstler reisten, um Techniken zu erlernen, Originale und bedeutende Kunstdenkmäler kennenzulernen oder bei Ausgrabungen antiker Schätze zu assistieren. Eine Fahrt nach Italien und die Romreise galten ab dem 16. Jahrhundert als höchstes Bildungsgut. Seit 1663 verlieh der französische Staat den jährlichen Rompreis.[3] Reisen, auch als Flucht und Vertreibung, verbreitete in Zuge der jahrhundertelangen religiösen Spannungen künstlerisches Wissen, wie zum Beispiel im Fall der französischen Hugenotten nach der Aufhebung des Edikts von Nantes 1685. Viele Künstler reisten ab dem 17. Jahrhundert auch als Tutoren reicher Adliger auf *Grand Tour* nach Italien, als Cicerones und Lehrer für Kunstgeschichte betreuten sie Kunstankäufe und stellten Kontakte her. Das folgende Zeitalter der Aufklärung markierte nicht nur den Beginn des modernen touristischen Reisens, sondern brachte eine ganze Reihe von Expeditionskünstlern hervor, welche bis zur Erfindung der Fotografie die notwendigen Aufzeichnungen und bildnerischen Dokumentationen auf Entdeckungs-, Handels- und Forschungsfahrten übernahmen.

KUNSTWERKE, DIE AUF REISEN ENTSTEHEN, TEILEN SOWOHL DEN BLICK DER ARCHIVIERUNG DES CHRONISTEN ALS AUCH DEN DER IMAGINÄREN SEHNSUCHTSORTE. William Hodges, künstlerischer Begleiter der zweiten Forschungsreise von James Cook, beeindruckte durch seine elegischen, großformatigen Landschaftsgemälde der Südsee, die die dargestellte Natur mit edlen Wilden belebte. Georg Forster, sein Vorgänger auf der ersten Reise, wägte an seinen Bildern kritisch ab, was Bericht und was dem Geschmack des heimischen Zielpublikums geschuldet sei.[4] Kamen also selbst die Expeditionskünstler nicht um das Imaginäre herum, so wurde seit dem Aufstieg der Reisebeschreibung zum literarischen Genre, seit der Erfindung der Laterna magica und den ersten Dioramen im ausgehenden 18. Jahrhundert

1 Vgl. Andreas Beyer, »Reisen als Teil der schönen Kunst betrachtet«, in: *Orte der Sehnsucht. Mit Künstlern auf Reisen,* hrsg. von Hermann Arnhold, Ausst.-Kat. LWL-Museum für Kunst und Kultur, Münster, Regensburg 2008, S. 24–30. Siehe auch: Joachim Rees, *Künstler auf Reisen. Von Albrecht Dürer bis Emil Nolde,* Darmstadt 2010, und Christoph Otterbeck, *Europa verlassen. Künstlerreisen am Beginn des 20. Jahrhunderts,* Köln / Weimar / Wien 2007.

2 Martin Warnke, *Hofkünstler. Zur Vorgeschichte des modernen Künstlers,* Köln 1985.

3 Ausst.-Kat. *Orte der Sehnsucht* 2008 (wie Anm. 1), und *Viaggio in Italia. Künstler auf Reisen 1770–1880,* hrsg. von Astrid Reuter, Ausst.-Kat. Staatliche Kunsthalle Karlsruhe, Berlin/München 2010.

4 Vgl. Rüdiger Joppien, »Die Künstler auf den Reisen des James Cook«, in: *James Cook und die Entdeckung der Südsee,* hrsg. von Hans Erich Bödeker, Christian Feest, Brigitta Hauser-Schäublin, Rüdiger Joppien, Adrienne L. Kaeppler, Gundolf Krügera, Ausst.-Kat. Kunst- und Ausstellungshalle der Bundesrepublik Deutschland, Bonn, Museum für Völkerkunde, Wien, Historisches Museum, Bern, München 2010, S. 112–118, Fußnote 9 und 11.

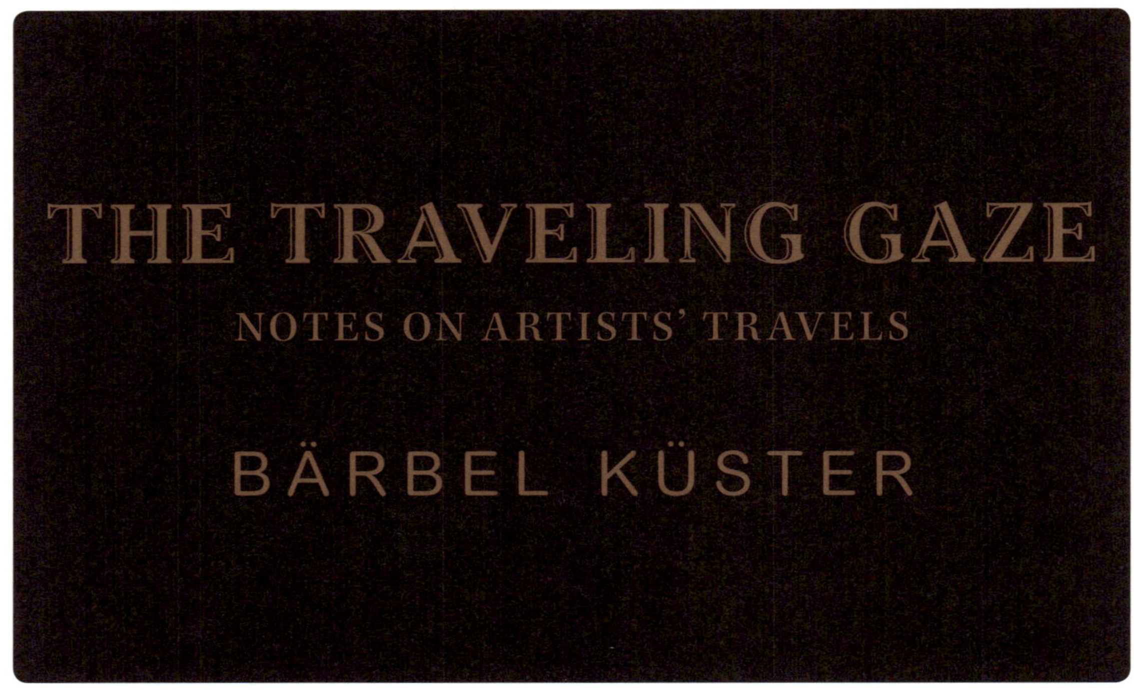

Mobility and exchange are fundamental motifs in European art history. Artists and works of art move through time and space—and each new era brings a refocusing of the lens through which the experience of foreign countries and objects is viewed. Although one might consider the reference to Antonello da Messina's presence in the Netherlands in the 15th century as a seminal document of the institution of the artist's journey, it does not mark the beginning of travel for artists.[1] Even in the Middle Ages members of guilds traveled as journeymen or itinerant craftsmen to find employment in foreign towns or with a locality's given ruler. Entire courts often moved between different residences. Artists traveled all across Europe and even as far as Asia in conjunction with the dynastic relationships between royal houses and states. Gentile Bellini, for example, was sent to Constantinople with an artistic delegation in 1479 to paint portraits of the local members of the court and teach Venetian artistic techniques. Albrecht Dürer's biography exemplifies the diverse nature of travel undertaken by artists, much in the way that the work of Peter Paul Rubens demonstrates the employment of court artists for the entertainment of individual rulers as well as the role of artists in diplomatic missions.[2] Artists traveled in order to learn techniques, to study original works of art and important artistic monuments, and to assist in the excavation of treasures from antiquity. Beginning in the 16th century, a trip to Italy or visit to Rome was considered a highly valuable educational asset. In 1663 the French state began awarding an annual Prix de Rome.[3] Travel, even when due to flight and expulsion, spread artistic knowledge in the wake of centuries of religious tensions, as for example in the case of French Huguenots after the repeal of the Edict of Nantes in 1685. During the 17th century, many artists began to travel to Italy as the tutors of rich nobility on the *Grand Tour.* As cicerones and art history teachers they acted as advisors in the purchase of art and facilitated contacts. The subsequent age of the Enlightenment marked not only the beginning of modern touristic travel, but it also produced a good number of expedition artists, who, until the discovery of photography, were responsible for the necessary recording and visual documentation of undertakings dedicated to exploration, trade, and research.

WORKS OF ART PRODUCED DURING A JOURNEY ENTAIL BOTH THE CHRONICLER'S ARCHIVAL GAZE AND THE GAZE OF DESIRE PROJECTED ONTO IMAGINARY PLACES. William Hodges, the attendant artist on James Cook's second research trip, impressed viewers with his elegiac, large-format landscape paintings of the South Seas, in which the depicted natural settings were populated with noble savages. Georg Forster, his predecessor on the first trip, tried to create a critical balance in his images between what was a reporting of fact and what was inspired by the taste of audiences back home.[4] Even if expedition artists were not able to avoid elements of the imaginary, home audiences were able to travel, at least through media, with the development of travel descriptions into a literary genre and with the invention of the laterna magica and

1 See Andreas Beyer, »Reisen als Teil der schönen Kunst betrachtet,« in *Orte der Sehnsucht. Mit Künstlern auf Reisen*, ed. Hermann Arnold, exhibit. cat. LWL-Museum für Kunst und Kultur, Münster (Regensburg, 2008), 24–30. See also Joachim Rees, *Künstler auf Reisen: Von Albrecht Dürer bis Emil Nolde* (Darmstadt, 2010); and Christoph Otterbeck, *Europa verlassen. Künstlerreisen am Beginn des 20. Jahrhunderts* (Cologne/Weimar/Vienna, 2007).

2 Martin Warnke, *Hofkünstler: Zur Vorgeschichte des modernen Künstlers* (Cologne, 1985).

3 *Orte der Sehnsucht* 2008 (see note 1); and *Viaggio in Italia: Künstler auf Reisen 1770–1880*, ed. Astrid Reuter, exhibit. cat. Staatliche Kunsthalle Karlsruhe (Berlin and Munich, 2010).

4 See Rüdiger Joppien, »Die Künstler auf den Reisen des James Cook,« in *James Cook und die Entdeckung der Südsee*, ed. Hans Erich Bödeker, Christian Feest, Brigitta Hauser-Schäublin, Rüdiger Joppien, Adrienne L. Kaeppler, and Gundolf Krügera, exhibit. cat. Kunst- und Ausstellungshalle der Bundesrepublik Deutschland, Bonn, Museum für Völkerkunde, Vienna, Historisches Museum, Bern (Munich, 2010), 112–118, footnotes 9 and 11.

Reisen auch dem heimischen Publikum zumindest medial ermöglicht.[5] Fremde Welten, Grusel, Belehrung und Unterhaltung entfalteten sich entlang von Handel, Forschung und Kolonialgeschichte und ihren Konfliktlinien. Die surrealistische Weltkarte von 1929, die die Kontinente verschiebt, steht in einer langen Tradition von Phantasmen der Welt, die Anspruch auf Realität erheben.[6] Die Verschiebungen zwischen Chroniken des Wissens und der Unmöglichkeit anzukommen bilden sich dabei in der vermeintlich objektiven Form der vermessenen Welt als Karte ab – ein Widerspruch, der die Fokussierung des Blicks auch bei reisenden Künstlern stets begleitet.

FOKUSSIERUNG DES BLICKS

Als Robert Hooke 1694 seine Abhandlung über die tragbare Camera obscura der Royal Society in London vorlegte (Abb. 1), hatte er nicht nur ein bestimmtes Modell der künstlerischen Mimesis vor Augen, sondern auch den reisenden Künstler. Stülpte sich jener die Camera obscura über Kopf und Schultern, war er gänzlich auf sein Auge reduziert: Allein durch das Loch fiel das Bild der Welt ins finstere Innere des Kastens, totale Abschottung war der Preis der Exaktheit. Zugleich stellt die Camera obscura, deren Urmodell ein kleines Haus war, eine Art der Behausung für das Auge dar. In Hookes Entwurf wurde dieses Haus mobil. Deutlicher kann man die Ausschnitthaftigkeit der mimetischen Kunstkonzeption nicht ins Bild setzen. Die in der Renaissance von Leon Battista Alberti ausgebildete abendländische Metapher des Gemäldes als Fenster ließ sich nun auch auf Reisen aufrechterhalten und wurde zu einem allgemeingültigen Modus der Bildwahrnehmung.

Mitte des 19. Jahrhunderts übernahm die Fotografie wichtige Funktionen der Reise- und Expeditionsdokumentation – die Orte, die Maxime Du Camp (Ägypten 1849) oder die Brüder Bisson (Montblanc 1859) besuchten, waren durch die Malerei visuell vorgeformt und bekamen nun neue fotografische Facetten. Fotografien der Campagna Romana lieferten Mitte des 19. Jahrhunderts den französischen Stipendiaten der Villa Medici in Rom die Vorlagen für ihre Landschaftsgemälde.[7] Die überkommenen Medien zeigen immer wieder, dass der reisende Künstler zwischen seinem Selbstverständnis als Chronist und der künstlerischen Bewältigung der bereits in Malerei, Literatur und Fotografie bekannten Kontaktzonen stand, die durch Mythen, Klischees und Vorurteile bestimmt waren.

Exotische Landschaften und fremde Objekte erneuerten die europäische Kunstgeschichte parallel zu den geopolitischen Ereignissen. Als Eugène Delacroix Anfang 1832 in Tanger ankam, begleitete er eine diplomatische Mission Frankreichs, die einen Konflikt mit den marokkanischen Stämmen und den in Nordafrika engagierten Briten entschärfen sollte, welcher durch die französische Besetzung Algeriens 1830 entstanden war. Orientalismus, Japonismus und schließlich Primitivismus, der auch auf koloniale Interessen in Afrika, Südostasien und Südamerika reagierte, verdichteten sich zu den großen formalen Neuerungen in den Kunstkonzeptionen der Moderne. Waren zunächst vor allem Dinge auf den Routen von Kolonialpolitik und Handel nach Europa gereist, folgte eine Welle des Reisens der Künstler hin zu den Ursprungsorten der nunmehr in Museen, Trödelläden und auf Weltausstellungen für Europa verfügbar gemachten Masken, Fetische und Tempelfiguren und ihrer medial vervielfältigten Abbilder. Eine Reise ist stets mit dem Bild verknüpft, das sich der Reisende zuvor von seinem Ziel macht. Sensationen und Erlebnisse sind somit medial bereits vorgeprägt. Abgebildete Sehnsuchtsorte sind Medienereignisse. Der Betrachter vor dem Bild, dessen penetrierender Blick[8] im Gemälde herumspaziert, als wäre es real, hat sein Pendant im reisenden Künstler, der in der Wirklichkeit herumspaziert, als sei sie ein Bild.

(BE-)HAUSEN IN DER FREMDE UND VERKOMMENE UFER

In der Fremde war das Hotel zunächst der Ort, an dem Reisenden Vertrautes begegnete. Wilhelm Gentz, gebürtiger Neuruppiner und einer der ersten deutschen Maler, der sich nach Stationen in Paris dem Orientalismus verschrieben hatte, reiste 1850/51 durch Ägypten bis in den heutigen Sudan. In Alexandria angekommen, reißen sich die Tagelöhner am Hafen um sein Gepäck, »so dass ich mit dem Stock zwischen fahren musste. Dazu konnte ich kein Wort verstehen. Man trug die Sachen zur Douane, wo ich sie endlich auf einen Esel packte und dann grad'aus in die Stadt ging, um ein europäisches Hotel zu suchen. – Die orientalischen Straßen sind wahre Labyrinthe. Pferde, Kamele, Ochsen, Menschen, Esel drängen sich durch die engsten Gassen hindurch, ich langte endlich an dem großen Platz an, wo die Konsuln wohnen und die Hotels sich befinden. Die Hotels sind sehr groß und schön, die *diners* ausgezeichnet. Der Preis aber ist in allem sehr teuer. Nachdem ich mich zum Frühstück zu Tische gesetzt hatte, fand ich gleich drei Deutsche, fünf Franzosen, Italiener und Griechen, die meistenteils von Ober-Ägypten zurückkamen, und von denen ich mir manche nützliche Unterweisung geben ließ.«[9]

Die Reisenden untereinander bildeten eine Klasse für sich. Da aber der weit gereiste Künstler eher mit Abenteuern und dem erlebten Exotischen zu Hause brillieren wollte, verwundert es wenig, dass Darstellungen des eher europäisch geprägten Lebens im Hotel nur selten überliefert sind. Gentz, ebenso wie vor ihm Georg Forster, verstand sich selbst als Berichterstatter aus der fremden Welt, seine Reisebeschreibungen verkauften sich glänzend.

5 *Die Welt in Reichweite. Imaginäre Reisen im 19. Jahrhundert,* hrsg. von Ursula Storch, Ausst.-Kat. Wien Museum, Wien 2009.

6 Vgl. Christine Buci-Glucksman: »Der kartographische Blick der Kunst«, in: *Atlas Mapping. Künstler als Kartographen. Kartographie als Kultur,* hrsg. von Paolo Bianchi, Sabine Folie, Ausst.-Kat. Offenes Kulturhaus Linz, Kunsthaus Bregenz, Wien 1997, und die Karte der Surrealisten: »Le monde aux temps des surrealistes«, in: *Variétés. Revue mensuelle illustrée de l'esprit contemporain,* Sonderheft, *Le Surrealisme en 1929,* Brüssel, Juni 1929, S. 26/27, sowie *Vermessung der Welt. Heterotopien und Wissensräume in der Kunst,* hrsg. von Katrin Bucher-Trantow, Hans Dieter Huber, Elke Krasny, Peter Pakesch, Ausst.-Kat. Kunsthaus Graz, Universalmuseum Joanneum, Köln 2011.

7 Françoise Heilbrun, »Die Reise um die Welt. Forscher und Touristen«, in: *Neue Geschichte der Fotografie,* hrsg. von Michel Frizot, Köln 1998, S. 148–173, hier S. 157.

8 Norman Bryson, *Das Sehen und die Malerei. Die Logik des Blicks,* München 2001.

9 Zit. nach: *Wilhelm Gentz. Briefe einer Reise nach Ägypten und Nubien 1850/1851,* hrsg. von Irina Röckel, Berlin 2004, S. 50 f.

the first dioramas in the late 18th century.[5] Foreign worlds, spine-chilling tales, instruction, and entertainment emerged together with the events surrounding trade, research, colonial history, and all their respective conflicts. The surrealist world map of 1929, which distorts the continents, belongs to a long tradition of phantasmas of the globe that lay claim to reality.[6] The disjunction between chronicles of the known world and the impossibility of arriving at the given destinations are represented in the supposedly objective form of a map of the world—a contradiction that is always present in the focusing of the gaze of traveling artists.

THE FOCUSING OF THE GAZE

When Robert Hooke presented his paper on the portable camera obscura (fig. 1) at the Royal Society in London in 1694, he not only had a specific model of artistic mimesis in mind but also the traveling artist. Anyone slipping the camera obscura over the head and shoulders was completely reduced to an eye: an image of the world came into the dark interior of the box only through the hole. Being completely sealed off was the price of precision. At the same time, the camera obscura was a kind of dwelling for the eye—its original model having had the form of a little house. In Hooke's design this house became mobile. There is hardly a more evocative illustration of the visual cut-out as inherent to the mimetic concept of art. The West's metaphor for painting as a window, cultivated in the Renaissance by Leon Battista Alberti, could then be perpetuated by the traveler and ultimately became a common mode of viewing images.

In the mid 19th century photography assumed an important function in the documentation of travel and expeditions. The places visited by Maxime Du Camp (Egypt 1849) or the Bisson brothers (Montblanc 1859), already having been shaped in the visual imagination by painting, now took on new facets through photography. In the mid 19th century photographs of the Campagna Romana provided models for the landscape painting of the French fellows of the Villa Medici in Rome.[7] The media that have been preserved repeatedly show that traveling artists were poised between their self-understanding as chroniclers and an artistic treatment of the areas which they encountered and which, having already been made familiar through painting, literature, and photography, were permeated by myth, cliché, and prejudice.

Exotic landscapes and foreign objects renewed European art history in parallel with geopolitical events. When Eugène Delacroix arrived in Tangiers in 1832, he was accompanying a diplomatic French mission that was trying to diffuse a conflict between Moroccan tribes and the British presence in North Africa, which had arisen due to the French occupation of Algeria in 1830. Orientalism, japonism, and ultimately also primitivism as responses to colonial interests in Africa, Southeast Aisa, and South America coalesced into major formal innovations in the modern concept of art. Whereas objects initially came to Europe via the routes of colonial politics and trade, a wave of artists later traveled to places where the masks, fetishes and temple figures—as well as reproducible media images thereof—available in Europe in museums, rummage shops, and at world fairs had originated. A journey is always associated with the traveler's initial mental image of the intended destination. Sensations and experiences are thus previously influenced by media. Depicted places of longing represent media events. The counterpart to the viewer, who stands before an image with a penetrating gaze[8] that wanders through the painting, is the traveling artist, who strolls through reality as if it were an image.

SHELTER IN FOREIGN TERRITORY AND REPROBATE SHORES

In unfamiliar lands the hotel initially served a place where travelers encountered familiar situations. Wilhelm Gentz, a native of Neuruppin and one of the first German painters to dedicate himself to Orientalism, traveled through Egypt in 1850/51 to what is today Sudan. When he arrived in Alexandria the locals fought over his baggage, »so that I was forced to intervene with my cane. Besides, I could not understand a word. The things were carried to the *douane,* where I finally packed them onto a donkey and went straight away into the city in order to find a European hotel. The oriental streets are veritable labyrinths. Horses, camels, oxen, people, and donkeys push their way through the narrowest lanes, and I finally arrived at a large square where the consuls live and where the hotels are situated. The hotels are very large and beautiful, the *diners* excellent. However, the price for everything is very expensive. After I had seated myself for breakfast, I immediately encountered three Germans, five Frenchmen, and Italians and Greeks, most of whom had come back from Upper Egypt and whom I allowed to brief me in a number of useful matters.«[9]

Travelers together represented a class unto themselves. However, given that widely traveled artists wished to dazzle those back at home with stories of adventure and exotic experiences, it is little wonder that depiction of the generally European-style life in the hotel was seldom recorded. Like Georg Forster before him, Gentz saw himself as a *rapporteur* from a foreign word. His travel descriptions sold brilliantly.

Since Orientalism, the topos of the (artist) journey has been defined by a freedom from social convention. »The Orient was almost a European invention,«[10] an imaginary realm that emerged in concert with travelogues, studies,

5 Ursula Storch, ed. *Die Welt in Reichweite. Imaginäre Reisen im 19. Jahrhundert,* exhibit. cat. Wien Museum (Vienna, 2009).

6 See Christine Buci-Glucksman, »Der kartographische Blick der Kunst,« in *Atlas Mapping. Künstler als Kartographen. Kartographie als Kultur,* eds. Paolo Bianchi and Sabine Folie, exhibit. cat. Offenes Kulturhaus Linz and Kunsthaus Bregenz (Vienna, 1997). For the map of the Surrealists see »Le monde aux temps des surréalistes,« in *Variétés. Revue mensuelle illustrée de l'esprit contemporain, special ed. Le Surréalisme en 1929* Brussels (June 1929), 26/27; and *Vermessung der Welt: Heterotopien und Wissensräume in der Kunst,* eds. Katrin Bucher-Trantow, Hans Dieter Huber, Elke Krasny, and Peter Pakesch, exhibit. cat. Kunsthaus Graz, Universalmuseum Joanneum (Cologne, 2011).

7 Françoise Heilbrun, »Around the World: Explorers, Travelers, and Tourists,« in *A New History of Photography,* ed. Michel Frizot (Cologne, 1998), 157.

8 Norman Bryson, *Vision and Painting: The Logic of the Gaze* (New Haven, 1983).

9 Quoted in *Wilhelm Gentz: Briefe einer Reise nach Ägypten und Nubien 1850/1851,* ed. Irina Röcker (Berlin, 2004), 50 f.

10 Edward W. Said, »Introduction,« in *Orientalismus* [1978] (New York, 1994), 1.

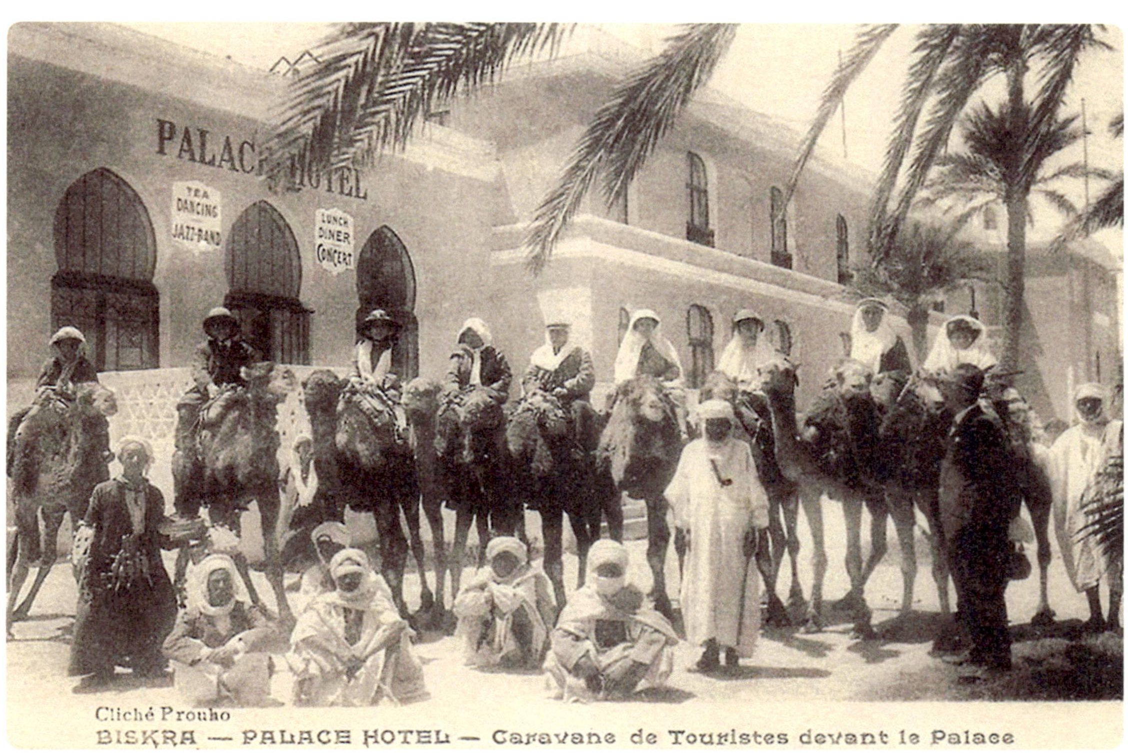

Abb. / Fig. 2

ANONYM: BISKRA IN ALGERIEN, PALACE HOTEL, TOURISTENKARAWANE VOR DEM PALACE, UM 1900, POSTKARTE
BISKRA IN ALGERIA, PALACE HOTEL, TOURIST-CARAVAN IN FRONT OF THE PALACE, C. 1900, POSTCARD

Der Topos der (Künstler-)Reise ist seit dem Orientalismus die Befreiung von gesellschaftlichen Konventionen. Der »Orient war beinahe eine Erfindung Europas« – als imaginärer Raum entstand er in Rückkopplung mit Reiseberichten, Forschungen und politischen Ereignissen.[10] Die Siedlungskolonie Algerien war bereits 1848 von Frankreich annektiert worden. Die Oase von Biskra, Wüstenstadt am nördlichen Rand der Sahara, gehörte schon Mitte des 19. Jahrhunderts zu den von romantischen Malern besuchten Orten erotischer Fantasie. Die berühmten Frauen des Stammes der Ouled Nail hielt Félix-Jacques Antoine Moulin bereits 1856 in einer Albuminserie fotografisch fest.[11] In den 1860er-Jahren eröffnete dann ein Fotostudio in Biskra und ab Ende des 19. Jahrhunderts reiste man in die als Kurort vermarktete Oase in der Wüste bequem per Bahn. 1898 residierte man im Hotel Royal oder Victoria und genoss den »Sommer, den ganzen Winter über«, wie der Werbeslogan eines Plakats versprach. Eine anonyme Postkarte aus der Zeit um 1900 (Abb. 2) zeigt eine Touristenkarawane vor dem Palace Hotel in Biskra, das am Eingang »Tea, Dancing, Jazzband, Lunch, Diner und Concert« annonciert. So wundert es nicht, wenn Henri Matisses erste Nordafrikareise 1906 mit einer Krise begann: Er fand kein Modell, war angesichts des anhaltenden Regens frustriert und klagte darüber, dass er die ganze Zeit wie ein Tourist unterwegs sei und keine Ruhe zum Malen finde.[12] Es ist zugleich eine Krise der Bilder, die hier überhaupt noch malbar waren. Denn um 1906 war Biskra künstlerisch bereits weitgehend eingenommen, der Wüstenort auch literarisch mehrfach beschrieben – unter anderem spielt hier André Gides Roman *L'Immoraliste* von 1902. Biskra wie auch Tanger waren nicht nur zu Festungen orientalistischer Malerei avanciert, sondern auch zu Orten erotischer Ausschweifungen europäischer Besucher in Nordafrika – »die Manilas und Bangkoks des ausgehenden 19. Jahrhunderts«.[13] Das verkommene Ufer des Kolonialismus wurde immer in der Ferne installiert: Gauguin beheimatete sich auf der polynesischen Insel Hiva Oa unter anderem dadurch, dass er sich ein junges Mädchen von 13 Jahren zur Frau nahm, Karl Hofer tat es ihm in Indien gleich – die Reise in die Fremde wurde gleichsam sexuell inkorporiert.[14]

FREIZEITGESELLSCHAFT

DER KÜNSTLER ALS TOURIST

Im ausgehenden 19. Jahrhundert waren die Bäder an der Küste der Normandie, etwa Trouville-sur-Mer und Deauville, oder an der Côte d'Azur (die englischen Seebäder schon im 18. Jahrhundert) zu Orten des mondänen Sommerlebens

10 Edward W. Said, *Orientalismus* (engl. Erstausgabe 1978), Frankfurt am Main 2009, Einleitung, S. 1.

11 Vgl. Moulins Album *Souvenir d'Algérie ou l'algérie photographié*, publiziert *1859/60.*

12 Vgl. Hilary Spurling, *Matisse. Eine Biographie*, 2 Bde., hier: Bd. 1 *Matisse 1898–1908*, Köln 2007, insbes. S. 365–368.

13 Roger Benjamin, *Orientalist Aesthetics: Art, Colonialism, and French North Africa (1880–1930)*, Berkeley / Los Angeles / New York 2003, S. 165.

14 Zu Gauguin vgl. Abigail Solomon-Godeau, »Going Native: Paul Gauguin and the Invention of Primitivist Modernism«, in: *The Expanding Discourse Feminism and Art History*, hrsg. von Norma Broude, Mary Garrad, New York 1992, S. 312–329; zu Karl Hofer: Otterbeck 2007 (wie Anm. 1), S. 187–195.

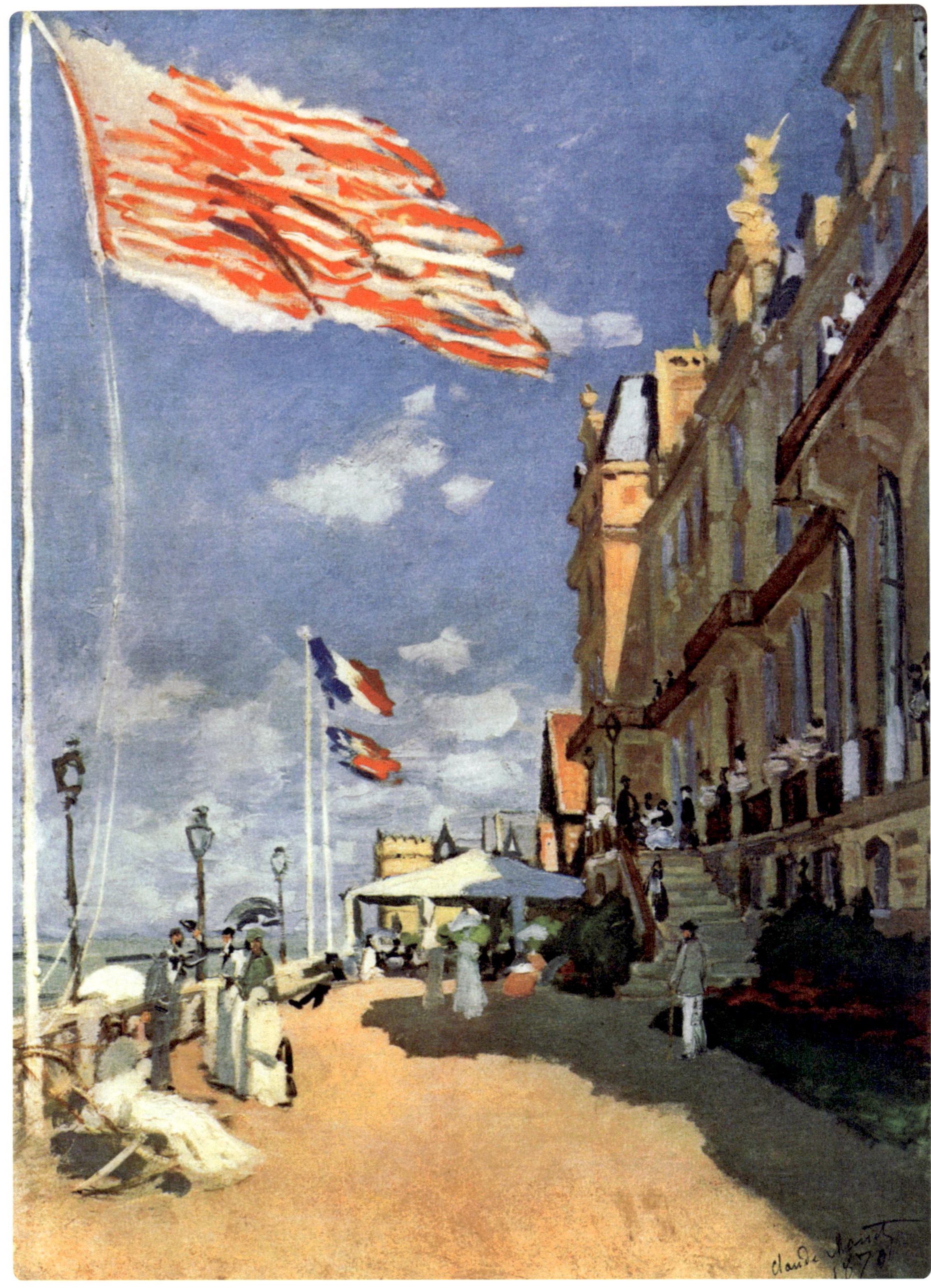

Abb. / Fig. 3 CLAUDE MONET

HOTEL DES ROCHES NOIRES. TROUVILLE

1870 (RF 1947–30), Öl auf Leinwand, Paris, Musée d'Orsay, Schenkung von Jacques Laroche für das Jeu de Paume-Museum im Jahr 1947 / 1870 (RF 1947–30), oil on canvas, Paris Musée d'Orsay, donation of Jacques Laroche for the Jeu de Paume Museum in 1947

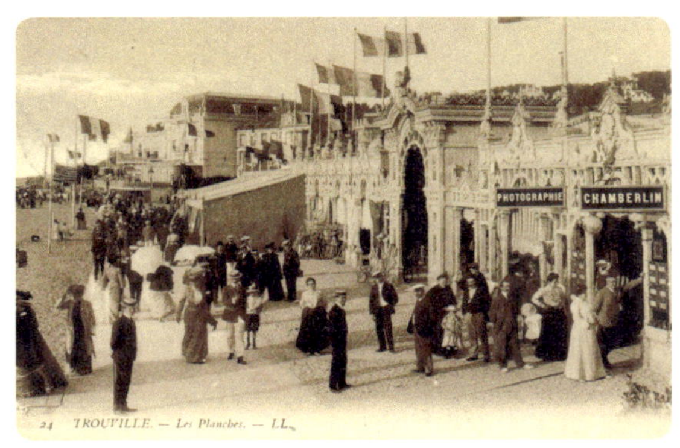

Abb. / Fig. 4

ANONYM: TROUVILLE CALVADOS, DER STRAND / THE BEACH

1908, Postkarte / Postcard

geworden. Künstler partizipierten an dieser neuen Welt der gepflegten Freizeitkultur, die der Kultursoziologe und Ökonom Thorstein Bunde Veblen schon 1899 aus einer Klasse des Müßiggangs, die ihrer Prestigesucht fröne, herleitete. Die Strandbilder und zahlreichen Ansichten von Strandpromenaden mit den großen Hotels, wie etwa Claude Monets Darstellung des HOTEL DES ROCHES NOIRES, wurden Legenden. Die Postkartenmotive nur eine Generation später bezeugen jedoch, wie dieses Lebensgefühl von Freiluft und Sommerfrische zur Massenveranstaltung geworden war (Abb. 3 und Abb. 4). Um 1900 bereits beklagten Zeitgenossen, dass man im August »tout Paris« in Trouville anträfe. Kein Wunder, dass Innenansichten von Hotels voller Pariser Nachbarn schwerlich zu finden sind.

DIE KÜNSTLERINNEN UND KÜNSTLER UM 1900 WAREN NOTORISCHE REISENDE, immer unterwegs in die Sommerfrische, zu den Kulturdenkmälern der Welt, zu abgelegenen Rückzugsorten oder Künstlerkolonien. Die reisende Moderne brachte Ernst Barlach und Henri Matisse nach Russland, Pablo Picasso fuhr nach Holland, zahlreiche Künstler zum Beispiel aus Osteuropa oder aus noch ferneren Gegenden wie Indien kamen im Gegenzug nach Paris, Emil Nolde und Max Pechstein machten sich in die Südsee auf. Die Vereinfachungen des Reisens hatten auch eine globale Internationalisierung der Moderne zur Folge.[15] Zwar schickten Galeristen ihre Künstler auch abseits der ausgetretenen Pfade, dennoch blieben Nordafrika, Ägypten und der Maghreb eine sichere Bank. Das erkannten auch die Kunsthistoriker Eduard Fuchs und Johannes Guthmann, die 1914 für Max Slevogt eine Reise nach Ägypten organisierten, der bereits zuvor zahlreiche orientalistische Sujets ohne eigene Reiseerfahrungen gemalt hatte. Fuchs stellte ihm sämtliche Materialien und Farben in einer großen Kiste zusammen, plante das Besuchsprogramm und organisierte auch die Modelle vor Ort: »Sofort hinter dem Hotelgarten ist ein elendes arabisches Dorf. Entlang der niedrigen Steinmauern hocken die schwarzgekleideten Weiber und schwarze Schafe sitzen im Sand.«[16] Slevogt vermied die großen Sehenswürdigkeiten in der Auswahl seiner Motive und konzentrierte sich mehr auf gedeckte Farbklänge, Figuren und Landschaftsimpressionen. Dass die Künstler der klassischen Moderne sich zunehmend auch auf andere Formen der Darstellung verlegten, hatte durchaus mit der Abgegriffenheit der bildlichen Repräsentation der Sujets und dem Gefühl zu tun, dass der Orientalismus nicht mehr zeitgemäß war. Paul Klee entwickelte die Farbstruktur der Bilder seiner Ägyptenreise 1929 nach der Cardinalprogression, mit der die kulturellen Spannungen in eine abstrakte mathematische Formel zur Farbgebung aufgelöst werden konnten.[17]

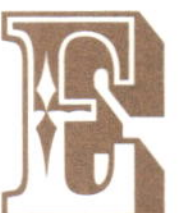
iner, der aus dem Koffer lebte, war der amerikanische Maler und gefeierte Porträtist John Singer Sargent. Er überlieferte auch, wie es aussah, wenn der Künstler im Hotelzimmer arbeitet: AN ARTIST IN HIS STUDIO zeigt seinen Freund Ambrogio Raffele beim Malen im Hotel im italienischen Purtud im August 1904 (Abb. 5). Raffele sitzt mit Pinsel und Palette im abendlichen Licht zwischen Bett und Fenster schräg auf einem Stuhl neben dem Bett. Dorthin hat er achtlos den Sonnenhut geworfen, um sich sogleich der Ausbeute des Tages zu widmen. Überall sind die Ölskizzen von unterwegs ausgebreitet und auf dem weißen Laken sowie dem Nachtschrank im Hintergrund lehnt ein frisches großformatiges Landschaftsgemälde an der Wand. Der Künstler hält in seiner Hand eine kleine Skizze (vielleicht auch eine Fotografie oder eine Postkarte?), in deren Anblick er versunken ist. Dieses beengte Hotelzimmer, so viel ist klar, wird nur zum Atelier umfunktioniert, wenn die Inspiration es absolut erfordert, die Singer Sargent hier zum Bildthema erhoben hat.

Der sichere Blick aus dem Fenster Während das Hotelinnere als Bastion europäischer Kultur in fernen Ländern nur selten Eingang in die Reisebilder gefunden hat, haben fast alle Künstler auf Reisen den Blick aus dem Fenster ihres (Hotel-)Zimmers festgehalten. Werke dieser Art bilden ein eigenes Genre der Reisebilder, die dem Hooke'schen Kasten als der provisorischen Behausung des Blicks in der tragbaren Camera obscura entsprechen. Das Hotelzimmer stellt das dunkle Futteral eines europäischen Innenlebens, von dem aus der Künstler zum Auge wird, um sich der draußen ihm zu Füßen liegenden Welt anzunähern. So malte Slevogt aus seinem Hotelzimmer in Assuan eine Nillandschaft, die seltsam unspezifisch wirkt (Abb. 6).

15 Vgl. den Reader *Modern Art in Africa, Asia and Latin America. An Introduction to Global Modernism,* hrsg. von Elaine O'Brian, Melissa Chiu, Mary K. Coffey, Benjamin Genocchio, Everlyn Nicodemus, Roberto Tejada, Oxford u. a. 2012, und z. B. *Amrita Sher-Ghil. Eine indische Künstlerfamilie im 20. Jahrhundert,* Ausst.-Kat. Haus der Kunst, München, München 2006.

16 So eine Beschreibung von Eugen Kahler, zit. nach: Otterbeck 2007 (wie Anm. 1), S. 140 f.

17 Vgl. Christoph Wagner, »Klees Reise ins Land der besseren Erkenntnis. Die Ägyptenreise und die Arbeiten zur ›Cardinalprogression‹ im kulturhistorischen Kontext«, in: *Paul Klee. Reisen in den Süden,* hrsg. von Uta Gerlach-Laxner, Ellen Schwinzer, Ausst.-Kat. Museum der bildenden Künste Leipzig, Gustav-Lübcke-Museum, Hamm, Ostfildern-Ruit 1997, S. 72–85, und Birgit Haehnel, »Gleißendes Licht über weißer Leinwand. Die Aneignung des Orients in der europäischen Malerei«, in: Ausst.-Kat. *Orte der Sehnsucht* 2008 (wie Anm. 1), S. 51–56.

and political events. The settler colony of Algeria was already annexed by France in 1848. Even in the 19th century the oasis of Biskra, a desert city bordering on the northern Sahara, was a place visited by romantic painters, which was infused with erotic fantasies. Félix-Jacques Antoine Moulin documented the famous women of the Ouled Naïl as early as 1856 in a volume of photographs.[11] A photography studio opened in Biskra in the 1860s, and by the late 19th century one could comfortably travel by rail to the oasis, which was marketed as a spa resort. In the year 1898 one would have stayed in the Hotel Royal or Victoria and enjoyed the »summer for the entire winter,« as promised by the advertising slogan on a poster. An anonymous postcard from the period around 1900 (fig. 2) shows a caravan of tourists in front of the Palace Hotel in Biskra, which advertises with »Tea, Dancing, Jazzband, Lunch, Diner and Concert« at the entrance. It is therefore no wonder that Henri Matisse's first North African trip in 1906 begins with a crisis. He could not find a model. He was frustrated by the continuous rain and complained that he was going about the whole time like a tourist and could not find any quiet time to paint.[12] His crisis is simultaneously a crisis about the kinds of images that were still paintable where he was. For the most part, Biskra had already been conquered artistically by 1906. The desert site had been described many times in literature, forming the backdrop for André Gide's novel *L' Immoraliste* from 1902, among others. Biskra as well as Tangiers had not only become strongholds of Orientalist painting but also places of erotic excess among European visitors to North Africa—the Bangkoks and Manilas of the late 19th century.[13] The depraved colonial shore was always situated far away. Gauguin made his home on the Polynesian island of Hiva Oa, also by taking a young girl of 13 as his wife. Karl Hofer did the same in India—the journey to foreign lands was incorporated sexually.[14]

LEISURE SOCIETY
THE ARTIST AS TOURIST

In the late 19th century the beach resorts on the coast of Normandy, such as Trouville-sur-Mer and Deauville, and those on the Côte d'Azur had become places of a sophisticated summer lifestyle (as had the English resorts already in the 18th century). Artists took part in this new world of cultivated leisure, which the sociologist of culture and economist Thorstein Bunde Veblen attributed already in 1899 to a class of the idle indulging its insatiable desire for prestige. Images of the beach and numerous views of boardwalks with immense hotels like Claude Monet's depiction of the HOTEL DES ROCHES NOIRES became legendary. The postcard motifs dating from just one generation later testify to what extent this taste for fresh air and summer resorts had become a mass phenomenon (fig. 3 and fig. 4). Around 1900 contemporary travelers complained of meeting »tout Paris« in Trouville in August. It is no surprise that interior views of hotels filled with neighbors from Paris are so difficult to find.

THE ARTISTS OF THE PERIOD AROUND 1900 WERE NOTORIOUS TRAVELERS, always visiting summer resorts, traveling to cultural monuments, distant places of retreat, or artist colonies. The modern era of travel took Ernst Barlach and Henri Matisse to Russia; Pablo Picasso traveled to Holland; in return numerous artists from Eastern Europe or even more distant regions such as India came to Paris; Emil Nolde and Max Pechstein headed to the South Seas. The simplification of travel brought about the global internationalization of the modern age.[15] Although gallery owners did send their artists to areas beyond the beaten path, North Africa, Egypt, and also the Maghreb always meant a return on the investment. Art historians Eduard Fuchs and Johannes Guthmann realized this when organizing a trip to Egypt in 1914 for Max Slevogt, who had already painted numerous Orientalist motifs without having any personal travel experience. Fuchs compiled all kinds of materials and paints for him in a large crate, planned the touring program, and organized models on site: »Just beyond the hotel garden is a miserable Arab village. Black-clad women and black sheep lie in the sand.«[16] Slevogt avoided major landmarks in his selection of motifs and focused instead on a muted palate, human figures, and impressions of the landscape. That the artists of the classical modern period increasingly shifted their focus to other forms of representation was certainly owed to the subject matter being visually exhausted and Orientalism being out of date. Paul Klee developed the color structure of the images from his Egypt trip in 1929 into a cardinal progression, through which cultural tensions could be replaced by an abstract mathematical formula for assigning colors.[17]

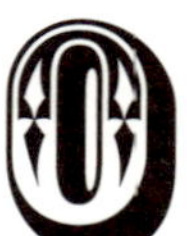

ne artist who lived out of his suitcase was the American painter and celebrated portrait artist John Singer Sargent, who has provided us with a picture of an artist working in a hotel room. AN ARTIST IN HIS STUDIO shows his friend Ambrogio Raffele while painting in a hotel in the Italian region of Purtud in August in 1904 (fig. 5). In the light of evening Raffele is sitting with his paintbrush and palette and is perched diagonally on a chair between the window and the bed, where he has carelessly thrown his hat to dedicate his attention to the spoils of the day. Sketches made while he was out are spread about. Balanced on the white sheet as well as the night table is a

11 See Moulin's album *Souvenir d'Algérie ou l'algérie photographié*, published 1859/60.

12 See Hilary Spurling, *Matisse: Eine Biographie*, vol. 1, *Matisse 1898–1908* (Cologne, 2007), 365–368.

13 Roger Benjamin, *Orientalist Aesthetics: Art, Colonialism, and French North Africa (1880–1930)*, (Berkeley/Los Angeles/New York, 2003), 171.

14 On Gauguin see Abigail Solomon-Godeau, »Going Native: Paul Gauguin and the Invention of Primitivist Modernism,« in *The Expanding Discourse Feminism and Art History*, eds. Norma Broude and Mary Garrad (New York, 1992), 312–329; on Karl Hofer see Otterbeck 2007 (see note 1), 187–195.

15 See the reader *Modern Art in Africa, Asia and Latin America. An Introduction to Global Modernism*, eds. Elaine O'Brian, Melissa Chiu, Mary K. Coffey, Benjamin Genocchio, Everlyn Nicodemus, and Roberto Tejada (Oxford et al, 2012); and for example, *Amrita Sher-Ghil. Eine indische Künstlerfamilie im 20. Jahrhundert*, exhibit. cat. Haus der Kunst, Munich (Munich, 2006).

16 As described by Eugen Kahler, quoted in Otterbeck 2007 (see note 1), 140 f.

17 See Christoph Wagner, »Klees Reise ins Land der besseren Erkenntnis. Die Ägyptenreise und die Arbeiten zur ›Cardinalprogression‹ im kulturhistorischen Kontext,« in *Paul Klee: Reisen in den Süden*, eds. Uta Gerlach-Laxner and Ellen Schwinzer, exhibit. cat. Museum der bildenden Künste Leipzig, Gustav-Lübcke-Museum, Hamm (Ostfildern-Ruit ,1997), 72–85; and Birgit Haehnel, »Gleißendes Licht über weißer Leinwand. Die Aneignung des Orients in der europäischen Malerei,« in *Orte der Sehnsucht* 2008 (see note 1), 51–56.

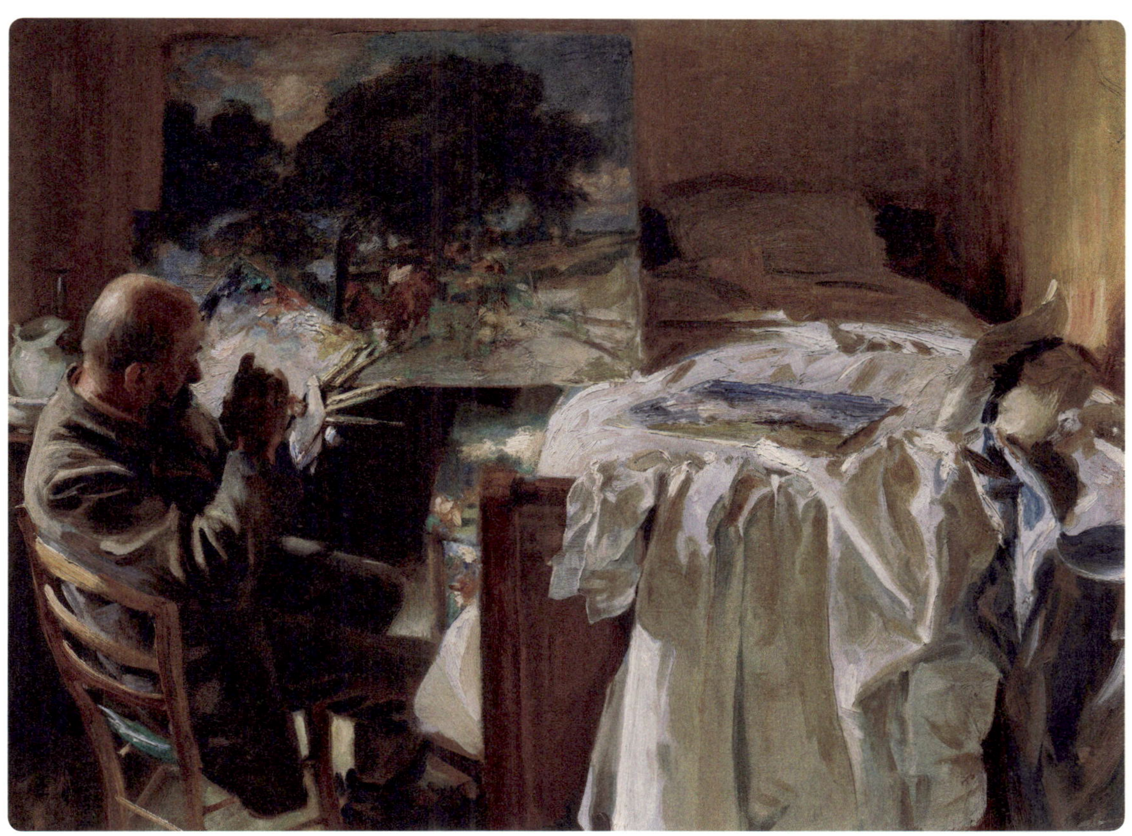

ABB. / *FIG.* *5* JOHN SINGER SARGENT
AN ARTIST IN HIS STUDIO
1904, Öl auf Leinwand, Museum of Fine Arts, Boston / 1904, oil on canvas, Museum of Fine Arts, Boston

Im Bild, das eine weitläufige Wasserlandschaft und die angrenzenden gelbtonig-kargen Ufer zeigt, findet das Auge keinen Halt; einziger Ankerpunkt ist das in ruhiger Bahn in der Mitte nach links gleitende Segelboot. Der Vordergrund ist topografisch kaum zu entschlüsseln und eine landschaftliche Stimmung stellt sich trotz der Betonung des gleißenden Lichtes und trotz der Tatsache, dass das Gemälde erst zu einem späten Zeitpunkt der Reise entstand, nicht ein.

Die Annäherung an das fremde Draußen durch den sicheren Hort eines Hotelzimmers ist ein *rite de passage,* welcher den ankommenden Maler zum Auge werden lässt. Henri Matisse war der Meister des Fensterblicks als Bildreflexion. Er führte ein rastloses Leben als Reisender und gerade das Provisorische des Quartiers im Hotel beflügelte seine Kreativität in Ajaccio, Collioure, Nizza und Tanger. In einer Schaffenskrise entschloss er sich mit 60 Jahren nach Tahiti zu fahren. Er hatte nur einen kleinen Reisemalkasten dabei und schuf auf der fünfmonatigen Reise von 1930 nicht ein einziges Bild – anders als sein Vorgänger Gauguin. Nach einer Skizze entstand nachträglich der Blick aus seinem Zimmer im Hotel Stuart in Papeete (Abb. 7). Matisse äußerte sich begeistert über die dortige Botanik, die Küche, das Kunsthandwerk und die Lebensweise, war aber entsetzt über das koloniale Gebaren der Europäer auf Tahiti, das in dieser Zeit noch nicht touristisch erschlossen war. Das Bild zeigt eine nachträgliche Betrachtung, ein wohl durchkomponiertes Farbflächenkonstrukt, das trotz der Abstraktion einen sinnlichen Eindruck zu vermitteln vermag. Matisse schließt zunächst Gelb aus dem Bild aus – das »breiige Licht« in Tahiti störte ihn[18] – und verspannt zwischen rostroten Himmelswolken und der gleichfarbigen Balkonbrüstung einen breiten königsblauen Streifen Wasser, auf dem im Vordergrund ein weißes Schiff mit kirchturmhohen Masten am Quai vor Anker liegt, flankiert von zwei ornamental emporrankenden grünen Baumbüscheln, die die wolkigen Formen des Himmels aufgreifen. Umrahmt von einem roten Strich und einer blau-weißen Blumenbordüre verfestigt Matisse das Bild optisch auf der Oberfläche. Allein die blaue, geblümte Gardine vorm Fenster bringt Verwirrung ins Spiel, denn sie ist auf Höhe des Himmels und des

18 Vgl. Spurling 2007 (wie Anm. 12), hier: Bd. 2 *Matisse – Der Meister. 1909–1954*, S. 325–334, hier S. 328.

fresh, large-scale landscape painting that leans against the wall. The artist holds a small sketch in his hand (maybe a photograph or a postcard?), which he is absorbed in studying. Clearly this cramped hotel room has been turned into a studio at the urgent demand of inspiration, the subject of Sargent's painting.

The Safe View from the Window

Although the interior of the hotel, a bastion of European culture in a foreign country, was seldom included among images of travel, almost all artists captured views out their (hotel) windows when traveling. Works of this kind form their own genre of travel pictures, which correspond to Hooke's box and the provisional dwelling of the eye in the form of the camera obscura. The hotel room represents the dark sheath of the European life within, from where the artist acts as an eye that is getting to know the world outside and below. For example, Slevogt painted a Nile landscape of a strangely non-specific character as seen from his hotel room in Aswan (fig. 6). Showing an expansive water landscape and a bordering yellow-toned and barren shoreline, the image offers no refuge for the eye. The only resting point is the sailboat in the middle of the image, which is calmly sailing towards the left. The foreground is topographically almost indecipherable, and a scenic atmosphere remains absent, despite the emphasis on glistening light and the fact that the painting was made at a later point during the trip.

Approaching the foreign world outside through the secure refuge of a hotel room is a *rite de passage,* which turns the newly arrived artist into an eye. Henri Matisse was a master of the view from the window as a form of reflecting on the image itself. He led a restless life as a traveler, and especially the makeshift quarters of a hotel nourished his creativity in Ajaccio, Collioure, Nice, and Tangiers. When faced with a creative crisis, he decided at age 60 to take a trip to Tahiti. He only took a small portable box of paints with him, and during his five-month trip in 1930 he did not paint a single picture—unlike his predecessor Gaugin. Only after the trip did he use a sketch to produce

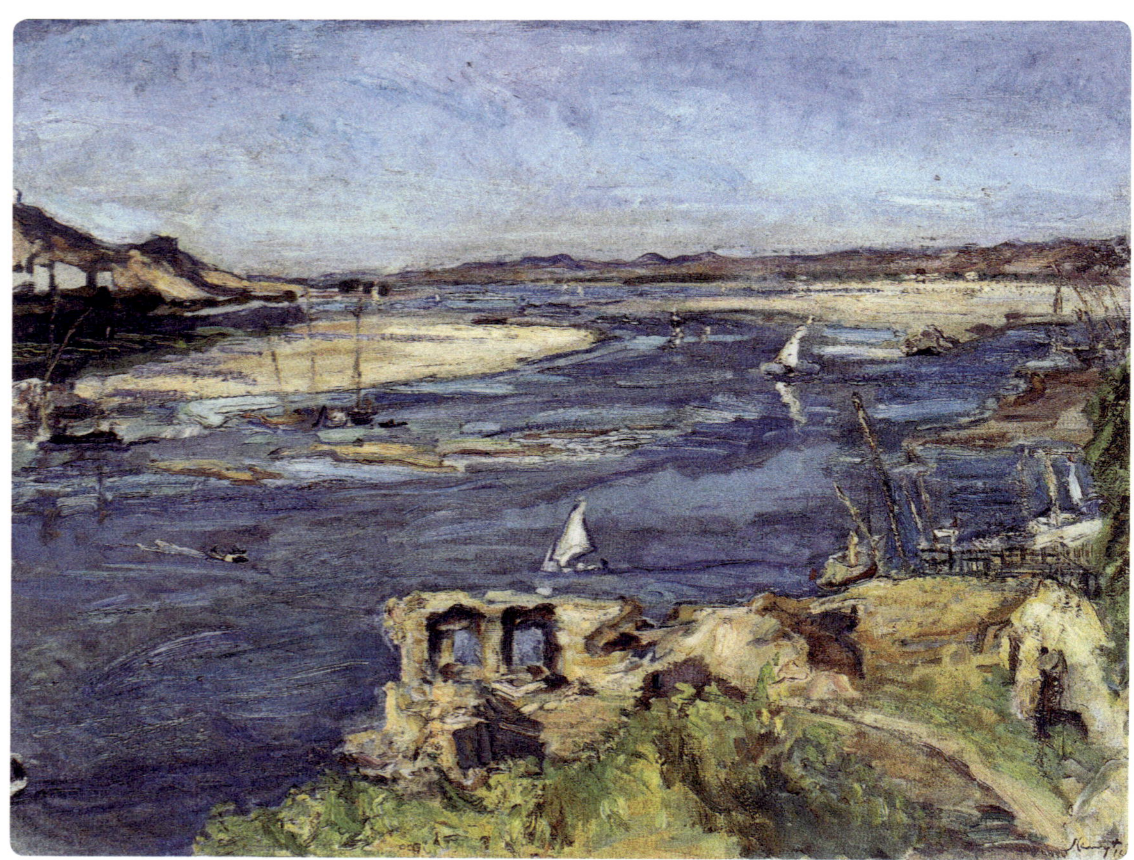

Abb. / Fig. 6

MAX SLEVOGT DER NIL BEI / THE NIL AT **ASSUAN / ASWAN**

1914, Öl auf Leinwand / Oil on canvas, Galerie Neue Meister, Staatliche Kunstsammlungen Dresden, SLUB Dresden/Deutsche Fotothek

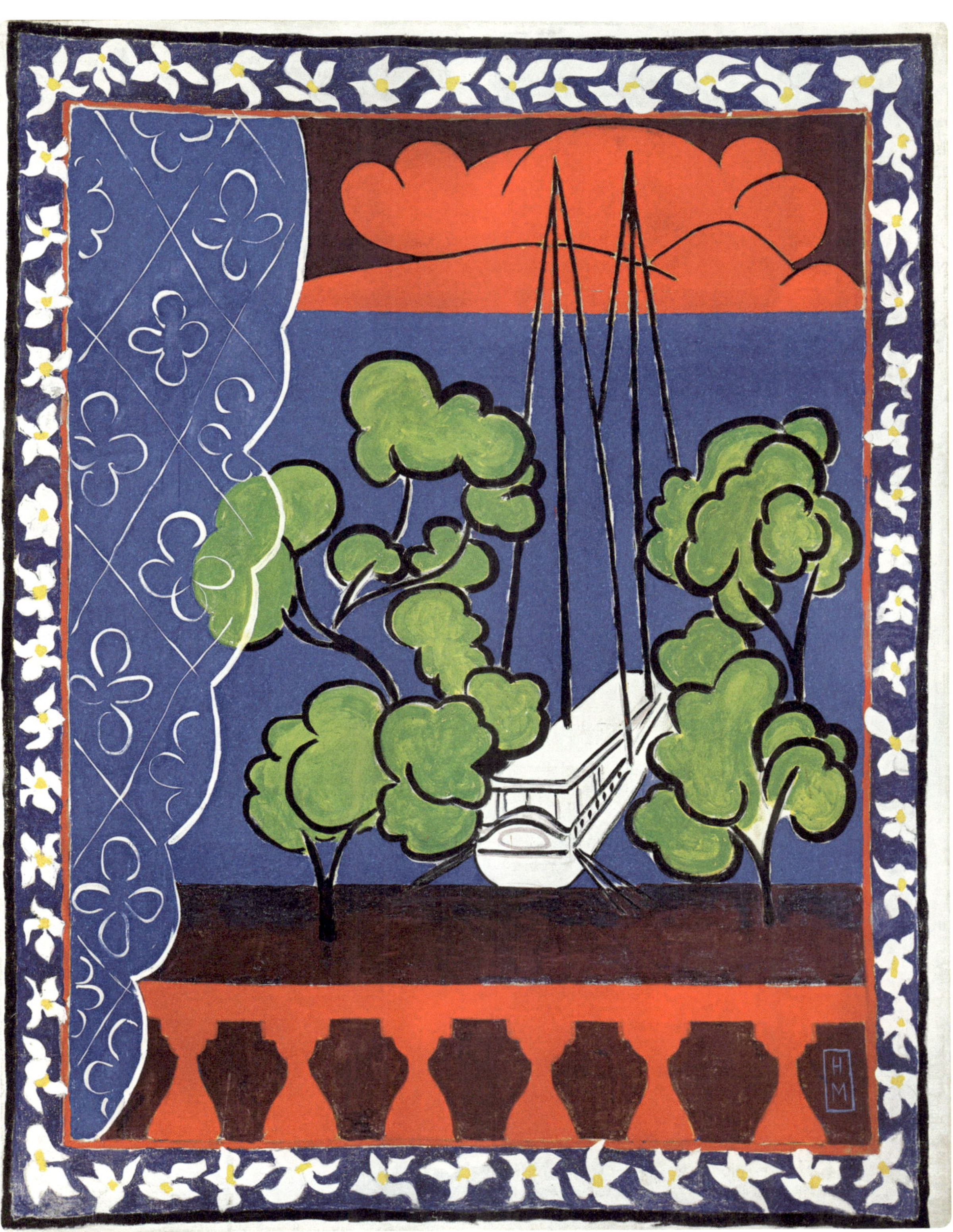

Abb. / Fig. 7

HENRI MATISSE FENSTER WINDOW IN TAHITI II

1932, Öl auf Leinwand / Oil on canvas, © Succession H. Matisse / VG Bild-Kunst, Bonn 2014

18 See Spurling 2007 (see note 12), vol. 2, *Matisse – Der Meister. 1909–1954*, 328.

the image of his view from his room in the Hotel Stuart in Papeete (fig. 7). Matisse expressed his enthusiasm for the local plant life, cuisine, crafts, and lifestyle, but he was appalled by the colonial conduct of the Europeans on Tahiti, which at the time had not yet become a tourist destination. The images presents a view painted after the fact, a carefully composed surface of colors, which despite its abstraction nevertheless creates a sensual impression. Matisse leaves yellow out of the picture, since the pasty light in Tahiti had bothered him,[18] spanning a wide strip of Prussian blue water between the rust-red clouds and the same-toned railing of the balcony. In the foreground is a white ship moored in the bay with masts as high as church towers; it is flanked by two green ornamental clumps of trees rising into the sky that echo the cloud formations above. Matisse optically anchors the image on the surface, which is framed by a red line and a blue and white floral border. Only the blue flower-patterned curtain in front of the window is a source of confusion, because at the height of the sky and balcony it is opaque, but over the water it becomes translucent and thus appears to be in motion. It contributes an element of uncertainty at the very site of the aesthetic interface between the image and the viewer. The pillow-like clouds, the well shaped balustrade, and the stereotypical view of a harbor merge as ornamentation that is rendered cool and distant due to the curtain and the cold colors. The ornamental surface reflects the paradisiacal projections of the viewer, who is only able to move through this image with the eyes.

Sven Johne's series of photographs taken from hotels on the Italian island of Lampedusa in 2012 draws on similar elements but within the context of late colonial events (fig. 8). Since 2009 the tourist island, which has the most beautiful beaches of Italy, has become an island of refugees. Since this period hundreds of thousand of refugees from Africa and the eastern Mediterranean have been heading for Europe's southern-most archipelago, which is situated in the Mediterranean between Sicily and Tunesia. On Lampedusa, tourism and displacement collide head-on at the guarded borders of Europe. Johne's photographs present quiet, unoccupied, well-situated hotels rooms, just like in a catalogue. The doors of the balconies are open to create a picture within a picture: sun, beach, sea, sailboat, and palms. The pillows on the interior signal reassuring comfort; the furnishings correspond to international everything-included tourism. The light flooding the photographs gives a sense of glistening heat outside as well as a clarity and brightness within. Alone the knowledge about the dramatic scenarios that play out with refugees before the island of Lampedusa, the inhuman border policies, the unconscionable conditions in the refugee camps on the island, and the political ineptitude of the Italian state and the entire European community make these matter-of-fact photographs almost unbearable. The image of the window with the longed-for beach idyll is deceptive. Not the camera but the knowledge of the world makes the photograph dubious. The traveling eye of the photographer records objectively but fundamentally calls the report of the chronicler into question. Johne forgoes showing the hotel room as a dwelling place; the interior is no longer depicted as an individual interpretation or a gaze of longing but instead it reflects the removed view of a touristic advertisement. Johne seeks out what many artist travelers since the 1900s have avoided—the replicated mass media image as a means of gauging its distance from reality. The traveler's eye is only capable of seeing what enters into its already focused lens in the form of light.

Balkons opak, vor dem Wasser jedoch transluzent, sodass sie sich optisch zu bewegen scheint. Sie bringt ein Moment des Ungewissen an genau der Stelle ein, wo die ästhetische Grenze zwischen Bild und Betrachter direkt hinter dem Rahmen verortet wird. Die kissenartigen Wolken, die wohlgeformte Balustrade und das stereotype Bild einer Hafenansicht gerinnen zum Ornament, von der Gardine und den kalten Farben kühl distanziert. Die ornamentale Oberfläche reflektiert die paradiesischen Projektionen des Betrachters, der in diesem Bild nur mit den Augen herumspazieren kann.

Sven Johnes Fotoserie von Hotels auf der italienischen Insel Lampedusa von 2012 greift ähnliche Aspekte unter den Vorzeichen spätkolonialer Ereignisse auf (Abb. 8). Die Touristeninsel mit Italiens schönsten Stränden ist seit 2009 zur Flüchtlingsinsel geworden. Den südlichsten Archipel Europas im Mittelmeer zwischen Sizilien und Tunesien steuerten seither Hunderttausende Flüchtlinge aus Afrika und dem östlichen Mittelmeerraum an. Tourismus und Flucht prallen hier an den bewachten Außengrenzen Europas zusammen. Johnes Fotos zeigen stille, unbewohnte, gut situierte Hotelzimmer wie aus dem Katalog. Die Balkontüren sind zu einem Bild im Bild geöffnet: Sonne, Strand, Meer, Segelboot und Palmen. Die Kissen im Interieur signalisieren wohlige Geborgenheit, die Ausstattung internationalen Pauschaltourismus. Das Licht, das die Fotos durchflutet, vermittelt draußen gleißende Wärme und drinnen klare Helligkeit. Allein das Wissen um die Flüchtlingsdramen im Meer vor Lampedusa, eine unmenschliche Grenzpolitik, die unhaltbaren Zustände im Auffanglager der Insel und um das politische Versagen des italienischen Staates und der gesamten europäischen Gemeinschaft machen die nüchternen Aufnahmen fast unerträglich. Das Bild des Fensters mit der ersehnten Strandidylle ist trügerisch. Nicht die Kamera, sondern unser Wissen um die Welt lässt das Foto obskur werden. Das reisende Auge des Fotografen zeichnete nüchtern auf, stellt den Bericht des Chronisten aber grundlegend infrage. Das Hotelzimmer als Ort der Behausung gibt er auf, das Innen ist nicht mehr individuelle Interpretation oder sehnsüchtiger Blick, sondern erzeugt die Distanz einer Touristikwerbung. Johne sucht damit auf, was viele reisende Künstler seit 1900 vermieden haben: das massenmediale Abziehbild, um die Entfernung von der Wirklichkeit zu vermessen. Das reisende Auge vermag nur zu sehen, was als Licht in seinen zuvor eingestellten Fokus fällt.

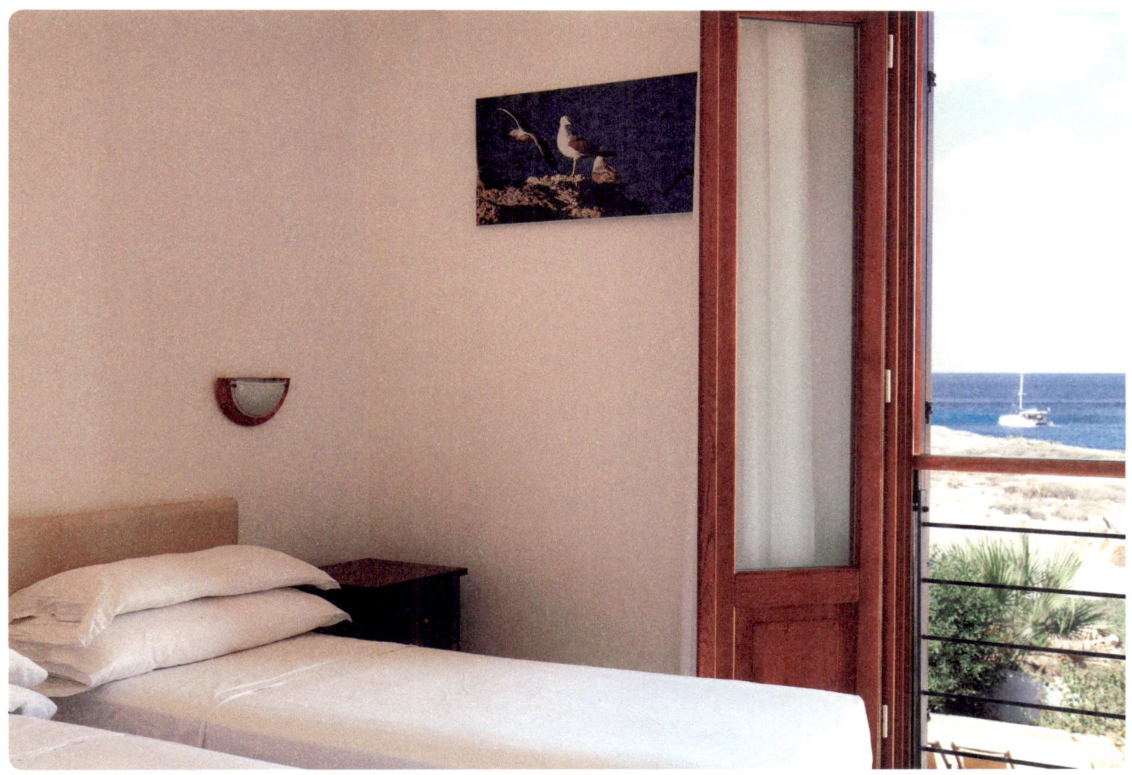

Abb. / Fig. 8

SVEN JOHNE DETAIL AUS DER SERIE **TRAUMHOTELS**
DETAIL FROM THE SERIES **DREAM HOTELS**

2012, Courtesy: Sven Johne, © Sven Johne, VG Bild-Kunst, Bonn 2014

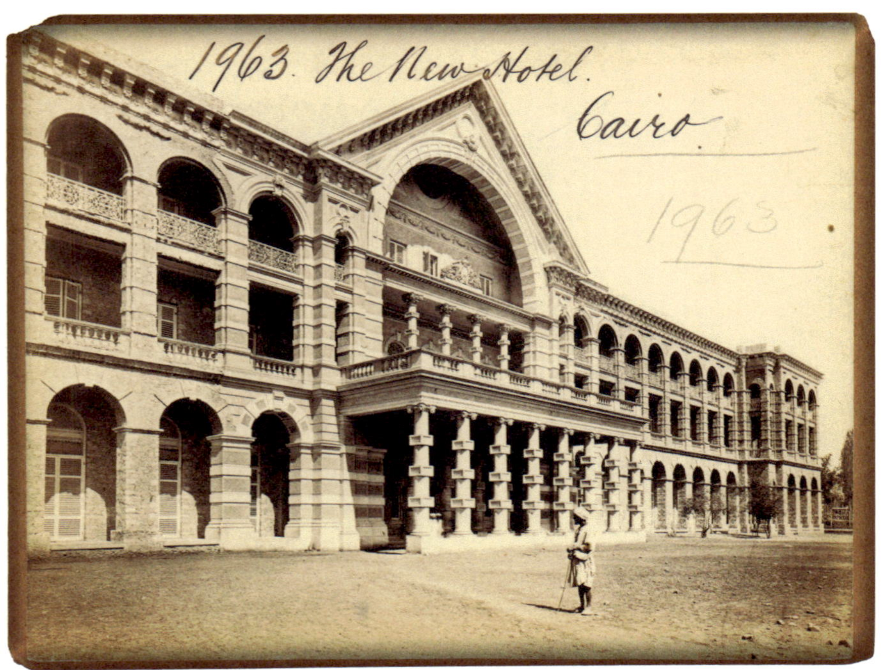

Abb. / Fig. 1

FRANCIS FRITH

THE NEW HOTEL CAIRO

1850 – 1870, Albumindruck, Sammlung Victoria und Albert Museum London, akquiriert von F. Frith and Company, 1954, © Victoria and Albert Museum, London 2014

1850 – 1870, Whole-plate albumen print, Collection Victoria and Albert Museum, London, acquired from F. Frith and Company, 1954, © Victoria and Albert Museum, London 2014

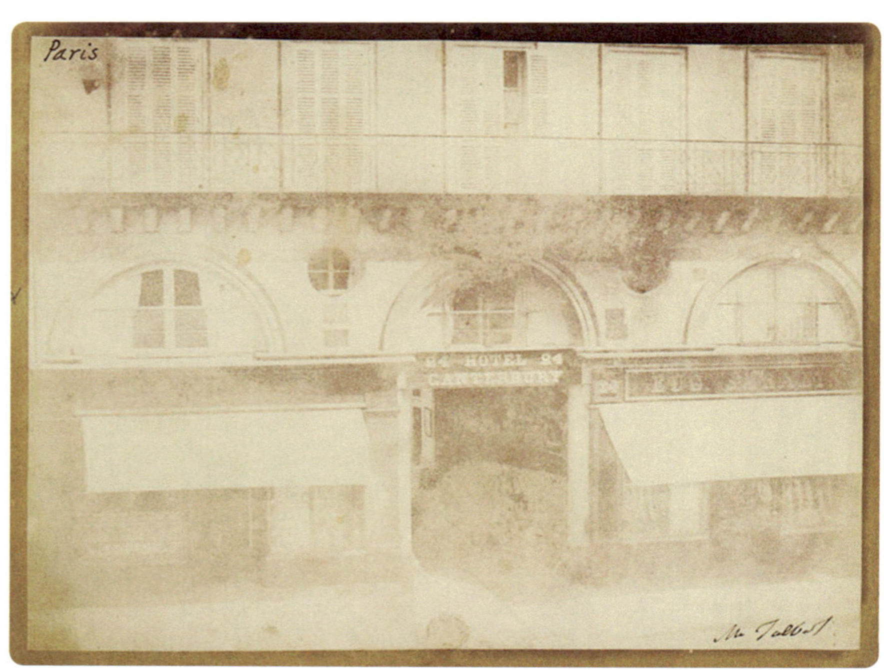

Abb. / Fig. 2

WILLIAM HENRY FOX TALBOT

RUE DE LA PAIX, HOTEL CANTERBURY

1843, Talbotypie-Negativ / Talbotype negative, Courtesy: National Media Museum / Science & Society Picture Library, © National Media Museum / Science & Society Picture Library, Bradford

FOTOGRAFIE UND ABENTEUER

KLAUS HONNEF

Francis Frith war ein reisefreudiger Mann. Als Brite gehörte er zu jenem Menschenschlag, der das Reisen als gesellschaftliche Vergnügungsform erfand. Auf der *Grand Tour* nach Rom entdeckten britische Reisende, vorwiegend Aristokraten und betuchte Bürger, auch den *romantischen Rhein*. Das *British Empire* erstreckte sich damals über den gesamten Globus, umfasste Territorien in Afrika, Amerika und Asien; Australien und Neuseeland zur Gänze. Die britische Königin Victoria, die ihrer Epoche den Namen gab, war seit dem 1. Januar 1877 überdies offiziell Kaiserin von Britisch-Indien. Reisen auf die fernen Kontinente dienten beinahe ausschließlich geschäftlichen und politischen Zwecken. Meistens waren beide miteinander verquickt; ebenso bei Unternehmungen, die vorgeblich Abenteuer und Erforschen verschiedenster Dinge zum Ziel hatten.

Francis Frith war zunächst weder reich noch war er von aristokratischer Abkunft. Er übte vielmehr ein Metier aus, das viele Züge eines Handwerks trug. Frith war Fotograf. Um den Anforderungen seines Berufs gerecht zu werden, war er stets mit viel Gepäck unterwegs. Voluminöse Plattenkameras darunter. Außerdem ein genügend umfangreicher Vorrat an großrahmigen Glasplatten. Darüber hinaus die notwendigen Chemikalien, um nach Aufkommen des lange gebräuchlichen Kollodiumverfahrens diese Glasplatten vorzubereiten, in feuchtem Zustand zu belichten und nach erfolgter Aufnahme sofort zu entwickeln. Die Resultate waren sogenannte Negative, von denen Positivabzüge auf Papier projiziert und fixiert wurden. Sonstiges technisches und persönliches Zubehör vergrößerte den Umfang der Bagage. Auf 1.100 Kilogramm belief sich etwa das Gepäck eines französischen Fotografen auf Reisen in Algerien. Zahlreiche Gehilfen und – über weite Strecken – Pferde- oder Ochsenwagen waren nötig, um die gewaltige Ausrüstung von einem Ort zum anderen zu schaffen. Gustave Flaubert, der den Fotografen und Verleger Maxime Du Camp auf einer Expedition nach Ägypten begleitete, notierte: »Die Fotografie zu erlernen ist leicht, aber die ganze Ausrüstung auf Maultieren, Kamelen und Trägern mitzuschleppen, ist ein schwieriges Problem.«

FRANCIS FRITH war also nicht der einzige Reisefotograf seiner Zeit. Sein berühmterer Landsmann Roger Fenton bereiste Russland und berichtete vom Krimkrieg; noch mit vergleichbar großer Zeitverzögerung. Samuel Bourne, ebenfalls Engländer, erkundete Indien und den Himalaja mit der Kamera. Die fotografischen Dokumente, die sie anfertigten, mussten erst per Hand in geeignete Vorlagen, etwa Holzschnitte oder Kupferstiche, umgewandelt werden, um sie drucktechnisch vervielfältigen zu können. Die Autotypie zur Herstellung von Druckklischees war noch nicht erfunden. Den Italiener Felice Beato und den Österreicher Baron Raimund von Stillfried-Rathenitz verschlug es bis nach Japan, wo Beato in Yokohama (1865) das erste Fotostudio des Landes gründete. Die US-amerikanischen Fotografen

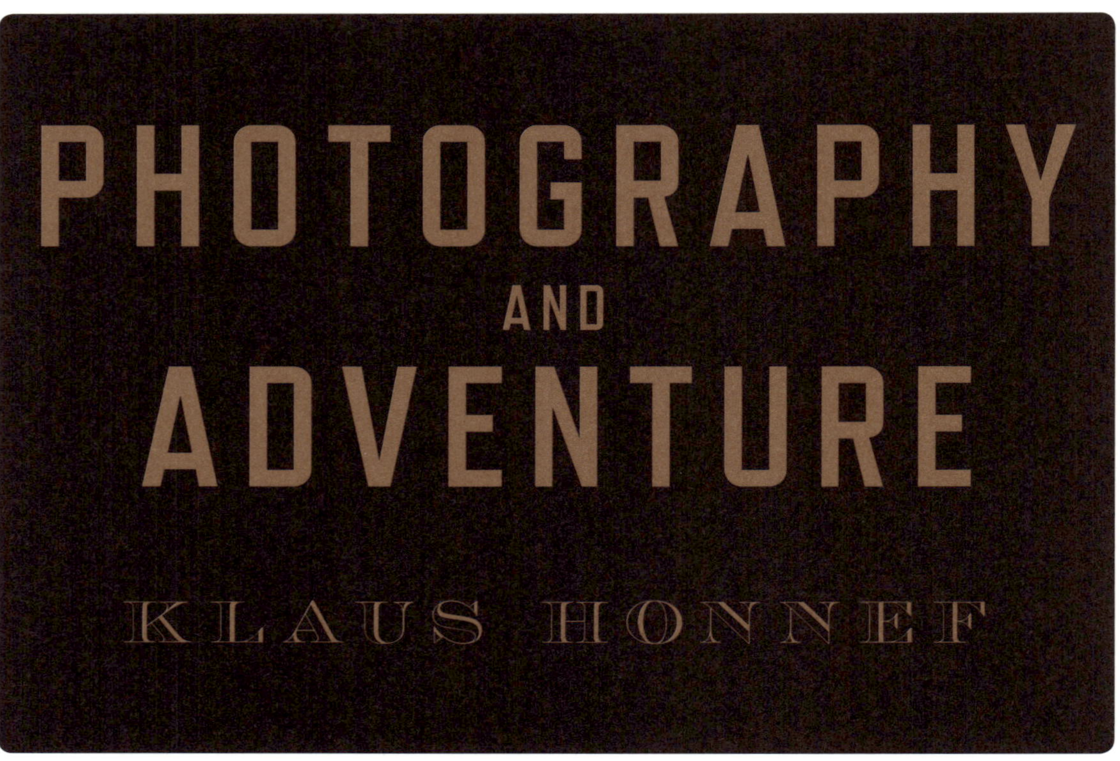

PHOTOGRAPHY AND ADVENTURE

KLAUS HONNEF

Francis Frith was a man who liked to travel. As a citizen of the British Empire, he originated from the nation that had invented traveling as a form of social leisure. On the *Grand Tour* to Rome, British travelers, for the most part aristocrats and the well-to-do, also discovered the »romantic Rhine.« At the time the British Empire extended across the entire globe and included territories in Africa, America, and Asia as well as all of Australia and New Zealand. The British Queen Victoria, the namesake of her epoch, officially ruled over British India as its empress from January 1, 1877 onward. Travel to distant continents was almost exclusively dedicated to business and political purposes, which were usually linked with one another; the same was true of undertakings that claimed to be for purposes of adventure or the study of a wide range of topics.

At the outset, Francis Frith was neither rich nor from an aristocratic background. Instead he practiced a métier that had many aspects of a skilled craft. Frith was a photographer. To meet the demands of his profession, he always traveled with a great deal of baggage, which contained voluminous plate cameras as well as a sufficient supply of large-format glass plates. In addition, he carried with him the necessary chemicals to prepare the glass plates in accordance with the collodion process—which remained in use for a long time—and to then expose the plates while still wet and immediately develop them after taking a successful photograph. The results were so-called negatives, of which positive images were projected and fixed onto paper. Other sundry technical and personal accessories added to the load of baggage. The luggage of one French photographer traveling through Algeria weighed in at 1,100 kg. Numerous porters and—when traversing longer distances—horses or oxen were required to transport this formidable amount of equipment from one place to another. Gustave Flaubert, who accompanied the photographer and publisher Maxime Du Camp on an expedition to Egypt, noted, »It is easy to learn photography, but carrying all the paraphernalia with mules, camels, and porters is a difficult problem.«

FRANCIS FRITH was thus not the only traveling photographer of his time. His famous countryman Roger Fenton visited Russia and reported on the Crimean War, still with a comparatively substantial time delay. Samuel Bourne, also British, explored India and the Himalayas with his camera. The photographic documents that these photographers produced had to be first transposed by hand into other reproducible media, such as woodcuts or cooper engravings, in order to replicate them in print. The use of the half-tone process for the production of printing plates had not yet been invented. The Italian Felice Beato and the Austrian Raimund Freiherr von Stillfried-Rathenitz went as far as Japan, where Beato founded the country's first photographic studio in Yokohama (1865). U. S. photographers conquered their own continent and laid the groundwork

eroberten ihren eigenen Kontinent und vermaßen ihn optisch als Teilnehmer zahlreicher Expeditionskorps in privatwirtschaftlichem und öffentlichem Auftrag und begründeten den US-amerikanischen Mythos. Letzten Endes waren die Reisefotografen auch die Wegbereiter des modernen Massentourismus.

Ob sie in den prachtvollen Luxushotels übernachtet haben, die zur gleichen Zeit in den europäischen Metropolen, den kolonialen Brennpunkten des indischen Subkontinents und den Kolonien Südostasiens aus dem Boden gestampft wurden, darf bezweifelt werden. Fotografen zählten nicht zur gesellschaftlichen Elite. Es sei denn, es handelte sich um die zahlreichen fotografischen Amateure aus der Militär- und Diplomatenkaste. Nur wenige der professionellen Fotografen verfügten über finanzielle Einkünfte, die ein verschwenderisches Leben erlaubten. Erst, als sie ihre Tätigkeit energisch kommerzialisierten, änderte sich die materielle Situation von einigen zum Besseren.

Francis Frith immerhin betrieb vor seinem Tod im südenglischen Reigate die größte Fotofirma Großbritanniens und unterhielt mehrere Filialen auf der Insel. Dass die Fotografen mit ihren Porträts der Notabeln und der schönen Frauen, die in den märchenhaften Luxushotels zu domizilieren pflegten, das Modell für die viel spätere *Promi-Society* entwarfen, in die sich einige ihrer berühmten Nachfolger dann nahtlos einreihten, ist eine der ironischen Wendungen der Geschichte. Unter die frühen fotografischen Modelle mischten sich auch die Neureichen des beginnenden Industriezeitalters und legten Zeugnis von ihrem Selbstbewusstsein ab. Die Porträtfotografie war die ergiebigste Quelle der beruflichen Existenz eines Kameramannes.

Selbst wenn Frith nicht in den prachtvollen Herbergen auf dem allmählich zusammenwachsenden Globus logierte – er hat zumindest in Europa, Afrika und Asien eine Menge dieser inzwischen legendären Hotels fotografiert (Abb. 1). Die imposantesten frontal oder übereck, die bescheideneren im jeweiligen Straßenkontext, um einen Eindruck von ihrer Dimension zu vermitteln, und anscheinend mit einer gewissen inhaltlichen Systematik. Die prächtigsten Gebäude paradieren in überladener Gründerzeitarchitektur, eine stilistische Mesalliance aus Tempel und Palast.

Für den privaten Gebrauch hat er die Hotels kaum fotografiert. Vielmehr darf vermutet werden, um die Bilder zu verkaufen; sei es an die Hotelgründer, -besitzer und -betreiber, meist noch in Personalunion, seltener mutmaßlich ans Personal, womöglich jedoch an die Reisenden, in der Mehrzahl Geschäftsleute, höhere Verwaltungsbeamte und Offiziere, die sie ihrem konkreten Erinnerungsschatz einfügten. Touristen waren auf den ziemlich beschwerlichen und risikoreichen Reiserouten außerhalb Europas noch selten. Vorwiegend in Gestalt von ein paar wagemutigen Forschern wie Alexander von Humboldt und Abenteurern und Zivilisationsflüchtigen wie dem Maler Paul Gauguin. Den anderen Zeitgenossen mussten voluminöse und dekorativ ausgestaltete Portfoliobände mit eingeklebten Originalabzügen oder manuell übertragenen Reproduktionen die unmittelbare Anschauung ferner Sehnsuchtsziele ersetzen. Ohnehin waren die für europäische Augen exotisch anmutenden Menschen der fremden Kulturen in ihren traditionellen Gewändern und die aus der mündlichen und schriftlichen Überlieferung bekannten kulturellen Monumente die attraktiveren Motive für die Fotografen. Das Hotel war und ist kein beherrschendes Thema der Fotografie.

DER KINOFILM SCHENKTE DEM SUJET GRÖSSERE AUFMERKSAMKEIT. Denn die anonyme Atmosphäre des Hotels bot die passende Kulisse für mysteriöse Affären und bösartige Intrigen. Das Hotel ist ein Narrativ an sich. Anders als Schiffsfotografen während der ersten Hälfte des 20. Jahrhunderts im Zeichen des aufblühenden Tourismus sind mir Hotelfotografen in der Geschichte der Fotografie nicht vertraut. Francis Frith scheint eine Ausnahme zu bilden. Da seine ausführliche Serie der Hotelpaläste nicht zu seinen bekannteren Arbeiten zählt, ist nicht auszuschließen, dass sich auch weitere Fotografen für das eigentümliche Motiv interessiert haben. Zumal zu den frühesten Beispielen fotografischer Praxis das Bild der Eingangszone des Hotels Canterbury in Paris zählt; allerdings nur als Negativ überliefert (Abb. 2). Es stammt vom Entdecker der modernen Papierfotografie: dem britischen Landedelmann und intensiven Naturforscher William Henry Fox Talbot, dem eigentlichen Wegbereiter des Massenmediums Fotografie. Während eines seiner Aufenthalte in der französischen Metropole hatte er das fotografische Bild aufgenommen. Ob auch seine erstaunliche Fotografie des Boulevard du Temple aus dem Fenster desselben Hotels realisiert wurde, steht dahin.

Zwischen Fotografie und Hotel entfalten sich frappierende Beziehungen. Hotels und fotografische Bilder wirken vertraut und fremd in einem. Hotels versprechen ein Zuhause auf Zeit, unterscheiden sich andererseits in signifikanter Weise vom heimischen Ambiente. Dieses Spannungsverhältnis ist programmatisch. Man fühlt sich umhegt, ist dennoch nicht in ein persönliches Verhältnis verstrickt. Fotografien versprechen ein authentisches Bild der sichtbaren Realität, verändern dennoch dabei die Sicht auf sie in entscheidendem Maße und implementieren ihre Optik in die menschliche Wahrnehmung.

Als fotografisches (literarisches und filmisches) Motiv erschöpfen sich Hotels aber keineswegs in den Besonder-

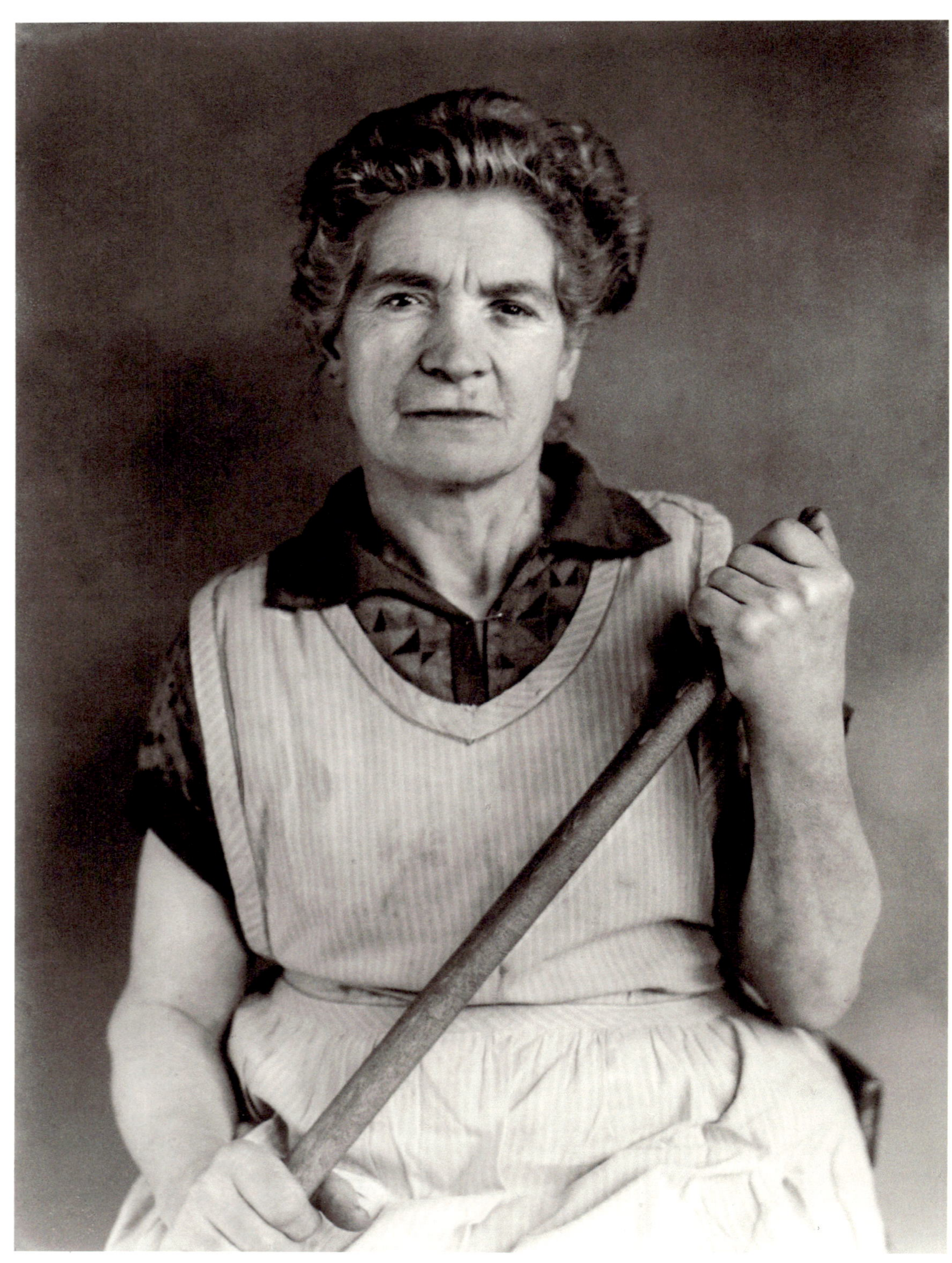

ABB. / FIG. 3 AUGUST SANDER **PUTZFRAU**

CLEANING WOMAN

Aus der Serie MENSCHEN DES 20. JAHRHUNDERTS, 1928, Gelatinesilberabzug, © Die Photographische Sammlung /SK Stiftung Kultur–August Sander Archiv, Köln / VG Bild-Kunst, Bonn 2014

From the series PEOPLE OF THE 20TH CENTURY, 1928, gelatin silver print, © Die Photographische Sammlung / SK Stiftung Kultur–August Sander Archiv, Köln / VG Bild-Kunst, Bonn 2014

heiten ihrer architektonischen Gehäuse. Besonders Luxushotels sind Phänomene spezifischer Art. Es sind Orte des exklusiven Wohlbefindens und des temporären Behütetseins. Den Gästen wird jeder Wunsch von den Lippen abgelesen, noch ehe diese sich geöffnet haben. Ihre Restaurants sind Orte üppiger wie erlesener Mahlzeiten, die Suiten in der Beletage vielleicht Orte berauschter Nächte und sozialer Kontakte in den mannigfaltigsten Variationen. Häufig geht es geheimnisvoll zu, zudem äußerst diskret; und gelegentlich, wenn etwas schief geht, bieten Hotels die Bühnen spektakulärer Skandale. Kurzum, sie liefern ergiebigsten Stoff für die Fantasie.

HINTER DEM FASZINIERENDEN SCHEIN DES KOSMOS DER HOTELLERIE VERBIRGT SICH EINE GLEICHERMASSEN GIGANTISCHE WIE KOMPLEXE MASCHINERIE. Verkörpert wird sie von einer bemerkenswerten Spezies Menschen: bestens darauf trainiert, anwesend und abwesend zugleich zu sein – analog zum strukturellen Wesen des fotografischen Bildes –, doch nie aufdringlich; dafür stets zur Stelle, wenn sie gebraucht werden, und in strenger Hierarchie gegliedert. Daneben spielen die unterschiedlichsten Einrichtungen und Utensilien eine markante Rolle sowie, maßgeblich, das Netzwerk perfekt aufeinander abgestimmter und eingespielter Systeme und Rituale.

Im Rahmen seines epochalen Sozialatlasses der Weimarer Republik mit dem Titel MENSCHEN DES 20. JAHRHUNDERTS warf der deutsche Fotograf August Sander einen nüchternen Blick hinter die Kulissen der Hotelszenerie. Er porträtierte eine Handvoll jener Frauen und Männer, die das gastliche Getriebe am Laufen halten: die Putzfrauen (Abb. 3), einen Schankkellner und einen Dienstmann, die Diener, die betuchten Reisenden ständig verfügbar waren, Wirtin und Wirt, eine Köchin, einen Handwerker und ein Kaffeehausmädchen. Aber lediglich sein Bild HOTELPERSONAL IN HAMBURG versammelt Angestellte einer Luxusherberge. Die übrigen Modelle repräsentieren das Personal von Gaststätten mit den üblichen Zimmerangeboten zwecks Übernachtung. Derlei Etablissements, häufig Kaschemmen und Spelunken, sorgten für Unterkünfte, ehe das erste Hotel, wahrscheinlich 1776 in London, auf den Plan trat. Immer en face, meist in voller Körpergröße, einige in Halbfigur oder Büste, präsentierten sich die dienstbaren Geister einzeln oder in Gruppen vor Sanders Kamera: der Querschnitt gesellschaftlicher Schichtung einer in seinem Mappenwerk nicht vom Fotografen eigens ausgewiesenen Berufskohorte unterhalb der oberen Etage der Gesellschaftspyramide, changierend zwischen Sozialtypus und individuellem Charakter, rangierend vom (klein)bürgerlichen Milieu bis zur Arbeiterklasse.

Die glanzvollste Zeit der mondänen Luxusherbergen war bereits vorbei, als Sander sich im Hotel- und Gaststättengewerbe umsah. Manche der berühmten Hotels illuminierten zwar noch die *Roaring Twenties* in Paris, Berlin und New York und verliehen ihnen einen morbiden Glamour. Politiker suchten sie auf, um zu konspirieren oder um wichtige Konferenzen abzuhalten. Doch das Beben des Ersten Weltkrieges hatte die bis dahin bekannte Welt umgewälzt. In allen Gegenden des Globus begannen sich die überkommenen sozialen Strukturen aufzulösen und die Gesellschaften gerieten in Bewegung. Namentlich den älteren dieser *Dienstleister* in Sanders Bildern scheinen die fürchterlichen Erfahrungen der anonymen »Menschenschlächterei« (Franz Rosenzweig) samt den Konvulsionen der unmittelbaren Nachkriegszeit mit Revolten, Hunger und horrender Inflation sichtbar ins Gesicht geschrieben. Verschärft mutmaßlich durch die Auswirkungen der Weltwirtschaftskrise im Kielwasser des *Schwarzen Freitags* 1929 an der Wall Street.

Siegfried Kracauer, einer der hellsichtigen Kritiker, der sich intensiv mit den neuen Massenmedien Fotografie und Film beschäftigte, widmete dem wachsenden Heer der neuen Angestellten anno 1930 eine exzellente soziologische Studie. Nur die herrschaftlichen Diener in Sanders prägnanten Bildern erinnern noch an die Belle Époque, die eine exquisite Hotelkultur erschaffen hatte.

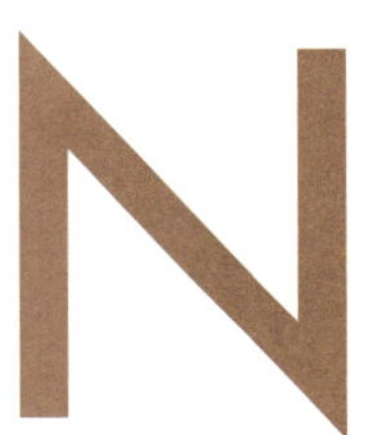

ach einem weiteren Weltkrieg ist diese Epoche nur noch nostalgischer Gegenstand von Romanen und Kinofilmen. Guy Tillim demonstriert in seinen Bildern den äußerlichen Wandel vom Nobelhotel des großbürgerlichen Industriekapitalismus zur Luxusabsteige des digital gesteuerten Kasinokapitalismus (Abb. 4). Verfallenden Palasthotels von einst, wahrscheinlich kurz vor dem Abriss, stellt er austauschbare Wolkenkratzerherbergen des 21. Jahrhunderts gegenüber. Letztere visiert er aus beträchtlicher Distanz an und vergegenwärtigt sie als selbstverständliche Bestandteile der modernen Stadtsilhouette. Unter den vielen ähnlich aussehenden Gebäuden der Millionenstädte stechen selbst die neuen Luxushotels nicht mehr hervor. Welch' ein Unterschied zu den prunkvollen architektonischen Wahrzeichen der Bilder von Francis Frith im Nahen und im Fernen Osten! Der Wandel betrifft nicht nur die äußere Erscheinung. In den monumentalen Zeugnissen einer grassierenden Investorenarchitektur drückt sich eine veränderte Einstellung gegenüber dem einzelnen Gast im Vergleich zu früheren Zeiten aus. Gekennzeichnet durch die Rationalität, die sich in der rationellen Bauweise spiegelt.

Im Inneren der genormten Gebäude, vor allem in den riesigen Eingangshallen, die bisweilen bis zum obersten

for the American myth by creating optical surveys of its landscape as members of the numerous expeditionary corps commissioned by both private and public sponsors. Ultimately, these travel photographers also paved the way for modern mass tourism.

It is doubtful whether these photographers stayed in the splendid luxury hotels that were sprouting up during the same period in major European cities and the colonial centers of the Indian subcontinent and of Southeast Asia. Photographers were not among the socially elite, excepting the numerous photography amateurs from the diplomatic and military castes. Only a small number of professional photographers were wealthy enough to be able to lead an extravagant lifestyle. Only once they had actively commercialized their field did the material situation of some photographers begin to improve.

Before his death, Francis Frith, for one, had established Britain's largest photography company in Reigate in southern England and maintained multiple branches across the country. One of the ironic turns of this story is how photographers of this epoch—with their portraits of the noteworthy individuals and beautiful women that tended to reside in the era's fairy-tale like luxury hotels—created a model for the much later »celebrity society,« into which their famous colleagues of subsequent eras readily inserted themselves. However, the people photographed by these early photographers also included the nouveau riche of the burgeoning industrial age, and these portraits clearly communicate their self-confidence. Portrait photography was one of the most lucrative sources of income in this profession.

Even if Frith himself did not stay in the magnificent lodgings found throughout world that was gradually becoming smaller, he did photograph a great number of these now legendary hotels, at least those in Europe, Africa, and Asia (fig. 1). The most imposing were depicted with a frontal shot or at a corner angle; the more modest were shown in the context of the street where they were located to give a sense of their dimensions; and overall his photographs demonstrated a certain systematic approach in terms of context. The most splendid buildings were overt displays of the most ornate Victorian architecture, a stylistic hodgepodge of the temple and the palace.

He certainly did not take these photographs of hotels for private reasons. It's likely that he intended to sell the photographs, either to the founder, owner, and operator of the hotel—at this time, all these roles were still unified in a single person—more seldom to members of the staff, but most likely to the travelers, for the most part business people, high-ranking officials, and military officers who wished to add the images to their concrete album of memories. At the time, tourists seldom undertook the quite arduous and risky routes of travel beyond Europe. Among those who did were a number of fearless scientists, such as Alexander von Humboldt, adventurers, and individuals fleeing the civilized world, like painter Paul Gauguin. Other contemporaries of this era had to reproduce the direct visual experience of sought-after, distant places by looking at massive, elaborately decorated portfolio albums with pages of glued-in photographs or reproductions thereof produced by hand. Certainly more attractive motifs for photographers were the peoples of foreign cultures in their traditional dress, exotic to the European eye, as well as cultural monuments known from written accounts. The hotel was and is not a predominant subject matter in photography.

AS A SUBJECT MATTER, THE HOTEL GARNERED A SUBSTANTIAL AMOUNT OF ATTENTION THROUGH CINEMA. The anonymous atmosphere of the hotel provided the appropriate backdrop for mysterious affairs and villainous intrigue. The hotel is a narrative unto itself. In contrast to the ship photographers active in the first half of the 20th century under the aegis of burgeoning tourism, I am not familiar with any other hotel photographers from the history of photography. Francis Frith seems to be an exception. Since his extensive series of hotel palaces are not among his best known works, it would be reasonable to assume that also other photographers were interested in this specific motif—especially since the image of the entry to the Hotel Canterbury in Paris is among the earliest examples of photography, although it has only been preserved as a negative (fig. 2). It stems from the inventor of modern paper-based photography, William Henry Fox Talbot, a member of the British landed gentry and a dedicated natural scientist, who actually paved the way for photography to become a mass medium. He took the photograph during one of his stays in the French capital. Whether his astounding photographs of the Boulevard du Temple were taken from the windows of this same hotel is unclear.

There are a number of surprising relationships between photography and the hotel. Both the hotel and the photographic image seem familiar and alien at the same time. Hotels offer the promise of a temporary home but differ significantly from a domestic environment. This inherent tension is a given; one feels protected and coddled, but one is not enmeshed in a personal relationship. Photographs promise an authentic image of a visible reality but alter the view of this reality to a significant extent, inserting their optic into human perception.

As a photographic (or literary or cinematic) motif, hotels are by no means limited to the unique qualities of

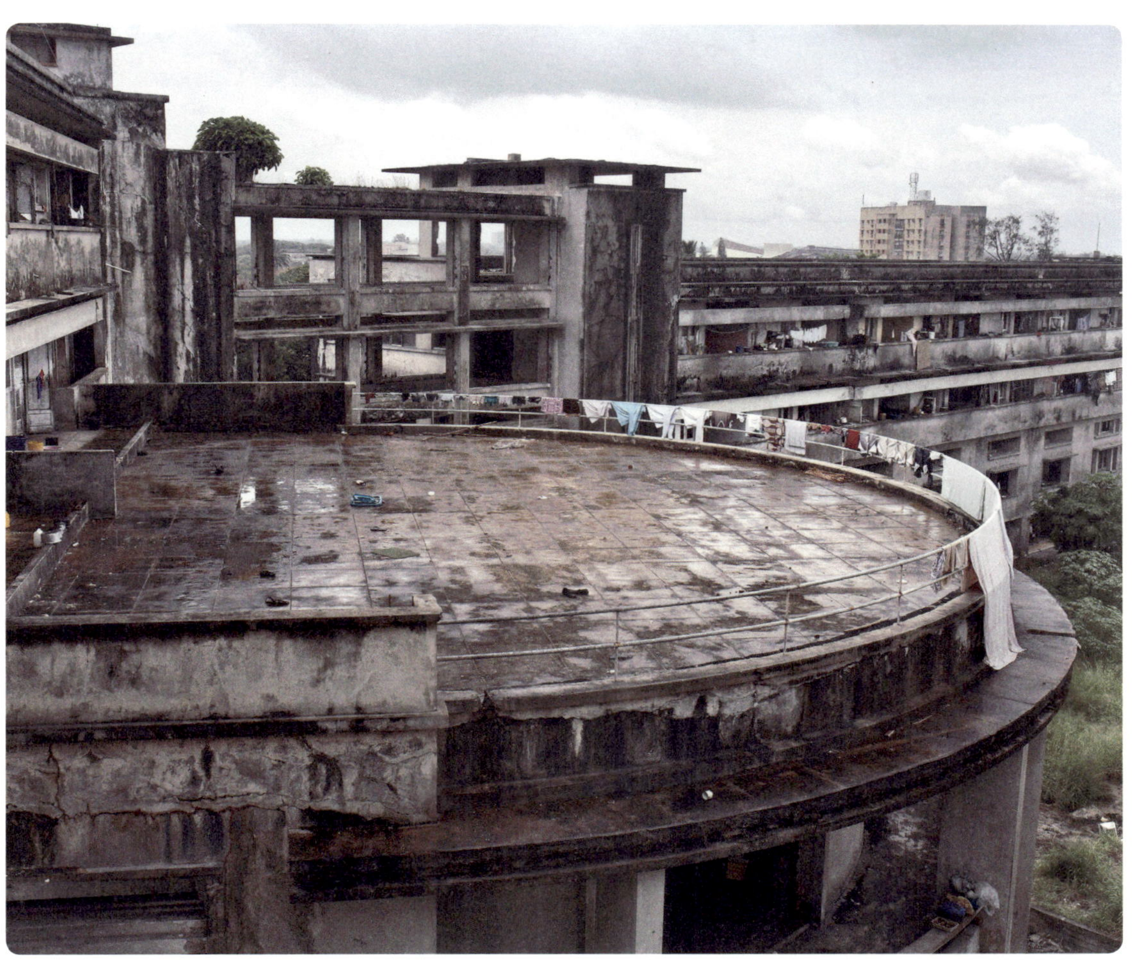

Abb. / Fig. 4

GUY TILLIM **GRANDE HOTEL BEIRA MOZAMBIQUE**

2008, Diptychon (links), Pigmentdruck, Courtesy: Privatbesitz, Berlin / Galerie Kuckei + Kuckei, Berlin, © Guy Tillim / 2008, diptych (left), pigment ink print, courtesy: private collection, Berlin / Gallery Kuckei + Kuckei, Berlin, © Guy Tillim

Geschoss hinaufreichen, ist alles auf Überwältigung angelegt. Durch schiere Größe, nicht wie einst durch Pomp. Wie diese Strategie die Hotelnutzer unmittelbar affiziert, transportieren die großformatigen Bilder von Andreas Gursky in denkbar verdichteter Intensität (Abb. 5). Die an Flughafenterminals gemahnenden Eingangshallen lassen die temporären Bewohner auf Ameisenmaß schrumpfen. Die in Schubladenform über verschiedene Etagen aufeinandergestapelte Zimmeranordnung besorgt das ihre zur Versachlichung. Unwillkürlich empfindet man sich als zahlendes Element in der Hotelmaschinerie und weniger als willkommener Gast. Selbst die routinierte Herzlichkeit der Concierges am Empfang und der übrigen dienstbaren Geister täuscht nicht darüber hinweg, dass in derlei Hallen kein Mittelständler zum gefühlten Fürsten promoviert wird wie in den Hotelpalästen der verblichenen Belle Époque. Den kalten Touch verstärkt Gursky mit pointierenden digitalen Eingriffen, um die Betrachter seiner Bilder einer vergleichbaren Gefühlslage auszusetzen wie die Nutzer der fotografierten Hotelinterieurs.

REAGIERT NICHT FLORIAN SLOTAWA MIT EINEM AKT DER SOUVERÄNITÄT AUF DIE SPÜRBARE ANONYMITÄT UND STANDARDISIERUNG DER HOTELS UND IHRER AUSSTATTUNG? Die Zimmer, die er jeweils bezieht, baut er nächtens um, verwandelt sie mit den verfügbaren Möbeln und Accessoires in persönliche Wohnhöhlen, fotografiert das Ergebnis seines massiven Eingriffs, um am Morgen alles in den vorherigen Zustand zurückzuversetzen. In seinen Bildern dokumentiert sich eine Gegenwelt zur sterilen Hotelszenerie: eigenwillig, individuell – ob wohnlicher, werden die Betrachter seiner Bilder entscheiden.

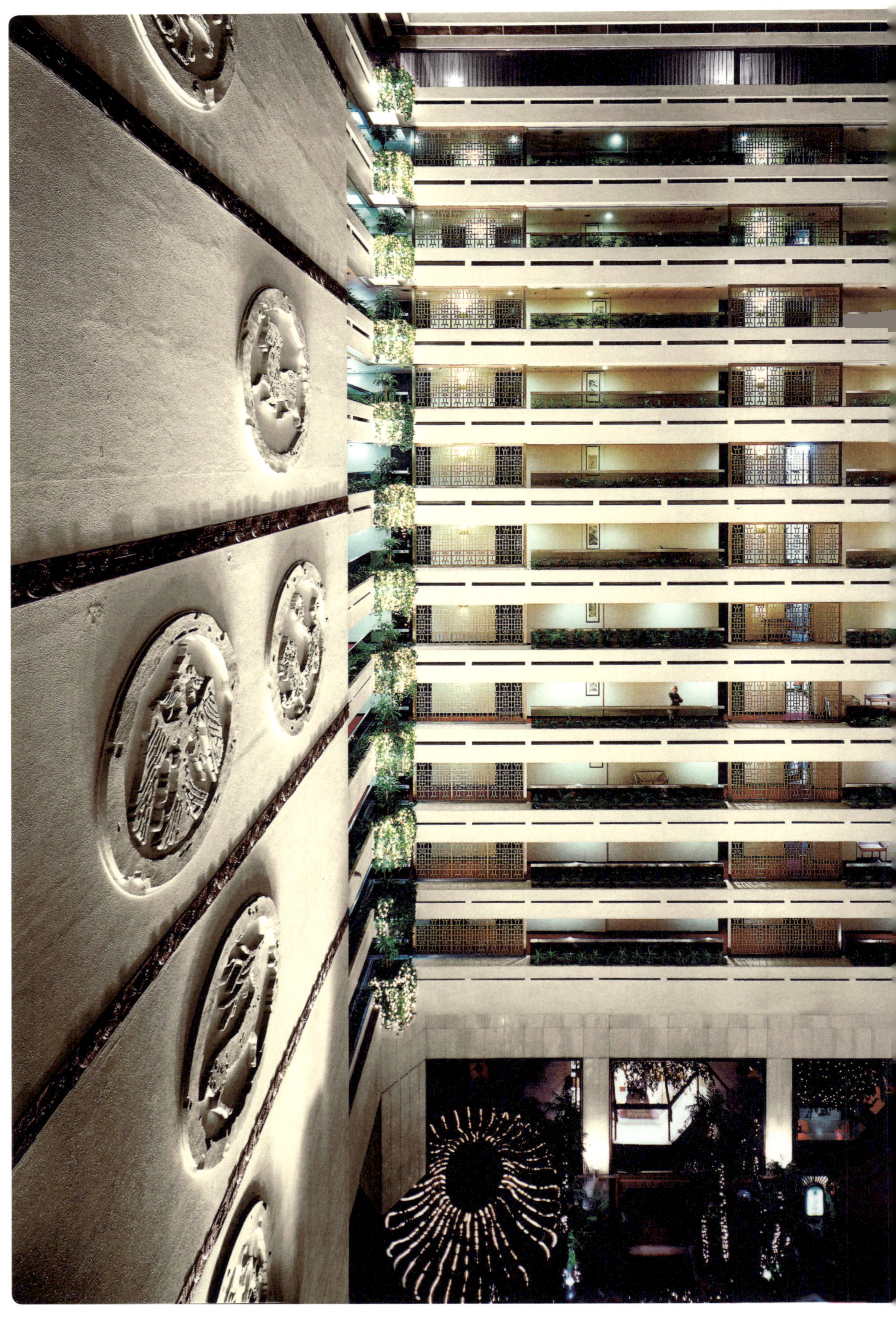

Abb. / Fig. 5 ANDREAS GURSKY

C-print, 1999, courtesy: Andreas Gursky, © Andreas Gursky, VG Bild-Kunst, Bonn 2014

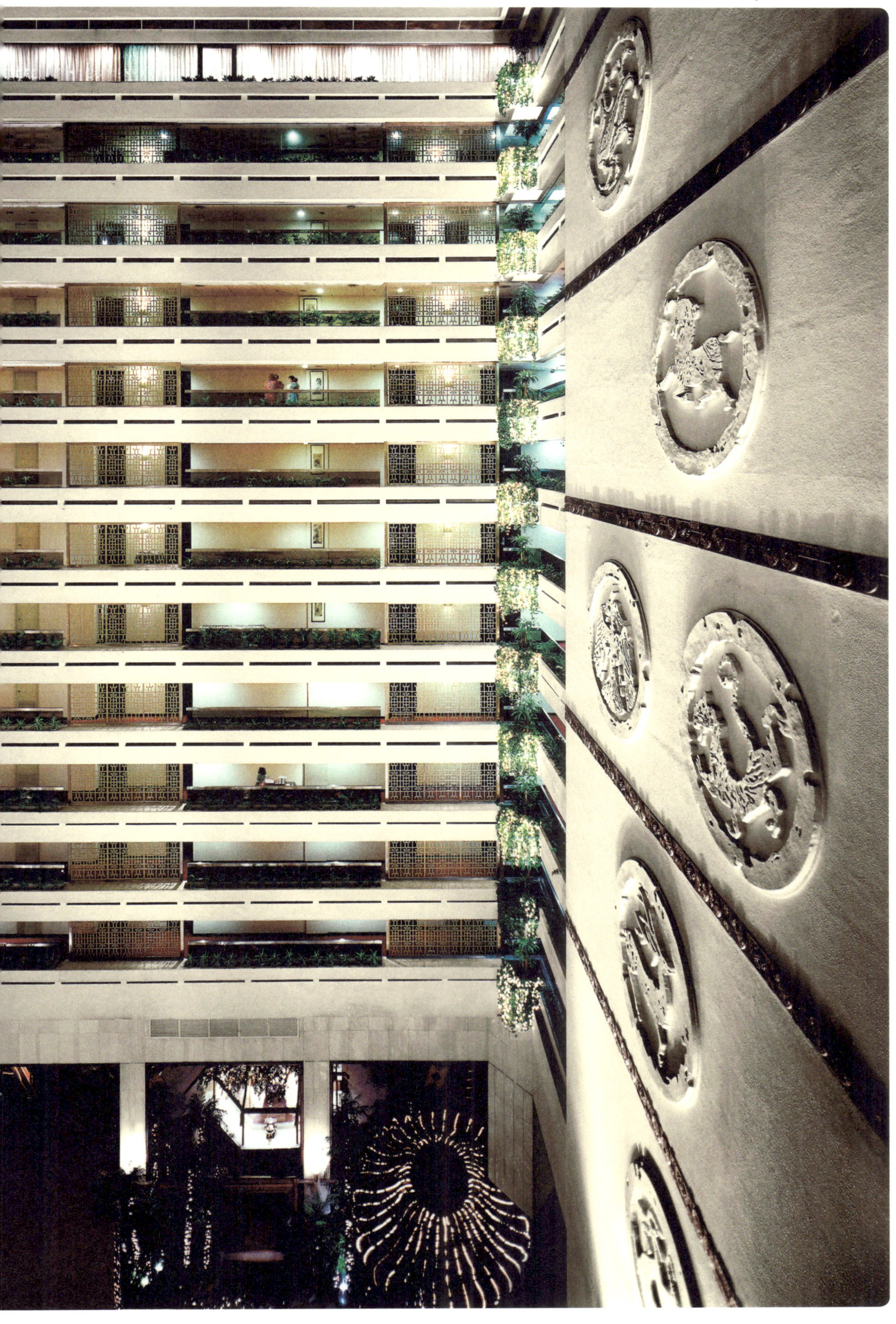

T A I P E I

C-Print, 1999, Courtesy: Andreas Gursky, © Andreas Gursky, VG Bild-Kunst, Bonn 2014

the architecture that houses them. Luxury hotels in particular are a special kind of phenomenon. These are places of exclusive well-being and temporary protective care. All the guests' wishes are read on their facees before they can even voice them. The restaurants are places of opulent and choice meals; the suites of the *bel étage* are perhaps places of intoxicated evenings and social contacts in endless variation. Often these goings-on are shrouded in secrecy and handled with great discretion; and sometimes, when everything goes wrong, hotels become the backdrop for spectacular scandals. In short, they provide a wealth of material for the imagination.

BEHIND THE FASCINATING AURA OF THE COSMOS OF THE HOTEL BUSINESS IS HIDDEN A MACHINERY AS GIGANTIC AS IT IS COMPLEX. It is populated by a remarkable species of human: optimally trained to be both present and absent at the same time—analogous to the structural essence of the photographic image—never overbearing but always at hand when needed, and organized in a strict hierarchy. In addition, various furnishings and utensils play a noticeable role as does, most significantly, a network of perfectly aligned and coordinated systems and rituals.

As part of his epochal social atlas of the Weimar Republic, MENSCHEN DES 20. JAHRHUNDERTS (People of the 20th Century), the German photographer August Sander took a matter-of-fact look behind the scenes of the hotel. He created portraits of a handful of the men and women who kept the business of hospitality running: cleaning women (fig. 3), a barman, and a porter, the servants on call around the clock for moneyed travelers, an innkeeper couple, a female cook, a skilled craftsman, and a coffeehouse waitress. Only his photograph HOTELPERSONAL IN HAMBURG (Hotel Staff in Hamburg) assembles the staff members of a luxury hotel. His other models represented workers from inns offering what were more common types of accommodations. Such establishments, often gin mills and drinking holes, offered lodgings before the first hotel appeared, probably in London in 1776. Individually or in groups, usually shown from top to toe or sometimes as a half-portrait or bust, these obliging souls always present themselves directly facing Sander's camera. They represent a social cross-section of a professional cohort that the photographer did not explicitly describe in his portfolio, a group situated below the upper echelons of the social pyramid and depicted in a manner alternating between social type and individual character, between a lower middle and working class milieu.

The dazzling era of the gentrified luxury hotel was already a thing of the past by the time Sander explored the hotel and guesthouse trade. Some of the famous hotels were still luminary institutions of the »Roaring Twenties« in Paris, Berlin, and New York, contributing their morbid glamour to the era. Politicians sought them out as places to conspire or hold important conferences. But the earth-shattering events of World War I had upset the world as it had been known up until that point. In all corners of the globe existing social structures began to break down and societies began to become more mobile. Seemingly written on the faces of particularly the elder »service providers« in Sander's photographs are the terrible experiences of the anonymous »human slaughterhouse« (Franz Rosenzweig) of World War I, including the convulsions of the subsequent post-war era with its revolutions, hunger, and horrendous inflation, all of which was presumably exacerbated by the effects of the economic crisis that occurred in the wake of Wall Street's »Black Friday« in 1929. Siegfried Kracauer, one of the most insightful critics to write intensively about the new mass media of photography and film, dedicated an excellent sociological study to the new growing army of employees in 1930. Only the stately servants in Sander's striking images still recall the Belle Époque, which had created an exquisite hotel culture.

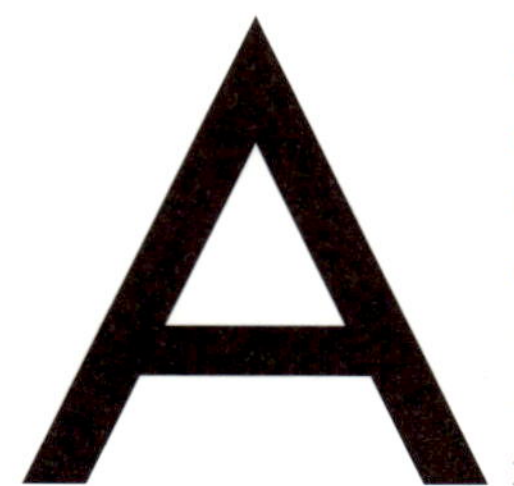fter an additional World War, this distant era survives only as the nostalgic subject matter of novels and films. In his photographs Guy Tillim demonstrates the external transformations of the first class hotel from the time of upper-class industrial capitalism to the luxury accommodations of digitally driven casino-capitalism (fig. 4). He juxtaposes the decrepit palaces of the past, probably about to be torn down, with the look-alike skyscraper hotels of the 21st century. Photographing the latter from a substantial distance, he portrays them as a natural component of the modern skyline. New luxury hotels no longer stand out among the many similar buildings in contemporary cities populated by millions of people. What a difference there is between these images and the ornately decorated architectural landmarks of Francis Frith's photographs from the Near and Far East! However, this change not only applies to the appearance of the exteriors. These monumental manifestations of rampant investor-style architecture are expressions of an altered attitude toward the individual guest in comparison to earlier times, which is marked by an efficiency mirrored in efficient forms of construction.

On the interior of the normed building and above all in the giant entry halls, which meanwhile extend to the top floor, everything is orchestrated to create a sense

Nichtsdestotrotz haben die Hotels nicht sämtliche Geheimnisse eingebüßt. Sophie Calle schlüpfte einmal in die Rolle eines Zimmermädchens und suchte anhand ihrer Hinterlassenschaften ein Profil einzelner Bewohner auf Zeit zu erstellen (Abb. 6). Diese erscheinen nur im Off; sind gleichzeitig abwesend und anwesend. Lediglich ihre *Eindrücke* in den Betten, ihre Koffer und deren Inhalte sowie ihre Notizen bezeugen, dass sie *da* waren: Ihre Spuren sind sichtbar. Wer sind sie (gewesen)? Sind es die Freaks, denen Diane Arbus Ausstrahlung und Würde verlieh? Sind es gewöhnliche Handelsreisende? In der Werkgruppe von Sophie Calle kristallisiert sich die Zentralfrage angesichts jedes fotografischen Porträts – fotografischer Bilder schlechthin: Wie präsent sind die Porträtierten im fotografischen Abbild überhaupt? Denn der Augenblick, in dem der Auslöser den fotografischen Prozess einleitet, ist stets schon Vergangenheit, wenn er sich dem lichtempfindlichen Sensor einsengt.

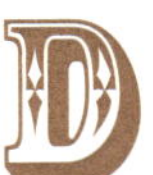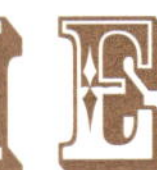 UNSICHTBAREN MODELLE DER KÜNSTLERIN SIND NICHT DIE GESCHÄFTIGEN MENSCHEN, die der deutsche Journalist Hanns Hubmann rund ein halbes Jahrhundert zuvor in ihren Hotelzimmern beim Ferngespräch fotografisch festgehalten hat; diese soignierten Herren, an deren Verhalten und Kleidung sich nicht der Diplomat vom Schriftsteller, der Unternehmer vom Musiker unterscheiden lässt. Telefonieren war noch Luxus. Aber womöglich hat jemand wie der einsame Mann auf dem Bett in William Egglestons fotografischem Meisterwerk für ein paar Minuten das Zimmer verlassen, das Sophie Calle durchmusterte.

Ein Aspekt ihrer Bilder springt förmlich ins Auge: jene Melange aus Spitzelei und Voyeurismus. Die französische Künstlerin spioniert Menschen nach, die nicht wissen, dass sie ausgespäht werden. Deuten die zerwühlten Betten vielleicht auf eine heimliche Affäre hin? Haben sich in den Räumen Menschen getroffen, die finstere Pläne schmiedeten? Schon die pure Insinuation ist eminent fotografisch. Calles Bilder werden jedoch nicht an die Betroffenen verkauft, sondern auf einem freien Markt als Kunstwerke gehandelt; in einem völlig anderen Register als Francis Friths Fotografien von einst. Wir Betrachter werden plötzlich zu unfreiwilligen Komplizen der Aktion.

Die rasant vorangeschrittene fotografische Technik arbeitete dem Voyeurismus entscheidend zu und machte das Ausspähen zum Habitus. Mit Friths Ausrüstung wäre Calles Vorhaben völlig unrealisierbar gewesen. Die Kameras sind im Laufe der vergangenen Dekaden immer kleiner geworden. Manche kann man sogar ins Knopfloch stecken. Dabei hat sich die visuelle Wiedergabequalität ständig verbessert, die Lichtempfindlichkeit der Filme oder der Chips enorm gesteigert. Thema und Technik korrespondieren. Wir werden unaufhörlich von Kameras überwacht. Insofern ist Sophie Calles Zyklus auch eine anschauliche Reflexion fotografischer Praxis und fotografischer Ästhetik – mit genügend Fingerzeigen in die Zukunft.

of being overwhelmed by the sheer size of building, in contrast to the pomp of earlier times. With an evocative and pointed intensity the large-format photographs of Andreas Gursky convey how this aesthetic strategy has a direct emotional impact on the hotel user. Recalling airport terminals, these entry halls shrink temporary inhabitants to antlike proportions (fig. 5). The arrangement of rooms, stacked on top of one another like a series of multiple-storey cabinet drawers, contributes even further to the guests' objectification. One involuntarily has the feeling of being a paying cog in the wheels of the hotel machinery rather than a welcome guest. Even the well-rehearsed friendliness of the concierges at the reception desks and the remaining service personnel does not obscure the fact that in these halls no middle class person is going to receive a royal and elevating kind of treatment, as in the hotel palaces of the faded Belle Époque. Gursky enhances this cold touch with strategic digital interventions to visually give the viewer the same feeling as the user of the photographed hotel interiors.

FLORIAN SLOTAWA'S RESPONSE TO THE PALPABLE ANONYMITY AND STANDARDIZATION OF HOTELS AND THEIR FURNISHINGS THUS SEEMS LIKE AN ACT OF SELF-ASSURANCE: at night he reconfigures the room that he has booked, using the given furniture and accessories of the room to transform it into a personal lair, photographing the results of his massive intervention, and putting everything back where it was in the morning. In his images he documents a world that runs counter to typically sterile hotel scenarios—idiosyncratic, individual but whether any more comfortable, that is left up to the viewer of his photographs.

Nevertheless, the hotel as such has not surrendered all its secrets. Slipping into the role of a chambermaid, Sophie Calle tried to reconstruct profiles of various temporary inhabitants by what they left behind in their room (fig. 6). These individuals appear in her photographs but only offstage; they are simultaneously present and absent. Only the impressions left in their beds, their suitcases, and the contents thereof as well as their notes affirm that they were in fact there; their traces are visible. Who are (or were) they? Are they the freaks that Diane Arbus surrounds with charismatic allure and dignity? Are they typical sales representatives? Within this series by Sophie Calle crystallizes the core question inherent to every photographic portrait, or even photographic images in general: How does the subject of the portrait present himself or herself in a photographic effigy? The moment in which the shutter initiates the photographic process immediately belongs to the past once it has been fixed onto the light-sensitive material.

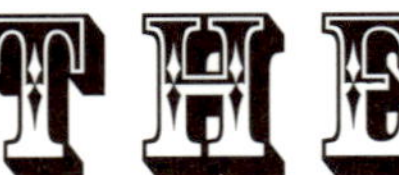

THE INVISIBLE MODELS OF THE ARTIST ARE NOT THE BUSY PEOPLE THAT THE GERMAN JOURNALIST HANNS HUBMANN PHOTOGRAPHED APPROXIMATELY A HALF A CENTURY EARLIER IN THEIR HOTEL ROOMS, photographically documenting them as they held a long-distance telephone conversations—dapper gentlemen whose clothing and bearing made it impossible to distinguish between the diplomat and the writer, the businessman and the musician. Making a telephone call was still a luxury. It was probably someone like the lonely man on the bed in one of William Eggleston's photographic masterpieces, who stepped out for a few minutes from his room, which Sophie Calle then riffled through.

One of the most overt aspects of Calle's images is the mixture of espionage and voyeurism. The French artist spies on people who do not know that they are being watched. Are the rumpled sheets a possible indication of a secret affair? Did people meet in these rooms to concoct an evil plan? Such pure insinuation is eminently photographic. However, Calle's images are not sold to the individuals in question but on the free market as works of art, a completely different set of circumstances than Francis Frith's photographs from a bygone age. In Calle's work we as viewers suddenly become unwilling accomplices to her actions.

Rapid development in photographic technology has decidedly aided and abetted voyeurism and has made spying a habit. Calle's undertaking would have been completely unrealistic with Frith's equipment. Cameras have become increasingly smaller over the course of the last decade. Some even fit into a buttonhole. Simultaneously the quality of the visual image has increased consistently, and the light sensitivity of the films or chips has been enhanced tremendously. Application and technology are perfectly aligned. We are continuously monitored by cameras, and in this sense Calle's series provides a vivid reflection on the practice and aesthetic of photography—also offering significant indication of what is to come.

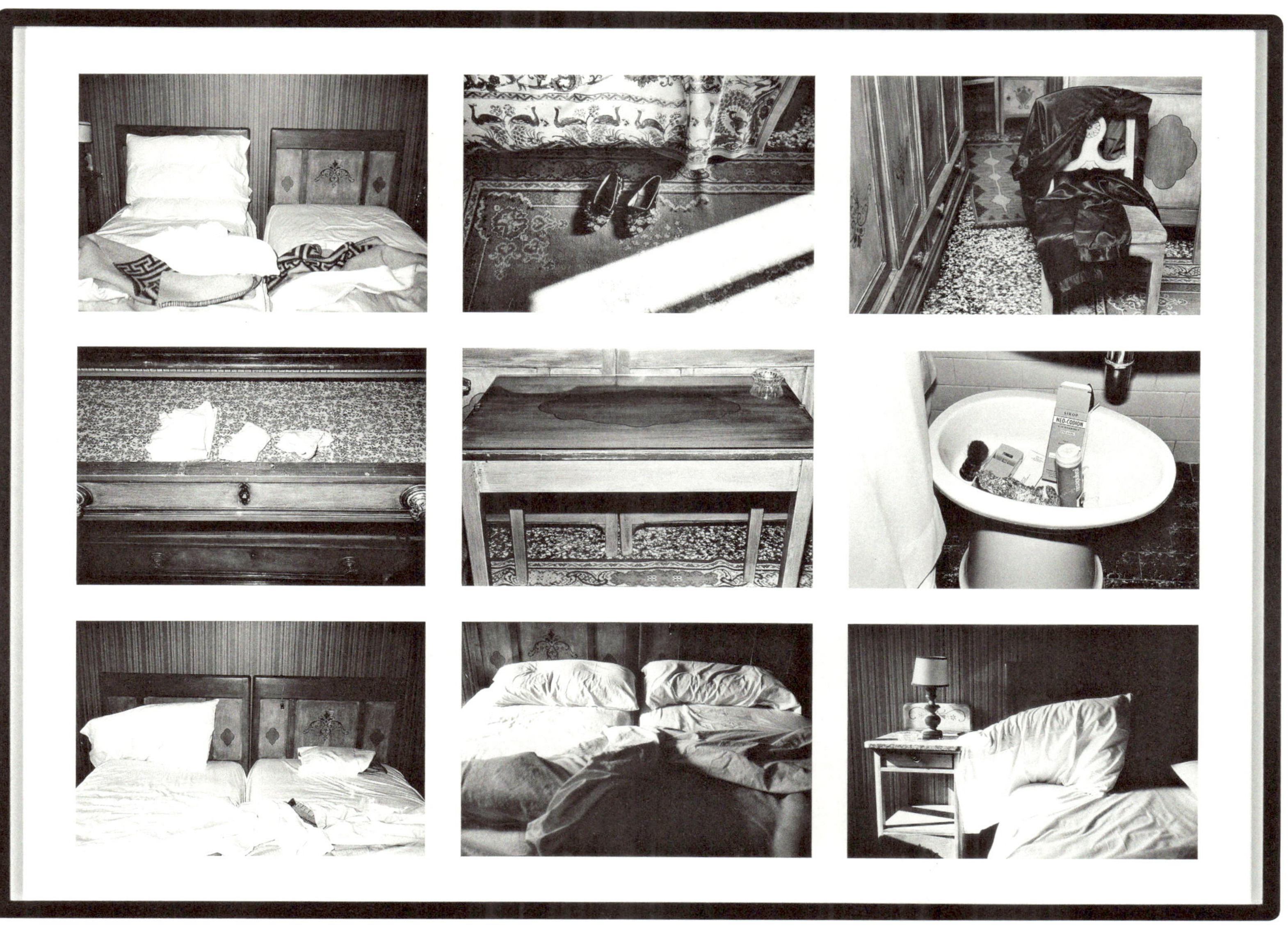

Abb. / Fig. 6

SOPHIE CALLE

THE HOTEL, ROOM 28, MARCH 3

1981, Dyptychon (oberer Teil), Aluminiumplatten mit Ektachrome-Druck und Text, S/W-Fotografien, Courtesy: Sophie Calle und Deichtorhallen Hamburg / Sammlung Falckenberg, © Sophie Calle / VG Bild-Kunst, Bonn 2014

Dyptych (upper part), aluminium plates with Ektachrome-print and text, b/w photographs, courtesy: Sophie Calle and Deichtorhallen Hamburg / Collection Falckenberg © Sophie Calle / VG Bild-Kunst, Bonn 2014

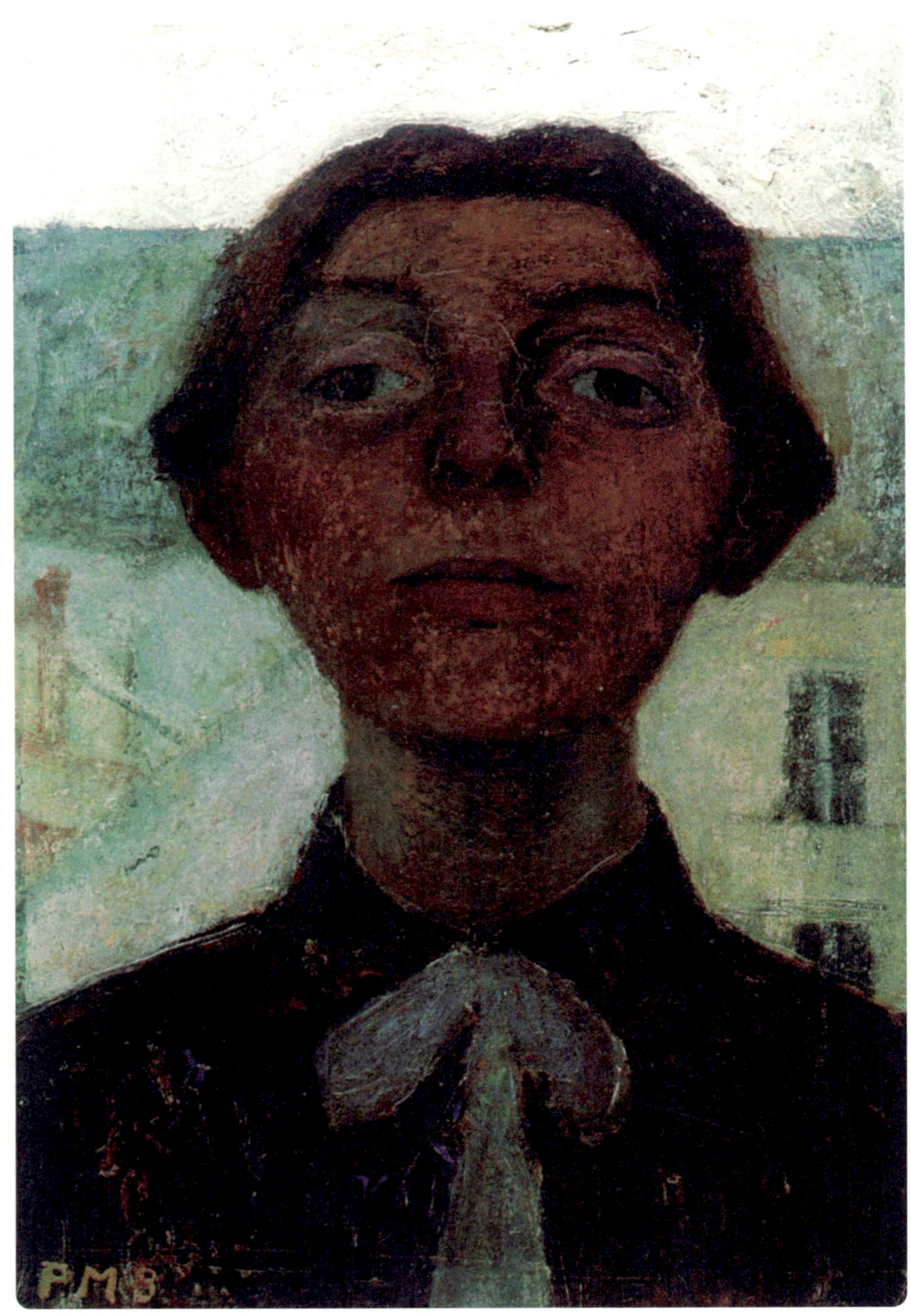

Abb. / Fig. 1

PAULA MODERSON-BECKER

SELBSTBILDNIS VOR FENSTERAUSBLICK AUF PARISER HÄUSER

SELF-PORTRAIT IN FRONT OF A VIEW OF PARISIAN HOUSES

1900, Öl auf Leinwand / Oil on canvas, Paula Modersohn-Becker-Stiftung, Bremen

BÜHNE DER MÖGLICHKEITEN

DAS HOTEL ALS ORT DES MODERNEN LEBENS IN KUNST UND LITERATUR AB 1840

HENDRIK BÜNDGE

Möchten doch die wahren Sucher uns im nächsten Jahr die einzigartige Freude bereiten, die Heraufkunft des Neuen zu feiern!«[1] Dieses Fazit zog der junge Charles Baudelaire über den Pariser Salon des Jahres 1845. Die Forderung nach der Darstellung des Neuen als Gegenentwurf zur klassischen Akademiemalerei wurde von ihm kurz vor seinem Tod in dem Aufsatz *Der Maler des modernen Lebens* (1863) als eine ästhetische Theorie der Moderne ausgearbeitet und zur programmatischen Auffassung einer jungen Künstlergeneration, die später – zunächst pejorativ – als Impressionisten bezeichnet wurde.[2] Die neuen Errungenschaften der industriellen Revolution haben in Werken dieser Künstler ihren Eindruck hinterlassen: Eisenbahnen durchschneiden die ländliche Idylle und überziehen sie mit grauschwarzen Rußschleiern. Die hohen Schornsteine der Fabriken entlang der Seine, in Le Havre oder in Rouen werden ebenso zu signifikanten Bildelementen von Landschaftsgemälden wie die Vergnügungs- und Freizeitaktivitäten des französischen Bürgertums. Stadtansichten mit ungewöhnlichen Blickwinkeln zeigen das gegenteilig Pittoreske und die Betrachtenden sind nunmehr dazu angehalten, das Bild durch eigene Sehleistung zu vollenden. In die unmittelbare Schaffenszeit jener Künstler – etwa Claude Monet, Armand Guillaumin, Édouard Manet, Camille Pissarro, Georges Seurat oder Gustave Caillebotte – fällt die Modernisierung des Stadtbildes von Paris durch Georges-Eugène Baron Haussmann.[3] Seine Neuerung war es, die Stadt erstmals in ihrer Gesamtheit den neuen baulichen Vorstellungen anzupassen, was einerseits zum Abriss der Elendsviertel und der mittelalterlichen *cité* führte, andererseits weiträumige und weitverzweigte Straßenzüge, Kanalisation und Gasbeleuchtung ermöglichte. Diese urbane Entwicklung sorgte dafür, dass am Stadtrand von Paris ein Industriegürtel entstand und sich das Zentrum zu einem Ort des Vergnügens entwickeln konnte: »Es gab Uferpromenaden, Cafés mit Blick auf neue Grünanlagen oder breite Bürgersteige an modernen Prachtstraßen, die nicht selten das Auge des Betrachters auf städtische Baudenkmäler lenkten. […] Für naturalistische Darstellungen der Stadt waren Panoramaaufnahmen gebräuchlich und akzeptiert. Dass ähnliche Kompositionen jetzt im Medium Malerei auftauchten, war ein Novum, aber es kam nicht überraschend.«[4] Die Anzahl der innerstädtischen Hotelbetriebe nahm ständig zu, um die wachsende Anzahl an Touristen aufnehmen zu können. Doch die künstlerische Darstellung von Hotels teilte ein ähnliches Schicksal wie die der Pariser Métro: »Im Gegensatz zur Eisenbahn, scheint der Bau der Metro die Maler nicht weiter beschäftigt zu haben.«[5]

Unter den Gemälden der Impressionisten und ihrer Nachfolger lassen sich zahlreiche Motive finden, die in Cafés, Ballsälen oder Nachtlokalen angesiedelt sind. Edgar Degas, Édouard Manet, Auguste Renoir oder Henri de Toulouse-Lautrec wählten ungewohnte Blickperspektiven und widmeten sich der Einsamkeit des Individuums in der Gesellschaft. Nicht nur in Paris war das Kaffeehaus bevorzugter Treffpunkt von Intellektuellen und beliebtes Sujet der Künstler. So galt etwa das Café des Grand Hotel in Kristiania (Oslo) als Sammelplatz der norwegischen Künstlerboheme.

1 Charles Baudelaire, »Der Salon 1845«, in: *Sämtliche Werke. Briefe*, Bd. 1, hrsg. von Friedhelm Kemp, Claude Pichois, München 1977, S. 127–184, hier S. 184.

2 Ders., »Der Maler des modernen Lebens«, in: ebd., Bd. 5, S. 213–228.

3 Er wurde 1853 als Präfekt des Département Seine von Napoleon III. ins Amt berufen.

4 Zit. nach: James H. Rubin, »Das impressionistische Stadtbild als Emblem der Moderne«, in: *Bilder einer Metropole. Die Impressionisten in Paris*, Ausst.-Kat. Museum Folkwang, Essen, Göttingen 2010, S. 69–82, hier S. 72 f.

5 Zit. nach: Robert Kopp, »Paris – Hauptstadt der zivilisierten Welt?«, in: ebd. S. 35–43, hier S. 42.

STAGE OF POSSIBILITIES

THE HOTEL AS A SETTING OF MODERN LIFE IN ART AND LITERATURE SINCE 1840

HENDRIK BÜNDGE

May next year true seekers grant us the unique pleasure of lauding the advent of novelty!«[1] The young Charles Baudelaire thus summarized the Paris Salon of 1845. He later developed this call for the presentation of the new as an alternative to classical academic painting into an aesthetic theory of the modern age in the essay *The Painter of Modern Life* (1863), which was written shortly before his death. The text became programmatic for a young generation of artists, which would later be called the Impressionists, initially with pejorative connotations.[2] The new achievements of the industrial revolution made their mark on the works of these artists. Railroads cut across rural idylls, covering them in veils of grey-black soot. The tall chimneys of the factories along the Seine, in Le Havre or Rouen, came to be featured as significant elements of landscape painting as did the depictions of the entertainment and leisure activities of the French bourgeoisie. Urban vistas from unusual perspectives presented a contrary notion of the picturesque, and henceforth viewers were then challenged to visually »connect the dots« of the images with their own eyes. In the very same period in which these artists—Claude Monet, Armand Guillaumin, Édouard Manet, Camille Pissarro, Georges Seurat, and Gustave Caillebotte, among others—were working, the urban image of Paris was being modernized by Georges-Eugène Baron Haussmann.[3] His innovations consisted of adapting the city in its entirety to new concepts of construction, which, on the one hand, led to the razing of slum areas and the medieval *cité* and which, on the other, made room for broad and far-branching streets, sewage lines, and gas illumination. This urban development caused an industrial belt to form around the outskirts of Paris, enabling the center to become a place for enjoyment: »There were boardwalks, cafés with views of new parks or broad sidewalks along modern boulevards, which often directed the gaze of the viewer towards the city's monuments . . . Panorama photographs were common and accepted as a naturalistic means of representing the city. That similar compositions began to appear in painting at the same time was a novelty but not a surprising development.«[4] The number of hotels in the city center increased steadily to accommodate the growing number of tourists. Nevertheless, artistic representations of hotels shared the same fate of those of the Paris subway: »In contrast to the railroad, the construction of the subway does not seem to have further interested the painters.«[5]

Numerous motifs set in cafés, ballrooms, or bars can be found in the paintings of the Impressionists and their successors. Edgar Degas, Édouard Manet, Auguste Renoir, and Henri de Toulouse-Lautrec chose unusual points of view and were concerned with portraying the loneliness of the individual in society. Not only in Paris was the coffeehouse a popular meeting point. For example, the café of the Grand Hotel Kristiania (Oslo) served as a gathering place for the Norwegian artistic bohème. In 1883 Edvard Munch produced a view of this hotel and its café, which through 1908 he used as the setting for numerous portrait paintings and lithographs of his friend Henrik Ibsen, a regular customer, who had died two years before. Solitary and framed by a

1 This is the translator's translation. For the original translation, see *Charles Buadelaire, Art In Paris 1845–1862 Salons And Other Exhibitions Reviewed By Charles Baudelaire*, ed. and trans. Jonathan Mayne (Ithaca, NY, 1981). Charles Baudelaire, »Der Salon 1845,« in *Sämtliche Werke. Briefe*, vol. 1, ed. Friedhelm Kemp, Claude Pichois (Munich, 1977), 127–184, 184.

2 Charles Baudelaire, »Der Maler des modernen Lebens,« in *Sämtliche Werke. Briefe*, vol. 5, ed. Friedhelm Kemp, Claude Pichois (Munich, 1977), 213–228.

3 In 1853 he was appointed Prefect of the Département Seine by Napoleon III.

4 Quoted in James H. Rubin, »Das impressionistische Stadtbild als Emblem der Moderne,« in *Bilder einer Metropole. Die Impressionisten in Paris*, exhibit. cat. Museum Folkwang, Essen (Göttingen, 2010), 69–82, 72 f.

5 Quoted in Robert Kopp, »Paris – Hauptstadt der zivilisierten Welt?« in ibid., 35–43, 42.

Edvard Munch fertigte bereits 1883 eine Ansicht des Hotels samt Café an, in dem er bis 1908 in mehreren Gemälden und Lithografien einen Stammgast und Freund porträtierte: den zwei Jahre zuvor verstorbenen Henrik Ibsen. Einsam, von schwarzen Gardinen umrahmt, blickt der Dramatiker zweifelnd dem Betrachter entgegen. Das Hotel als geheimnisumwitterter Ort von Gastlichkeit ist hier lediglich Kulisse. Munchs Augenmerk ruht auf der inneren Verfasstheit des prominenten Porträtierten, den er bewusst vom betriebsamen Geschehen jenseits des Fensters draußen auf der Straße ablöst.

ES WAREN WOHL VOR ALLEM DIE KÜNSTLERTOURISTEN, DIE FÜR WENIGE TAGE ODER WOCHEN IN EINEM DER PREISWERTEN HOTELS UNTERKAMEN. Paula Modersohn-Becker bezieht auf ihrer ersten Parisreise im Jahr 1900 Unterkunft in einem Hotel und porträtiert sich darin. Doch wird nicht das Hotelzimmer selbst zum Sinnbild der Reise, sondern die pittoreske Aussicht aus dem Fenster (Abb. 1). Daran lässt sich ein künstlerischer Typus ausmachen, der bereits mit Joseph Mallord William Turner im ersten Drittel des 19. Jahrhunderts seinen Anfang nimmt (Abb. S. 138–140). Bereits zwanzig Jahre vor Modersohn-Becker hält Adolph Menzel auf einer Reise in München zeichnerisch ebenfalls einen Ausblick fest (Abb. S. 145). Hätte Menzel indes nicht rechts oben auf der kleinformatigen Zeichnung den Titel notiert – MÜNCHEN VOM BALKON DES HOTEL DETZER –, lieferte allein das dargestellte geschäftige Treiben auf dem Platz im unteren Teil des Blickfeldes keinen Hinweis auf den Ort, an dem das Blatt entstand: das Hotel. Dieses bleibt Mittel zum Zweck. So findet auch mit der Blütezeit der Grand Hotels kaum eine bildkünstlerische Auseinandersetzung statt. Eine mögliche Erklärung liefert jene soziologische Betrachtung: An den öffentlichen Plätzen der Metropolen präsentiert sich der Bürger in seiner öffentlichen Rolle. Der Einbruch des Privaten – zumal in der Fremde – ist an diesen Orten des modernen Lebens nicht auszumachen. Dies erschwert Künstlern offenbar die Darstellung, da die Herausforderung für sie gerade darin besteht, einen Blick hinter die Maske der gesellschaftlichen Rolle der Porträtierten zu werfen und einzufangen. Diese ist mit dem Eintritt in das Hotelgebäude, so scheint es, in Auflösung begriffen. Der rote Teppich ist meist so ausgelegt, dass er von dem öffentlichen Bereich des Bürgersteigs in das Semiprivate des Hotels hineinreicht. Als »verführerisches Angebot, in diesen exquisiten Kreis von Gästen als vergangenheitsloser und zukunftsfreier Mensch einzutreten«.[6] Es ist mithin die Auslöschung des Alltags und das Privileg des Gastes, die – einer Verwandlung gleich – neue Machverhältnisse schaffen. Der Alltag bleibt den Angestellten überlassen. Der Gast ist König.

In der Literatur nimmt das Hotel als Handlungsort im 20. Jahrhundert mit dem 1902 publizierten Roman *The Grand Babylon Hotel* von Arnold Bennett seinen Anfang.[7] Nachdem einem amerikanischen Millionär das Verhalten des Oberkellners missfällt, erwirbt er kurzerhand das gesamte Hotel. Die Folgen dieses Kaufes für ihn und seine Tochter erzählt Bennett in einem unterhaltsamen kriminalistischen Plot: Hotelangestellte verschwinden und prominente Gäste, die sich ankündigen, tauchen nie auf. Das Hotel wird zu einem Ort mysteriöser Möglichkeiten verklärt, der scheinbar mit dem alltäglichen Leben nicht viel gemein hat. Der französische Maler Auguste Chabaud fängt in seinem Gemälde HOTELFLUR von 1907/08 die düstere Atmosphäre der labyrinthartigen Gänge im Hotel ein (Abb. S. 158). Erst auf den zweiten Blick entdeckt man einen nach oben verschwindenden rechten Fuß auf der Treppe, durch die Tür von Zimmer Nr. 12 fällt ein Lichtschein durch den Türschlitz. Der Schlüssel steckt jedoch von außen. Nur mit wenigen bildlichen Details skizziert Chabaud so eine Narration, die dem Hotel eine geheimnisvolle Atmosphäre verleiht. Siegfried Kracauer untersucht das Hotel als literarische Bühne möglicher krimineller Machenschaften in seinem Essay *Die Hotelhalle*.[8] In jenem laufen mehrere potenzielle Ereignisstränge, unterstützt durch vielfach interessante Psychogramme der Gäste und des Personals, zusammen, die möglicherweise zu erhellen vermögen, warum Schriftsteller wie Joseph Roth, Franz Werfel oder Marcel Proust ihre Erzählungen in Hotels spielen lassen.[9] Im Gegensatz zur Malerei können in der Literatur zudem olfaktorische und auditive Eigenschaften der Wahrnehmungen des Hotellebens atmosphärisch beschrieben werden.

THOMAS MANN LÄSST IN GLEICH DREI BÜCHERN SEINE PROTAGONISTEN AUF DER PSYCHOLOGISCH VIELSCHICHTIGEN BÜHNE DES HOTELS AUFTRETEN.[10] Die Figur des Hochstaplers Felix Krull lässt er nach dem Tod des Vaters eine Stelle als Liftjunge im Pariser Luxushotel Saint James and Albany an der Rue Saint-Honoré antreten.[11] Dieser transitorische Ort zieht Hasardeure geradezu magisch an, da die Bereitschaft zur Verführung dank der Scheinwelt des Luxushotels unter den Gästen exponentiell scheint.[12] Im Gegensatz zu den anderen Angestellten betrachtet Krull sein eigenes Leben als Schauspiel. Ihm gelingt nach und nach der berufliche Aufstieg zum Oberkellner, wobei Mann für Krulls Auffassung dieser Arbeitswelt um 1900 die Möglichkeit des Rollenwechsels wählt: »Es war der Gedanke der Vertauschbarkeit. Den Anzug, die Aufmachung gewechselt, hätten sehr vielfach die Bedienenden ebensogut Herrschaft sein und hätte so mancher von denen, welche, die Zigarette im Mundwinkel, in den tiefen

6 Zit. nach: Cordula Seger, *Grand Hotel. Schauplatz der Literatur*, Köln / Weimar / Wien 2005, S. 316.

7 Arnold Bennett, *The Grand Babylon Hotel*, London 1902.

8 Siegfried Kracauer, »Die Hotelhalle«, in: ders., *Das Ornament der Masse. Essays*, Frankfurt am Main 1963, S. 157–170. Dieser Aufsatz entstammt einem unveröffentlichten Traktat über den Detektivroman von 1922.

9 Auszugsweise Franz Kafkas *Der Verschollene (Amerika)* (1911–1914, unvollendet, 1927 postum veröffentlicht), Joseph Roths *Hotel Savoy* (1924), Arthur Schnitzlers *Fräulein Else* (1924), Franz Werfels *Die Hoteltreppe* (1927), Stefan Zweigs *Untergang eines Herzens* (1927) und *Rausch der Verwandlung* (1931 begonnen, 1982 aus dem Nachlass veröffentlicht), Vicki Baums *Menschen im Hotel* (1929), Hugo von Hofmannsthals letztes Libretto für die Oper *Arabella* (1929 beendet) oder Erich Kästners *Drei Männer im Schnee* (1934).

10 *Die Bekenntnisse des Hochstaplers Felix Krull* (1954), *Der Tod in Venedig* (1912) und *Der Zauberberg* (1924).

11 Die Idee dazu hatte Mann bereits 1905. Von 1910 bis 1913 schrieb er die Geschichte ausführlich nieder, schloss die fiktiven Memoiren jedoch erst 1954 ab.

12 »Felix Krull verdoppelt die Illusion des Grand Hotels durch die Scheinhaftigkeit seiner eigenen Existenz. Die Maskenlust der Hotelgäste ist in Krulls Erscheinung vervollkommnet.« Zit. nach: Seger 2005 (wie Anm. 6), S. 247.

black curtain, the playwright encounters the viewer with a doubtful expression. In this image the hotel merely serves as a backdrop—as a place of conviviality shrouded in secrecy. Munch's attention is focused on the internal constitution of his prominent model, whom he intentionally sets apart from the bustling activity outside the window on the street beyond.

IT WAS LARGELY ARTIST-TOURISTS WHO LODGED FOR A FEW DAYS OR WEEKS IN MORE ECONOMICAL HOTELS. During one of her first trips to Paris in 1900 Paula Modersohn-Becker stayed in a hotel where she produced a self-portrait. However, the hotel room itself did not become emblematic of her trip, but instead the picturesque view from the window (fig. 1). This composition can be identified as a typology that was introduced by Joseph Mallord William Turner in the first third of the 19th century (fig. pp. 138–140). Almost twenty years before Modersohn-Becker, Adolph Menzel also made a drawing of a view out the window during a trip to Munich (fig. p. 145). Had Menzel not noted this on the above right corner of the small drawing, MÜNCHEN VOM BALKON DES HOTEL DETZER (Munich from the Balcony of Hotel Detzer), alone the busy activity on the square on the lower half of the image would not have given any indication of the place where the drawing originated. The hotel thus remains a means to the end. Also in the heyday of the grand hotel one hardly finds any artistic interest in the subject matter. A sociological observation offers a possible explanation: When presenting themselves in a public capacity the middle class tended to occupy the public spaces of major cities. And here one did not find incursions of the private sphere—particularly not among visitors to a foreign environment. This apparently made it more difficult for artists to portray people in public space, since the challenge they faced was precisely managing to look behind the mask of the social role assumed by those depicted and capture what it revealed. As soon as one enters a hotel this begins to dissipate, or so it seems. The red carpet is usually positioned to lead from the public space of the sidewalk into the semi-private space of the hotel—as »a tantalizing offer to enter this choice circle of guests as a person without a past and free of any future.«[6] It is thus the obliteration of the everyday and the privilege enjoyed by the guest that—like a transformation—create new power relationships. Everyday business is left to the hotel staff. The guest receives the royal treatment.

The hotel begins to serve as a backdrop for works of literature with Arnold Bennett's *The Grand Babylon Hotel* published in 1902.[7] An American millionaire is displeased by the behavior of the head waiter and subsequently buys the entire hotel at the drop of a hat. The consequences of this purchase for himself and his daughter unfold through the entertaining plot of a criminal mystery in Bennett's narrative: Hotel employees disappear, and prominent guests who announce their arrival never turn up. The hotel is romanticized a place of perplexing possibilities, which seem to have little in common with everyday life. In his painting HOTELFLUR (Colouir d'hotel) from 1907/08 the French painter Auguste Chabaud captures the dark atmosphere of the labyrinthine passageways in a hotel (fig. p. 158). Only at second glance does one discover a right foot disappearing up the stairs; a crack of light shines through an opening in the door of room number 12, but the key is in the lock. Merely through the use of a few visual details Chabaud provides the outlines a narrative that lends the hotel a secretive aura. In his essay *Die Hotelhalle* (The Hotel Lobby) Siegfried Kracauer investigates the hotel as a backdrop in literature for potential criminal intrigue.[8] In this essay various potential plotlines of events are brought together, supported by various interesting psychological analyses of the guest and staff, which in sum offer a probable explanation as to why authors such as Joseph Roth, Franz Werfel, or Marcel Proust have written stories that play out in hotels.[9] In contrast to painting, literature enables atmospheric descriptions of the olfactory and auditory aspects of the experience of hotel life.

IN THREE OF HIS BOOKS THOMAS MANN HAS HIS PROTAGONISTS ACT OUT THEIR ROLES ON THE PSYCHOLOGICALLY VERSATILE STAGE OF THE HOTEL.[10] He has Felix Krull, the figure of the confidence man, take a job as an elevator operator in the luxury hotel of the Saint James and Albany on Rue Saint-Honoré in Paris after the death of his father.[11] This transitory place magically attracts conmen, since the guests seem to possess an exponential degree of willingness to be swindled, thanks to the world of appearances that constitutes the luxury hotel.[12] In contrast to the other employees, Krull views his own life as a theater play. Gradually he manages to advance professionally to head waiter, and Mann gives Krull a view of this working environment as offering the potential to change roles. Mann was interested in the idea of exchangeability. »With a change of clothes and make-up, the servitors might often just as well have been the masters, and many of those who lounged in the deep wicker chairs smoking their cigarettes might have played the waiter. It was pure accident that the reverse was the fact, an accident of wealth.«[13] The aspect of shifting roles determines the relationship been appearance and reality in the hotel. At the same time, the hotel itself becomes a springboard for Krull's professional rise. »That Krull's art, his ability to play a role, is equatable to his life—this constitutes the fundamental evil of this decadent artist.

6 Quoted in Cordula Seger, *Grand Hotel. Schauplatz der Literatur,* (Cologne, Weimar and Vienna, 2005), 316.

7 Arnold Bennett, *The Grand Babylon Hotel* (London, 1902).

8 Siegfried Kracauer, »Die Hotelhalle,« in *Das Ornament der Masse. Essays,* (Frankfurt am Main, 1963), 157–170. For the English translation see: Siegfried Kracauer, »The Hotel Lobby« in *The Mass Ornament. Weimar Essays,* ed. and trans. Thomas Y. Levin (Cambridge, MA and London, 1995), 173–185. This essay stems from an unpublished manuscript dating from 1922 on the detective novel.

9 Among others, Franz Kafka's *Der Verschollene (Amerika)* (1911–1914, unfinished, published posthumously in 1927), Joseph Roth's *Hotel Savoy* (1924), Arthur Schnitzler's *Fräulein Else* (1924), Franz Werfel's *Die Hoteltreppe* (1927), Stefan Zweig's *Untergang eines Herzens* (1927) and *Rausch der Verwandlung* (begun in *1931*, published in 1982 from his papers), Vicki Baum's *Menschen im Hotel* (1929), Hugo von Hofmannsthal's final libretto for the opera *Arabella* (completed in 1929), and Erich Kästner's *Drei Männer im Schnee* (1934).

10 *Die Bekenntnisse des Hochstaplers Felix Krull* (1954), *Der Tod in Venedig* (1912), and *Der Zauberberg* (1924).

11 Mann had the idea for the story already in 1905. He wrote the story out in detail from 1910 to 1913 but only completed the fictional memoires in 1954.

12 »Felix Krull doubles the illusion of the grand hotel through the illusory nature of his own existence. The hotel guests' appetite for disguises is fully realized in the guise of Krull.« See Seger 2005 (see note 6), 247.

13 See Thomas Mann, *Gesammelte Werke in dreizehn Bänden,* vol. 9 (Frankfurt am Main, 1990), 491 f. English translation quoted in Egon Schwarz, »Felix Krull,« in *A Companion to the Works of Thomas Mann,* eds. Herbert Lehnert and Eva Wessel (London, 2004), 268.

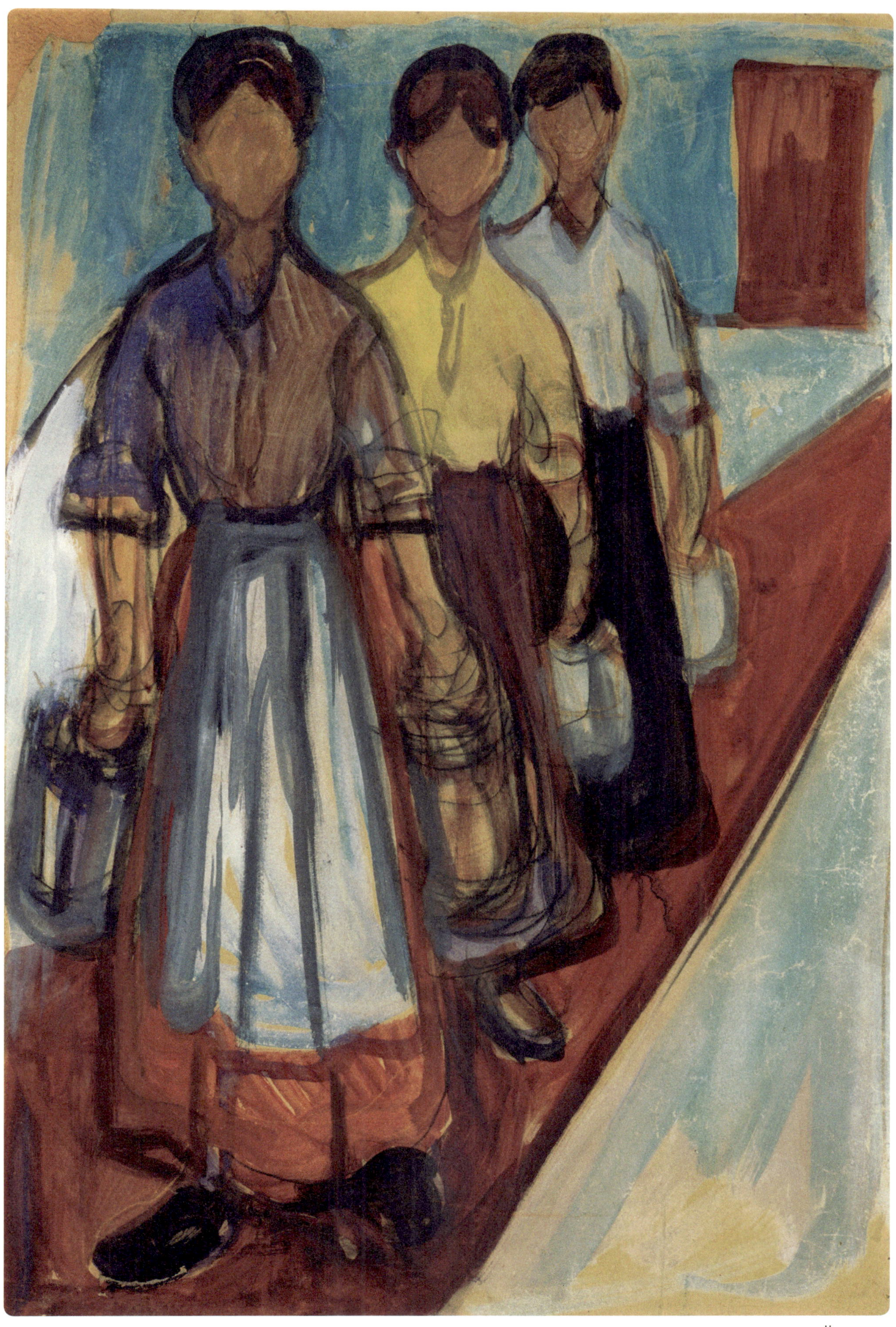

ABB. FIG. 2 EDVARD MUNCH PUTZFRAUEN IM / CHARWOMEN AT THE MUTIGER RITTER HOTEL IN KÖSEN

1906, Gouache und Kreide auf Papier, befestigt auf Papier, Munch Museum, Oslo / 1906, gouache and crayon on paper, mounted on cardboard, Munch Museum, Oslo © Munch Museum / Munch-Ellingsen Group / VG Bild-Kunst, Bonn 2014

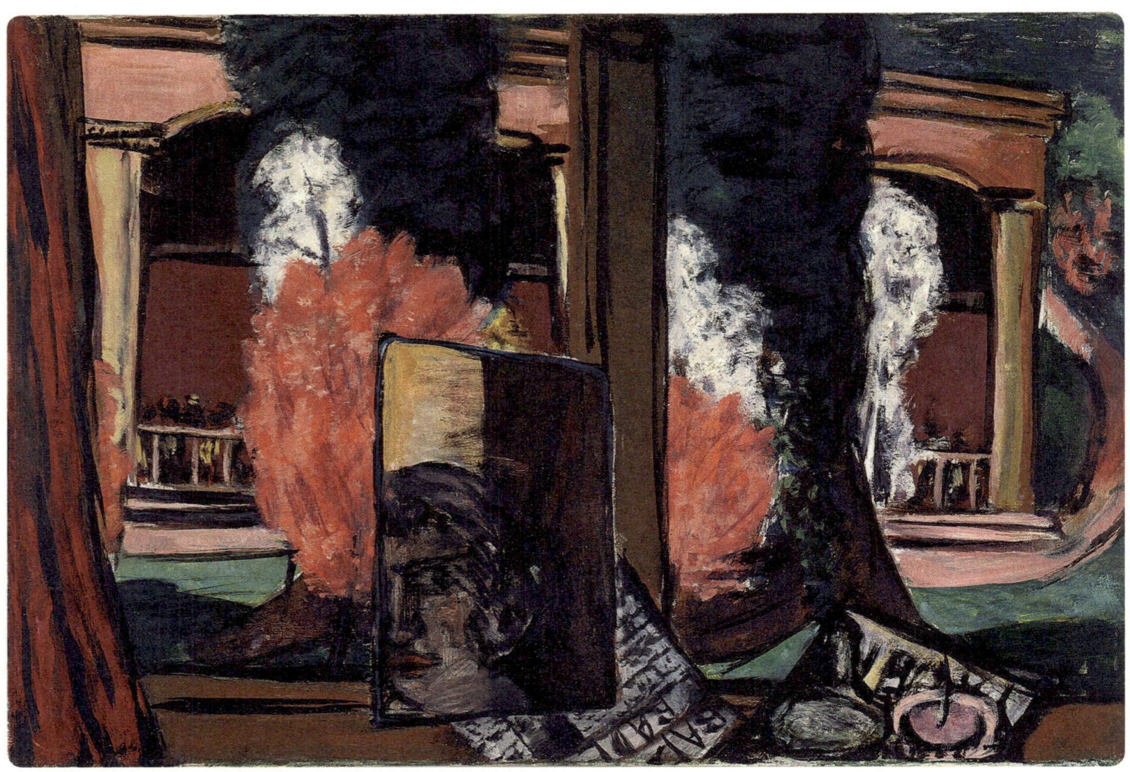

ABB. FIG. 3 MAX BECKMANN BLICK AUS DEM FENSTER VIEW OUT OF THE WINDOW IN BADEN-BADEN
1936, Öl auf Leinwand / Oil on canvas, Courtesy: Museum Frieder Burda, Baden-Baden

Krull is a master of effect, who shapes his life on the basis of the supernatural allure of his outer appearance, through simulating an ability to speak other languages, imitating an aristocratic habitus, and repeating scientific knowledge that he has heard.«[14]

In the mid 1920s the Belarus painter Chaïm Soutine created a number of portraits of hotel employees; the artist portrays elevator operators, waiters, pages, cooks, and chambermaids, usually set apart from any precisely defined spatial setting and placed in front of dark, semi-monochrome backgrounds. Alone the poses and gestures, expressions, or position of the hands offer insights into the state of mind of the depicted hotel staff (fig. p. 160). His artistic interest in this subject matter is marked by two elements in particular: the uniforms and the exhaustion written on the individuals' faces, an indication of the exploitation they suffered on the job. Soutine's series was inspired by his fascination for the daily lives of the lower classes of society: »And the uniform has the effect of hiding individuality, depersonalizing, masking uniqueness by means of anonymity.«[15] In his phenomenological study *Die Angestellten* (The Salaried Masses) (1930) Kracauer attests to the fact that the salary-earning employees of the Weimar Republic did not possess any revolutionary willingness to improve their situation and, like Thomas Mann, he reveals their idle impulses toward relentless pleasure and entertainment as chasing after an illusion and a mirage, as a kind of business trip to paradise for the salaried worker.[16] In the sense of Kracauer, the hotel servants in Soutine's images were human manifestations of the functional components typical of the industrial society of the day. The portraits indicate the necessary and complex organization of the hotel business, which would not function without the strict and rigid adherence to a given hierarchy. This is visible in the various pseudo uniforms that he portrays.

The motifs of Soutine's paintings are prefigured in gouaches by Edvard Munch, who stayed at the Mutiger Ritter (in English: Courageous Knight) resort hotel in the Thuringian town of Bad Kösen. One of the works on paper shows three cleaning women lined up in a row on a red carpet in a hallway of the hotel; they wear different colored blouses and aprons and carry buckets and rags in each hand (fig. 2). Aspects of their physiognomy, such as their eyes, noses, and mouths, are lacking completely. Here the anonymization of the hotel employees is obvious; like invisible fairies they ensure the cleanliness of the *sacred halls of the*

14 See Uta Buttkewitz, *Das Problem der Simulation am Beispiel der Bekenntnisse des Hochstaplers Felix Krull und der Tagebücher Thomas Manns*, (Rostock, 2002), 89 f.

15 Quoted in Maurice Tuchman, »Chaim Soutine (1893–1943),« in *Chaïm Soutine 1893–1943*, exhibit. cat. Westfälisches Landesmuseum für Kunst und Kulturgeschichte, Münster, Kunsthalle Tübingen, Hayward Gallery, London, and Kunstmuseum Luzern (Stuttgart, 1981), 47–71, 62.

16 Siegfried Kracauer, *Die Angestellten: Aus dem neuesten Deutschland* (Frankfurt am Main, 1971), 98.

Korbstühlen sich rekelten – den Kellner abgeben können. Es war der reine Zufall, daß es sich umgekehrt verhielt – der Zufall des Reichtums; denn eine Aristokratie des Geldes ist eine vertauschbare Zufallsaristokratie.«[13] Das Moment des Rollentauschs bestimmt das Verhältnis von Sein und Schein im Hotel. Zugleich wird das Hotel selbst zum Sprungbrett für Krulls beruflichen Aufstieg. »Daß Krulls Werk, seine Selbstinszenierung, mit seinem Leben gleichzusetzen ist, kann man als das Grundübel des dekadenten Künstlers ansehen. Krull ist ein Wirkungskünstler, der auf der Basis der übernatürlichen Wirkung seines Äußeren durch Simulation von Sprachkenntnissen, Imitation von aristokratischem Habitus sowie Repetition von gehörten wissenschaftlichen Erkenntnissen sein Leben gestaltet.«[14]

Mitte der 1920er-Jahre wendet sich der weißrussische Maler Chaïm Soutine in gleich mehreren Porträts der Belegschaft des Hotelgewerbes zu: Liftjungen, Kellner, Pagen, Köchinnen und Zimmermädchen werden von ihm, losgelöst von einer genauen räumlichen Verortung, vor meist dunklen, partiell monochromen Hintergründen dargestellt. Allein Posen und Gesten, Mimik und Haltung der Hände geben Aufschluss über die Befindlichkeit des dargestellten Hotelpersonals (Abb. S. 160). Besonders zwei Merkmale charakterisieren das künstlerische Interesse: Uniformierung und die in die Gesichter eingeschriebene Erschöpfung, Zeichen der Ausbeutung durch ihren Beruf. Es ist die Faszination des Alltäglichen der niederen Gesellschaftsschichten, die Soutine zu diesen Serien anregte. »Und die Uniform bewirkt, daß Individualität versteckt, daß ent-persönlicht, daß Einzigartigkeit mit Anonymität überdeckt wird.«[15] Dem Angestelltendasein der Weimarer Republik bescheinigt Kracauer in seiner phänomenologischen Studie *Die Angestellten* (1930) keine Revolutionsbereitschaft zur Verbesserung der eigenen Lage und enttarnt wie schon Thomas Mann den müßiggängerischen Drang zur Genuss- und Vergnügungssucht als Illusion und Schein – als »Geschäftsreisen für Angestellte ins Paradies.«[16] Im Sinne Kracauers werden die Bediensteten des Hotelbetriebs bei Soutine zu fleischgewordenen Funktionselementen der Industriegesellschaft. In den Porträts deutet sich die notwendige und komplexe Organisation der Hotellerie an, die ohne die streng festgelegte Einhaltung von Hierarchien – sichtbar in den verschiedenen Fantasieuniformen – nicht funktionieren würde.

Soutines Gemälde haben motivische Vorläufer in Gouachen von Edvard Munch, der im Jahr 1906 im Kurhotel Mutiger Ritter im thüringischen Bad Kösen logierte. Ein Blatt zeigt auf dem roten Teppich des Hotelflurs drei Putzfrauen hintereinander aufgereiht, in unterschiedlich farbige Blusen und Schürzen gekleidet, Putzeimer und -lappen in beiden Händen (Abb. 2). Physiognomische Merkmale wie Augen, Nasen und Münder fehlen hingegen. Hier bricht sich die Anonymisierung der Hotelangestellten Bahn, die wie unsichtbare Heinzelmännchen für die Sauberkeit in den *heiligen Hotelhallen* sorgen, ohne von den Hotelgästen bemerkt zu werden.[17] »Die Hoteldirektion verschweigt daher den Gästen fürsorglich die realen Geschehnisse, die den schlecht-ästhetischen Zustand tilgen könnten, der jenes Nichts verkleidet.«[18] Nicht nur die Arbeitswelt, auch das Hotelleben selbst wird von Kracauer als Schein und Illusion einer theatralischen Inszenierung entlarvt, die einzig und allein auf das Wohlbefinden des Gastes innerhalb seines zeitlich begrenzten Aufenthalts zielt.

UNIFORMEN IM WEITESTEN SINNE SPIELEN IM WERK VON MAX BECKMANN EINE ZENTRALE ROLLE. In zahlreichen Selbstporträts trägt er »Cut, Smoking, Frack, Ensemble mit weißer, grauer Weste: es sind Tarnhüllen, die unsichtbar machen, die ihn in Bars, Theatern, Hotelhallen, Badeorten ungestört jenen Jahrmarkt der Eitelkeit, des Begehrens, der betriebsamen Leere studieren lassen, als den er die menschliche Existenz entlarvt hat«.[19] Selbstreflexion im Hotel bestimmt Beckmanns erstes Blatt seiner Grafikmappe BERLINER REISE (Abb. S. 159). Doch welches Selbst sehen wir? Zum einen den zeichnenden Maler, mit dem Skizzenblock an einem Tisch sitzend, den Stift in der Hand. Dahinter arrangiert sind zwei Spiegel, die ihn zugleich von hinten und im Seitenprofil erkennen lassen. Doch nicht nur der Raum des Hotels löst sich so multiperspektivisch auf: »Das Selbst jedenfalls ist in verschiedene Einheiten zerfallen, es hat sich im Wortsinne vermehrt.«[20] Seit 1928 entstehen mehrere Gemälde, die den Typus des Ausblicks variieren.[21] 1936 bildet in BLICK AUS DEM FENSTER IN BADEN-BADEN (Abb. 3) das Hotel Europäischer Hof mit Aussicht auf die gegenüberliegende Trinkhalle das Motiv. Ein auf dem Fenstersims eingeblendetes Frauengesicht, vermutlich ein Spiegelbild, bricht die bislang angeführten Beispiele des Ausblicktypus auf. Der Maler konstruiert eine verwirrende Räumlichkeit im Inneren des Hotels als komplexe Scheinwelt im Spannungsfeld zwischen dem Privaten und Öffentlichen. Es ist diese Unsicherheit des Raumes – des Hotelraumes zumal –, die das Œuvre Beckmanns auszeichnet und die seine Ausblicksdramaturgie in bis dato unbekannter Weise steigert. Den genauen Aufenthaltsort Beckmanns auf einer Reise nach Monte Carlo verraten drei Zeichnungen, die er auf dem Briefpapier des Cap Martin Hôtel auf Vorder- und Rückseite anfertigt und die als Vorgriff auf Martin Kippenbergers schelmisch-charmante Hotelzeichnungen des vermeintlich vielreisenden Künstlers in den 1980er-Jahren verstanden werden können (Abb. S. 182–185).

13 Zit. nach: Thomas Mann, *Gesammelte Werke in dreizehn Bänden*, Bd. IX, Frankfurt am Main 1990, hier S. 491 f.

14 Zit. nach: Uta Buttkewitz, *Das Problem der Simulation am Beispiel der Bekenntnisse des Hochstaplers Felix Krull und der Tagebücher Thomas Manns*, Rostock 2002, S. 89 f.

15 Zit. nach: Maurice Tuchman, »Chaïm Soutine (1893–1943)«, in: *Chaïm Soutine 1893–1943*, Ausst.-Kat. Westfälisches Landesmuseum für Kunst und Kulturgeschichte, Münster, Kunsthalle Tübingen, Hayward Gallery, London, Kunstmuseum Luzern, Stuttgart 1981, S. 47–71, hier S. 62.

16 Zit. nach: Siegfried Kracauer, *Die Angestellten: Aus dem neuesten Deutschland*, Frankfurt am Main 1971, S. 98.

17 Ich beziehe mich hier auf Kracauers Gleichsetzung von Gotteshaus und Hotelhalle, in der ebenfalls eine »Ablösung vom Alltag« erfolgt, deren Gäste »statt auf das Gottesverhältnis« sich dem »Verhältnis zum Nichts« annähern. Zit. nach: Kracauer 1963 (wie Anm. 8), S. 161 ff.

18 Ebd. S. 170.

19 Zit. nach: Günter Metken, »Max Beckmann im Spiegelkabinett. Ein Selbstbildnis aus Selbstporträts«, in: *Max Beckmann. Gemälde 1905–1950*, Ausst.-Kat. Museum der bildenden Künste Leipzig, Städelsches Kunstinstitut, Frankfurt am Main, 2. Aufl., Stuttgart 1990, S. 19–25, hier S. 21.

20 Zit. nach: Sebastian Karnatz, *Eine Szene im Theater der Unendlichkeit. Max Beckmanns Dramen und ihre Bedeutung für seine Bildrhetorik*, Göttingen 2011, S. 146.

21 Z.B. SCHEVENINGEN, FÜNF UHR FRÜH (1928), GOLFPLATZ BADEN-BADEN (1937) oder SOUVENIR CHICAGO (1948).

hotel but go unnoticed by the hotel guests.[17] »The hotel management therefore thoughtfully conceals from its guests the real events which could put an end to the false aesthetic situation shrouding that nothing.«[18] Not only the working world but also hotel life itself are revealed as conveying the kinds of illusionary appearances found in a theatrical production, which is solely oriented towards making guests feel comfortable during the limited period of their stay.

UNIFORMS IN THE BROADEST SENSE OF THE WORD PLAY A CENTRAL ROLE IN THE WORK OF MAX BECKMANN. In his numerous self-portraits he wears a »cutaway, tuxedo, white tie and tails, ensembles with white or grey vests. These are mantles of camouflage that make him invisible, so that in bars, theaters, and hotel lobbies he can study the carnival of vanities, the desires, and the bustling emptiness that he depicts as constituting human existence.«[19] His mirror-image in a hotel is the first work in his portfolio of prints entitled BERLINER REISE (Trip to Berlin) (fig. p. 159). But what kind of image of the self are we confronted with? On the one hand we see the painter making a drawing, sitting at a table with his sketchbook, a pencil in his hand. Behind him is an arrangement with two mirrors, which enable us to see him simultaneously from the back and in profile. Not only the space of the hotel is broken down into multiple perspectives: »In any case the self has disintegrated into different components; it has literally replicated itself.«[20] From 1928 onward he produced a number of paintings that were variations on the typology of the view from the window.[21] In 1936 the work BLICK AUS DEM FENSTER IN BADEN-BADEN (View from the Window in Baden-Baden) (fig. 3) features a motif looking out from the Hotel Europäischer Hof to the opposite drinking hall. A female face, possibly a reflection in a mirror, is superimposed on the windowsill and adds a new element to the examples of the view-from-the-window typology mentioned above. The painter constructs a confusing sense of space within the interior of the hotel as a complex, illusory world poised between the private and the public realm. It is this uncertainty of space—the hotel space in particular—that distinguishes Beckmann's oeuvre and adds unprecedented drama to his window views. Three drawings reveal where Beckmann stayed on a trip to Monte Carlo. Made on the front and back of Cap Martin Hôtel stationary, they can be viewed as anticipating Martin Kippenberger's mischievously charming hotel drawings produced by the reputedly much-traveled artist in the 1980s (fig. pp. 182–185). Beckmann addresses the foreignness of hotel life in the painting HOTEL LOBBY, completed in 1950, the year of his death. Rendered in dark colors and thrust close together, the guests individually remain in their own worlds. However, before attempting to capture these complex structures of hotel life in painting, he tried his hand at presenting them in the literary form of a drama in four acts in 1920, *Das Hotel* (The Hotel).[22] Unpublished during his lifetime, the manuscript can be interpreted as an agglomeration of his personal experiences as well as his observation and studies of hotel guests and staff.

The loneliness engendered by the anonymity of the hotel is also conveyed in many paintings by the American painter Edward Hopper produced in the same period as Beckmann's work. Rendered in muted colors, hotel rooms and lobbies set the stage and characterize the heterotopic site of the hotel. This temporary home away from home becomes something uncanny, which Hopper views as having a special quality, in which the foreignness of the surroundings assume an existential dimension. In his work the collective space of the hotel is no longer a place of possibility. The setting of the hotel ultimately becomes an abstraction, a stage where real people perform their roles as actors in a theater play without feeling as such. Whereas in Europe many hotels are committed to preserving tradition, in the New World the focus is instead placed on the conquest of the new: Hopper's paintings convey the American experience of *being on the road,* in which the hotel stay is reduced to its absolute barest necessities. As a transit stop for the motorized guest arriving by car, the motel is used for one night, instead of multiple days or a week (fig. 4). The complex and lavish representation of the would-be stage of the grand hotel is absent; the interior decor of the motel is reduced to a minimum; superfluous details have been done away with.

In the 1930s European hotels became places of refuge for numerous people in exile. With World War II the reign of sophistication came to a temporary end. Apart from written or painted testimonies, the hotel played an important role in the life of numerous writers and artists, and the stories that have been handed down about them certainly rival works of art. It is said that Salvador Dalí regularly turned his hotel room, the Royal Suite in the Hotel Le Meurice in Paris, into a *gesamtkunstwerk:* he painted the walls, ceiling, curtains, and sheets, and the suite was destroyed by his pet, an ocelot.[23] Food poisoning caused Alfred Otto Wolfgang Schulze, better known as Wols, to be admitted to a Paris hospital in August 1951. In contrast to Joseph Roth, the self-proclaimed *hotel citizen,* who died in a hospital for the indigent in Paris, Wols had his wife take him to the five-star hotel Montalembert a few days later. The next morning he died there and was unobtrusively removed through a back exit.[24] Discretion and rumor are ultimately the most reliable currencies for a hotel—the material for the making of legends.

17 See Kracauer 1995 (see note 8), 175 f. I am referring to Kracauer's equation of the church and the hotel lobby, in both of which one is »detached from the everyday.« (176). Instead of encountering »a relation to God,« the hotel guest experiences »a relation to nothing« (179).

18 Ibid., 184.

19 Günter Metken, »Max Beckmann im Spiegelkabinett. Ein Selbstbildnis aus Selbstporträts,« in *Max Beckmann. Gemälde 1905–1950,* exhibit. cat. Museum der bildenden Künste Leipzig, Städelsches Kunstinstitut, Frankfurt am Main, 2nd ed. (Stuttgart, 1990), 19–25, 21.

20 Sebastian Karnatz, *Eine Szene im Theater der Unendlichkeit. Max Beckmanns Dramen und ihre Bedeutung für seine Bildrhetorik,* (Göttingen, 2011), 146.

21 For example, SCHEVENINGEN, FÜNF UHR FRÜH (Scheveningen, Five O' Clock in the Monring) (1928), GOLFPLATZ BADEN-BADEN (Golf Course Baden-Baden) (1937), or SOUVENIR CHICAGO (1948).

22 Max Beckmann, *Das Hotel,* ed. Gerd Udo Feller (Munich, 1984).

23 See Silke Behl and Eva Gerberding, *Drehtür in die große Welt: die 50 schönsten Grandhotels in Europa,* (Cologne, 1998), 159 f.

24 See Claire van Damme, »Das trunkene Schiff. Kritische und dokumentierte Biographie des Künstlers WOLS (1913–1951),« in *WOLS. Sa vie ...,* exhibit. cat. Goethe-Institut, Paris (Paris, 1986), n. p.

Der Fremdheit des Hotellebens widmet Beckmann noch im Jahr seines Todes, 1950, das Gemälde HOTEL LOBBY. In dunklen Farben, dicht zusammengedrängt, bleiben die Gäste jeder für sich. Bis Beckmann jedoch diese komplexen Strukturen des Hotellebens malerisch einfangen konnte, erprobte er sie ab 1920 literarisch in dem Drama in vier Akten *Das Hotel.*[22] Das zu Lebzeiten unveröffentlichte Manuskript kann als Verdichtung seiner persönlichen Erfahrungen und Beobachtungsstudien, die er von Hotelgästen und -personal betrieb, verstanden werden.

Einsamkeit in der Anonymität des Hotellebens scheint zeitgleich zu Beckmann auch der US-amerikanische Maler Edward Hopper in mehreren Gemälden festzuhalten. Hotelzimmer und Lobby bilden dafür die Bühne und bestimmen in zurückgenommen Farben den heterotopen Ort des Hotels: Das Heim auf Zeit wird zum Un-Heimlichen, dessen Besonderheit Hopper darin sieht, dass die Fremdheit der Umgebung eine existenzialistische Dimension erhält. Der kollektive Raum des Hotels wird bei ihm nicht mehr zum Möglichkeitsort. Die Bühne des Hotels wird endgültig eine Abstraktion, auf der reale Personen wie in einer Theaterinszenierung als Schauspieler agieren, ohne sich als solche zu fühlen. Während gerade in Europa viele Hotels der Wahrung der Tradition verpflichtet sind, rückt in der Neuen Welt die Eroberung des Neuen in den Fokus: In Hoppers Gemälden kommt bereits das amerikanische *Unterwegs-Sein* zum Ausdruck, mit dem der Hotelaufenthalt aufs Nötigste verkürzt wird. Statt mehrerer Tage oder Wochen wird das Motel zur motorisiert angesteuerten Durchgangsstation für eine Nacht (Abb. 4). Die aufwendige und verschwenderische Repräsentation der vermeintlichen Bühne Grand Hotel ist hier aufgehoben; die Inneneinrichtung der Motels ist auf ein Minimum reduziert, alles Überflüssige verbannt.

In den 1930er-Jahren werden europäische Hotels zum Zufluchtsort zahlreicher Exilanten. Mit dem Zweiten Weltkrieg endet vorerst die Dominanz des Mondänen. Abgesehen von den schriftlichen und malerischen Zeugnissen spielt das Hotel im Leben zahlreicher Literaten und Künstler eine wichtige Rolle und die kolportierten Ereignisse können durchaus mit den Kunstwerken konkurrieren. So ist von Salvador Dalí überliefert, dass er sein Hotelzimmer, die Royal Suite im Hotel Le Meurice in Paris, regelmäßig in ein Gesamtkunstwerk verwandelte: Wände, Decken, Vorhänge, Bettwäsche wurden von ihm bemalt und die Suite von seinem Haustier, einem Ozelot, zerstört.[23] Eine Lebensmittelvergiftung sorgte dafür, dass Alfred Otto Wolfgang Schulze, besser bekannt als Wols, im August 1951 in ein Pariser Krankenhaus eingeliefert wird. Im Gegensatz zum *Hotelbürger* Joseph Roth, der in einem Armenhospital in Paris stirbt, lässt sich Wols einige Tage später von seiner Frau in das Fünfsternehotel Montalembert bringen. Am nächsten Morgen stirbt er dort und wird dezent durch den Hinterausgang entfernt.[24] Diskretion und Kolportage sind letzten Endes die verlässlichsten Währungen für ein Hotel. Sie sind der Stoff aus dem seine Legenden gewoben sind.

22 Max Beckmann, *Das Hotel*, hrsg. von Gerd Udo Feller, München 1984.

23 Vgl. Silke Behl, Eva Gerberding, *Drehtür in die große Welt: die 50 schönsten Grandhotels in Europa*, Köln 1998, S. 159 f.

24 Vgl. Claire van Damme, »Das trunkene Schiff. Kritische und dokumentierte Biographie des Künstlers WOLS (1913–1951)«, in: *WOLS. Sa vie ...*, Ausst.-Kat. Goethe-Institut, Paris, Paris 1986, o. S.

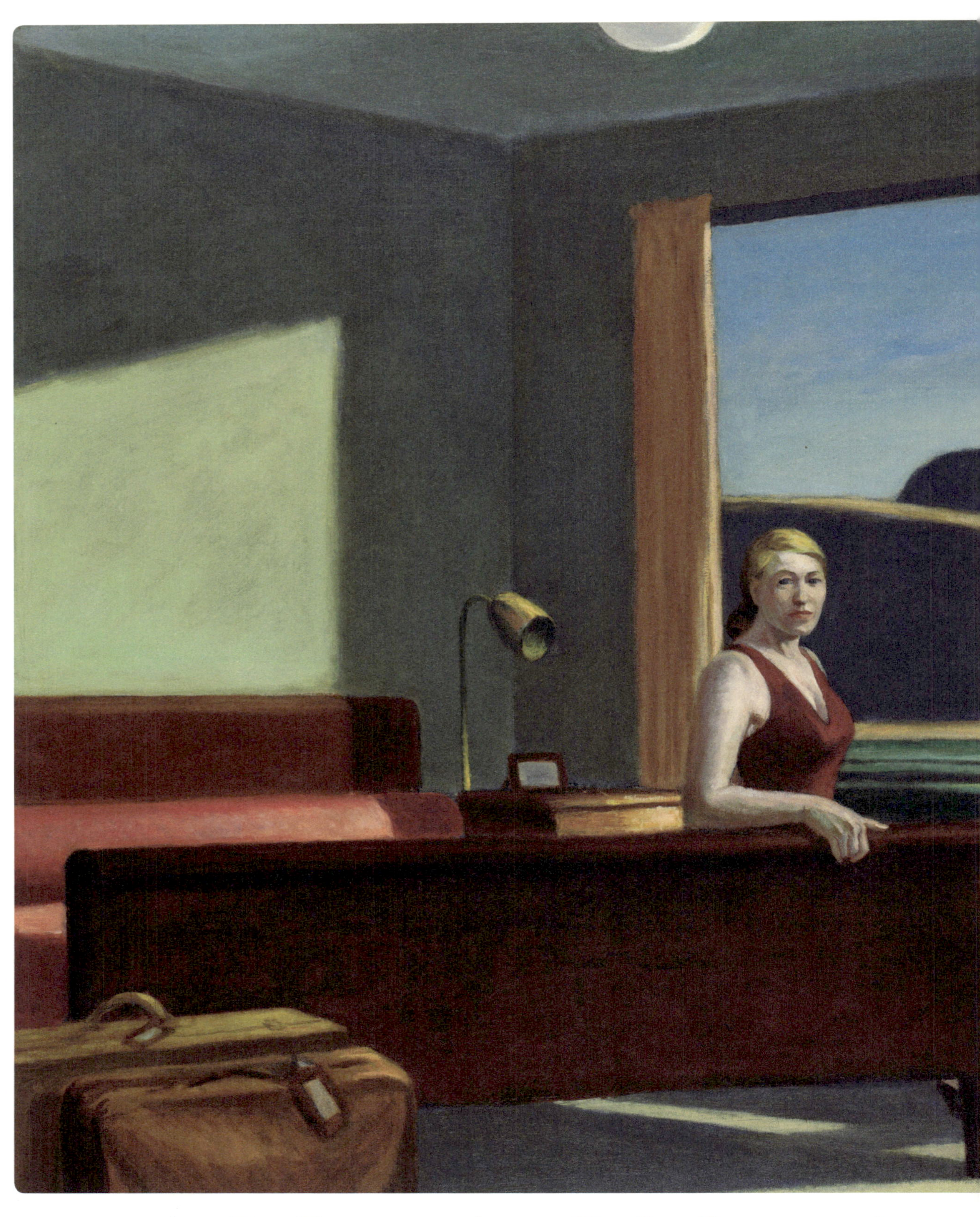

ABB. / FIG. 4

WESTERN

1957, oil on canvas, The Yale University Art Gallery, New Haven

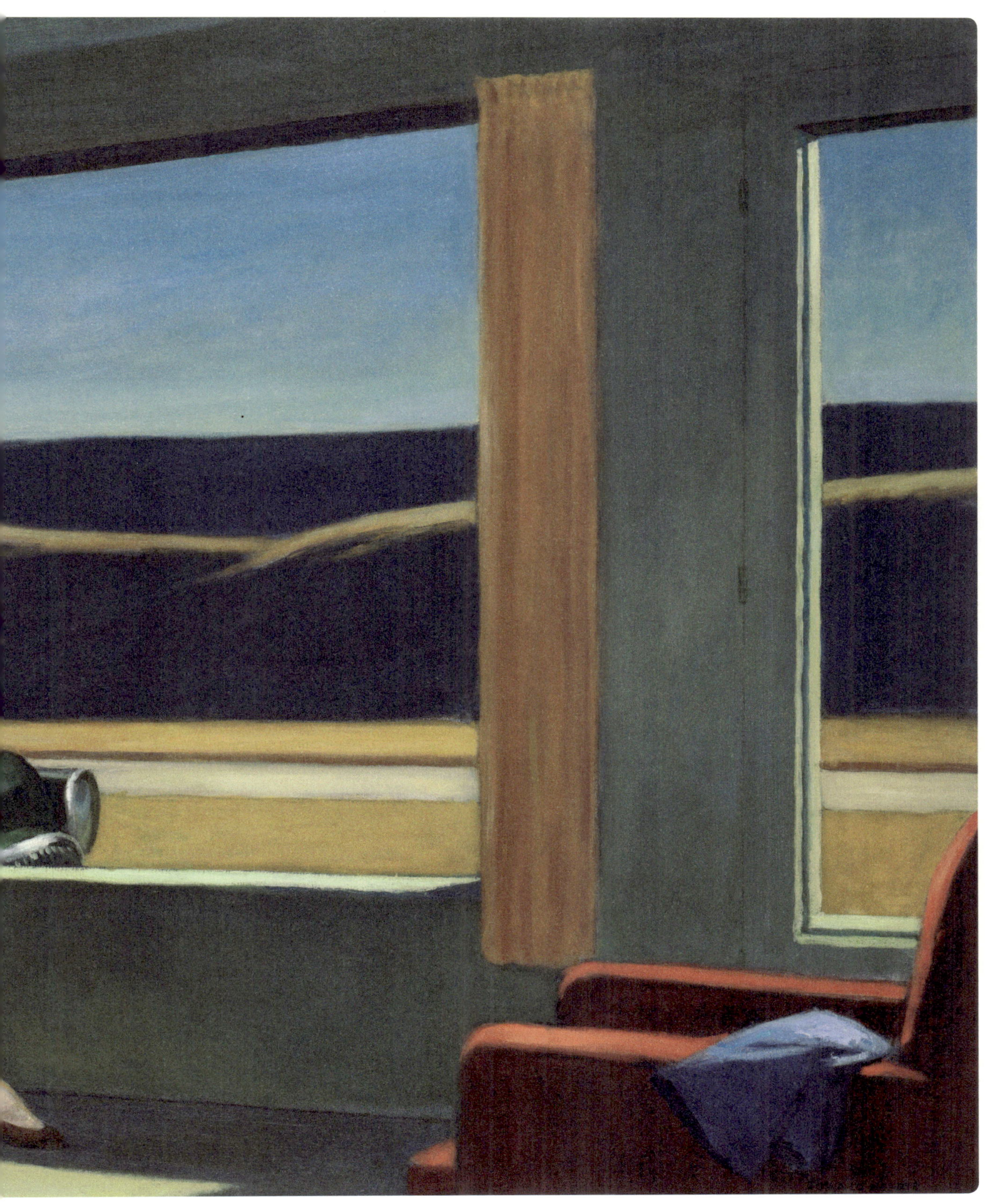

EDWARD HOPPER
MOTEL

1957, Öl auf Leinwand, The Yale University Art Gallery, New Haven

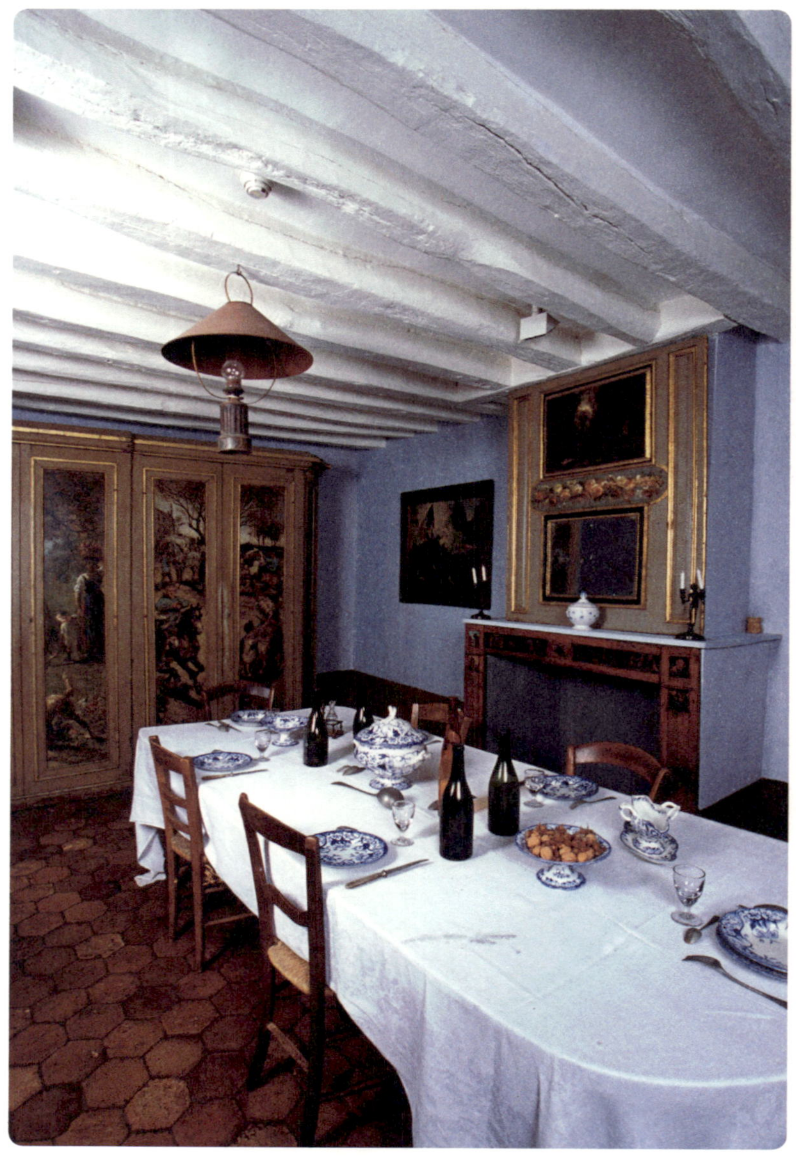

Abb. / Fig. 1

SPEISESAAL IN DER
DINING ROOM AT THE **AUBERGE GANNE**

Barbizon, Frankreich / France

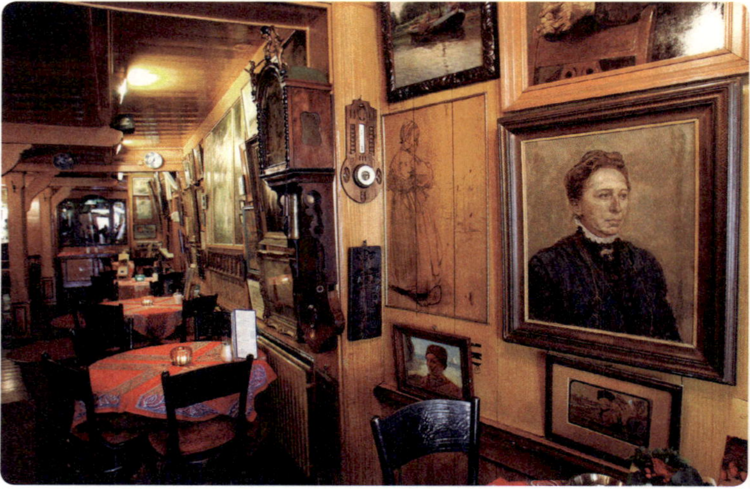

Abb. / Fig. 2

SPEISESAAL IM HOTEL
DINING ROOM AT THE HOTEL **SPAANDER**

Volendam, Niederlande / The Netherlands

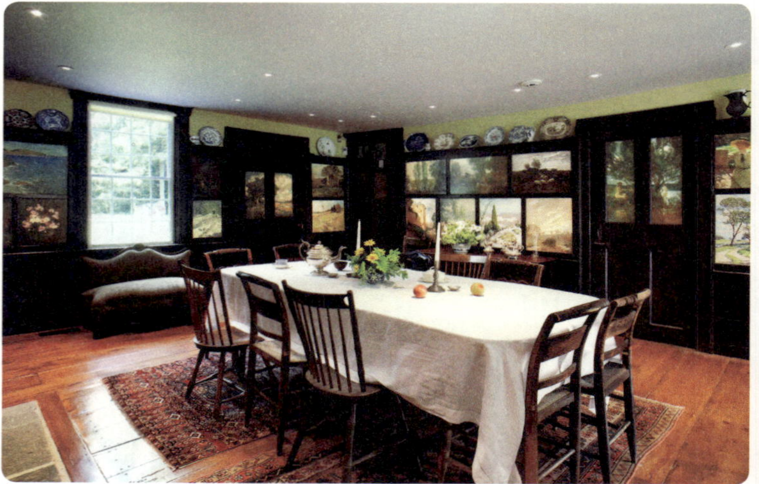

Abb. / Fig. 3

SPEISESAAL IM
DINING ROOM AT THE **FLORENCE GRISWOLD HOUSE**

Old Lyme, CT, USA

DAS HERZ DER GEMEINSCHAFT

BRØNDUMS SPEISESAAL

METTE BØGH JENSEN

IM Skagens Museum, ganz im Norden von Jütland in Dänemark, befindet sich ein ganz außerordentlicher Raum, bekannt als *Brøndums Speisesaal.* Mit seinen dunkel gebeizten Paneelen und den installierten Gemälden sieht er völlig anders aus als alle anderen Räume im Haus, aber er ist nichtsdestotrotz ein zentraler Teil des Museums und seiner Sammlung. Der Raum umfasst und verkörpert die Geschichte jener Künstlerkolonie, die wiederum der Grund dafür ist, dass es dieses Museum überhaupt gibt. Aber warum sieht der ehemalige Hotelspeisesaal so aus, wie er aussieht? Wer hat diesen außergewöhnlichen Raum geschaffen? Und warum um alles in der Welt befindet er sich heute in einem Museum?

Künstlerische Ausschmückungen von Speisesälen beziehungsweise Räumen in Wirtshäusern oder Hotels wurden gegen Ende des 19. Jahrhunderts wieder sehr populär, als auch das Phänomen von Künstlerkolonien mehr oder weniger häufig in ganz Europa und Nordamerika aufzublühen begann. Dort versammelten sich Künstler – üblicherweise in kleineren Städten und häufig in der Nähe von Wäldern oder dem Meer –, weil sie sich oft danach sehnten, einer informellen Gemeinschaft anzugehören, und weil viele von ihnen sich außerdem ausgiebig der Freilichtmalerei widmeten. Über das Gefühl der Solidarität und der gegenseitigen Kameradschaft hinaus, das in den Künstlerzirkeln kultiviert wurde, und neben anderen Ähnlichkeiten hatten viele dieser Kolonien gemein, dass die teilnehmenden Künstler sich oft in bestimmten ausgewählten Hotels oder Wirtshäusern am Ort trafen und meist auch eines oder mehrere Werke dorthin verschenkten. In vielen dieser Lokale wurden diese Geschenke der Künstler oft in einem einzelnen Zimmer versammelt und fungierten somit als eine kumulierte Dekoration. Diese kunstvoll ausgeschmückten Räume bildeten wiederum den Rahmen für die gesellschaftlichen Aktivitäten der Künstler und es sind eben diese speziellen Räume, die dann später die Touristen anlocken sollten, die den Künstlern nachfolgten. In künstlerischer Manier markierten die Schaffenden so den Punkt, an dem sich ihre Gemeinschaft üblicherweise zusammenfand. Meist waren diese Hotels zudem die ersten Ausstellungsräume, wo von den Künstlern vor Ort geschaffene Werke gezeigt wurden.[1]

INTERNATIONALE KÜNSTLERKOLONIEN

Heute sind etliche solcher Arrangements leider vollkommen verschwunden. Im Lauf der Zeit, als immer mehr der einst von Künstlern frequentierten Gasthäuser und Hotels ihre Besitzer wechselten, wurden die Werke verkauft und die Dekorationen auseinandergerissen und verstreut. Im französischen Barbizon dagegen, wo in der ersten Hälfte des 19. Jahrhunderts einige der ersten Künstlerkolonien entstanden waren, hatte sich die L'auberge Ganne zu einem ganz selbstverständlichen Versammlungsort für viele Künstler entwickelt, die dort bereitwillig Möbel und Wände dekorierten. In den letzten Jahren nun wurde das Gasthaus umfassend und mit dem Ziel restauriert, dem Mobiliar und dem übrigen Inventar wieder das ursprüngliche Erscheinungsbild zurückzugeben. 2010 wurde es schließlich als Museum wiedereröffnet (Abb. 1). Andernorts war es nicht notwendig, die Innenausstattung zu restaurieren, um eine klare Vorstellung davon zu bekommen, was die Beiträge

1 Dieser Artikel behandelt zum Großteil Themen, mit denen ich mich auch in meinem Buch *Brøndum's dining room: in gratitude for happy days*, Skagen 2011, sowie in meinem Artikel »Brøndum's dining room – an international meeting place«, in: hrsg. von Marianne Saabye, *KRØYER: An International perspective*, Ausst.-Kat. Den Hirschsprungske Samling, Kopenhagen, Skagens Museum, Skagen, Skagen 2011, beschäftigt habe.

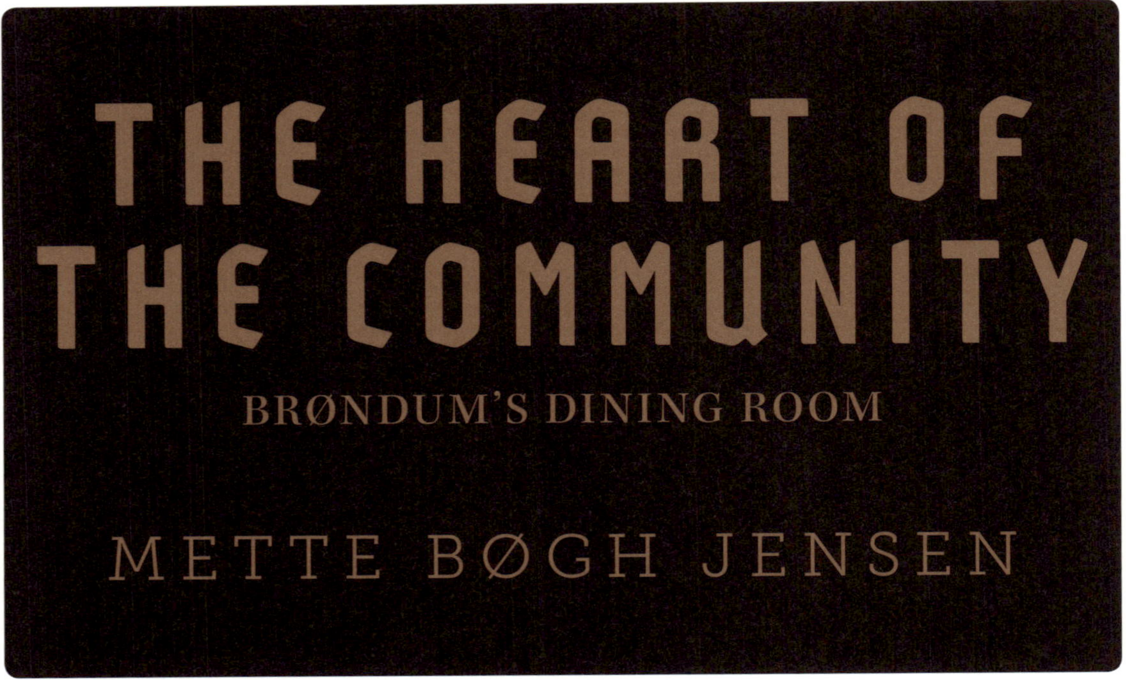

THE HEART OF THE COMMUNITY

BRØNDUM'S DINING ROOM

METTE BØGH JENSEN

AT Skagens Museum, located in the northernmost part of Jutland, there is a most extraordinary room that is known as *Brøndum's dining room.* With its dark-stained panels and paintings installed in the space, this room does not look anything like what one finds in the rest of the museum. Nevertheless, it is a central part of the museum and its collection. The room encompasses and embodies the story of the artist colony that formed the basis for the existence of this museum in the first place. But why does the dining room look like it does? Who created this unusual room? And why on earth is it now situated *inside* a museum?

The decoration of dining halls or rooms inside inns and hotels by artists saw a marked resurgence in the late 19th century, when the phenomenon of artist colonies started to flourish more or less prevalently in many parts of Europe and North America. At such sites, typically in smaller towns and often close to the woods or to the seaside, artists gathered together, because they yearned to be part of an informal creative community and also because many devoted themselves extensively to the practice of *plein air* painting. Above and beyond the sense of solidarity and mutual camaraderie that was cultivated in artist colonies and many other similarities between such places, what many of the colonies had in common was that the participating artists would typically gather at certain hotels or inns and that these artists would often donate one or more of their works to this establishment. At many of these places the artists' donations were brought together in a single room and accordingly came to function as an aggregate *in-situ* decoration. These ornately adorned rooms in turn provided the setting for the artists' social activities, and, as a rule, it was these rooms in particular that later attracted the tourists who followed in the wake of the artists. In this way the artists made their mark on the place where their community had its natural point of rendezvous. Moreover, the hotels were some of the first exhibition spaces to show the art being created by the artists who were living there.[1]

INTERNATIONAL ARTISTS COLONIES

Today, unfortunately, several of these *in-situ* decorations have disappeared in their entirety. In the course of time, as more and more of these inns and hotels changed hands, the works of art were sold off and the decorations were divided up and scattered. In Barbizon in north-central France, where some of the first artist colonies arose in the first half of the 19th century, the inn Auberge Ganne became a natural gathering spot for many artists, who willingly decorated pieces of furniture and the walls. In recent years the inn has undergone a major restoration, with the aim of bringing the furniture and the rest of the inventory back to their original appearance, and in 2010 Auberge Ganne was re-opened as a museum (fig. 1). Elsewhere it has not been necessary to reconstruct the interiors in order to get a clear idea of what the artists' contributions to the decorations of the rooms in question were. In the town of Volendam, an old fishing camp located in northwestern Holland, we find the Hotel Spaander, which opened in 1881 as the first hotel in the town. The hotel quickly became a gathering place for the steadily increasing stream of artists who came

1 This article is based, to a great extent, on themes that I have also been dealing with in my book, *Brøndum's Dining Room: In Gratitude for Happy Days,* (Skagen: Skagens Museum, 2011) and in my article, »Brøndum's dining room – an international meeting place,« in *KRØYER: An International Perspective,* ed. Marianne Saabye, exhibition catalogue, Den Hirschsprungske Samling [The Hirschsprung Collection] and Skagens Museum (Copenhagen and Skagen, 2011).

der Künstler zur Ausschmückung der fraglichen Räume waren. In der Stadt Volendam, einer alten Fischersiedlung im Nordwesten Hollands, befindet sich das Hotel Spaander, das 1881 als das erste seiner Art in der Stadt eröffnet wurde. Das Hotel zog sehr bald einen immer stärker werdenden Strom von Künstlern an, die das Fischerdorf besuchten. Bereits im Verlauf der 1880er-Jahre war das Haus voller Kunstwerke.[2] Die Familie Spaander erkannte rasch, wie man am besten von den Künstlerbesuchen profitieren würde, und richtete sogar einige der Zimmer als Ateliers ein.[3] Heute gehört das Hotel zwar nicht mehr der Familie, aber auch der heutige Besitzer hat die Kunstsammlung erhalten und noch immer sind die Wände voller Kunst (Abb. 2).

Viele der Künstler, die Mitte und Ende des 19. Jahrhunderts nach Europa – insbesondere nach Frankreich – kamen, waren Amerikaner und etliche von ihnen partizipierten rege an dem Gemeinschaftsgefühl in einer oder gleich in mehreren Künstlerkolonien. Dies war gewiss bei Henry Ward Ranger (1858–1916) und Willard Leroy Metcalf (1858–1925) der Fall. Zu Anfang des 20. Jahrhunderts waren diese beiden Maler, nachdem sie einige Jahre in Europa gelebt hatten, schließlich an der Gründung einer Künstlerkolonie in Old Lyme in Connecticut/USA, beteiligt. Hier bot eine Pension, das Florence Griswold House, den gesellschaftlichen Aktivitäten der Künstler den Rahmen und auch hier war der Speisesalon schon bald mit Kunstwerken geschmückt (Abb. 3). Wenn man die Frage stellt, woher ursprünglich jeweils die Idee stammte, ein bestimmtes Zimmer mit der Kunst einer vor Ort angesiedelten Künstlerkolonie zu gestalten, variieren die Geschichten von einem Hotel zum nächsten sehr. Manchmal waren es die Besitzer oder Gastwirte, die den Vorschlag machten – vielleicht von anderen Häusern inspiriert, wo sie ähnliche Dekorationen gesehen hatten –, während in anderen Fällen die Künstler selbst auf die Idee kamen. In bestimmten Konstellationen wurde mittels Kunst auch das Gästezimmer oder aber das verzehrte Essen und die Getränke bezahlt. Dies war beispielsweise in Skagen der Fall, wo es die Tradition gab, dass der Wirt des Brøndums Hotel, Degn Brøndum (1856–1932), den Künstlern immer Runden von Schnaps ausgab, wenn ein neues Gemälde aufgehängt wurde.[4] Diese Tradition trug ganz gewiss zum Wachsen der Kunstsammlung bei. Heute ist Brøndums Speisesaal von allen ornamentalen Esszimmern in Hotels des späten 19. Jahrhunderts eines der am besten erhaltenen.

DIE KÜNSTLERKOLONIE IN SKAGEN

Als die Künstler begannen, in den 1870er-Jahren in erheblicher Anzahl nach Skagen zu strömen, war die Stadt relativ überschaubar und abgelegen: Es lebten dort weniger als 2.000 Menschen. Von 1859 bis 1884 gab es auch nur ein einziges Hotel vor Ort, das Brøndums Hotel. Und doch war es eben diese Herberge, die eine entscheidende Bedeutung für die internationale Künstlerkolonie bekommen sollte, die in der Stadt aufkeimte.[5] Sie wurde zum Versammlungsort für all diejenigen Künstler, die sich aus den europäischen Metropolen auf die Reise an die Spitze von Jütland gemacht hatten. Von den meisten, die nach Skagen kamen, sind Beschreibungen überliefert, wie gut sie in Brøndums Hotel empfangen wurden, oder auch davon, wie das Gefühl, zusammen mit anderen Künstlern in die Gemeinschaft aufgenommen zu werden, eine entscheidende Rolle dafür spielte, dass ihr Aufenthalt hier ein Erfolg wurde – oder eben auch nicht. Während die Künstlerkolonie als solche bereits in den 1870er-Jahren Wirklichkeit wurde, sollte es aber noch bis 1882 dauern, als der Maler Peder Severin, auch P. S. Krøyer (1851–1909) nach Skagen kam, dass sie ihren eigenen Treffpunkt bekam. Danach spielte genau dieser eine wichtige Rolle, um andere internationale Künstler nach Skagen zu locken: Es ging ihnen nun nämlich um die ästhetische Dekoration von Brøndums Speisesaal.

P. S. KRØYER – EIN INTERNATIONAL ANERKANNTER KÜNSTLER IN SKAGEN

P. S. Krøyer war einer der ersten Maler in Skagen mit internationaler Ausrichtung. Er stellte seine Arbeiten immer wieder sowohl in Dänemark selbst, aber auch im Ausland aus. Krøyer hatte seine Studien an der Königlichen Akademie der Schönen Künste (dän. Det Kongelige Academie for de skjønne Kunster) in Kopenhagen im Jahre 1870, kurz vor seinem neunzehnten Geburtstag abgeschlossen und galt als eines der vielversprechendsten künstlerischen Talente seiner Generation. In den Jahren 1877 bis 1881 unternahm er eine ausgedehnte Auslandsreise, die ihn nach Frankreich, Spanien und Italien führte. Diese Reise hatte in vielerlei Hinsicht großen Einfluss auf seine Entwicklung als Künstler; in Frankreich etwa hörte Krøyer von verschiedenen Künstlerkolonien. Am wichtigsten für die Geschichte von Brøndums Speisesaal war wohl Krøyers Aufenthalt im Hôtel Margat im kleinen französischen Dorf Cernay-la-Ville, 30 Kilometer von Paris entfernt. Unter den Stammgästen war dieses Hotel als Chez Léopold bekannt, benannt nach seinem Besitzer Léopold Lequesne (1839–1914). Aller Wahrscheinlichkeit nach war er es, der die Idee hatte, seine Künstlergäste einzuladen, ein Werk im Hotel zu hinterlassen. Hier nun malte Krøyer sein erstes Bild einer Künstlergemeinschaft und hier – so lässt sich mutmaßen – sah er auch zum ersten Mal ein Zimmer, das mit Werken von Künstlern geschmückt war, die als Gäste im Hotel gewohnt hatten. Auch Krøyer selbst trug zur Ausschmückung des Hauses bei, indem er Lequesne das Gemälde schenkte, das er während

2 Wilhelm Peters, *Hvad jeg saa og hvem jeg mødte. Erindringer fra et kunstnerliv*, Kristiania (Oslo)/Kopenhagen 1914, S. 184.

3 Brian Dudley Barrett, *Artists on the Edge. The Rise of Coastal Artists' Colonies, 1880–1920*, Amsterdam 2011, S. 258.

4 Jensen 2011 (wie Anm. 1), S. 94.

5 Von 1859 bis 1891 hieß das Brøndums Hotel eigentlich Brøndums gæstgiveri (dt. Brøndums Gasthaus). Nachdem die Räumlichkeiten 1891 vergrößert worden waren, hieß das Gasthaus schließlich Brøndums Hotel. In diesem Essay verwende ich durchgängig diesen Begriff, auch wenn ich mich auf die Zeit vor 1891 beziehe.

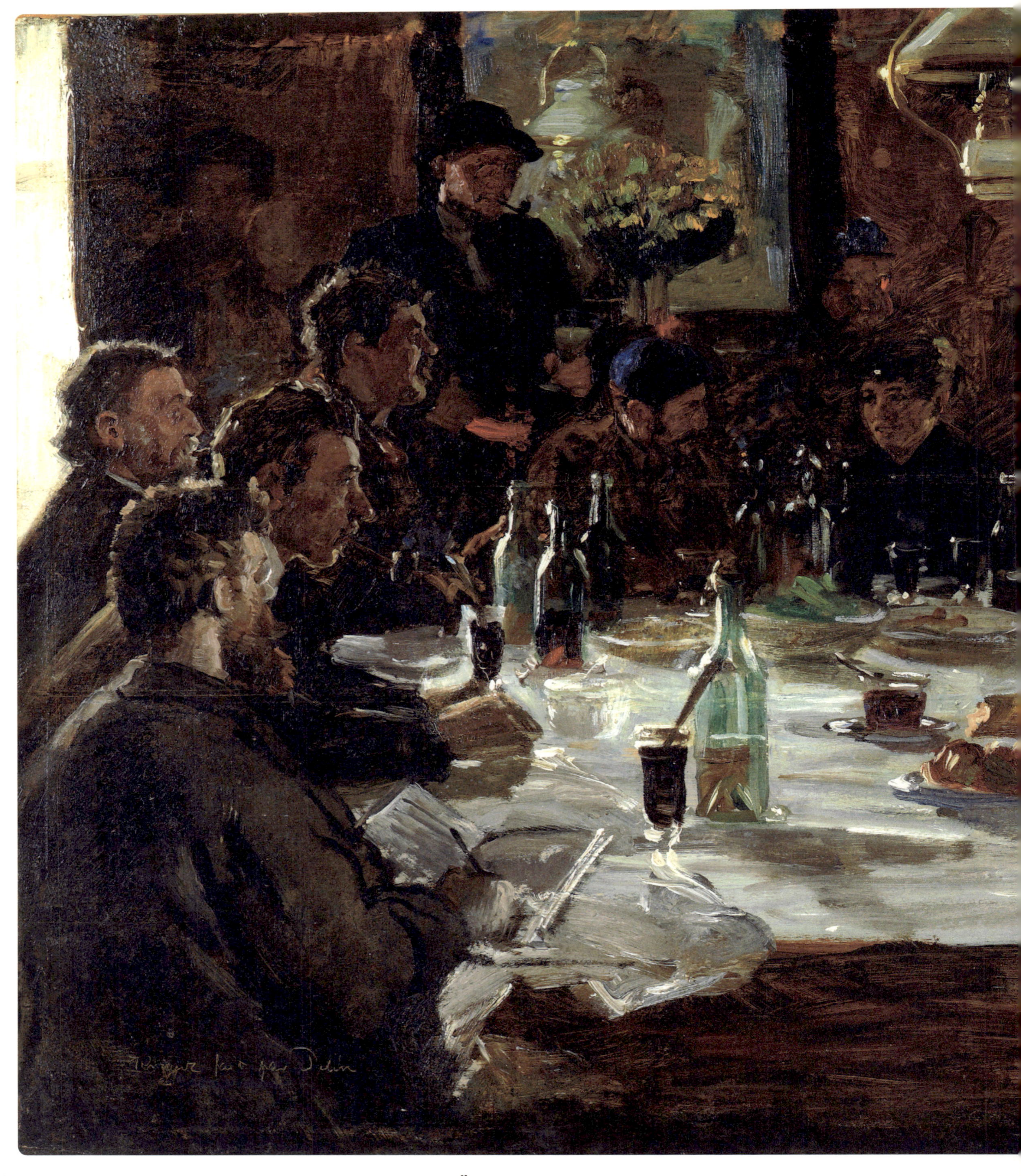

ABB. 4 PEDER SEVERIN KRØYER
FIG.

KÜNSTLER BEIM MITTAGESSE
ARTISTS' LUNCH

1879, oil on wood, Skagens Museum

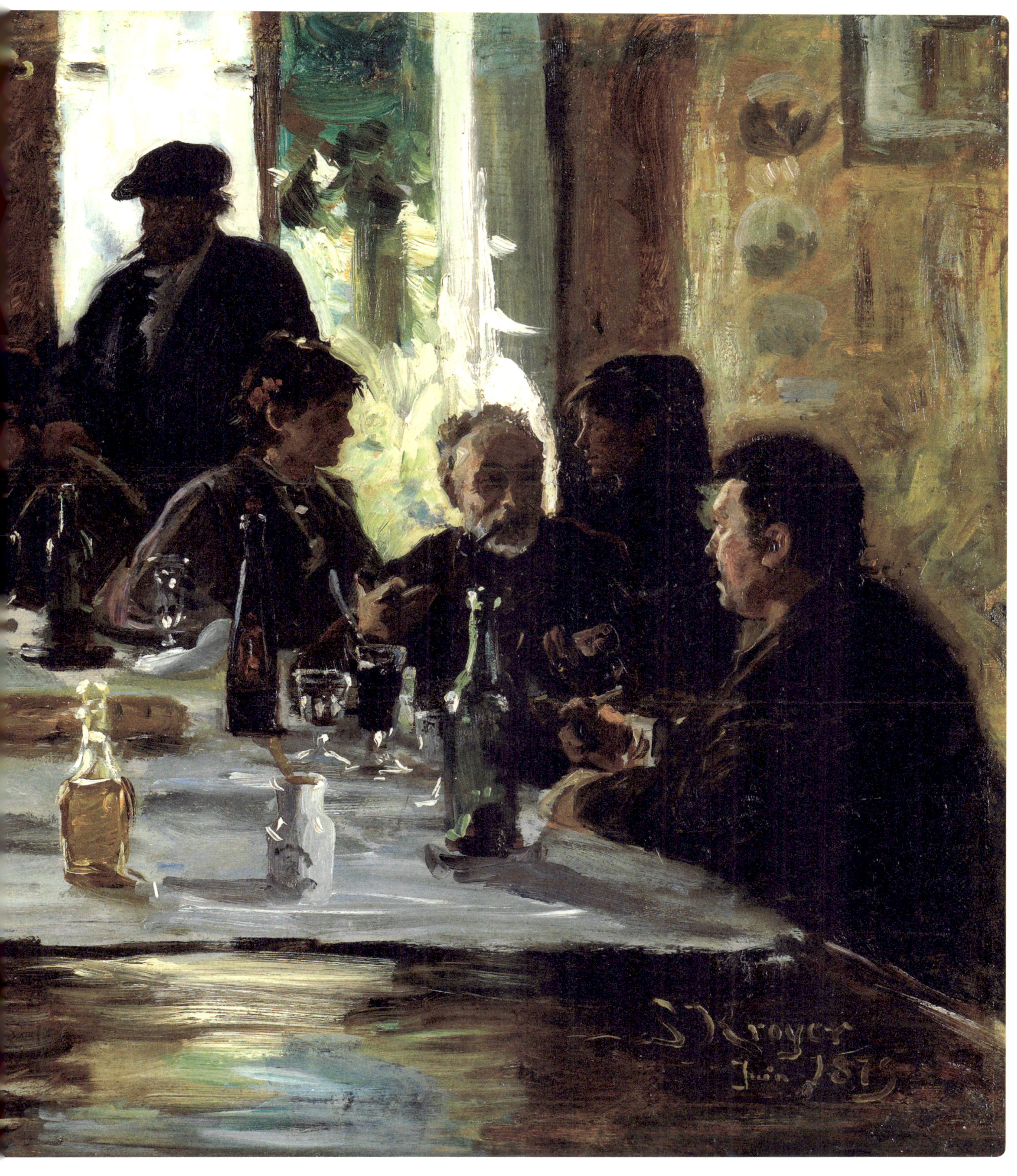

N CERNAY-LA-VILLE

1879, Öl auf Holz, Skagens Museum

2 Wilhelm Peters, *Hvad jeg saa og hvem jeg mødte. Erindringer fra et kunstnerliv* (Kristiania and Copenhagen, 1914), 184.

3 Brian Dudley Barrett, *Artists on the Edge. The Rise of Coastal Artists' Colonies, 1880–1920* (Amsterdam: Amsterdam University Press, 2011), 258.

4 Mette Bøgh Jensen (see note 1), 94.

5 From 1859 until 1891 Brøndum's Hotel [Brøndum's Hotel] was actually named *Brøndums gæstgiveri* [Brøndum's Inn]. After the premises were enlarged in 1891 the inn came to be known as *Brøndum's Hotel*. Throughout this entire article I use the term *hotel* even when referring to the period before 1891.

to visit the fishing hamlet. The hotel's walls already filled with artworks over the course of the 1880s.[2] The Spaander family understood how to make the most of the artists' visits and furnished several rooms as studios.[3] Today the hotel is no longer owned by the Spaander family, but the current owner has preserved the art collection, and the walls of the hotel are still full of art (fig. 2).

Many of the artists who came to Europe—and especially to France—in the middle and late 19th century were Americans, and a number of them were active participants in the communal atmosphere of one or multiple artist colonies. This was certainly the case with Henry Ward Ranger (1858–1916) and Willard Metcalf (1858–1925). At the beginning of the 20th century these two artists—after having spent some years living in Europe—took part in establishing an art colony in Old Lyme, Connecticut, USA, where a boarding house, the Florence Griswold House, provided the framework for the artists' social activities, and its dining room was soon embellished with works of art (fig. 3). When it comes to the question as to the origin of the idea to enliven a particular room with a particular room with art, stories vary widely from one establishment to the next. Sometimes it was the hotel proprietor/innkeeper who came up with the idea, perhaps inspired by having seen other hotels with similar *in-situ* decorations. In other cases the idea may have come from artists themselves. In certain instances the donations served as payment for the stay or for food and drink. This was the case in Skagen, for example, where there was a tradition that the innkeeper at Brøndum's Hotel, Degn Brøndum (1856–1932), would treat the artists to rounds of liquor whenever a new painting was mounted in the dining room.[4] This was a tradition that certainly contributed to the expansion of the collection of artworks. Today, of all the ornamental dining rooms from the late 19th century, Brøndum's dining room is one of the best preserved.

THE ARTIST COLONY IN SKAGEN

At the time when artists started flocking to Skagen in considerable numbers in the 1870s the city was relatively secluded. It contained less than 2,000 inhabitants. From 1859–84 there was only one hotel in town, Brøndum's Hotel, and these accommodations took on a crucial importance for the international artist colony that was burgeoning in the town.[5] The hotel became a gathering place for all the artists who ventured from Europe's metropolises all the way to the northern tip of Jutland. Most of the artists who came to Skagen described how they were very well received at Brøndum's Hotel and how the feeling of being admitted into the community of other artists bore crucially on whether or not their stay in Skagen eventually was a success. Although the artist colony established itself in the 1870s, it was not until the painter P.S. Krøyer (1851–1909) arrived in Skagen in 1882 that the colony gained its own meeting spot, which subsequently came to play an important role in attracting other international artists to Skagen: Brondum's dining room with its artistic decor.

KRØYER—AN INTERNATIONALLY RENOWNED ARTIST IN SKAGEN

Krøyer was among the most internationally oriented of the Skagen painters. Throughout the course of his life he exhibited his works both in Denmark and abroad. Krøyer completed his studies at The Royal Academy of Fine Arts in Copenhagen in 1870, just before his 19th birthday, and he was considered one of his generation's most promising artistic talents. In the years 1877–81 he made an extended trip abroad, which took him to France, Spain, and Italy. In many ways this trip had an epoch-making impact on his development as an artist. It was in France that Krøyer heard about a number of artist colonies. Most relevant to the story of Brøndum's dining room was Krøyer's sojourn at the Hôtel Margat in the small French village of Cernay-la-Ville, situated 30 kilometers outside Paris. This hotel was called Chez Léopold by the regular patrons, taking its name from the hotelkeeper Léopold Lequesne (1839–1914), who, in all likelihood, was also the originator of the idea of inviting visiting artists to contribute with a work of art. It was here that Krøyer painted his first picture of an artists' community, and it was here that, from what we can surmise, he first witnessed a room adorned with works created by the artists who had come to stay at the hotel. Krøyer himself contributed to the decoration of the hotel, giving Lequesne the picture that he had painted during his stay (fig. 4). The painting delineates a scene that was to reappear a number of times in Krøyer's later depictions of the artists' community in Skagen: a circle of artists and cultural figures who have gathered together around a table. In this particular painting the table with its food and drink fills the greater part of the foreground, whereby it is difficult to identify the people, especially because Krøyer has painted the figures in backlight, with the result that they appear almost as silhouettes. Krøyer himself is seated on the left side of the picture and is busily absorbed in sketching.

IN 1883 KRØYER RETURNED TO SKAGEN, AND DURING THIS PARTICULAR YEAR AN EXTRAORDINARILY LARGE NUMBER OF ARTISTS AND WRITERS CROWDED TOGETHER IN THE COLONY. It was Krøyer who hit upon the idea of embellishing the dining room with paintings and portraits of the artists and cultural

seines Aufenthalts gemalt hatte (Abb. 4). Dieses zeigt eine Szene, die später noch öfter in Krøyers Darstellungen der Skagener Künstlergemeinschaft auftauchen sollte: einen Kreis von Künstlern und Kulturschaffenden, die sich um einen Tisch versammelt hatten. In jenem Bild aus Frankreich ist es vor allem der Tisch mit Speisen und Getränken, der den Großteil des Vordergrunds ausfüllt, während es schwer ist, einzelne Personen zu identifizieren. Dies liegt insbesondere daran, dass Krøyer hier das Licht von hinten einfallen lässt und die Figuren somit fast nur als Silhouetten erscheinen. Er selbst sitzt, ins Zeichnen vertieft, links im Bild.

1883, IN EINEM JAHR, IN DEM SICH AUSSERGEWÖHNLICH VIELE KÜNSTLER UND SCHRIFTSTELLER IN DER HIESIGEN KOLONIE ZUSAMMENDRÄNGTEN, KEHRTE KRØYER NACH SKAGEN ZURÜCK. Er war es, der nun die Idee hatte, das Speisezimmer des Brøndums Hotel mit Malereien und Porträts derjenigen Künstler und Kulturschaffenden auszuschmücken, die es besuchten. Der dänische Maler Carl Locher (1851–1915), der ebenfalls Mitglied der Künstlerkolonie war, erinnert sich folgendermaßen: »Es war Krøyer, der die Idee hatte, dass unser Treffpunkt im Speisesaal im Brøndums eine Bildergalerie mit unseren Porträts und von uns gemalten Bildern sein sollte. Diese Sammlung sollte den Ort als unser Wohnzimmer markieren. Jedes Mal, wenn ein Bild fertig war und es als würdig erachtet wurde, in der Sammlung aufgehängt zu werden, wurde ein Fest gegeben, für das der Hotelier Gastgeber und Wirt sein musste.«[6] VED FROKOSTEN (dt. BEIM MITTAGESSEN) war das erste Gemälde, das speziell für diesen Raum gemalt wurde (Abb. 5). Hierin stellt Krøyer eine Gruppe von hauptsächlich norwegischen und schwedischen Künstlern dar, die in demselben Zimmer, das später mit den Kunstwerken geschmückt werden sollte, um einen Tisch herum sitzt. Dieses Gemälde ist einerseits eine der zentralen Arbeiten des Speisesaals, es fungiert aber darüber hinaus gleichzeitig als eine Art Manifest für das starke Gemeinschaftsgefühl innerhalb der Kolonie, erkennbar daran, dass Krøyer alle Namen der dargestellten Künstler unten im Bild festgehalten hat. 1909, als das Original nach Venedig verschickt werden sollte, um dort auf der Biennale gezeigt zu werden, schuf Krøyer sogar eigens eine Kopie als Kreide- und Kohlezeichnung auf Papier. Es gab neben diesem Beispiel durchaus auch eine Reihe von anderen Werken in diesem Speisesaal, die während Degn Brøndums Zeit für diverse Ausstellungen verliehen wurden; die Leerstellen an den Wänden wurden allerdings oft mit anderen Arbeiten gefüllt, bis das ursprüngliche Bild wieder *nach Hause* zurückkehrte.

Die meisten Werke in diesem Zimmer sind Darstellungen von Motiven aus Skagen. Nur zwei von ihnen wurden andernorts gemalt und Degn Brøndum erst später geschenkt. Seine Sammlung zeichnet sich aus durch eine Mischung aus Freiluftmalerei, Stillleben, Marinebildern und Interieurs. Insgesamt fungierten diese Gemälde fast wie ein Katalog aller Motive, die Skagen zu bieten hatte. Im Jahr 1884 wurde der Speisesaal schließlich mit seiner dunkel gebeizten Holzvertäfelung ausgestattet, in deren einzelnen Paneelen die Gemälde in einer Art Petersburger Hängung mit relativ wenig Abstand zwischen den Bildern präsentiert wurden (Abb. 6). Ab dem Jahr 1891 wurden die Paneele zudem mit schwarzen Ornamenten versehen, die von einem der berühmtesten Vertreter des Jugendstils in Dänemark geschaffen worden waren, dem Architekten und Kunsthandwerker Thorvald Bindesbøll (1846–1908).

DIE FAMILIE BRØNDUM

Während es stimmt, dass es ohne die Künstler wohl nie eine Künstlerkolonie in Skagen gegeben hätte, ist es ebenso unbestritten, dass die Familie Brøndum eine zentrale Rolle bei der Gründung dieser Kolonie spielte. Zu Anfang war es der Vater der bekannten Malerin Anna Ancher (1859–1935), Erik Brøndum (1820–1890), der die Künstler willkommen hieß und dabei behilflich war, ihnen Kontakt zu potenziellen Modellen in der Stadt zu verschaffen. Es heißt, Erik sei ein Mann weniger Worte gewesen, der an den Künstlerfesten kaum teilnahm. Wenn es um Spaß und Ausgelassenheit ging, waren eher die beiden Brüder von Anna, Degn and Johan Henrik (1862–1918), stets gern zur Stelle. Beide ließen sich auch für den Porträtfries in Brøndums Speisesaal malen. Annas Mutter und drei weitere Schwestern waren hingegen sehr fromm und stark in der sogenannten Indre Mission (dt. Innere Mission) engagiert, einer kirchlichen Bewegung, die ihre Hochzeit am Ende des 19. Jahrhunderts vor allem in vielen ländlichen Amtsbezirken Dänemarks hatte. Dementsprechend nahmen sie nicht an den diversen Festivitäten der Künstler teil, obgleich zwei von Annas Schwestern ihren Eltern zusammen mit Degn im Hotelbetrieb halfen. Keines der übrigen Geschwister war verheiratet oder hatte eigene Kinder, nur Anna war als einzige von ihnen vermählt: 1880 gab sie Michael Ancher (1849–1927), einem zu Besuch weilenden Künstler, der bereits einige Jahre zuvor nach Skagen gekommen war, das Jawort. Drei Jahre später bekam das Paar seine Tochter Helga (1883–1964). Nach Erik Brøndums Tod 1890 stürzte sich Degn voll in die Arbeit und kümmerte sich um die Bedürfnisse der Gäste. Seinen Einstand als neuer Besitzer eines der erfolgreichsten Hotels der Stadt gab er, indem er einen Anbau errichtete. Dieser Annex wurde 1891 nach Plänen des dänischen Architekten Ulrik Plesner (1861–1933) gebaut und war der erste von letztendlich fünf Anbauten, die alle von ihm entworfen wurden. Die Erweiterung von 1891 führte auch zu

6 Zit. nach: Carl Locher, »Fra Krøyers Ungdom«, in: *Illustreret Tidende*, Nr. 12, 19. Dezember 1909, Kopenhagen, S. 152–153.

7 Siehe auch: Jensen 2011 (wie Anm. 1), S. 206–225.

6 Carl Locher, *Fra Krøyers Ungdom*, *Illustreret Tidende*, Copenhagen (December 19, 1909), 153.

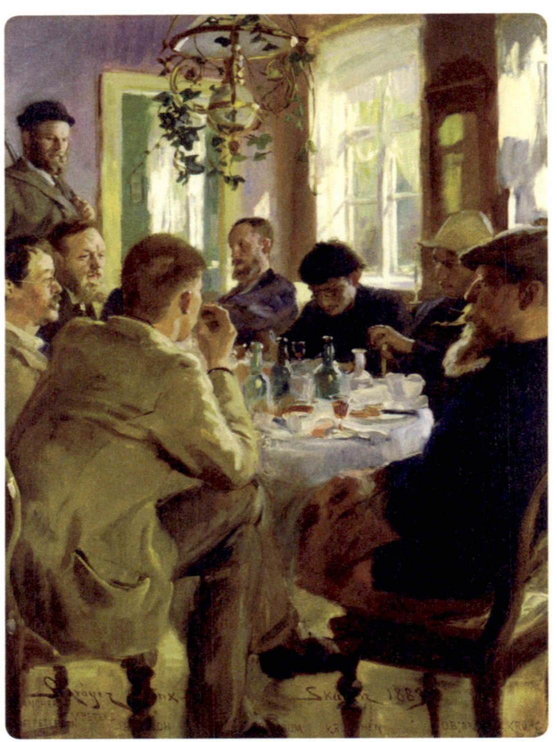

Abb. / Fig. 5
PEDER SEVERIN KRØYER
BEIM MITTAGESSEN
AT LUNCH
1883, Öl auf Holz / Oil on wood, Skagens Museum

figures visiting Brøndum's Hotel. The Danish painter Carl Locher (1851–1915), who was also a member of the artist colony, describes the situation as follows: »It was Krøyer who came up with the notion that our meeting spot in the dining room at Brøndum's ought to serve as a picture gallery, with our portraits and with paintings that we had made. This collection was supposed to mark the place as our living room. Every time such a painting was finished and deemed worthy of being hung in the collection, a party was thrown, for which the hotelkeeper functioned as host and proprietor.«[6] VED FROKOSTEN (Artists' Luncheon at Brøndum's Hotel, alternatively known as The Artists' Luncheon at Skagen) was the very first picture painted expressly for the room (fig. 5). Here, Krøyer depicted a company of primarily Norwegian and Swedish artists sitting around a table in the room that would later come to be decorated with the artists' works. This painting is one of the dining room's central works, and it simultaneously functions as a kind of manifesto for the strong sense of community in the colony, seeing as Krøyer inscribed all of the artists' names at the bottom of the painting. In 1909 when the original oil painting was about to be shipped off and placed on exhibition at the Venice Biennial, Krøyer created a replica of the luncheon painting in charcoal and chalk on paper. There were a number of paintings in this room that were lent out for various exhibitions during Degn Brøndum's lifetime. The empty spaces thus created were often filled by other paintings until the work on loan was brought back home to the dining room.

Most of the paintings in this room are depictions of motives from Skagen. There are only two works that were painted elsewhere and subsequently presented as gifts to Degn Brøndum. The pictures amount to a mixed assortment of *plein air* paintings, still lifes, maritime paintings, and interiors. As a whole, they functioned as a virtual catalogue of the motives that Skagen had to offer. In 1884 the dining room was fitted with dark-stained wood paneling, within the panels of which the paintings and portraits were arranged in a kind of salon-style hanging with the pictures being hung relatively close together (fig. 6). From the year 1891 onward the panels were decorated with black ornaments designed by one of the most famous figures of Danish Art Nouveau, the architect and craftsman Thorvald Bindesbøll (1846–1908).

THE BRØNDUM FAMILY

While it is true that there would never have been an artist colony in Skagen without the artists, the Brøndum family indisputably played a vital role in the establishment of the colony. In the beginning it was the renowned painter Anna Ancher's (1859–1935) father, Erik Brøndum (1820–1890), who welcomed the artists and who was instrumental in putting them in contact with some of the potential models in the town. By all accounts Erik was a man of few words, who did not readily take part in the artists' parties to any significant extent. When it came to fun and high spirits, Anna Ancher's two brothers, Degn and Johan Henrik (1862–1918) were always game. Both brothers had their likenesses painted for the portrait frieze in Brøndum's dining room. Anna's mother and three sisters were very religious and were deeply involved in the Indre Mission (The Inner Mission), a church-based movement popular largely in rural Danish districts that had its heyday in the late 19th century. Accordingly these women did not take part in any of the artists' festivities, although two of Anna's sisters helped their parents run the hotel, together with Degn. None of Anna's siblings were married or had any children; Anna was the only one of the Brøndum children who married. In 1880 she wed Michael Ancher (1849–1927), one of the visiting artists who had arrived in Skagen a few years earlier. Three years later the couple had a daughter, Helga (1883–1964). After Erik Brøndum died in 1890, Degn dedicated himself to servicing the needs of the guests at the

einer deutlichen Vergrößerung des Speisesaals und dementsprechend gab es nun ebenso mehr Platz für Bilder.

DER PORTRÄTFRIES

Ein zentraler Teil der Dekoration in Brøndums Speisesaal ist ein Porträtfries, der sich im oberen Teil der Saalwände rund um den Raum zieht und bis fast zur Decke reicht (Abb. 7). Von allen Elementen im Speisesaal hat sich der Fries über die Jahre am meisten verändert. Das erste Bildnis für ihn malte P. S. Krøyer 1883 und im Lauf der nächsten 20 Jahre wurden viele weitere von den Künstlern der Gemeinschaft geschaffen – das letzte wurde 1935 aufgehängt. Insgesamt wurden 73 Porträts gemalt, allerdings sind von ihnen heute nur noch 51 vorhanden. Dies liegt vor allem daran, dass sich der Fries ständig veränderte und ab und zu Bilder entfernt wurden, um Platz für andere zu schaffen. Die meisten der aus der Reihe entnommenen Arbeiten wurden andernorts im Hotel aufgehängt, während manche Porträts auch verschenkt oder von Künstlern gekauft wurden.[7] Andere gingen leider ganz verloren wie etwa 17 Porträts, die aus dem Speisesaal in ein Zimmer in Brøndums Hotel gehängt wurden, das 1954 abbrannte. Die letzten Veränderungen erfuhr der Fries, als der gesamte Speisesaal von Brøndums Hotel ins Skagens Museum kam: Von dem Moment an, als das Museumsgebäude 1928 fertiggestellt und bereit war, wurde ein besonderer Raum speziell dafür vorgesehen, eines Tages den Speisesaal zu beherbergen. Degn Brøndum vermachte ihn einschließlich aller seiner Kunstwerke und Möbel offiziell 1929 an das Skagens Museum, allerdings mit dem Vorbehalt, dass der Saal noch so lange im Hotel verbleiben sollte, bis auch die letzte seiner Schwestern gestorben wäre. Dies geschah 1945. Im darauf folgenden Jahr wurde schließlich der gesamte Speisesaal mit all seinem Inventar vom Hotel ins Museum verbracht. Degn Brøndums großzügige Schenkung und die Tatsache, dass der Museumsvorstand darauf bestand, dass der Speisesaal Teil des Skagens Museums sein sollte, ist es zu verdanken, dass das Ensemble bis zum heutigen Tage intakt geblieben ist.[8] Nach wie vor ist es außerordentlich schwierig, die Veränderungen nachzuvollziehen, die im Verlauf der Zeit innerhalb des Porträtfrieses stattgefunden haben, und noch schwieriger ist es, herauszufinden, wer einst entschied, welche Werke wo hingehängt werden sollen, da dies offenbar nie dokumentiert wurde.[9] Die jeweiligen Arrangements der Bilder an den beiden Längswänden des Saals unterscheiden sich insgesamt auf frappierende Weise. Der Porträtfries an der Hauptwand, die man gleich sieht, wenn man den Raum betritt, ist dabei der geordnetere von beiden. Außerdem ist dies ist die Wand, an der die wenigsten Veränderungen vorgenommen worden sind. In der Mitte befindet sich ein rundes Porträt von Degn Brøndum, das genau über dem bereits erwähnten Gemälde VED FROKOSTEN (dt. BEIM MITTAGESSEN) hängt. Links wird es von den Bildnissen von Michael und Anna Ancher und rechts von denen Maries und P. S. Krøyers flankiert. Auf der gegenüberliegenden Längswand hingegen lässt sich kein vergleichbares Ordnungsprinzip erkennen und es gibt auch keinen betonten Mittelpunkt. Dies ist außerdem der Teil des Frieses, der über die Zeit am meisten verändert wurde.

Nach und nach wurden in die Reihe nicht nur Porträts bildender Künstler eingegliedert. Es gab auch Sänger, Schriftsteller, Musiker und, wie bereits erwähnt, Anna Anchers zwei Brüder, die sich extra für den Fries haben malen lassen. Später kamen noch Bilder von König Christian X. (1870–1947) und Königin Alexandrine (1879–1952) hinzu, die oft ihre Ferien in Skagen verbrachten und sogar etliche Jahre eine eigene Wohnung im Hotel hatten. Insgesamt sind die meisten der in der Bildnisgalerie des Frieses Porträtierten aber bildende Künstler und mit ihnen wurden zugleich diverse Nationalitäten – von Dänemark, Norwegen, Schweden bis hin zu Österreich und England – repräsentiert.

Über die Erinnerung oder Hommage an die Künstler und Kulturschaffenden hinaus, die Teil dieser Gemeinschaft waren, bezeugen die Porträts in diesem Raum zugleich auch einen Akt der Freundlichkeit der Künstler gegenüber ihrem Wirt Degn Brøndum, der sie willkommen hieß und sich stets verpflichtet und inspiriert genug fühlte, sie alle immer dann einzuladen – oft zu einen Punsch –, wenn ein neues Gemälde oder Porträt im Speisesaal aufgehängt wurde. Hätte Degn Brøndum den Künstlern nicht erlaubt, den Raum mit ihren Arbeiten zu schmücken, hätte es nie einen so kunstvollen Speisesaal gegeben, wie wir ihn heute kennen. Gleichwohl hatte die Familie natürlich auch ein kommerzielles Motiv dafür, die Künstler einen Raum im Hotel dekorieren zu lassen. Es war absehbar, dass viele Touristen den Spuren der Künstler würden folgen wollen, um selbst die Orte zu sehen, die jene in ihren Werken dargestellt hatten, und vielleicht auch, um dem einen oder anderen Maler aus der Skagen-Gemeinschaft persönlich zu begegnen, für die das Hotel und insbesondere der Speisesaal eine zentrale Rolle spielte.

PERSONENKULT DER ZEIT

Es ist kein Zufall, dass die kunstvoll geschmückten Speisesäle von Hotels oder Gastwirtschaften, die sich in Verbindung mit vielen europäischen Künstlerkolonien entwickelten, am Ende des 19. Jahrhunderts entstanden. Ziemlich genau zu dieser Zeit erreichte der besonders starke Kult und das Interesse an den Künstlern als Personen einen Höhepunkt. Dies manifestierte sich unter anderem im Anstieg von Zeitungsartikeln und Pressemeldungen in diversen Zeit-

8 Degn Brøndum war von 1908 bis 1932 selbst Vorstandsmitglied des Museums.

9 Siehe auch: Jensen 2011 (wie Anm. 1), S. 97.

7 See Mette Bøgh Jensen (see note 1), 206–225.

8 Degn Brøndum himself was a member of the museum's board of directors from 1908 until 1932.

9 See also, Mette Bøgh Jensen (see note 1), 97.

hotel, and he launched his career as proprietor of one of the town's most successful hotels by having an extension built. Brøndum's Hotel was thus expanded with an annex designed by the architect Ulrik Plesner (1861 – 1933) in 1891. This marked the beginning of what eventually came to be five extensions of the hotel, all designed by Plesner. The expansion of 1891 resulted in making the dining room considerably larger and accordingly providing more room for paintings.

THE PORTRAIT FRIEZE

A central part of the in-situ decoration in Brøndum's dining room is the portrait frieze, which runs all the way around the upper portion of the room's walls and extends almost to the ceiling (fig. 7). Of all the elements in the dining room, the frieze has changed the most over the years. Krøyer painted the first portrait for the room in 1883, and more portraits were created by artists in the community over the course of the next 20 years—with the last the portraits being installed in 1935. A total of 73 portraits were painted, although today only 51 portraits hang in the room. This is due to the fact that the portrait frieze underwent constant change; portraits were removed from time to time to make room for others. Most of the portraits that were removed from the frieze were placed elsewhere in the hotel, while other portraits were eventually presented as gifts or purchased by other artists.[7] Seventeen of the portraits that had been replaced by others were hung in a room at Brøndum's Hotel that burned down in 1954. The last alteration to the frieze took place when the entire dining room was moved from Brøndum's Hotel to Skagens Museum. With the completion of the museum building in 1928, a special space was created and expressly reserved for the purpose of presenting the dining room. Degn Brøndum had bequeathed the dining room, including all its artworks and furnishings to Skagens Museum in 1929, with the stipulation that the dining room was not to be removed from the hotel until the last of his sisters had died, which occurred in 1945. In the following year the dining room, with all contents, was taken from the hotel and transferred to the interior of the museum. Degn Brøndum's generous donation and the museum's board of directors' insistence that the room be part of Skagens Museum are why the dining room has remained intact today.[8] It remains extraordinarily difficult to track the changes that took place in the portrait frieze over time, and it is even harder to determine who decided what portraits should be hung where, since this was evidently never recorded.[9] There is a striking difference between the respective arrangements of the portraits on each of the two side walls. The portrait frieze on the main wall, which one sees first when entering the room, is the better ordered of the two. It is also the wall to which the fewest changes have been made. At the center of this wall is the circular portrait of Degn Brøndum that hangs just above ARTISTS' LUNCHEON at Brøndum's Hotel and is flanked by the portraits of Michael and Anna Ancher, on the left, and the portraits of Marie and P. S. Krøyer, on the right. A similar organization is not found on the opposite wall of the room, which seems to have no natural center. This is the wall to which most changes have been made.

It was not only visual artists who had their portraits incorporated into the frieze. There were singers, writers, and musicians as well. As mentioned earlier, Anna Ancher's two brothers also had their portraits painted expressly for the frieze. Later, portraits of King Christian X (1870 – 1947) and Queen Alexandrine (1879 – 1952) were installed; the couple often spent their holidays in Skagen and even had their own apartment at the hotel for a good many years. However, most of the individuals portrayed in the portrait gallery of the frieze now or at one time were visual artists of various nationalities—including Denmark, Norway, Sweden, Finland, Austria, and England.

The portraits in this room not only serve as a remembrance or an homage to the artists and cultural figures who were part of the community; they also represented expressions of friendship towards the host Degn Brøndum, who welcomed the artists and who felt sufficiently compelled and inspired to serve refreshments—often a punch—whenever a new painting or portrait was hung in the dining room. Had Degn Brøndum not given the artists permission to embellish the room with their works and portraits, there would never have been the ornate dining room as we know it today. However, the family also had commercial motives for letting the artists decorate a room at the hotel. It was foreseeable that many tourists would want to follow the artists, to see for themselves the very places that they had depicted in their works, and to maybe even get a chance to rub shoulders with artists from the Skagen community, in which the hotel and especially its dining room played a central role.

THE PERSONALITY CULT OF THE DAY

It is no coincidence that the ornately decorated dining rooms associated with many of European artist colonies came into being at the close of the 19th century. It was precisely during this time that the cult of and interest in the artistic persona was at its height. This was manifested by a flood of newspaper articles and reports in various journals, by features on artists' homes, and by the publication of artist-biographies, artist-memoirs, caricatures, and fictional

schriften, in Berichten über die Wohnungen und Häuser von Künstlern sowie in der Veröffentlichung von Künstlerbiografien, Künstlermemoiren, Karikaturen oder auch Erzählungen und Romanen, deren Hauptfiguren Künstler waren.[10] All das führte auch zu einem wachsenden Interesse an deren Ateliers, da man damals der Ansicht war, man würde jemanden am besten kennenlernen, wenn man seine häusliche Umgebung studiert und bei Künstlern insbesondere das Atelier.[11] Betrachtet man vor diesem Hintergrund die Ausschmückungen in vielen der Künstlerkolonien, wird deutlich, dass der Speisaal im Gastlokal teilweise den Status des Ateliers übernommen hatte – hier konnte man den Künstlern nahekommen. Zudem waren diese Dekorationen in situ manchmal der einzige Ort, wo man ihre Werke ausgestellt sehen konnte. Natürlich hatten die Hoteliers und Gastwirte ein ökonomisches Interesse daran, Künstler einen oder mehrere Räume genau dort gestalten zu lassen, wo sie sich versammelten. Und wir können sicher sein, dass in Skagen auch die Künstler selbst daran interessiert waren, sich und damit ihre Werke zu zeigen und zugänglich zu machen. Der ständig wachsende Strom von Touristen konnte hier eine Ausstellung von Werken sehen, die zum Großteil vor Ort gemalt worden waren und eine nicht unerhebliche Rolle dabei spielten, die Karrieren jener Künstler zu befördern, die Teil der Kolonie waren. Die erste Ausstellung der Skagen-Künstler, die in der Stadt, aber außerhalb von Brøndums Hotel stattfand, wurde erst 1907 gezeigt. Ansonsten war es in Skagen nur in diesem Speisesaal möglich, die Bilder dieser Künstler zu sehen, denn in der Tat waren die meisten von ihnen schon bald damit beschäftigt, ihre Werke aus Skagen in den europäischen Metropolen zu zeigen. In diesem Licht sollte man auch den Porträtfries betrachten: Er ist nicht nur eine Erinnerung an die Maler und andere Kulturschaffende, die einmal Teil der Gemeinschaft dieser Kolonie waren. Als die Künstler noch lebten, fungierte er im Grunde auch als eine Art *Ruhmeshalle,* wo die Bildnisse aller bekannten (und auch der weniger bekannten) Persönlichkeiten von einem stets interessierten Aufgebot an Besuchern genau studiert werden konnten. Es war also nicht nur die Kunst, sondern es waren auch die Künstler selbst, die das große Interesse erregten. Jenen war das sehr wohl bewusst und im Allgemeinen waren sie bereit und willens etwa für Interviews für diverse Zeitschriften zur Verfügung zu stehen, in denen dann auch Fotos aus ihren Häusern und Ateliers erschienen.

FÜR DIE FAMILIE BRØNDUM war es von unschätzbarem Wert, dass ihr Hotel im Mittelpunkt des gesellschaftlichen Lebens der Skagener Künstlerkolonie stand. Die Gäste- und Übernachtungszahlen schossen in die Höhe, weil viele Touristen sich danach sehnten, die Künstler ganz nah zu erleben. Das Verlangen nach Nähe zu ihnen führte zu einem stetigen Strom von Besuchern, die nach Skagen reisten, insbesondere nach 1890, als die Bahnlinie bis in die Stadt fertiggestellt war. Es gab hier inzwischen durchaus auch andere Hotels, die von der künstlerischen Ausschmückung in Brøndums Speisesaal inspiriert waren und die nach einer Weile ihre eigenen Dekorationen bekamen, aber es blieb doch das Original, das den Großteil der Künstler und Kulturschaffenden anzog.

Brøndums Hotel gibt es übrigens immer noch und bis zum heutigen Tage ist es ein sehr beliebtes Hotel mit vielen Gästen, obwohl sein legendärer Speisesaal seit 1946 ein zentraler Teil des Skagens Museums ist.

10 Rachel Esner, »In the Artist's Studio with L'Illustration«, in: *RIHA Journal 0069,* 18. März 2013, S. 1–2 (http://www.riha-journal.org/articles/2013/2013-jan-mar/esner-lillustration).

11 Ebd., S. 2.

10 Rachel Esner, *In the Artist's Studio with L'Illustration* RIHA Journal 0069 (March 18, 2013), 1–2. Online: *http://www.riha-journal.org/articles/2013/2013-jan-mar/esner-lillustration.*

11 Ibid., 2.

stories with an artist as the main character.[10] It also resulted in an increased interest in artists' studios, because people of the day were of the opinion that the best way of getting to know somebody was to study his or her surroundings—or in the case of the artist, his or her studio.[11] In examining the decorative embellishments of dining rooms in many artist colonies, it is clear that the dining room in part assumed the status of the studio as a place where one could get close to artists. In addition, the arrangement of in-situ decorations sometimes served as the only place in an artist colony where one could actually see the artists' pieces on display. Of course, hotel proprietors and innkeepers had a vested economic interest in letting artists decorate one or more of the rooms at the places where they gathered. And one can be sure that in Skagen the artists themselves were interested in presenting their work and making it accessible, along with themselves. Here the ever-increasing flow of tourists could see an exhibition of works that were largely painted in Skagen and served to promote the artists who were part of the colony. It was not until 1907 that an exhibition of works by Skagen painters was mounted in the town outside the premises of Brøndum's Hotel. Apart from this, the dining room was the only place in Skagen where anyone could actually see such works, since most of the artists were also busy exhibiting their works from Skagen in major European cities. This sheds a special light on the portrait frieze. It not only serves as a memorial to the artists and cultural figures who were part of the colony's community at one time or another; but also while the artists were still alive, the portrait frieze actually functioned as a *Hall of Fame,* where all the portraits of well-known (and lesser-known) personalities could be closely studied by a continuous array of interested spectators. Not merely art but also artists were the source of all the interest. The artists themselves were quite conscious of this, and they were generally ready and willing to make themselves available for interviews with various magazines, which also included photographs of their homes and studios.

IT WAS OF INESTIMABLE VALUE TO THE BRØNDUM FAMILY that Brøndum's Hotel was the heart and center of the social life in the artist colony. The hotel experienced an upsurge in the number of visitors and overnight guests, since many tourists genuinely yearned to personally experience the artists up close. The appetite for being near the artists resulted in a steady stream of tourists traveling to Skagen, especially after 1890 when a railway line was built that went directly to Skagen. There were other hotels in Skagen that were inspired by the artistic decoration in Brøndum's dining room and eventually managed to obtain their own decorations, but it was always Brøndum's Hotel that attracted the major portion of artists and cultural figures.

Brøndum's Hotel does still exist, and it remains a popular hotel with a lot of visitors, even though the dining room has been a central feature of the Skagens Museum since 1946.

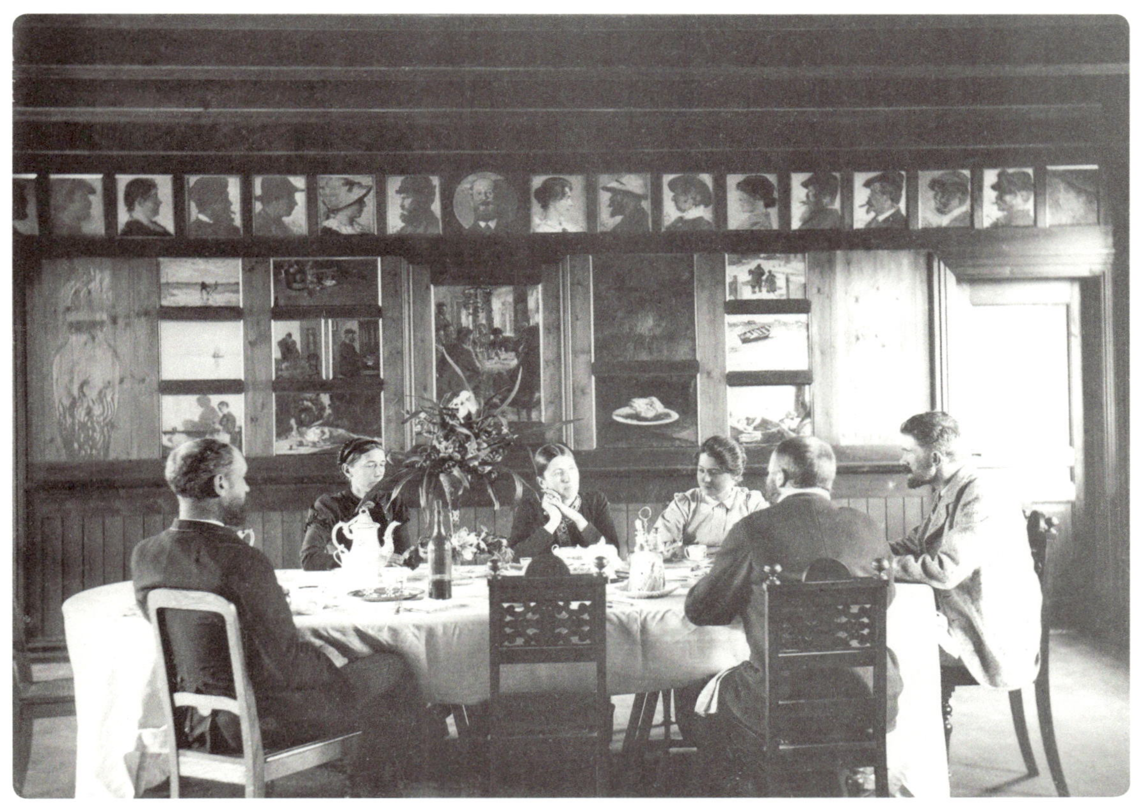

Abb. / Fig. 6 PEDER SEVERIN KRØYER

BRØNDUMS SPEISESAAL
DINING ROOM

1890er-Jahre / 1890s, Skagens Museum

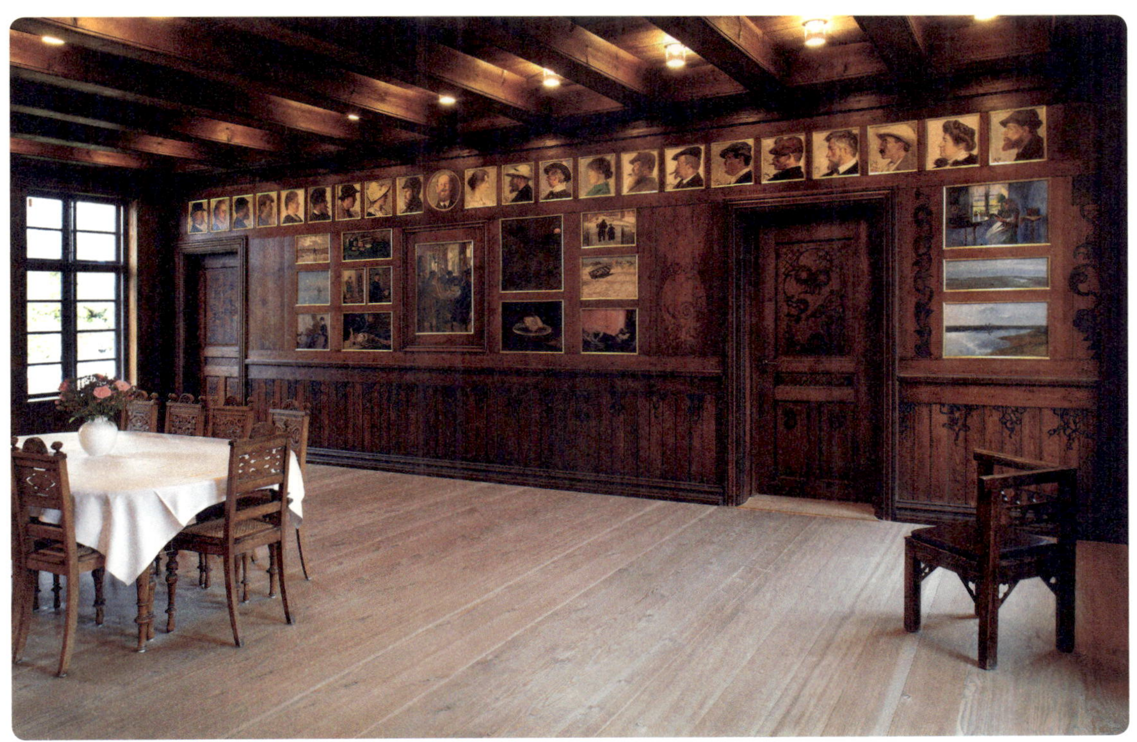

Abb. / Fig. 7

DER PORTRÄTFRIES
THE PORTAIT FRIEZE

Brøndums Speisesaal, 2010 / Brøndums dining room, 2010

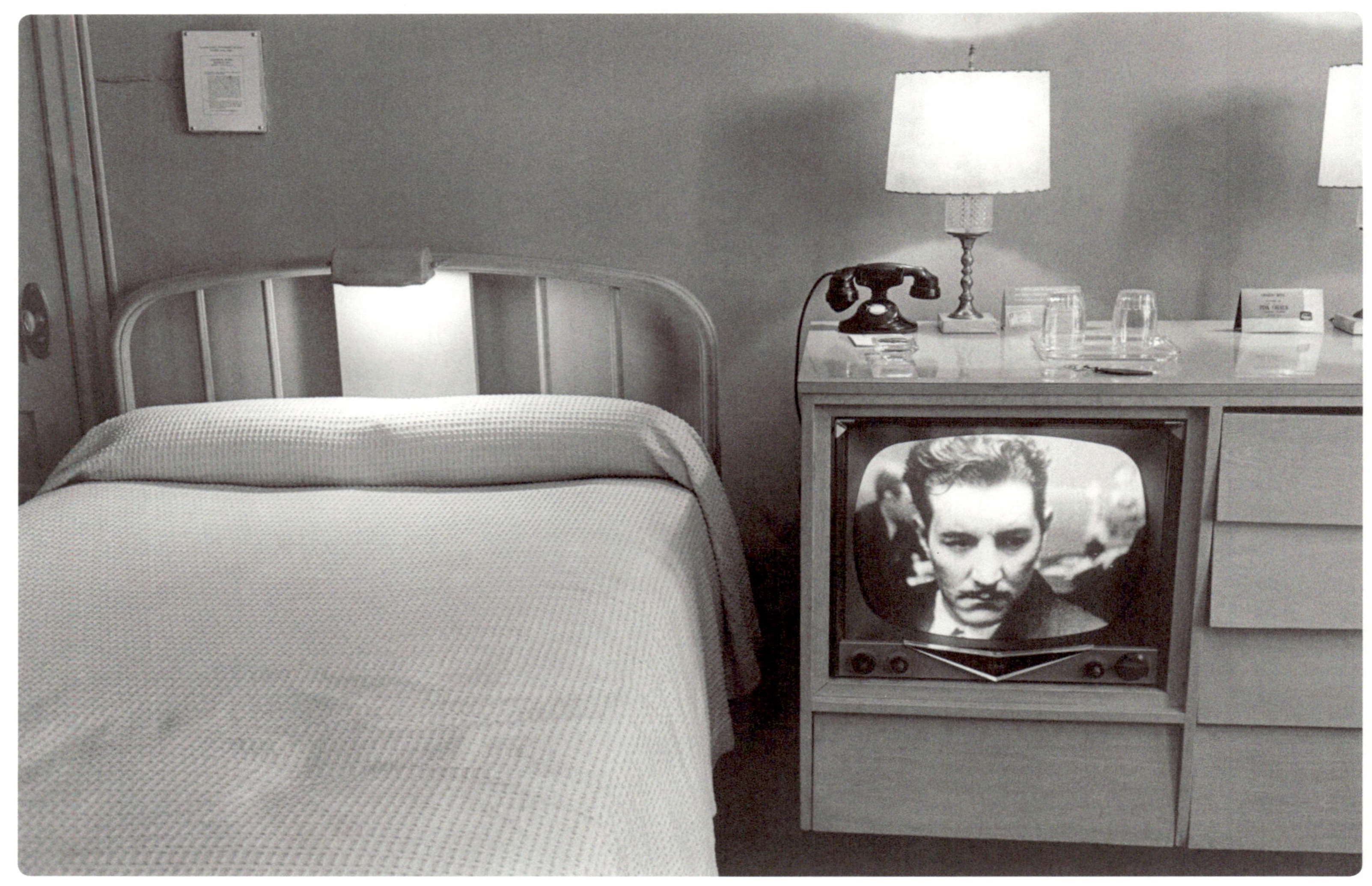

ABB. / FIG. 1 **LEE FRIEDLANDER**

BALTIMORE, MARYLAND

1962, Silbergelatinabzug / Gelatin silver print, Courtesy: Fraenkel Gallery, San Francisco, © Lee Freedlander

VERORTEN IN DER FREMDE

ANEIGNUNGEN DES HOTELS IN DER KUNST SEIT DEN 1960ER-JAHREN

LUISA HEESE

Ein Hotelzimmer. Das Kingsize-Bett ragt schräg in den Raum hinein, der synthetisch-glatte Überwurf glänzt im künstlichen Licht, das sich von der Decke aus über die kahlen Wände verteilt. Am Fußende sitzt ein Mann, den Körper abgewandt, den Kopf leicht in Richtung der Kamera gedreht. Er hält inne in seiner Pose, wirkt erschöpft, in sich zusammengesunken, ein Whiskyglas in den Händen haltend. Der leere Blick suggeriert Einsamkeit. Auf dem Sideboard aus dunklem Holz liegt ein geöffneter Koffer, das Neonlicht über dem Spiegel der kleinen Nasszelle glimmt gegen die eigene Nichtigkeit an. Die Tür des Zimmers steht offen, doch die Schwelle führt nur in die Dunkelheit. Das Interieur des Zimmers scheint zum Spiegel der Seele zu werden, mit wenigen Utensilien ausgestattet, deren pragmatische Funktion des Übernachtens eindeutig identifizierbar ist und somit Vertrautheit implizieren soll, die in ihrer Zusammenstellung jedoch fremd bleiben. Abgeschlossen von der Außenwelt zwischen blassgelben Wänden, samtig-rotem Teppich und quadratischer Deckenvertäfelung findet sich der Protagonist in einer leblosen Umgebung wieder, die ein bestimmtes soziales und kulturelles Verhalten einfordert. Für den weniger erfahrenen Gast ist dieses noch schriftlich in der Hausordnung festgehalten, die mahnend an der Wand lehnt. Diese Szene hält der Fotograf William Eggleston 1970 in Huntsville, Alabama/USA, fest und schafft damit ein ikonisches Bild des *Homo ambulans* in der anonymisierten Maschinerie des modernen Reisens, der Gefahr läuft, sich in ihr zu verlieren (Abb. S. 173). Die Aufnahme fällt in eine Zeit, in der die westliche Welt eine zunehmende Mobilität und Demokratisierung des Reisens erlebt.[1] Das Hotelwesen, Teil der Infrastruktur dieses Unterwegs-Seins, entfaltet sich zu einem globalen Netzwerk, dem zunehmend gleichförmige basale Strukturen professionalisierter und standardisierter Hospitalität zugrunde liegen.

Es bietet Reisenden einen temporären Aufenthalt an einem mutablen Ort, der bestimmten Regeln des halböffentlichen Raumes folgt. Dieser birgt die Möglichkeit des Rückzugs in eine vorgebliche Privatheit, die jedoch an der Türschwelle des Hotelzimmers endet und in jene Räume mündet, in denen Menschen verschiedenster Herkunft und sozialen Hintergrunds aufeinandertreffen. Der Aufenthalt im Hotel wird zu einer kollektiv wirksamen gesellschaftlichen Erfahrung, in der das soziale Gefüge einem eigenen heterotopischen Prinzip folgt und »Lücken in der Ordnung der Dinge«[2] ausbildet, die außerhalb dieser Institution herrschen. Es ist ein Raum »zwischen Arbeit und Freizeit, zwischen Alltag und Reise, zwischen Wünschen und Wirklichkeiten«.[3] Dieses Konglomerat teilweise konträrer Sphären und Protagonisten macht das Hotel zu einem vielschichtigen zivilisatorischen Phänomen, das sich auch in

1 Vgl. Hasso Spode, »Eine kurze Geschichte des Hotels. Zur Industrialisierung der Gastlichkeit«, in: *Das Hotel. Voyage. Jahrbuch für Reise- & Tourismusforschung 2011*, Bd. 9, hrsg. von Nikola Langreiter, Klara Löffler, Hasso Spode, Berlin 2011, S. 10–31, hier S. 23.

2 Gerrit Confurius, »Die Hotelhalle als Lücke«, in: *Daidalos. Architektur – Kunst – Kultur*, Heft 62: *Übernachten / Sleeping out*, Gütersloh 1996, S. 142–147, hier S. 147.

3 Nikola Langreiter, Klara Löffler, Johanna Rolshoven, »Das Hotel, das Reisen und der Alltag – im Dreieck besehen«, in: Langreiter/Löffler/Spode 2011 (wie Anm. 1), S. 170–189, hier S. 170.

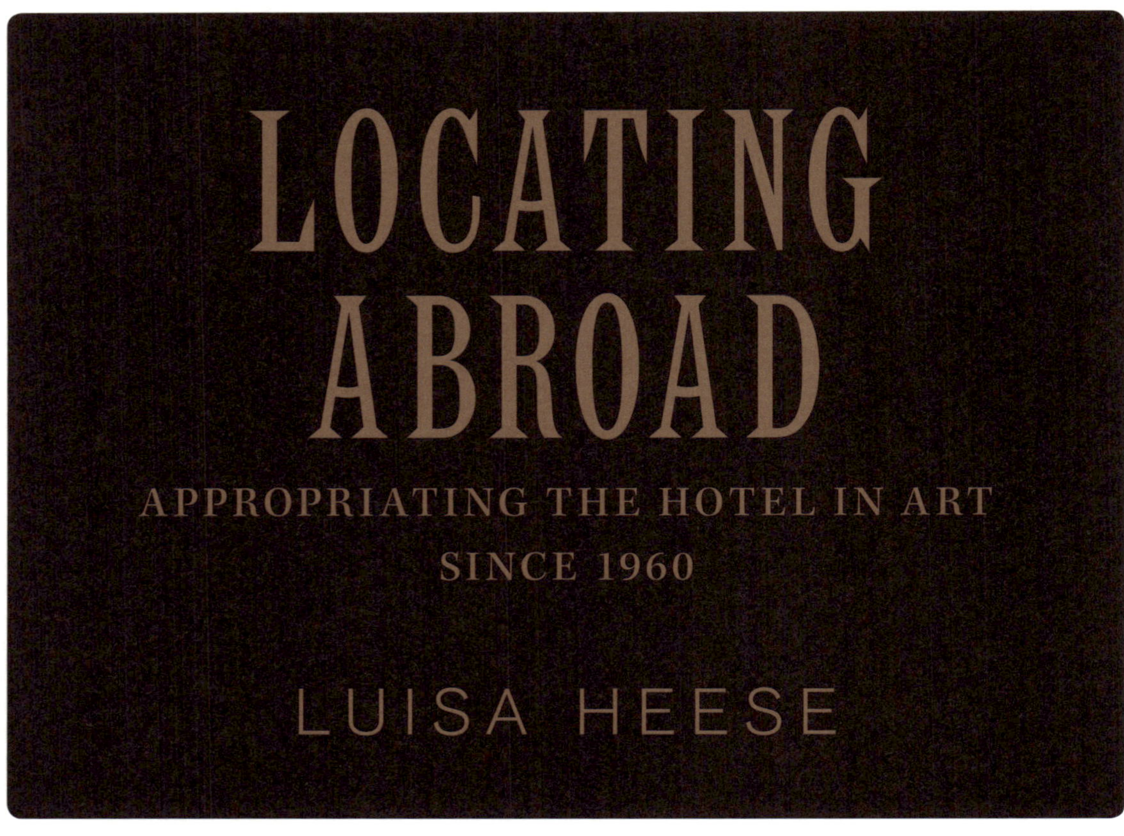

A hotel room. The king-sized bed juts diagonally into the image, the synthetic-smooth overthrow shines in the artificial light strewn from the ceiling over the cool walls of the room. A man sits at the end of the bed, his body turned away, with his head tilted slightly towards the camera. He takes pause in his pose, looks exhausted, collapsed, holding a whiskey glass in his hand. His empty gaze suggests loneliness. On the dark wooden sideboard lies an open suitcase, the fluorescent light over the mirror of the classical vanity glows against its own irrelevance. The door of the room is open, yet the threshold leads only to darkness. The interior of the room seems to become a mirror of the soul, outfitted with only a few utensils whose pragmatic function of the overnight stay is clearly identifiable, thus implying familiarity, and yet it remains unfamiliar as a joint ensemble. Closed off from the outer world inside these pale yellow walls, with the velvety red carpet and square ceiling panels, the protagonist finds himself in lifeless surroundings that call for a certain social and cultural behavior. For the less experienced guest, the expectations are recorded in the house rules hanging on the wall. The scene was captured by the photographer William Eggleston in 1970 in Alabama, who created an iconic image of *Homo ambulans* in the anonymous machinery of modern travel, in which he is in danger of getting lost (fig. p. 173). The shot was taken during a time in which the Western world was experiencing increasing mobility and the democratization of travel.[1] Hotels, part of the infrastructure of mobility, developed into a global network based on increasingly uniform basic structures of professionalized and standardized hospitality.

Hotels offer travelers a temporary stay in a mutable location that follows certain rules of semi-public space. This offers the possibility of a retreat to a pretend privacy, which however ends at the threshold of the hotel room, leading to spaces where people from all origins and social backgrounds encounter one another. The stay in a hotel becomes a social experience with a collective impact in which the social structure follows its own heterotopic principle and forms »gaps in the order of things«[2] that dominates outside this institution. It is a space »between work and free time, between everyday life and travel, between wishes and realities.«[3] This conglomeration of in part contrary spheres and participants makes the hotel a multi-layered cultural phenomenon that leaves its mark on contemporary cultural production: beginning with the golden age of the grand hotel around 1900, it primarily attracted writers and filmmakers as a backdrop of social studies and great narratives.[4]

After 1945 the myths and functions of the hotel increasingly came to be explored in the fine arts as well. Together with the political sense of a new beginning in Western

1 See Hasso Spode, »Eine kurze Geschichte des Hotels: Zur Industrialisierung der Gastlichkeit,« in *Das Hotel. Voyage. Jahrbuch für Reise- & Tourismusforschung 2011*, vol. 9, eds. Nikola Langreiter, Klara Löffler, and Hasso Spode (Berlin, 2011), 23.

2 Gerrit Confurius, »Die Hotelhalle als Lücke,« *Daidalos: Architektur, Kunst, Kultur* 62 (1996), 147.

3 Nikola Langreiter, Klara Löffler, and Johanna Rolshoven, »Das Hotel, das Reisen und der Alltag – im Dreieck besehen,« in Langreiter/Löffler/Spode 2011 (see note 1), 170.

4 See the contributions of Hendrik Bündge and Andreas Kilb in this catalog.

der zeitgenössischen kulturellen Produktion niederschlägt: Seit der goldenen Ära der Grand Hotels um 1900 zieht es vorrangig Schriftsteller und Filmemacher als Kulisse für Sozialstudien und große Erzählungen an.[4]

Nach 1945 werden die Mythen und Funktionen des Hotels neben den sprachbasierten Künsten vermehrt auch in den bildenden Künsten thematisiert. Einhergehend mit der politischen Aufbruchstimmung in den westlichen Gesellschaften suchen Künstler verstärkt nach Wegen, durch erweiterte kreative Ausdrucksmöglichkeiten die Dominanz eines selbstreferenziellen Werkbegriffs aufzubrechen, der sich in Nordamerika vor allem im abstrakten Expressionismus und in Europa in Strömungen wie dem Informel manifestiert hatte. Unter Schlagwörtern wie Fluxus, Happening, Minimalismus, Situationismus, Performance und vielen anderen, die meist unter dem weitläufigen Begriff der Concept-Art zusammengefasst werden, werden die Grenzen zwischen den Gattungen zunehmend durchlässig, ebenso die Distinktion zwischen Kunst und Leben: Vorgefundene Gegenstände, Themen und Orte der realen Welt und des Alltags halten vermehrt Einzug in künstlerische Äußerungen.

Dass das Hotel als Habitat auf Zeit ebenso zum Gegenstand verstärkter Auseinandersetzung wird, ist wenig verwunderlich. Mit der Ausweitung des Kunstbegriffs vollzieht sich fast zwangsläufig auch eine »Entauratisierung und Veralltäglichung« des Ateliers – es entwickelt sich das »Bild des reisenden nomadisierenden Künstlers, der kein Atelier im herkömmlichen Sinne mehr unterhält, sondern in der (Kunst-)Welt umherzieht, um seine Projekte an wechselnden Schauplätzen zu verwirklichen«.[5] Das Hotel als Einrichtung und Idee nimmt innerhalb des Beziehungsgeflechts zwischen Künstler, Werk und Rezipient verschiedene Rollen ein. Im Zuge seines Unterwegs-Seins dient es Künstlern nicht mehr nur als Herberge und Atelier auf Zeit im pragmatischen Sinne, sondern avanciert bisweilen selbst zum künstlerischen Sujet oder Material. Vermehrt laufen diese beiden Sphären zusammen – etwa im genau dafür berühmt gewordenen New Yorker Chelsea Hotel. Ab den 1950er-Jahren verstärkt von der lokalen und internationalen Boheme frequentiert, findet es in zahlreichen Kunstwerken Niederschlag, wobei als berühmtestes Beispiel wohl der Experimentalfilm THE CHELSEA GIRLS von Andy Warhol und Paul Morrissey gelten mag, der 1966 sowohl in Räumen des Chelsea Hotels als auch in Warhols berüchtigter Factory gedreht wird und zufallsgenerierte Geschichten verschiedener fiktiver Bewohnerinnen des Chelsea Hotels erzählt, gespickt mit provokativen Bildern ausschweifenden Drogenkonsums und freimütig ausgelebter Sexualität. Einige der Darstellerinnen wie Nico residieren zu dieser Zeit tatsächlich als Dauergäste in ebenjenem Hotel, sodass sich im Film verschiedene Realitätsebenen überlagern. Das Werk sorgt schließlich trotz – oder womöglich gerade wegen – durchwachsener Kritiken nicht nur für den kommerziellen Erfolg Andy Warhols und seiner mit dem Begriff Pop-Art bezeichneten Kunstpraxis, sondern unterstützt auch das Image des Chelsea Hotels als verwegenen Hort der New Yorker Künstlerkaste.

AUCH DER SCHWEIZER KÜNSTLER DANIEL SPOERRI RESIDIERT 1965 IM CHELSEA HOTEL UND FUNKTIONIERT SEIN ZIMMER KURZERHAND ZUM AUSSTELLUNGSRAUM UM: In ROOM NO. 631 AT THE CHELSEA HOTEL öffnet er seinen Atelier- und Wohnraum dem Publikum und steuert damit nicht zuletzt einen weiteren Schritt zur Überwindung eines hermetischen Werk- und Atelierbegriffs bei.[6] Doch ist das Chelsea Hotel nicht die einzige Herberge auf Zeit, die Eingang in Spoerris Werk fand: Vor seinem Aufenthalt in New York bewohnte der Mitbegründer des *Nouveau Réalisme* zwischen 1959 und 1965 ein Zimmer im Pariser Hotel Carcassonne und entwickelt dort, mit und aus den spezifischen Gegebenheiten des Ortes heraus, die ersten seiner später berühmten FALLENBILDER. Das zufällige Arrangement alltäglicher Gegenstände auf einer Tischplatte, das benutzte Geschirr eines ausgiebigen Frühstücks zum Beispiel, wird hierbei fixiert und in ein dreidimensionales Stillleben verwandelt, das, um 90 Grad gedreht, vorerst an der Wand des kleinen Zimmers Platz findet. Die Ortsspezifik greift Spoerri viele Jahre später wieder auf und repliziert dieses Hotelzimmer, das für ihn den »Geburtsort meiner Künstleridentität«[7] darstellt, als einen musealisierten Erinnerungsraum in dem sowohl einige der damals angefertigten als auch neue Arbeiten Platz finden. Die Rekonstruktion des Zimmers führte unversehens auch zu Komplikationen, als Spoerri der erneute Zugang in das Hotel zum Maßnehmen verwehrt bleibt: Die Hausdame verübelte ihm noch immer sowohl die unzähligen an ihn adressierten Postsendungen nach seinem Weggang als auch jene Schaulustigen, die das Hotel in den vergangenen Jahrzehnten nur betreten hatten, um einen Blick in das *Spoerri-Zimmer* zu erhaschen.[8] So bedient sich Spoerri schließlich allein seiner Erinnerungen und Fotografien, um den Raum zwischen 1998 und 2000 nachzubauen. Ein wichtiges Dokument stellt hierfür die fotografische Collage dar, die 1962 nach Spoerris Vorgaben von seiner Frau Vera Mertz erstellt wurde (Abb. S. 168 – 169.). In einem kubistisch anmutenden Stil bietet diese Arbeit eine in 50 Einzelbilder unterteilte Sicht auf die Räumlichkeit sowie die zahlreichen Dinge und Fundstücke, mit denen das kleine Zimmer angefüllt war – von einem Standpunkt aus fotografiert. Spoerri versieht sie später mit einem Paar

4 Siehe hierzu die Beiträge von Hendrik Bündge, S. 75 ff., und Andreas Kilb, S. 127 ff., in diesem Katalog.

5 Heinz Knobeloch, »Porträt des Künstlers als Nomade und Bastler«, in: *Was ist ein Künstler? Das Subjekt der modernen Kunst*, hrsg. von Martin Hellmold, München 2003, S. 213 – 228, hier S. 213.

6 Vgl. Michael Glasmeier, »Von der Staffelei zum Schreibtisch. Episoden einer Historie des Atelierschwunds«, in: *Mythos Atelier. Von Spitzweg bis Picasso, von Giacometti bis Nauman*, hrsg. von Ina Conzen, Ausst.-Kat. Staatsgalerie Stuttgart, München 2012, S. 226 – 235, hier S. 231.

7 Daniel Spoerri, *Anekdotomania. Daniel Spoerri über Daniel Spoerri*, Ausst.-Kat. Museum Tinguely, Basel, Ostfildern-Ruit 2001, S. 271.

8 Vgl. ebd., S. 272.

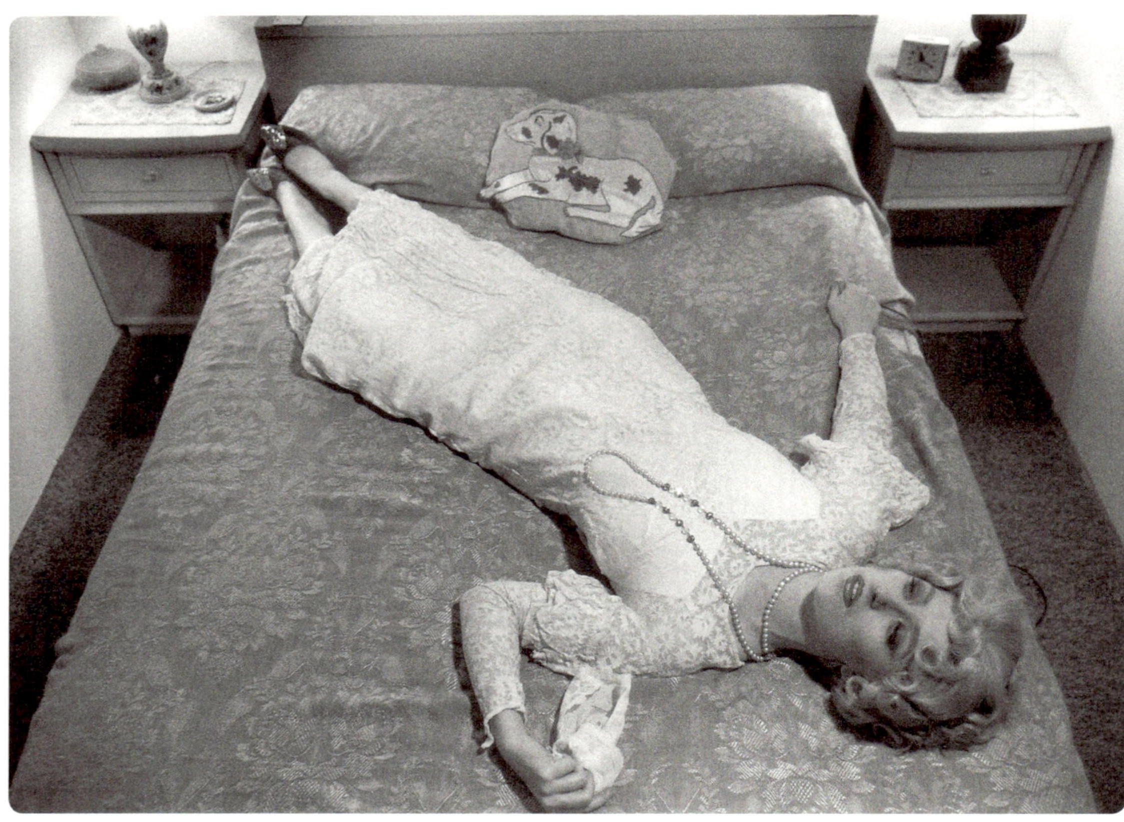

Abb. / Fig. 2

CINDY SHERMAN **UNTITLED FILM STILL #11**

1978, S/W-Fotografie, Courtesy: Die Künstlerin und Metro Pictures, New York, © Cindy Sherman
1978, b/w photography, courtesy of the artist and Metro Pictures, New York, © Cindy Sherman

societies, artists increasingly looked for ways to break up the domination of a self-referential concept of art, represented primarily by Abstract Expressionism in North America and by currents like Art Informel in Europe, through expanded creative possibilities of expression. With key terms like Fluxus, happenings, minimalism, situationism, and performance art, usually grouped under the broader term of conceptual art, the lines separating the genres became more and more permeable, as did the distinction between art and life: found objects, subjects, and places in the real world and everyday life increasingly found their way into artistic statements.

IT is not surprising that the hotel also started to become a subject of interest as a temporary habitat. The expansion of the concept of art almost automatically entailed a »deauratization and increasing ordinariness« of the studio, the »image of the itinerant, nomadic artist develops, who has no studio in the standard sense, but who moves around in the (art) world to realize his or her projects in various locations.«[5] The hotel as an institution and an idea took on various roles in the relationship between the art, the work, and the recipient. Since artists were also constantly on the move, the hotel no longer served just as a dwelling and temporary studio in the pragmatic sense, but advanced to become an artistic subject or material. Increasingly, these two spheres combined, as in the case of New York's Chelsea Hotel, which became famous for this. Increasingly frequented by local and global bohemians in the 1950s, it played a role in numerous artworks, perhaps the most famous being the experimental film THE CHELSEA GIRLS by Andy Warhol and Paul Morrissey, which was filmed both at the Chelsea Hotel and at Warhol's infamous *Factory* and tells chance-generated stories of various fictional residents of the Chelsea Hotel, filled with provocative images of excessive drug consumption and freely lived sexuality. Some of the performers in the film, like Nico, were actually living as permanent guests at the hotel at the time, so that various layers of reality overlap in the film. Despite, or perhaps because of the mixed reviews, the work not only ensured the commercial success of Andy Warhol and his artistic practice, called Pop Art, but also supported the image of the Chelsea Hotel as the decadent home of the New York artist caste.

5 Heinz Knobeloch, »Porträt des Künstlers als Nomade und Bastler,« *Was ist ein Künstler? Das Subjekt der modernen Kunst*, ed. Martin Hellmold (Munich, 2003), 213.

Pantoffeln, die er auf der Bildfläche montiert und die dem Bild einen heimeligen Charakter geben.

Die Fotografie erlebt in der Kunstwelt ab 1960 einen rasanten Aufstieg. Ihre besondere Relation zur Wirklichkeit ist hierfür ausschlaggebend: Ausgehend von dem Einsatz als dokumentierendes Medium für ephemere Kunstwerke, Aktionen und Performances entwickelt sich schon bald ein Bewusstsein für eine eigene fotografische Bildsprache und -logik, die das Sichtbare hinterfragt und mit den Mitteln der eigenen Medialität seine inhärenten Metaebenen reflektiert. Strategien zunächst kunstferner Strömungen, etwa die der Reportagefotografie, halten zunehmend Einzug in die künstlerische Praxis, wovon nicht zuletzt das eingangs erwähnte Werk von William Eggleston zeugt. Auch Lee Friedlander nutzt das fotografische Bild, um die spezifische Atmosphäre von Motels einzufangen (Abb. 1). Er fotografierte stets die flimmernden Fernsehgeräte in jenen Zimmern, in denen er selbst als Gast abstieg. Die Gesichter auf diesen Bildschirmen scheinen die einzige Verbindung vom Inneren des isolierten, in einer gewissen Zeitlosigkeit verharrenden Zimmers zur sozialen Außenwelt zu sein – wobei diese Aufnahmen vor allem durch ihre Serialität zum signifikanten Ausdruck eines gesellschaftlichen Befindens werden. Aus den Bildern formt sich ein gesichtsloses, übergeordnetes Transitnetz, dem auch das unpersönliche Motel als materialisierte Komponente angehört, welches so, kulturkritisch betrachtet, zum Sinnbild einer zunehmenden Entindividualisierung und »Industrialisierung der Gastlichkeit«[9] wird. Das Fernsehgerät deutet überdies auf eine Künstlergeneration, die mit der vereinfachten Zugänglichkeit der neuen Medien wie Fotografie, Film und Fernsehen aufgewachsen ist und gleichermaßen eine verstärkte Reflexivität ihnen gegenüber entwickelt hat.

DIESER Generation angehörend, wählt Cindy Sherman aktiv den Rückgriff auf mediale Artefakte und konstruierte Bilder der Populärkultur wie Kinofilme, Fernsehen, Illustrierte oder auch Werbung. Anders als Andy Warhol nutzt oder reproduziert sie diese Bilder jedoch nicht direkt, sondern eignet sich ihre massenkulturellen Codierungen und Stereotypen an, um eigene Bilder mit sich selbst als stilisierter Protagonistin zu generieren. 1977 beginnt sie die Serie der UNTITLED FILM STILLS, die, wie der Name bereits indiziert, an die Bildsprache von Hollywoodfilmen angelehnt ist, ohne auf ein ganz konkretes filmisches Vorbild zu rekurrieren. Bereits unter den ersten Bildern dieser Serie finden sich auch Anlehnungen an die Örtlichkeit eines Hotelzimmers, dessen symbolische Zuschreibungen für die Bilderzählung genutzt werden: UNTITLED FILM STILL #11 etwa zeigt eine herausgeputzte Dame in einem Brautkleid, die erschöpft auf einem Doppelbett liegt und in der Hand ein zerknittertes Taschentuch umfasst. Ihr Gesichtsausdruck in Kombination mit ihrer Aufmachung und der Umgebung vermittelt ein persönliches Drama, das die Figur im Moment der Aufnahme durchlebt. Das Geheimnis um die Hintergründe dieser Szene wird jedoch nicht gelüftet (Abb. 2). Durch die spezifische *Mise en Scène* deutet Cindy Sherman eine Situation lediglich an, die durch den bewussten Bezug auf das Hotel als Schauplatz unzähliger Kriminalfilme und Melodramen die hiermit verbundenen Narrative und Assoziationen heraufbeschwört. Viele Jahre später greift Sherman erneut auf dieses bedeutungsbeladene Setting zurück: Hierbei nutzt sie jedoch nicht das standardisierte Mittelklassehotel als Ort des Geschehens, sondern suggeriert den Eindruck ausladender Empfangshallen in vornehmen Grand Hotels, um so eine ironisch zugespitzte Milieustudie der alternden Bourgeoisie zu schaffen. Damen der besseren Gesellschaft posieren hier herausgeputzt und vornehm drapiert für die Kamera. Im verfallenden, fratzenhaften Antlitz der fiktiven Figuren spiegelt sich nunmehr nicht nur der eigene Drang nach jugendlicher Schönheit und gesellschaftlichem Status, sondern ebenso der verblassende Glanz jener luxuriösen Hotel-paläste, die ihre Blütezeit bereits weit hinter sich gelassen haben.

Die Beschäftigung mit verschiedenen Gesellschaftsschichten zieht sich nicht nur quer durch die Geschichte der Fotografie, sondern auch durch die Bildgeschichte des Hotels. Ist es die Halbwelt, die Brassaï in den Hinterzimmern der Pariser Hotels fotografiert, sind es bei August Sander die Hotelangestellten selbst, die in seinem umfänglichen Werk MENSCHEN DES 20. JAHRHUNDERTS abgelichtet sind (Abb. S. 64, 157). In den 1960er-Jahren greift Diane Arbus wieder das Hotelzimmer als diskreten Ort auf, an dem sich gesellschaftliche Randfiguren, die durch ihre Lebensart oder körperliche Physiognomie als *andersartig* gelten, ungestört tummeln können. Auf einem ihrer dokumentarisch intendierten Bilder posiert ein kleinwüchsiger Herr, lediglich bekleidet mit Hut und Handtuch, lässig und mit einem leichten Lächeln auf dem Bett eines Hotelzimmers (Abb. S. 167). Er wirkt entspannt und in wohlwollender Relation zur Kamera und Fotografin. Das Bild zeugt von einem intimen Moment und vermittelt das Hotelzimmer als positiv konnotierten Zufluchtsort.[10] Diskretion als hohes Gut des Hotels, das sich frei von moralisierenden Elementen gibt, um seinen Gästen einen eskapistischen Möglichkeitsraum offenzuhalten, liefert der Künstlerin Sophie Calle wiederum den Anreiz für eine Sozialstudie anderer Art. Sie eignet sich das Hotel nicht nur als Kulisse, sondern seine innere Organisationsstruktur an: 1981 lässt sie sich für drei Wochen in einem

9 Spode 2011 (wie Anm. 1), S. 10.

10 In diesem Zusammenhang sei ebenso auf die Künstlerin Nan Goldin verwiesen, die ihr persönliches Umfeld mit der Kamera in intimen und schonungslosen Fotografien festhält und damit auch ein durchdringendes Bild des sie umgebenden Milieus schafft. U.a. in ihrer Serie THE BALLAD OF SEXUAL DEPENDENCY von 1986 taucht das Hotel immer wieder als Schauplatz auf.

6 See Michael Glasmeier, »Von der Staffelei zum Schreibtisch. Episoden einer Historie des Atelierschwunds,« *Mythos Atelier: Von Spitzweg bis Picasso, von Giacometti bis Nauman*, ed. Ina Conzen, exhibit. cat. Staatsgalerie Stuttgart (Munich, 2012), 231.

7 Daniel Spoerri, *Anekdotomania: Daniel Spoerri über Daniel Spoerri*, exhibit. cat. Museum Tinguely, Basel (Ostfildern-Ruit, 2001), 271.

8 Ibid., 272.

9 Spode 2011 (see note 1), 10.

THE SWISS ARTIST DANIEL SPOERRI ALSO LIVED IN THE CHELSEA HOTEL IN 1965 AND SWIFTLY TRANSFORMED HIS ROOM INTO AN EXHIBITION SPACE. In ROOM NO. 631 AT THE CHELSEA HOTEL, he opened his studio and living space to the audience, thus helping to overhaul the hermetic concept of the work and the studio.[6] And yet the Chelsea Hotel is not the only temporary residence that found its way into Spoerri's work. Before his stay in New York, the co-founder of *Nouveau Réalisme* lived in a room at the Paris Hotel Carcassonne, where he developed the first of his famous FALLENBILDER, using the specific attributes of the location. The accidental arrangement of everyday objects on a table, the used tableware of a long breakfast for example, was fixed and transformed into a three-dimensional still life, that, turned 90 degrees, first was placed on the wall of the small room. Many years later Spoerri returned to site specificity and replicated this hotel room, which for him represents »the birthplace of my identity as an artist,«[7] as a museumified space of memory in which both some of the works created then as well as new ones can find their place. The reconstruction of the room immediately led to complications, since Spoerri was refused entrance to the hotel to take the dimensions of the room. The hotel housekeeper was cross with the artist about the endless supply of mail sent to him at the hotel after his departure as well as the many curious people who only came to the hotel in later decades to capture a glimpse of the »Spoerri Room.«[8] So Spoerri only used his memories and photographs to reconstruct the room between 1998 and 2000. An important document here was a photographic collage, made by his wife Vera Mertz according to Spoerri's instructions in 1962 (fig. pp. 168–169). In a cubistic style, this work offers a view of the space divided into 50 individual images as well as of the numerous things and found objects with which the small room was filled, photographed from a single standpoint. Spoerri later added a pair of slippers that he montaged onto the image surface, giving the image a homey character.

As of 1960, photography quickly gained in importance in the art world. Its special relationship to reality was crucial in this context. Based on its use as a documentary medium for ephemeral artworks, actions, and performances, an awareness soon developed for a unique visual language and logic that questioned the visible and reflected its inherent metalevels by means of its own mediation. Strategies of initially non-artistic currents like reportage photography increasingly found their way into artistic practice, as is attested to by the aforementioned work of William Eggleston. Lee Friedlander also used the photographic image to capture the specific atmosphere of motels (fig. 1). He took photographs of the flickering television screens in all the rooms he stayed in. The faces on these screens seem to be the only link from the inside of the isolated room, caught in a certain timelessness, to the outer social world, while these shots, especially due to their seriality, become a significant expression of a social state of mind. The images form a faceless, overarching transit network to which the impersonal motel belongs as a materialized component, which, seen from the perspective of cultural criticism, becomes an emblem of an increasing de-individualization and »industrialization of hospitality.«[9] The television furthermore points to an artist generation that grew up with the simplified accessibility of new media such as photography, film, and television, and that simultaneously developed a strong reflexive attitude toward them.

Belonging to this generation, Cindy Sherman actively makes use of media artifacts and constructs images of popular culture like movies, television, magazines, or advertising. Unlike Andy Warhol, however, she does not use or reproduce these images directly, but appropriates their mass cultural codings and stereotypes to generate her own images with herself as a stylized protagonist. She began the series UNTITLED FILM STILLS in 1977. As the title suggests, the series is based on the visual language of Hollywood film stills, without taking recourse to any actual film. The very first images of this series borrow from the locale of the hotel room, whose symbolic attributes are used for visual narrative. UNTITLED FILM STILL #11, for example, shows a woman wearing a wedding dress, lying exhausted on a double bed, and holding a crumbled handkerchief in her hand. Her facial expression in combination with her get up and the surroundings communicate a personal drama that the figure is living through in the moment the picture was taken. And yet the secret behind this scene is not revealed (fig. 2). Through the specific *mise en scène* Cindy Sherman alludes merely to a situation that by the concrete reference to the hotel as the setting for countless mystery films and melodramas evokes related narratives and associations. Many years later, Sherman returned to this setting, laden with meaning. Here, however, she does not use the standardized middle-class hotel as the site of action, but suggests the impression of expansive foyers in exquisite grand hotels, creating an ironic study of the milieu of the aging bourgeoisie. The figures posing in these images are women from high society, all done up and elegantly draped for the camera. The decaying, grimacing countenance of the fictional figures reflects not only their own desire for youthful beauty and social status, but also the tattered glamour of those luxurious hotel palaces that have long left their best days behind them.

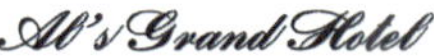

7175 Sunset Boulevard / Hollywood, California 90046 / (213) 656-5500

Allen Ruppersberg/President and Managing Director

Dear Sirs:

As you can see by the letterhead there is a new hotel coming to the Los Angeles area. I would like to take this opportunity to formally announce the opening of Al's Grand Hotel at 7175 Sunset Boulevard in Hollywood.

The grand opening is scheduled for May 7 and 8. It will be, as Al's Cafe, in all respects a full operational hotel, including bar, comfortable, relaxing lobby, music, continental breakfast, daily maid service, souvenirs and adjusted rooms for your sleeping comfort. For six weeks it will be open Friday and Saturday nights from eight o'clock; check-out time will be noon the following day. All rooms are fitted with a double bed, linen changed daily, and a full bathroom down the hall. The rates will be fifteen through thirty dollars a night depending on your choice of room.

The rooms are as follows:

The "B" Room	15.00
The Day Room	20.00
The Ultra Violet Room	25.00
The Breakfast Room	25.00
The Al Room	30.00
The Jesus Room	30.00
The Bridal Suite	30.00

Since it will be open only six weeks, I am taking reservations in advance. You may either phone or mail your checks to me at 7507 Sunset Boulevard #2, Hollywood, 90046. Your reservations will be confirmed by phone if you wish to include your telephone number.

The rooms will be open for inspection until midnight, however, everyone is welcome to come, have a drink, and enjoy the luxurious atmosphere whether or not you stay the night. I hope everyone will be comfortable and able to experience the piece by spending one or many nights, so please make your reservations early.

See you at The Grand Hotel,

Sincerely,

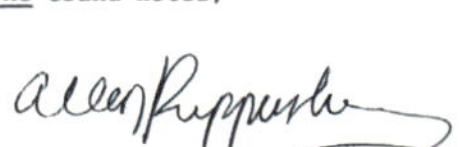

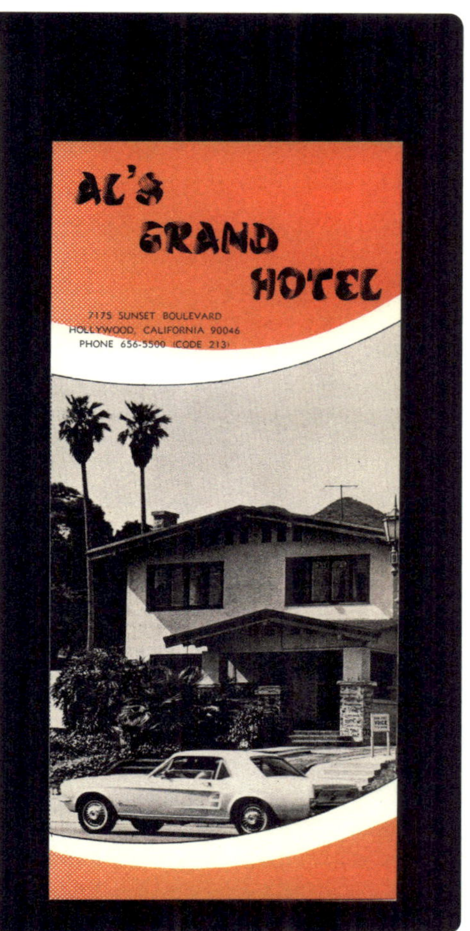

Abb. / Fig. 3 **ALLEN RUPPERSBERG**

Brief und Broschüre für Al's Grand Hotel, 2. Mai 1971, gestaltet von Allen Ruppersberg, Offsetlithografie, getippter und unterzeichneter Brief, © Allen Ruppersberg

Letter and brochure for Al's Grand Hotel, May 2, 1971, designed by Allen Ruppersberg, offset lithograph brochure, typed letter (signed), © Allen Ruppersberg

venezianischen Hotel als Zimmermädchen anstellen. Dort agiert sie an den Übergängen der sichtbaren und unsichtbar gehaltenen Orte des Hotels und dringt detektivisch in die Privatsphäre seiner Gäste ein. Während ihrer Dienste führt sie minutiös Buch über die persönlichen Gegenstände und sichtbaren Nutzungsspuren in den Zimmern, fotografiert diese und notiert ihre eigenen Annahmen zu den Personen, denen sie persönlich höchstens im Vorbeigehen begegnet. Calle nimmt mit L'HÔTEL eine Position innerhalb des Getriebes ein, um von dieser aus ihren Handlungsradius auszuloten (Abb. S. 178–181).

In Bezug auf die Aneignung von Organisationsstrukturen übernehmen Künstler gelegentlich sogar den gesamten funktionalen Rahmen der Hotelinstitution. Allen Ruppersberg bewegt sich Ende der 1960er-Jahre im Umfeld der zunehmend als konzeptuell bezeichneten Kunstszene in Los Angeles. Wie viele Künstler seiner Generation beschäftigt er sich mit der Frage, »wie man außerhalb des Ateliers und jenseits der Herstellung von Objekten an die Dinge herangehen«[11] und alternative Präsentationsmodi zu klassischen Ausstellungen erproben könnte. Eine Möglichkeit bietet für ihn das selbstverlegte Künstlerbuch: 1968 veröffentlicht er 23 PIECES, darauf folgt 1970 24 PIECES. Ersteres enthält 23 abgedruckte Fotografien von unterschiedlichen Schauplätzen in und um Los Angeles, darunter auch einige Aufnahmen von weitgehend menschenleeren Hotels: Sie zeigen vereinsamte Haustelefone im Embassador Hotel, die weitläufige Lobby des Century Plaza Hotels und im Bild aus dem Hollywood Roosevelt Hotel tritt Ruppersberg selbst, sitzend auf einem der ausladenden Sofas, in Erscheinung. In 24 PIECES wird dem Hotel als Schauplatz dezidierter nachgegangen. Auf Doppelseiten im Buch werden jeweils auf der linken Seite Aufnahmen von verschiedenen

11 Allen Ruppersberg, zit. nach: Ann Goldstein, »Eine demokratischere Art des Kunstobjekts«, in: *Allen Ruppersberg. One of Many – Origins and Variants*, Ausst.-Kat. Kunsthalle Düsseldorf, Köln 2006, S. 27–54, hier S. 29.

10 In this context, consider the artist Nan Goldin, who captured her personal circle with the camera in intimate and brutal photographs, thus creating a penetrating image of the milieu around her. In her 1986 series THE BALLAD OF SEXUAL DEPENDENCY, for example, the hotel repeatedly emerges as a showplace.

11 Allen Ruppersberg, quoted in: Ann Goldstein, »A More Democratic Kind of Art Object,« *Allen Ruppersberg. One of Many: Origins and Variants,* exhibit. cat. Kunsthalle Düsseldorf (Cologne, 2006), 29.

12 Allen Ruppersberg, quoted in Goldstein 2006 (see note 11), 35.

13 Annemarie Sauzeau, *Alighiero Boetti's One Hotel, 100 Notizen, 100 Gedanken, dOCUMENTA 13),* No. 025 (Ostfildern, 2012), 21 f.

14 Ibid., 19.

AN engagement with various layers of society not only runs through the entire history of photography but the visual history of the hotel as well. While Brassaï photographs the demimonde in the back rooms of Parisian hotels, in August Sander's photographs the hotel employees themselves are depicted in his extensive work MENSCHEN DES 20. JAHRHUNDERTS (fig. pp. 64, 157). In the 1960s, Diane Arbus returns to the hotel room as a discreet location where marginal social figures, considered »different« due to their lifestyle or their physiognomy, can cavort freely. In one of her documentary-style images, a very short man, merely dressed with a hat and a towel, poses nonchalantly with a slight smile on the bed of a hotel room (fig. 167). He seems relaxed and friendly in relation to the camera and the photographer. The image attests to an intimate moment and depicts the hotel room as a place of escape with a positive connotation.[10] Discretion as the hotel's greatest good and the apparent freedom from moralizing elements that allows its guests an escapist space of possibility—this inspires the artist Sophie Calle to create a social study of a different kind. She adapts the hotel not just as a stage set but also uses its organizational structure. In 1981 she worked for three weeks in a Venetian hotel as a maid. There she used the transitional spaces between the visible and invisible parts of a hotel and penetrated the private spheres of its guests like a detective. During her work, she kept a record of the personal objects and visible traces of use in the rooms, taking pictures and noting her own assumptions about the people that she only met in person in passing. In L'HÔTEL Calle takes a position within the apparatus of hospitality to explore it from her own radius of action (fig. pp. 178–181).

In reference to the appropriation of structures of organization, artists occasionally take on the entire functional frame of the hotel as an institution. During the late 1960s, Allen Ruppersberg was active in the circles of the increasingly conceptual art world of Los Angeles. Like many artists of his generation, he is concerned with the question of »how to approach things outside of the studio and object making,«[11] exploring alternative modes of presentation to classical exhibitions. He saw the self-published artist's book as one promising possibility. In 1968 he published 23 PIECES, followed by 24 PIECES in 1970. The first contains 23 reproduced photographs of various locations in and around Los Angeles, including several shots of largely empty hotels. They show abandoned in-house telephones at the Ambassador Hotel, the wide-open lobby of the Century Plaza Hotel, whereas the image of the Hollywood Roosevelt Hotel shows Ruppersberg himself sitting on one of the huge sofas. In 24 PIECES, the hotel is used more decisively as a showplace. The left images on double spreads present shots of various hotel rooms where small interventions have been undertaken. They are usually juxtaposed with exterior shots on the right that also show traces of human intervention. The image pairings generate narrative feedback. Whereby the left-hand image, for example, shows a clean room in the Hyatt House Hotel, where a large suitcase stands ready to be unpacked or for departure, the image on the right side shows a collection of empty bottles piled up on the edge of a concrete block on sandy ground. Immediately this raises questions: does the owner of the suitcase have anything to do with the bottles? Is this a kind of consumption critique? It seems a logical consequence of Ruppersberg's interest in the hotel as a showplace for photographic interventions that the artist finally opened his own hotel in 1971, AL'S GRAND HOTEL (fig. 3). From May 7 to June 12, on Friday and Saturdays guests could stay overnight in one of the seven rooms of the two-storey house on 7175 Sunset Boulevard, or attend concerts or readings. All the rooms are designed individually by Ruppersberg according to different themes, so there's the *The Al Room, The Ultra Violet Room, The Jesus Room,* and *The Bridal Suite,* in which all the objects are available for purchase. AL'S GRAND HOTEL can thus be understood as a performative installation with which Ruppersberg tries »to introduce an audience to a social reality rather than the context of a gallery—switching contexts without anyone knowing it.«[12]

ITALIAN artist Alighiero Boetti was also working as a hotelier at virtually the same time. In 1971, after several stays in Afghanistan and having become famous as a representative of Arte Povera, Boetti decided to open a hotel in Kabul together with his friend Gholam Dastaghir in 1971. The small residence in which One Hotel was located can be found in a central part of Kabul and largely housed merchants from the surrounding countries and provinces and a few lone travelling hippies. Boetti himself used One Hotel several times a year for longer stays in a »happy state of hyperactivity, even if appearing idle.« When Boetti was absent, Dastaghir took over running the hotel.[13] In Kabul, Boetti organized the production of his MAPS, large format political world maps that he had made by embroiderers on site as wall hangings. In contrast to Allen Ruppersberg's AL'S GRAND HOTEL, One Hotel for Boetti does not represent an autonomous art work per se, and yet it is a fixed component in his artistic practice, which beginning in the 1960s increasingly focuses on the collective production of his ideas (fig. 4). For Boetti, ultimately »creativity also means opening a hotel in Kabul.«[14] Another art project that Boetti continued in Kabul was his LAVORI POSTALI, for which he uses the postal system as

Hotelzimmern gezeigt, in denen kleine Interventionen vorgenommen wurden. Ihnen sind auf der rechten Seite meist Außenaufnahmen gegenübergestellt, die ebenfalls Spuren von menschlichem Eingreifen zeigen. Zwischen den Bildpaaren entwickeln sich narrative Rückkopplungen: Während die linke Aufnahme beispielsweise ein säuberlich hergerichtetes Zimmer im Hyatt House Hotel zeigt, in dem ein großer Koffer zum Auspacken respektive zur Abreise bereit steht, zeigt die Abbildung auf der rechten Seite eine Ansammlung leerer Flaschen, die sich am Rande eines Betonblocks auf erdigem Boden auftürmen. Sofort stellen sich Fragen ein, ob der Besitzer des Koffers etwas mit den Flaschen zu tun hat? Oder ob es sich um eine Art Konsumkritik handelt? Es erscheint als logische Konsequenz aus Ruppersbergs Beschäftigung mit dem Hotel als Schauplatz für fotografisch festgehaltene Eingriffe, dass der Künstler 1971 mit AL'S GRAND HOTEL schließlich ein eigenes Hotel eröffnet (Abb. 3). Vom 7. Mai bis 12. Juni können freitags und samstags Gäste in einem der sieben Zimmer des zweistöckigen Hauses am 7175 Sunset Boulevard in Hollywood nächtigen sowie Konzerten und Lesungen beiwohnen. Alle Zimmer sind von Ruppersberg individuell thematisch gestaltet, so gibt es unter anderem *The Al Room, The Ultra Violet Room, The Jesus Room* und *The Bridal Suite,* in denen alle Einrichtungsgegenstände auch käuflich zu erwerben sind. AL'S GRAND HOTEL ist demnach als eine performative Installation zu verstehen, mit der Ruppersberg versucht, »[...] das Publikum eher an eine soziale Realität als an den Kontext einer Galerie heranzuführen – indem ich die Kontexte austauschte, ohne dass es jemandem klar war.«[12]

FAST **zeitgleich betätigt sich der italienische Künstler Alighiero Boetti ebenfalls als Hotelier.** Bekannt geworden als Vertreter der Arte Povera beschließt Boetti nach mehreren Aufenthalten in Afghanistan gemeinsam mit seinem Freund Gholam Dastaghir 1971 ein Hotel in Kabul zu eröffnen. Die kleine Villa, in der das One Hotel einquartiert wird, liegt in einem zentralen Stadtteil Kabuls und beherbergt vor allem Händler aus den umliegenden Ländern und Provinzen sowie vereinzelt einige Hippies auf der Durchreise. Boetti selbst besucht das One Hotel mehrmals im Jahr für längere Aufenthalte, versetzt »in eine[n] glückseligen Zustand der Hyperaktivität, wenn auch dem Anschein nach müßig«. In seiner Abwesenheit übernimmt Dastaghir die Leitung des Hauses.[13] In Kabul organisiert Boetti die Produktion seiner MAPPE, großformatigen politischen Weltkarten, die er von Näherinnen vor Ort als Wandbehänge umsetzen lässt. Im Gegensatz zu AL'S GRAND HOTEL von Allen Ruppersberg stellt das One Hotel für Boetti kein eigenständiges Kunstwerk per se dar, ist aber dennoch fester Bestandteil seiner Kunstpraxis, die ab den 1960er-Jahren verstärkt auf kollektive Produktionsmöglichkeiten seiner Ideen abzielt (Abb. 4). So bedeutet für Boetti letztlich »Kreativität auch, ein Hotel in Kabul aufzumachen«.[14] Ein anderes Kunstprojekt, das Boetti in Kabul weiterführt, sind seine LAVORI POSTALI: Hierfür nutzt er das postalische Versendungssystem als Spielfeld der Beziehungen zwischen Regel und Zufall. Briefumschläge, Briefmarken und der Adressstempel des One Hotels dienen als Grundelemente für grafische und numerische Permutationen, die im Sinne mathematischer Sequenzen auf Briefumschlägen kombiniert und auf die Reise durch das Postsystem geschickt werden. Boetti arbeitet hier oft mit nicht existenten Empfängeradressen und überlässt es dem Zufall, ob die Sendungen ihren Weg zurück zu ihrem Absender in das One Hotel finden. 1977 muss das Hotel aufgrund der sich zuspitzenden politischen und wirtschaftlichen Situation des Landes schließlich seine Pforten schließen – nur wenige Jahre vor der sowjetischen Machtübernahme in Afghanistan.

D**ie Versendung von Lebenszeichen aus der Fremde in Form von Briefen oder Postkarten ist eng verknüpft mit der Kulturgeschichte des Reisens.** Sie fungierten als touristische Statusmeldungen lange bevor dieses Vokabular von Social-Media-Plattformen aufgegriffen wurde. Und die Hotelindustrie ist seit jeher bestens darauf eingestellt: Postkarten sind oft in den Eingangshallen zu erwerben, jedes größere oder namhafte Hotel bietet sogar eigenes Briefpapier auf jedem Zimmer, stets mit dem Logo des Hauses versehen. Niedergeschriebene Nachrichten können direkt an der Rezeption abgegeben werden, um auf schnellstem Wege in die Heimat oder voraus in die Ferne geschickt zu werden. Oft geht es in diesen Mitteilungen nicht so sehr um anspruchsvolle Inhalte, sondern eher um eine Geste der Aufmerksamkeit, der Wertschätzung. Diese touristische Kulturtechnik des Sich-und-andere-Vergewisserns nutzt On Kawara, ein nomadischer Künstler par excellence, für ein Projekt, das er 1968 beginnt und bis 1979 ohne Unterbrechung fortführt: Täglich versendet er zwei Bildpostkarten seines jeweiligen Aufenthaltsortes an Freunde und Bekannte, versehen mit der Adresse sowie dem Aufdruck »I got up at« und der genauen Zeitangabe des Momentes, an dem er am jeweiligen Tag aufgestanden ist. (Abb. S. 170–171) Er konzeptualisiert eine alltägliche Handlung – den Moment des Erwachens, die Aufnahme geistiger Aktivität – und agiert somit im Grenzbereich zwischen subjektivem und objektivierendem Handeln. Er greift zudem die direkten Wechselverbindungen zwischen Ort und Werk aufgrund der spezifischen Produktionsbedingungen des nomadischen Künstlerlebens auf: Ausgehend von seinem Lebenswandel in diesen Jahren finden sich unzählige Adressen von Hotels auf den Karten, die als Markierungen in einer

12 Allen Ruppersberg, in »Interview mit Frédéric Paul« in: *Allen Ruppersberg: Books, Inc.* Ausst.-Kat. FRAC Limousin, Limoges 1999, S. 47, zit. nach: Goldstein 2006 (wie Anm. 11), S. 37.

13 Annemarie Sauzeau, *Alighiero Boetti's One Hotel,* aus der Reihe *100 Notizen – 100 Gedanken* zur *dOCUMENTA 13),* No. 025, Ostfildern 2012, S. 21 f.

14 Ebd., S. 19.

15 See Paolo Bianchi, »K. reist ...,« *Atlas der Künstlerreisen*, ed. Paolo Bianchi, *Kunstforum International* 137 (1997), 50.

16 Diedrich Diederichsen, »Das Prinzip der Verstrickung: Kippenberger und seine Rezeptionen,« *Texte zur Kunst* 26 (June 1997), 75–83.

17 Allan Kaprow, »The Artist as a Man of the World,« (1964) in: *Allan Kaprow: Essays on the Blurring of Art and Life*, ed. Jeff Kelley (Berkeley, 1993), 58.

a playing field of relations between rule and chance. Envelopes, letters, and the address stamps of One Hotel serve as basic elements for graphic and numeric permutations that are combined like mathematical sequences on letter envelopes and sent on a journey through the postal system. Here Boetti often works with non-existing recipient addresses, leaving it to chance whether or not the missives find their way back to their sender at One Hotel. In 1977, just a few years before the Soviet invasion, the hotel had to close its doors due to the increasingly dramatic political and economic situation of the country.

Sending signs of life from abroad in the form of letters or postcards is closely linked to the cultural history of travel. They served as tourist status reports long before this vocabulary was taken up by social media platforms. And the hotel industry has since adapted to this. Postcards can often be acquired in the entrance foyers, and all large or prominent hotels offer their own notepaper in each room, always featuring the logo of the hotel in question. Reports written can be given to the reception directly, to be sent home or ahead abroad as soon as possible. Often, these messages are less about profound content and more about a gesture of attention, of value. On Kawara, nomadic artist par excellence, used this touristic cultural technique of reassuring oneself and others for a project that he began in 1968 and continued without interruption until 1979. Each day he sent two picture postcards from the place where he was staying to friends and acquaintances, featuring the address and a stamped »I got up at,« with the precise time when got out of bed on the day in question (fig. pp. 170–171). He conceptualized an everyday act, the moment of waking up, the start of intellectual activity, and thus intervened in the realm between subjective and objectivizing action. He also takes up the direct mutual linkages between the location and the work based on the specific conditions of production of the nomadic artist life. Based on his lifestyle in these years, countless addresses of hotels on the cards serve as markings in the artist's individualized global topography. Fleeting fragments of Kawara's personal life are translated into a permanently materialized form and recorded; the descriptions printed with rubber stamps stand in a direct relationship to his person, the respective location as well as the recipient. The recipient receives the postcard as part of a serial artwork, and yet in On Kawara's selection there is certainly a social valuation—similar to the function of postcards sent from a vacation.

Martin Kippenberger in turn took the act of self-reassurance and location as an occasion to playfully subvert this gesture. The artist, who also travelled frequently, explores his role as a guest by using hotel stationary for sketches, project ideas, or as a medium for small-format artworks. He plays consciously with the suggestion that he resided in the hotels in question at the time when these works were made—something that was seldom the case (fig. pp. 182–185). Unlike On Kawara or Hans-Peter Feldmann, who since 1975 documented usually banal views from his hotel rooms in photographs (fig. pp. 174–175), with his hotel drawings Klippenberger created a fictional auto-geograph,[15] which would only lead to failure if used to track his (supposed) stays. He makes this play with references, following the »principle of entangling«[16] art and life, into his trademark, and plays with the new type of artist that Allan Kaprow described in his 1964 essay »The Artist as a Man of the World.« According to Kaprow, the artist no longer moves on the margins but increasingly in the midst of society and is forced to adjust to the social practices of competition and attention. Furthermore, he increasingly makes his private life public and finds inspiration in his experiences as a wanderer, a beggar, a dandy, or a tourist.[17] Art is thus understood as an inherent part of society, and since the early 1960s it developed into an increasingly pluralistic concept of creativity and artistry, as also became clear in artistic approaches to the hotel. As a location, structure, and theme, it offered numerous points of departure, since it contained the overarching, globalized idea of professional hospitality as well as the cultural shaping of a specific location, always in close relationship to the various life models of the society to which it belonged. It is no accident that as early as 1927 in his book *The Mass Ornament,* Siegfried Kracauer compared the hotel hall with a church space and thus emphasized the relevance of this special kind of temple of his time, an attribution that has hardly lost any of its validity today.

individualisierten globalen Topografie des Künstlers fungieren. Flüchtige Fragmente des persönlichen Lebens Kawaras werden in eine dauerhaft materialisierte Form übersetzt und festgehalten – die mit Gummistempeln aufgedruckten Beschreibungen stehen in direkter Beziehung zu seiner Person, dem jeweiligen Ort als auch dem Empfänger. Dieser erhält die Postkarte zwar als Teil eines seriellen Kunstwerks, in On Kawaras Auswahl liegt jedoch durchaus eine soziale Wertung – ähnlich der Funktion von Postkarten, die aus dem Urlaub verschickt werden.

Den Akt der Selbstvergewisserung und Verortung nimmt Martin Kippenberger wiederum zum Anlass, diesen spielerisch zu unterlaufen. Der ebenfalls vielreisende Künstler thematisiert seine Rolle als Gast durch die Nutzung von Hotelbriefbögen für Skizzen, Projektideen oder als Bildgrund für kleinformatige Kunstwerke. Er spielt bewusst mit der Suggestion, in den jeweiligen Hotels zur Zeit der Entstehung dieser Arbeiten residiert zu haben – was wiederum kaum je der Fall war (Abb. S. 182–185). Anders als bei On Kawara oder auch Hans-Peter Feldmann, der seit 1975 meist profane Blicke aus seinen Hotelzimmern fotografisch dokumentiert (Abb. S. 174–175), erstellt Kippenberger mit seinen Hotelzeichnungen eine vor allem fiktive Autogeografie[15], anhand derer der Nachvollzug seiner (vermeintlichen) Aufenthaltsorte scheitern muss. Er erhebt das Spiel mit Verweisen nach dem »Prinzip der Verstrickung«[16] von Kunst und Leben zu seinem Markenzeichen und spielt mit dem neuen Künstlertypus, den Allan Kaprow 1964 in seinem Essay »The Artist as a Man of the World« beschreibt: Demnach bewege der Künstler sich nicht mehr am Rande, sondern zunehmend in der Mitte der Gesellschaft und sei gezwungen, sich auf die gesellschaftlichen Usancen des Wettbewerbs um Aufmerksamkeit einzustellen. Er stelle ferner sein Privatleben zunehmend zur öffentlichen Disposition und finde seine Inspiration in der unmittelbaren Selbsterfahrung als Wanderer, Bettler, Dandy oder Tourist.[17] Kunst wird hier begriffen als inhärenter Teil der Gesellschaft und entwickelt sich seit den frühen 1960er-Jahren zu einem zunehmend pluralistischen Begriff von Kreativität und Künstlertum, was auch an den exemplifizierten künstlerischen Umgangsformen mit dem Gegenstand Hotel deutlich wird. Als Schauplatz, Struktur und Thema bietet es zahlreiche Anknüpfungspunkte, da es sowohl die übergeordnete, globalisierte Idee von professioneller Hospitalität in sich trägt, als auch die kulturelle Prägung eines spezifischen Ortes – stets in enger Beziehung zu den unterschiedlichen Lebensentwürfen einer Gesellschaft, deren Teil es ist. Nicht von ungefähr hat Siegfried Kracauer bereits 1927 in seinem Buch *Ornament der Masse* die Hotelhalle mit einem Kirchenraum verglichen und damit die Relevanz dieser besonderen Art des Tempels seiner Zeit herausgestellt. Eine Zuschreibung, die bis auf den heutigen Tag kaum an Gültigkeit eingebüßt hat.

15 Vgl. Paolo Bianchi, »K. reist …«, in: *Atlas der Künstlerreisen*, hrsg. von Paolo Bianchi, *KUNSTFORUM International*, Bd. 137, Ruppichteroth 1997, S. 49–53, hier S. 50.

16 Diedrich Diederichsen, »Das Prinzip der Verstrickung. Kippenberger und seine Rezeptionen«, in: *Texte zur Kunst*, Nr. 26: *Alte Schule*, Juni 1997, S. 75–83.

17 Allan Kaprow, »The Artist as a Man of the World. (1964)«, in: *Allan Kaprow, Essays on the blurring of art and life*, hrsg. von Jeff Kelley, Berkeley / Los Angeles / London 1993, S. 46–58, hier S. 58.

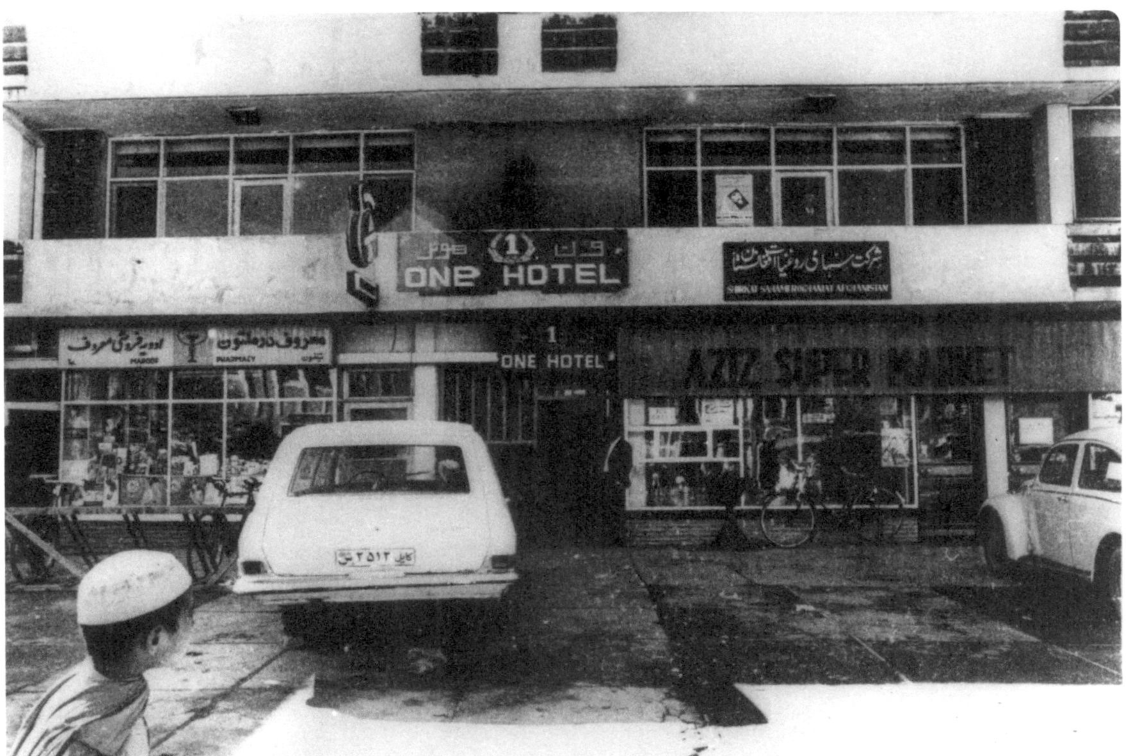

Abb. / Fig. 4 ALIGHIERO BOETTI **ONE HOTEL** © VG Bild-Kunst, Bonn 2014

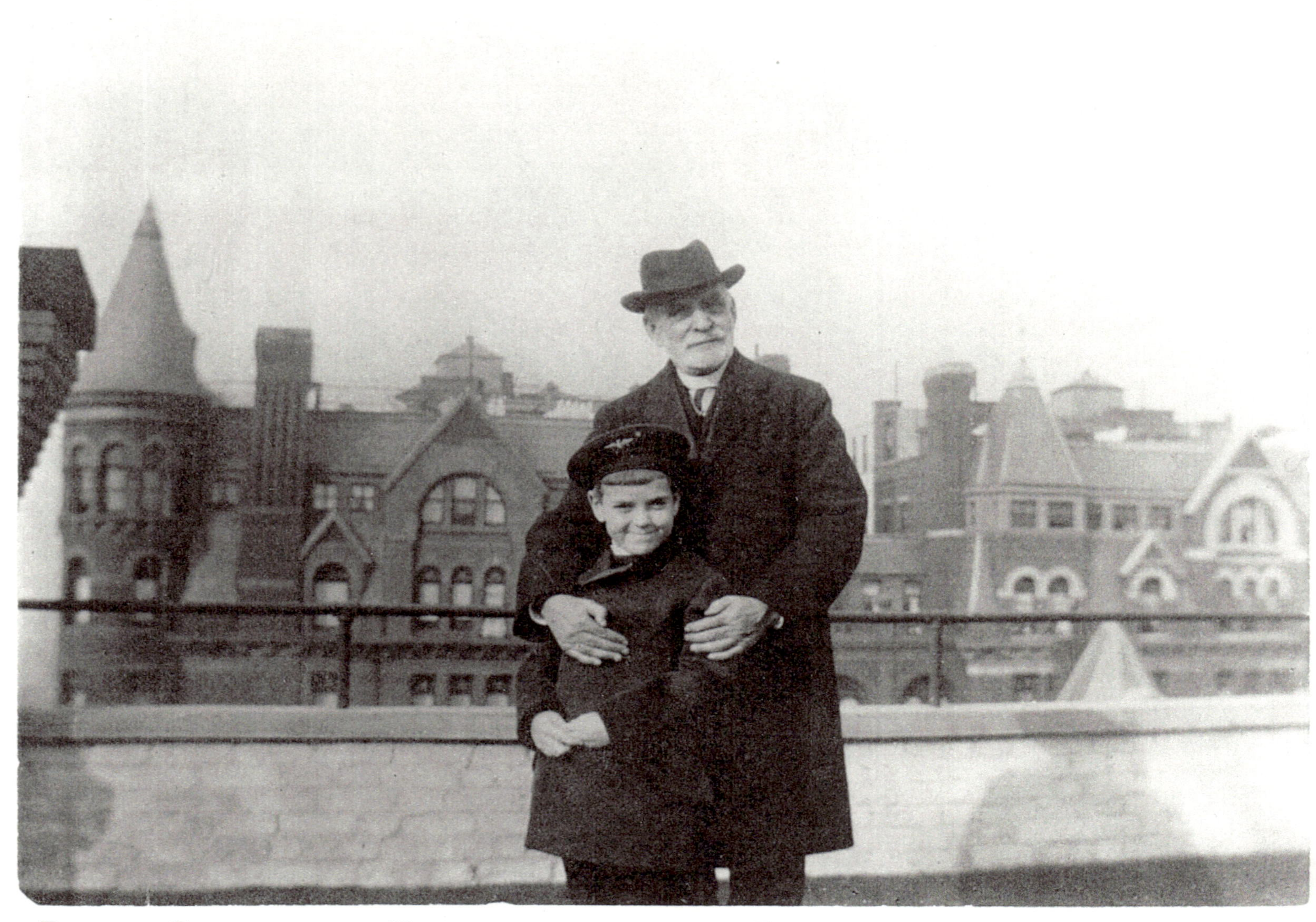

PHILIP GENGEMBRE HUBERT MIT SEINEM ENKEL LOUIS HENRY FROHMAN
PHILIP GENGEMBRE HUBERT WITH HIS GRANDSON LOUIS HENRY FROHMAN

© Philip G. Hubert Archives, Cornelia Frohman Santomenna

DAS CHELSEA HOTEL

NEW YORKS ÄLTESTER KREATIVER NEXUS

SHERILL TIPPINS

WAS IST ES, DASS SO VIELE KÜNSTLER AN HOTELS ANZIEHT? Wie kann ein vorübergehender Aufenthalt die Kreativität anregen und, auf lange Sicht, ein kreatives Leben ermöglichen? Ganz gewiss kann man Inspiration in den nur angedeuteten Geheimnissen im Blick eines Fremden finden oder in der Fähigkeit, die Vergangenheit abzulegen und eine neue Rolle anzunehmen. Aber kann die Architektur eines Hotels selbst dazu beitragen, die Fantasie von Künstlern zu beflügeln?

Philip Gengembre Hubert, ein französischer Emigrant, der jenes Gebäude entwarf, welches später das New Yorker Chelsea Hotel werden sollte, beabsichtigte ganz sicher nicht, ein Zuhause speziell für Künstler zu schaffen, aber er hatte durchaus das Ziel, das kreative Leben mitten im *Goldenen Zeitalter* dieser – seiner – Stadt zu unterstützen. Huberts Vater, Colomb Gengembre, ebenfalls Architekt und Adept des utopischen Philosophen Charles Fourier, hatte einst die erste Fourieristische Gemeinschaft in Frankreich entworfen. Daher war Hubert von Kindesbeinen an mit Fouriers Traum einer Gesellschaft vertraut, die so strukturiert sein sollte, dass sie individuelle Leidenschaften fördert und sich jede menschliche *Stimme* stark und wahrhaftig mit anderen verbindet, um eine Sinfonie kreativen Ausdrucks zu erschaffen. Als 1848 ein Aufstand die Fourieristen dazu zwang aus Frankreich in die Vereinigten Staaten von Amerika zu fliehen, betrachteten sie New York City als den idealen Boden, um ihre Saat utopischen Denkens auszubringen. Philip Hubert war selbst ein Künstler – Maler und Schriftsteller –, aber praktischer veranlagt als sein idealistischer Vater. Fouriers Idee von *Struktur* war für ihn reizvoller als dessen Traum eines irdischen Paradieses. Wie ermöglicht man kreativen Austausch innerhalb einer Gesellschaft, fragte sich Hubert – und insbesondere in der Gesellschaft einer atomisierten, hoffnungslos provinziellen und unbezahlbaren Stadt, die wild entschlossen war, die nächste Hauptstadt der Welt zu werden?

Seine Antwort: Man muss die Menschen zusammenbringen. In diesem Sinne präsentierte Hubert 1880 seinen Entwurf für eine ganz neue Art von Wohnbauten, die er *Hubert's Home Clubs* nannte – gewaltige, genossenschaftliche Wohnhäuser, deren größenbedingter Kostenvorteil die Baukosten senken und deren Dimensionen den New Yorkern zu einem interessanteren Leben verhelfen würde. Obgleich die Amerikaner den sozialistischen Implikationen von Hubert's Home Clubs sehr misstrauisch begegneten, erwies sich ihr Einsparpotenzial als unwiderstehlich und schon bald entstanden in der ganzen Stadt derartige Genossenschaften. Aber Hubert war unzufrieden, denn die Home Clubs spalteten sich entlang ökonomischer Klassen auf.

Das Chelsea Association Building, Huberts Home Club von 1884, war ein verbesserter Entwurf. Im Herzen des Theaterbezirks sollte dieses Gebäude Bewohner anziehen, die Lust auf Abenteuer hatten. Eine bequeme Lobby, eine zentrale Küche, Gemeinschaftsspeisesäle sowie Dachgärten und Räume für Aufführungen luden die Bewohner dazu ein, miteinander in Kontakt zu kommen. Mit den vorhandenen Zwölf-Zimmer-Wohnungen neben kleinen, preiswerten Apartments in jedem Stockwerk wurde das Chelsea Association Building das erste New Yorker Wohnhaus, in dem

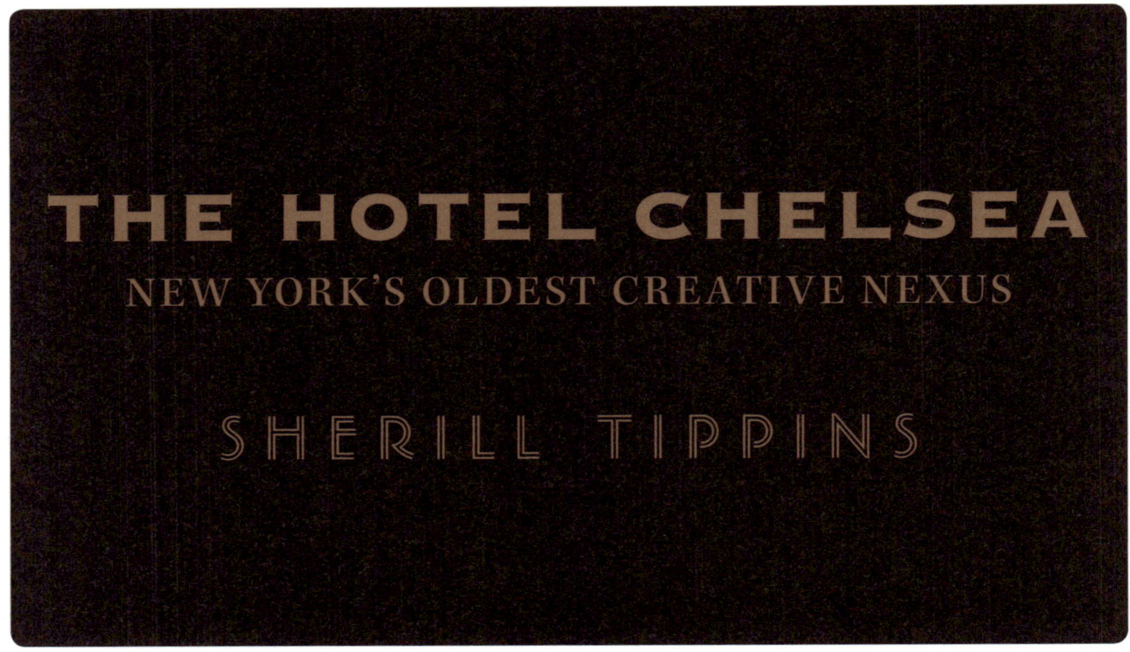

THE HOTEL CHELSEA

NEW YORK'S OLDEST CREATIVE NEXUS

SHERILL TIPPINS

WHAT IS IT ABOUT HOTELS THAT ATTRACTS SO MANY ARTISTS? How does a transient residence stimulate creativity and, over the long term, facilitate a creative life? Certainly one can find inspiration in the secrets implied by a stranger's gaze and in an ability to shed the past and assume a new persona. But can a hotel's physical design help drive artists' imaginations?

Philip Gengembre Hubert, the French émigré who designed the building that later became New York's Chelsea Hotel, did not intend to create a home specifically for artists, but he was intent on facilitating creative life in the midst of that city's Gilded Age. Hubert's father, Colomb Gengembre, an architect and follower of the utopian philosopher Charles Fourier, had designed the first Fourierist community in France. As a result, Hubert had been schooled from infancy in Fourier's dream of a society structured to facilitate individual passions, so that each human »voice,« ringing powerful and true, would combine with others to create a symphony of creative expression. When the 1848 uprising forced the Fourierists to flee France for the United States, they saw New York City as the perfect ground for planting their seeds of utopian thought.

Philip Hubert was an artist—a painter and a writer—but more practical than his idealist father. Fourier's *structure* appealed to him more than the philosopher's dreams of an earthly paradise. How does one facilitate creative interaction in any society, Hubert wondered—particularly in a socially atomized, hopelessly provincial, and unaffordable city determined to become the next capital of the world? His answer: bring people together. In 1880 Hubert presented his design for a new kind of housing that he called *Hubert's Home Clubs*—large, cooperative residences whose economy of scale would lower construction costs and whose size would push New Yorkers toward a more stimulating life. Leery as Americans were of the socialist implications of Hubert's Home Clubs, the savings proved irresistible, and cooperatives soon sprang up throughout the city. Still, Hubert remained unsatisfied as the Home Clubs continued to self-segregate by economic class.

The Chelsea Association Building, Hubert's 1884 Home Club, was a corrective design. Located in the heart of New York's theater district, it would attract residents of an adventurous frame of mind. A comfortable lobby, a central kitchen and shared dining rooms, and roof gardens and performance spaces invited residents to mingle. And with twelve-room flats placed beside small, inexpensive apartments on each floor, the Chelsea Association Building became the first residence where New Yorkers of significantly different economic classes lived side by side. Following Fourier's dictates, Hubert selected from a wealth of Home Club applicants a core population of practical individuals—the contractors who built the Chelsea and the men of finance who would oversee its business affairs. The young artists occupying the fifteen top-floor art studios as well as the writers and musicians in the soundproof apartments below would see to the community's *spiritual needs.*

The Chelsea thus began as a residential cooperative—but its social diversity gave it the feel of a grand hotel

Menschen aus vollkommen unterschiedlichen ökonomischen Klassen nebeneinander lebten. In Anlehnung an das Diktat Fouriers wählte Hubert aus den vielen Bewerbern eine Kerngruppe von zukünftigen Bewohnern mit vor allem praktischen Fähigkeiten aus – einerseits jene, die das Chelsea bauten, und daneben Finanzfachleute, die das Geschäftliche erledigen konnten. Die jungen Künstler, die die fünfzehn Ateliers im obersten Stockwerk bezogen, wie auch die Schriftsteller und Musiker in den schallisolierten Wohnungen darunter, sollten sich um die *geistigen Bedürfnisse* der Gemeinschaft kümmern. Das Chelsea begann also als Wohnungsgenossenschaft, doch seine soziale Vielfalt verlieh ihm von Anfang an etwas von einem Grand Hotel. Schon der große US-amerikanische Romancier William Dean Howells konstatierte die bemerkenswerte Atmosphäre des Hauses, als er und seine Frau 1888 dort wohnten. Das lebendige und offene Klima erinnerte ihn an *Looking Backward 1887–2000,* den neuen Roman eines seiner Protegés, Edward Bellamy (unter dem deutschen Titel *Rückblick aus dem Jahre 2000 auf das Jahr 1887* erschienen). Dieser erzählt von einem jungen Mann, der im Boston des 19. Jahrhunderts einschläft und in einer utopischen Metropole des 20. Jahrhunderts wieder aufwacht. Mit seinem täglichen Betrieb von Geschäftsleuten, die mit Theatervolk und Schriftstellern Umgang pflegten, war das Chelsea, als wäre *Looking Backward* wahr geworden.

Vor allem waren es die jungen Künstler im Chelsea, die William Dean Howells am meisten faszinierten. Vom Beginn des Home Clubs an hatten seine lichtdurchfluteten Ateliers eine Gruppe von tonalistischen Malern angezogen, die fest entschlossen waren, einen Ort für die US-amerikanische Kunst zu etablieren. Dies war durchaus ein schwerer Kampf: John Francis Murphy, der Sohn eines Farmers, verkaufte nur ein oder zwei Gemälde pro Jahr an eurozentrische Sammler; Charles Melville Dewey lebte vor allem vom Lehrgeld seiner Schüler. Howells bewunderte sowohl ihren Ehrgeiz als auch ihre nebligen Landschaften, obwohl er sich wünschte, sie würden viel mehr das urbane Leben um sie herum malen. Er selbst war fest davon überzeugt, dass die amerikanischen Menschen das beste Rohmaterial für eine spezifisch amerikanische Kunst seien.

1892 gewann Howells einen starken Verbündeten, als der Komponist Antonin Dvořák nach New York kam, um das neue National Conservatory of Music of America zu leiten. Fasziniert von der Metropole drängte Dvořák seine Studenten dazu, die »Stimmen der Menschen« der Stadt in ihre Musik zu integrieren – die pfeifenden Jungs, die Drehorgelspieler, ganz gleichgültig, wie »unbedeutend« oder »niedrig« diese Quellen auch sein mochten. Seine Begeisterung verzehnfachte sich noch, nachdem er den afroamerikanischen Bariton Henry »Harry« Thacker Burleigh hörte, wie dieser das Spiritual *Let My People Go* sang. Dvořák erklärte, genau hier sei das Material, aus dem sich ein amerikanischer Kanon bilden ließe – was er mit seiner eigenen Sinfonie *Aus der neuen Welt* unter Beweis stellte.

Im Chelsea bemühte sich Dvořáks hochgeschätzte Schülerin Laura Sedgwick Collins eine *Musik des Volkes* zu komponieren, aber als Angehörige der weißen New Yorker Mittelschicht wusste sie herzlich wenig über die Lieder der afroamerikanischen *Sharecropper* (Landpächter). Es war klar, dass das Chelsea noch eine sehr vielschichtigere Mischung an Bewohnern brauchte, damit seine Künstler der Bevölkerung vor der Tür eine authentische Stimme würden verleihen können. Man könnte es fast als Vorsehung betrachten, dass eine weitere massive Rezession zur Jahrhundertwende die Stadt erfasste, die schließlich zum Bankrott des Chelsea Buildings, aber damit zur Gründung des Chelsea Hotels führte.

Schon seit ihren Anfängen ist die Stadt New York für ihre Fähigkeit bekannt, ihre Vergangenheit enorm schnell zu vergessen. Und tatsächlich: Auch im Chelsea Hotel war bereits in den 1920er-Jahren jede Erinnerung an die Utopisten, die tonalistischen Maler und *Volkskomponisten* der ursprünglichen Chelsea Association des 19. Jahrhunderts verblasst. Aber die Patina dieser Erfahrung sollte dennoch über ein weiteres Jahrhundert lang ohne Unterlass ungewöhnliche und intuitive Menschen anziehen.

Für den Schriftsteller Sherwood Anderson zeugten die labyrinthartigen Korridore des Hotels, die Gerüche, die in seinen Fluren hingen, die Musik und das Gelächter, die im Treppenhaus widerhallten, von einem komplexen Gewebe aus Impulsen und Begehren, das auch seine berühmte Erzählsammlung *Winesburg, Ohio* prägte. Wenn er von seinem Balkon aus die Packard- und Pierce-Arrow-Automobile betrachtete, die auf der West 23rd Street entlangfuhren, dann schätzte Anderson das Chelsea als ein beruhigendes Gegengift zum ungezügelten Kommerz der Stadt. Innerhalb seiner Mauern wurde man an die wirklich wichtigen Dinge erinnert: freundliche Nachbarn, Respekt für die Privatsphäre und niedrige Mieten, die ein produktives Leben ermöglichten. Doch als Hotel erwarb sich das Chelsea auch noch eine ganz andere Art von Geschichte: Der Horror des Selbstmords von Etelka Graf etwa, der Frau eines Konzertpianisten, die sich nur kurz vor Andersons Ankunft ihre eigene Hand abschlug (die schließlich von ihrer Tochter gefunden wurde) und dann aus dem Fenster sprang; die Überdosis von Miss Almyra Wilcox, deren Leiche man neben einem angefangenen Liebesbrief fand, oder der Tod des Künstlers

from the very beginning. The great novelist William Dean Howells took note of its curious ambience, when he and his wife lived there in 1888. The lively, open atmosphere called to mind *Looking Backward,* a new novel by one of Howells's protégés, Edward Bellamy, which told of a young man who falls asleep in 19th-century Boston and wakes up in a utopian 20th-century metropolis. With its bustle of businessmen mixing with theater professionals and writers, the Chelsea was like *Looking Backward* come true.

But it was the young artists at the Chelsea who most fascinated William Dean Howells. From the Home Club's inception, its light-flooded studios had attracted a coterie of tonalist painters determined to stake out a place for American art. The struggle was a grim one: John Francis Murphy, a farmer's son, sold only one or two paintings per year to Eurocentric collectors; Charles Melville Dewey subsisted on students' fees. Howells admired their ambition—and their misty rural landscapes—

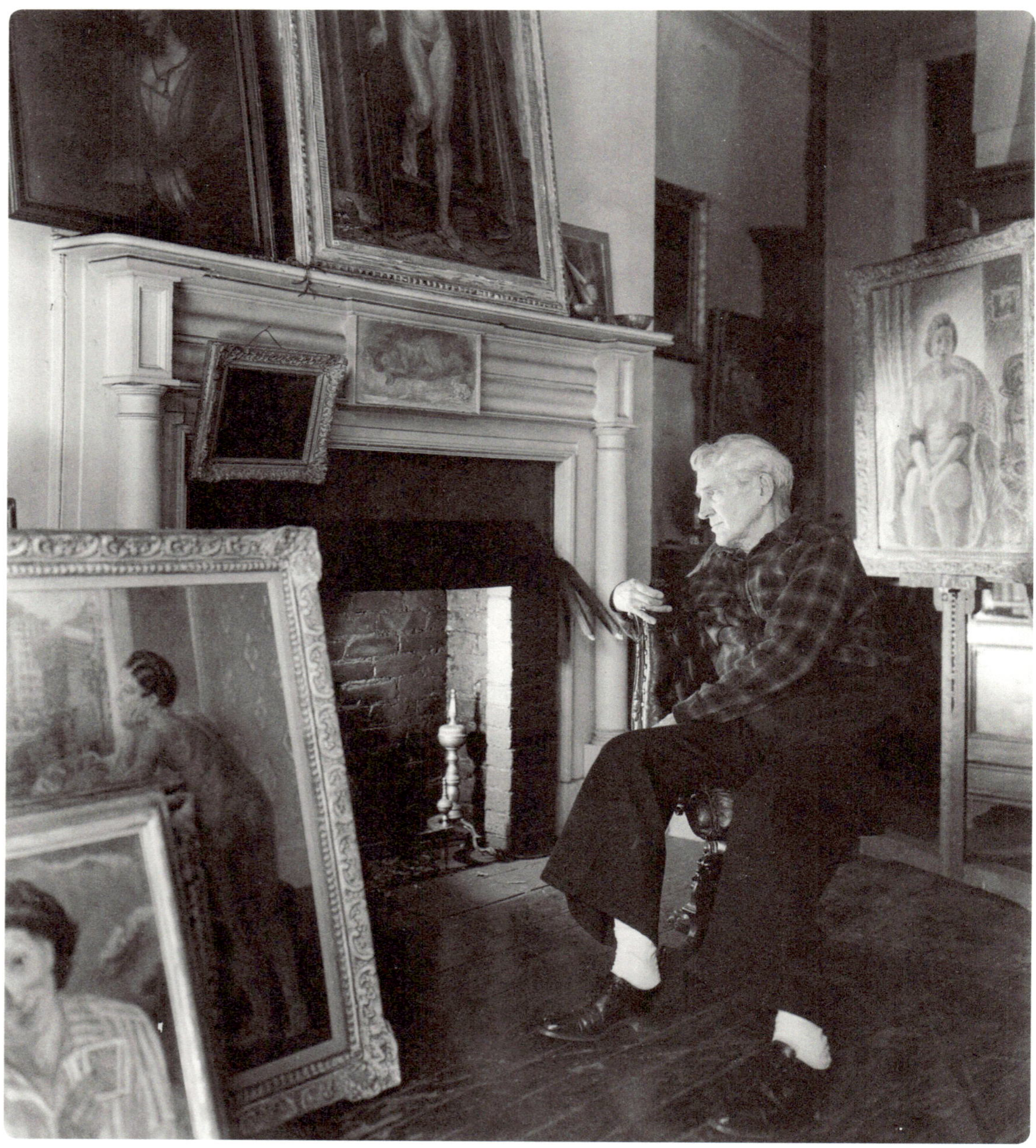

BERENICE ABBOTT JOHN SLOAN IN SEINEM CHELSEA-ATELIER
JOHN SLOAN IN HIS CHELSEA STUDIO

1948, John Sloan Manuscript Collection, Delaware Art Museum, Willmington, Schenkung von / Gift of Helen Farr Sloan, 1978, © Berenice Abbott/Commere Graphics

Frank Kavecky, der eines Tages ins Hotel eincheckte und sich dann in seinem Zimmer eine Kugel in den Kopf jagte.

ES war wohl diese eher groteske Geschichte des Hauses, dieses Gefühl, dass es dort eine geheime Vergangenheit gab, auf die der Künstler Arthur B. Davies reagierte, als er fünf Jahre später im Chelsea ankam – vielleicht auch deshalb, weil er so seine eigenen Geheimnisse hatte. Dieser symbolistische Maler, heute vor allem bekannt als Hauptorganisator der New Yorker ARMORY SHOW von 1913, wurde maßgeblich von seiner Frau, einer Ärztin, finanziert, die sich auf dem Lande um ihre Familie kümmerte, während er schon lange in der Stadt eine geheime zweite Ehe mit seinem Lieblingsmodell, einer rothaarigen Tänzerin namens Edna Potter, führte. Nachdem aus dieser Verbindung ein Baby auf die Welt gekommen war, wurde es Davies allerdings zu anstrengend, seine zweite Familie zu verstecken, weshalb er sie 1926 nach Europa schickte, aus den Augen der New Yorker Öffentlichkeit. Er bezog dann ein Eckatelier im obersten Stock des Chelsea, füllte es mit Arbeiten von Picasso, Cézanne und Seurat, und inmitten all dieser Schätze stellte er eine Staffelei auf, um Ednas Nachfolgerin zu malen, eine geschmeidige junge Sängerin namens Wreath.

Abigail Aldrich (»Abby«) Rockefeller und Lizzie P. Bliss, die Mäzeninnen, die bereits die ARMORY SHOW unterstützt hatten und von denen Davies immer noch abhing, fanden diese ganze Szenerie unwiderstehlich. Wenn sie mit dem quietschenden Aufzug in Davies' Atelier fuhren, fühlten sie sich, als würden sie hinter einen künstlerischen Schleier treten. Hier erklärte ihnen ihr gut aussehender Gastgeber Picabia, Man Ray und Duchamp und versetzte sie so in die Lage, sich als Kunstspekulantinnen hervorzutun, während ihre Männer in ihren Kreisen mit Öl und Stahl Imperien erschufen. »Ohne das Selbstvertrauen, das mir seine Zustimmung gab«, schrieb Abby Rockefeller später, »hätte ich mich nie in die Welt der modernen Kunst getraut.«

Leider war diese idyllische Situation nicht von langer Dauer. Davies starb 1928 und sein Doppelleben wurde offenbart. Während hingegen seine Ehefrau noch mit der Existenz der Geliebten Edna Potter zu kämpfen hatte, brüteten Rockefeller und Bliss bereits einen neuen ehrgeizigen Plan aus: Zum Gedenken an Davies wollten sie ein Museum für moderne Kunst in New York gründen. Aber im Oktober 1929, nur zwei Wochen vor der ersten Ausstellung des angedachten Museums of Modern Art, beendete der große Börsenkrach das ambitionierte Vorhaben – und brachte den Anfang von etwas Neuem.

Die Weltwirtschaftskrise bescherte dem Chelsea Hotel aber noch weitere Schwierigkeiten. Die ursprünglichen Wohnungen wurden nun in kleine Einheiten unterteilt, die man preiswert für eine Nacht oder einen Monat mieten konnte. Problematisch daran war, dass für die Kulturschaffenden, die das Hotel in wachsender Zahl anzog, die 1930er-Jahre eine Blütezeit der Produktivität darstellten. »Ich kann gar nicht sagen, wie *reich* alle waren«, erinnert sich ein Künstler an die Zeit, als die sogenannte Works Progress Administration, die Arbeitsbeschaffungsbehörde der USA, wöchentlich Stipendien an Menschen vergab, die überall im Land in Theatern, Ateliers, Varietétheatern und an Schreibmaschinen arbeiteten. So komponierte im Chelsea Virgil Thomson die Musik für den nur mit schwarzen Schauspielern besetzten Streifen *Macbeth* des *Wunderkind*-Regisseurs George Orson Wells, hier lehrte er Paul Bowles, schrieb die atemberaubende Musik für die Dokumentarfilme über die Dust Bowl genannten Staubstürme und war Gastgeber eines Salons, der zu einer nachhaltigen Wandlung der amerikanischen Musikkultur beitrug.

Der auf das Wesentliche fokussierende New Yorker Maler John French Sloan und der Dichter Edgar Lee Masters, berühmt geworden durch seine *Spoon River Anthology*, sollten während dieser Zeit ebenfalls den Weg ins Chelsea Hotel finden. Masters überredete den jüngeren Schriftsteller Thomas Clayton Wolfe dort 1937 eine Ecksuite zu mieten, als jener unter großem Druck stand, einen neuen Roman zu schreiben, der seinem *Of Time and the River* ebenbürtig sein würde. Er schaffte zwei Kisten halb fertiger Manuskripte in seine neue Bleibe und arbeitet dort jede Nacht an dem großen runden Tisch, fest entschlossen, irgendwie seinem Gefühl Ausdruck zu verleihen, dass sich das amerikanische Volk in der Herrlichkeit des wirtschaftlichen Aufschwungs der 1920er-Jahre und dem schrecklichen Zusammenbruch, der darauf gefolgt war, verirrt hatte. Im Verlauf der Monate gewöhnten sich Wolfes Nachbarn an den Klang seiner tiefen Stimme mit Südstaatenakzent, die stets im Flur zu hören war, wenn er sich seine geschriebenen Worte laut vorlas. Gelegentlich lud Edgar Lee Masters den Schriftsteller auch auf einen abendlichen Drink zu sich ein. Er fand es faszinierend, Wolfe zuzusehen, wie dieser auf und ab ging und aus dem Gedächtnis Szenen nachspielte. Dieser Mann schien ihm eine Naturgewalt zu sein, »besoffen von Worten und Gedanken, und vom Leben elektrisiert«.

Im Mai 1938, als die Sommerhitze bereits so stark war, dass Wolfe sicher war, er könne »alle sieben Millionen Bewohner von New York riechen«, ergriff er die Gelegenheit, an die Westküste zu reisen. Er übergab das Manuskript seinem Lektor – überzeugt, eine Geschichte geschrieben zu haben, die als »eine Art Legende« über Amerika gelten würde – und rannte los, um seinen Zug noch zu bekommen.

but he wished they would apply themselves to recording the city life around them. The American people were the best raw material for American art, Howells believed.

In 1892, Howells gained a powerful ally when the composer Antonin Dvořák arrived to direct the new National Conservatory of Music. Dazzled by New York, Dvořák urged his students to integrate into their music the city's »voice of the people«—the whistling boys, the organ grinders—no matter how »low« or »insignificant« the source. His excitement expanded tenfold after hearing the African-American baritone Harry Thacker Burleigh sing *Let My People Go.* Here was the material from which to create an American canon, Dvořák proclaimed—as he demonstrated by his own *New World Symphony.*

At the Chelsea, Dvořák's prized pupil Laura Sedgwick Collins struggled to produce an American *music of the people,* but as a white, middle-class New Yorker she knew little about the songs of African-American sharecroppers. It was clear that the Chelsea required an even more diverse population, if its artists were to give voice to the life outside its doors. It could almost be described as Providence, when another massive recession washed over the city at the turn of the century, bankrupting the Chelsea and leading to the creation of the Chelsea Hotel.

From the beginning, New York has been known for an ability to forget its past with extraordinary speed. At the Hotel Chelsea, all memory of the Chelsea Association's 19th-century utopians, tonalist painters, and *people's* composers had faded by the 1920s. Yet a patina of that experience would continue to attract the intuitive and the curious for a century to come.

For the writer Sherwood Anderson, the hotel's labyrinthine passageways, its lingering odors, the music and laughter sifting down the stairwell spoke to the intricate mesh of impulses and desires that had informed his acclaimed *Winesburg, Ohio.* Gazing down from his balcony at the Packards and Pierce-Arrows cruising along West 23rd Street, Anderson cherished the Chelsea as a reassuring antidote to the city's rampant commercialism. Within its confines, one was reminded of the things that mattered: friendly neighbors, respect for privacy, and rents low enough to allow for a productive life. Yet, as a hotel, the Chelsea was acquiring another kind of history as well: the horror, shortly before Anderson's arrival, of the suicide of a concert pianist's wife named Etelka Graf, who cut off her own hand, left it for her daughter to find, and leaped out her window; the overdose of Miss Almyra Wilcox, found dead with an unfinished love letter beside her; and the demise of the artist Frank Kavecky, who checked into a room one day and shot himself in the head.

IT was this more grotesque history, this sense of a secret past, to which the artist Arthur B. Davies responded upon his arrival at the Chelsea five years later—perhaps because he had secrets of his own. This Symbolist painter, best known as the principle organizer of the 1913 New York ARMORY SHOW, was supported by a physician wife who tended their family in upstate New York, but he had long maintained a clandestine second marriage in the city with his favorite model, a red-haired dancer named Edna Potter. After a baby was born, Davies had found the strain of hiding his second family burdensome, and in 1926 he moved them to Europe, out of sight. Taking a corner studio on the Chelsea's top floor, he filled it with works by Picasso, Cézanne, and Seurat, and in the midst of these treasures set up an easel on which to paint Edna's replacement, a lithesome young singer named Wreath.

Abby Rockefeller and Lizzie Bliss, the patronesses who had backed the ARMORY SHOW and on whom Davies still depended, found the setting irresistible. Riding the creaky elevator up to Davies' studio, they felt as if they were being ushered behind an artistic veil. Here, their handsome host tutored them on Picabia, Man Ray, and Duchamp, enabling them to make their mark as art speculators, as the men of their set were creating empires from oil and steel. »Without the confidence which his approval gave me,« Abby Rockefeller wrote, »I should never have dared venture into the field of modern art.«

Sadly, this idyllic situation did not last long. Davies died in 1928, and his double life was revealed. As his first wife struggled with the news of Edna Potter's existence, Rockefeller and Bliss hatched an ambitious plan: to memorialize Davies by creating a museum of modern art in New York. But in October 1929, two weeks before the Museum of Modern Art's first show, the stock market crash brought an end to the era of the museum's birth and the beginning of something new.

The Great Depression brought more hardship to the Hotel Chelsea. The original apartments were chopped up into small units that could be rented cheaply by the night or the month. But for the artists who were drawn to the hotel in increasing numbers, the 1930s represented a heyday of productivity. »I can't begin to tell you how *rich* everybody was,« one artist recalled of that period when the Works Progress Administration issued weekly stipends to those working in theaters, in art studios, in music halls, and at typewriters across America. At the Chelsea, the composer Virgil Thomson contributed to *wunderkind*-director Orson Welles' all African-American production of *Macbeth,* mentored Paul Bowles, provided stunning scores for Dust Bowl documentaries, and hosted a salon that would help transform American musical culture for decades to come.

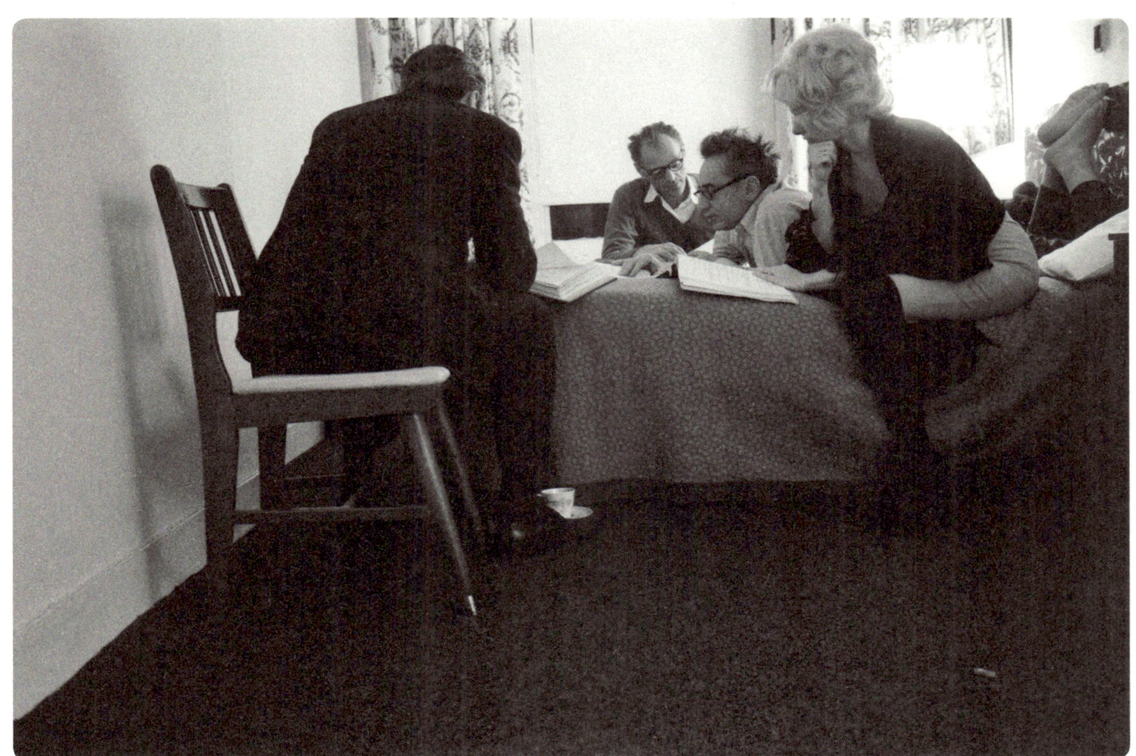

INGE MORATH ARTHUR MILLER UND BESETZUNG LESEN *AFTER THE FALL*
ARTHUR MILLER AND THE CAST READ *AFTER THE FALL*
1963, © Inge Morath Foundation, Magnum Photos

Das Chelsea Hotel sollte Thomas Wolfe nie wieder sehen. Nur vier Monate später starb er mit 37 Jahren an einer Hirnerkrankung. Nun blieb es seinem Lektor überlassen, seine großen postum veröffentlichten Romane *The Web and the Rock* und *You Can't Go Home Again* zusammenzustückeln.

»ALLES IST PERFEKT«, **erklärte David Bard, der neue Direktor und Mitinhaber des Chelsea Hotels,** als er 1960 den Dramatiker Arthur Miller in eine der oberen Suiten des Hauses führte. Unbeirrt von Millers entsetztem Gesichtsausdruck beim Betrachten des billigen Mobiliars und der schmutzigen Fensterbretter fügte er stolz hinzu: »Das Zimmermädchen kommt jeden Tag. Aber passen Sie in der Dusche auf: Kalt ist bei uns heiß, und heiß ist kalt.«

Der Zustand des Chelsea Hotels hätte Miller eigentlich nicht überraschen sollen. Inge Morath, die Freundin, die ihm das Hotel empfohlen hatte, hatte es ihm als die Art bequeme, zweitklassige Herberge beschrieben, wie man sie in jeder großen europäischen Stadt finden würde. Und so heruntergekommen, wie es war, war das Chelsea der wohl letzte Ort, an dem Reporter Miller vermuten würden, der vor allem Ruhe suchte und sich von seiner gescheiterten Ehe mit Marilyn Monroe erholen wollte. Fast gegen seinen Willen war Miller von Bards eigentümlich beiläufiger Gastlichkeit und auch von der klassenlosen Gesellschaft im Chelsea angetan. Er mietete eine Suite, heiratete bald darauf Inge Morath und begann mit der Arbeit an einem Theaterstück, das er *After the Fall* nannte. Miller selbst beschrieb das Stück als eine objektive Betrachtung der moralischen Verantwortung eines Unbeteiligten für die Selbstzerstörung eines Mitmenschen. Aber natürlich war es für alle offensichtlich, dass das eigentliche Thema seine Beziehung zu Monroe war – insbesondere, als er wenige Tage nach deren Selbstmord beschloss, seine Heldin im zweiten Akt sterben zu lassen. Millers Weigerung zuzugeben, dass es im Stück um Monroe ging, machte später die Atmosphäre bei den Proben zu einer »Schlangengrube«, wie sich ein Teilnehmer erinnert – insbesondere immer dann, wenn die Hauptdarstellerin Barbara Loden zu Lesungen im Chelsea mit einer blonden Marilyn-Monroe-Perücke erschien. Die öffentliche Reaktion auf *After the Fall* stellte sich dann als genauso empört heraus, wie alle außer Miller selbst das erwartet hatten. Dass der Dramatiker seine Protagonistin als »für die meisten Menschen ein Witz« bezeichnete, erschien so kurz nach Monroes Tod besonders anstößig. Das Publikum identifizierte sich mit Marilyn; es war nur folgerichtig, dass sie wollten, dass Monroe und

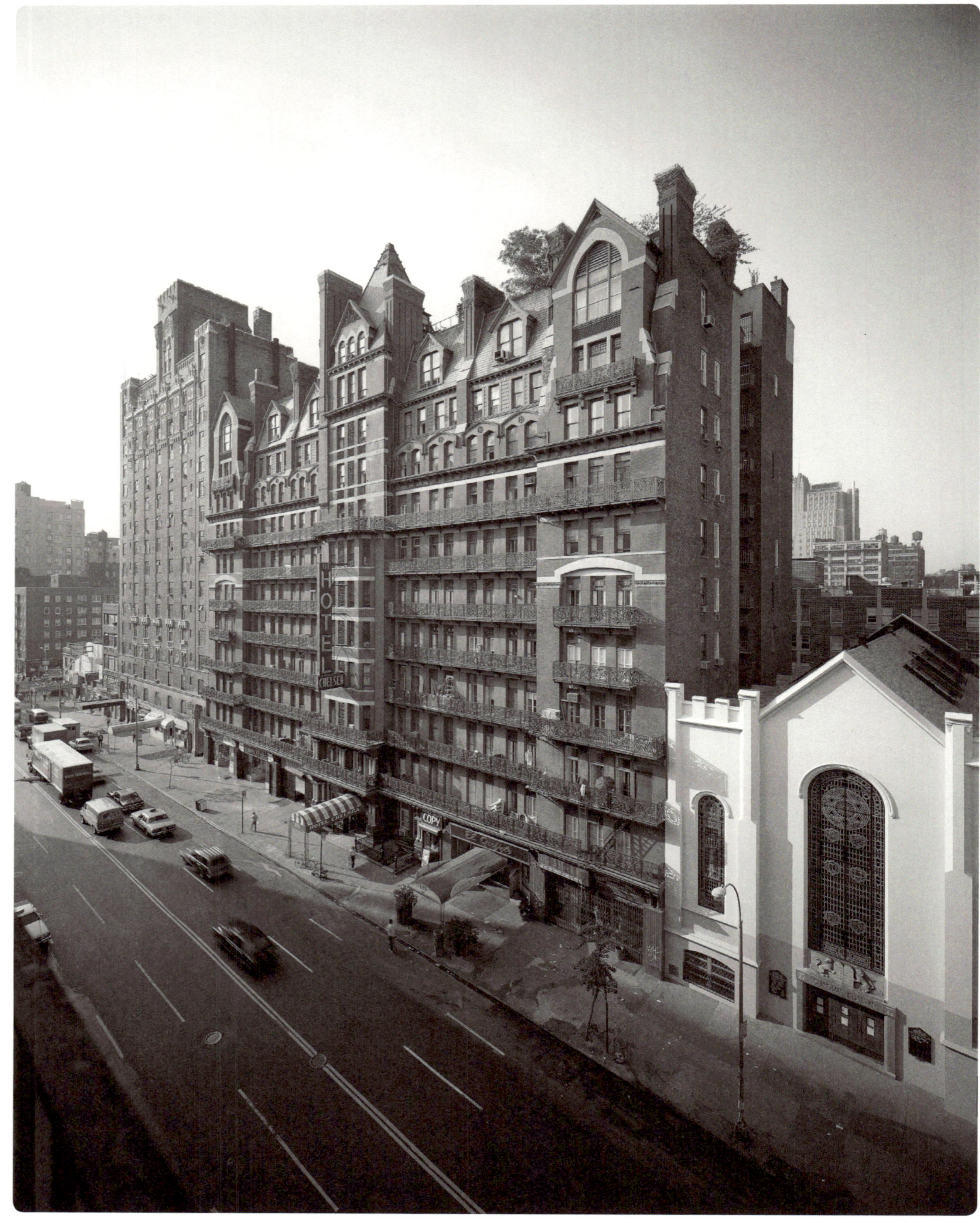

ENRICO FERORELLI

DAS THE CHELSEA HOTEL

1966, © Ferorelli/Agentur FOCUS 2014

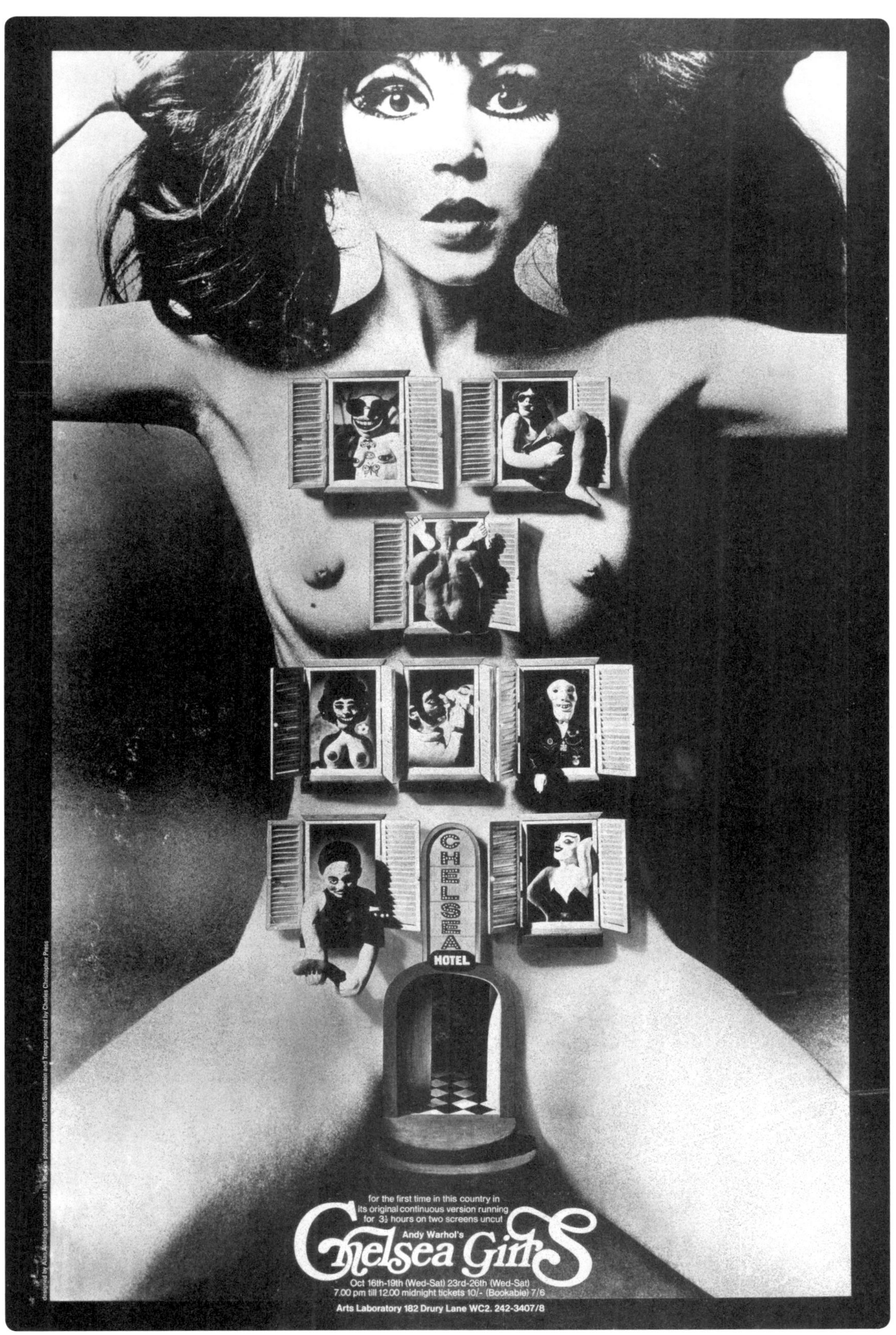

ALAN ALDRIDGE

CHELSEA GIRLS

1966, Poster, © Alan Aldridge. Courtesy of Alan Aldridge

The quintessential New York painter John Sloan and the poet Edgar Lee Masters of *Spoon River Anthology* fame would also find their way to the Hotel Chelsea during this time. It was Masters who persuaded the younger novelist Thomas Wolfe to rent a corner suite there in 1937, when Wolfe was under pressure to produce a novel worthy of following *Of Time and the River.* Moving two crates full of half-finished manuscripts into his rooms, Wolfe worked night after night at the big round table, determined to express his sense that somehow, in the glory of the 1920s economic boom and the horrible collapse that followed, the American people had lost their way.

As the months passed, Wolfe's neighbors grew accustomed to the sound of his deep, Southern-accented voice drifting into the corridor as he read his own words aloud. Occasionally Edgar Lee Masters invited the novelist down to his own rooms for a nightcap. He found it fascinating to watch Wolfe pacing back and forth, reenacting scenes from memory. The man seemed a force of nature, »drunk with words and thoughts and electric with living.«

In May, 1938, with the summer heat already so intense that Wolfe was sure »he could smell all seven million inhabitants« of New York, the writer seized on an opportunity to travel to the West Coast. He handed his manuscript over to his editor—a story that he believed would stand as »a kind of legend« about America—just moments before racing to catch his train.

That was the last anyone at the Chelsea would ever see of Thomas Wolfe. Four months later—struck down by a brain malady—Wolfe died at age thirty-seven. It would be left to his editor to piece together his great posthumous novels *The Web and the Rock and You Can't Go Home Again.*

»EVERYTHING IS PERFECT,« announced the Hotel Chelsea's new manager and co-owner, David Bard, as he ushered the playwright Arthur Miller into an upstairs suite in 1960. »A maid comes every day,« Bard added proudly, oblivious to Miller's appalled expression as he took in the room's cheap furniture and grimy windowsills. »But be careful in the shower, the cold is hot and the hot is cold.«

Miller shouldn't have been surprised by the Chelsea's condition. Inge Morath, the friend who had recommended the hotel, had described it as the kind of comfortable, second-rate hostel one found in every large European city. Shabby as it had become, the Chelsea was the last place reporters would look for the playwright as he tried to recover from his failed marriage to Marilyn Monroe.

Almost in spite of himself, Miller was charmed by Bard's vaguely distracted hospitality and by the classless society existing within the Chelsea's walls. Renting a suite, he soon married Inge and set to work on a play he called *After the Fall.* Miller described the play as an objective examination of the bystander's moral culpability for a fellow individual's self-destruction, but it was obvious to everyone that he was recreating his relationship with Monroe—particularly when, days after Monroe's suicide, he decided to have his heroine die in the second act. Miller's refusal to admit Monroe's presence in the play made the atmosphere at rehearsals »a snake pit,« one participant recalled—especially when the lead actress Barbara Loden attended readings at the Chelsea in a blonde Marilyn Monroe wig.

The public response to *After the Fall* proved to be as scandalized as everyone but Miller had predicted. The playwright's summing-up of his protagonist as »a joke to most people« seemed particularly offensive so soon after Monroe's death. Audiences identified with Marilyn; it was clear that they were ready for Monroe, and other objects of artists' fascination, to speak up for themselves.

No one understood this transformation in artistic viewpoint better than Andy Warhol. Setting up his camera to observe New Yorkers in his *Screen Tests* and other cinematic experiments, he worked several years on dissolving the barrier between the artist and the subject. By 1966, when more and more of his *Factory* superstars were staying at the Chelsea, Warhol obtained permission from David Bard's son Stanley, who had taken over as manager, to record their performances on location. With his collaborator Paul Morrissey, Warhol experimented with ways to throw his subjects emotionally off-guard—repeating a nasty rumor about them or asking an intrusive personal question just before turning on the camera—in order to capture the raw authenticity he wanted. The strung-out New Yorkers produced some riveting performances: a lesbian torture fantasy, an intimate confession, a hyped-up impersonation of a drug dealer so convincing that a member of the hotel staff called the police. Meanwhile, the hotel's mystery and magic caught Warhol's imagination; when he was invited to present his filmed scenes at the *Filmmakers' Cinémathèque* in September, he gave the collected sequences the name THE CHELSEA GIRLS.

THE CHELSEA GIRLS gave the hotel a different kind of celebrity that drew a new type of bohemian tourist. Once it was released, »It was all over for the Chelsea Hotel. You might as well have burned it down,« remarked Bob Dylan, who had experienced the first glimmerings of *Blonde on Blonde* in a suite on the third floor.

Certainly, the utopian dream underlying the Chelsea's conception had taken a beating. In the decades to come, its idealistic spirit would be further crushed by the weight of a rising corporate culture, the Vietnam War, and

andere Objekte der Faszination für Künstler besser für sich selber sprechen sollten.

Niemand verstand diese Wandlung in der künstlerischen Perspektive besser als Andy Warhol. Als er seine Kamera aufstellte, um in seinen *Screen Tests* und anderen Filmexperimenten Menschen in New York zu beobachten, arbeitete er mehrere Jahre daran, die Barriere zwischen Künstler und Sujet aufzulösen.

1966, als immer mehr von seinen Factory-Superstars im Chelsea wohnten, erhielt Warhol die Erlaubnis von David Bards Sohn Stanley, der inzwischen als Direktor übernommen hatte, ihre Performances vor Ort aufzuzeichnen. Mit seinem Koregisseur Paul Morrissey experimentierte Warhol, wie er die Menschen vor der Kamera emotional aus der Fassung bringen könnte. Dies gelang etwa, indem er kurz bevor er die Kamera einschaltete ein hässliches Gerücht wiederholte oder eine aufdringliche, indiskrete persönliche Frage stellte, um dann die ungeschönte Authentizität einzufangen, auf die er aus war. Die häufig vollkommen fertigen New Yorker produzierten so einige fesselnde Auftritte: eine lesbische Folterfantasie, eine intime Beichte, eine aufgeputschte Imitation eines Drogendealers, die so überzeugend war, dass ein Hotelmitarbeiter die Polizei rief. Das Geheimnisvolle und Magische des Hotels befeuerte Warhols Fantasie; als er schließlich eingeladen wurde, seine gefilmten Szenen im September im Rahmen der Veranstaltungsreihe *Filmmakers' Cinémathèque* zu präsentieren, gab er den gesammelten Sequenzen den Titel THE CHELSEA GIRLS.

THE CHELSEA GIRLS verlieh dem Hotel eine andere Art von Berühmtheit, die ihm wiederum einen neuen Typus Touristen, nämlich den Bohemien, bescherte. Nachdem dieser Film veröffentlicht worden war, »war alles aus für das Chelsea Hotel. Man hätte es auch abfackeln können«, sagte etwa Bob Dylan, der hier die Anfänge seines Albums *Blonde on Blonde* in einer Suite im dritten Stock erlebt hatte.

Gewiss hatte der utopische Traum, der einmal dem Konzept des Chelsea zugrunde gelegen hatte, inzwischen ziemlich gelitten. In den folgenden Jahrzehnten wurde sein idealistischer Geist zunehmend vom Gewicht einer aufsteigenden Unternehmenskultur, dem Vietnamkrieg oder später der schmerzlichen Stagnation der 1970er-Jahre erdrückt. Es war eine resignierte Janis Joplin – deprimiert, weil ihr Plattenlabel sie unter Druck setzte, ihre Band zu feuern –, die an einem Winterabend im Aufzug auf einen gleichermaßen missmutigen Leonard Cohen traf, woraus sich ein Stelldichein ergab, das Cohen später mit seinem Song *Chelsea Hotel No. 2* unsterblich machte. Es war eine wütende Germaine Greer, die die Fotografin Diane Arbus aus ihrem Hotelzimmer hinauswarf, weil diese versuchte, sie der Öffentlichkeit als feministisches Monster darzustellen – genau wie das Modell Viva aus dem Chelsea Hotel Arbus angedroht hatte, sie zu verklagen, weil sie sie vier Jahre zuvor als Junkie porträtiert hatte. In den 1970er-Jahren begann der experimentelle Filmemacher Harry Smith, Brechts und Weills *Aufstieg und Fall der Stadt Mahagonny* mit Hotelbewohnern zu adaptieren, also die Geschichte einer Traumstadt, »in der alles erlaubt ist« und wo die einzige Sünde ist, kein Geld zu haben. Zum Ende des Jahrzehnts schließlich hatte der Fotograf William Eggleston, auch er ein Besucher des Hotels, ein Druckverfahren aus der Werbeindustrie verwendet, um Bilder vom Niedergang des amerikanischen Traums zu schaffen.

DAS LEBEN im Chelsea Hotel bildete als Mikrokosmos immer den Zustand vor seinen Türen ab. Daher war es kaum eine Überraschung, als im Oktober 1978, in der Hochzeit der Punk-Ära, der Portier einen Anruf mit der Information bekam: »In Zimmer 100 gibt es ein Problem« – genau dem Zimmer, das Sid Vicious, der Bassist der Band Sex Pistols, mit seiner Freundin Nancy Spungen teilte. Als dann ein Hotelpage Spungens leblosen Körper auf dem Badezimmerboden fand, schien dies das Ende des kreativen Lebens im Chelsea Hotel zu sein.

»Davon wird sich das Hotel nie mehr erholen«, erklärte Stanley Bard rundweg, selbst noch Jahre nach dem Mord an Spungen. Doch bereits bei der Hundertjahrfeier des Chelsea Hotels 1983 waren Zeichen der Wiedergeburt in den Dichterlesungen und musikalischen Ehrungen, die von den Bewohnern des Hotels aus diesem Anlass veranstaltet wurden, zu spüren. Während der Jahrzehnte seitdem versammeln sich noch immer Künstler in dieser Backsteinfestung – jüngere Künstler kümmern sich um die älteren, ältere Künstler beraten die jüngeren. Immer mehr ließen sich kreative Gäste auch vom Chelsea selbst inspirieren – Beispiele dafür sind Ethan Hawkes Film *Chelsea Walls,* der Roman *Chelsea Horror Hotel* des Punkgitarristen Dee Dee Ramone oder die zahlreichen Sammlungen von Fotografen, die dem Hotel gewidmet sind.

Kürzlich wurde das Hotel von neuen Besitzern erworben, die es für Renovierungen geschlossen haben. Touristen lesen nun auf einem Schild, dass aktuell allen mit Ausnahme der noch verbliebenen Bewohner der Zutritt verwehrt wird. Für das Frühjahr 2015 ist die Wiedereröffnung geplant. Ob das Chelsea Hotel danach noch der Ort für eine Künstler-Community sein wird, ist vollkommen offen. Aber dank des utopischen Traums von Philip Hubert sind eigentlich alle Bedingungen dafür vorhanden. Und für eine Wiedergeburt im Herzen New Yorks sind die Menschen ganz gewiss auch bereit.

the painful stagflation of the 1970s. It was a weary Janis Joplin, depressed by her record label's pressure to fire her band, who bumped into an equally morose Leonard Cohen in the elevator one winter's night and embarked on a tryst later to be immortalized in Cohen's *Chelsea Hotel No. 2.* It was a furious Germaine Greer who ejected the photographer Diane Arbus from her Chelsea Hotel room for trying to objectify her to the public as a feminist monster—just as the Chelsea's Viva had threatened to sue Arbus for portraying her as a junkie four years before. In the 1970s, using hotel denizens as subjects, experimental filmmaker Harry Smith began adapting Bertolt Brecht's and Kurt Weill's *Rise and Fall of the City of Mahagonny,* the story of a dream city where »everything is allowed« and the only sin is to have no money. By the end of that decade Chelsea Hotel visitor William Eggleston had made use of an advertising-industry printing process to create images of the American dream's demise.

ALWAYS, life within the Chelsea expressed in microcosm the state of things outside its doors. So it was hardly a surprise when, at the height of the punk era in October, 1978, a call to the Chelsea's front desk clerk informed him, »There's trouble in Room 100«—the room shared by the Sex Pistols bass player Sid Vicious and his girlfriend Nancy Spungen. When a bellman found Spungen's lifeless body on the bathroom floor, it seemed surely the end of the creative life of the Chelsea Hotel.

»The hotel will never get over it,« Stanley Bard stated flatly, even decades after Spungen's murder. Yet, by the Chelsea's centennial celebration in 1983, signs of rebirth were evident in the poetry recitations and musical tributes created for the occasion by hotel residents. Throughout the decades since, artists have continued to congregate in the redbrick fortress—younger artists tending the elderly, older artists mentoring the young. Increasingly, guests began to take inspiration from the Chelsea itself—as reflected in actor Ethan Hawke's film *Chelsea Walls,* punk guitarist Dee Dee Ramone's novel *Chelsea Horror Hotel,* and numerous photographers' collections featuring the hotel.

Recently, the Chelsea has been acquired by new owners, who have shut it down for renovations. Tourists now arrive to find a notice forbidding entry to anyone but remaining residents. A re-opening is scheduled for spring, 2015. Whether the Chelsea will remain an artists' community is anyone's guess. But thanks to the Philip Hubert's utopian dream, the conditions are there, and the people are there for a rebirth in the heart of New York.

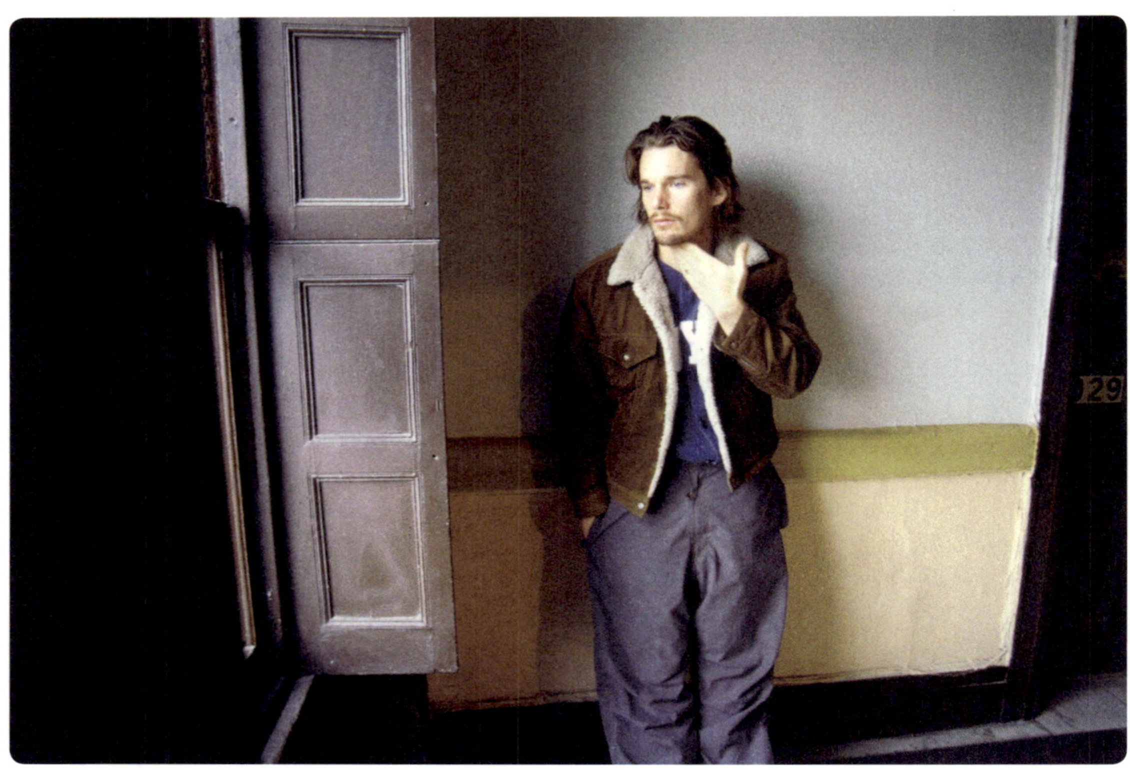

LINDA TROELLER

ETHAN HAWKE, CHELSEA HOTEL, 2001, NEW YORK

© Linda Troeller

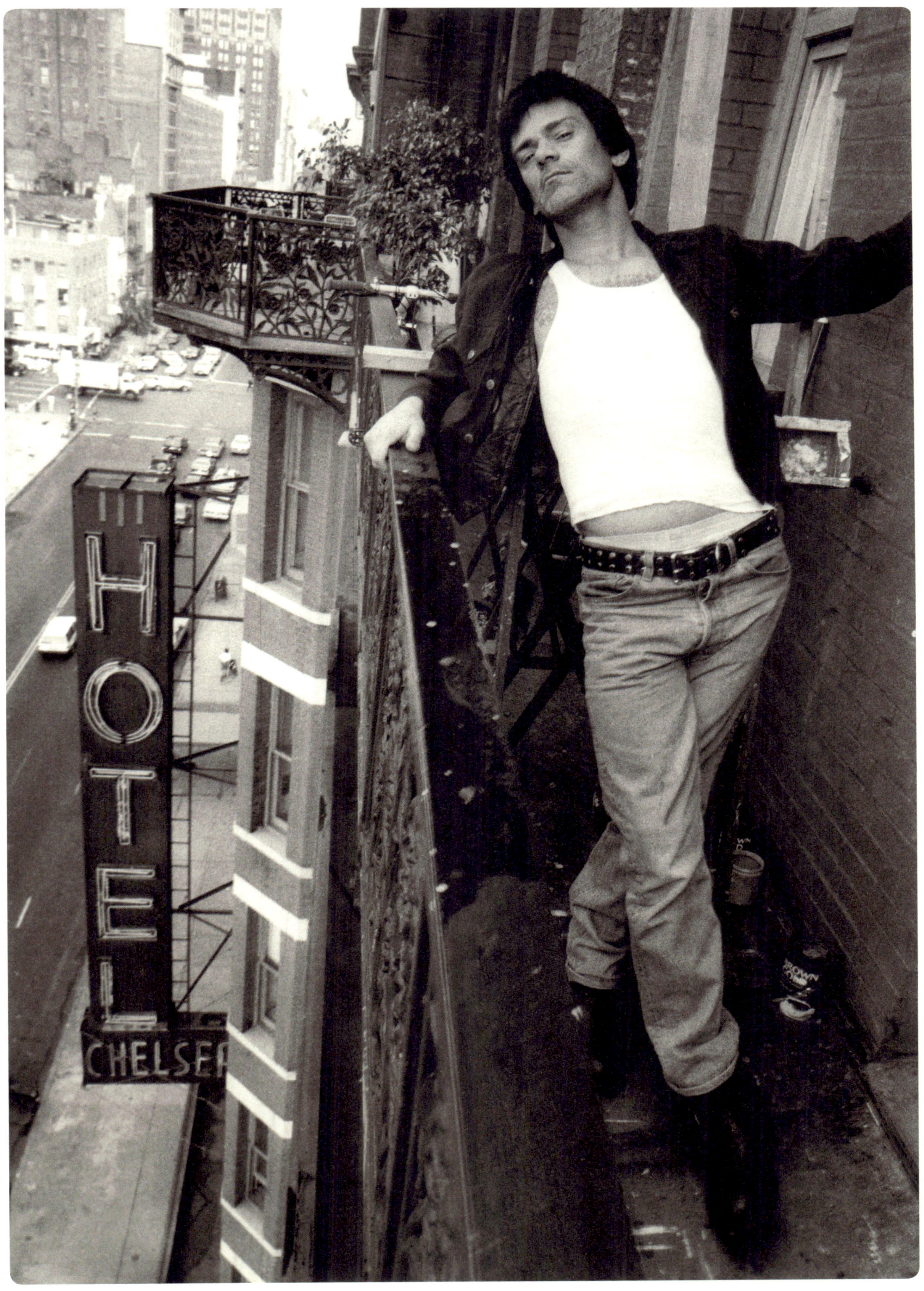

KEITH GREEN

DEE DEE RAMONE AUF DEM BALKON DES CHELSEA HOTELS
DEE DEE RAMONE ON THE BALCONY OF THE CHELSEA HOTEL

1993, © Keith Green, Alle Rechte vorbehalten / All rights reserved

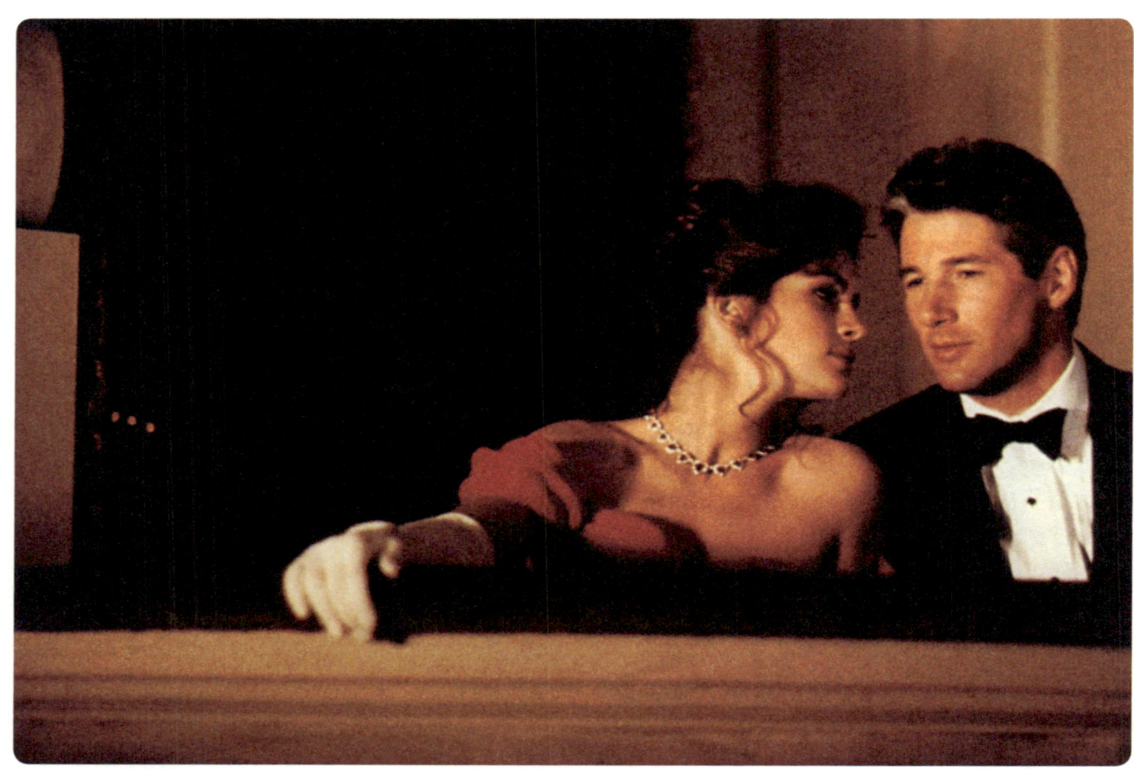

PRETTY WOMAN
Abb. / Fig. 1
Regie / Directed by: Gary Marshall, 1990, © Collection Christophel

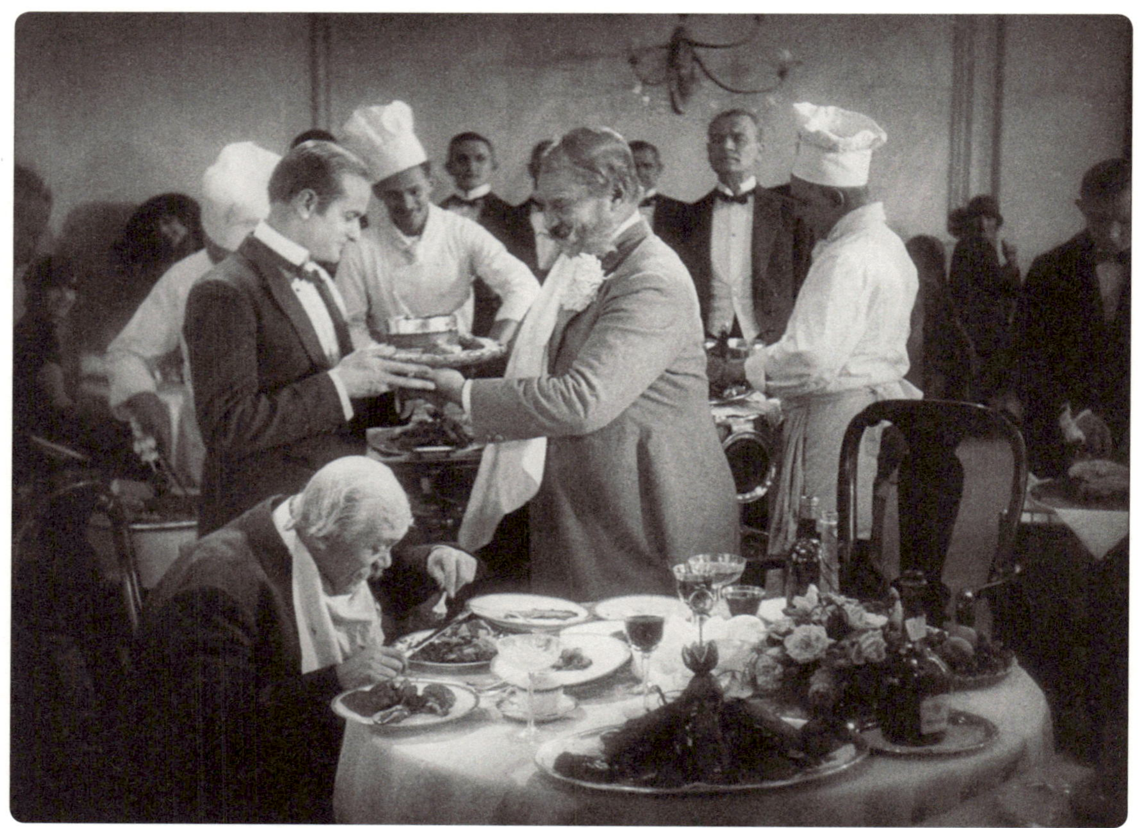

Abb. / Fig. 2
DER LETZTE MANN / THE LAST LAUGH
Regie / Directed by: Friedrich Wilhelm Murnau, 1924, © Friedrich-Wilhelm-Murnau Stiftung, Wiesbaden

DAS HOTEL IN DER FILMGESCHICHTE

SCHICKSALSRAUM, HAUS DER SCHRECKEN, ABENTEUERSPIELPLATZ

ANDREAS KILB

Hotels begrenzen unseren Blick. Sie engen ihn ein, aber sie geben ihm auch Halt. Wie alle filmischen Räume funktionieren sie auf zweierlei Art: als Angst- wie als Traummaschinen, als Stätten des Schreckens, der Exzesse, der Einsamkeit und des Todes, aber auch als Orte der Sehnsucht, der Verwandlung, des Glücks und der Geborgenheit. Mit ihren klar gegliederten Strukturen und Hierarchien, ihrer Trennung von Funktions- und Repräsentationsräumen, von Empfangshalle, Treppenhaus, Suiten, Einzelzimmern und Dienstbotenkammern, haben sie aber noch einen anderen Effekt: Sie geben den Geschichten, denen sie als Rahmen dienen, Formen, Bewegungen und Sujets vor. Kein Hotelfilm, der nicht mehr oder weniger explizit von Macht, Rang und Geltung, von sozialen und finanziellen Klassenunterschieden handelte, der nicht mit den Möglichkeiten vertikaler Trennung und horizontaler Verflüssigung von Räumen, Charakteren und Perspektiven, die der Schauplatz ermöglicht, sein ästhetisches Spiel triebe. Das Hotel Regent Beverly Wilshire in Los Angeles beispielsweise, in dem die »Pretty Woman« Julia Roberts in Garry Marshalls Film ihre märchenhafte Liebesgeschichte mit dem Investmentmanager Richard Gere erlebt, ist zugleich der Schauplatz ihres gesellschaftlichen Aufstiegs: Als Straßenprostituierte betritt sie zum ersten Mal seine Lobby, als Lady verlässt sie sie zum Schluss (Abb. 1).

Erst da, wo die klassische Vertikalität des Hotels zum flachen Patchwork amerikanischer Motels einschrumpft, verliert auch die hierarchische Ordnung der Figuren ihren Sinn. In *No Country for Old Men,* dem Thrillermeisterwerk der Coen-Brüder von 2007, geht es nur mehr darum, in welchem Motelzimmer das Geld der toten Drogenbosse versteckt ist, nicht darum, wer es gerechterweise beanspruchen darf. Dennoch kann auch der größte aller Motelfilme, Alfred Hitchcocks *Psycho* (1960), nicht ganz auf vertikal gegliederte Räume verzichten: Der Weg zu Norman Bates' Geheimnis, der toten Mutter, führt über die Treppen der alten Familienvilla, hinab in den Keller, wo der zweite visuelle Schock nach der Duschszene auf uns wartet.

Im Spartenangebot der Kinogenres hat der Hotelfilm von Anfang an seinen Platz. Schon 1897 gibt es einen Film der Edison Manufacturing Company namens *Hotel Vendome, San Jose, Cal.;* bis zum Ende des Ersten Weltkrieges entstehen unter anderem *The Haunted Hotel* (1907), ein *Hôtel du silence* (1908), ein *L'Hôtel de la gare* (1914, Regie: Louis Feuillade), ein *Hotel Paradis* (1917, nach einem Skript von Carl Theodor Dreyer) und ein *Globe Hotel* (1918, mit Oliver Hardy in einer seiner ersten Rollen), dazu *The Mystery of the Sea View Hotel* (1914), *Mysteries of the Grand Hotel* (1915) und *Das unruhige Hotel* (1917). D. W. Griffith, damals noch nicht der Meister von *Intolerance* (1916) dreht 1913 den One-Reeler *Love in an*

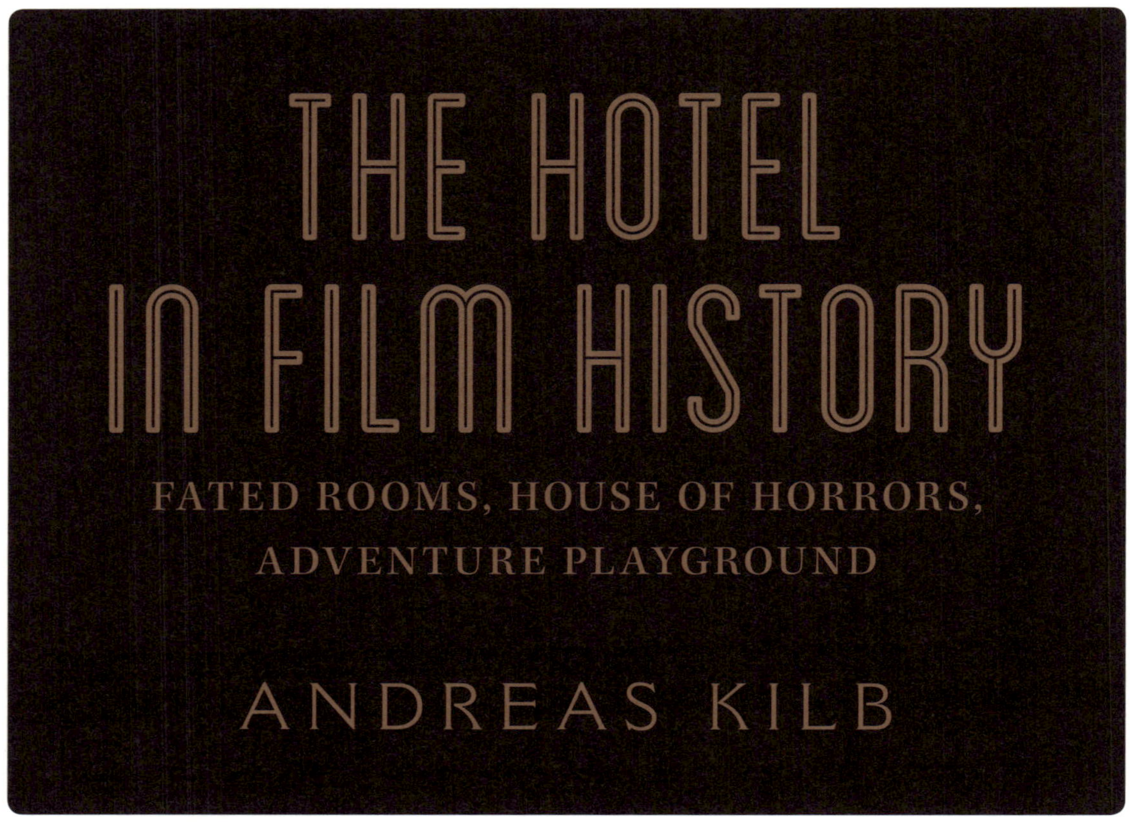

THE HOTEL IN FILM HISTORY

FATED ROOMS, HOUSE OF HORRORS, ADVENTURE PLAYGROUND

ANDREAS KILB

Hotels limit our gaze, not only narrowing it but also giving it structure. Like all filmic spaces, hotels have a dual function: as machines of fears and dreams, sites of horror, excess, loneliness, and death, but also as places of longing, transformation, happiness, and sanctuary. With their clearly ordered structures and hierarchies, their separation between functional and representational spaces, between the entry hall, stairwell, suites, singles rooms, and porters' vestibule, hotels have an additional effect; they grant the stories set within their walls a certain form, a set of movements, and a subject. For example, the Hotel Regent Beverly Wilshire in Los Angeles is where Julia Roberts experiences her fairytale love story with the investment manager played by Richard Gere in Garry Marshall's *Pretty Woman;* it is also the backdrop for her social rise. She enters the lobby for the first time as a street prostitute and ultimately leaves the hotel as a lady (fig. 1).

Only where the classical verticality of the hotel is reduced to the flat patchwork of the American motel does the hierarchical order among characters lose its significance. In *No Country for Old Men,* the Coen Brothers' masterpiece thriller from 2007, the key question boils down to which motel room contains the hidden money of the dead drug lord and not who is entitled to the cash. However, even the most famous motel film of all, Alfred Hitchcock's *Psycho* (1960), cannot completely forgo the use of vertically organized spaces. The way to Norman Bates' secret, his dead mother, leads down the stairs of the old family villa into the cellar, where the second visual shock—after the shower scene—awaits us.

The hotel film has had its place within the spectrum of film genres from the very beginning. As early as 1897 a film produced by the Edison Manufacturing Company was entitled *Hotel Vendome, San Jose, Cal.;* up through the end of World War I hotel film productions included *The Haunted Hotel* (1907), *Hôtel du silence* (1908), *L'Hôtel de la gare* (1914, directed by Louis Feuillade), *Hotel Paradis* (1917, after a script by Carl Theodor Dreyer), *Globe Hotel* (1918, with Oliver Hardy in one of his first roles) as well as *The Mystery of the Sea View Hotel* (1914), *Mysteries of the Grand Hotel* (1915), and *Das unruhige Hotel* (1917). D. W. Griffith, who at the time had not yet created his masterful *Intolerance* (1916), created the one-reel film *Love in an Apartment Hotel* in 1913, in which a pair of lovers is interrupted by a thief during an amorous tryst. The scenario of the hotel with its structured sequences of various floors and interiors perfectly suits the requirements of the early silent film, which depended on strong lighting and a stage-like clarity of setting.

Still, it was not until 1924 that the first truly major hotel film was created, Friedrich Wilhelm Murnau's *Der*

Apartment Hotel, in dem ein Liebespaar beim Schäferstündchen von einem Dieb gestört wird. Die Hotelkulisse mit ihren gegliederten Sequenzen von Stockwerken und Innenräumen entspricht geradezu ideal den Bedürfnissen des frühen Stummfilms, der auf starke Lichtsignale und eine bühnenhafte Übersichtlichkeit angewiesen ist.

Trotzdem dauert es bis 1924, bis der erste wirklich große Hotelfilm entsteht, Friedrich Wilhelm Murnaus *Der letzte Mann* (Abb. 2). Es ist, wie für die Krisenzeit der 1920er-Jahre passend, eine Parabel über die Wechselhaftigkeit des Glücks: »Heute bist Du der Erste, geachtet von Allen, ein Minister, ein General, vielleicht sogar ein Fürst – weißt Du, was Du morgen bist?!«, fragt der Vorspann. Der namenlose Hotelportier des »Atlantic«, unsterblich verkörpert von Emil Jannings, erlebt dieses Auf und Ab zwischen dem Heute und Morgen am eigenen Leib: Vom allenthalben geachteten Funktionsträger steigt er nach einem Schwächeanfall zum traurigen Hüter der Herrentoilette ab, der sich nur nach Feierabend in seiner alten Prachtuniform noch einmal als Respektsperson aufspielen kann. Als die Wahrheit ans Licht kommt und die Welt des »letzten Mannes« endgültig zusammenbricht, greifen Murnau und sein Drehbuchautor Carl Mayer zu einem ebenso durchschaubaren wie wirkungsvollen Kinotrick: Sie setzen auf die ausweglose Fabel ein märchenhaftes Happy End. Der heruntergekommene Alte wird von einem reichen Kunden, der in seiner Toilette stirbt, als Alleinerbe eingesetzt und kann fortan sein Vermögen an den Tischen des Hotelrestaurants verprassen.
Im *Letzten Mann* ist das Motivrepertoire des klassischen Hotelfilms bereits vollständig entwickelt. Die Eingangsszene führt in einer einzigen langen Plansequenz durch die verschiedenen Stockwerke und die Lobby des Hotels bis auf den Vorplatz, den der alte bärtige Portier mit der raumgreifend-allegorischen Präsenz eines antiken Meergottes beherrscht. Als er später die Uniform ablegen muss, wird er zum Gespött seiner Kollegen, wie er zuvor das Objekt ihrer Ehrfurcht war. Die Gäste, vom kleinen Gernegroß bis zum amerikanischen Nabob, erscheinen nur als Staffage im hierarchischen Wettkampf der Hotelangestellten. Eine Besonderheit des Films, die ihn aus allen späteren Beispielen des Genres heraushebt, ist die Verschränkung von öffentlicher Berufs- und privater Lebenswelt. Denn der Portier wohnt nicht im Hotel, sondern haust mit seiner Familie in einem städtischen Wohnblock. Auch dort ereilt ihn die Verachtung der Nachbarn, als sein Uniformschwindel auffliegt. Das Theater des modernen Lebens spielt bei Murnau auf zwei parallelen Bühnen, die beide auf die gleiche bewusstlose Weise der Herrschaft des Scheins über das Sein huldigen.

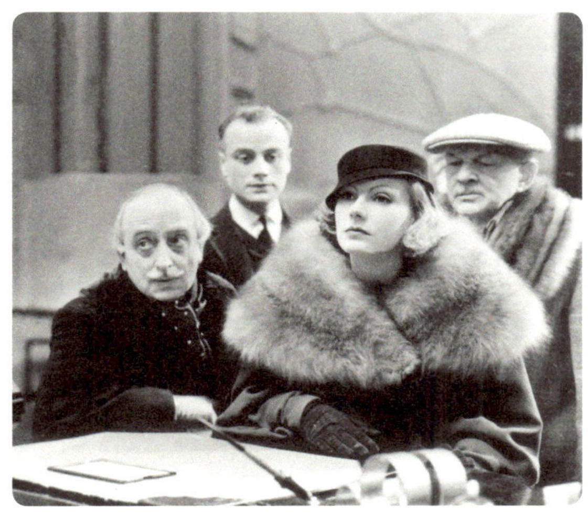

Abb. / Fig. 3
MENSCHEN IM HOTEL
GRAND HOTEL
Regie / Directed by: Edmund Goulding, 1932,
© Metro-Goldwyn-Mayer

In Edmund Gouldings *Grand Hotel* (1932), der auf Deutsch *Menschen im Hotel* heißt (wie der Roman von Vicki Baum, nach dem er entstand), kehrt sich die Perspektive auf das Geschehen hinter den Hotelfassaden um (Abb. 3). Hier stehen die Gäste, ihre Macht- und Liebesverhältnisse im Mittelpunkt, das Personal ist nur Statisterie. Sein Motto legt der Film zu Beginn einem Stammgast des Grand Hotels in den Mund: »Menschen kommen, Menschen gehen. Nie passiert etwas.« Was natürlich umgehend widerlegt wird. Ein Bonvivant (John Barrymore), der von Diebereien lebt, ein vom Bankrott bedrohter Firmendirektor (Wallace Beery), eine Stenotypistin (Joan Crawford), ein unheilbar kranker Büroangestellter (Lionel Barrymore) und eine lebensmüde Ballerina (Greta Garbo) – sie treffen auf den Gängen, in den Suiten und an den Spieltischen des Hotels aufeinander, begehren und bestehlen, betrügen und verlieben sich, finden ihr Glück oder den Tod. *Grand Hotel* ist ein unbestrittener Klassiker des Genres, nicht nur wegen der Eleganz der Kulissen und Dekors (der Film spielt wie *Der letzte Mann* in Berlin, wurde aber in den MGM-Studios in Hollywood gedreht), sondern auch, weil er perfekt die Balance zwischen individuellem und kollektivem Schicksal hält: Weltwirtschaftskrise, Klassenkampf, verkommene Aristokratie, aufsteigendes Proletariat, modernes *taedium vitae,* alles ist da. Und der Schauplatz, das Hotel, gibt allem einen gemäßen Raum: der Groteske und der Tragödie, der Liebe wie der Langeweile.

VON hier aus führt eine Entwicklungslinie in die Welt Ernst Lubitschs mit ihren Meisterdieben (*Ärger im Paradies,* 1932) und eleganten Betrügerinnen (*Angel,* 1937), weiter über Alfred Hitchcocks *Über den Dächern von Nizza* (1955) und Blake Edwards *Der rosarote*

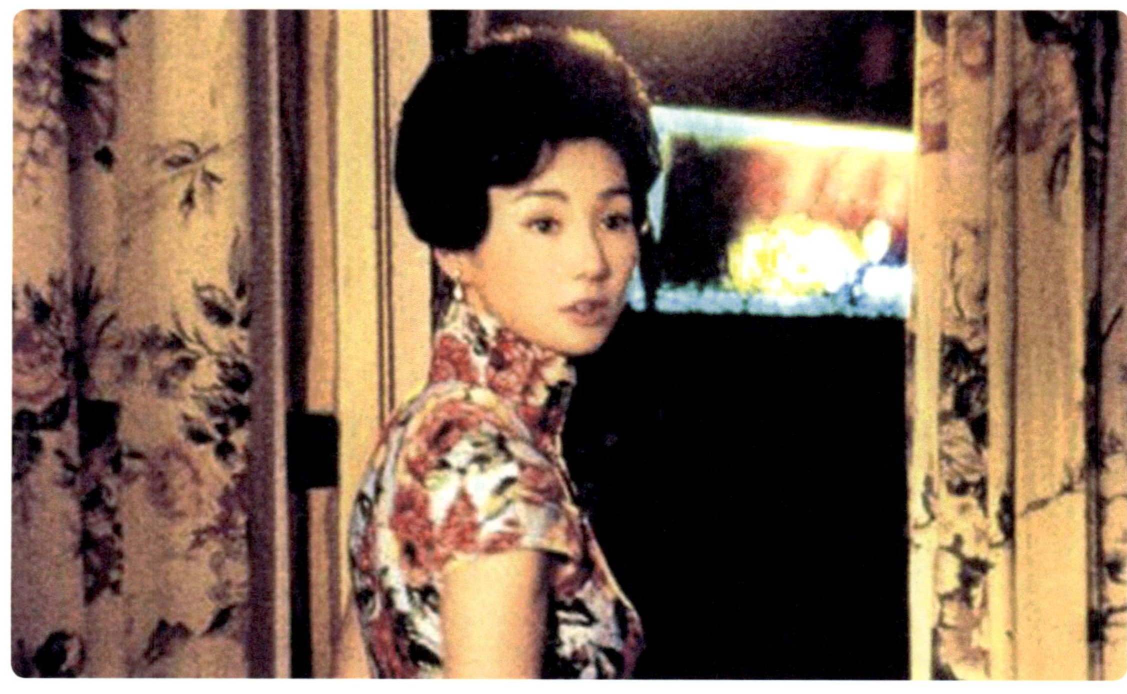

Abb. / Fig. 4

IN THE MOOD FOR LOVE

Regie / Directed by: Wong Kar-Wai, 2000, © action press / Everett Collection

letzte Mann (The Last Laugh, fig. 2). In correspondence with the 1920s as a period of crisis, the film is a parable of the vicissitudes of good fortune: »Today you are at the very top, respected by everyone, a minister, a general, perhaps even a prince—do you know what you will be tomorrow?!« is the question posed in the opening credits. The anonymous hotel porter of the Atlantic, immortalized by actor Emil Jannings, personally experiences the ups and downs that can occur from one day to the next. After a dizzy spell he falls from his position as a generally respected official to the sad position of men's toilet attendant, and only after work can he again assume the role of a respected figure by donning the pomp of his old uniform. When the truth comes out and the world of this »last man« finally falls apart, Murnau and his screenplay writer Carl Mayer turn to a film trick that is as transparent as it is effective: they slap a fairytale-like happy end onto this seemingly hopeless story. The decrepit old man is named sole heir by a rich guest who dies in the men's toilet, and from then on he is able to squander his money at the tables of the hotel restaurant.

In *Der letzte Mann* the repertoire of motifs characterizing the classic hotel film is already fully developed. The introductory scene leads through the various floors and the lobby of the hotel in an extended sequence shot, which leaves out the vestibule where the old, bearded porter sits while exuding the allegorically expansive presence of an antique sea god. When he later is forced to take off his uniform, he becomes an object of ridicule among his colleagues to the same extent that he had formerly enjoyed their respect. The guests, from insignificant social climbers to the American zillionaire, appear only as accessories within hierarchical competition among the hotel employees. A special aspect of this film, which makes it stand out among later examples of this genre, is the combination of the public, professional realm with the private and domestic, for the porter does not live in the hotel but resides with his family in an urban apartment building. There too, he suffers the disdain of the neighbors once his uniform farce is revealed. Murnau allows the theater of modern life to play out on two parallel stages, both of which unconsciously celebrate the triumph of appearances over reality in the same manner.

In Edmund Goulding's *Grand Hotel* (1932), the perspective on the events occurring behind the hotel façade is inverted (fig. 3). In this case the guests and their power and love relationships are the focus, and the hotel personnel are merely extras. The motto of the film is expressed early on by a regular guest of the hotel: »People come, people go. Nothing ever happens.« Of course, this statement is subsequently contradicted. A bon vivant (John Barrymore) who lives from thievery, a company director (Wallace Beery)

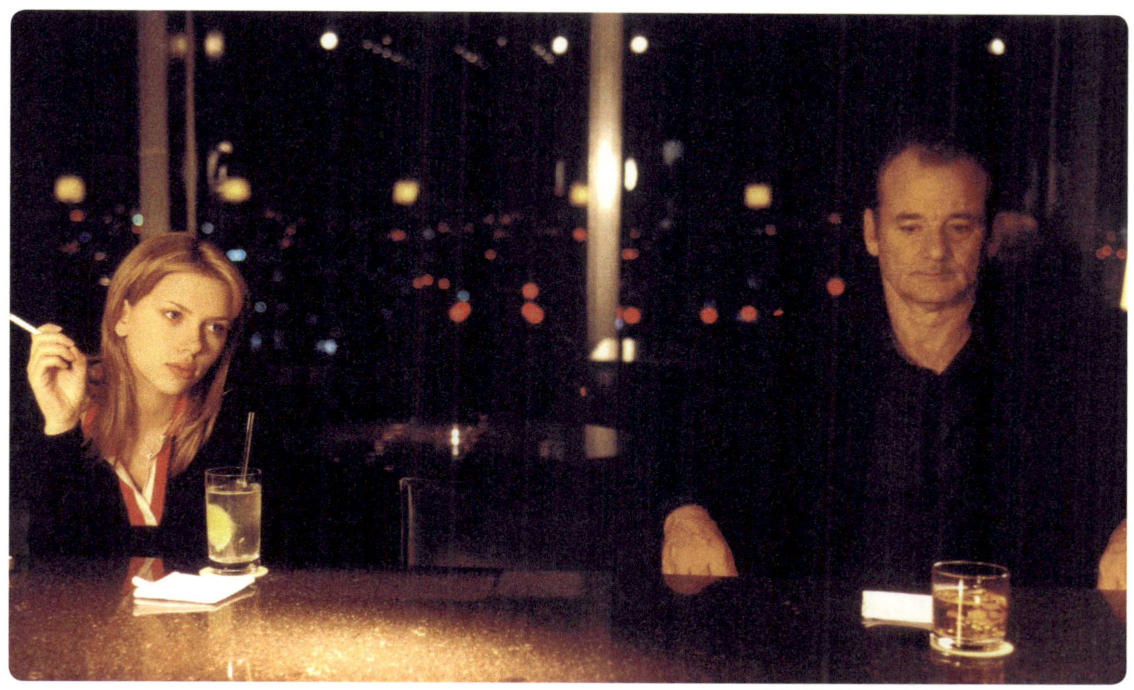

Abb. / Fig. 5
LOST IN TRANSLATION
Regie / Directed by: Sofia Coppola, 2003, © action press / Munawar Hosain

Panther (1963) bis zu den Filmen der *Ocean's*-Trilogie von Steven Soderbergh (2001, 2004 und 2007), deren vertrackte Plots ohne die prächtigen, den Blick des Zuschauers zugleich blendenden wie lenkenden Hotel- und Kasinokulissen kaum funktionieren würden. Eine andere führt zu jenen Kinoromanzen, in denen das Hotel nicht bloß eine beiläufig rahmende, sondern eine thematische Rolle spielt. In *Pretty Woman* (1990) ist es der Transitraum zwischen käuflicher und romantisch-authentischer Liebe, in Wayne Wangs *Manhattan Love Story* (2002) dient es als gesellschaftliche Drehbühne, auf der das alleinerziehende Zimmermädchen (Jennifer Lopez) unter falschem Namen den berühmten Politiker (Ralph Fiennes) kennenlernt, sein Glück dann aber gegen die reiche Rivalin (Natasha Richardson) und die eigenen Skrupel bis zum guten Ende verteidigen muss. In Wong Kar-Wais *In the Mood for Love* (2000, Abb. 4) ist ein Hotel der Ort, an dem das Liebespaar, das keines sein will (Maggie Cheung und Tony Leung Chiu-Wai), gemeinsam Romane schreibt, während es in der Fortsetzung *2046* (2004) den Rahmen für eine aussichtslose Affäre bildet, in der der vereinsamte Journalist die im ersten Teil versäumte Erfüllung mit einer Lebedame (Zhang Ziyi) nachzuholen versucht. Die originellste Variation des Themas aus den letzten Jahren aber ist zweifellos Sofia Coppolas *Lost in Translation* von 2003. Hier treffen Bill Murray und Scarlett Johansson, die beide aus je unterschiedlichen Gründen in Tokio gestrandet sind, in einem der dortigen Hoteltürme aufeinander und erleben gemeinsam fast alles, was zu einer solchen Begegnung gehört, außer jenem körperlichen Vollzug, der sonst zum Mainstreamstandard gehört (Abb. 5). Das Gefühl, fremd in den Städten, unter den Menschen und auf der Welt überhaupt zu sein, hat seit Antonionis großen Filmen der 1960er-Jahre kaum einen schöneren Ausdruck gefunden.

Eine besondere Variante des Hotels ist das Landhotel. In Stanley Kubricks *Shining* (1980) nach dem Roman von Stephen King steht es als gewaltiger hölzerner Kasten auf einer Hügelkuppe in den Rocky Mountains und wird Gefäß für Geschichten, Träume und Geister (Abb. 6). Der Schriftsteller Jack Torrance alias Jack Nicholson, der es mit seiner Familie einen Winter hindurch bewohnen und pflegen soll, wird in die Leere des Overlook Hotels hineingesogen und die Bewegungen der Steadicam, die Kubrick als erster Regisseur der Filmgeschichte über ganze Sequenzen hin benutzte, ziehen den Betrachter mit in diese Leere hinein: in die endlosen Flure, auf denen Jack und sein kleiner Sohn einer toten Frau und ihren Kindern begegnen, in die große leere Hotelhalle, in der der Schriftsteller tagelang immer wieder denselben Satz in seine Schreibmaschine hackt, und in die Bar, in der er in eine Traumzeit eintritt, die mit seiner Gegenwart nichts mehr zu tun hat. Das Overlook

facing the threat of bankruptcy, a stenographer (Joan Crawford), a terminally ill office employee (Lionel Barrymore), and a world-weary ballerina (Greta Garbo)—they encounter one another in the hallways and suites and at the gambling tables of the hotel; they desire and steal from one another, betray each other and fall in love, ultimately finding happiness or death. *Grand Hotel* is an uncontested classic of the genre, not only because of the elegance of the sets and décor (like *Der letzte Mann,* the film is set in Berlin but was filmed at the MGM studios in Hollywood) but also because it maintains a perfect balance between individual and collective fates. The world economic crisis, class struggle, a faded aristocracy, an emerging proletariat, and a modern *taedium vitae*—it's all there. And the site of the action, the hotel, lends everything the appropriate atmosphere, grotesqueness and tragedy, love and boredom.

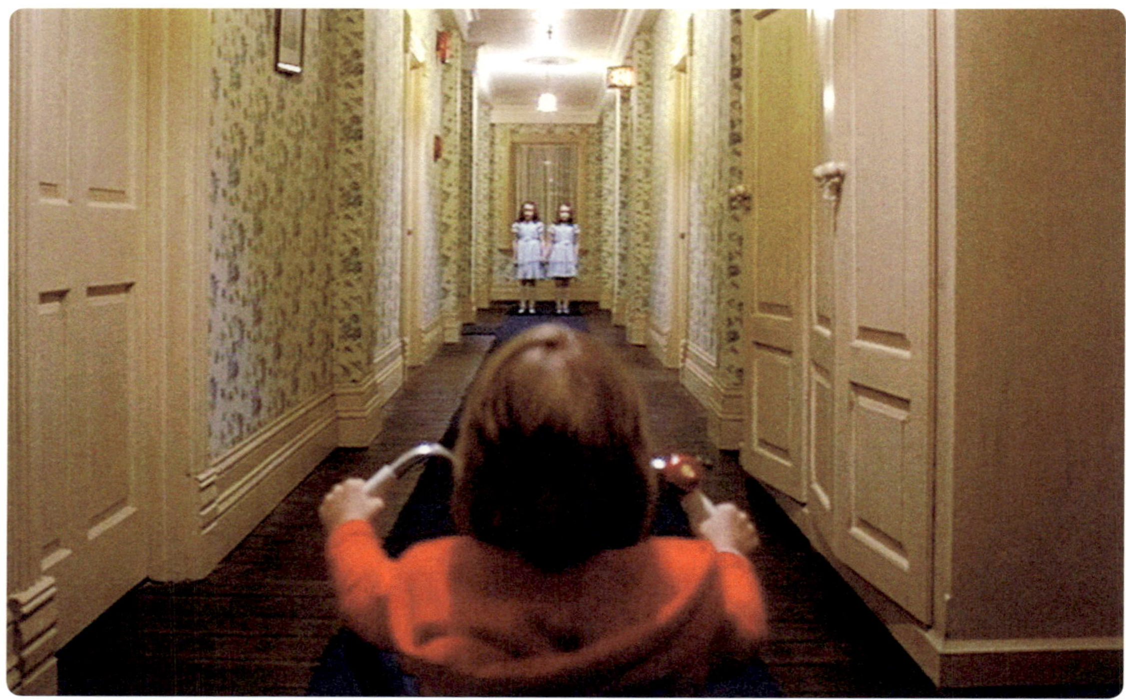

Abb. / Fig. 6

THE SHINING

Regie / Directed by: Stanley Kubrick, 1980, © action press / Everett Collection

FROM here one line of development takes us to the world of Ernst Lubitsch with its master thieves *(Trouble in Paradise,* 1932) and elegant female swindlers *(Angel,* 1937) and on through Hitchcock's *To Catch a Thief* (1955) and Blake Edwards' *The Pink Panther* (1963), continuing into the films of Steven Soderbergh's *Ocean's*-trilogy (2001, 2004, and 2007), the entwined plots of which would hardly function without the hotel and casino scenarios that both dazzle and steer the gaze of the viewer. An alternate thread leads to romance films in which the hotel does not merely serve to randomly frame the plot but has a thematic purpose. In *Pretty Woman* (1990) this is the transition between bought love and romantic-authentic love. In Wayne Wang's *Manhattan Love Story* (2002) the hotel is a revolving social stage, where a single-parent chambermaid (Jennifer Lopez) meets a famous politician (Ralph Fiennes) under a false name and is then forced to defend her happiness against a rich rival (Natasha Richardson) while going against her own scruples. In Wong Kar-Wai's *In the Mood for Love* (2000, fig. 4) the hotel is a place where a pair of reluctant lovers (Maggie Cheung and Tony Leung Chiu-Wai) write novels together, whereas in the sequel *2046* (2004) it provides the setting for a hopeless affair, where the lonely journalist tries to make up for the fulfillment that escaped him in the first film with a girl about town (Zhang Ziyi). The most original variation on this theme from recent years is undoubtedly Sofia Coppola's *Lost in Translation* from 2003. In this film Bill Murray and Scarlett Johansson, both stranded in Tokyo for different reasons, meet in one of the city's hotel towers and experience almost everything fitting to such an encounter,

Hotel ist in *Shining* mehr als ein Gebäude, es ist, jedenfalls für Jack Torrance, ein lebendiger Organismus, der Visionen ausbrütet und aufbewahrt und ihm am Ende, wie wir in der letzten Einstellung sehen, eine Art Unsterblichkeit schenkt, ein Überleben im Bild.

Die Coen-Brüder haben von Kubricks Bildfantasien gezehrt, als sie John Turturro als Drehbuchschreiber Barton Fink in dem gleichnamigen Film in die feuchtheiße Hölle des Hotels Earle unterhalb der Hügel von Hollywood schickten, in dem sich die Tapeten von den Wänden lösen, Ungeziefer im Ausguss lauert und ein gesuchter Serienmörder im Nebenzimmer wohnt.

Das Hotel, dieses Transitorium der Sehnsüchte und Schrecken, der Individuen und Ideologien, ist auch ein Kinoschauplatz, an dem sich Zeitgeschichte bündeln, in dem sich historische Verhältnisse exemplarisch spiegeln lassen. In Cristian Mungius *4 Monate, 3 Wochen und 2 Tage,* dem Siegerfilm von Cannes 2007, steht das Stadthotel, in dem die Hauptfigur Otilia für ihre Freundin Gabita ein Zimmer mietet, damit Gabita dort eine illegale Abtreibung vornehmen lassen kann, beispielhaft für den Muff und die erstarrten Machtverhältnisse der Ära Ceauşescu, für die Korruption und Verlogenheit, die die Beziehungen der Menschen untereinander regeln. In Leander Haußmanns *Hotel Lux* (2011) ist es eine Art Schaukasten der deutschen Emigration, in dem eine erfundene Figur, der unter falschem Namen reisende Kabarettist Hans Zeisig (Michael »Bully« Herbig), auf allerlei historisch verbürgte Charaktere trifft, darunter Walter Ulbricht, Wilhelm Pieck, Johannes R. Becher und Kurt Funk alias Herbert Wehner. Uli Edels jüngst ausgestrahlter Fernsehdreiteiler *Das Adlon* (2013) entfaltet mit der Geschichte des Berliner Adlon-Hotels zugleich eine deutsche Chronik des 20. Jahrhunderts, von der Entstehung des Hotels im Kaiserreich über die Bombennächte des Zweiten Weltkriegs bis zu seiner Wiedererrichtung nach dem Fall der Mauer. Wim Wenders Film *The Million Dollar Hotel* (2000) hält neben seiner Krimihandlung, die sich rings um eine von Drogensüchtigen und anderen Außenseitern bewohnte Absteige in Downtown Los Angeles entwickelt, die Stimmung im sozial gespaltenen Amerika der späten 1990er-Jahre fest. Selbst Luchino Viscontis berühmte Thomas-Mann-Verfilmung *Tod in Venedig* (1971) besitzt inzwischen, wenn auch ungewollt, den Rang eines historischen Dokuments, denn das Grand Hotel des Bains am Lido, in dem die Novelle und der Film spielen, ist dabei zu verschwinden (Abb. 7). Der Investor, der das Gebäude gekauft hatte, um seine Räume in Luxusapartments umzuwandeln, ist bankrott; das monumentale Bauwerk, durch hohe Metallzäune abgesperrt, sieht einem langsamen Verfall entgegen. Der Speisesaal, in dem Thomas Manns Aschenbach in der von Visconti gewählten Gestalt von Dirk Bogarde seinen Tadzio erblickte und in dem man noch bis vor Kurzem frühstücken konnte, ist endgültig Geschichte.

HOTELS waren immer – um einen Romantitel von Italo Calvino abzuwandeln – Orte, an denen sich Schicksale kreuzen. Das hat in *Grand Hotel* und in Jim Jarmuschs virtuos mit den Mythen der Popkultur spielender Träumerei *Mystery Train* (1998) funktioniert, und das klappt auch in John Maddens *Best Exotic Marigold Hotel,* einer englischen Komödie von 2011, die das bewährte Muster geschickt für die Generation der Best Ager zuschneidet, indem sie eine gute Handvoll beruflich oder privat gescheiterter Briten in eine gemeinsame Unterkunft im indischen Jaipur fliegen lässt, wo jeder für sich ein neues Lebensglück findet. Und auch die dramaturgische Grundformel des *Letzten Manns* ist aus dem Kino nicht verschwunden: Sie taucht etwa in Rodrigo Garcías Theateradaption *Albert Nobbs* von 2011 wieder auf, in der Glenn Close einen als Mann verkleideten weiblichen Butler in einem Dubliner Hotel der vorletzten Jahrhundertwende spielt.

Manchmal ist ein Hotel auf der Leinwand auch nur ein kunterbunter Abenteuerspielplatz. Als die drei Helden von Todd Phillips Erfolgskomödie *Hangover* (2009) am Morgen nach ihrem ersten Abend in Las Vegas in ihrer Suite erwachen, ist der Boden mit Essenresten, Verpackungen und Kleidungsstücken übersät, ein Huhn pickt auf dem Teppich herum, im Badezimmer sitzt ein Tiger, im Schrank liegt ein Baby mit nasser Windel und eine der Matratzen aus dem Zimmer wird sich später auf einer Statue an der Hotelfassade wiederfinden (Abb. 8). Das Luxushotel als Readymade eines entgleisten Junggesellenabends, das ist nicht die schlechteste Variation eines Motivs, das in immer neuen Verwandlungen durch die Filmgeschichte spukt.

except for the physical consummation that is a standard in mainstream films (fig. 5). The feeling of being out of place in cities, among people, and in the world has hardly been expressed so beautifully since Antonioni's major films of the 1960s.

A particular kind of hotel is the country hotel. Based on the novel by Stephen King, Stanley Kubrick's *The Shining* (1980) is set in a hotel that stands at the summit of a hill in the Rocky Mountains and becomes a receptacle for stories, dreams, and ghosts (fig. 6). The writer Jack Torrance, alias Jack Nicholson, who is supposed to live in and care for the hotel over the winter, gets sucked into the emptiness of the Overlook Hotel. The movements of the Steadicam—which Kubrick was the first director to use for entire sequences—pull the viewer into the void along with him: into the endless hallways where Jack and his little son meet a dead woman and her children, into the great, empty hall of the hotel, where the writer repeatedly hammers the same sentence into his typewriter, and into the bar where he enters a dream-time that has nothing to do with the present. In *The Shining* the Overlook Hotel is more than a building. At least for Jack Torrance, it is a living organism, which gives birth to and preserves visions. In the end, as we see in the last shot, it gives him a kind of immortality, a form of survival in an image. The Coen Brothers fed on Kubrick's visual imagination in the movie *Barton Fink* by sending John Turturro as the title character into the steamy, hot hell of Hotels Earle, situated below the hills of Hollywood. There the wallpaper peels from the walls, vermin lurk in the drains, and a wanted serial murderer lives in the room next door.

The hotel, this transitory space of longing and horror, of individuals and ideologies is also a film scenario that is tied to recent historical events and that can exemplify historical situations. In Cristian Mungiu's *4 Months, 3 Weeks and 2 Days,* the winning film in Cannes in 2007, the main character Otilia rents a room in a city hotel for her friend Gabita, so that the latter can have an illegal abortion. The hotel becomes a symbol of the staleness and rigid power relationships of the Ceauşescu era, of the corruption and dishonesty that determine interpersonal relationships. In Leander Haußmann's *Hotel Lux* (2011) the hotel is a kind of showcase of German emigration, in which an invented character, a cabaret artist travelling under the false name of Hans Zeisig (Michael »Bully« Herbig), encounters all sorts of authentic historical personages, including Walter Ulbricht, Wilhelm Pieck, Johannes R. Becher, and Kurt Funk alias Herbert Wehner. Uli Edel's recently broadcast three-part television series *Das Adlon* (2013) tells the story of the history of the Berlin Adlon-Hotel but simultaneously also serves as a chronicle of the 20th century, from the beginnings of the hotel in imperial Germany, to the nights of bombings during World War II, and reconstruction after the fall of the Wall. In addition to its crime-thriller plot Wim Wenders' film *The Million Dollar Hotel* (2000) captures the mood of a socially divided America in the late 1990 as the film unfolds around a sleazy hotel in downtown Los Angeles that is inhabited by drug addicts and other outsiders. Even Luchino Visconti's famous adaptation of Thomas Mann's *Death in Venice* (1971) now occupies the unintended status of a historical document. The Grand Hotel des Bains on the Lido, where the novella and the film are set, is about to disappear (fig. 7). The investor who purchased the building for the purpose of transforming its rooms into luxury apartments is bankrupt, and the monumental building, now surrounded by a high metal fence, is facing the prospects of gradually rotting to the ground. The dining hall where Thomas Mann's Aschenbach, who Visconti cast with Dirk Bogarde, sees his Tadzio and where until only recently one could have breakfast is now finally history.

HOTELS have always been places where destinies cross, to borrow from the title of an Italo Calvino novel. This was served in *Grand Hotel* as well as in Jim Jarmusch's *Mystery Train* (1998), a musing film that virtuously plays with myths of pop culture. It also worked well in John Madden's *Best Exotic Marigold Hotel,* a British comedy from 2011, which tailors a tried and true formula to the best-ager generation by having a good handful of British travelers, all of whom had failed somehow either professionally or personally, fly to joint accommodations in Jaipur, India, where each one discovers a new form of personal happiness. And also the fundamental dramaturgical formula of the *Der Letzte Mann* has not disappeared from the cinemas. It reappears, for example, in Rodrigo Garcías' theatrical adaptation of *Albert Nobbs* from 2011, in which Glenn Close plays a female butler in a Dublin hotel of the past turn of the century, who is disguised as a man.

Sometimes the hotel on the silver screen is merely a jumbled adventure playground. When the three heroes of Todd Phillips' successful comedy *Hangover* (2009) wake up in the morning after their first night in Las Vegas, they find the floor littered with scraps of food, packaging, and pieces of clothing; a chicken is pecking at the carpet, and a tiger is sitting in the bathroom; in the cupboard lies a baby with wet diapers, and one of the mattresses from the room is later found on a statue on the hotel façade (fig. 8). The luxury hotel as a readymade of an out-of-hand bachelor party is not such a bad variation on a motif that continues to haunt the history of film in continually shifting forms.

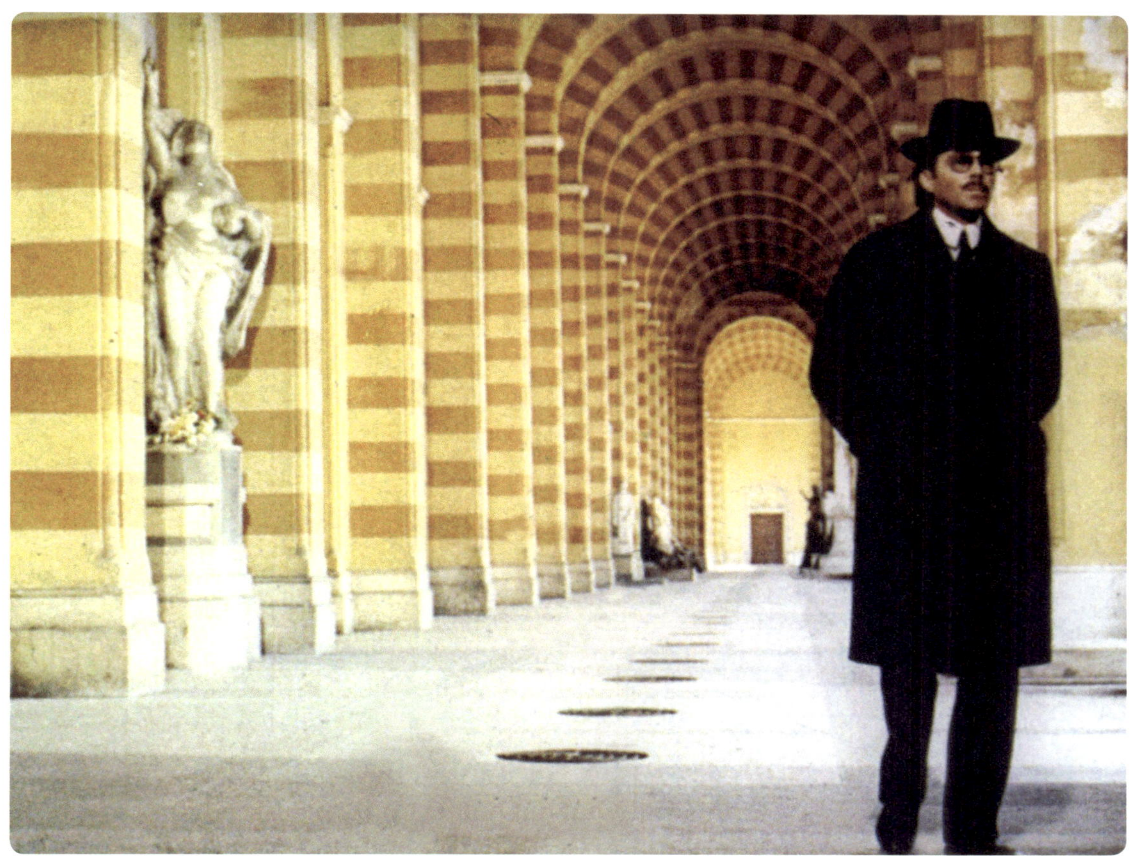

Abb. / Fig. 7

TOD IN VENEDIG / DEATH IN VENICE

Regie / Directed by: Luchino Visconti, 1971, © action press / Everett Collection

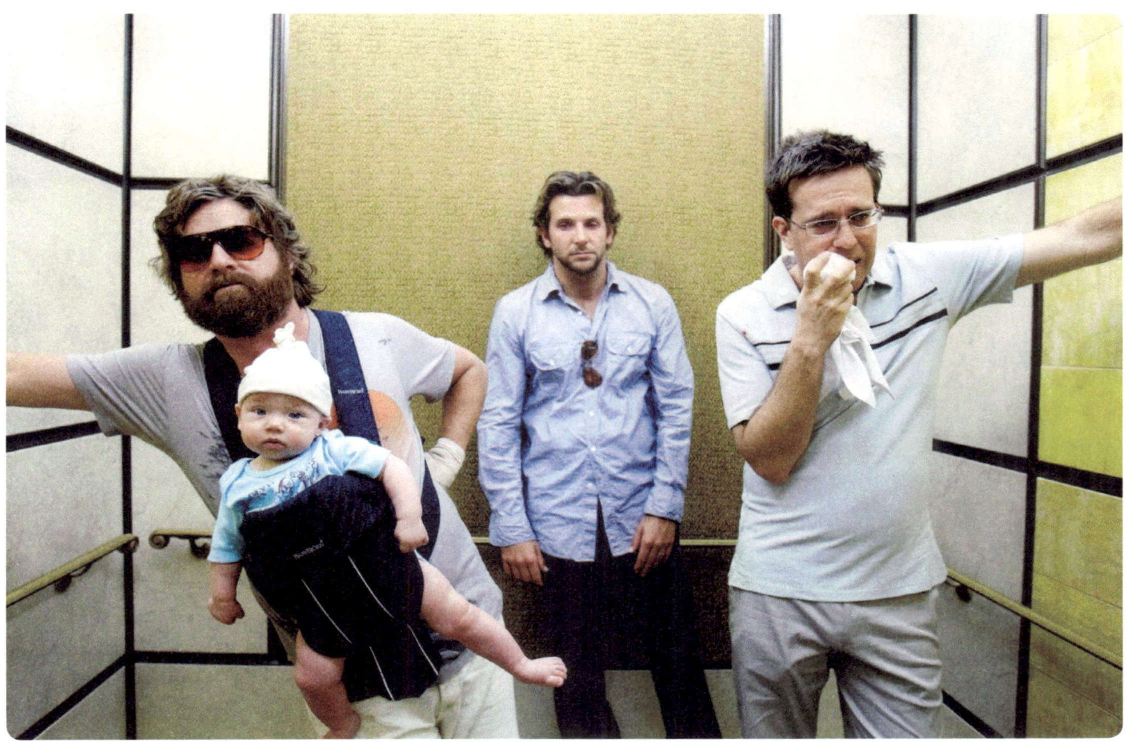

Abb. / Fig. 8

HANGOVER

Regie / Directed by: Todd Phillips, 2009, © Collection Christophel

AUSSTELLUNG / EXHIBITION STAATLICHE KUNSTHALLE BADEN-BADEN

MIT ARBEITEN VON / WITH WORKS BY

Joseph Mallord William Turner | John Constable

William Henry Fox Talbot | Honoré Daumier

Adolph Menzel | Francis Frith

Michael Ancher | Christian Krohg

Laurits Tuxen | Oskar Björck

Valdemar Schønheyder Møller

Peder Severin Krøyer | Laurits Schmidt-Nielsen

Georg Hering | Paul Signac

Paul Riess | George Stephenson

Carl Windels | Johan Marinus ›Mari‹ Ten Kate

Otto Albert Koch | Hugo Degenhard

Julius Reith | August Sander

Auguste Chabaud | Max Beckmann

Chaïm Soutine | George Grosz

Hans Meyboden | Henri Cartier-Bresson

Hanns Hubmann | Diane Arbus

Daniel Spoerri | On Kawara

William Eggleston | Hans-Peter Feldmann

Candida Höfer | Sophie Calle

Martin Kippenberger | Thomas Schütte

Andreas Gursky | Olaf Nicolai

Guy Tillim | Thomas Demand

Eberhard Havekost | Sven Johne

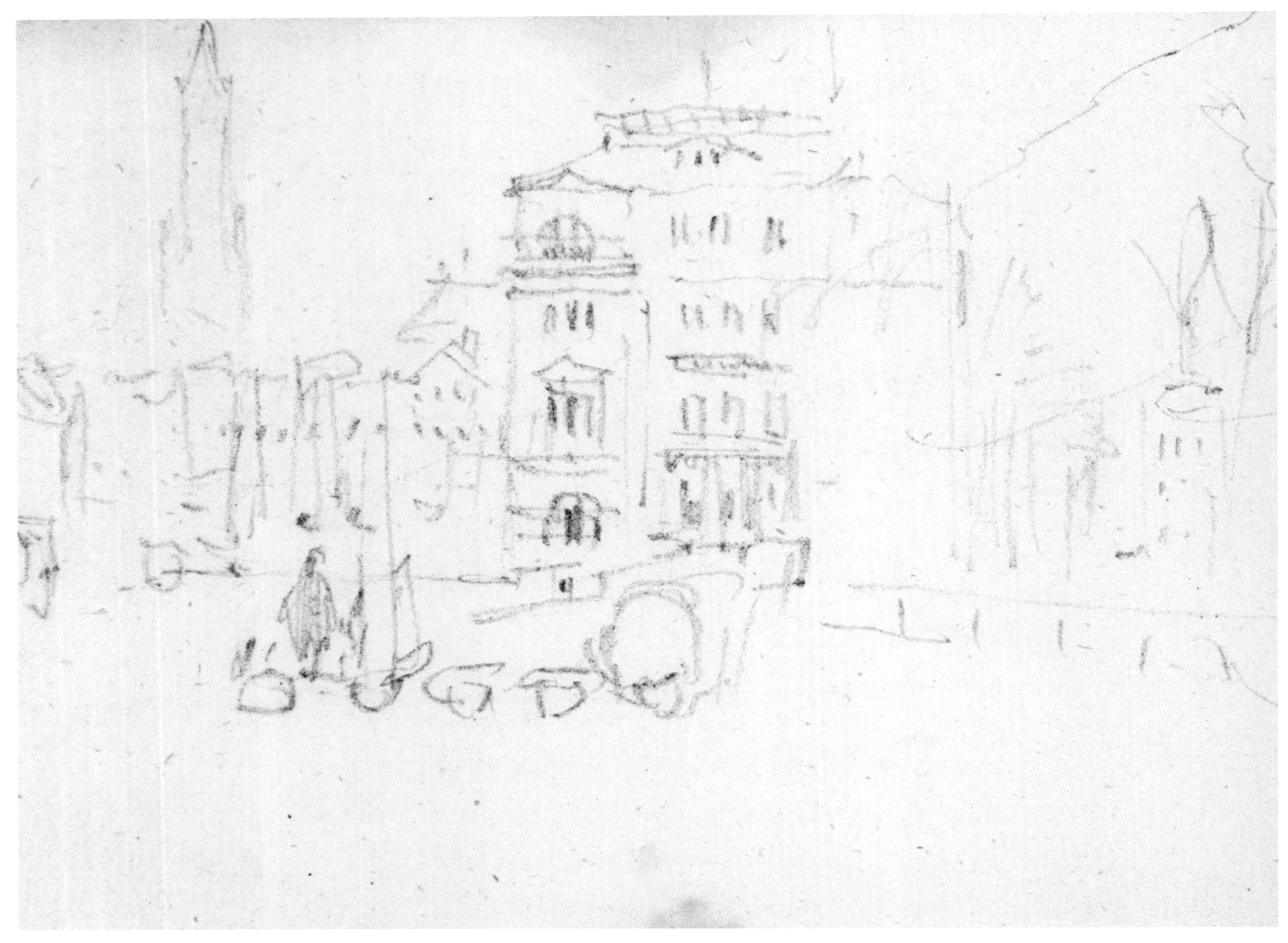

Joseph Mallord William Turner (1775–1851)
HAMBURG: BLICK ÜBER DEN JUNGFERNSTIEG AUF DAS HOTEL BELVEDERE MIT DEN TÜRMEN DER JACOBIKIRCHE UND DER PETRIKIRCHE DAHINTER /
HAMBURG: VIEW ALONG THE JUNGFERNSTIEG TO HOTEL BELVEDERE WITH THE SPIRES OF THE JACOBIKIRCHE AND PETRIKIRCHE IN THE BACKGROUND, 1835

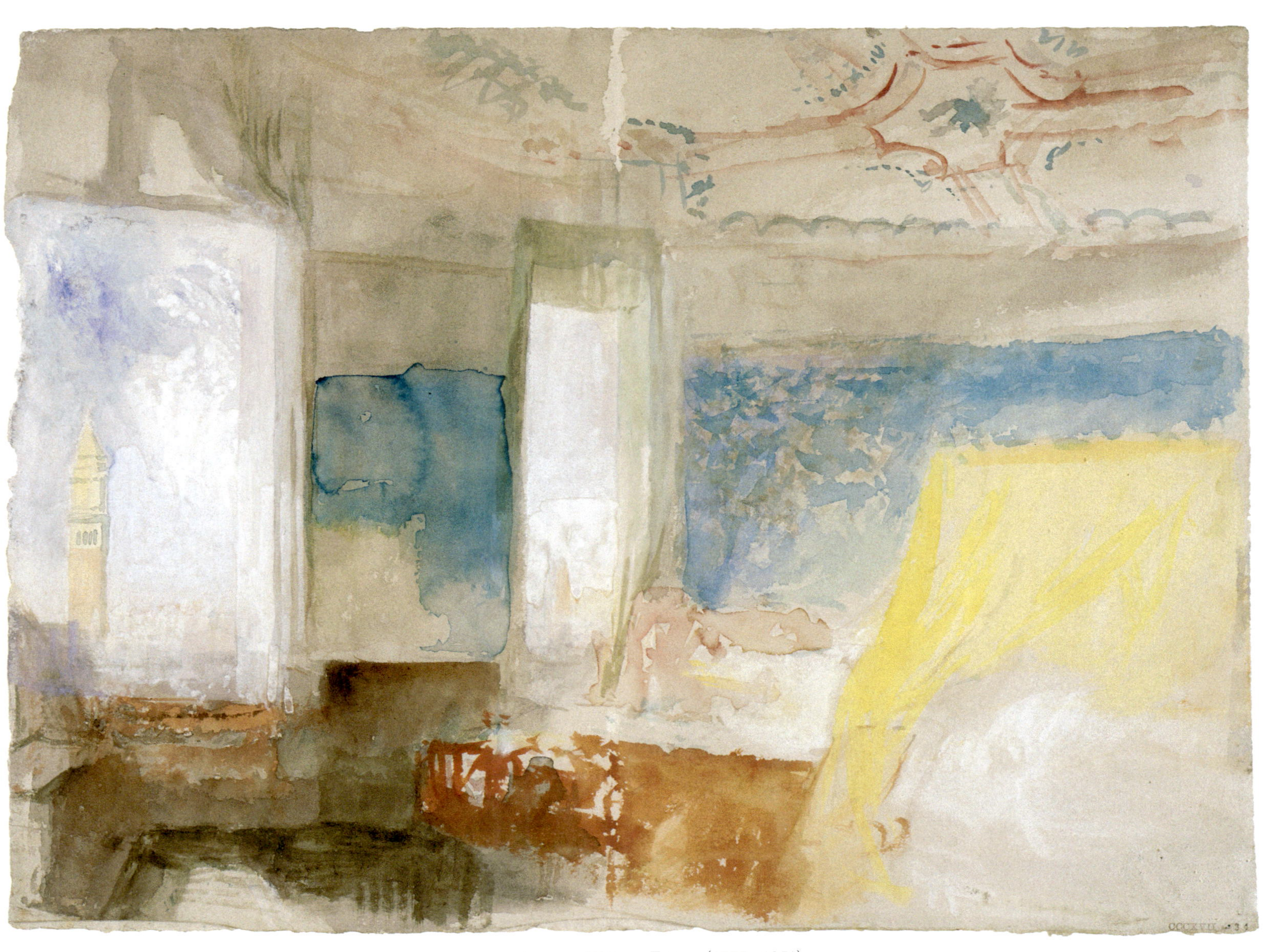

Joseph Mallord William Turner (1775–1851)
TURNERS SCHLAFZIMMER IM PALAZZO GIUSTINIAN (HOTEL EUROPA), VENEDIG / TURNER'S BEDROOM IN THE PALAZZO GIUSTINIAN (HOTEL EUROPA), VENICE, um / c. 1840

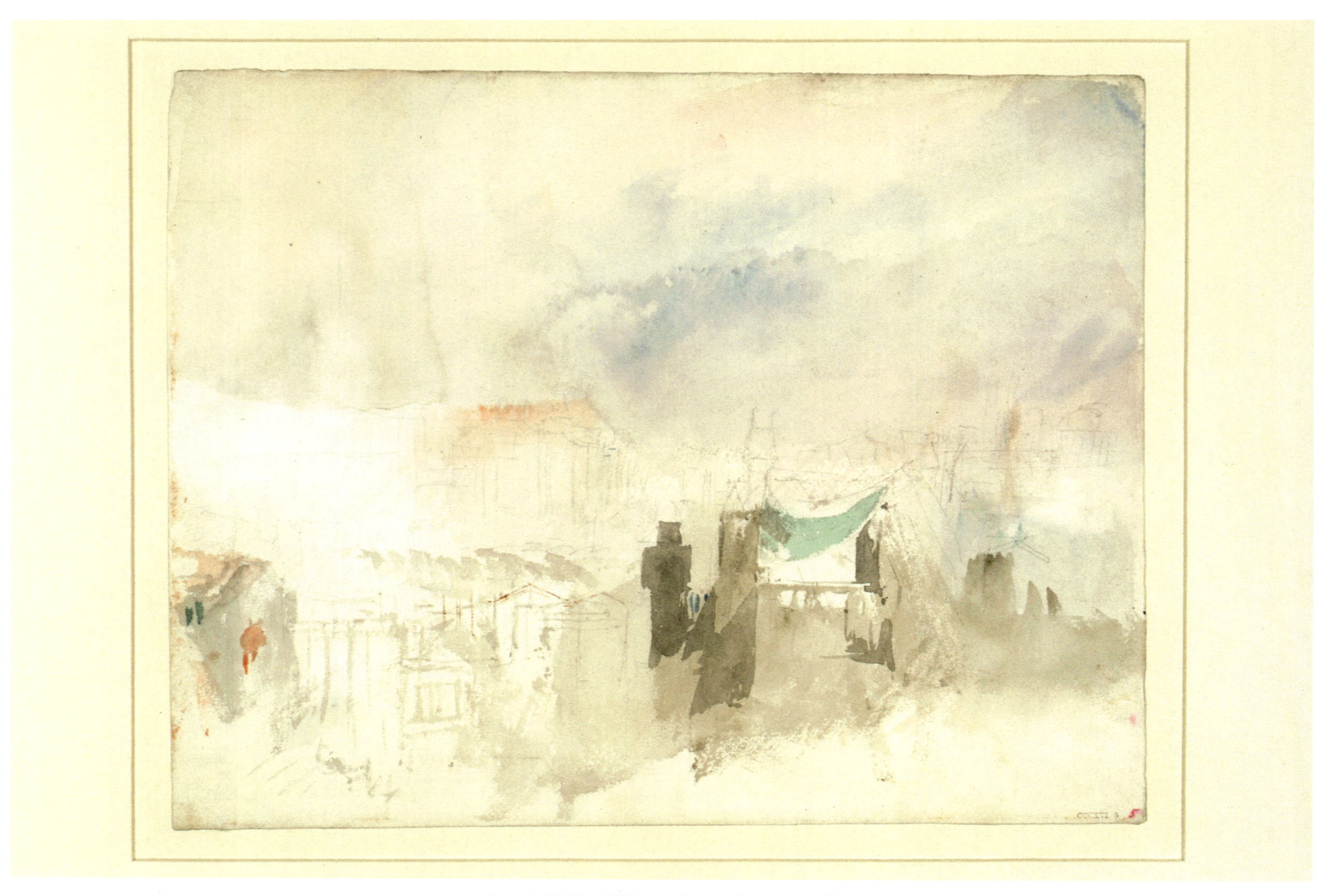

Joseph Mallord William Turner (1775–1851)
VENEDIG: BLICK ÜBER DIE DÄCHER VOM HOTEL EUROPA AUS / VENICE: VIEW ACROSS THE ROOFTOPS FROM HOTEL EUROPA, 1840

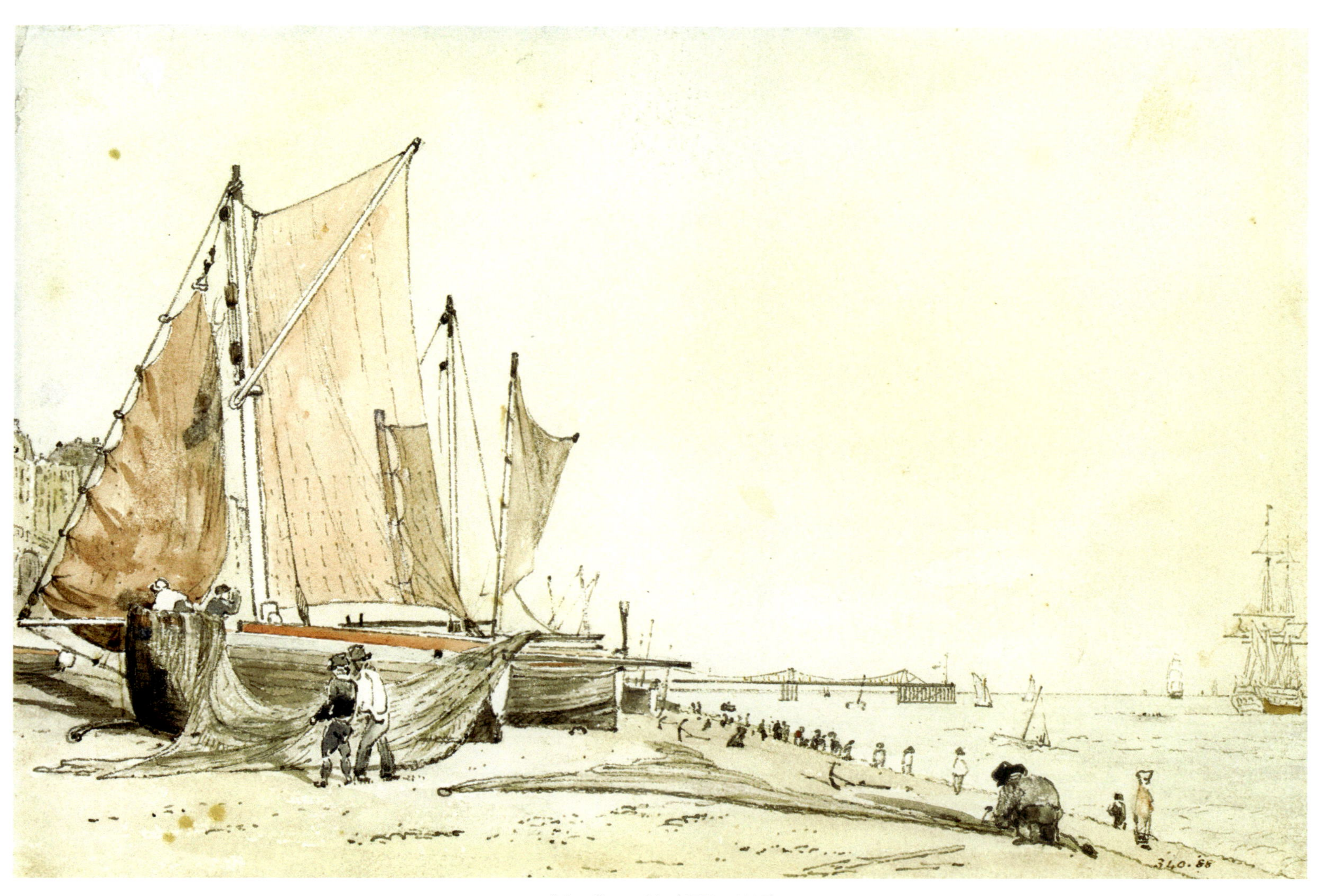

John Constable (1776–1837)
DER STRAND VON BRIGHTON, MIT FISCHERBOOTEN UND DEM CHAIN PIER / BRIGHTON BEACH, WITH FISHING BOATS AND THE CHAIN PIER, um / c. 1824

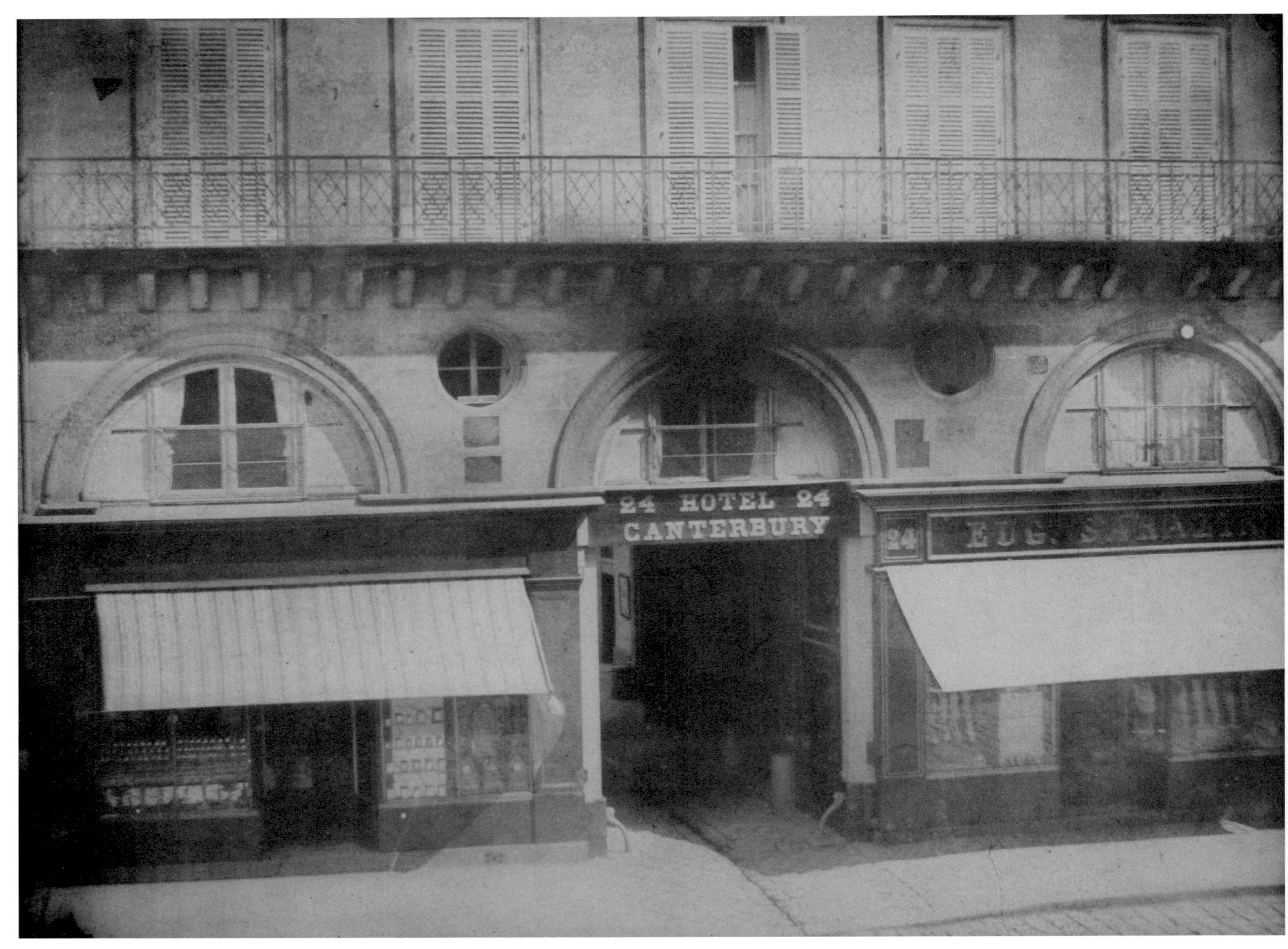

William Henry Fox Talbot (1800–1877)
RUE DE LA PAIX, HOTEL CANTERBURY, 1843

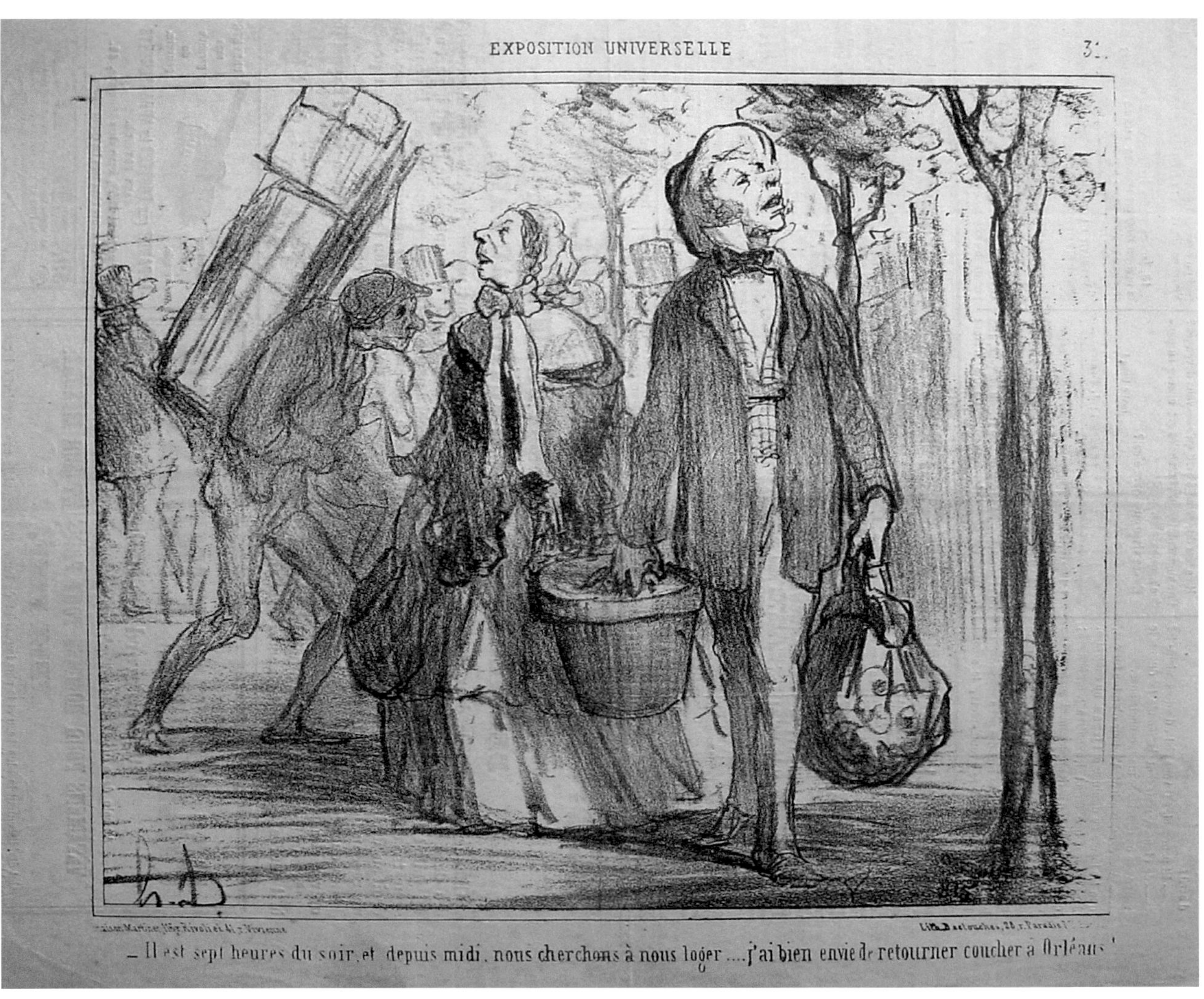

Honoré Daumier (1808–1879)
EINE VORÜBERGEHENDE BEHAUSUNG / A TEMPORARY LODGING, 1854

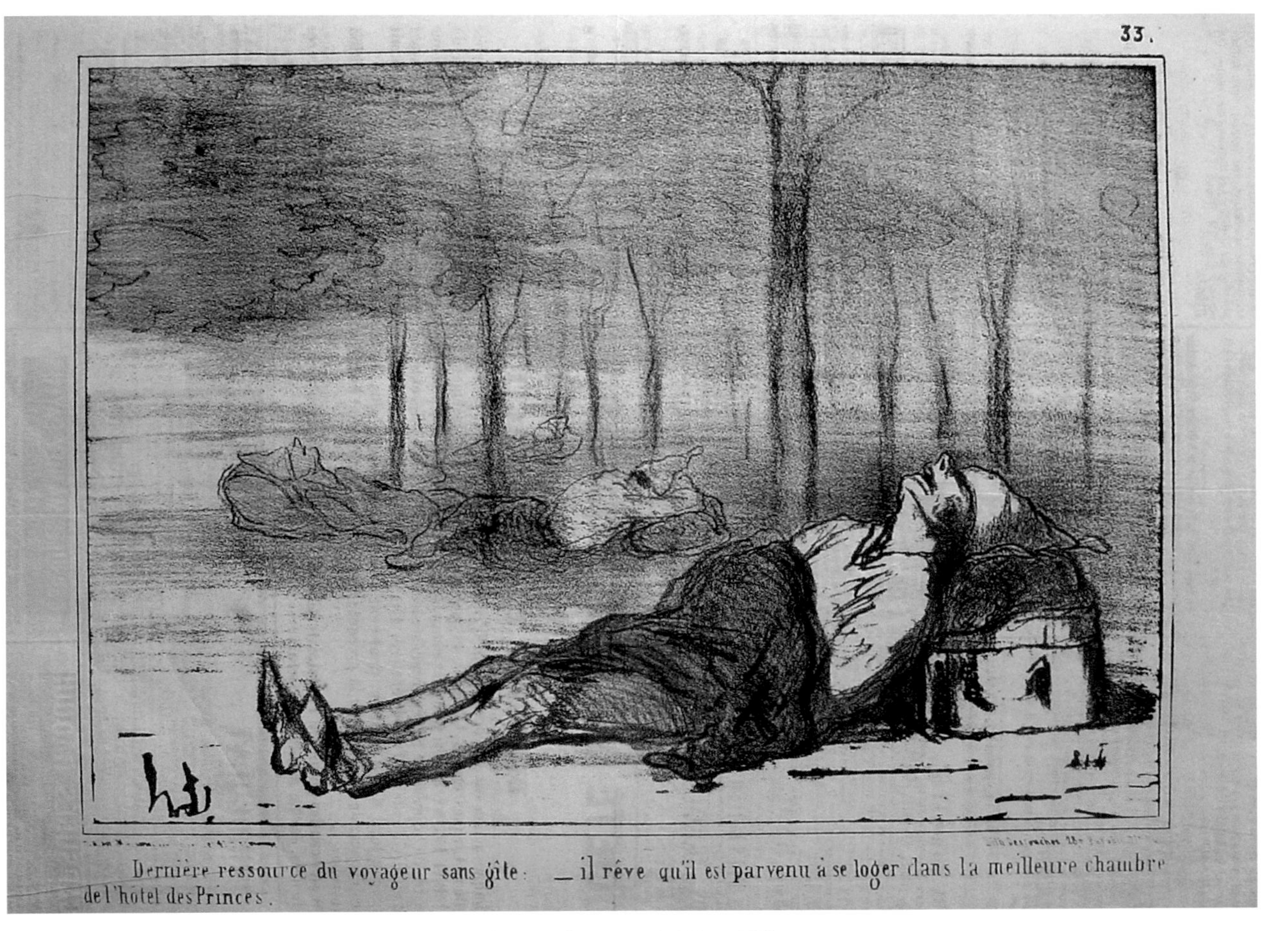

Honoré Daumier (1808–1879)
DIE LETZTE ZUFLUCHT FÜR BESUCHER OHNE ZIMMER. ER TRÄUMT DAVON, IM BESTEN ZIMMER DES HOTEL DES PRINCES ZU NÄCHTIGEN / THE LAST RESORT FOR TRAVELERS WITHOUT LODGINGS. HE DREAMS ABOUT SLEEPING IN THE BEST ROOM OF THE HOTEL DES PRINCES, 1855

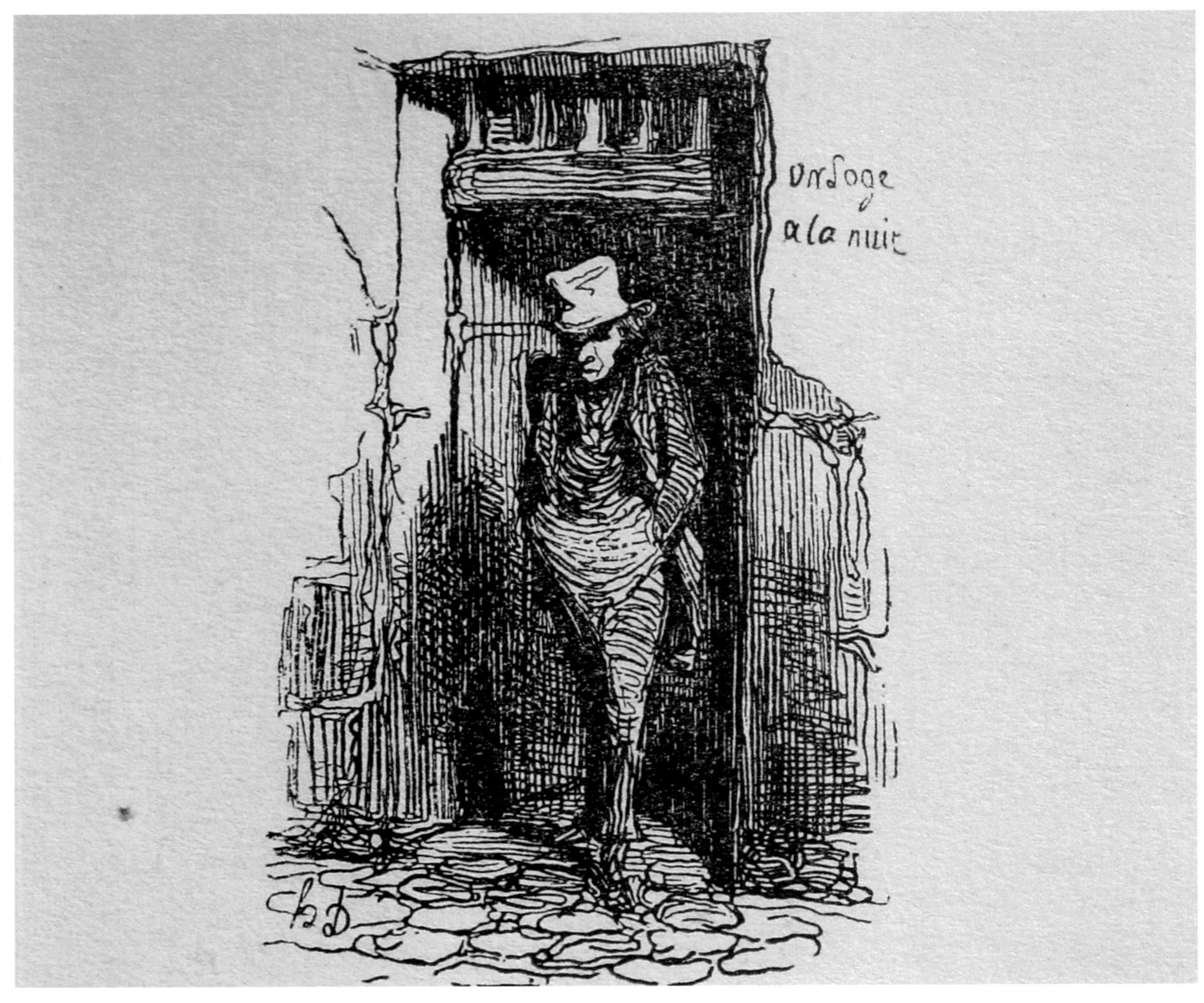

Honoré Daumier (1808–1879)
DAS NACHTASYL / SHELTER FOR THE NIGHT, 1842–1843

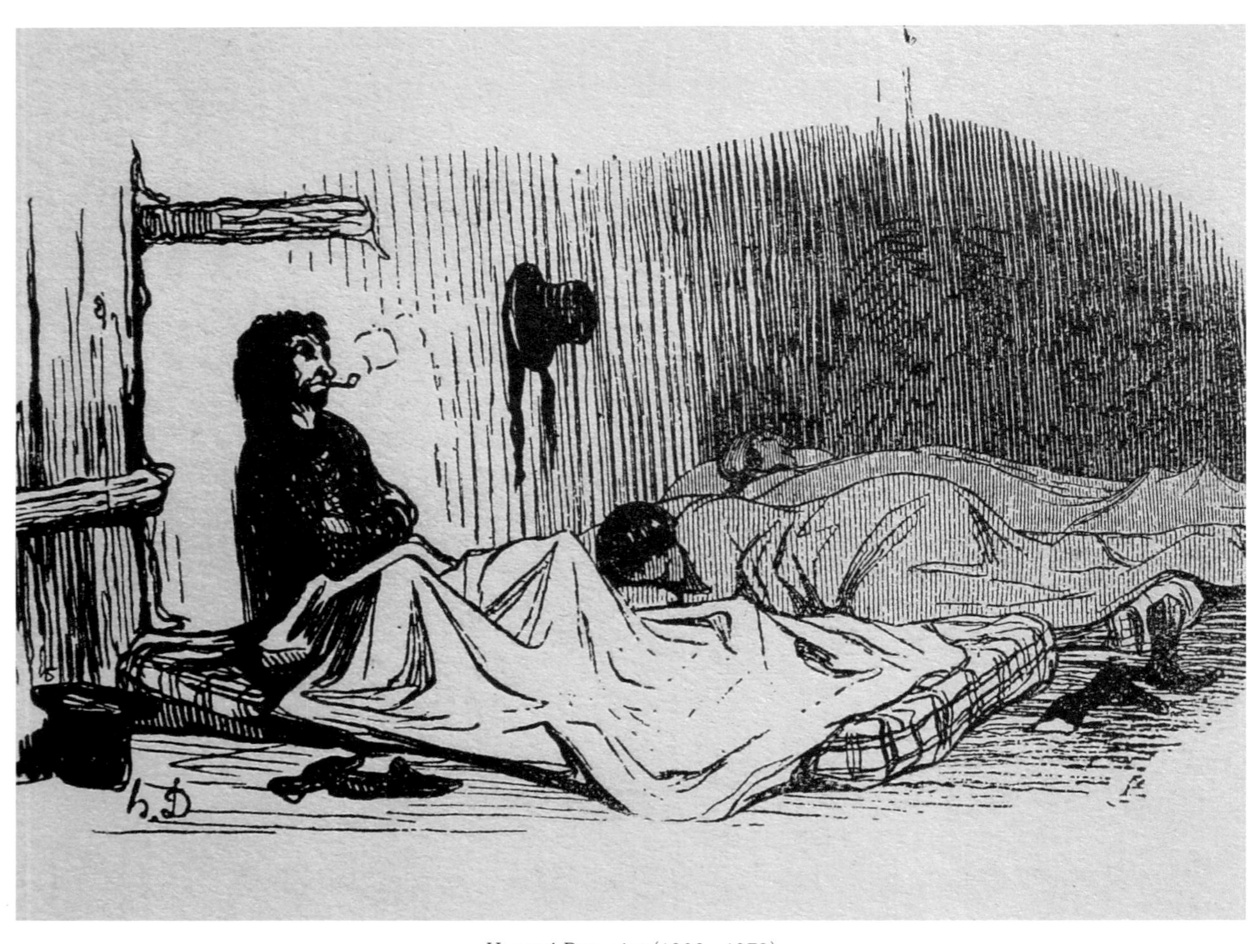

Honoré Daumier (1808–1879)
EIN HOTEL GARNI / A CHEAP PLACE TO SLEEP, 1842–1843

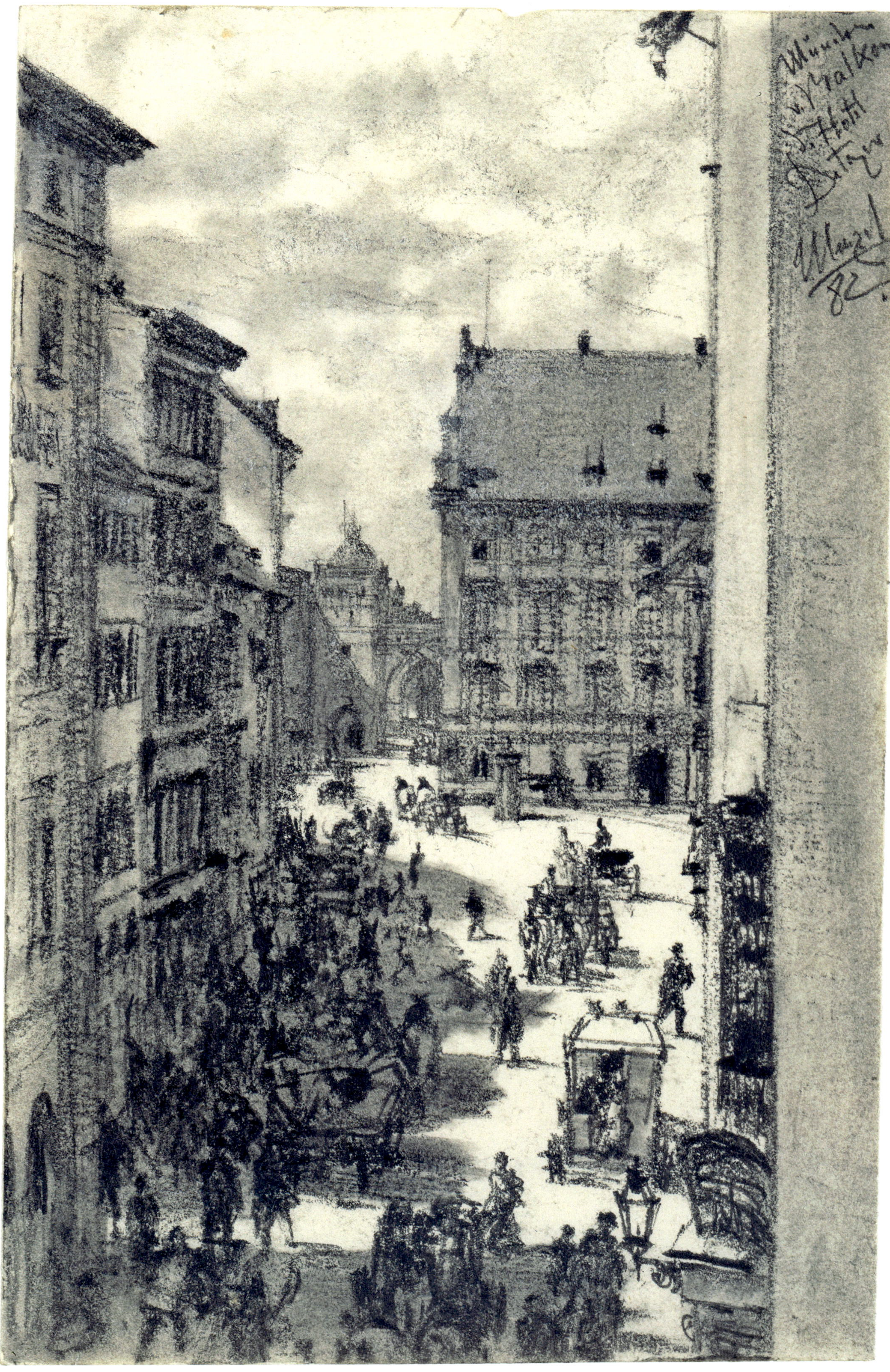

Adolph Menzel (1815–1905)
BLICK VOM BALKON DES HOTELS DETZER AUF DEN INNSBRUCKER PLATZ IN MÜNCHEN / VIEW FROM THE BALCONY OF HOTEL DETZER ON INNSBRUCKER SQUARE IN MUNICH, 1882

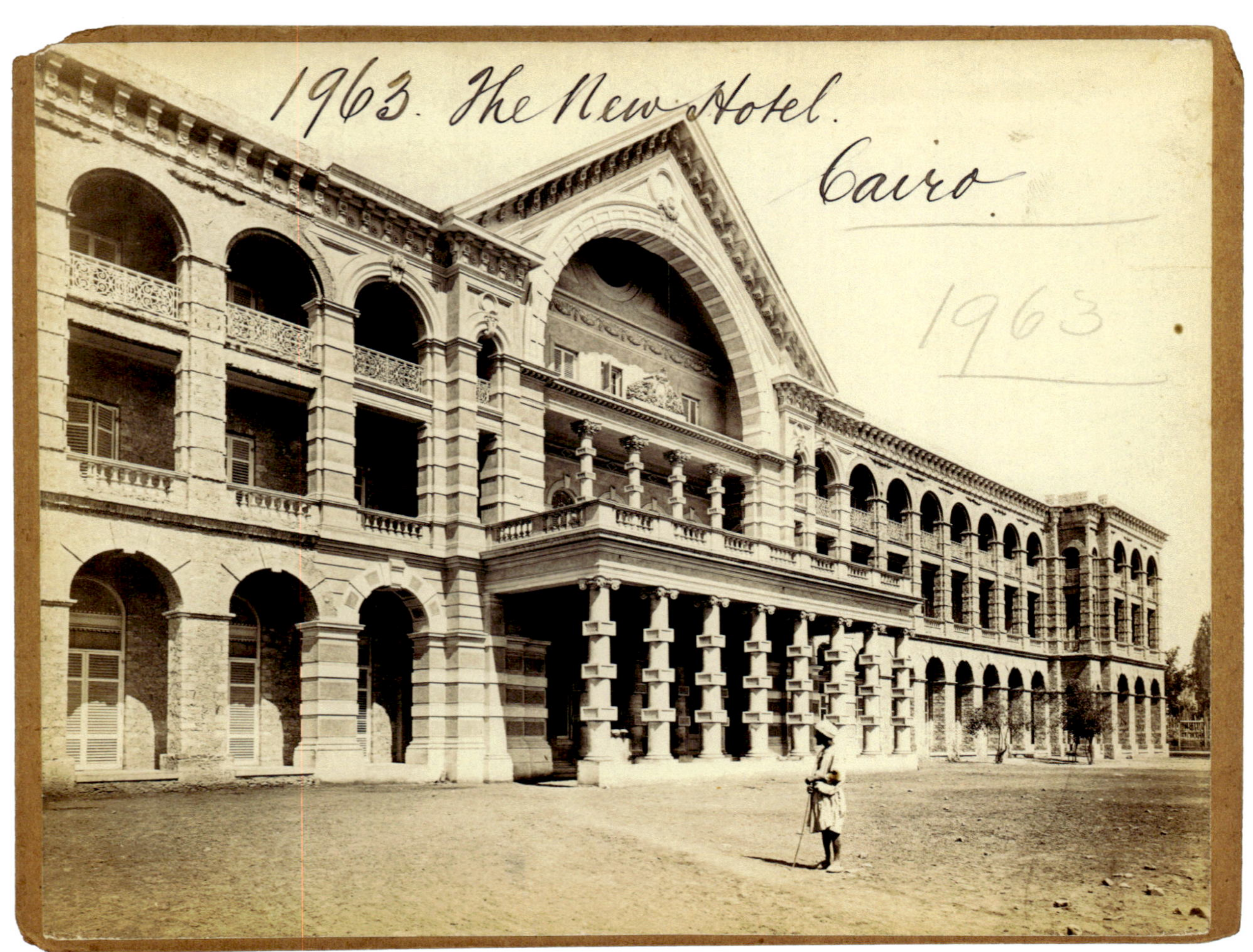

Francis Frith (1822–1898)
THE NEW HOTEL. KAIRO / THE NEW HOTEL. CAIRO, 1850–1870

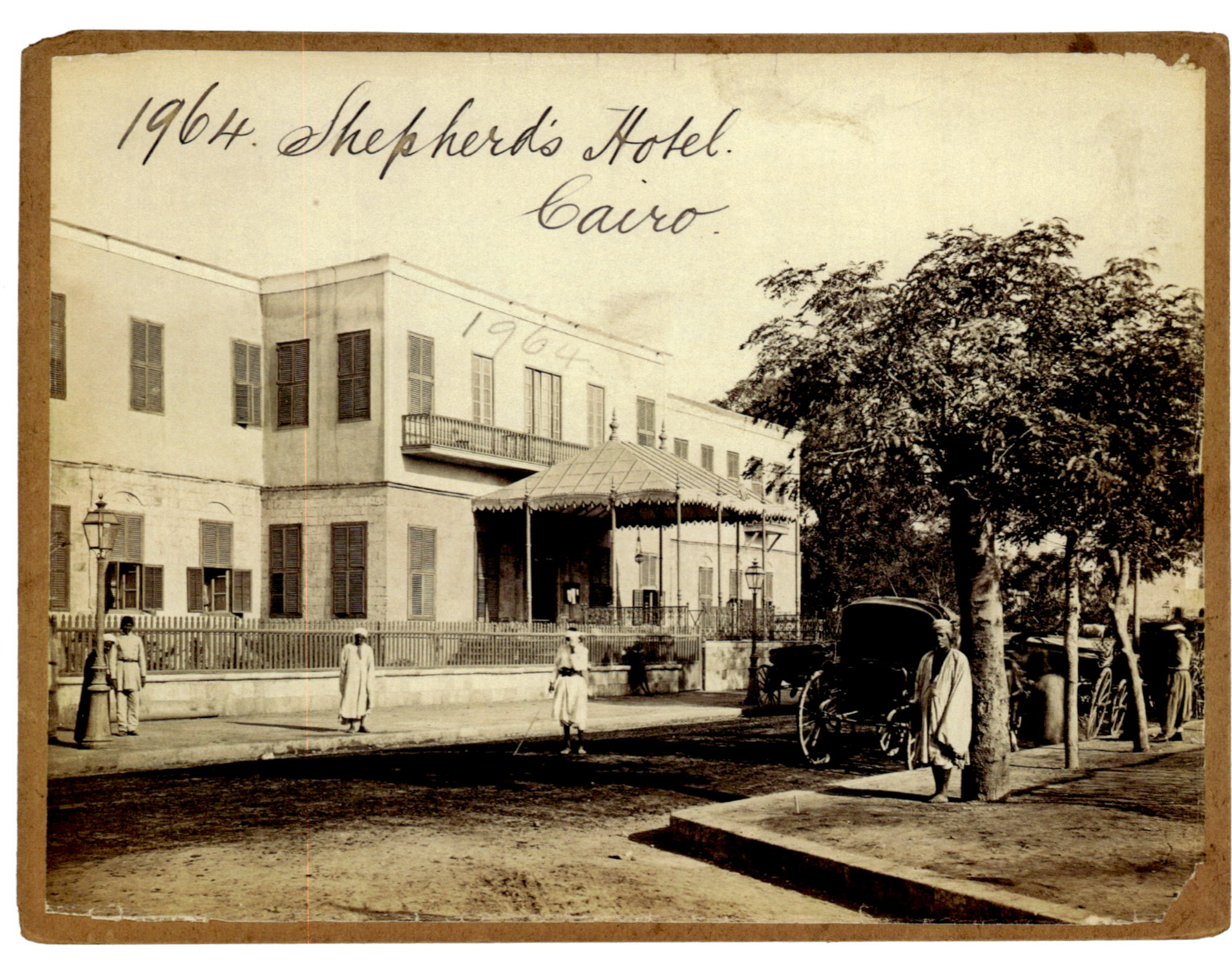

Francis Frith (1822–1898)
SHEPHERD'S HOTEL. KAIRO / SHEPHERD'S HOTEL. CAIRO, 1850–1870

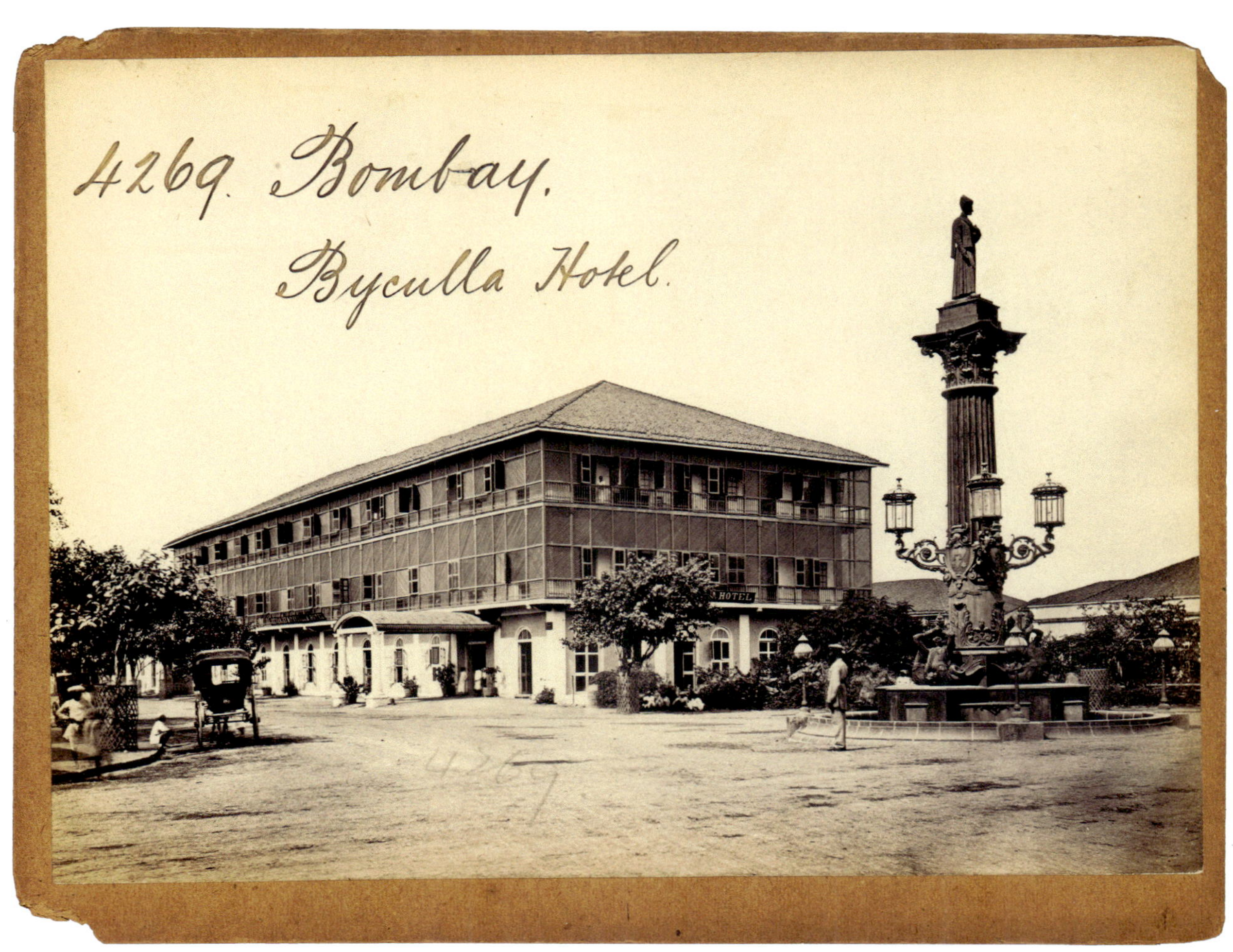

Francis Frith (1822–1898)
BOMBAY, BYCULLA HOTEL, 1850–1870

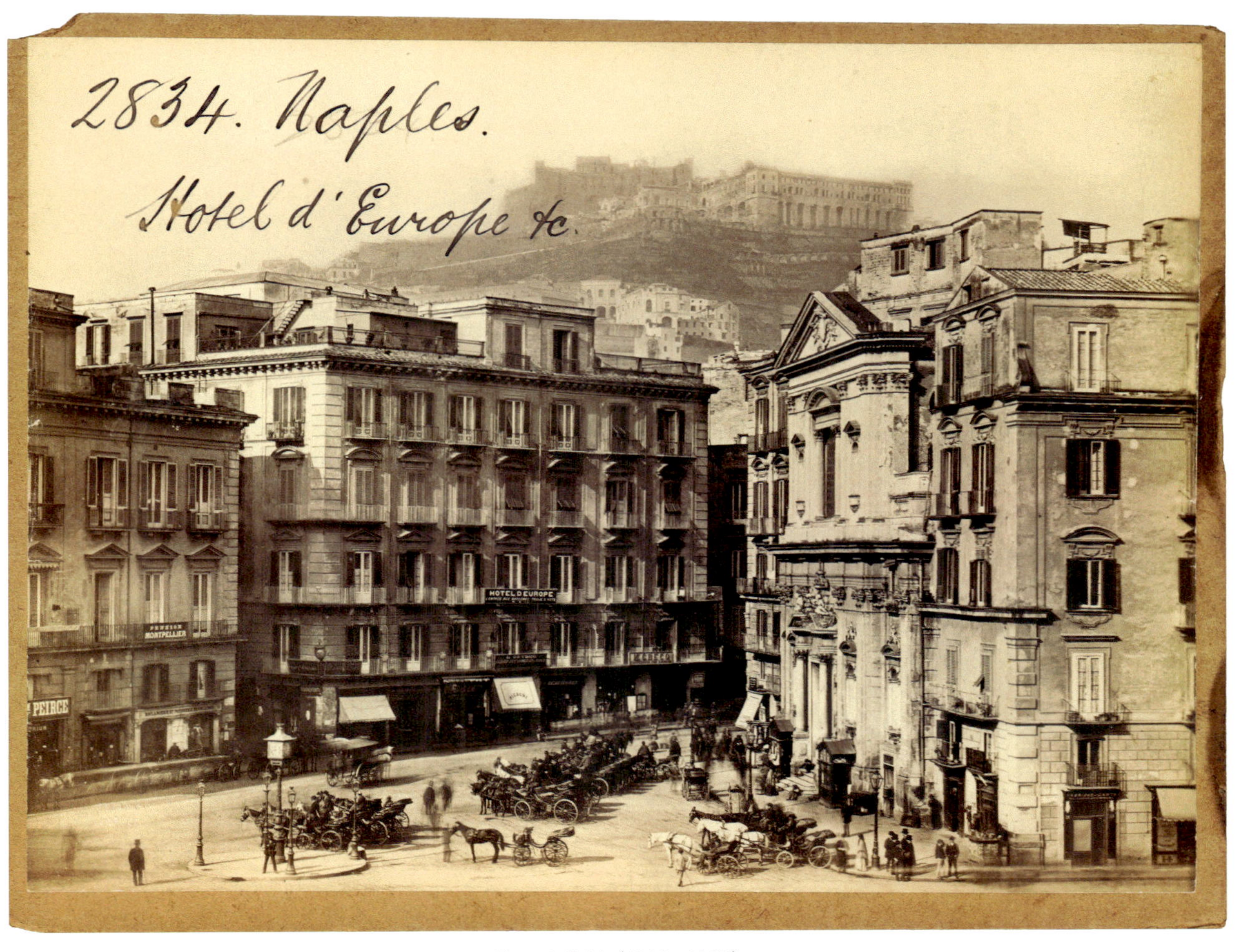

Francis Frith (1822–1898)
NEAPEL. HOTEL D'EUROPE ETC. / NAPLES. HOTEL D'EUROPE ETC., 1850–1870

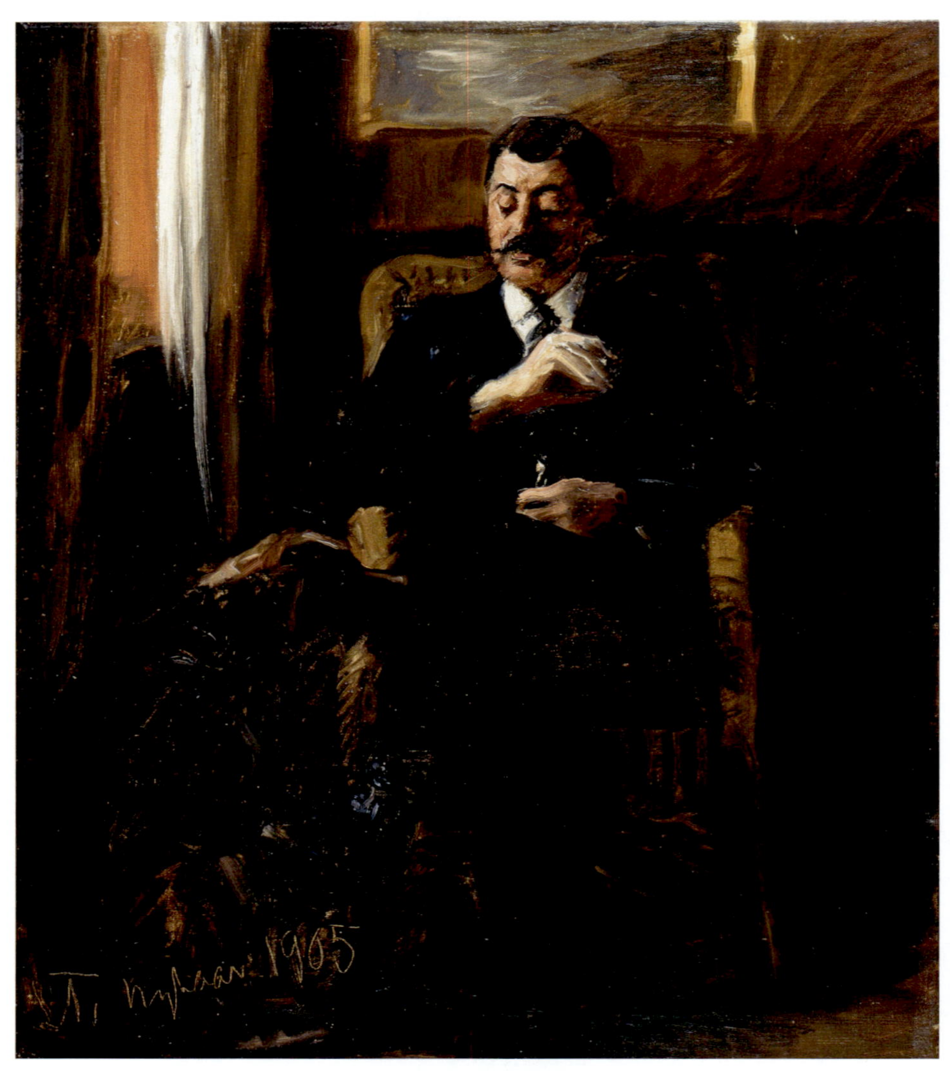

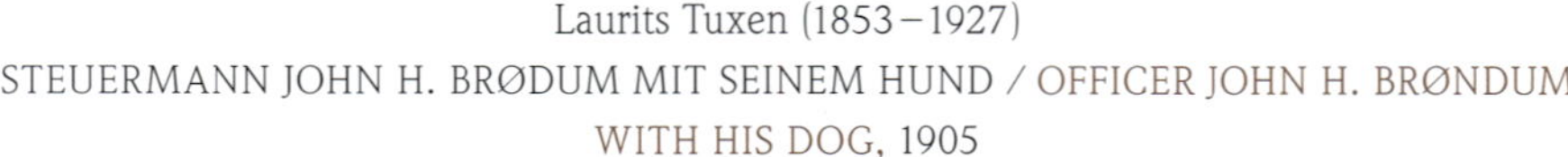

Laurits Tuxen (1853 – 1927)
STEUERMANN JOHN H. BRØDUM MIT SEINEM HUND / OFFICER JOHN H. BRØNDUM WITH HIS DOG, 1905

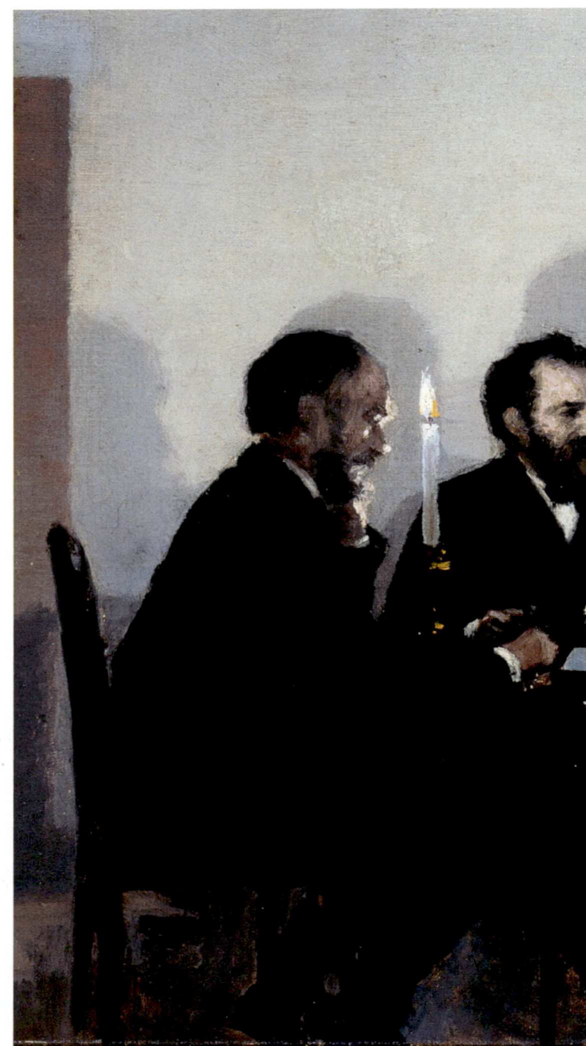

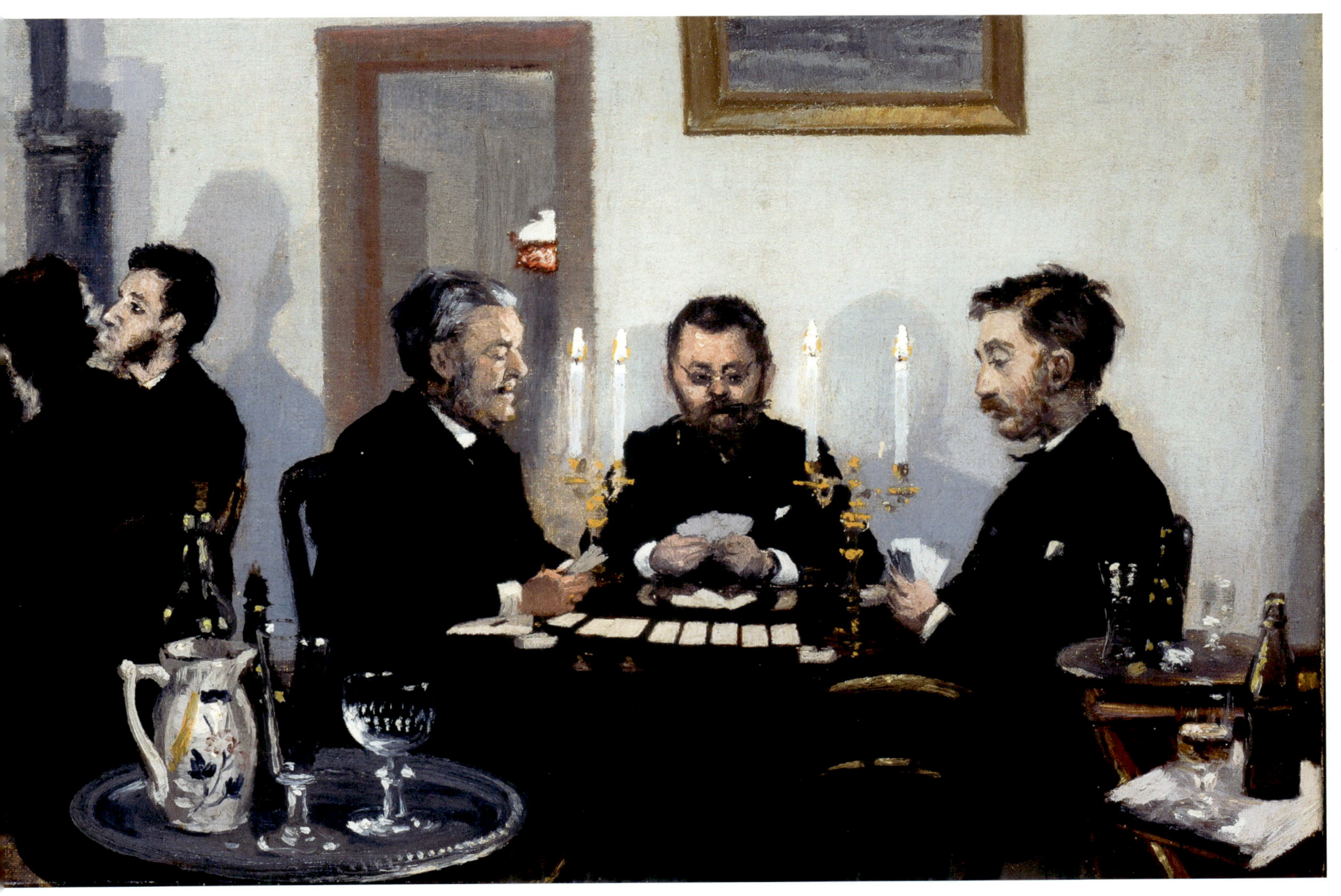

Valdemar Schønheyder Møller (1864–1905)
KARTENCLUB AN DEN SPIELTISCHEN IN DER WEISSEN STUBE DES BRØNDUMS HOTELS /
E »SKAGENS KLUB« AT THE GAMBLING TABLES IN THE WHITE ROOM AT BRØNDUMS HOTEL, 1891/1893

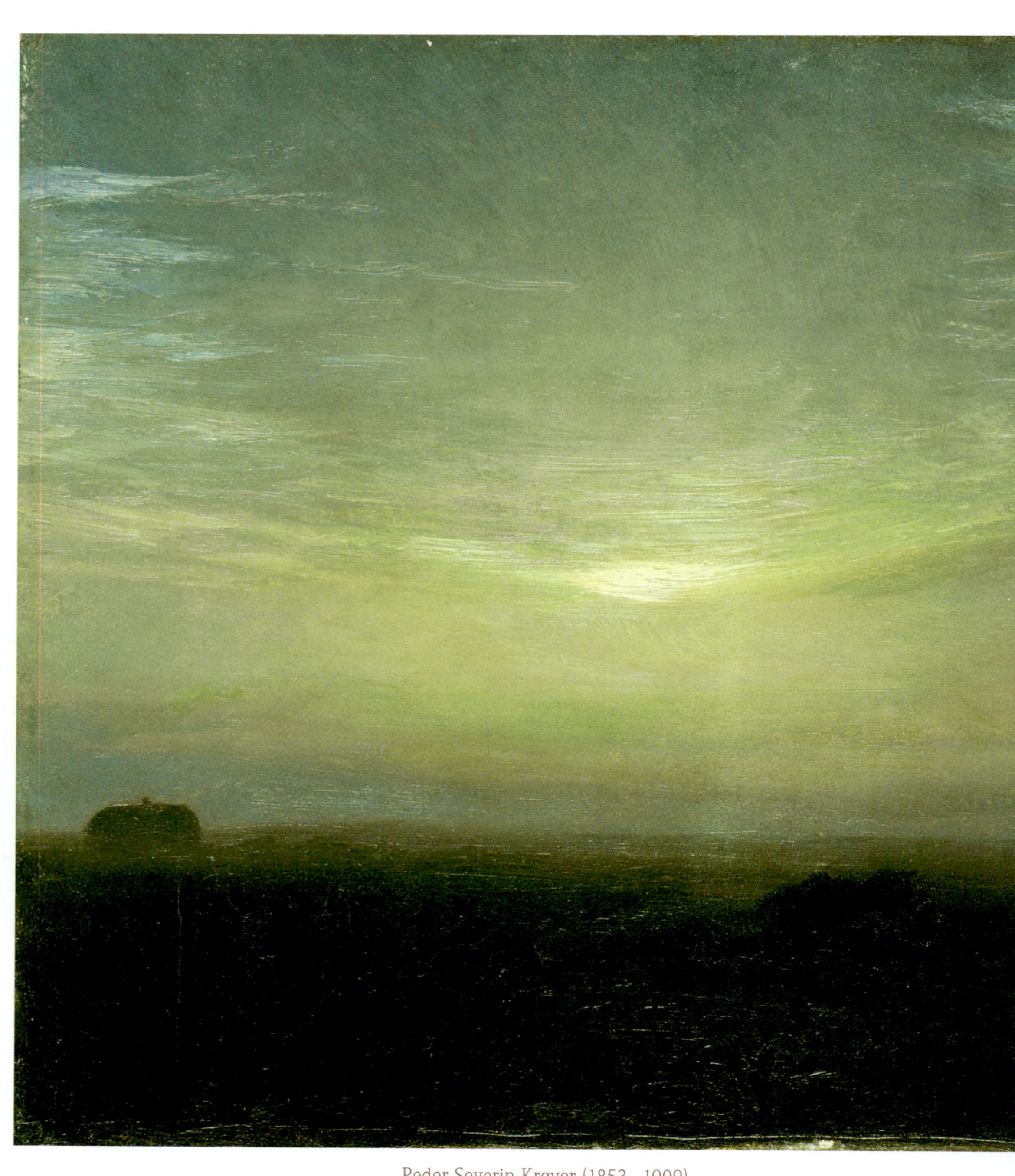

Peder Severin Krøyer (1853–1909)
FROM THE MOORS NORTH OF SKAGEN. MIDNIGHT, 6 JULY, 1885

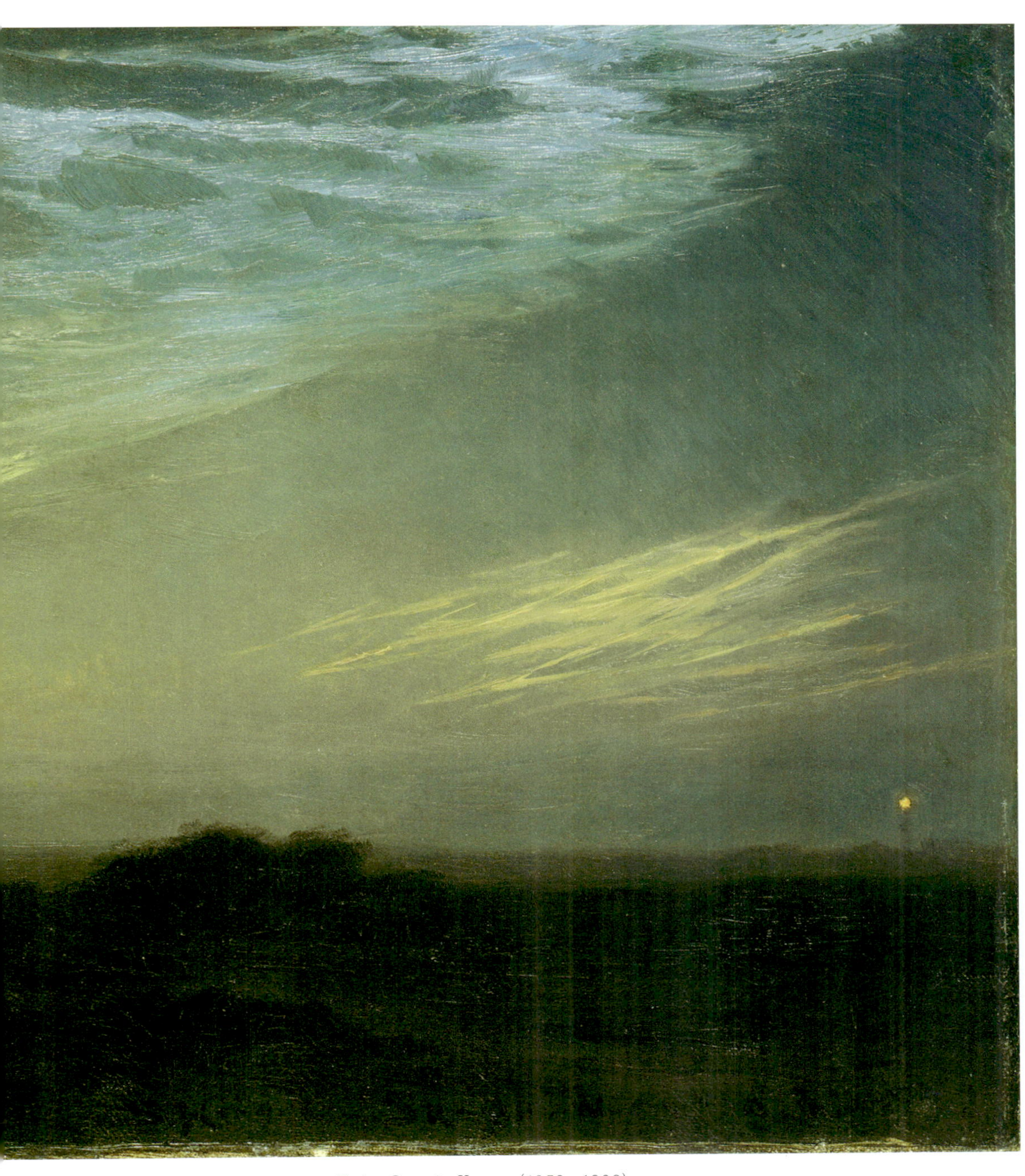

Peder Severin Krøyer (1853–1909)
VON DER HEIDE NÖRDLICH VON SKAGEN. MITTERNACHT, 6. JULI 1885

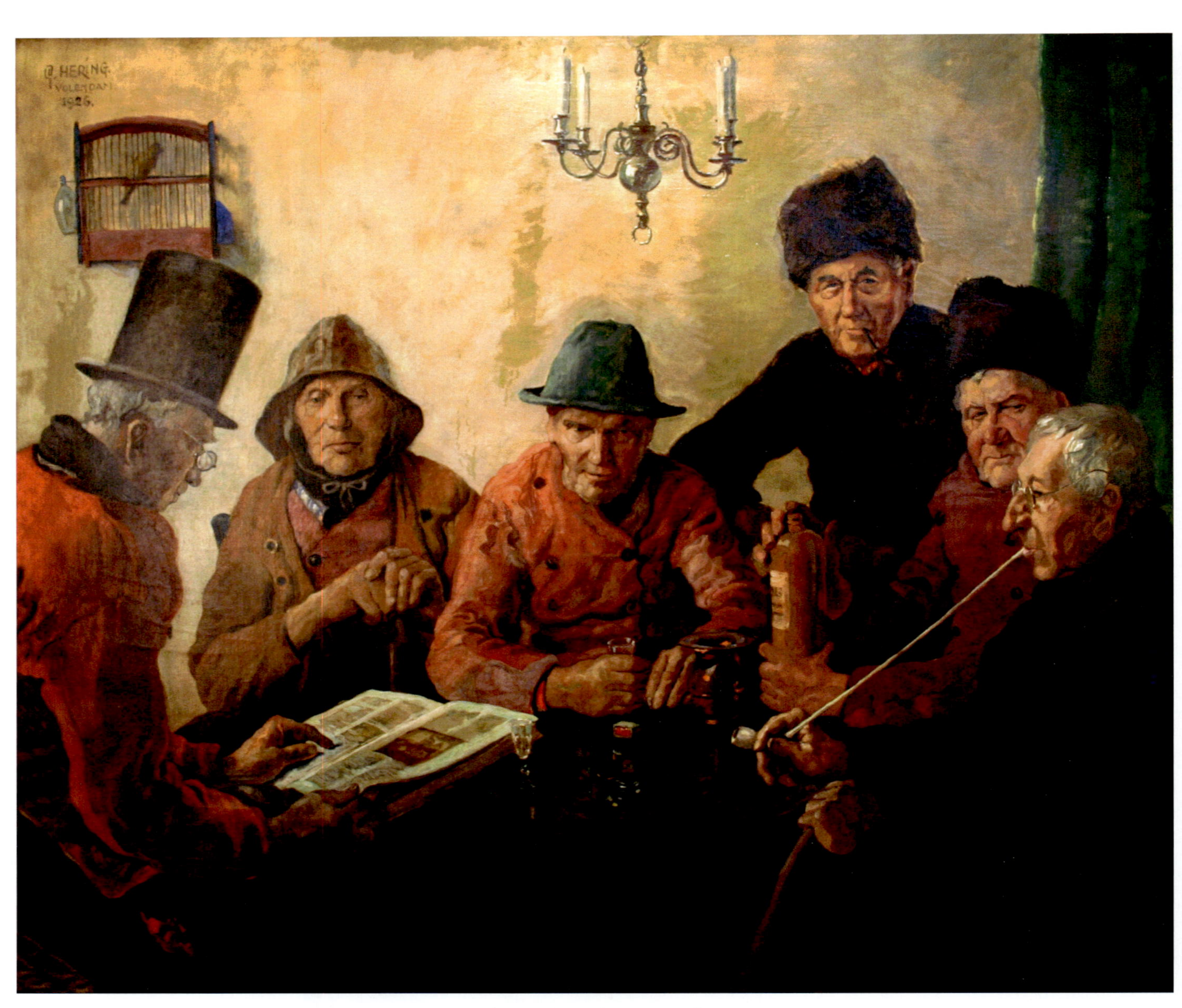

Georg Hering (1884–1936)
IN DER ALTEN HERBERGE / IN THE OLD INN, 1926

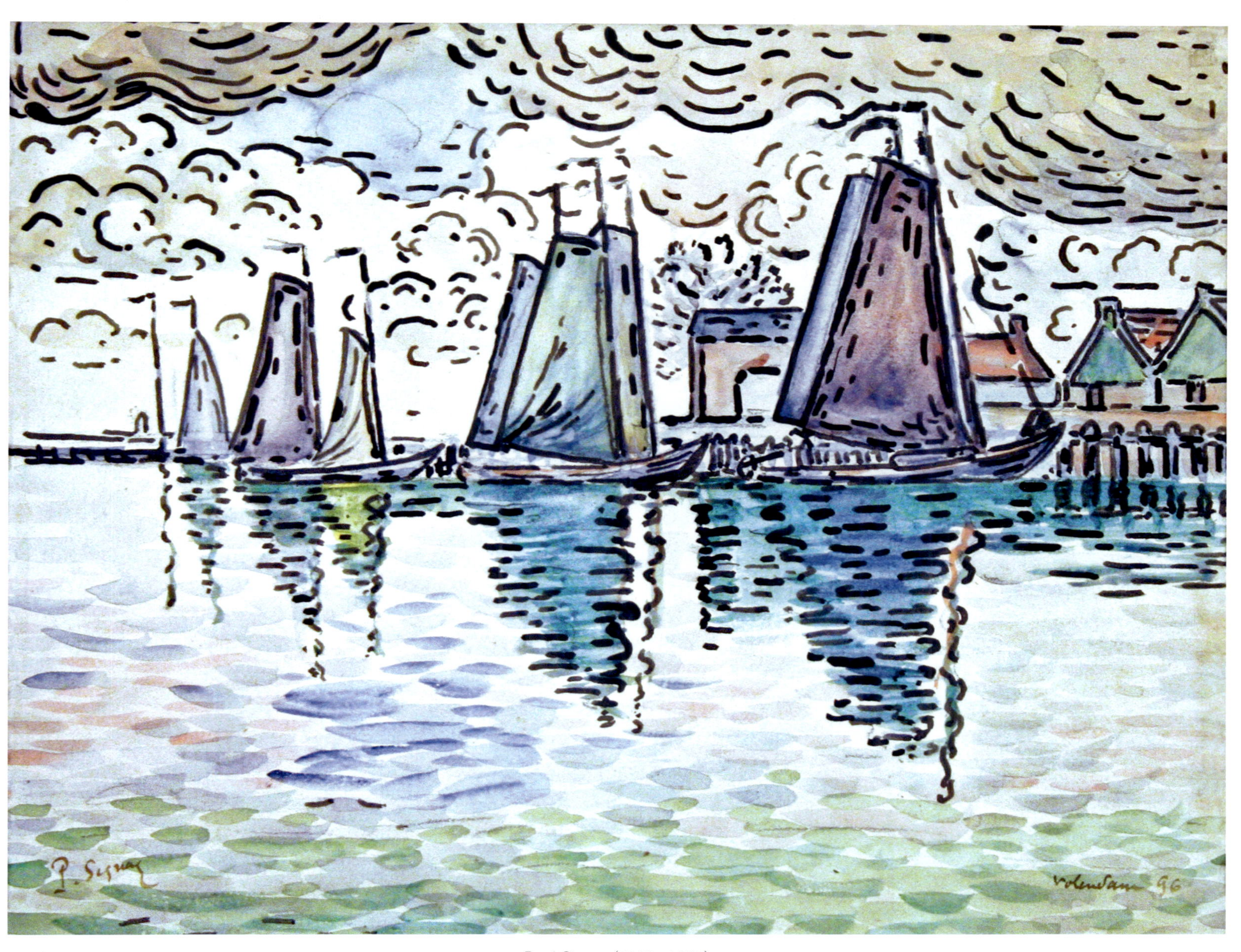

Paul Signac (1863–1935)
SEESTÜCK / SEASCAPE, 1896

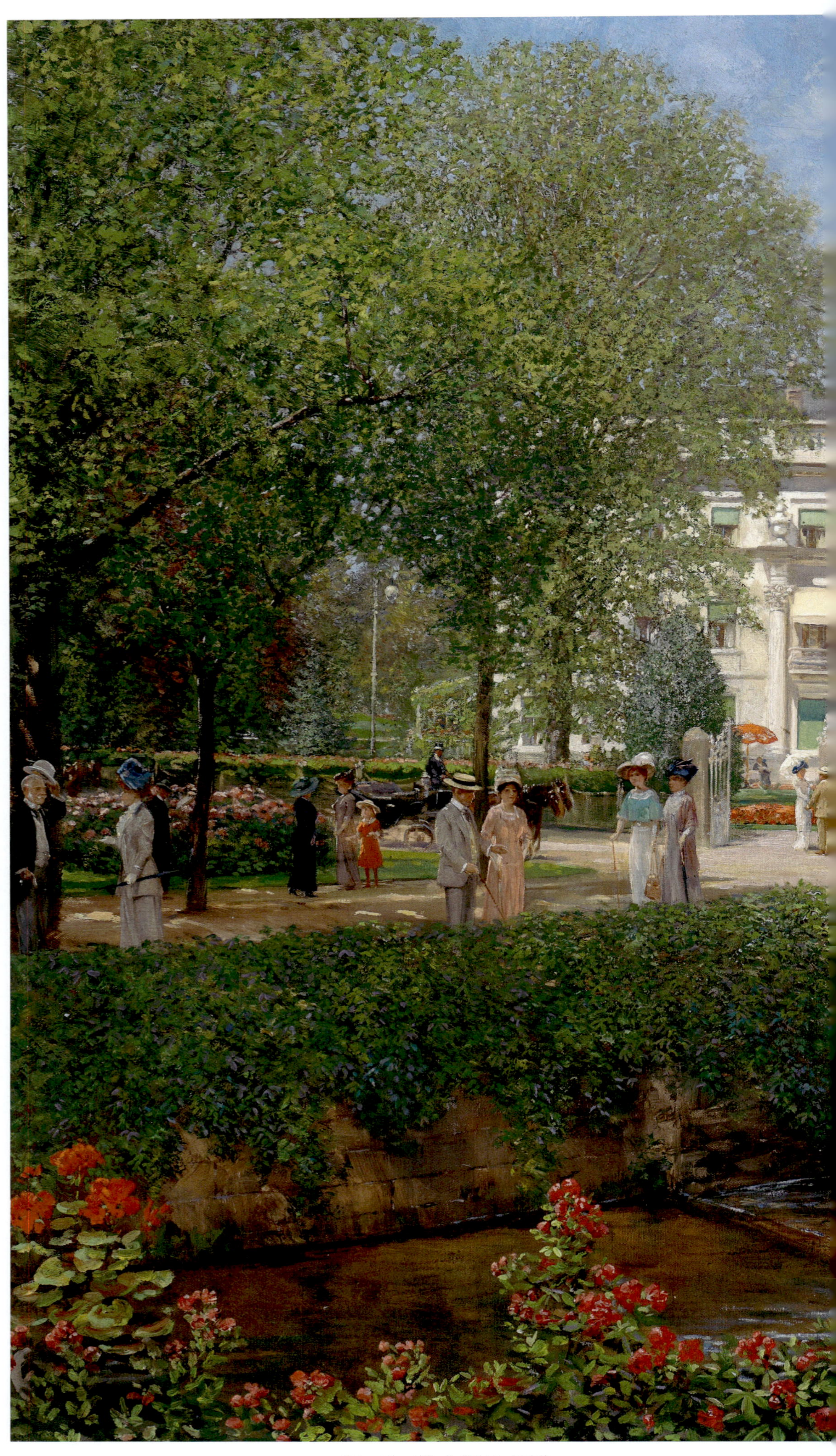

Otto Albert Koch (1866–1920)
VIEW OF THE SPA HOTEL IN BADEN-BADEN, 1911

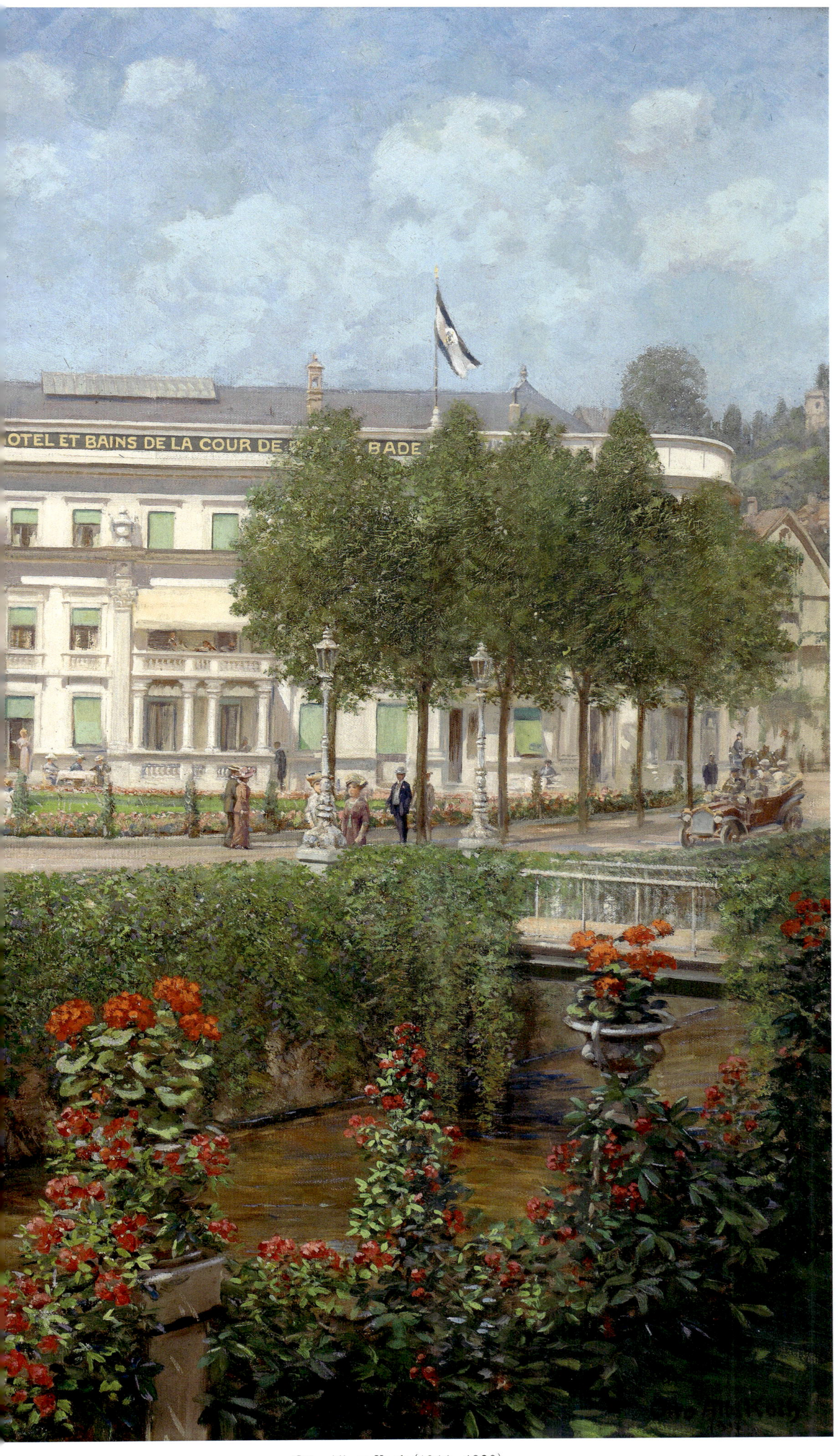

Otto Albert Koch (1866–1920)
BLICK AUF DAS KURHOTEL IN BADEN-BADEN, 1911

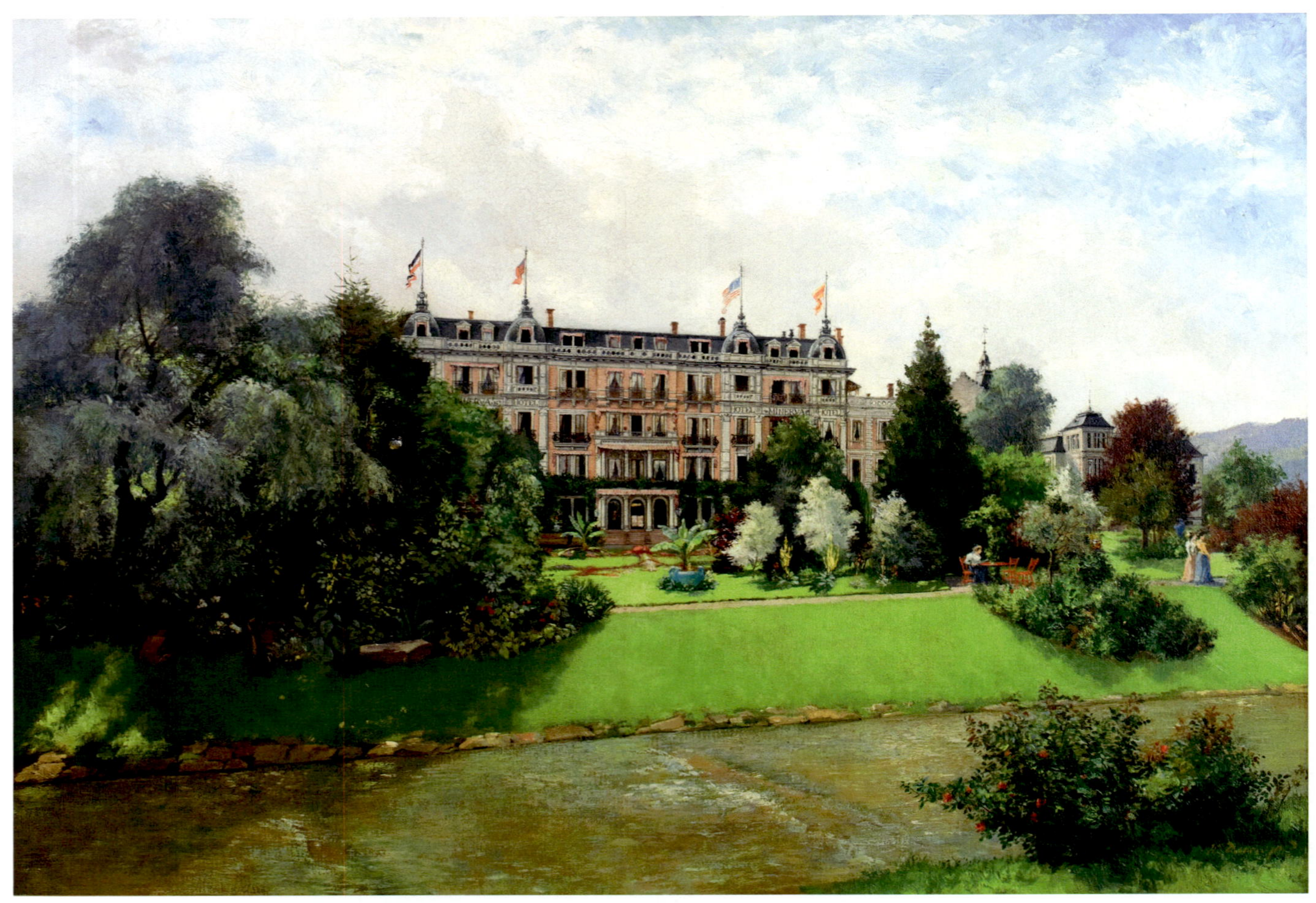

Hugo Degenhard (1866–1901)
HOTEL MINERVA, um / c. 1890

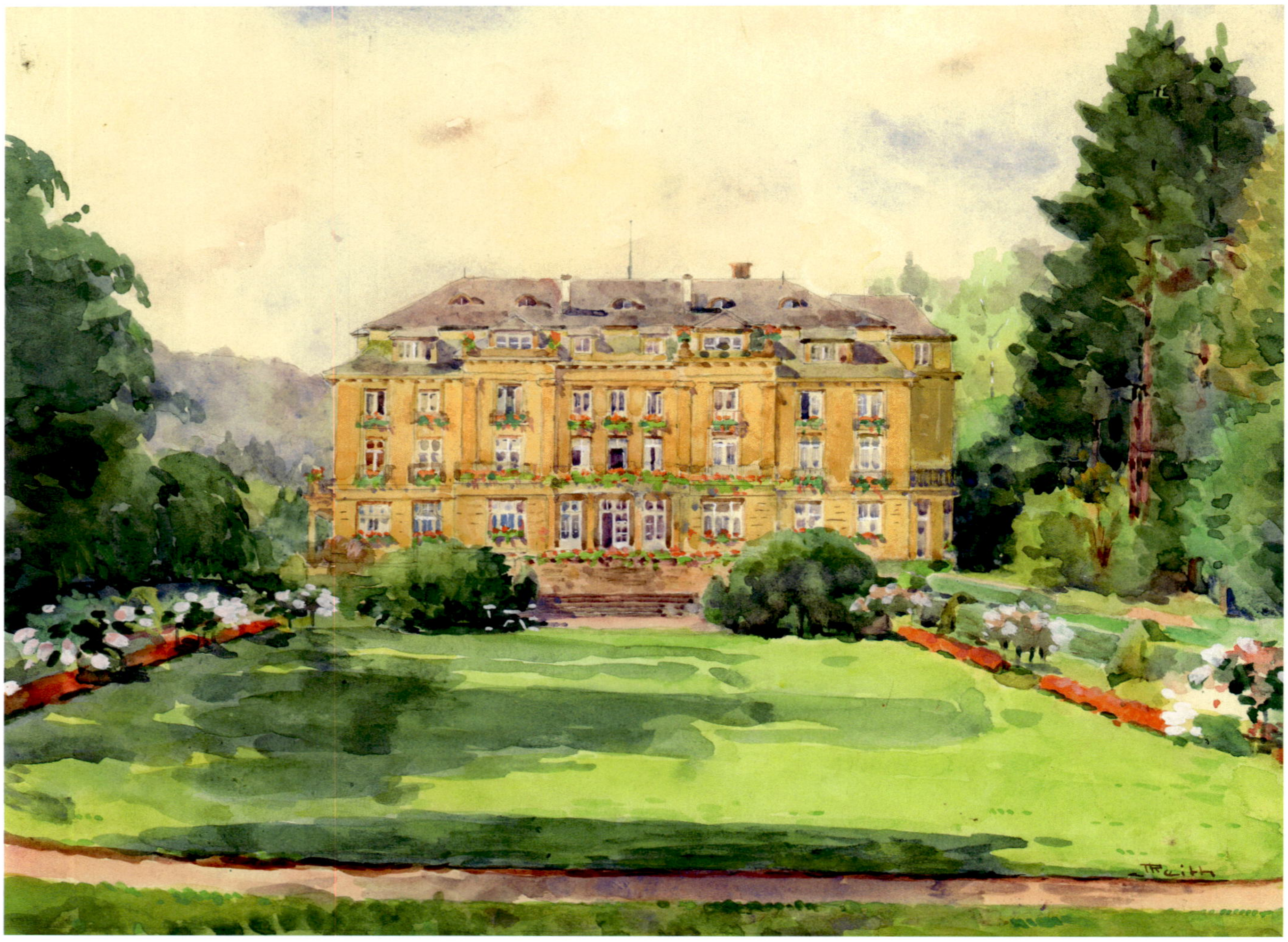

Julius Reith
HOTEL RUNKEWITZ, 1950

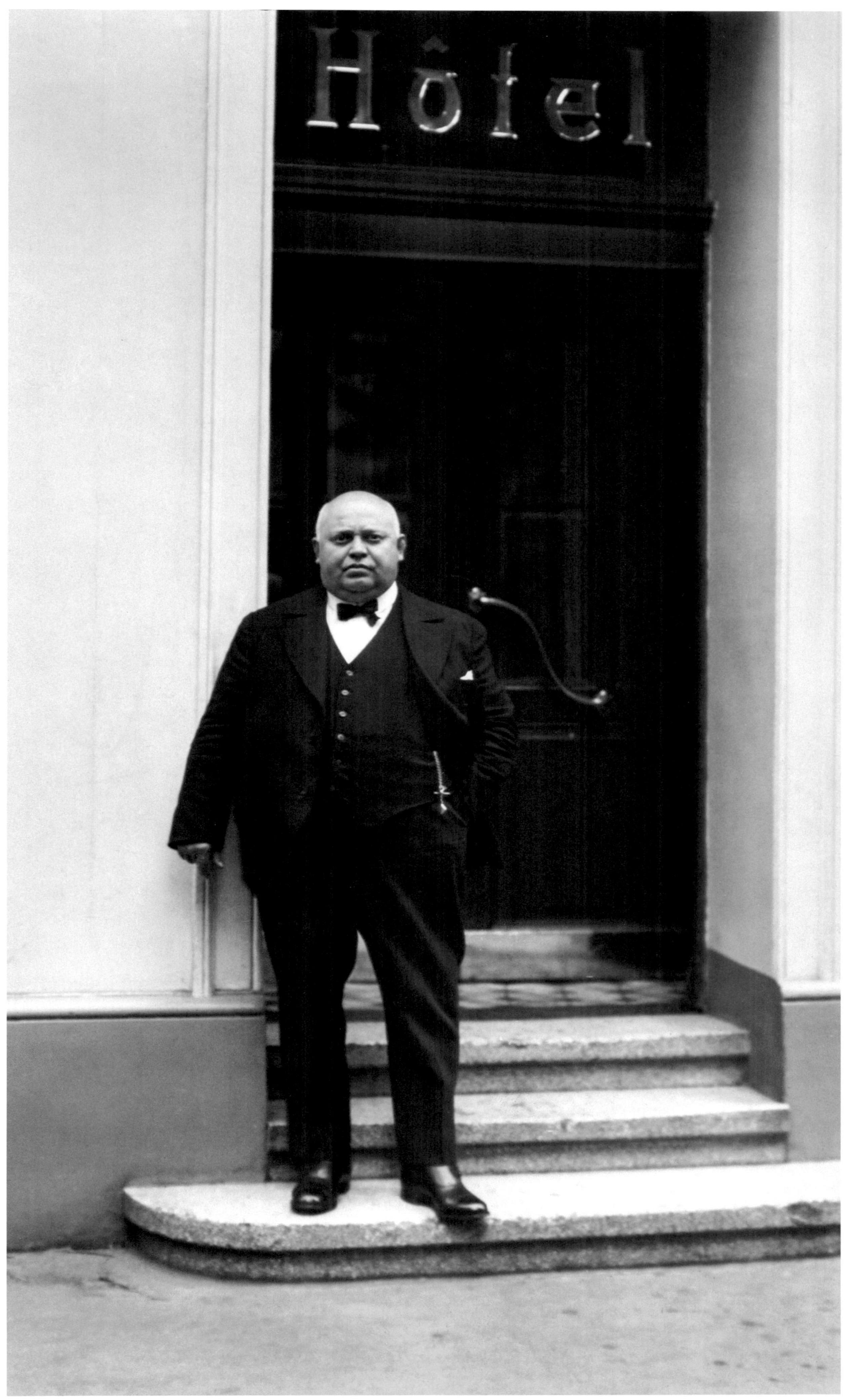

August Sander (1876–1964)
HOTELIER / HOTEL OWNER, 1930

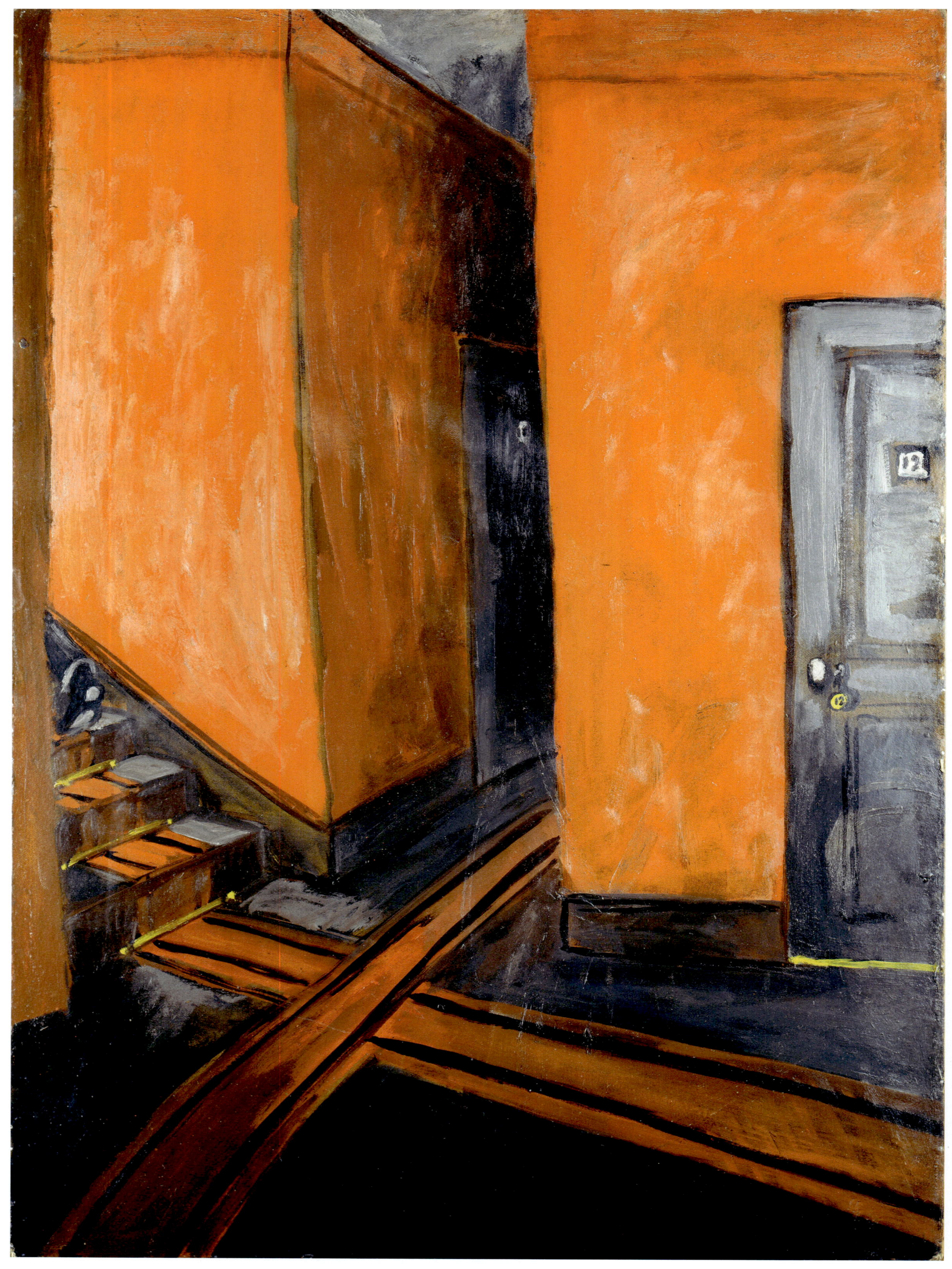

Auguste Chabaud (1882 – 1955)
HOTELFLUR (COULOIR D'HOTEL) / HOTEL CORRIDOR (COULOIR D'HOTEL), 1907/08

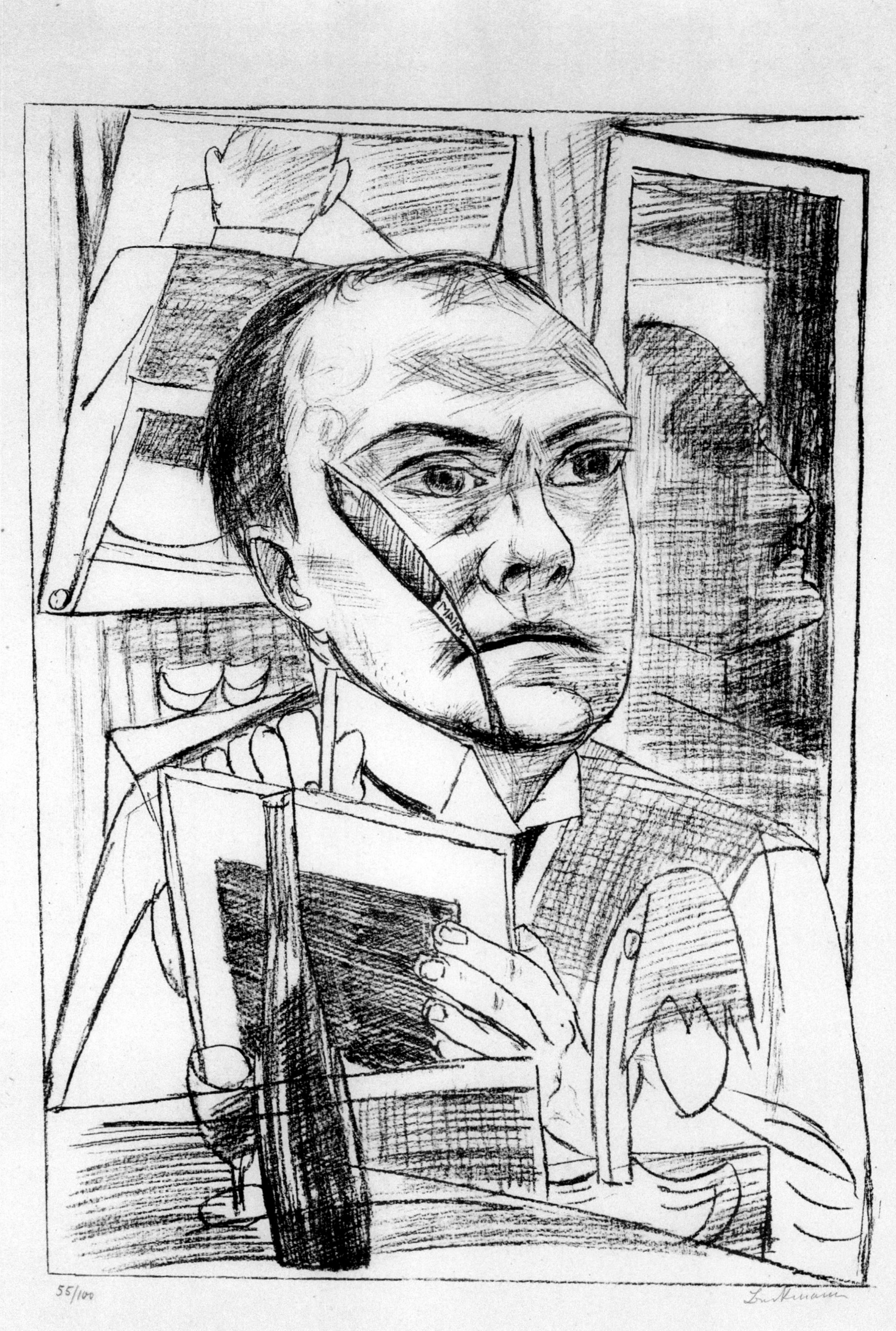

Max Beckmann (1884–1950)
SELBST IM HOTEL / SELF-PORTRAIT IN THE HOTEL, 1922

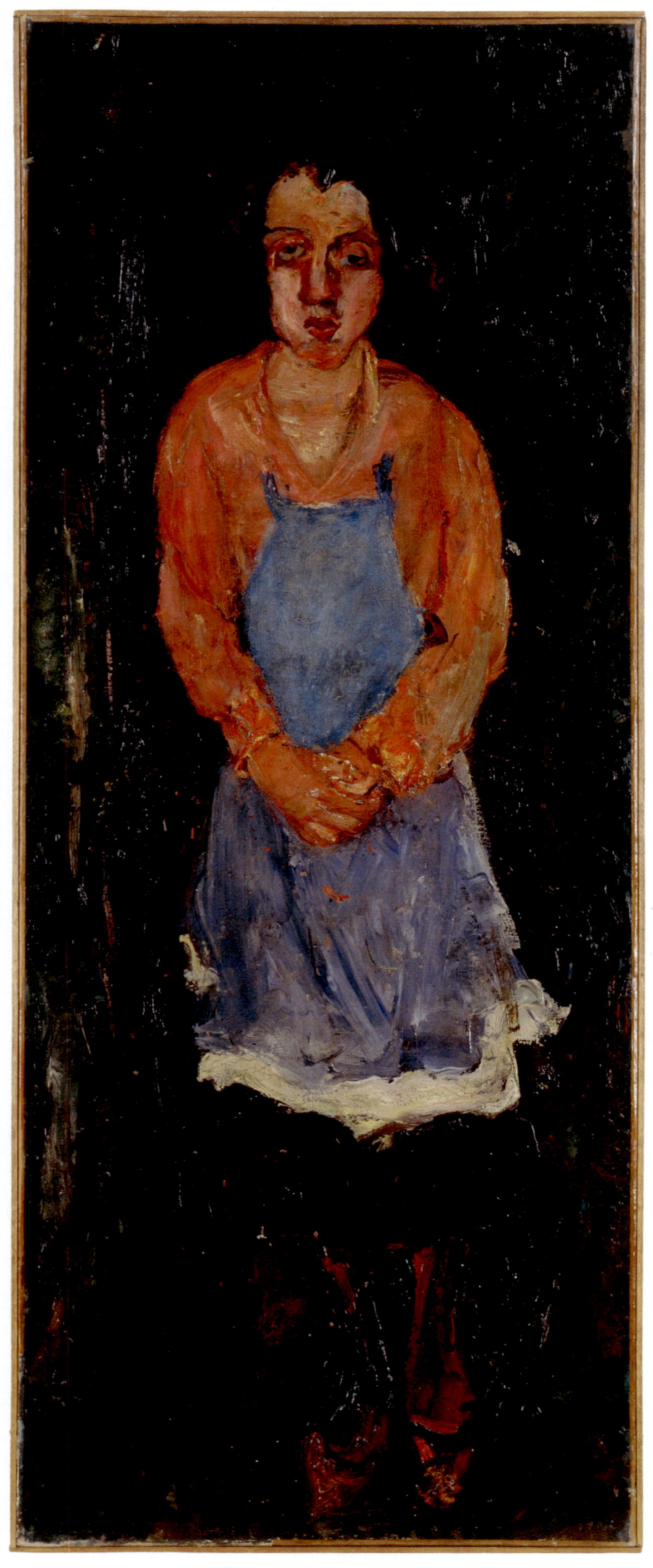

Chaïm Soutine (1893–1943)
DIE KÖCHIN MIT BLAUER SCHÜRZE / COOK WITH BLUE APRON,
um / c. 1930

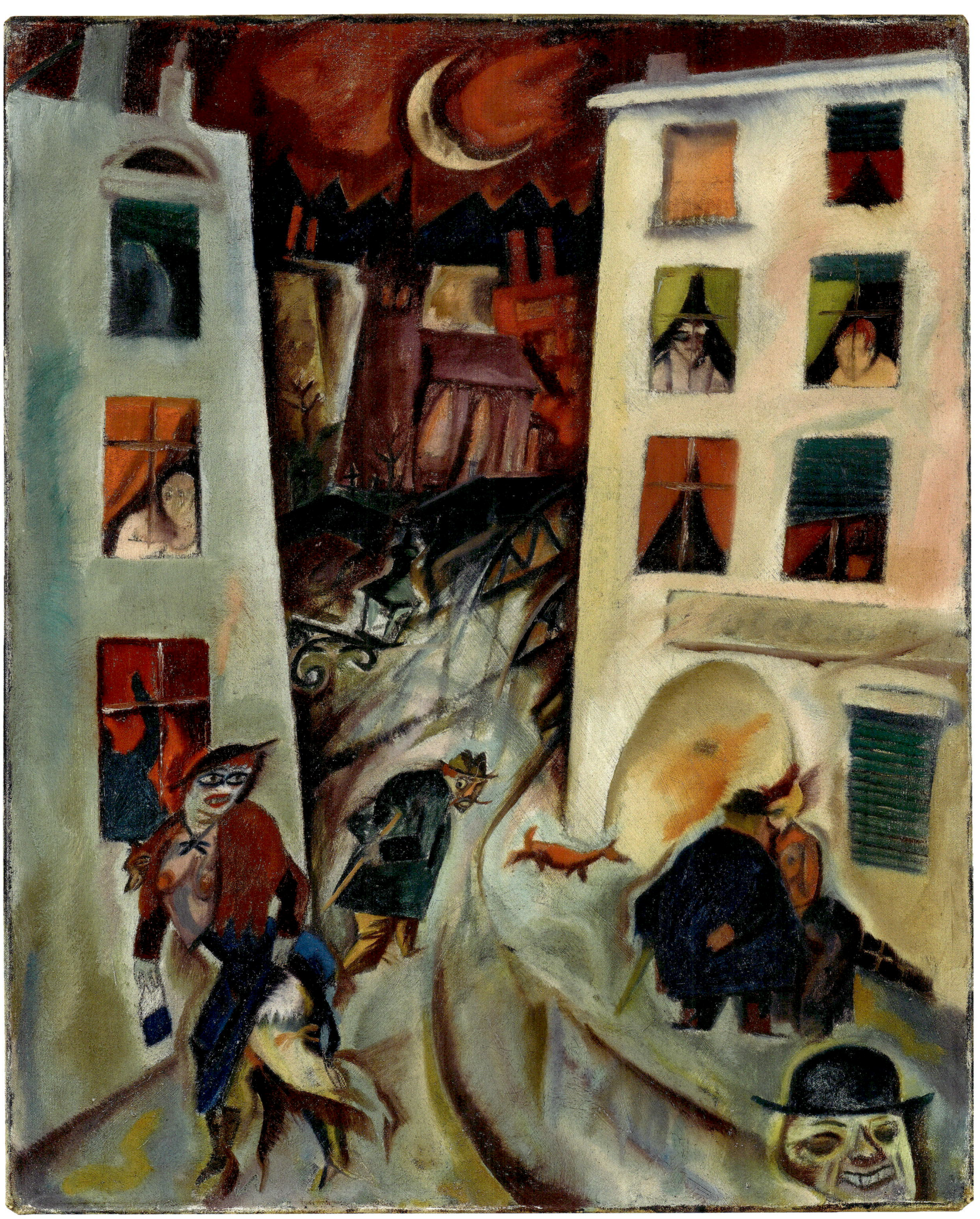

George Grosz (1893–1959)
DIE STRASSE / THE STREET, 1915

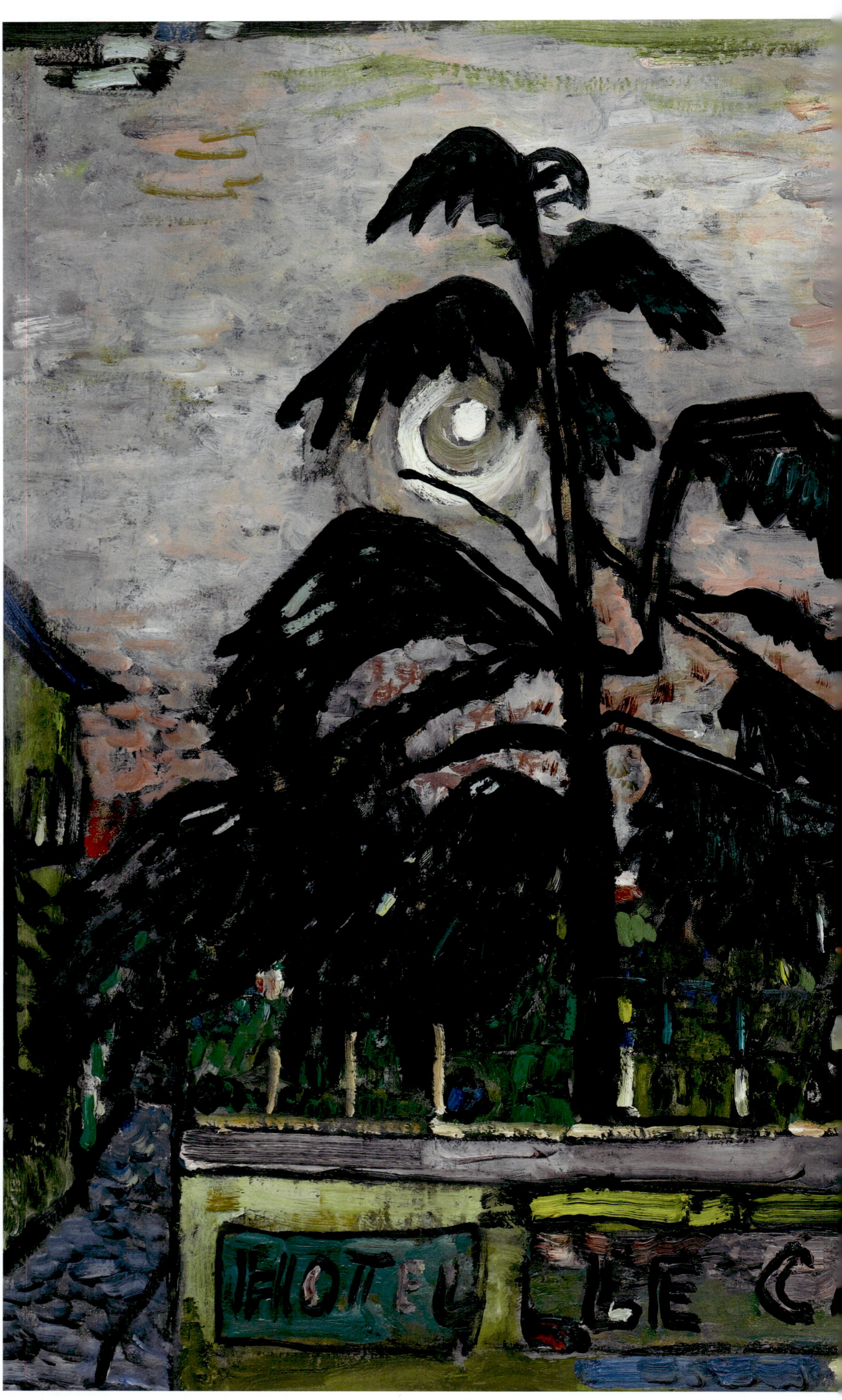

Hans Meyboden (1901–1965)
HOTEL PROVENCE, 1963

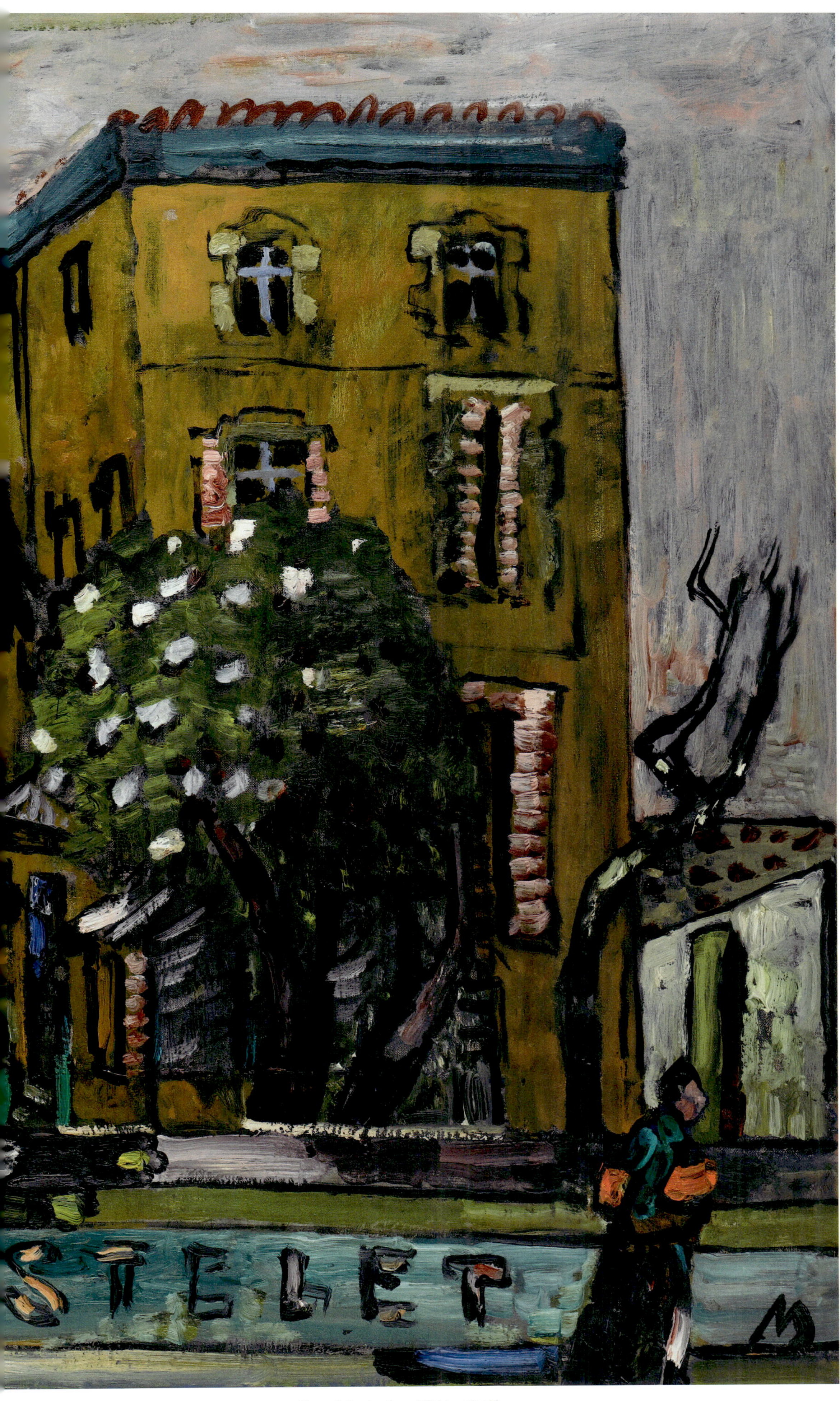

Hans Meyboden (1901–1965)
HOTEL PROVENCE, 1963

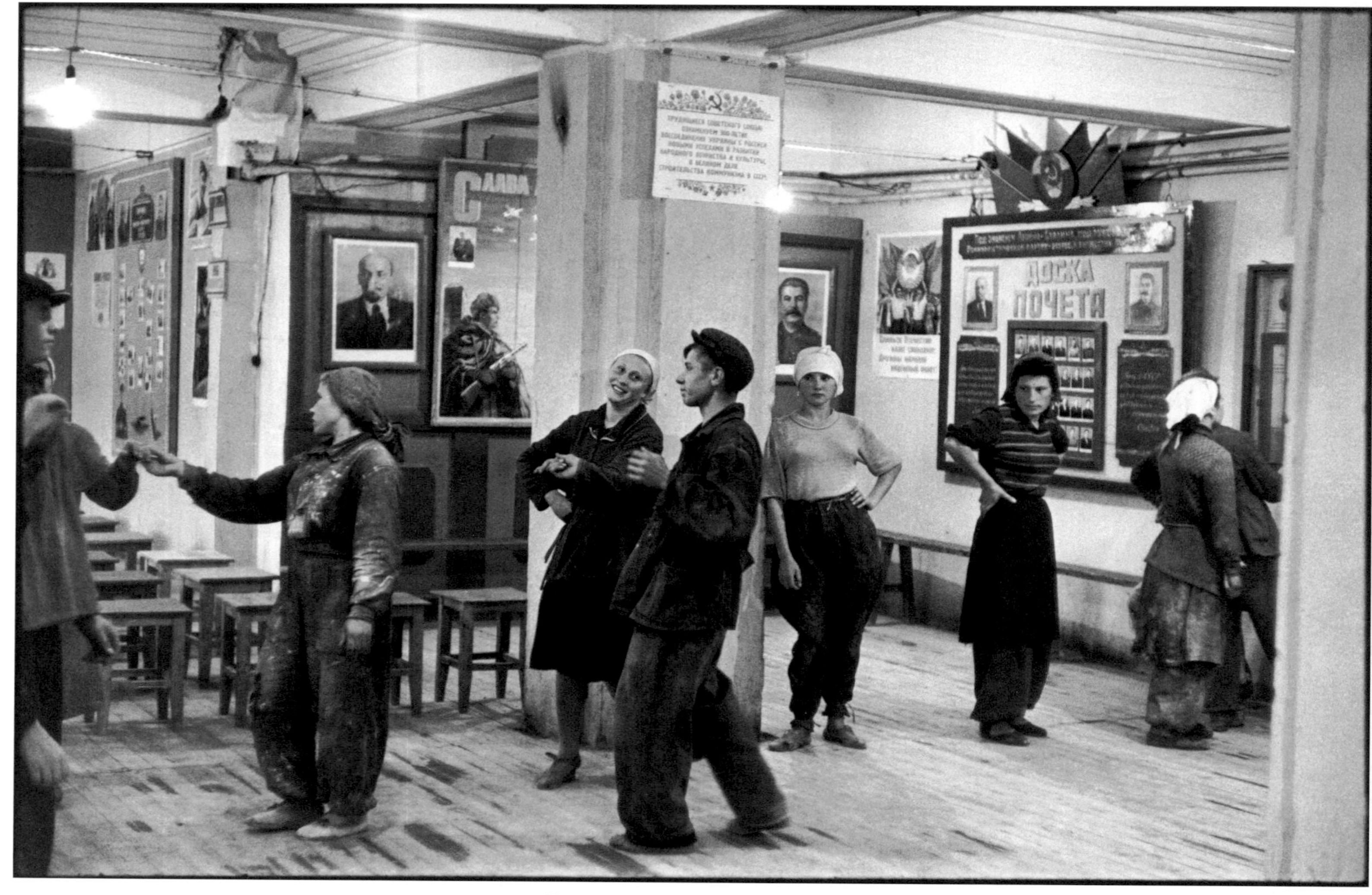

Henri Cartier-Bresson (1908–2004)
SOWJETUNION. MOSKAU. 1954. KANTINE FÜR BAUARBEITER DES HOTELS METROPOL / SOVIET UNION. MOSCOW. 1954. CANTEEN FOR WORKERS BUILDING THE HOTEL METROPOL, 1954

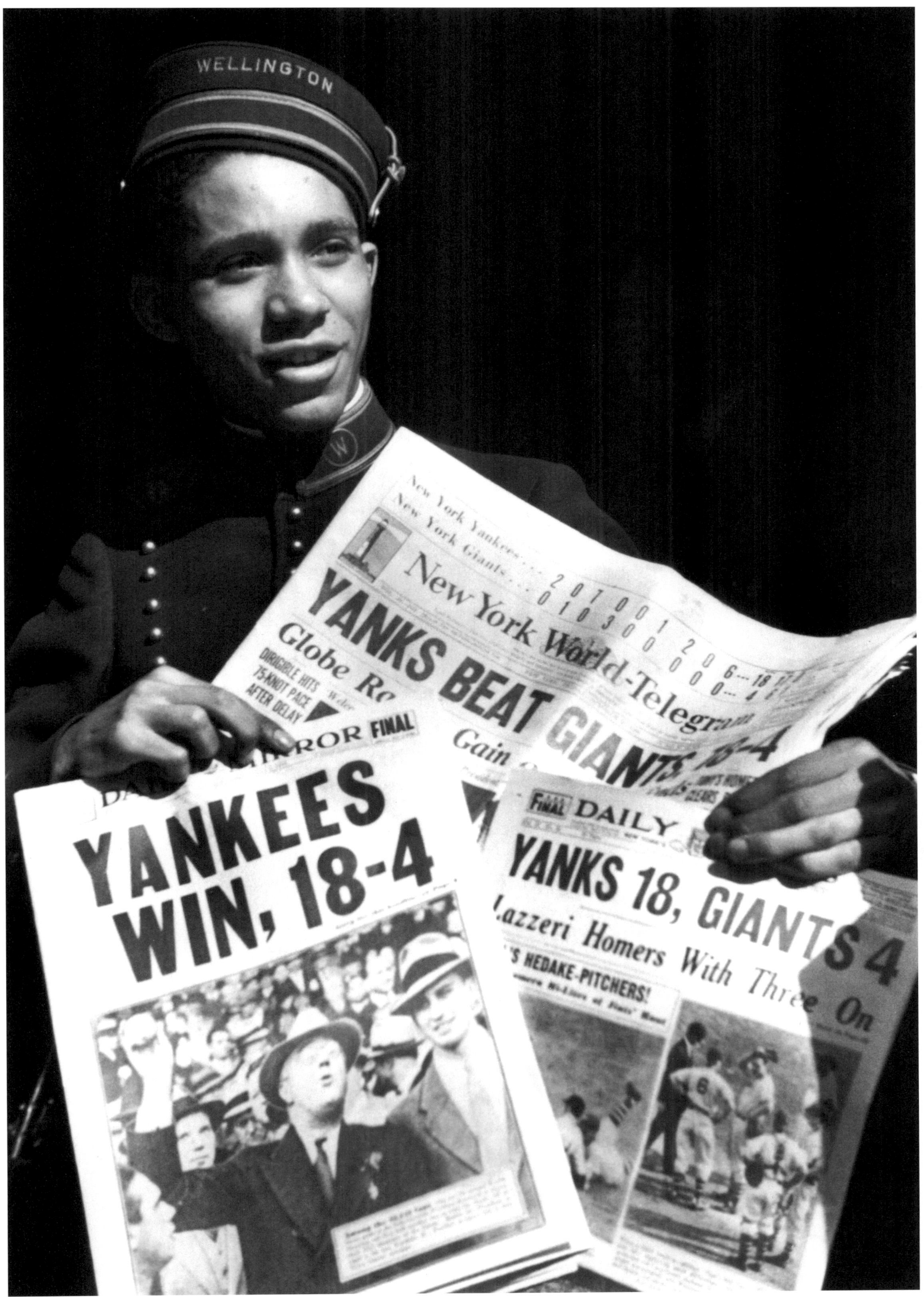

Hanns Hubmann (1910–1996)
PAGE DES HOTELS WELLINGTON MIT ZEITUNGEN ZUM BASEBALL-ENDSPIEL / MESSENGER BOY OF THE HOTEL WELLINGTON WITH NEWSPAPERS FEATURING THE BASEBALL CHAMPIONSHIPS, 1936

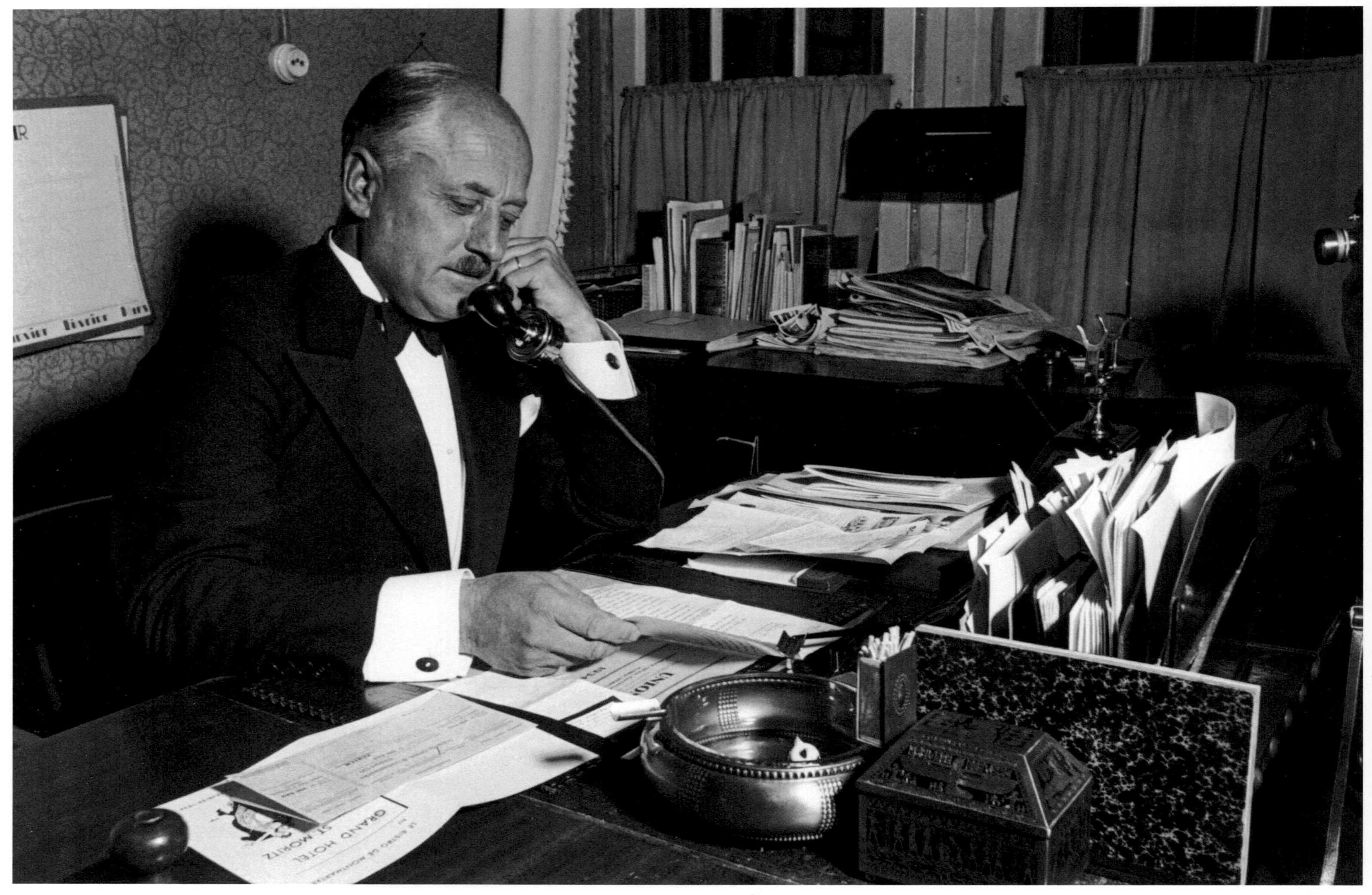

Hanns Hubmann (1910 – 1996)
DER HOTELDIREKTOR DES GRAND HOTELS IN ST. MORITZ AN SEINEM SCHREIBTISCH BEIM TELEFONIEREN / HOTEL MANAGER OF THE GRAND HOTEL IN ST. MORITZ TALKING ON THE PHONE AT HIS DESK, 1934

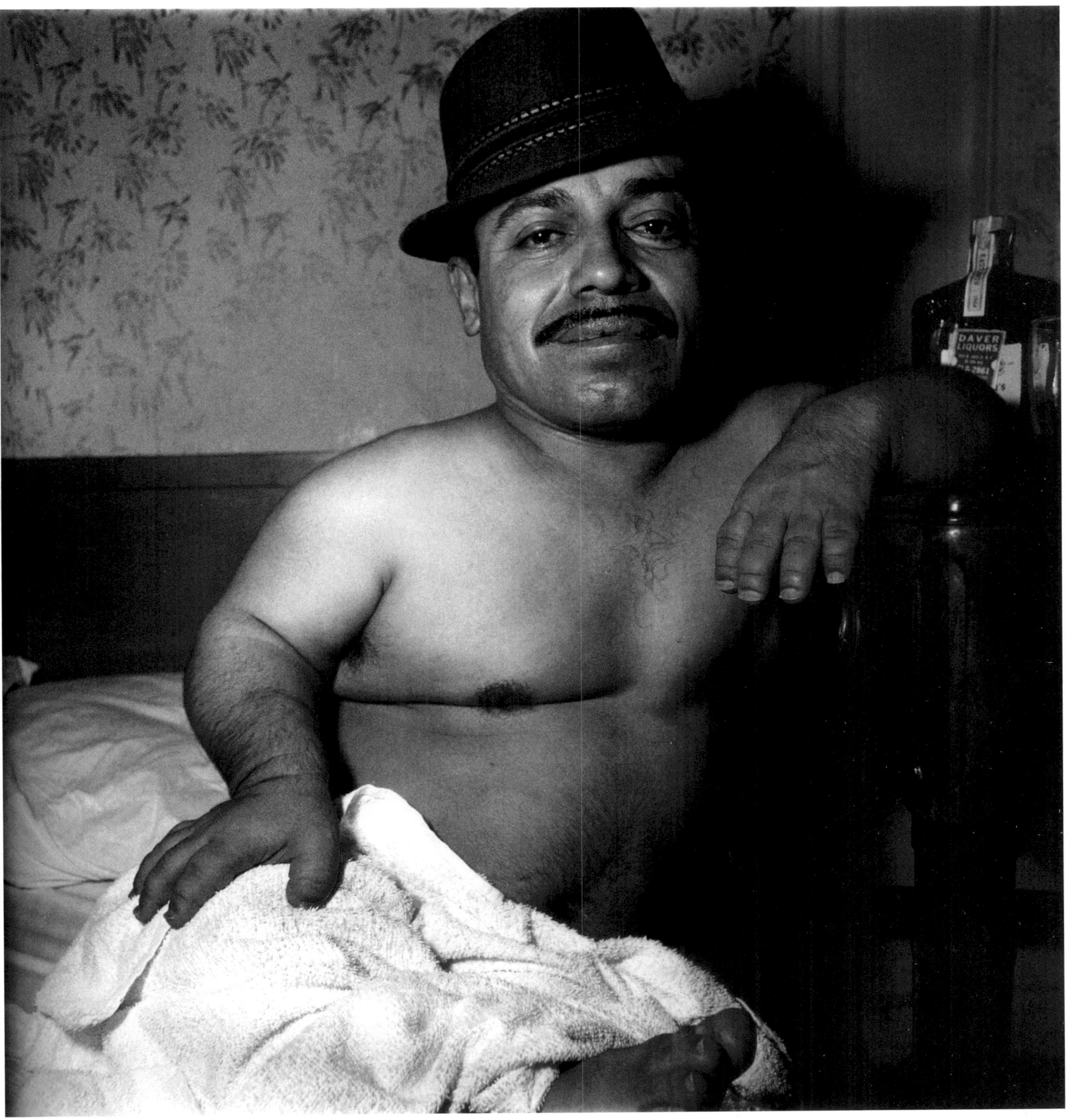

Diane Arbus (1923–1971)
MEXIKANISCHER LILIPUTANER IN SEINEM HOTELZIMMER IN NEW YORK CITY / MEXICAN DWARF IN HIS HOTEL IN NEW YORK CITY, 1970

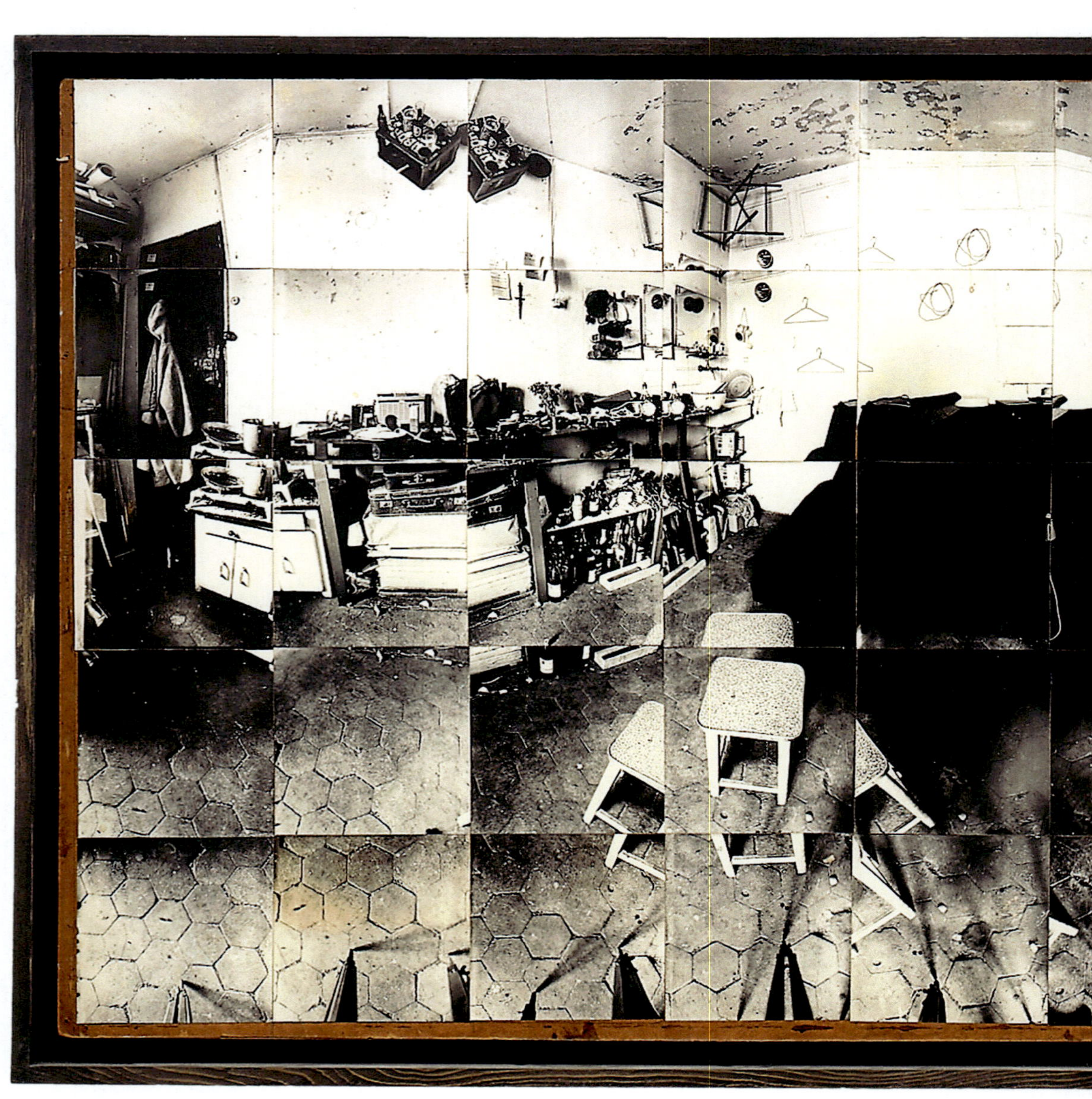

Daniel Spoerri (*1930)
VUE CUBISTE DE MA CHAMBRE NO 13 DE L'HÔTEL CARCASSONNE, 24 RUE MOUFFETARD, 1961

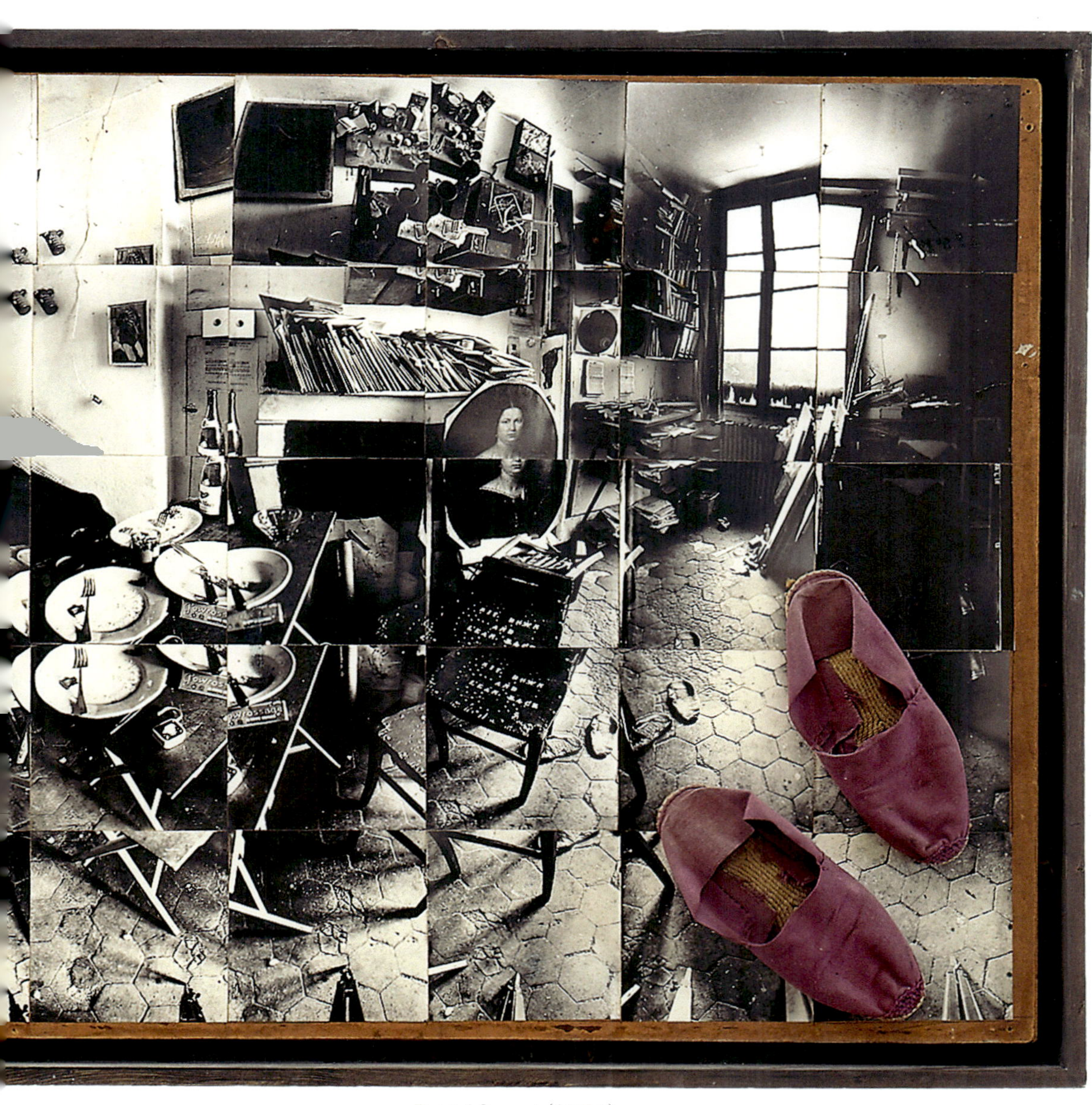

Daniel Spoerri (*1930)
VUE CUBISTE DE MA CHAMBRE NO 13 DE L'HÔTEL CARCASSONNE, 24 RUE MOUFFETARD, 1961

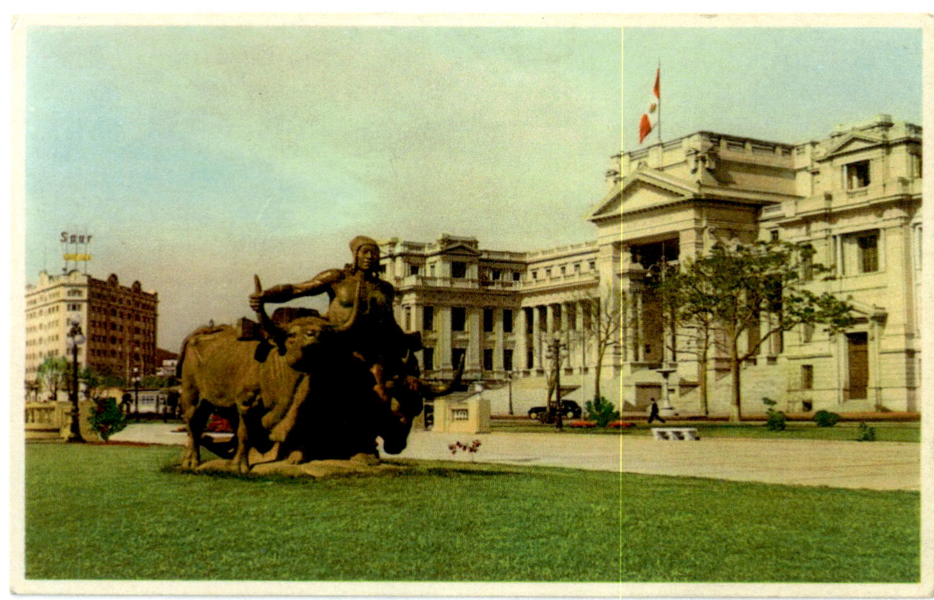

On Kawara (*1933)
I GOT UP, 1968

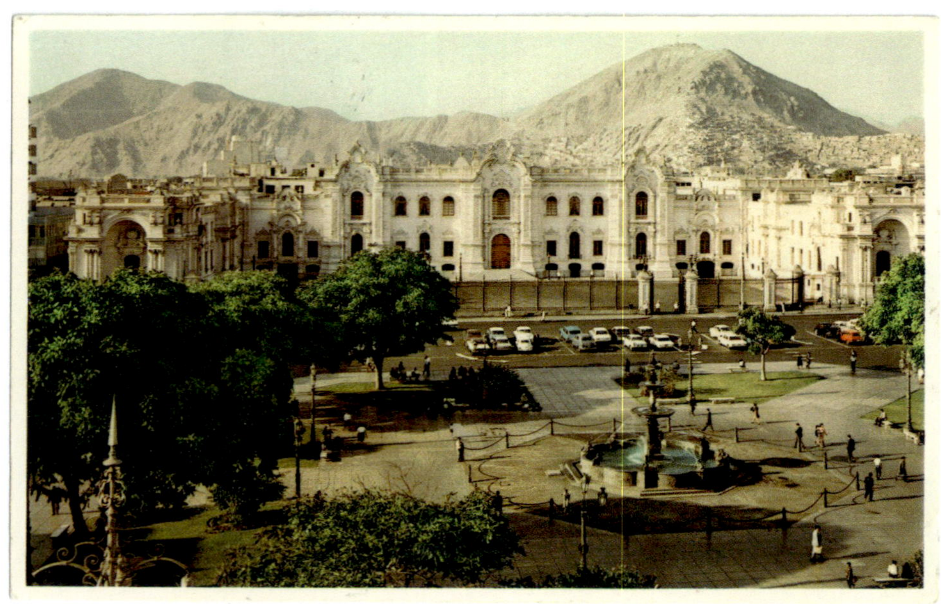

On Kawara (*1933)
I GOT UP, 1968

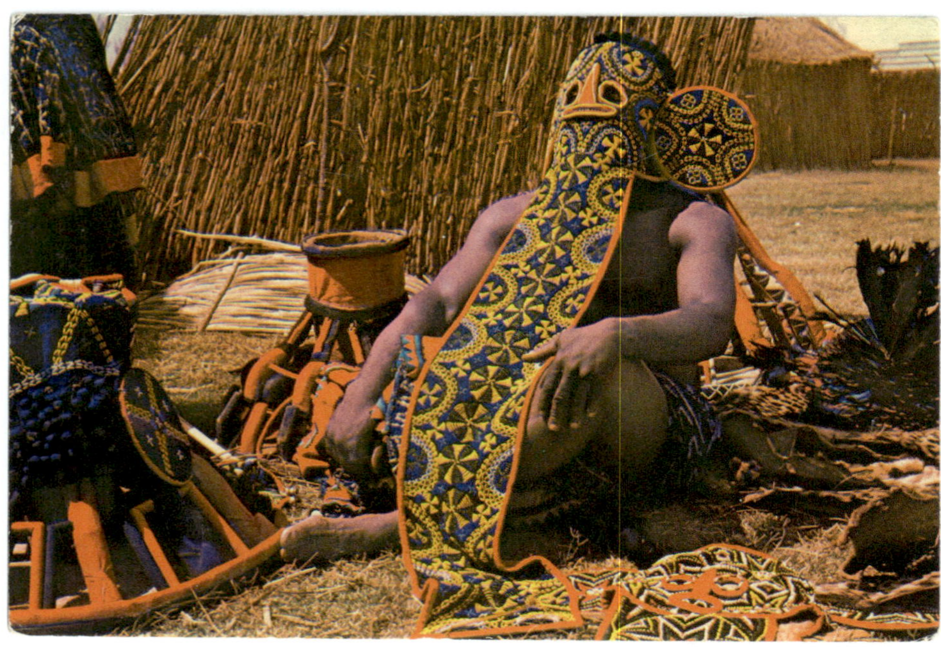

On Kawara (*1933)
I GOT UP, 1973

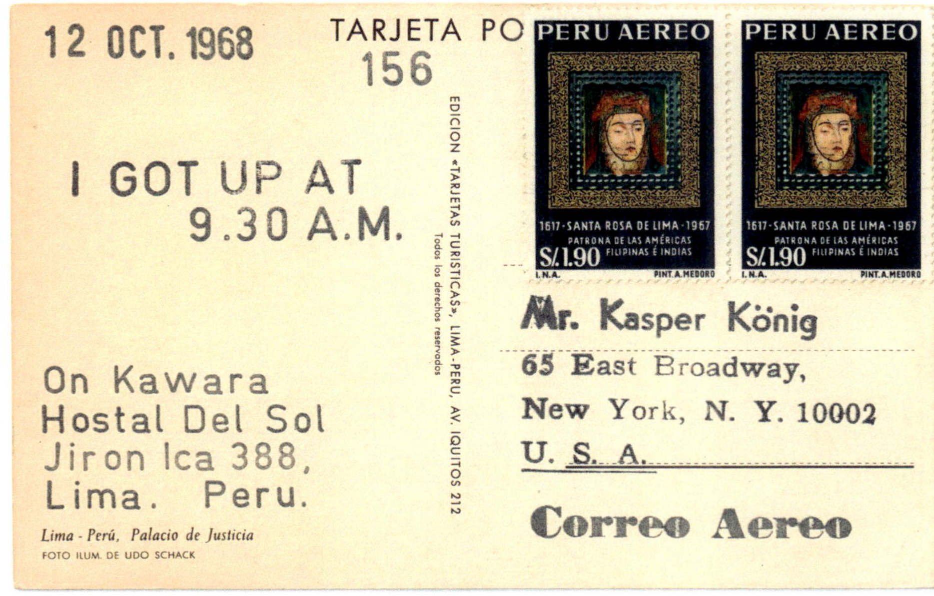

On Kawara (*1933)
I GOT UP, 1968

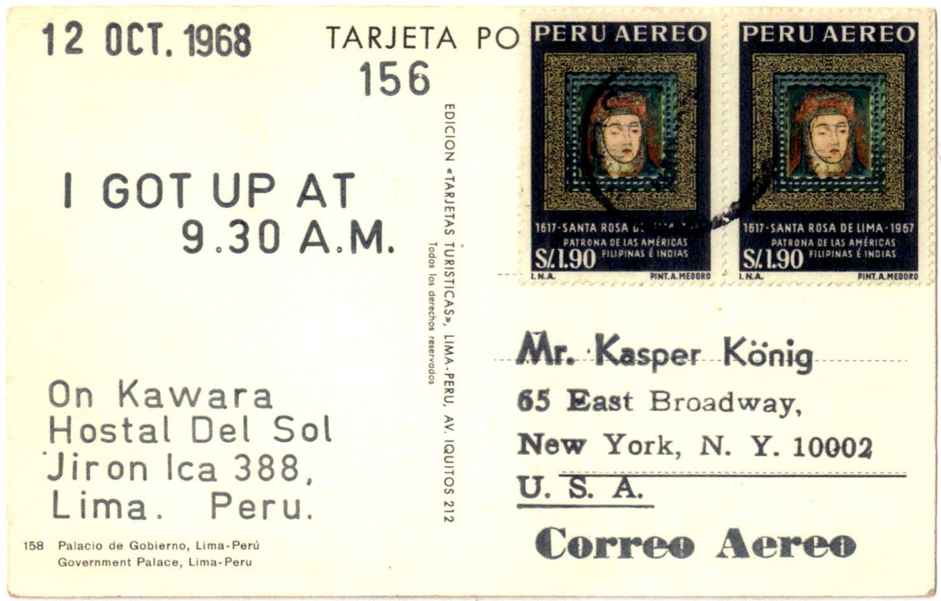

On Kawara (*1933)
I GOT UP, 1968

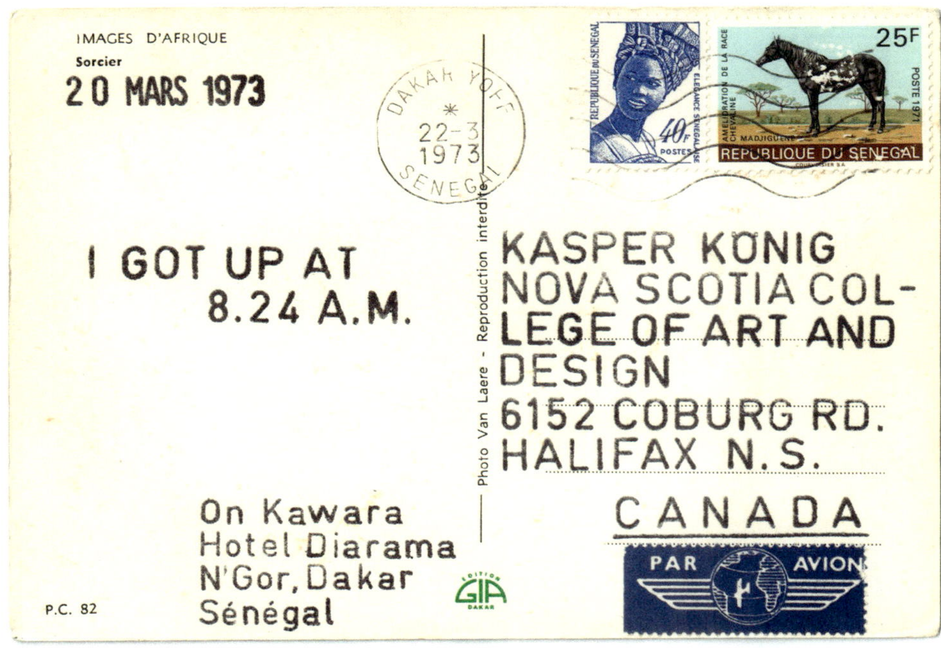

On Kawara (*1933)
I GOT UP, 1973

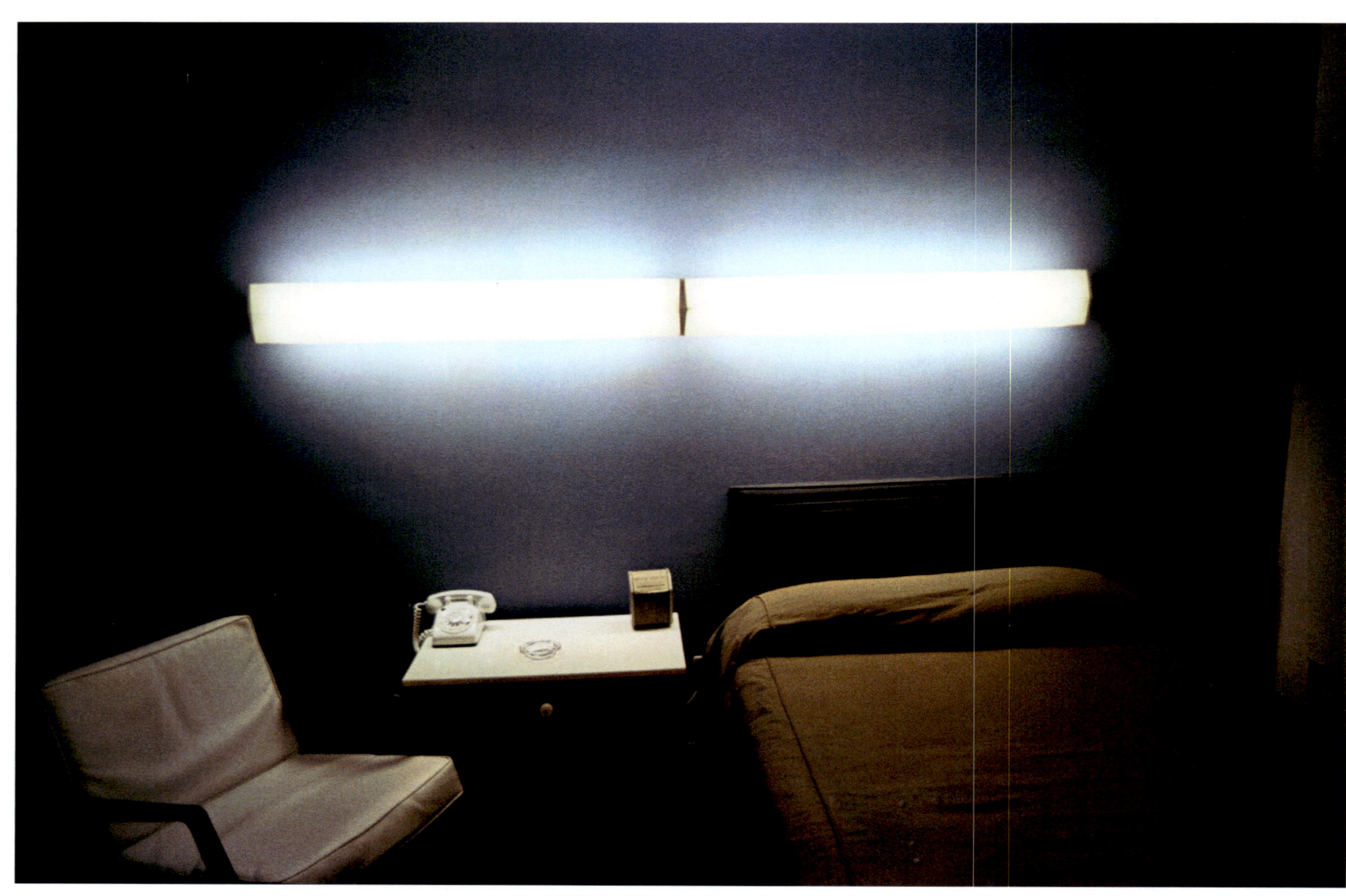

William Eggleston (*1939)
UNTITLED (MOTEL ROOM WITH FLUORESCENTS), 1965–1968

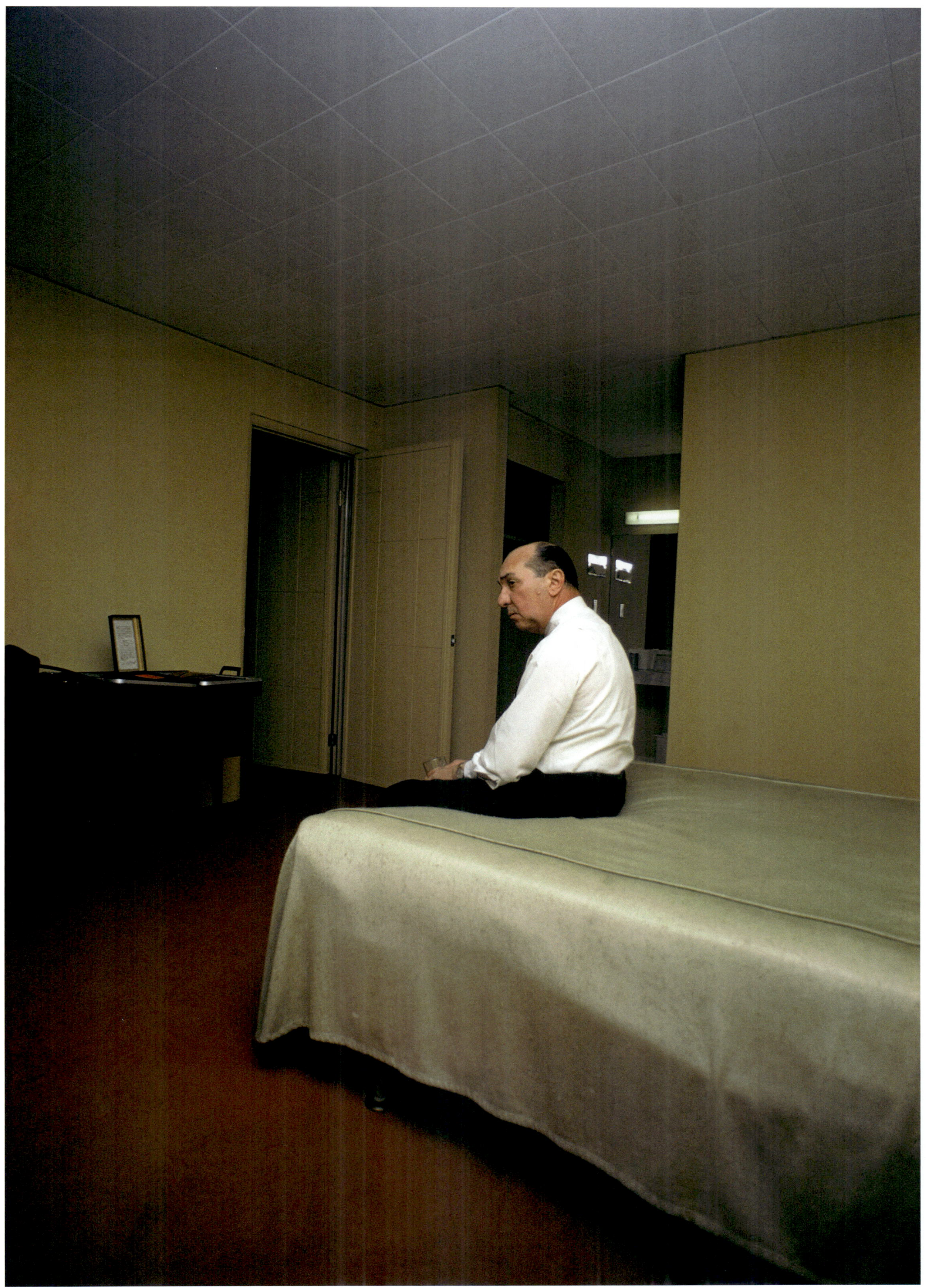

William Eggleston (*1939)
UNTITLED (HUNTSVILLE, ALABAMA), 1969/70

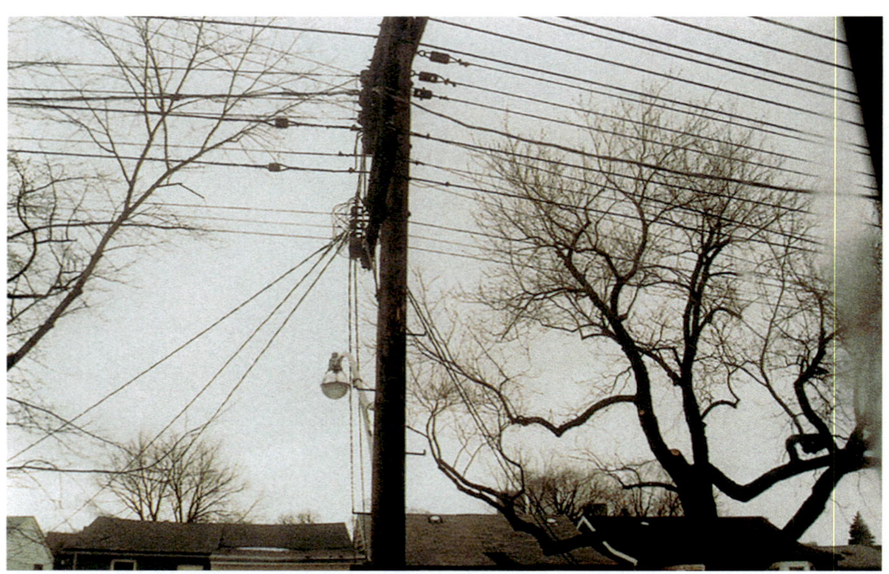

Hans-Peter Feldmann (*1941)
TORONTO, KANADA / TORONTO, CANADA, 1982–2002

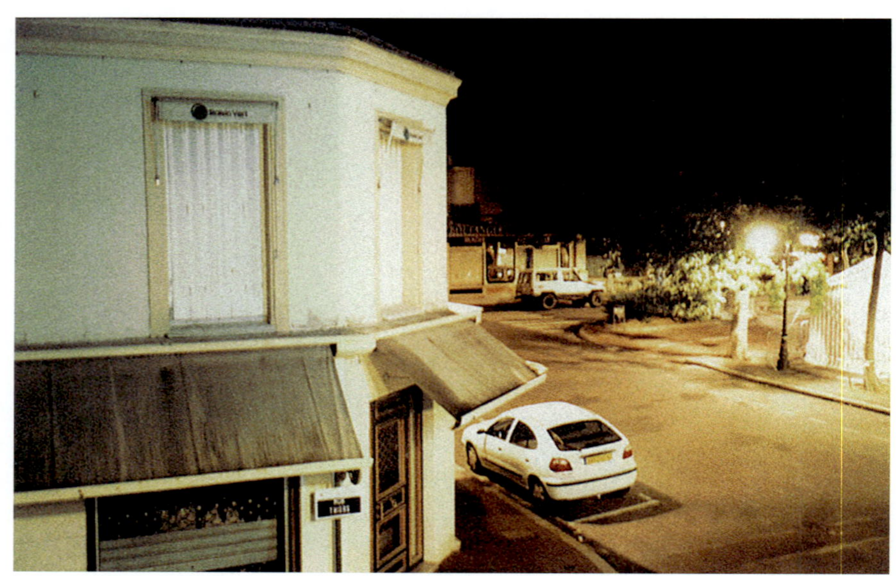

Hans-Peter Feldmann (*1941)
LE VÉSINET, FRANKREICH / LE VÉSINET, FRANCE, 1982–2002

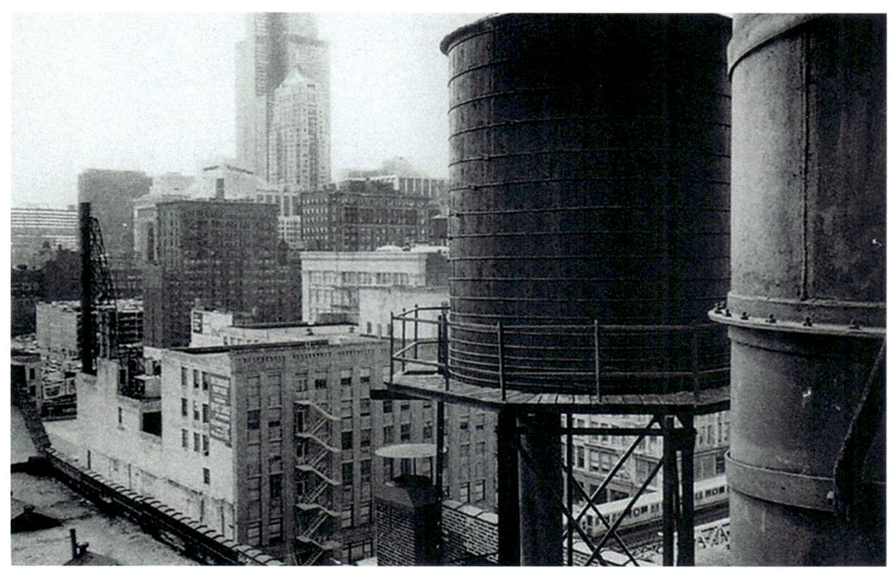

Hans-Peter Feldmann (*1941)
CHICAGO, USA, 1982–2002

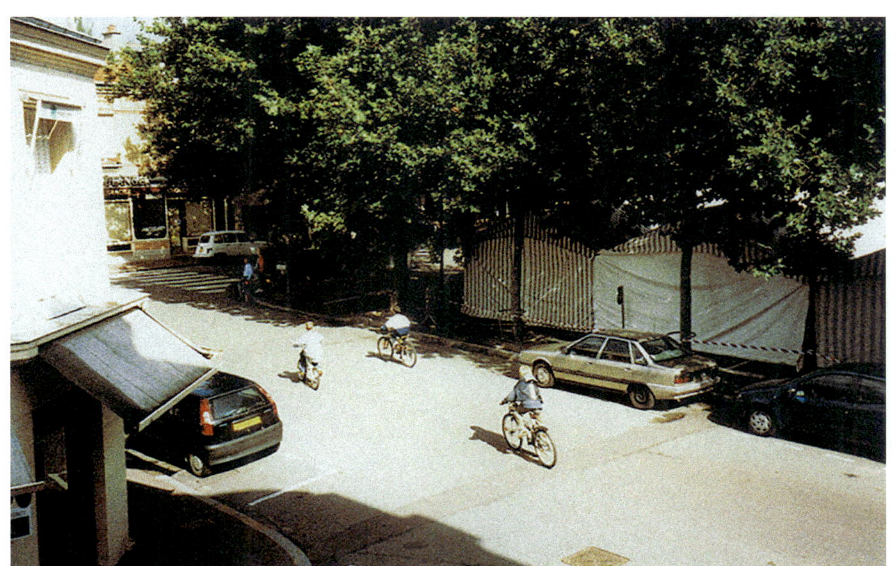

Hans-Peter Feldmann (*1941)
LE VÉSINET, FRANKREICH / LE VÉSINET, FRANCE, 1982–2002

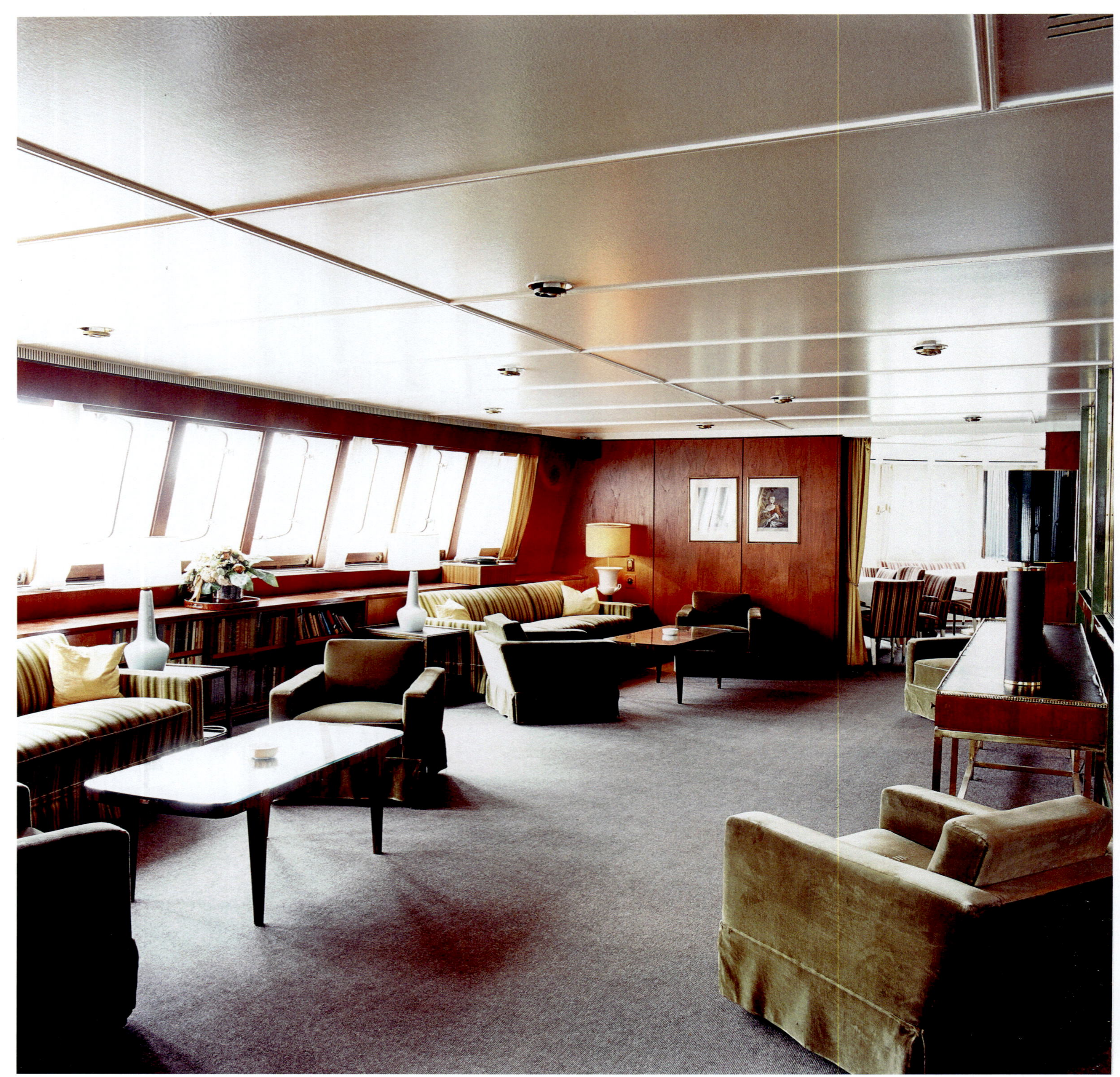

Candida Höfer (*1944)
CAP SAN DIEGO, HAMBURG V, 2000

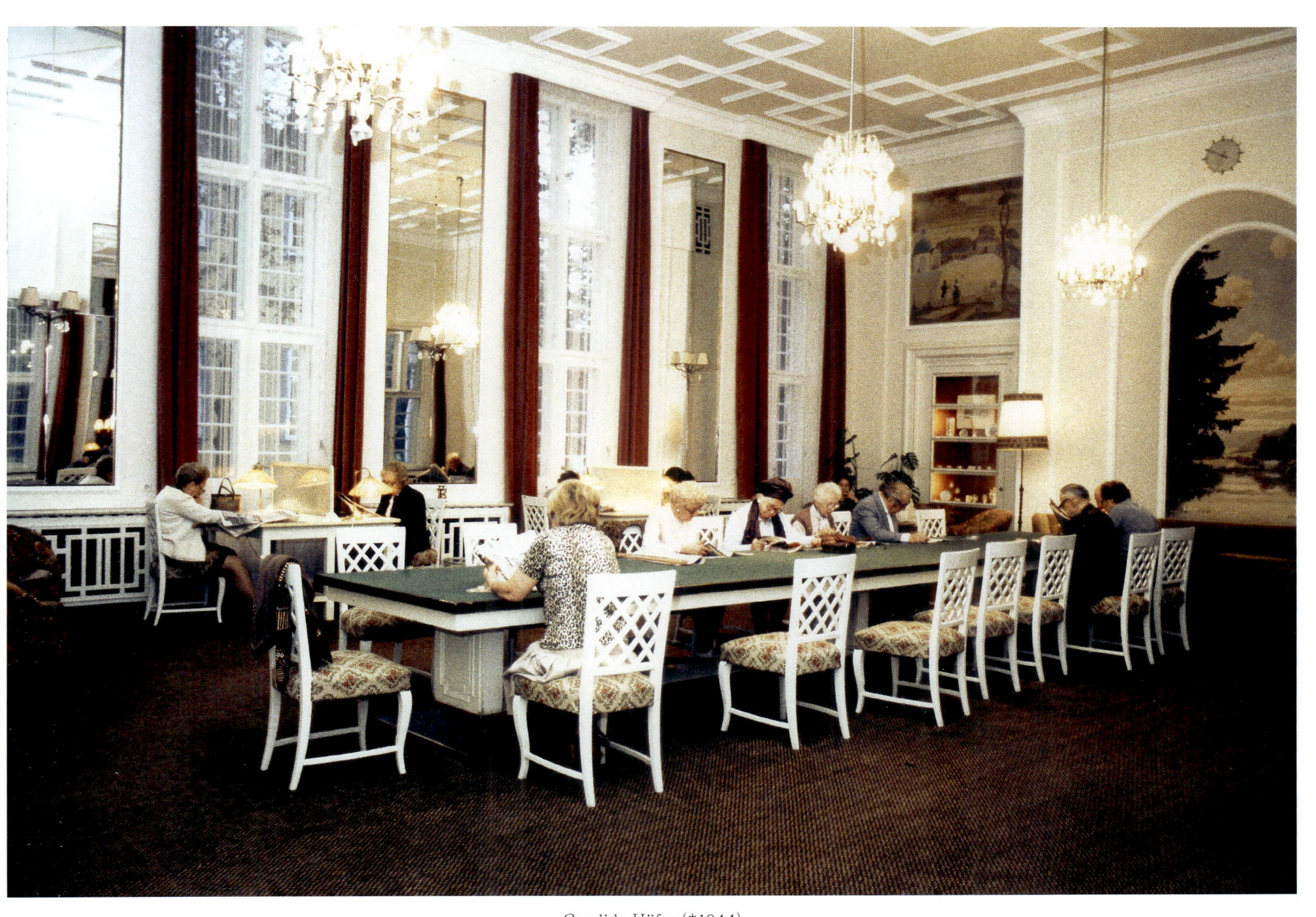

Candida Höfer (*1944)
KURANLAGE BADEN-BADEN, 1981

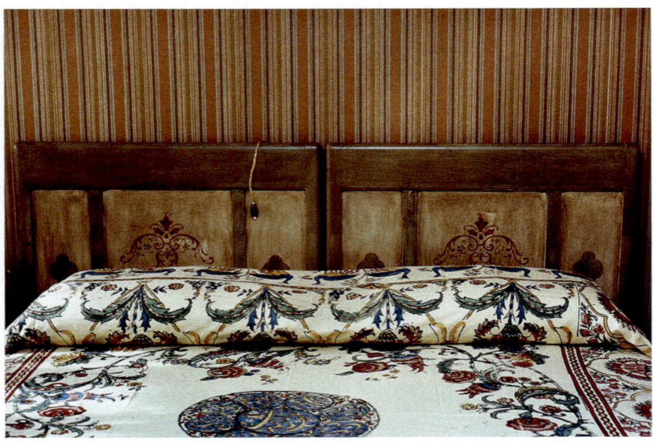

ROOM 28

Tuesday March 3, 1981. *9:15a.m. I enter room 28. The twin beds are unmade. The person on the left sleeps with two pillows; the one on the right, with none. I notice men's red-and-black silk pajamas on the chair and embroidered babouche-type slippers (size 38). These are the only visible signs of occupancy along with a suitcase and traveling bag, both locked. The wardrobe is empty except for some white underwear (two pairs of underpants and a vest) in the top drawer of the chest, a few toiletry items (razors, shaving brush...) and some medicine in the bidet in the bathroom. There is nothing else to see. I clean the room and leave.*

Wednesday 4. *10:00a.m. The suitcases are still locked shut. The babouches and pajamas in their respective places. Today, the occupant of the right-hand bed made a little pillow out of a cushion from the sofa, covered with a towel. On the left, there is now only one pillow. I notice that the bedside table has been turned around so that the drawer is lodged against the bed. I set it straight. The drawer is, in fact, empty.*

Thursday 5. *9:00a.m. Two pairs of boots (sizes 38 and 42) have appeared. The suitcases are still locked shut. The three pieces of underwear have not moved. And still in the same place are the babouches and pajamas. For once, the pillows have remained as I arranged them. They have not touched the table.*

Friday 6. *10:00a.m. The situation is the same (pajamas, babouches, suitcases, bathroom, table, underclothes, boots). It's my last day of work at the Hotel C. I leave it up to my successor to observe the variations on the pillows in room 28. Today, the one on the left, falling off the bed slightly, bears the rounded imprint of a presence. I see this as a farewell signal.*

Sophie Calle (*1953)
THE HOTEL, ROOM 28, MARCH 3, 1981

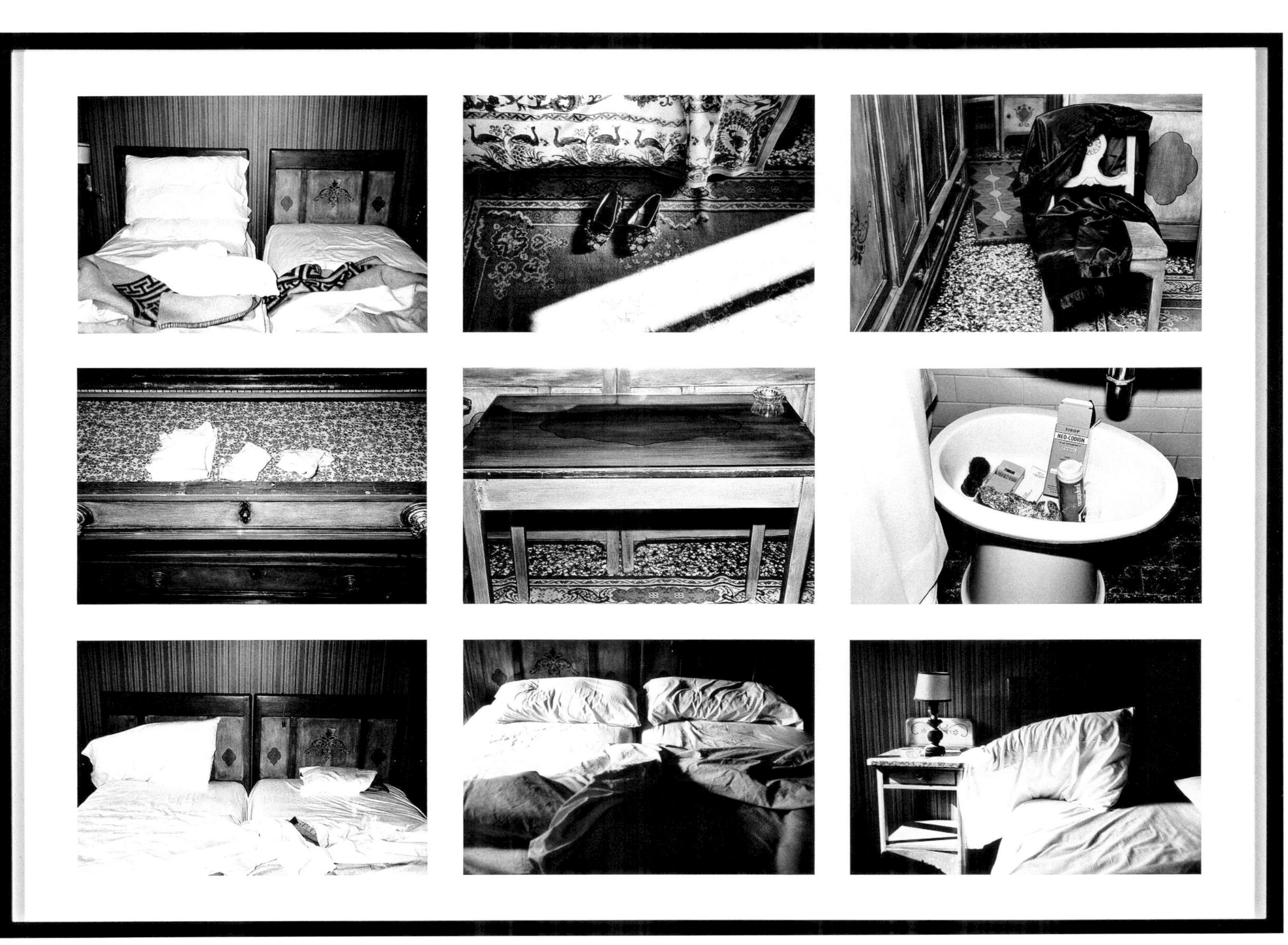

Sophie Calle (*1953)
THE HOTEL, ROOM 28, MARCH 3, 1981

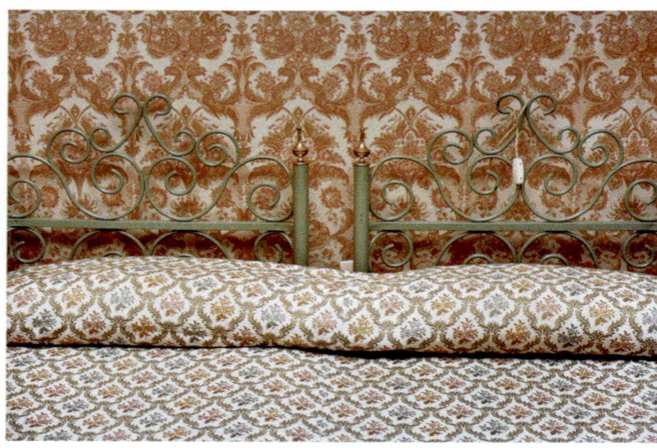

ROOM 30

Thursday March 5, 1981. *10:00 a.m. I go into room 30. The twin beds are unmade. On the luggage stand is a red suitcase, half-open; inside, a heap of clothes that I don't touch. On top are men's pajamas, brown flannelette, some hair curlers, a scarf, a woolen bonnet. I open the wardrobe: men's and women's clothing, among which is a black nylon nightgown. In the bathroom, a big load of laundry is drying on the rail of the shower curtain. The toiletries and make-up are still in an overnight case. A name is printed on it: Mrs. John D. She lives in Boulder, Colorado. A little case filled with fake pearls has been set on the soap dish. I go back into the bedroom. On the table, some Marlboros, a book,* American Women's Club in Denmark. *Some of the names are underlined in red. There's also an almost empty glass (I take a sip: it's Coca-Cola), an address book, nine postcards of Venice. They haven't been addressed yet. Here's what they say: "Dear Anna and John, We said hello to your friends in the leather shop and George bought your gloves at the glove shop but we didn't find the shop that sells red pajamas. The trip has been great. See you soon. Liz." "My dear friends, We are having a wonderful trip and the H. are fun companions. We had good weather in Germany, rain in Switzerland and Florence. Now we are in the sun, in Venice, to make it even more beautiful. Next stop is Vienna. Good bye. Liz." "The goodies arrived. The stockings are great, thank you very much, my dear Christina and Oliver and Bob. We are having a wonderful trip. Everything is beautiful with the sun shining to make the water sparkle. Our friends have been charming traveling companions. Next stop will be Vienna. I bought Italian boots and a Pierrot… Love, Liz." "The Christmas nuts arrived. We ate the whole thing. Delicious. Thank you dear Bernard and Monique. We are having a great trip with your friends. We have been to Germany, Switzerland, Florence and now Venice. It rained in Florence but we have sun in Venice to make it even more beautiful. Our next stop is Vienna. Liz." "Dear Ruth, We are having a wonderful trip through Europe with friends. Now we are in beautiful Venice. Next we go to Vienna. I love seeing these places. Love, Liz." "Dear Francis, Dad loves the Alfa-Romeo Bar – we drove by the factory. We are in magical Venice with sunshine to make the water sparkle. Next stop will be Vienna. Much love, Mom and Dad." "Dear Johanna. It's a really beautiful cathedral and Florence is still medieval. Now we are in Venice near the highly ornate St. Mark's. I wish you could visit the churches of Europe. Love. Liz." "Dear Deborah and Jennifer. We have been to Germany, Switzerland, Florence and now Venice. I hope Jennifer will visit all the beautiful places when she is grown up. Next stop will be Vienna where we'll hear the boys. Love. Liz." "Dear Emily. Now we are in beautiful Venice with the sun shining to make the water sparkle. We hope to see you soon at the end of the month. Love. Liz." As I read Liz's letters, the rain continues to come down. It hasn't stopped for three days. I make the bed and leave.*

Friday 6. *9:30 a.m. Signs of departure: their things have been tidied up, the bathroom is empty. In the wardrobe there's still a skirt in its garment bag. On the chair in a plastic bag is a selection of objects to be kept to hand: an umbrella, two pairs of boots, a pair of men's underpants, a bottle of Martini Bianco, a flask of Johnny Walker.*

Sophie Calle (*1953)
THE HOTEL, ROOM 30, MARCH 5, 1981

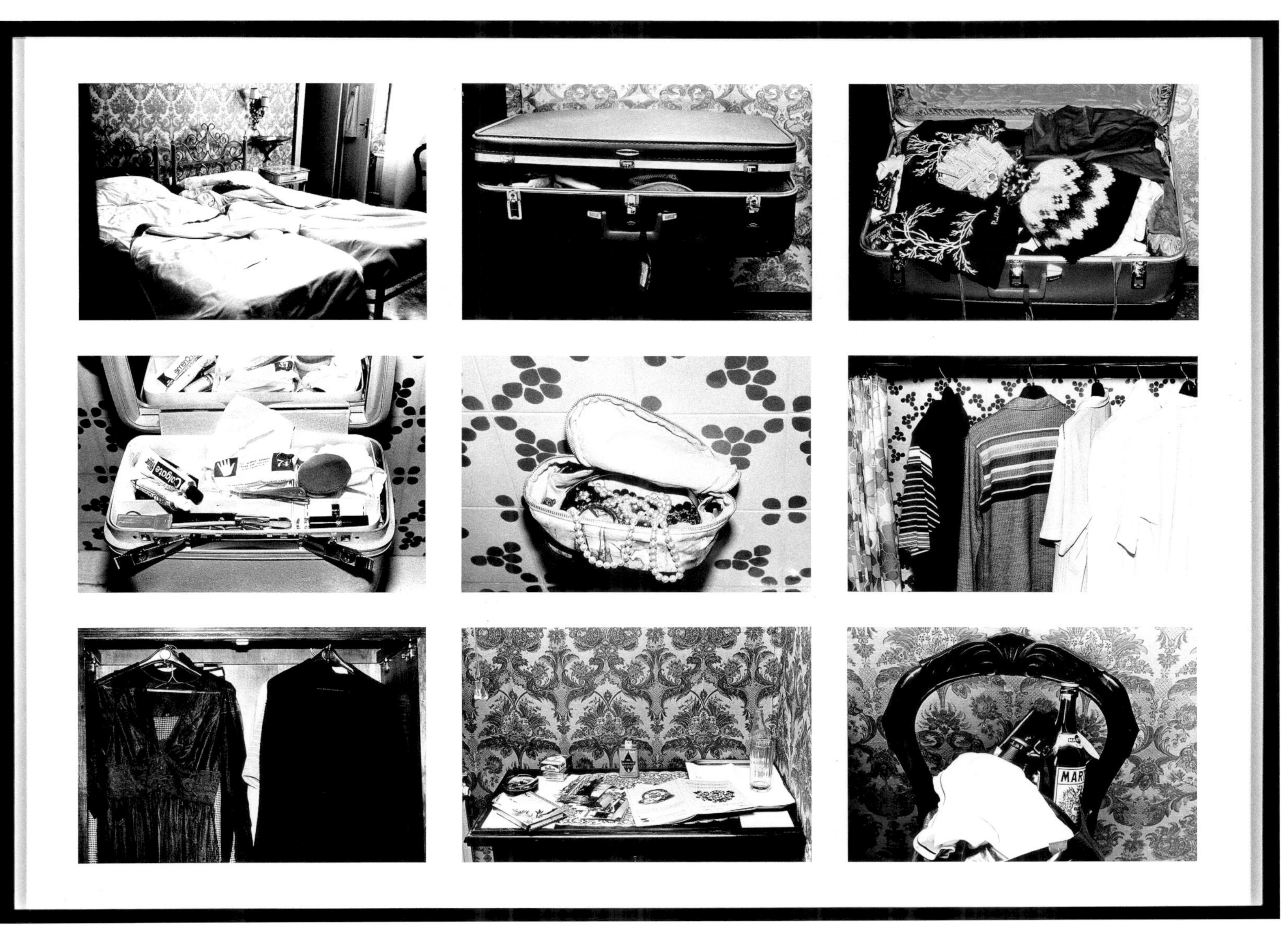

Sophie Calle (*1953)
THE HOTEL, ROOM 30, MARCH 5, 1981

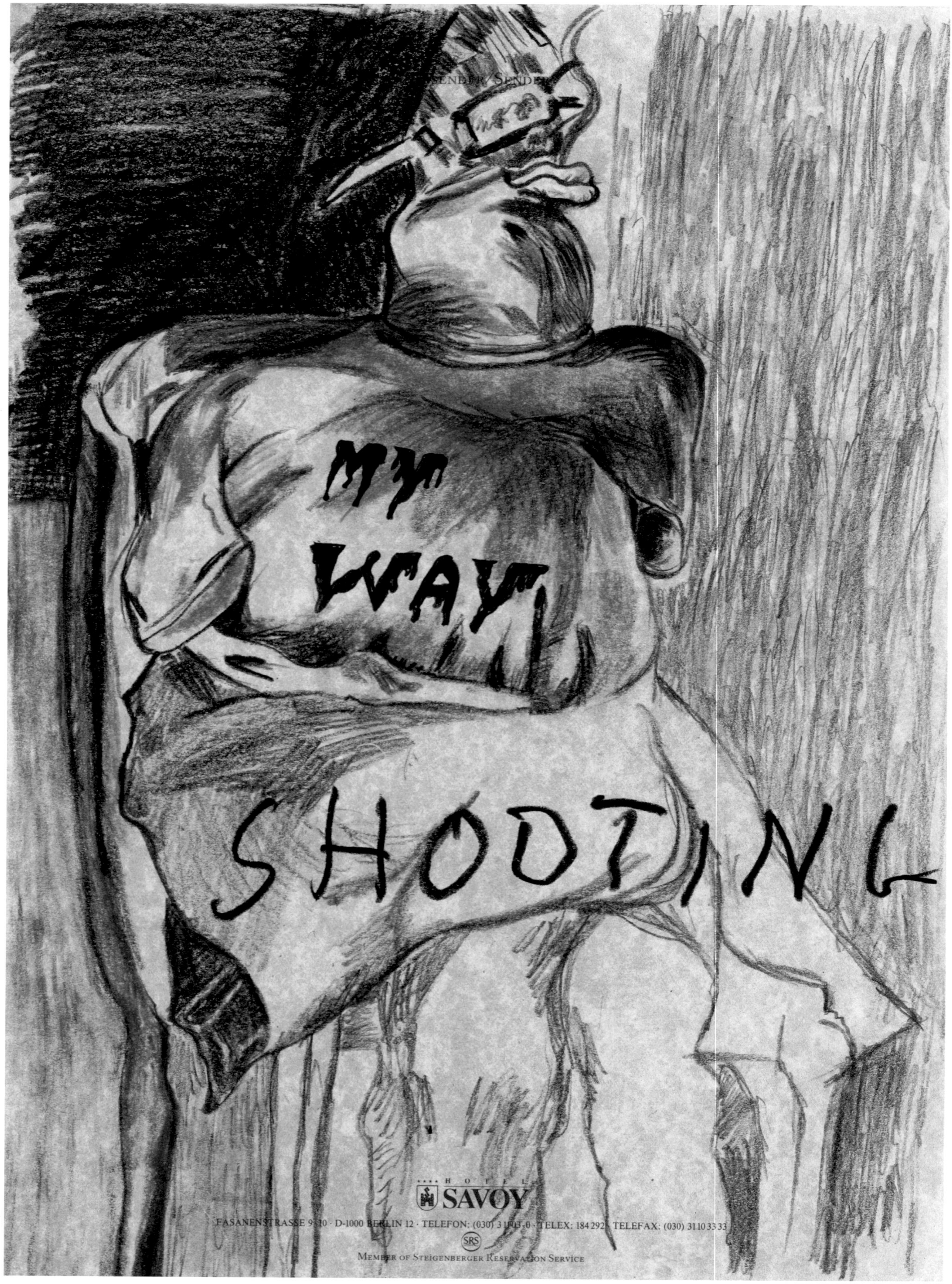

Martin Kippenberger (1953–1997)
OHNE TITEL (MY WAY SHOOTING / HOTEL SAVOY BERLIN) / UNTITLED (MY WAY SHOOTING / HOTEL SAVOY BERLIN), 1992

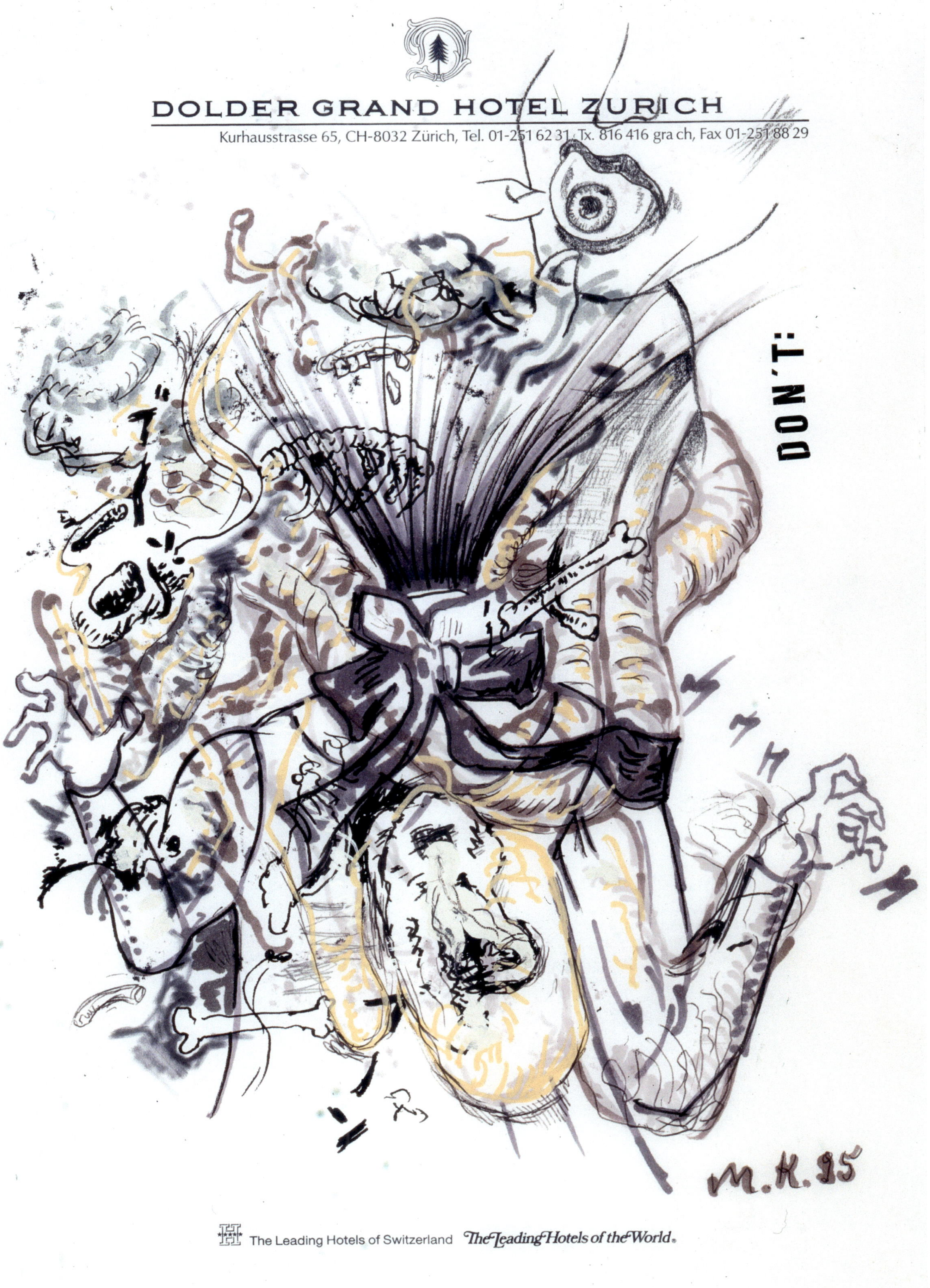

Martin Kippenberger (1953–1997)
OHNE TITEL (DOLDER GRAND HOTEL, ZÜRICH) / UNTITLED (DOLDER GRAND HOTEL, ZURICH), 1995

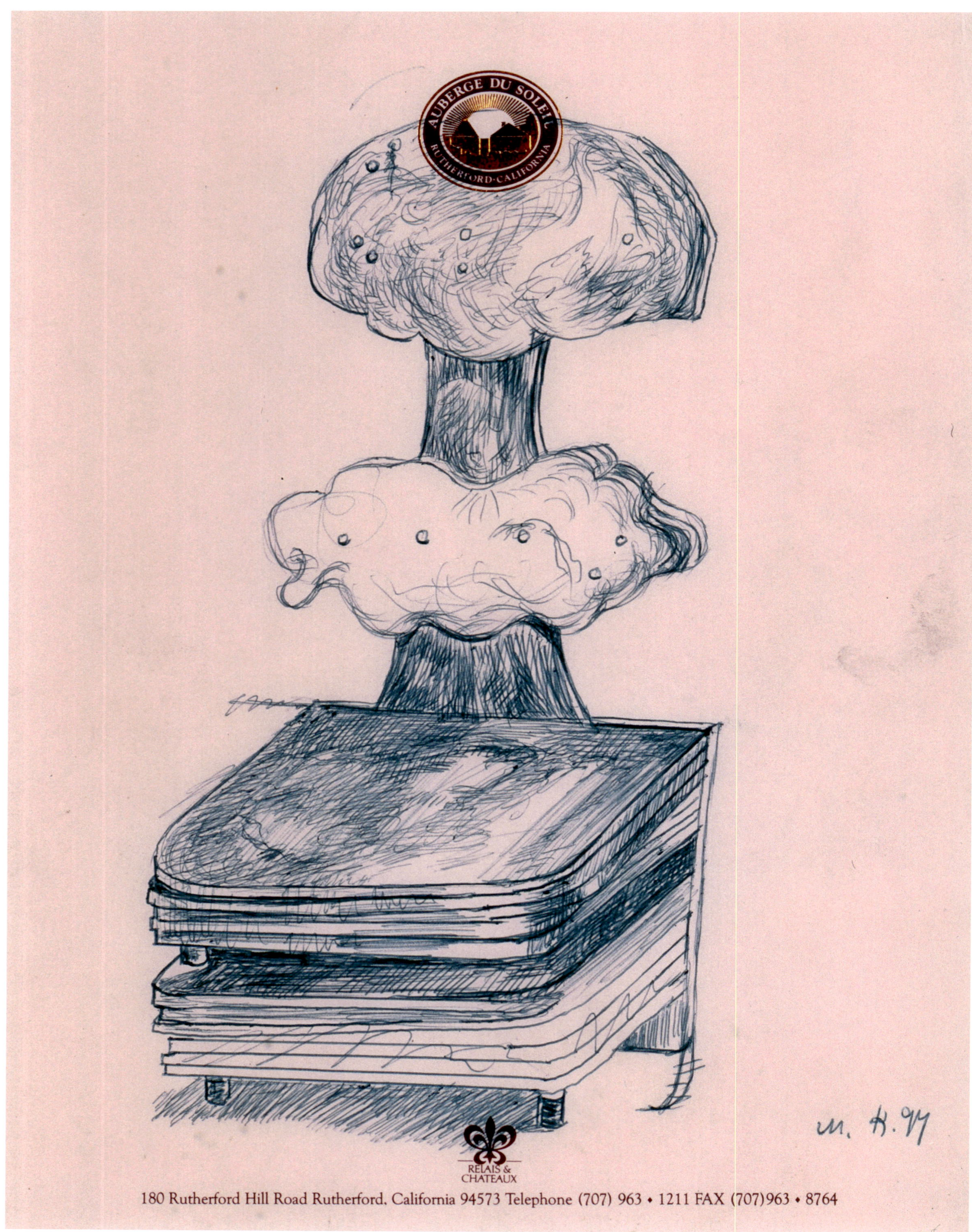

Martin Kippenberger (1953–1997)
OHNE TITEL (AUBERGE DU SOLEIL, RUTHERFORD CA) / UNTITLED (AUBERGE DU SOLEIL, RUTHERFORD CA), 1994

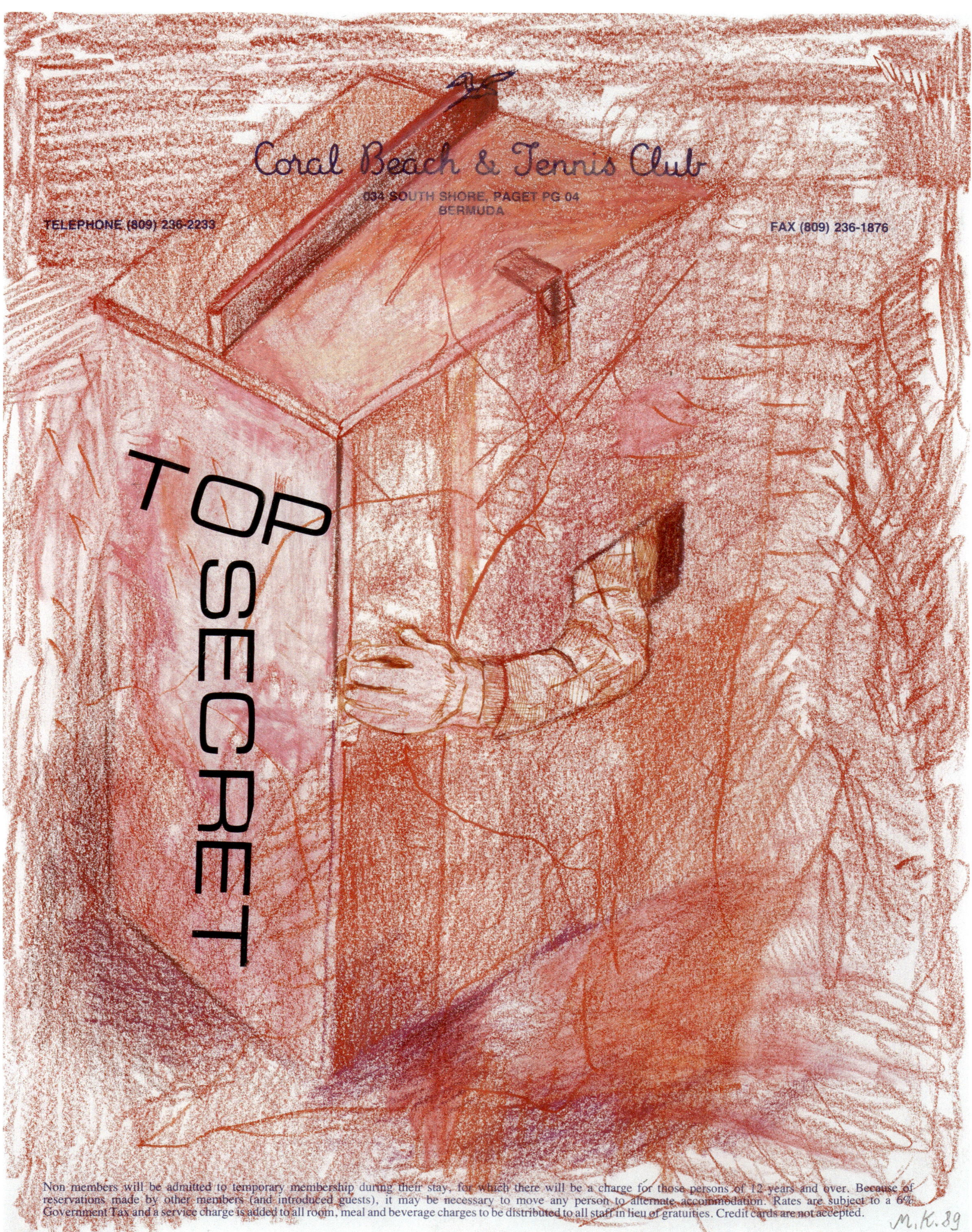

Martin Kippenberger (1953–1997)
OHNE TITEL (TOP SECRET) / UNTITLED (TOP SECRET), 1989

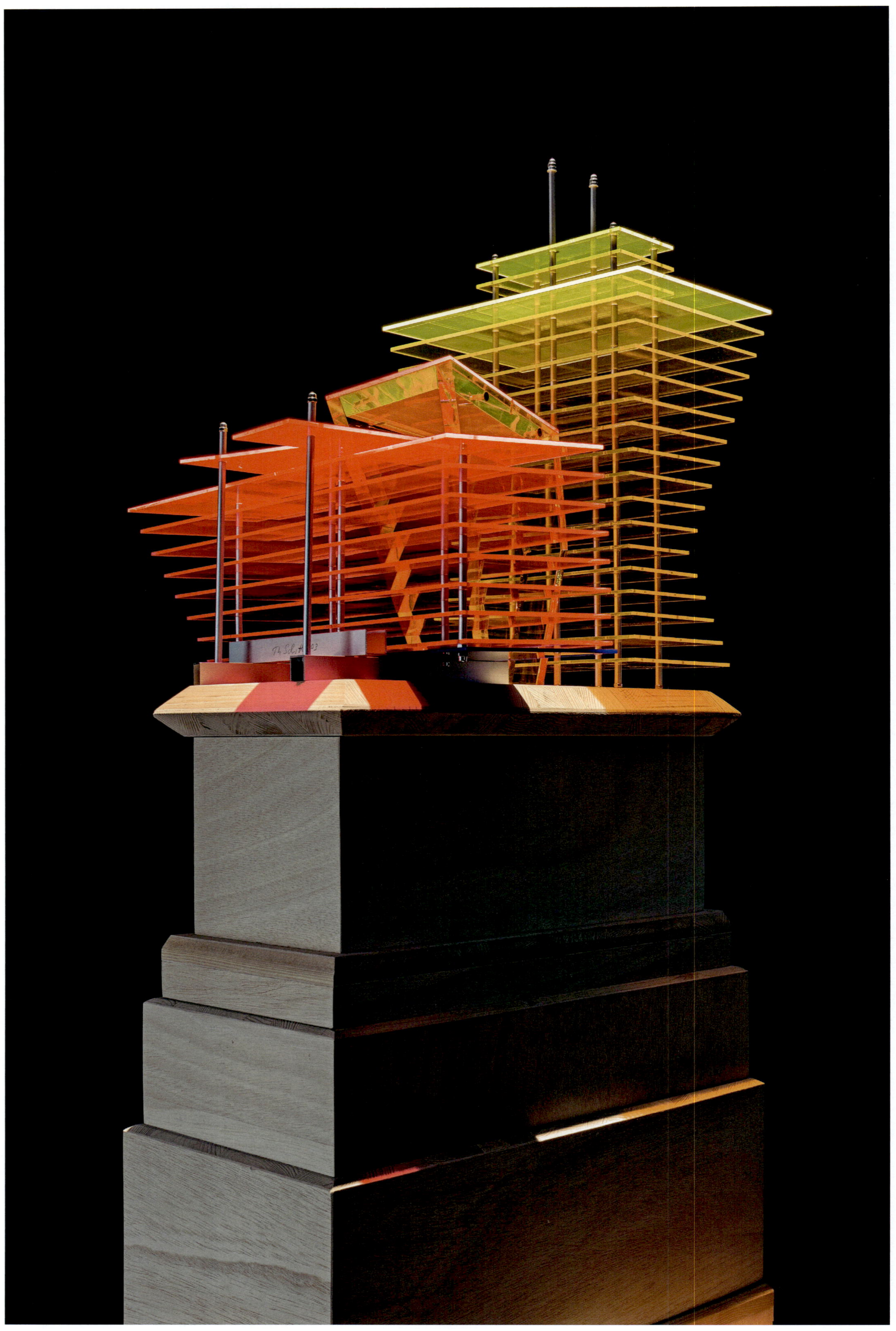

Thomas Schütte (*1954)
HOTEL FOR THE BIRDS, 2003

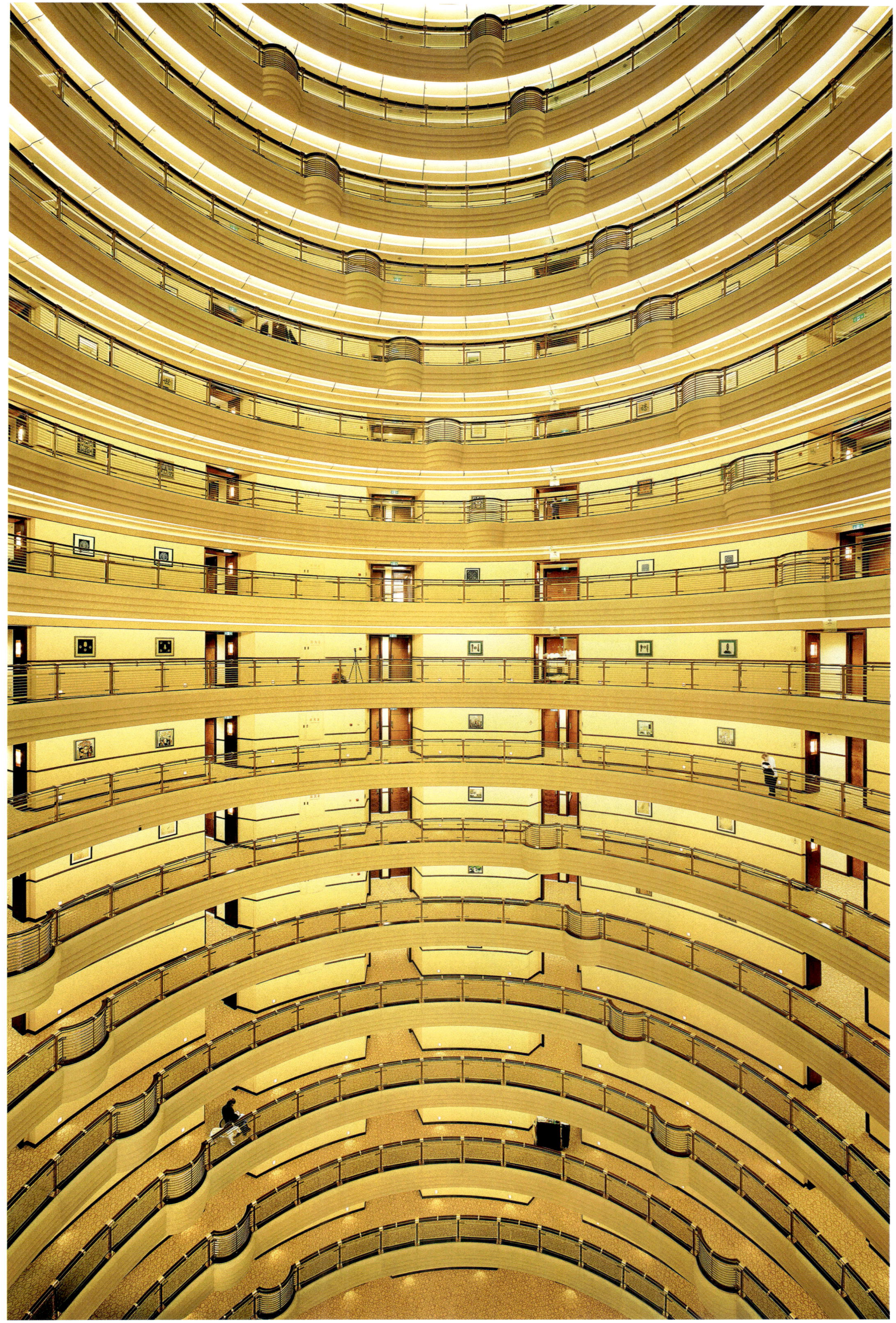

Andreas Gursky (*1955)
SHANGHAI, 2000

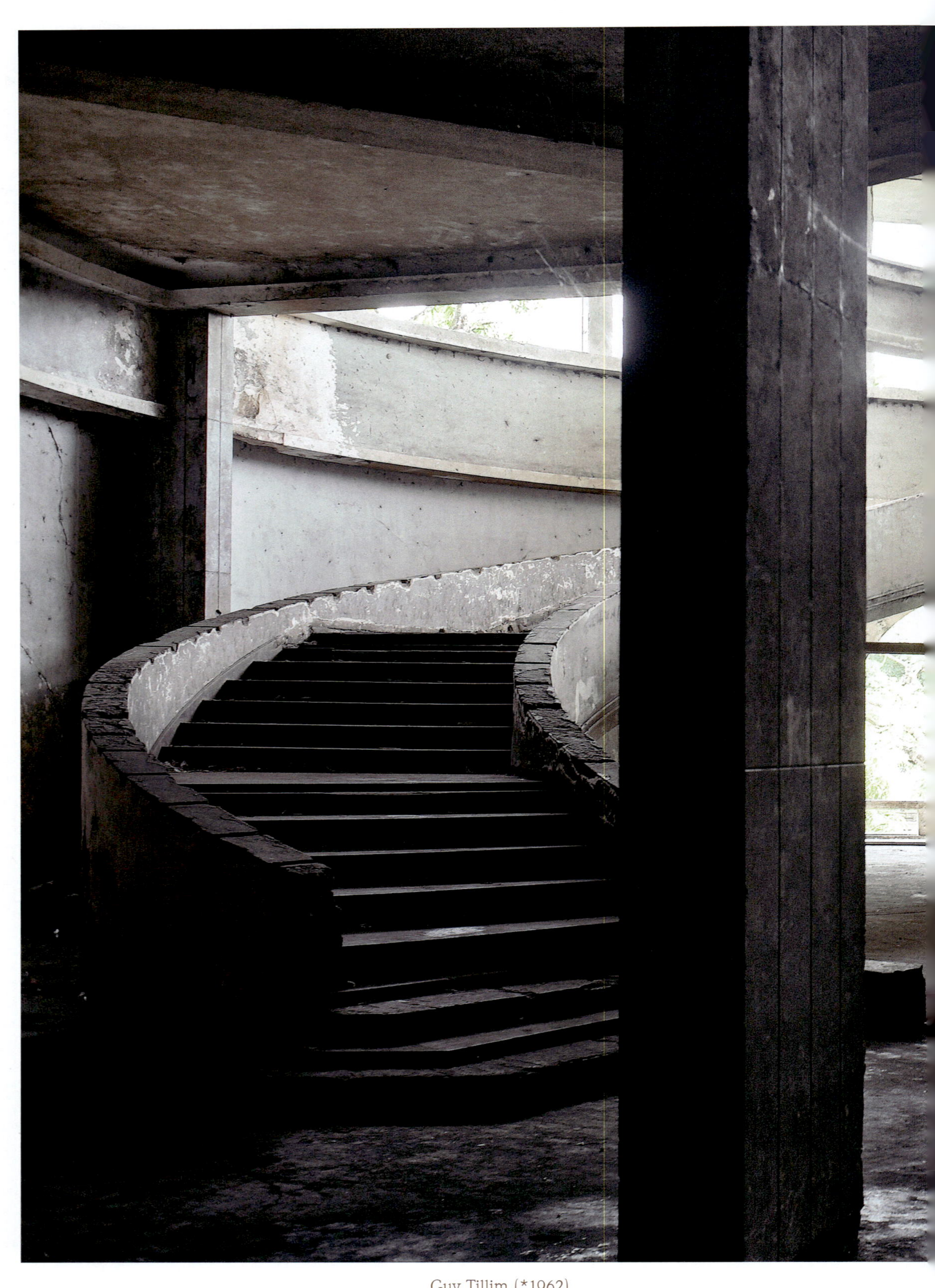

Guy Tillim (*1962)
GRANDE HOTEL, BEIRA, MOZAMBIQUE, 2008

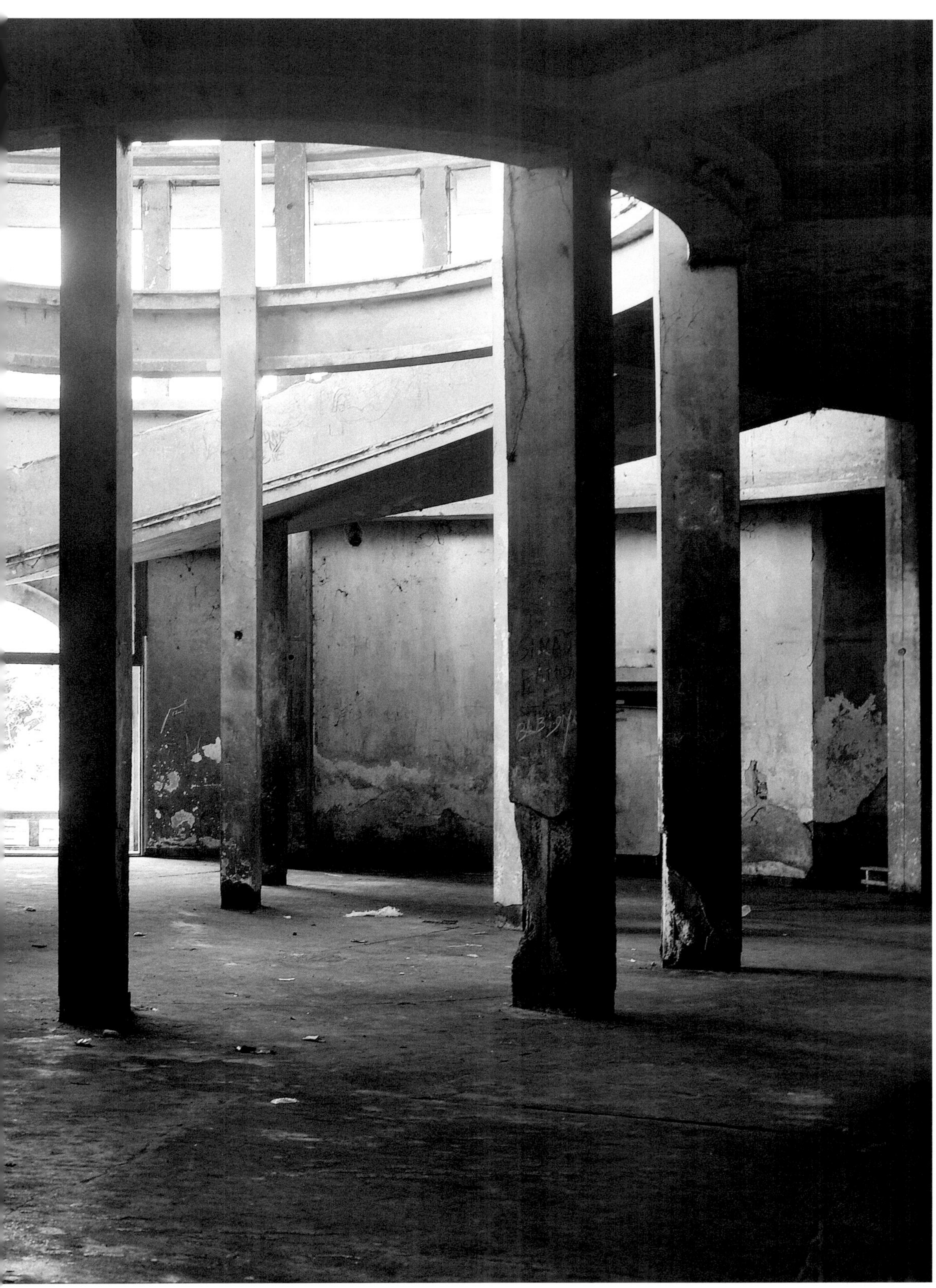

Guy Tillim (*1962)
GRANDE HOTEL, BEIRA, MOZAMBIQUE, 2008

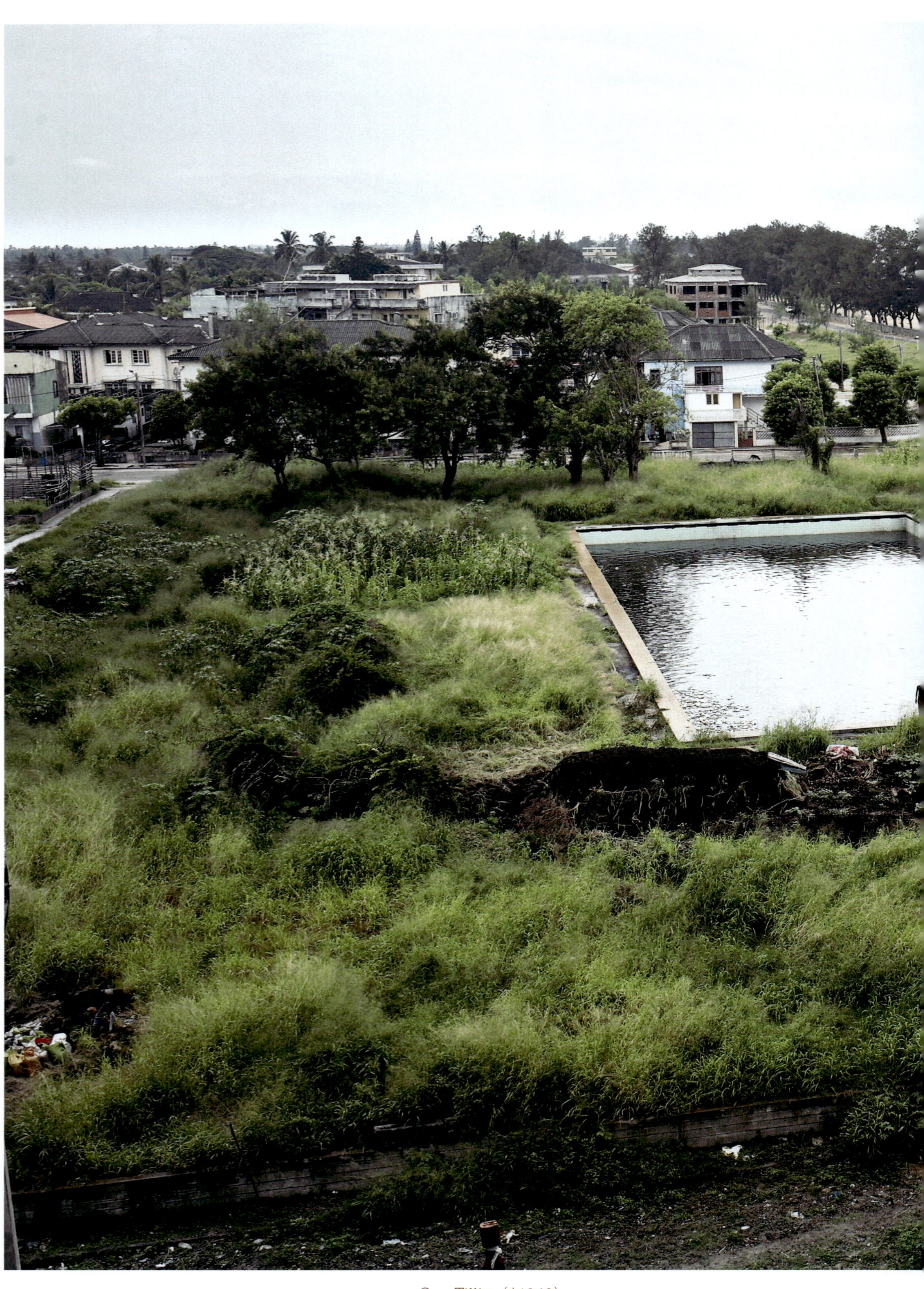

Guy Tillim (*1962)
GRANDE HOTEL, BEIRA, MOZAMBIQUE, 2008

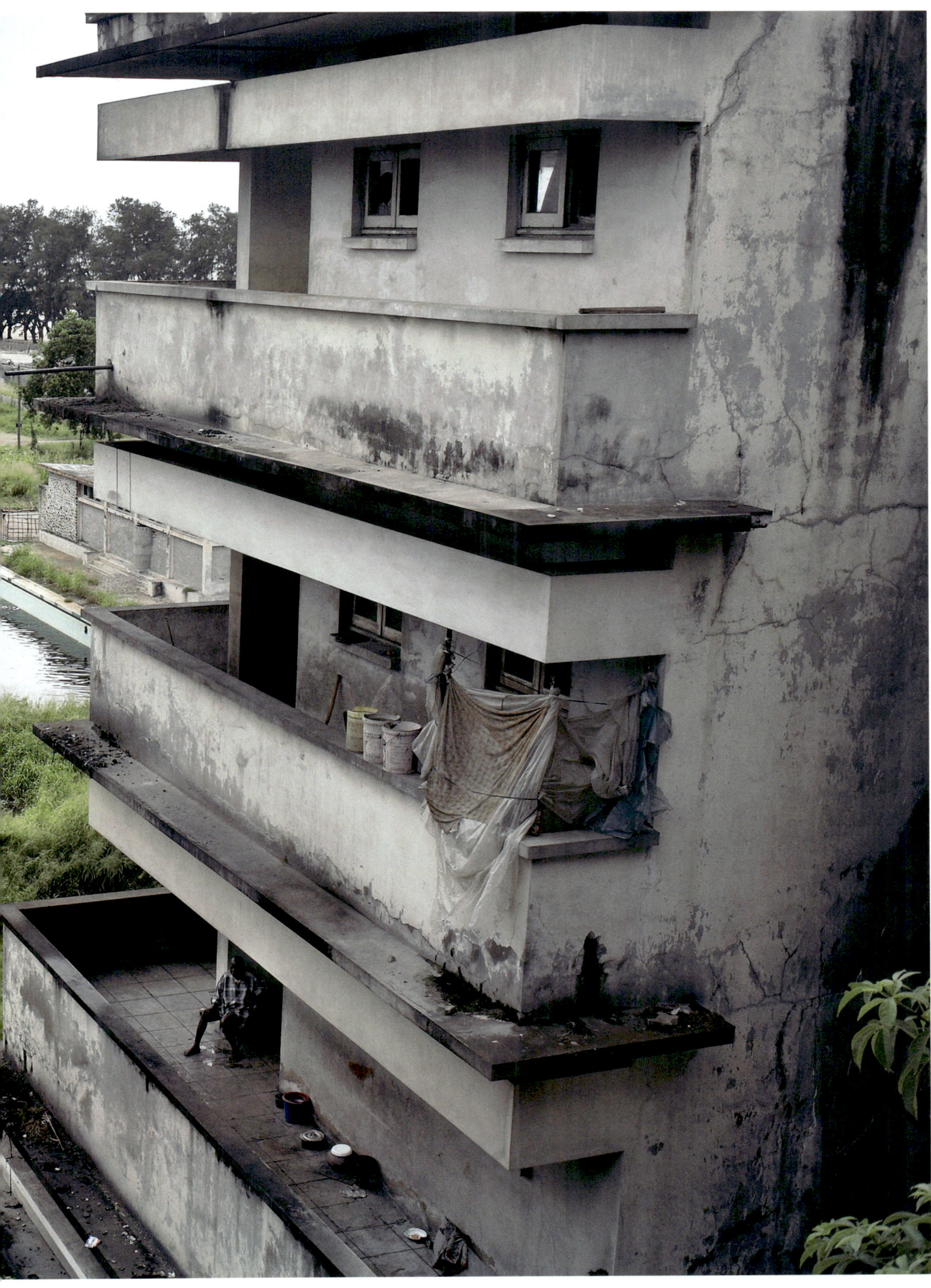

Guy Tillim (*1962)
GRANDE HOTEL, BEIRA, MOZAMBIQUE, 2008

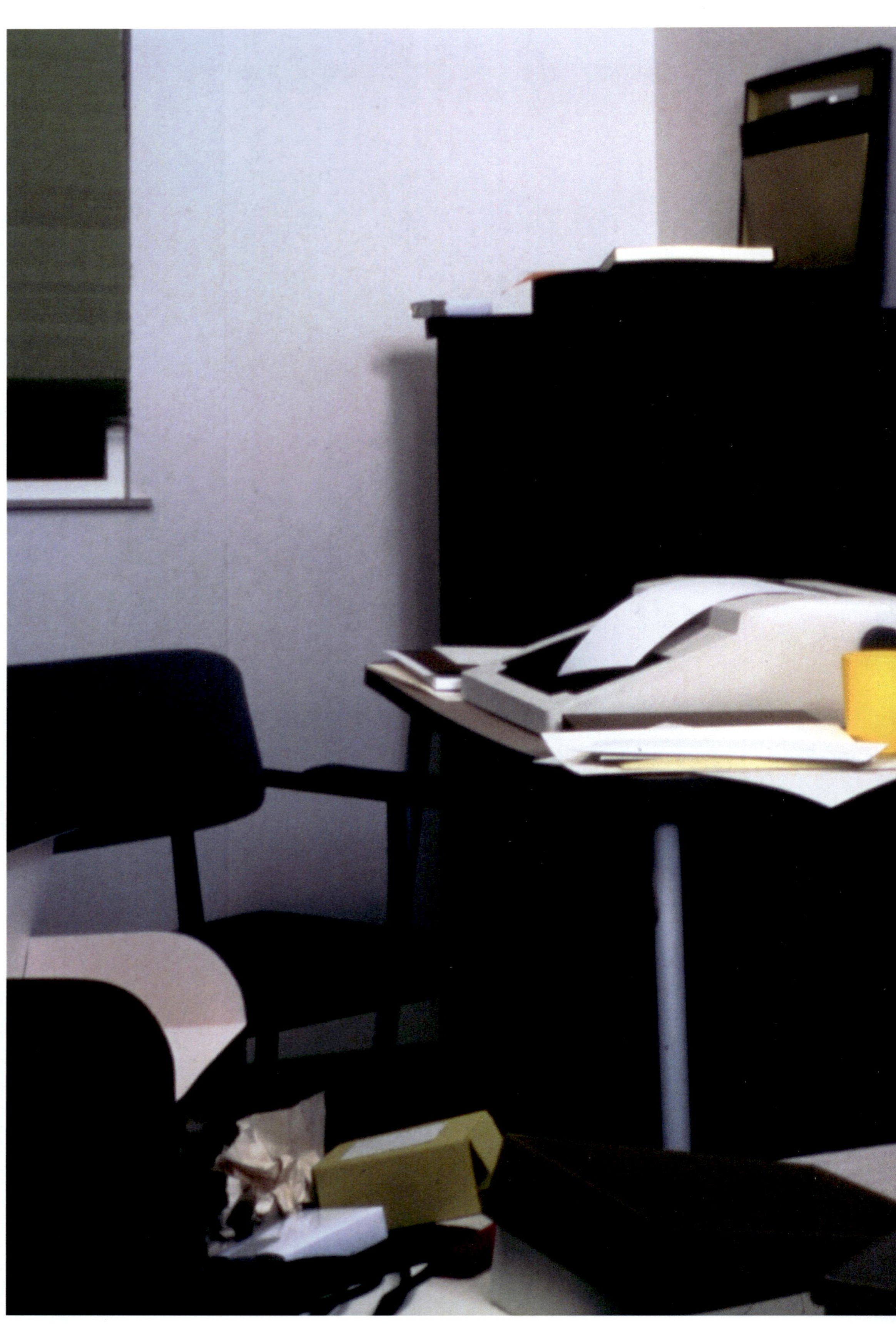

Thomas Demand (*1964)
ZIMMER/ROOM, 1996

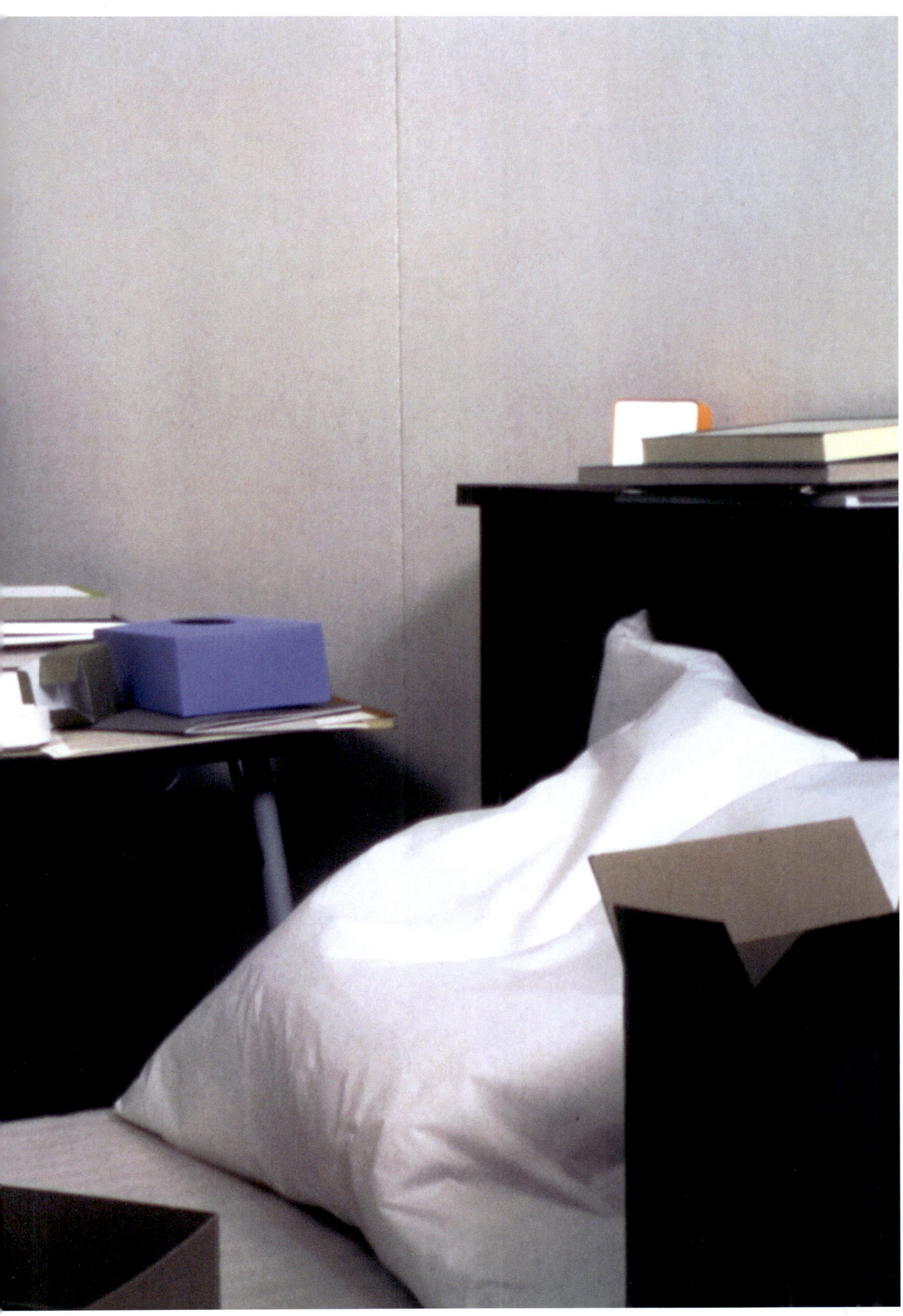

Thomas Demand (*1964)
ZIMMER/ROOM, 1996

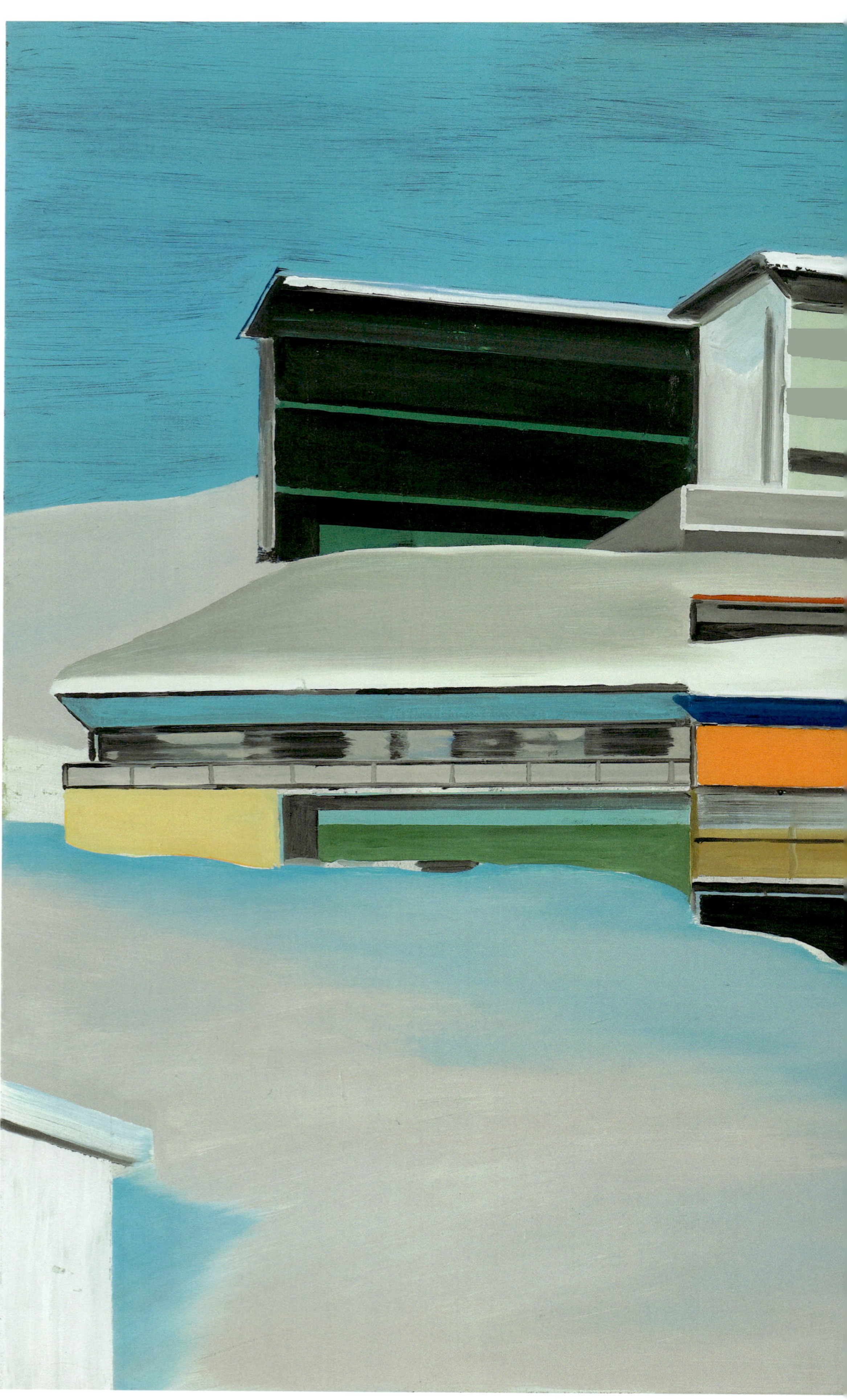

Eberhard Havekost (*1967)
SKIHOTEL, 1996

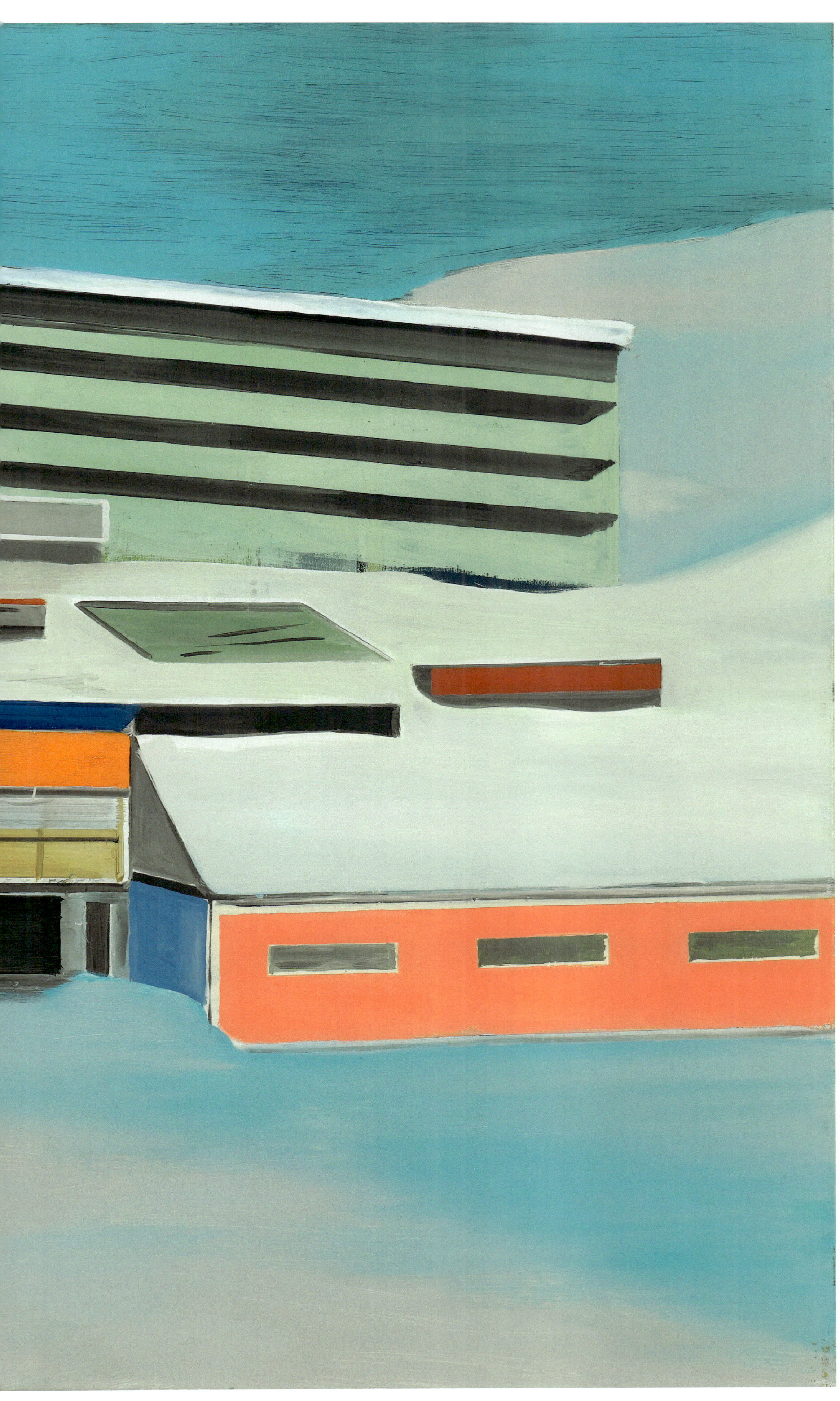

Eberhard Havekost (*1967)
SKIHOTEL, 1996

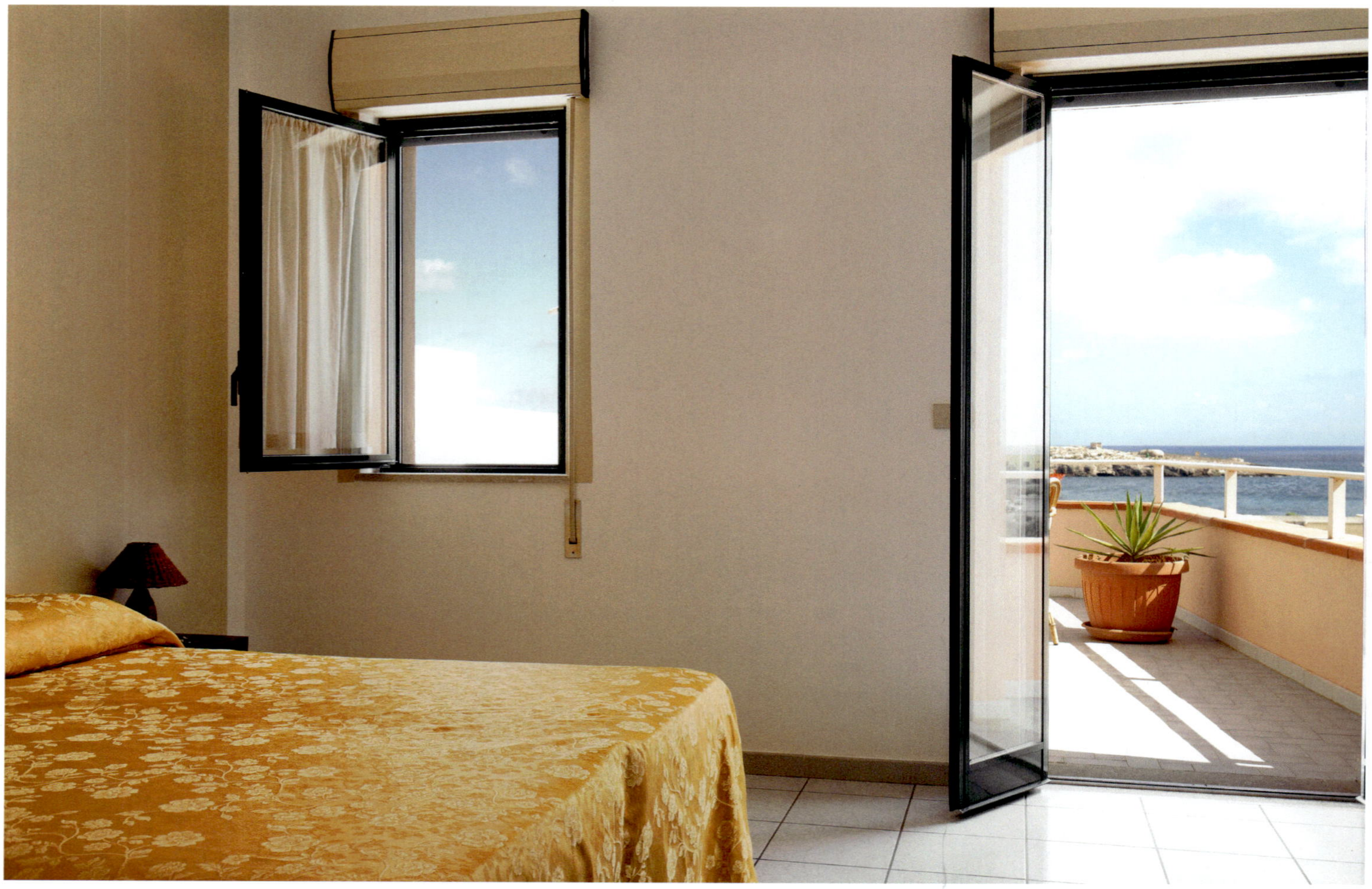

Sven Johne (*1976)
Detail aus der Serie TRAUMHOTELS / Detail from the series DREAM HOTELS, 2012

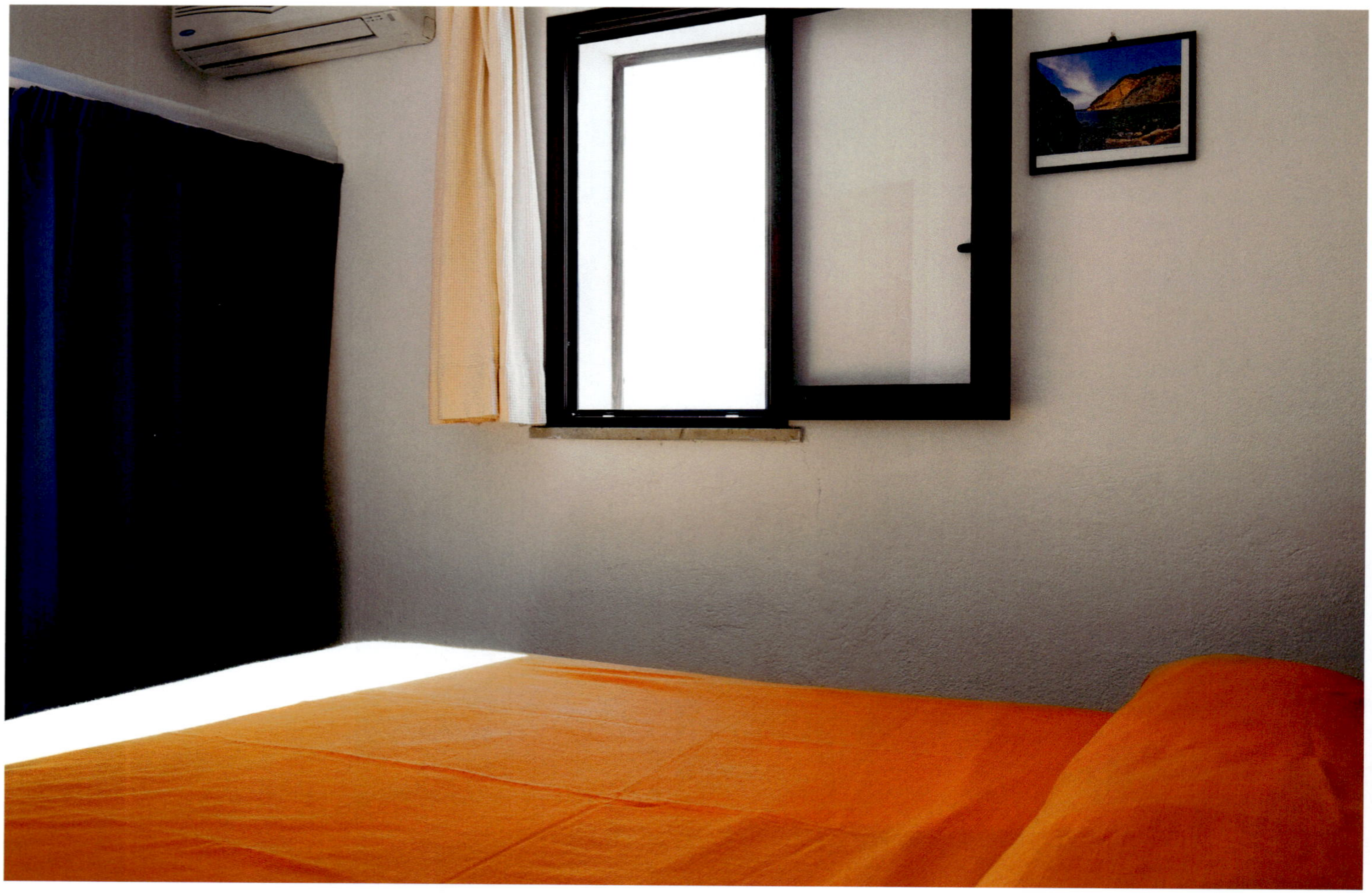

Sven Johne (*1976)
Detail aus der Serie TRAUMHOTELS / Detail from the series DREAM HOTELS, 2012

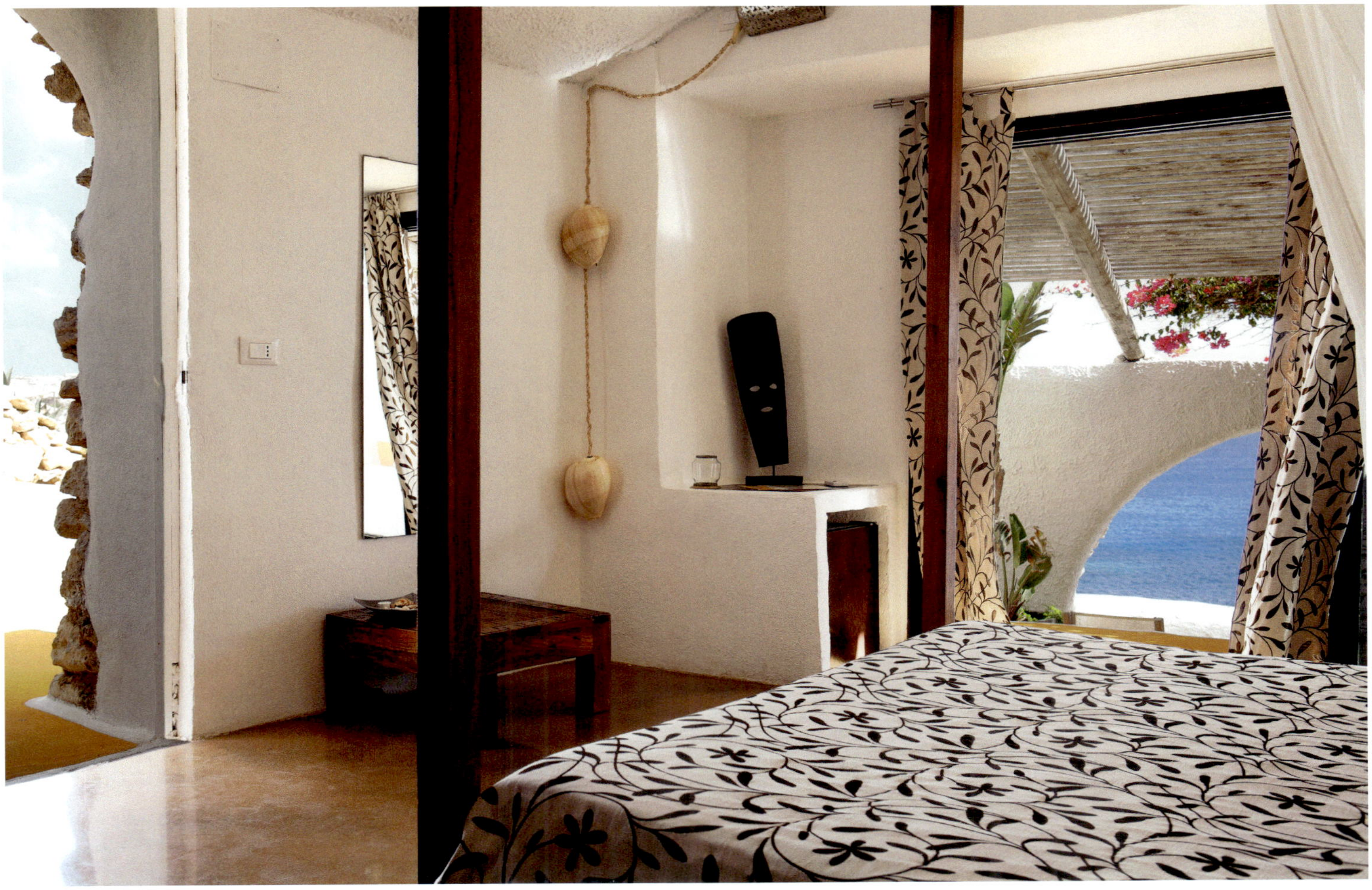

Sven Johne (*1976)
Detail aus der Serie TRAUMHOTELS / Detail from the series DREAM HOTELS, 2012

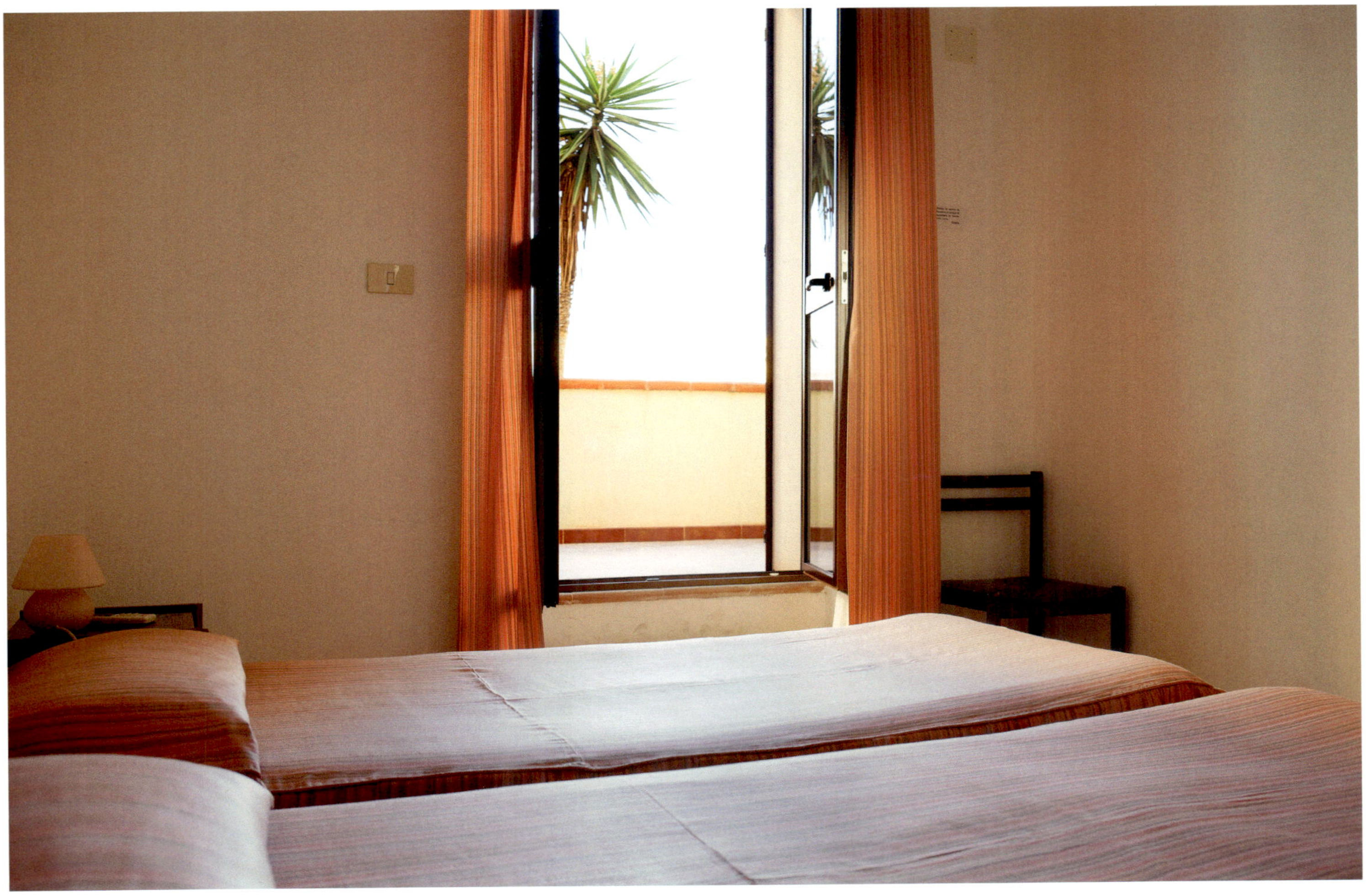

Sven Johne (*1976)
Detail aus der Serie TRAUMHOTELS / Detail from the series DREAM HOTELS, 2012

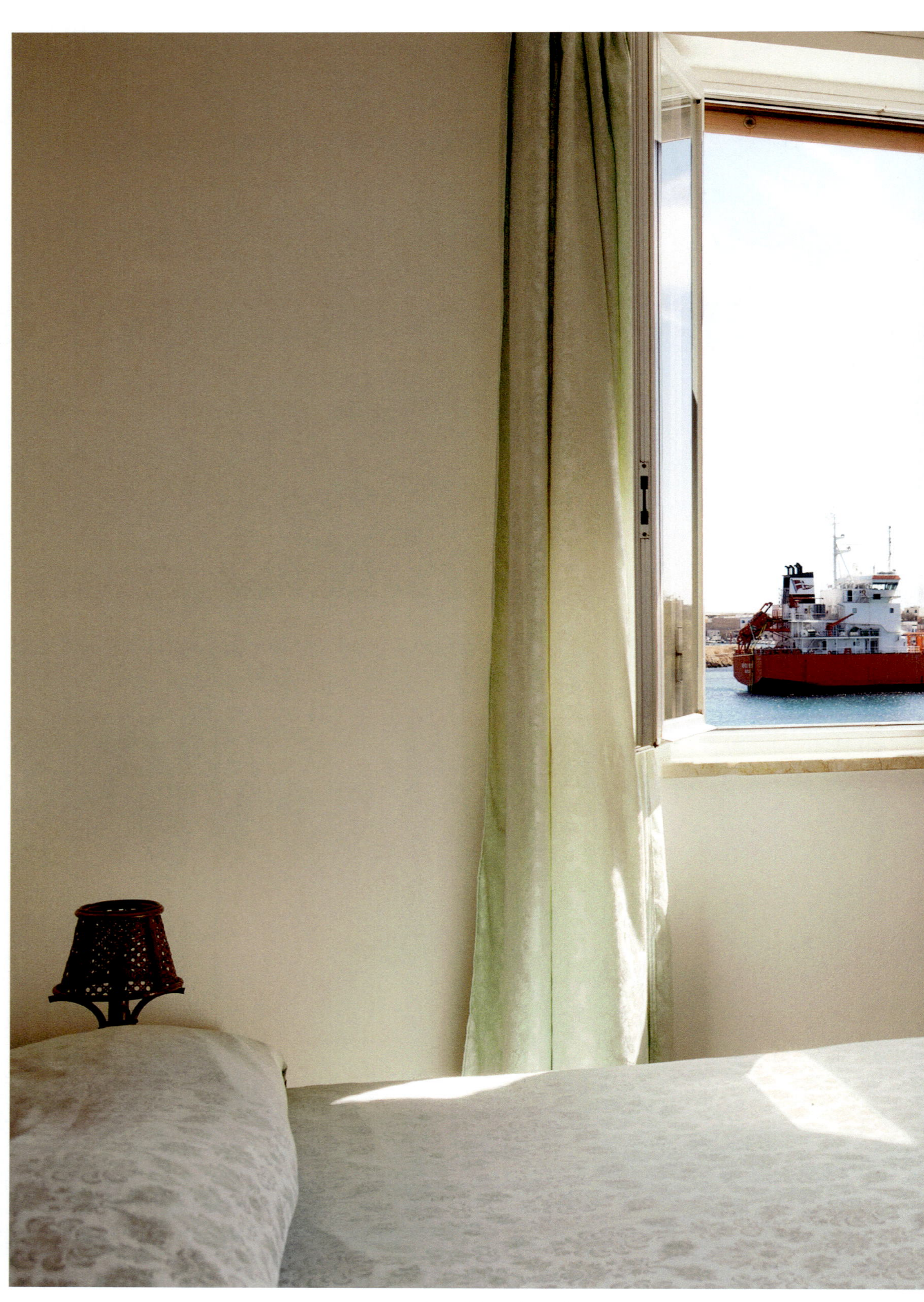

Sven Johne (*1976)
Detail from the series DREAM HOTELS, 2012

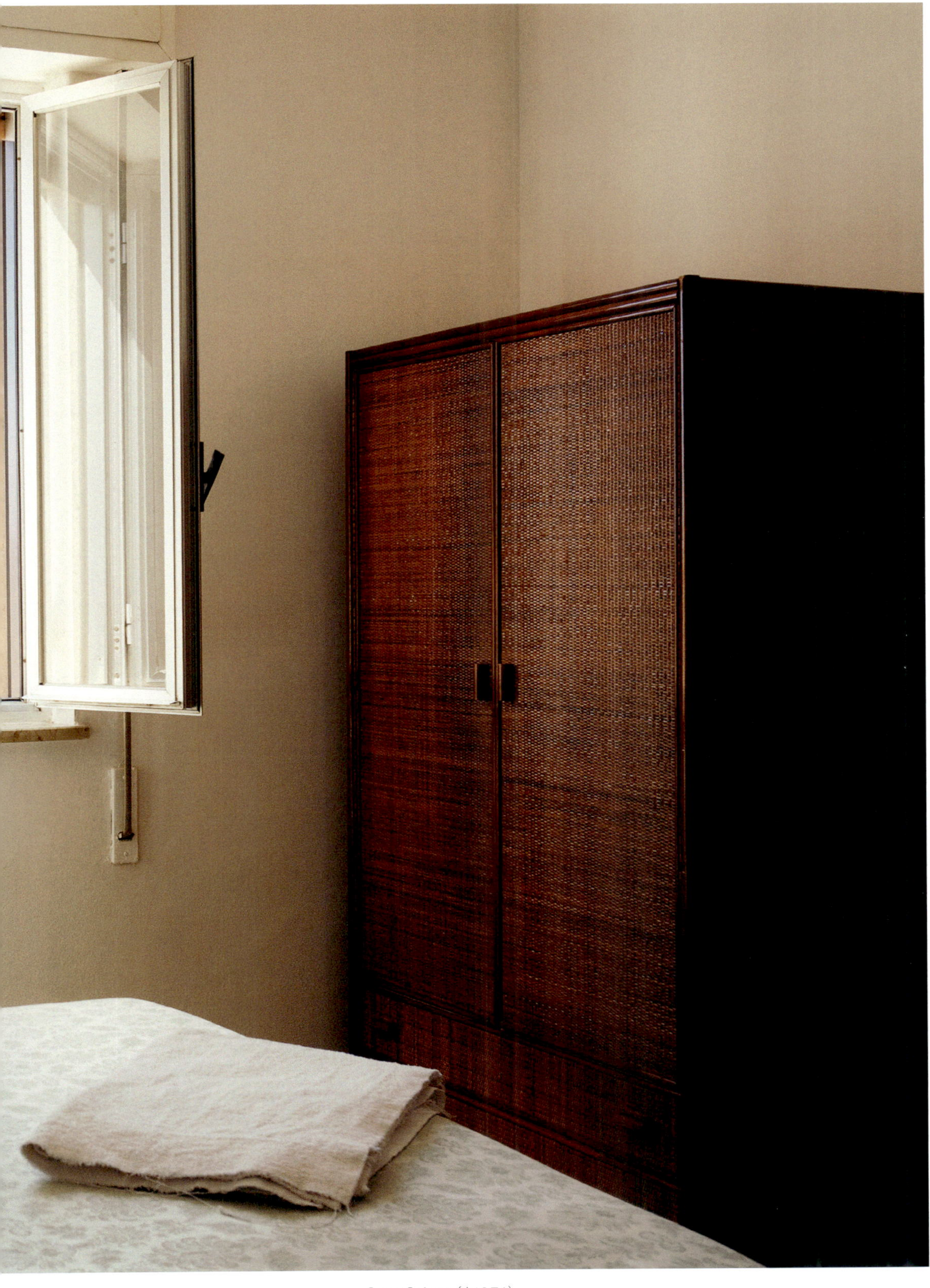

Sven Johne (*1976)
Detail aus der Serie TRAUMHOTELS, 2012

AUSSTELLUNG / EXHIBITION
ATLANTIC PARKHOTEL

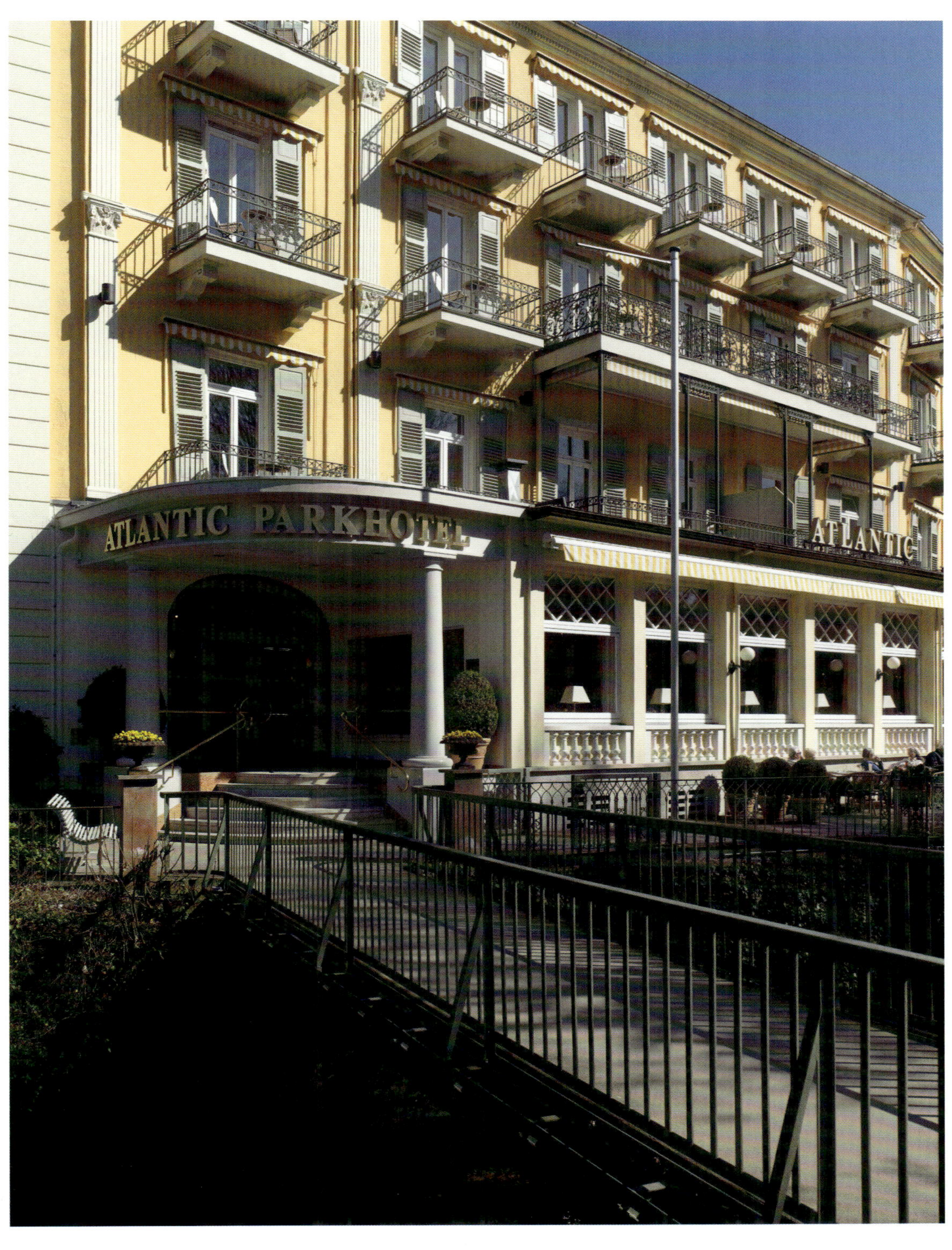

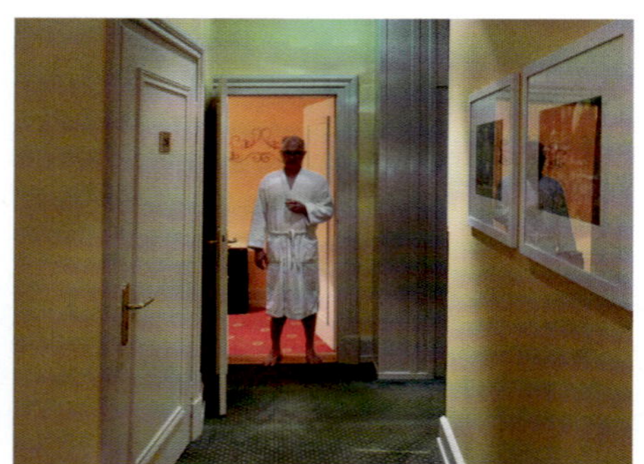

Christian Andersson

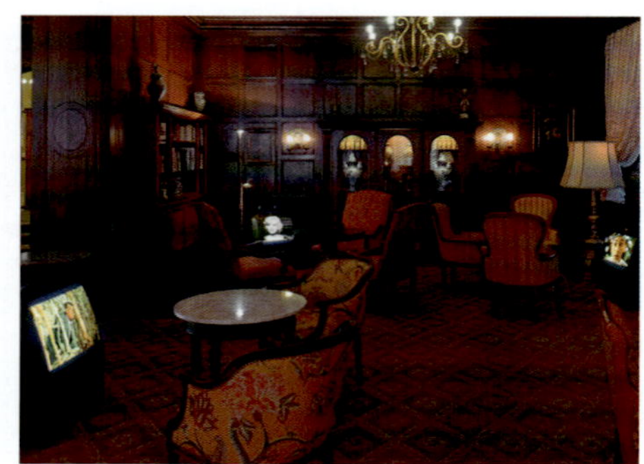

Bücher- und Filmarchiv
zur Ausstellung
Book and Film Archive
Accompanying the Exhibition

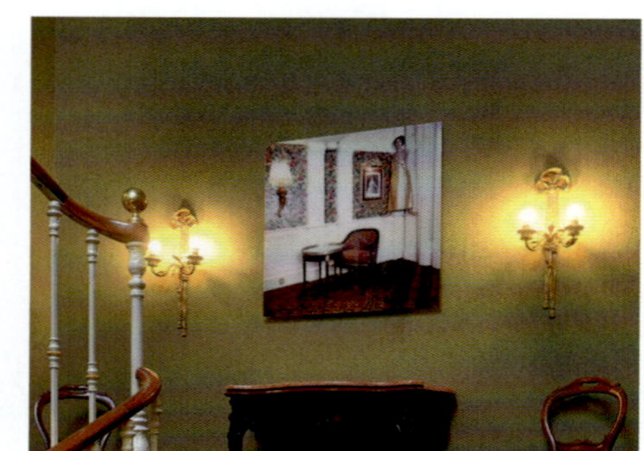

Kunstsammlung des Hotels
Castell, Zuoz
Art Collection of the Hotel
Castell, Zuoz
Mit Werken von / With works by
Fischli/Weiss | Andreas Gursky
Tobias Madison | Chantal Michel
Gabriel Orozco | Roman Signer

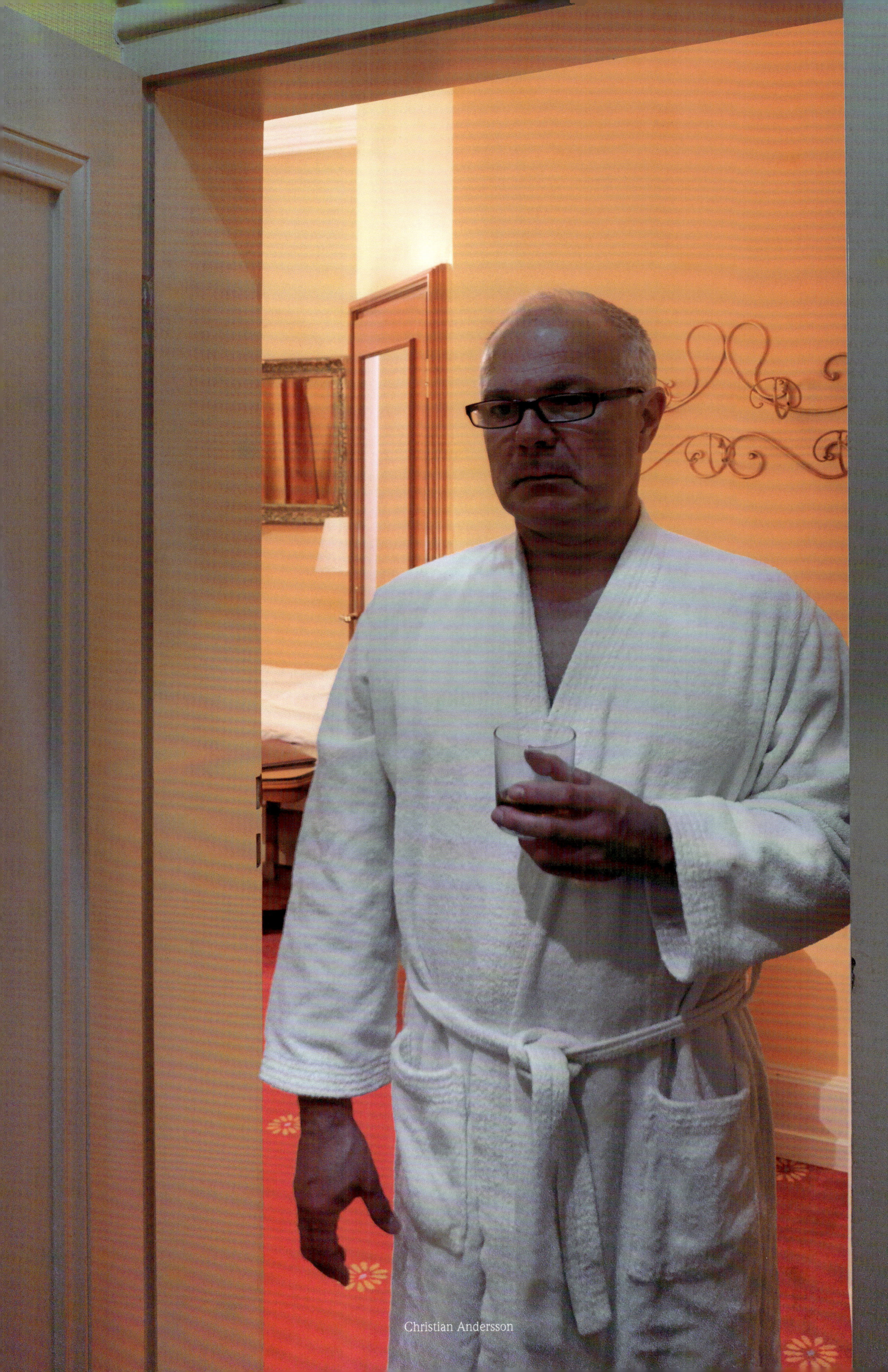

Christian Andersson

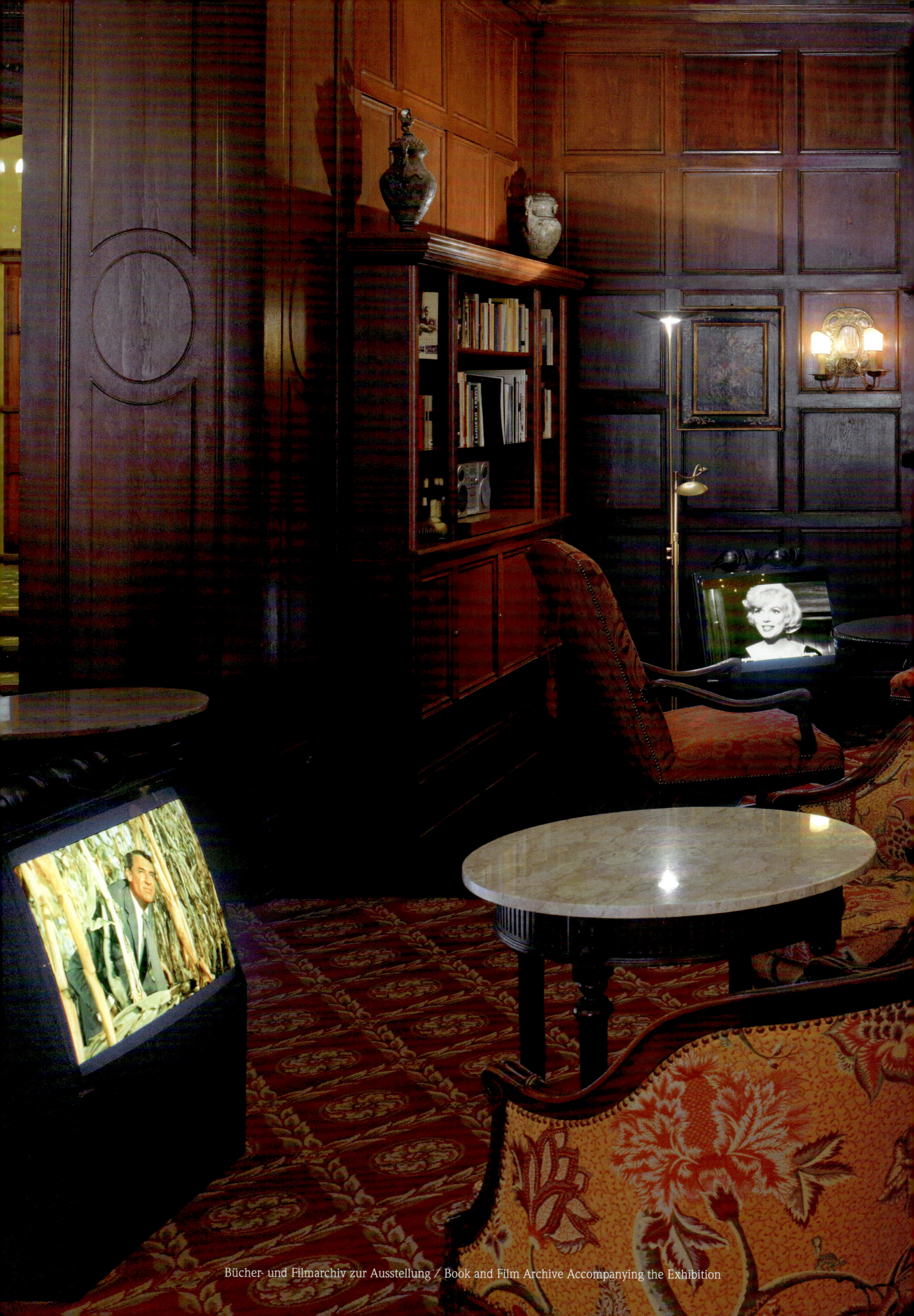

Bücher- und Filmarchiv zur Ausstellung / Book and Film Archive Accompanying the Exhibition

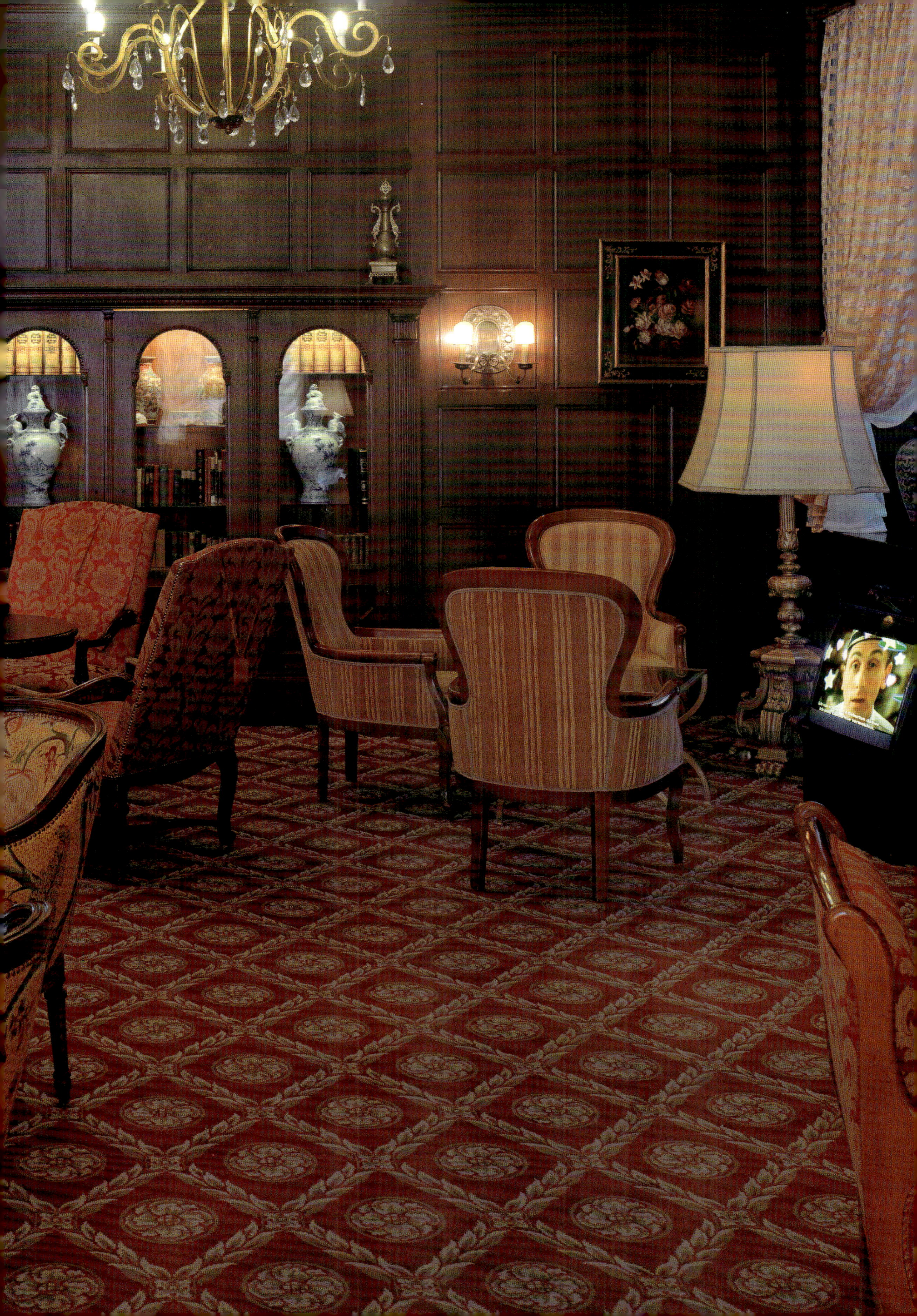

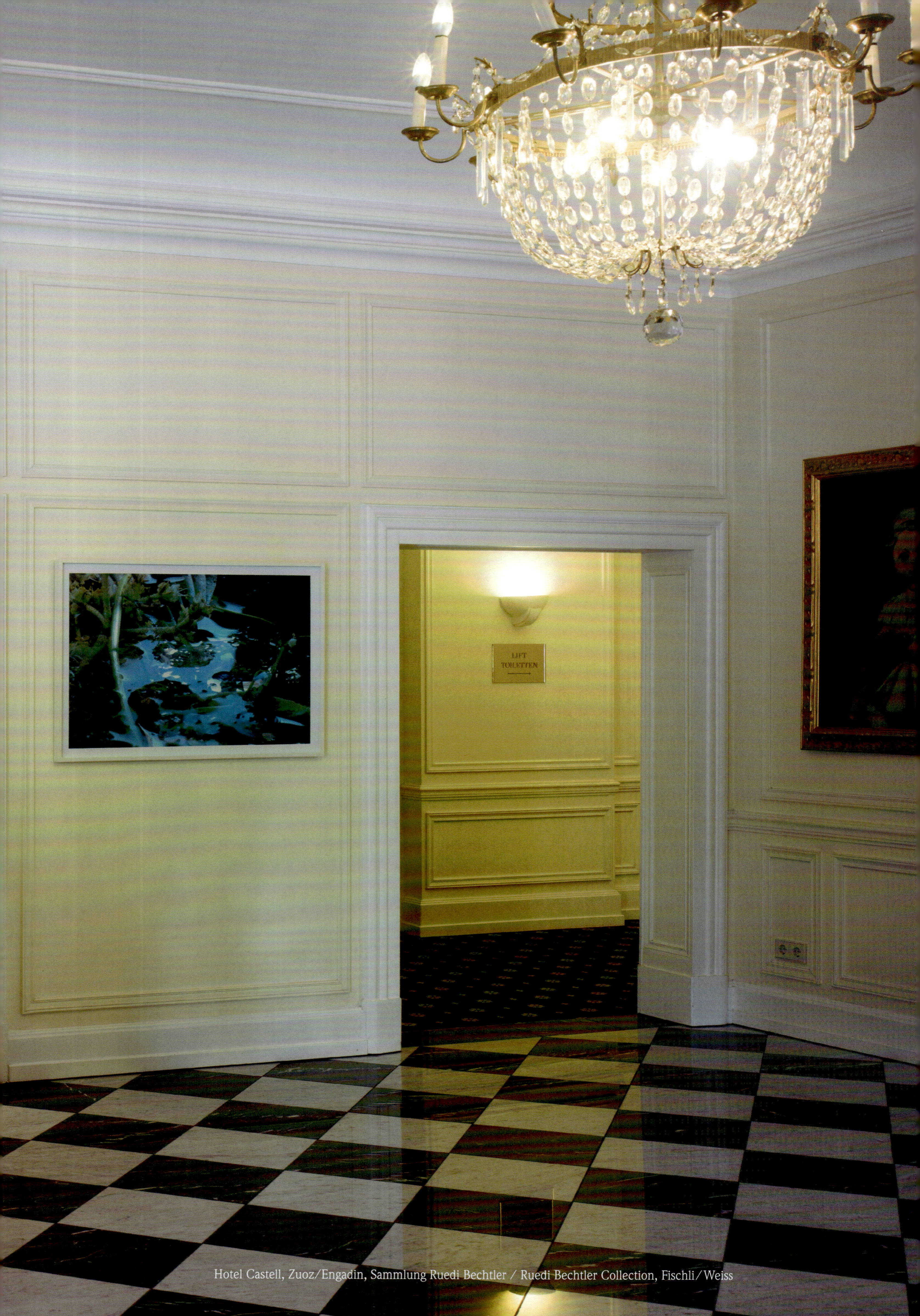

Hotel Castell, Zuoz/Engadin, Sammlung Ruedi Bechtler / Ruedi Bechtler Collection, Fischli/Weiss

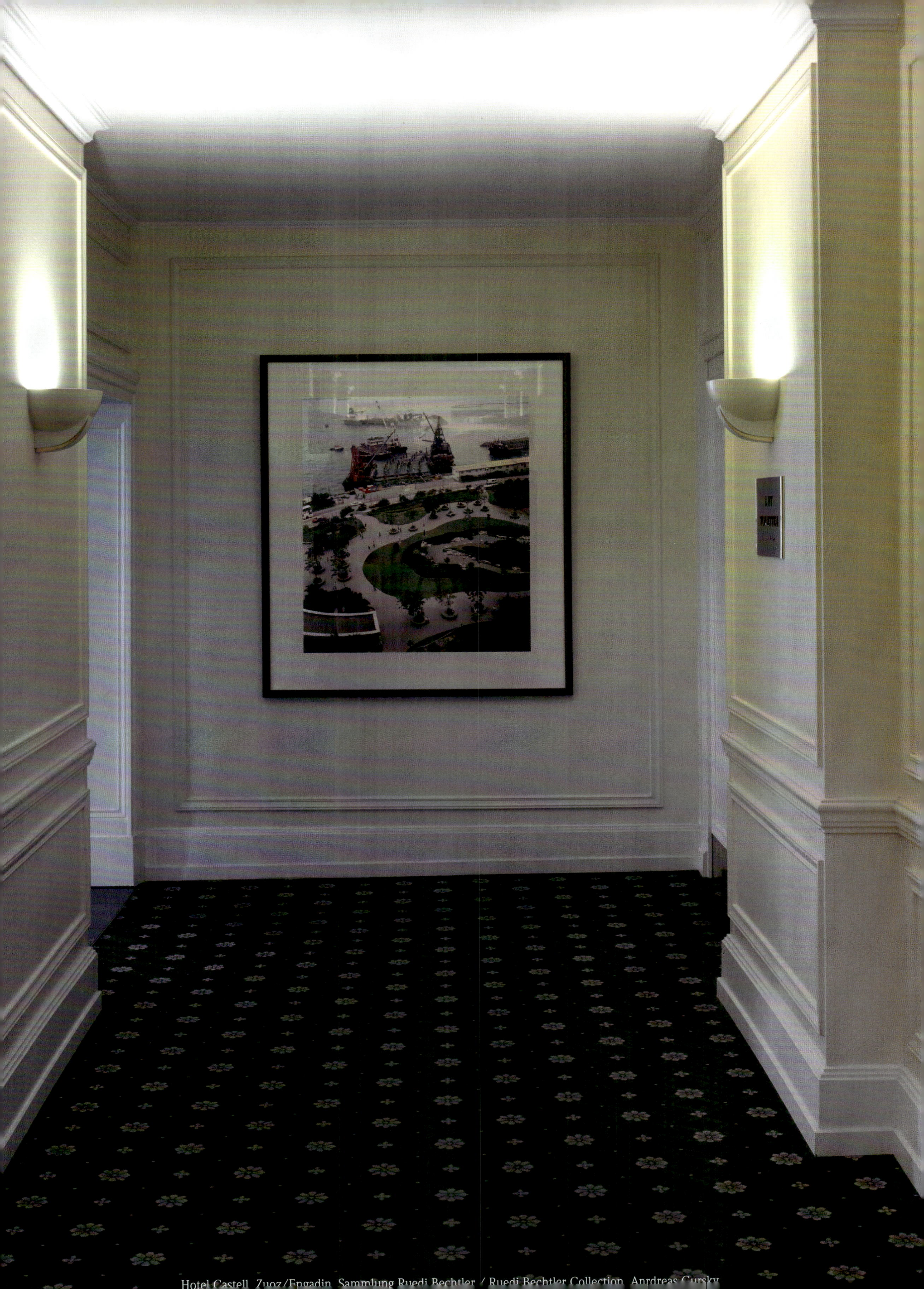

Hotel Castell, Zuoz/Engadin, Sammlung Ruedi Bechtler / Ruedi Bechtler Collection, Anrdreas Gursky

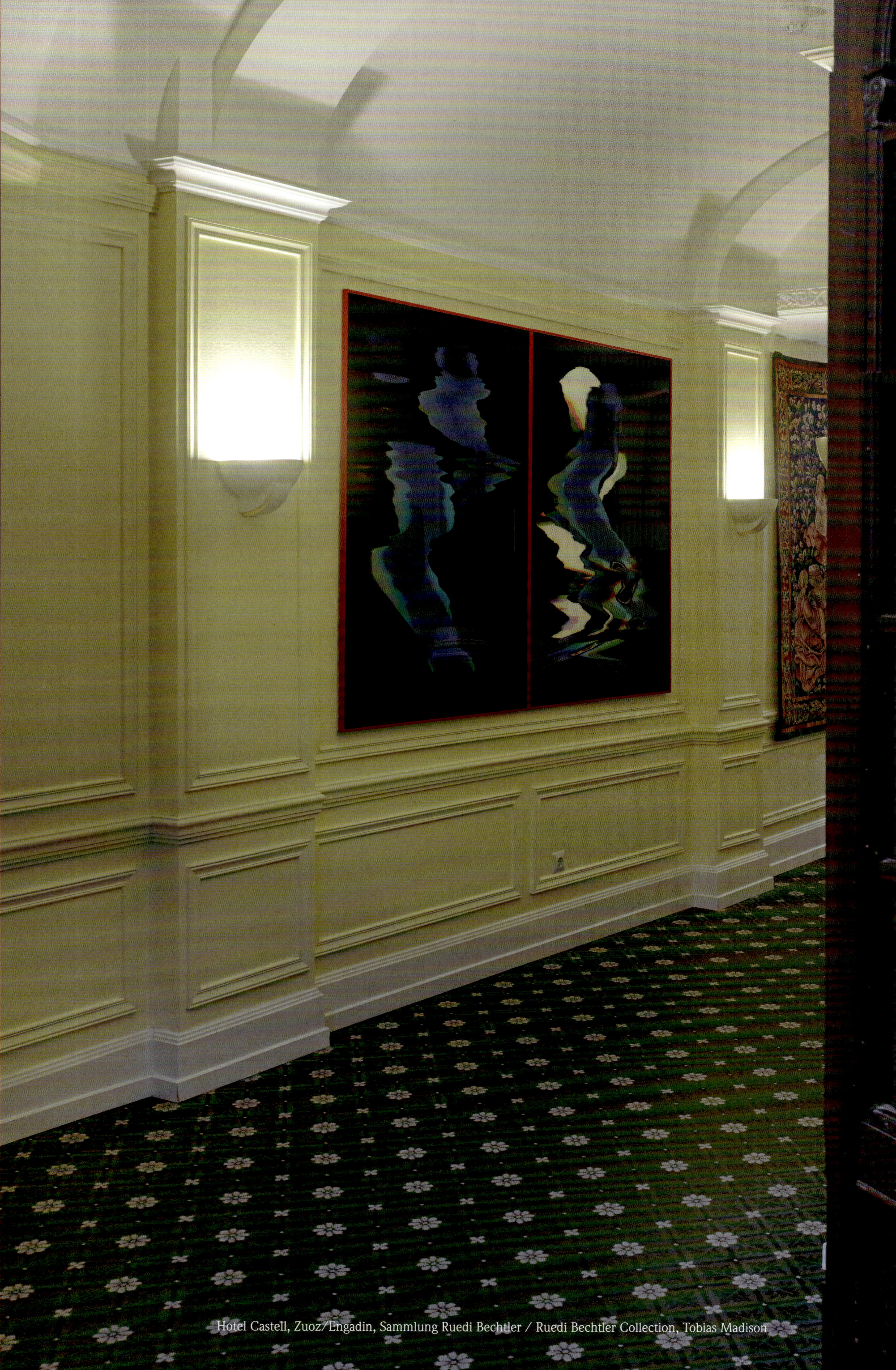

Hotel Castell, Zuoz/Engadin, Sammlung Ruedi Bechtler / Ruedi Bechtler Collection, Tobias Madison

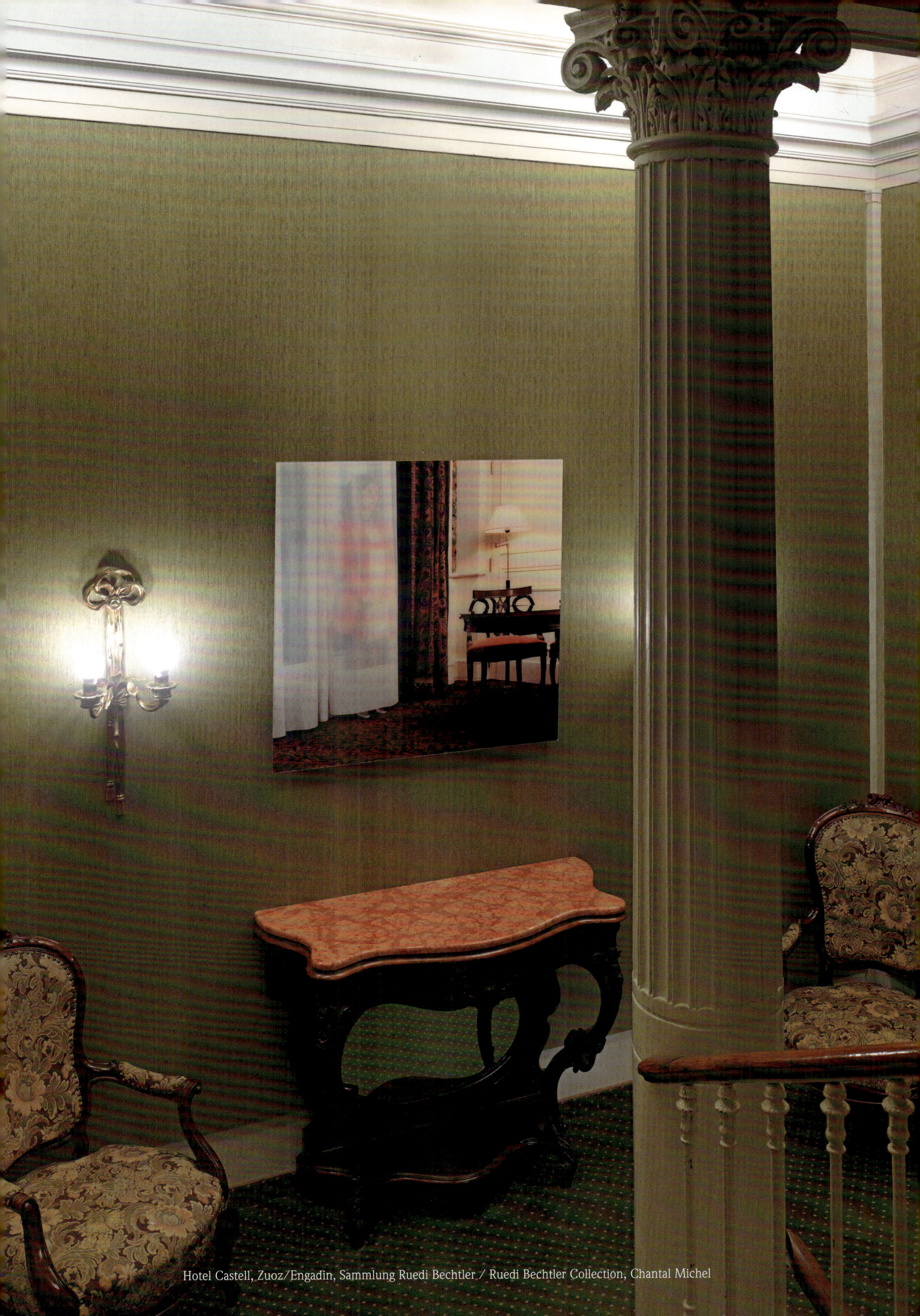

Hotel Castell, Zuoz/Engadin, Sammlung Ruedi Bechtler / Ruedi Bechtler Collection, Chantal Michel

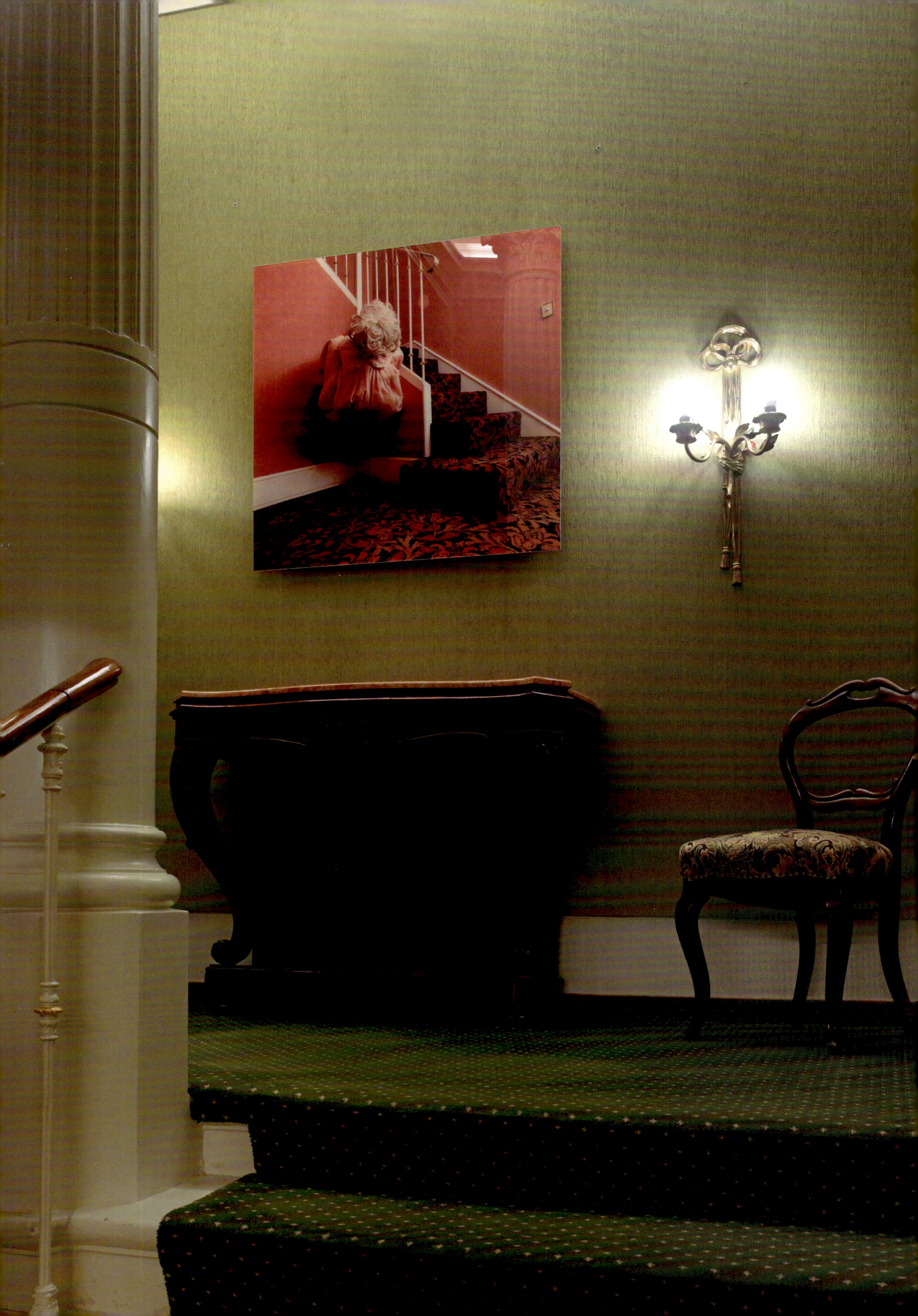

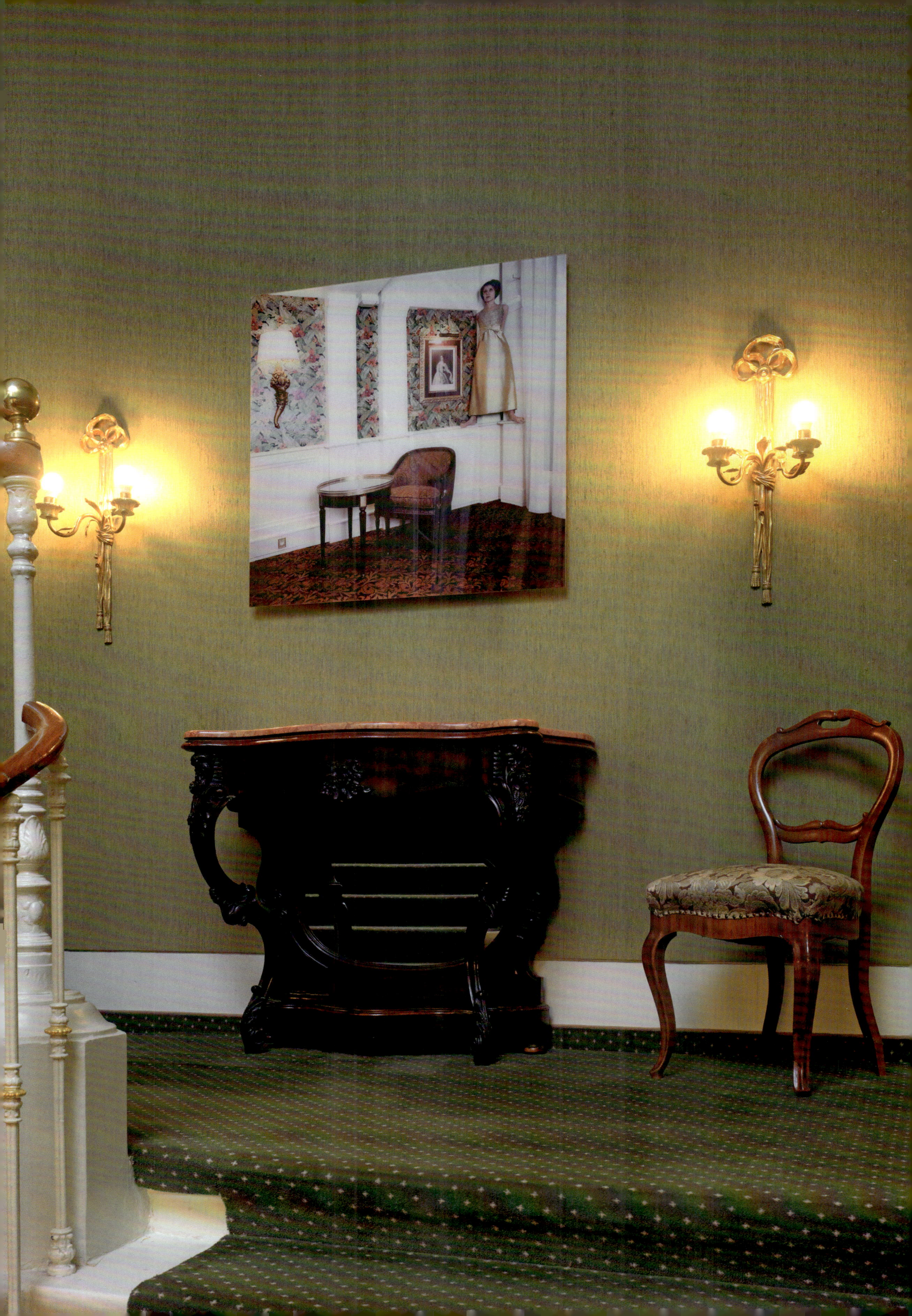

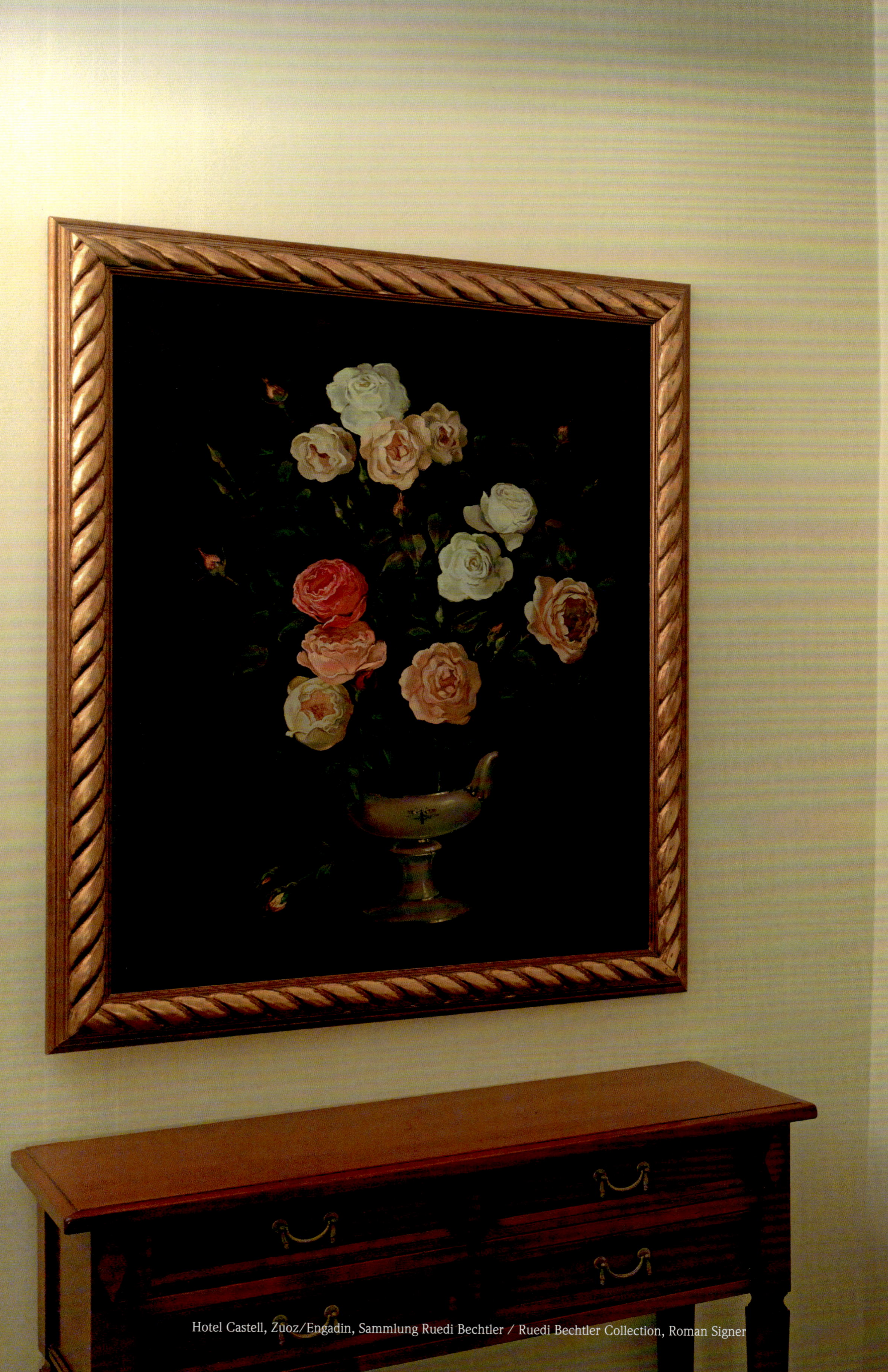

Hotel Castell, Zuoz/Engadin, Sammlung Ruedi Bechtler / Ruedi Bechtler Collection, Roman Signer

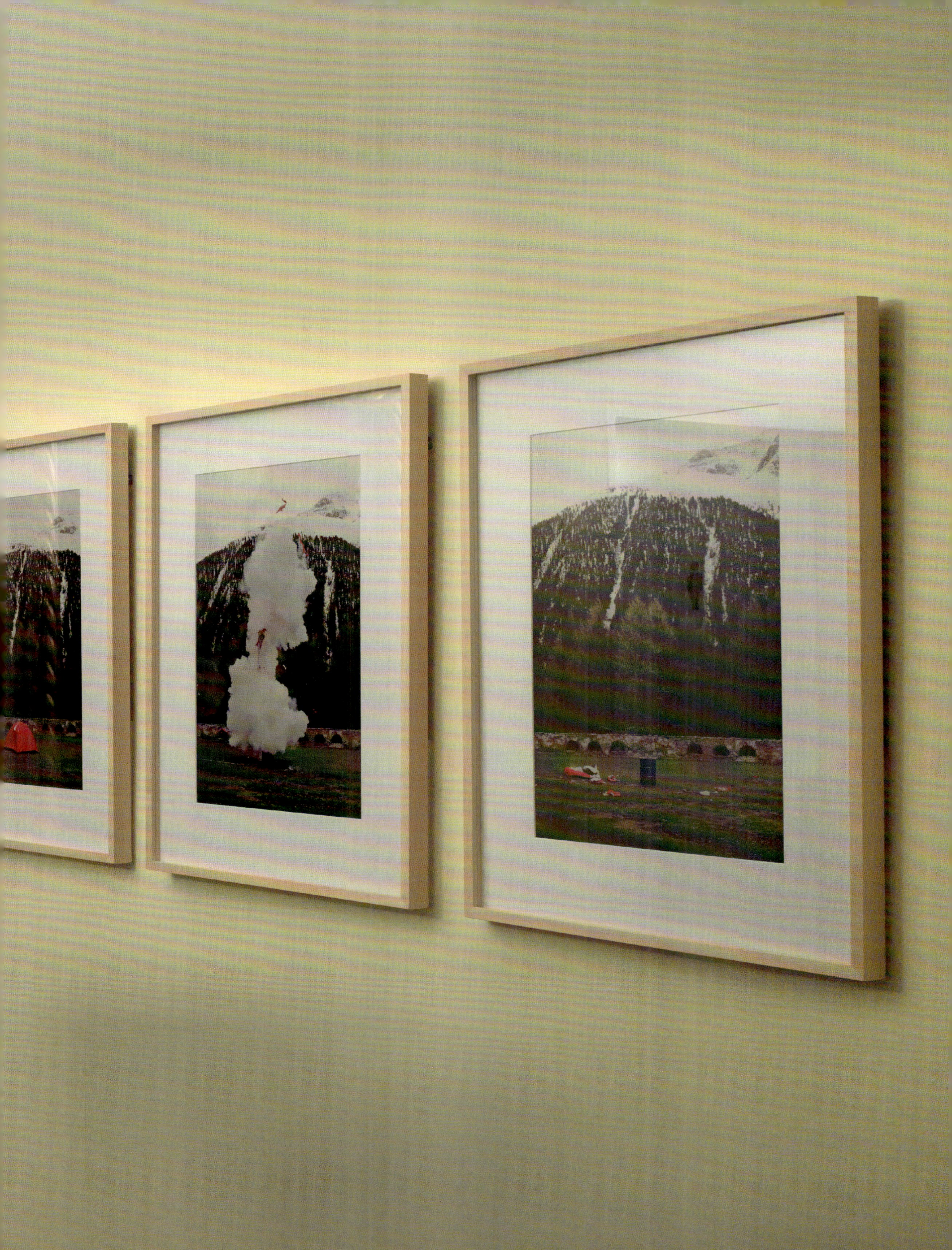

AUSSTELLUNG / EXHIBITION
HOTEL BELLE EPOQUE

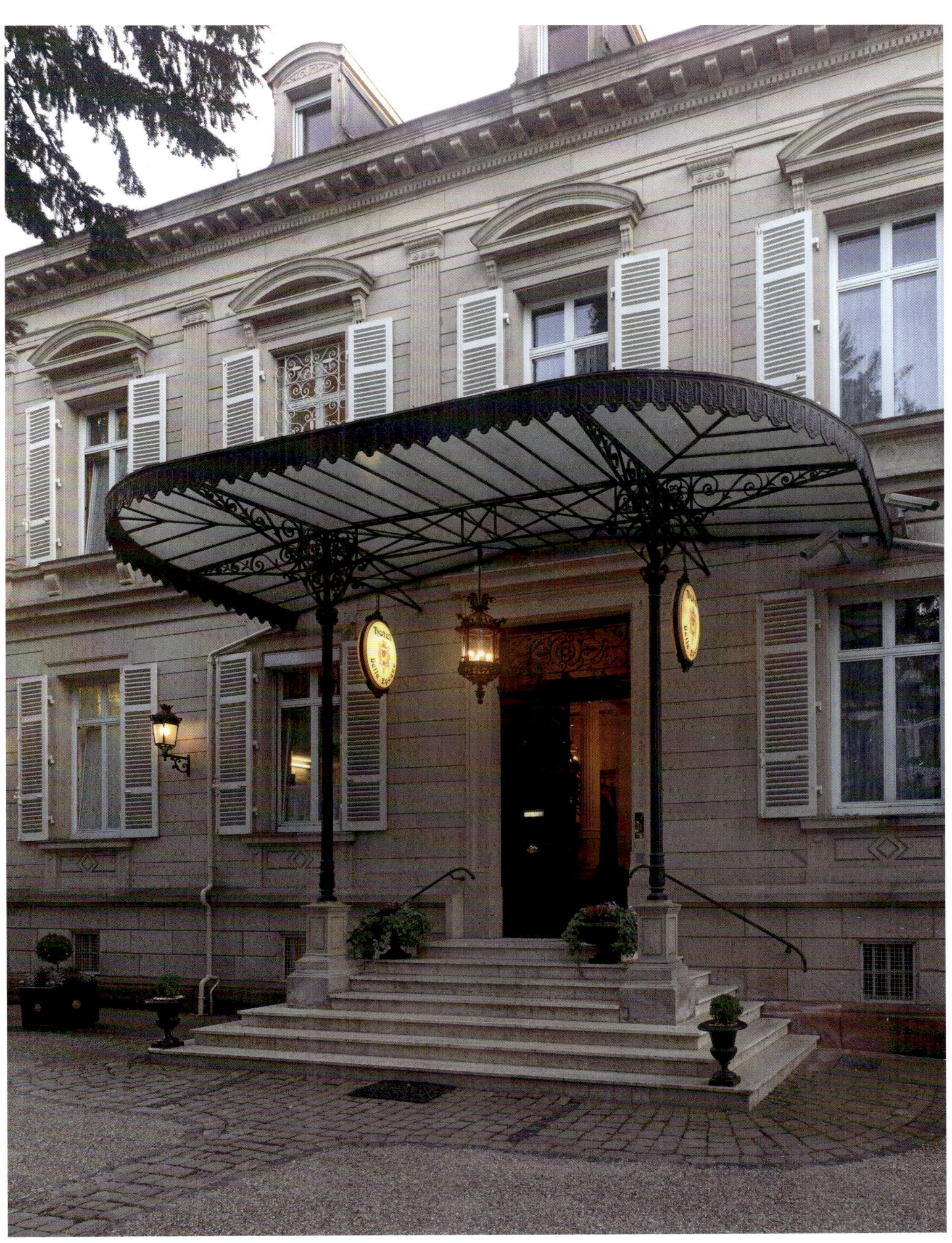

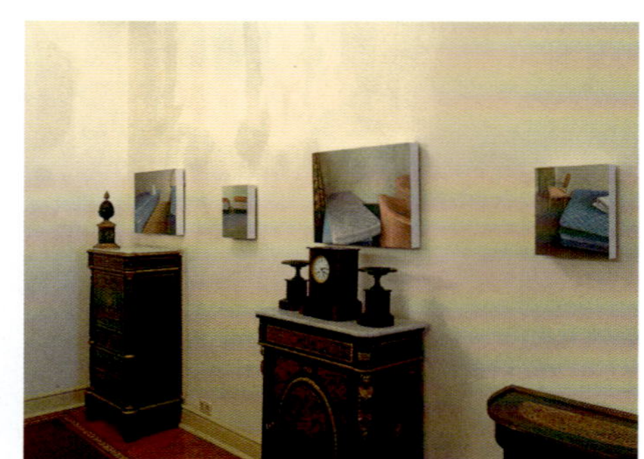

Jenny Brillhart

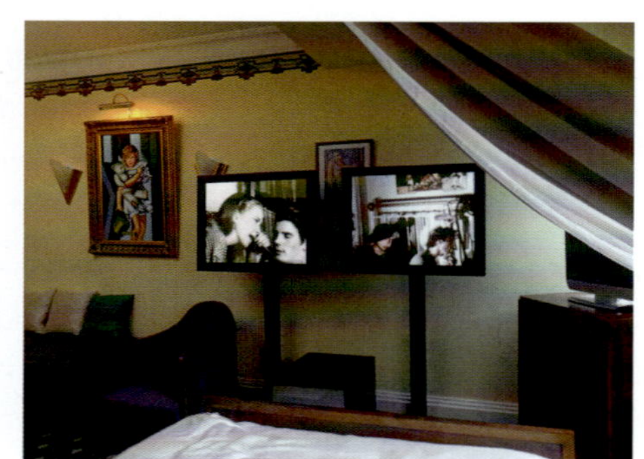

Andy Warhol

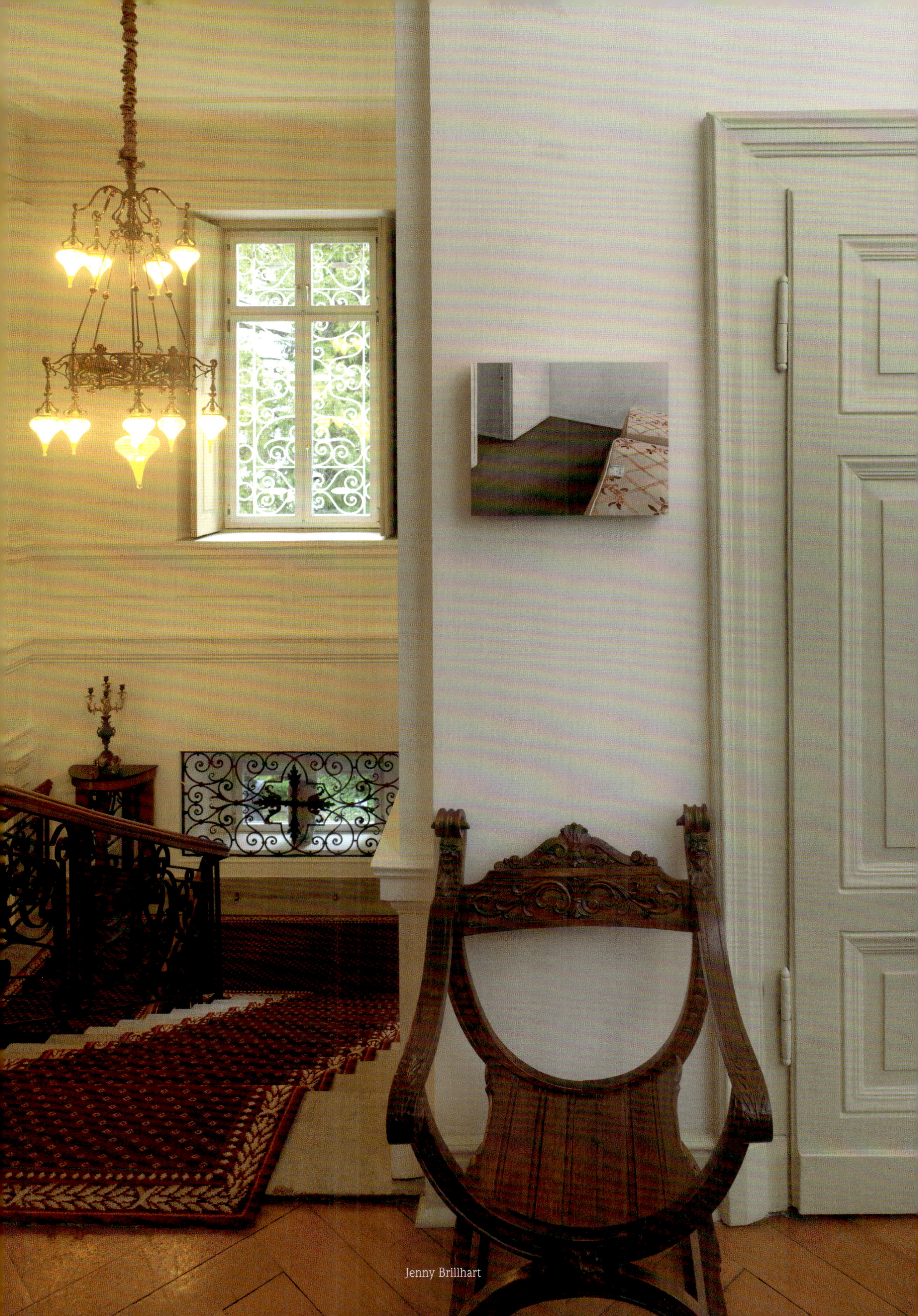

Jenny Brillhart

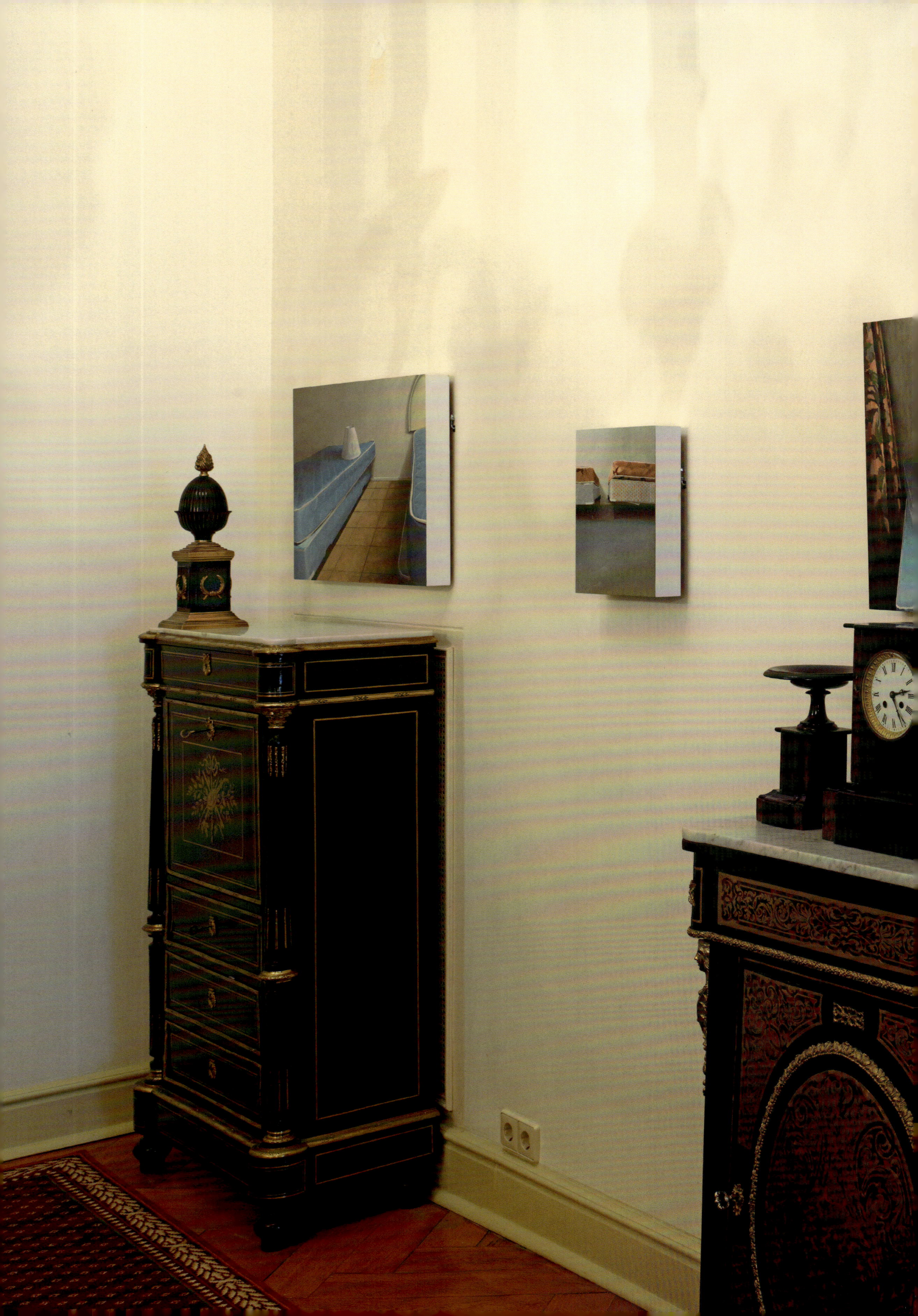

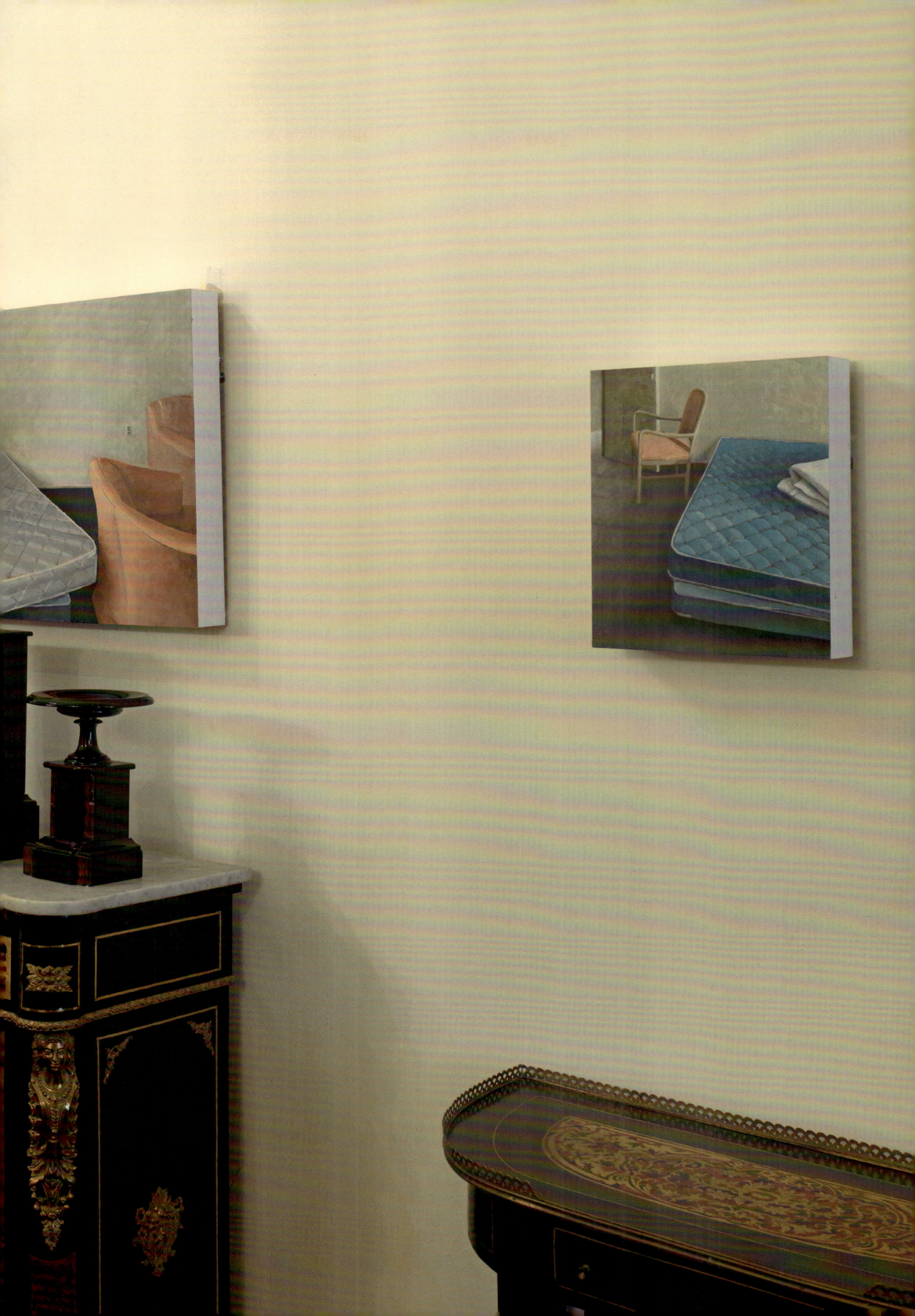

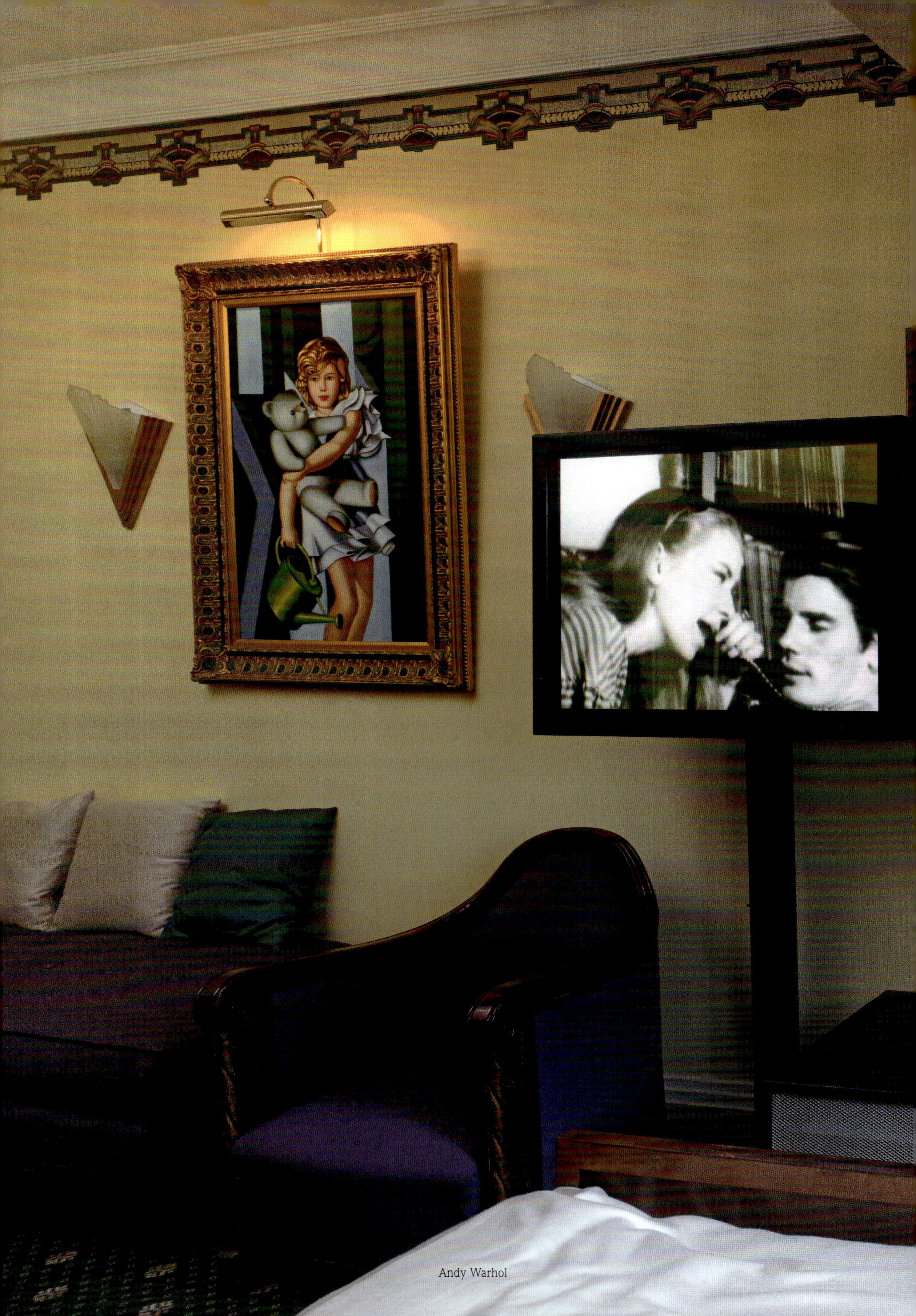

Andy Warhol

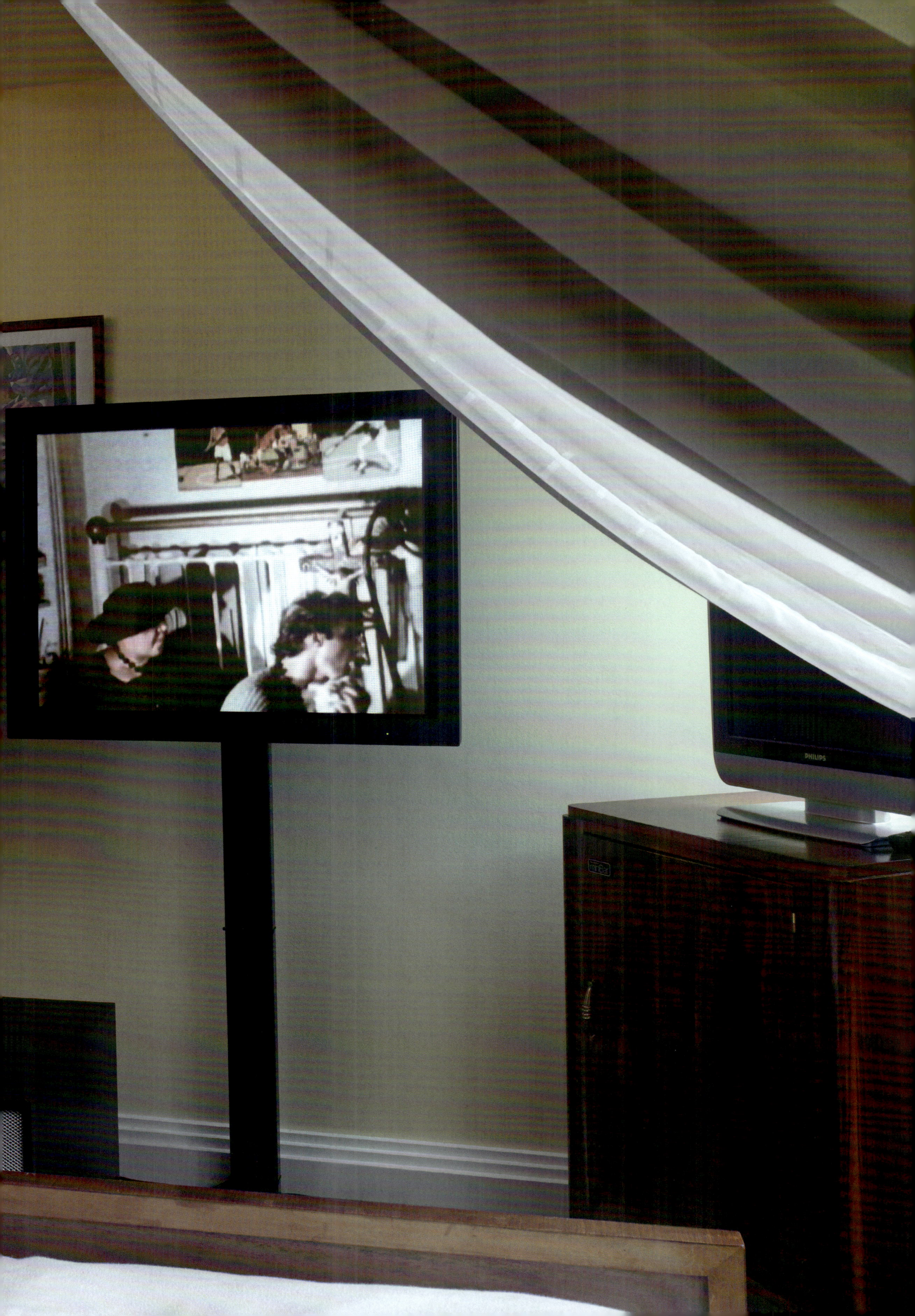
PHILIPS

AUSSTELLUNG / EXHIBITION
BRENNERS PARK-HOTEL & SPA

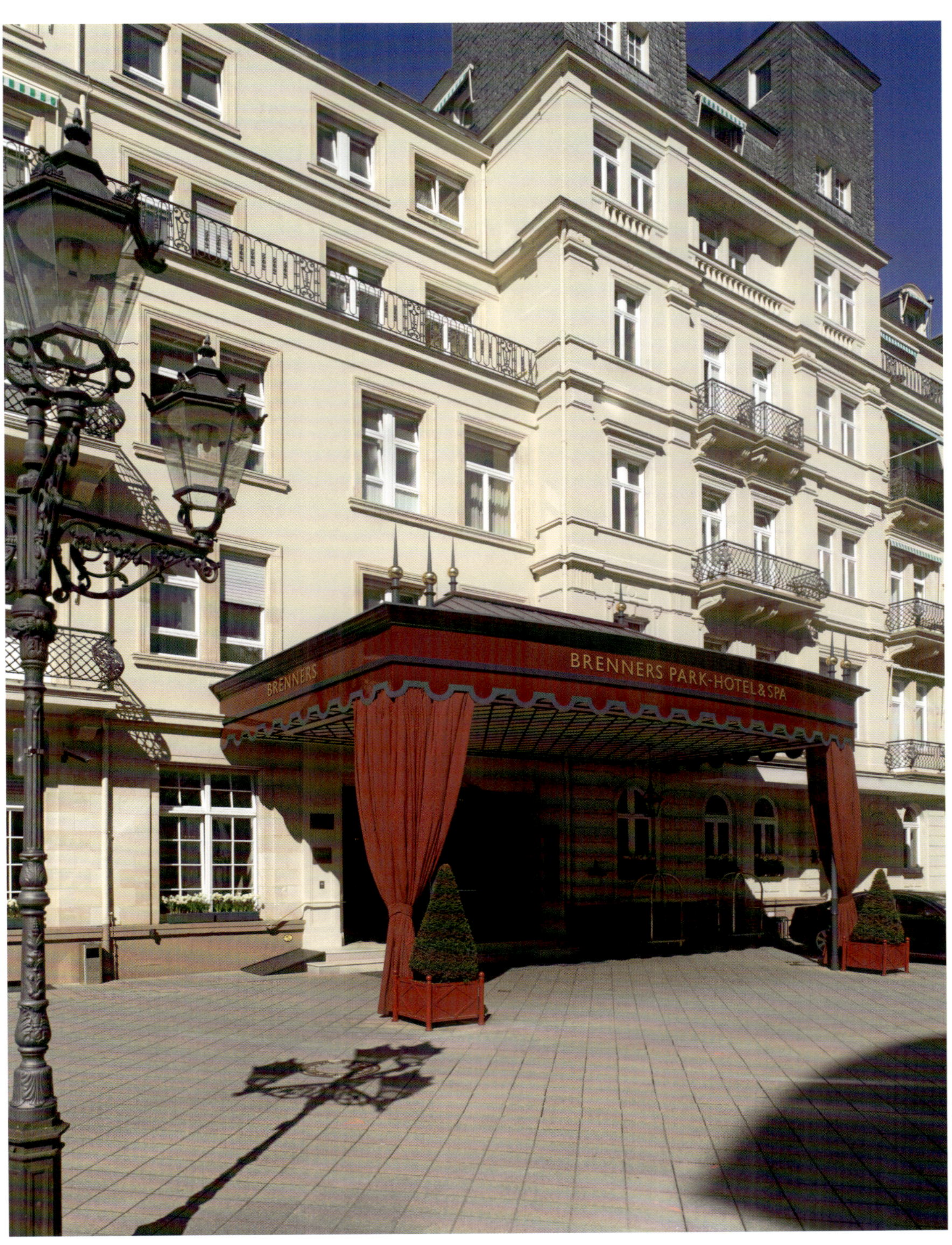

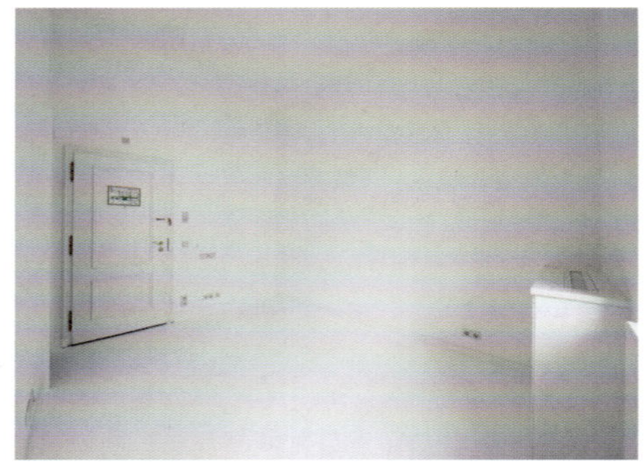
Christian Jankowski

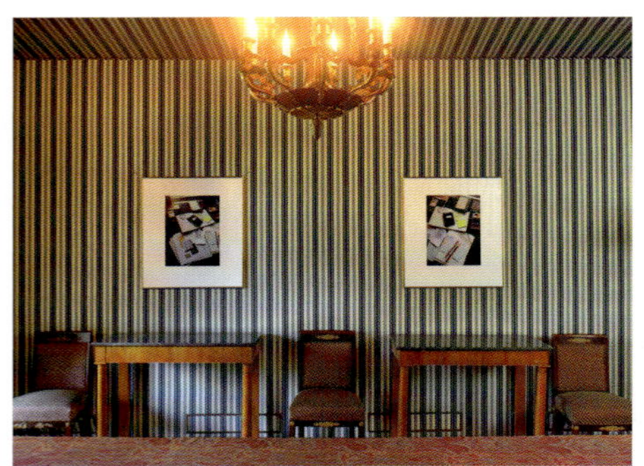
Ian Wallace

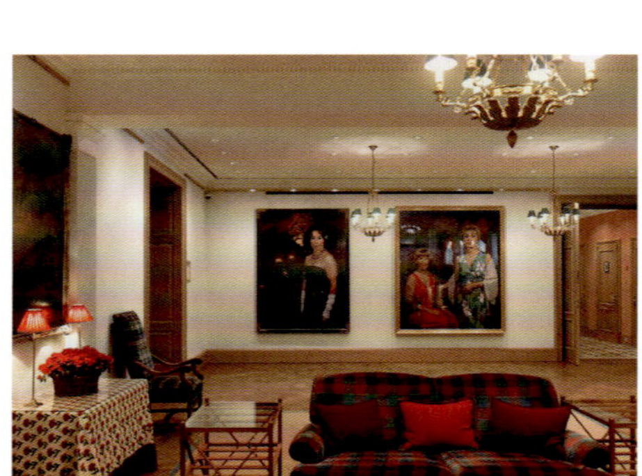
Cindy Sherman

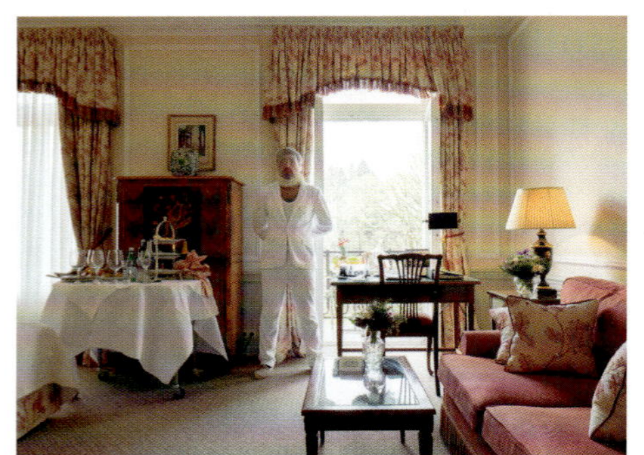
Naneci Yurdagül

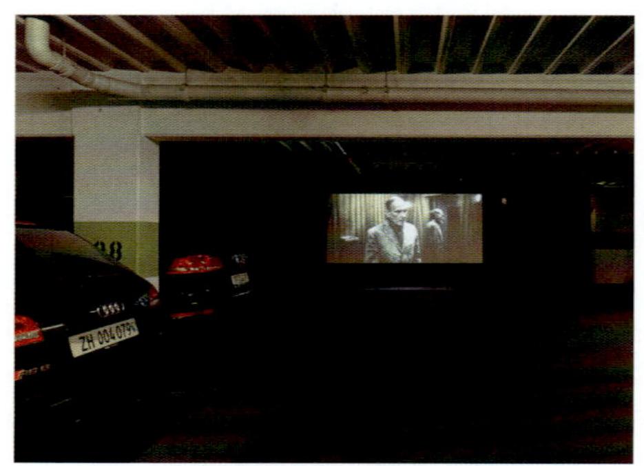
Markus Schinwald

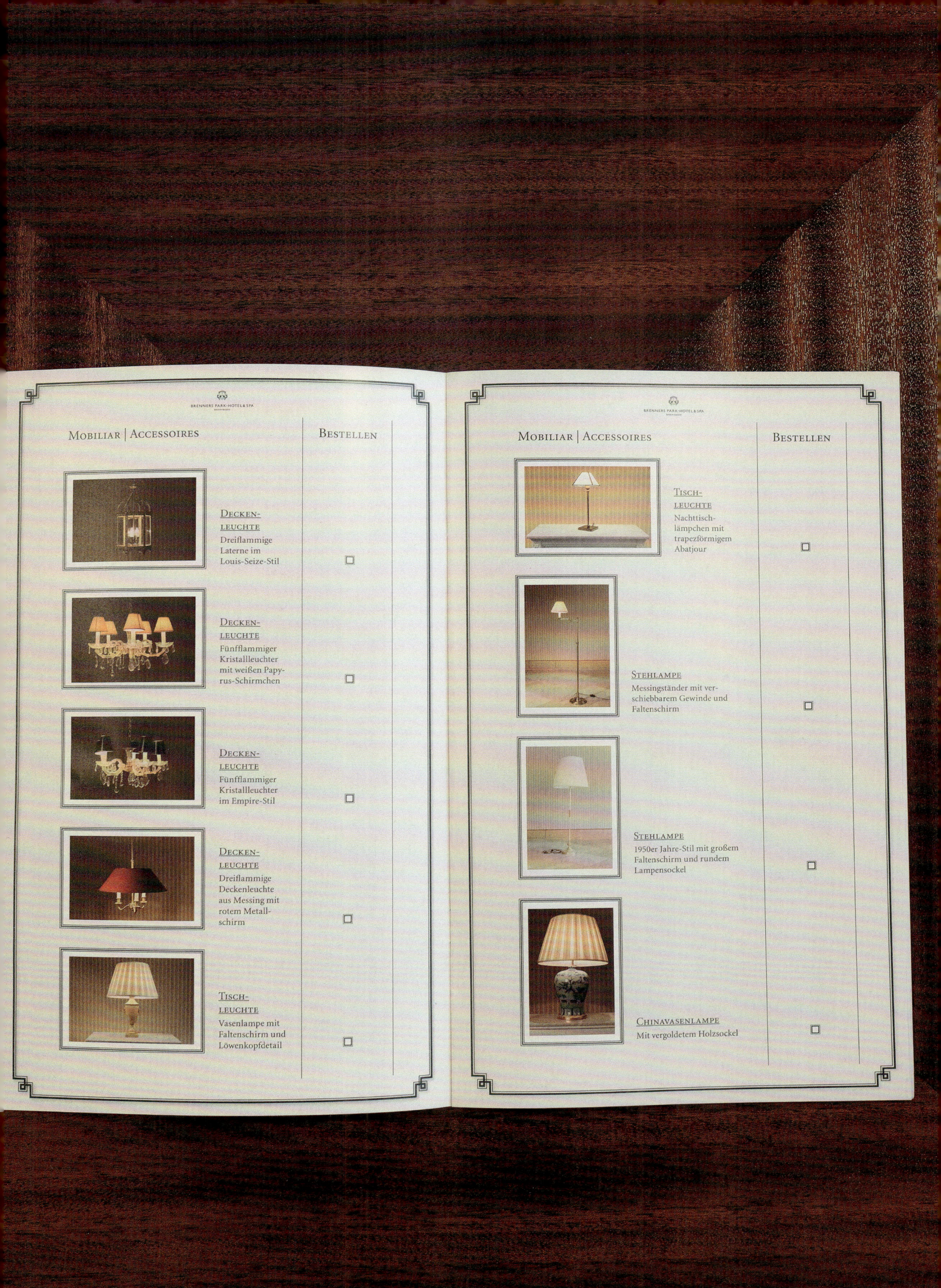

Mobiliar | Accessoires

Bestellen

Decken-leuchte
Dreiflammige Laterne im Louis-Seize-Stil ☐

Decken-leuchte
Fünfflammiger Kristallleuchter mit weißen Papyrus-Schirmchen ☐

Decken-leuchte
Fünfflammiger Kristallleuchter im Empire-Stil ☐

Decken-leuchte
Dreiflammige Deckenleuchte aus Messing mit rotem Metallschirm ☐

Tisch-leuchte
Vasenlampe mit Faltenschirm und Löwenkopfdetail ☐

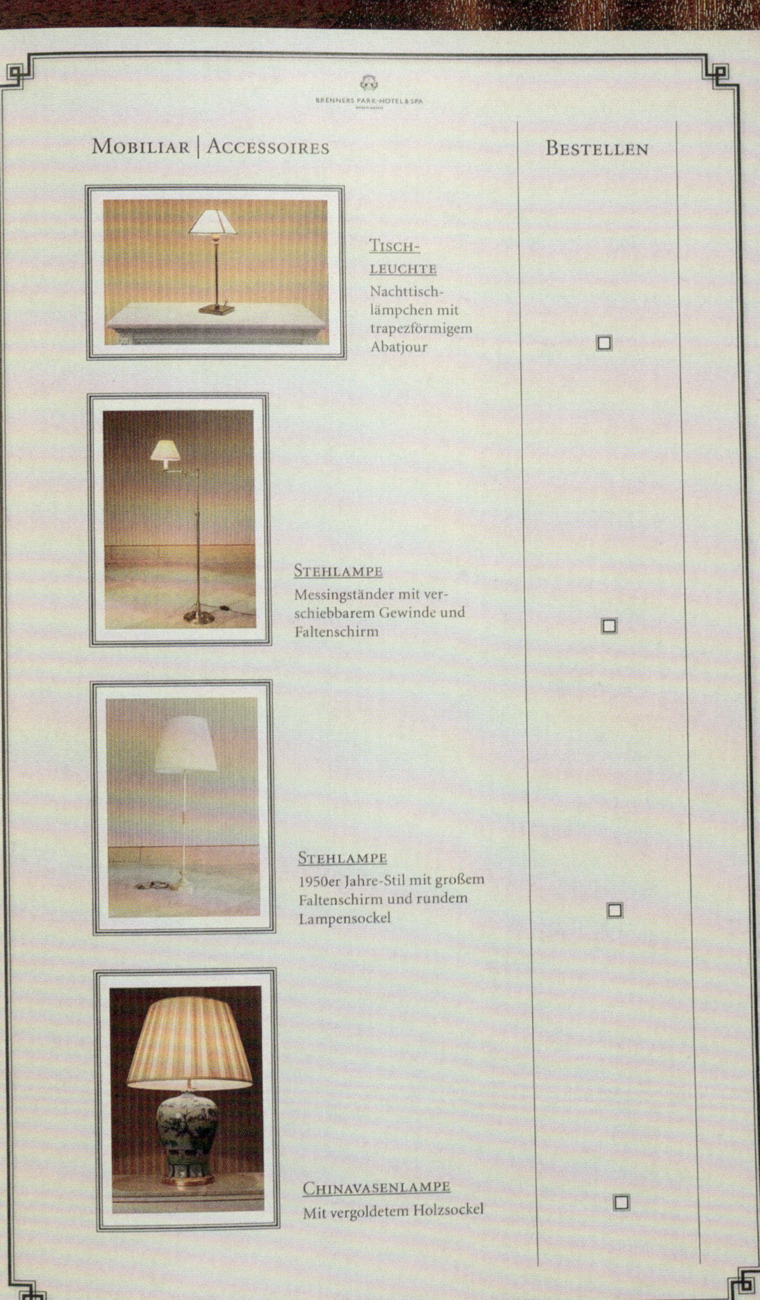

Christian Jankowski

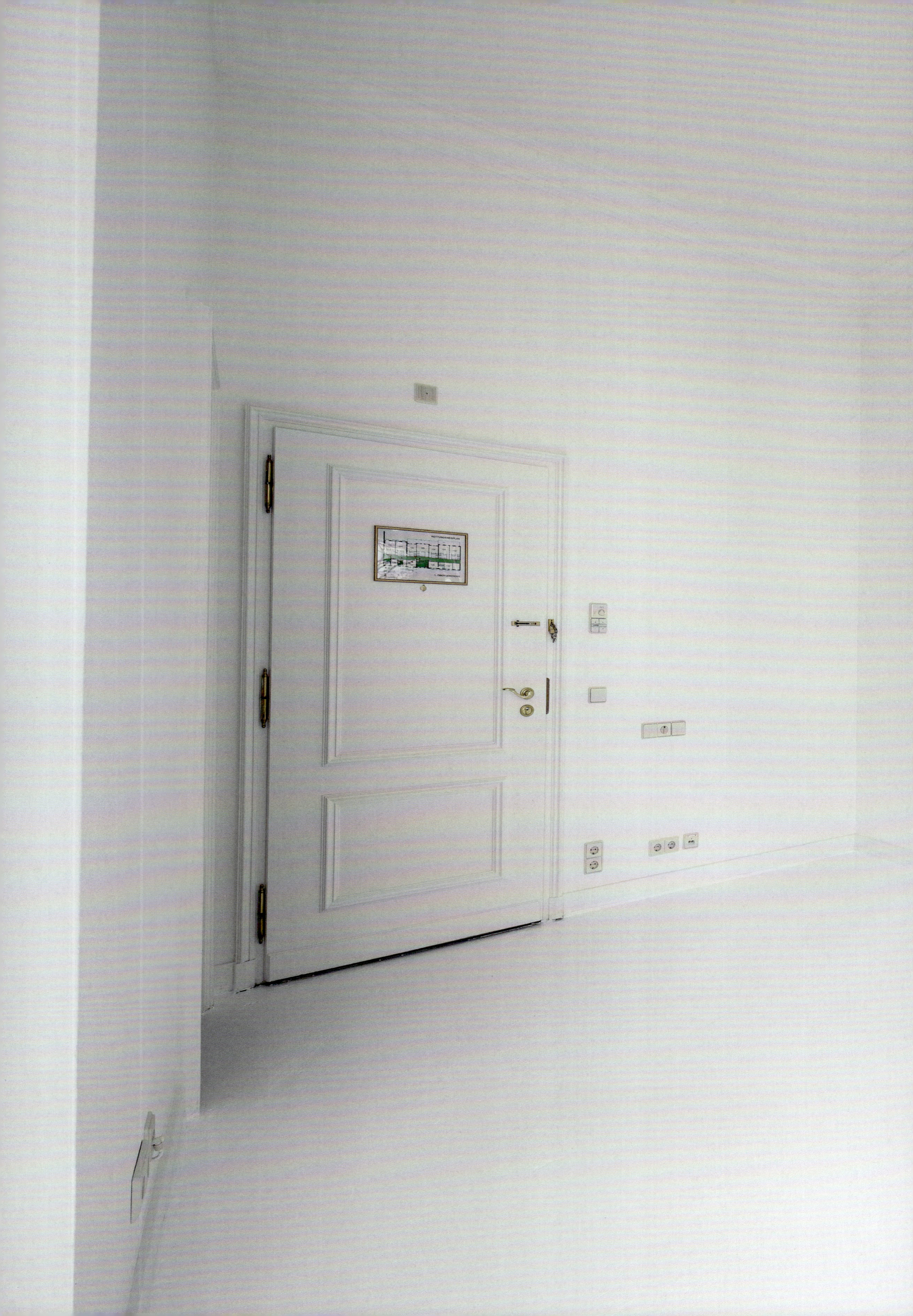

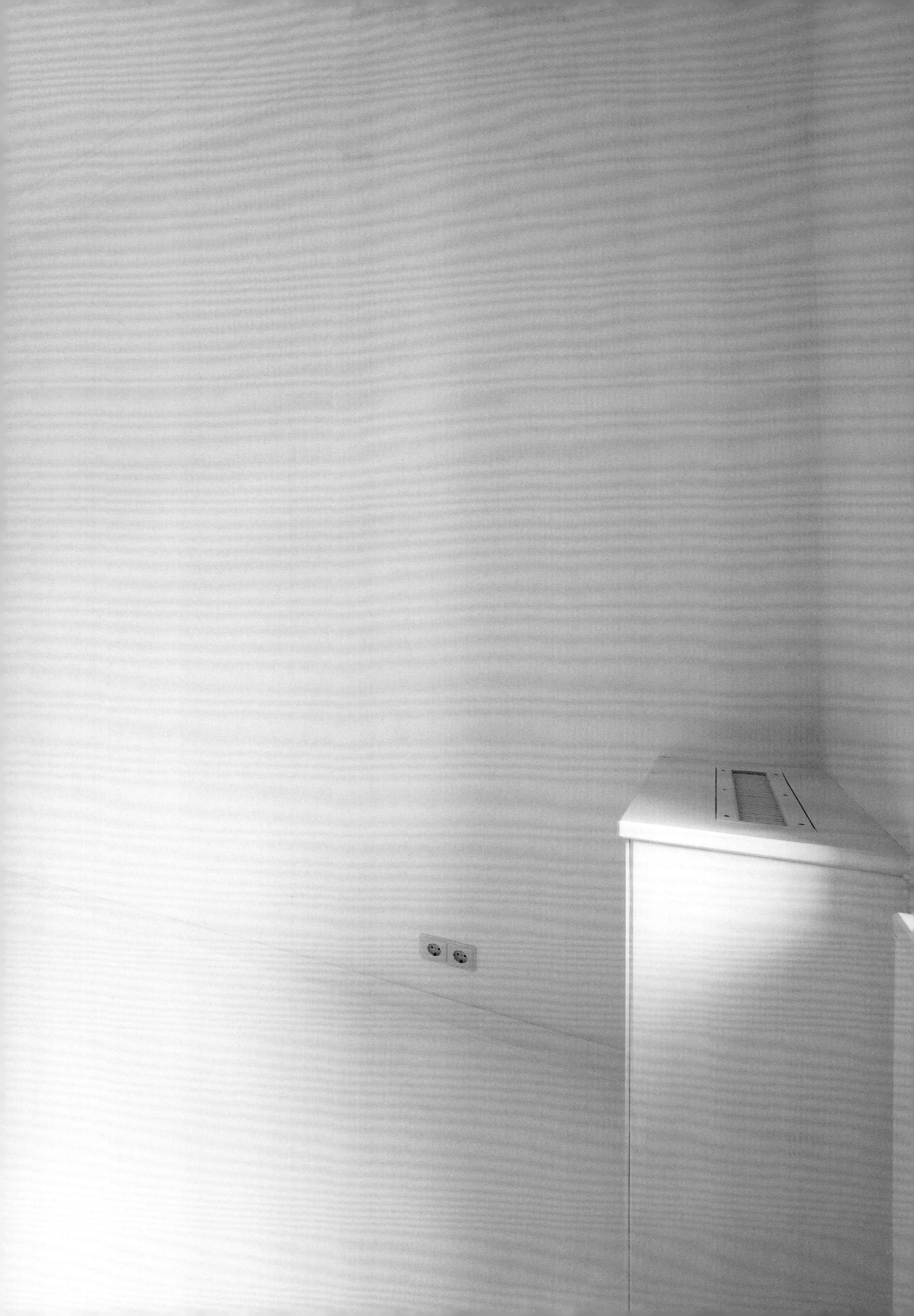

BRENNERS PARK-HOTEL & SPA
BADEN-BADEN

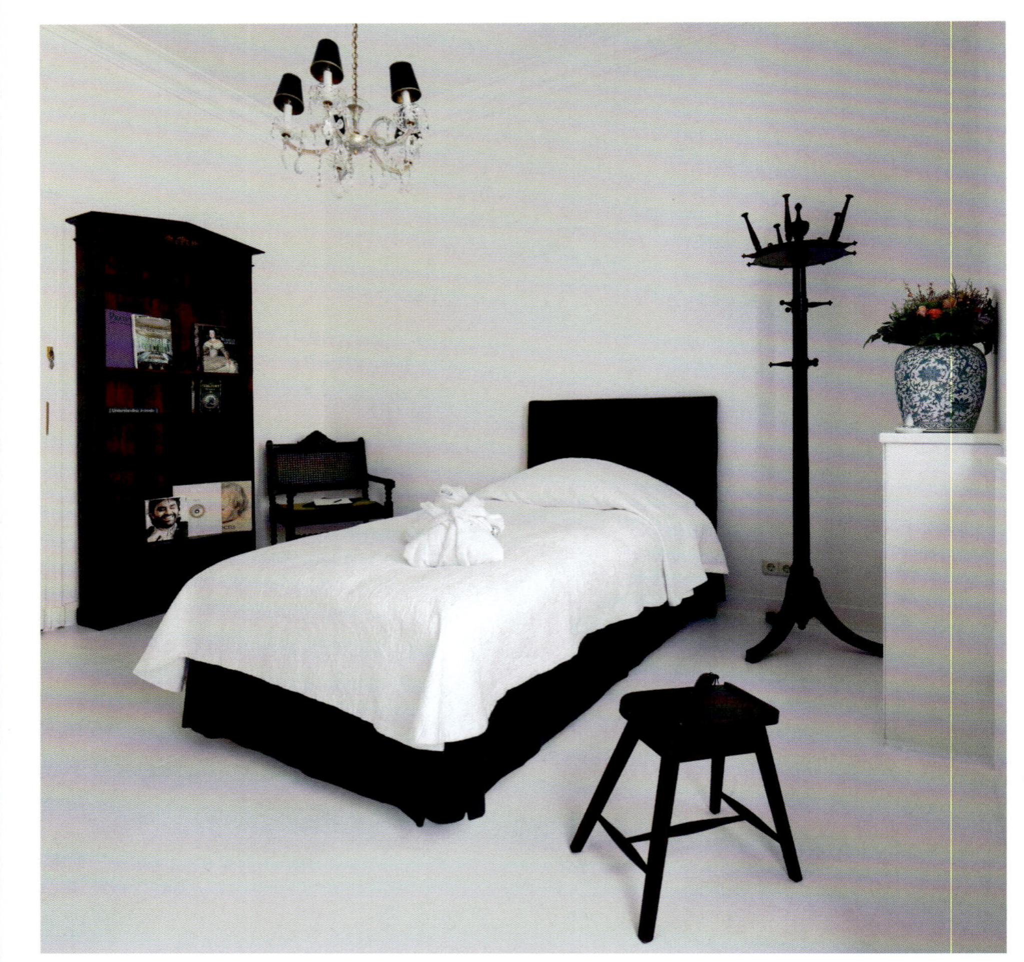

» Nicht nur einmal, sondern alle drei Monate möchte ich mich zurückziehen, um auf diese Weise Entscheidungen zu treffen. «
Wert: 350,– €

Bett komplett, Bademantel, Kristalleuchter im Empire-Stil, Barockstuhl, Biedermeierregal, Schuhbänkchen, Garderobenständer, Wellness-Armenities, Deckelvase

Der kleine Entscheidungsraum
Gast Nr. 1 | 16.–17.03.2014

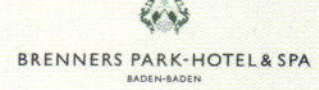

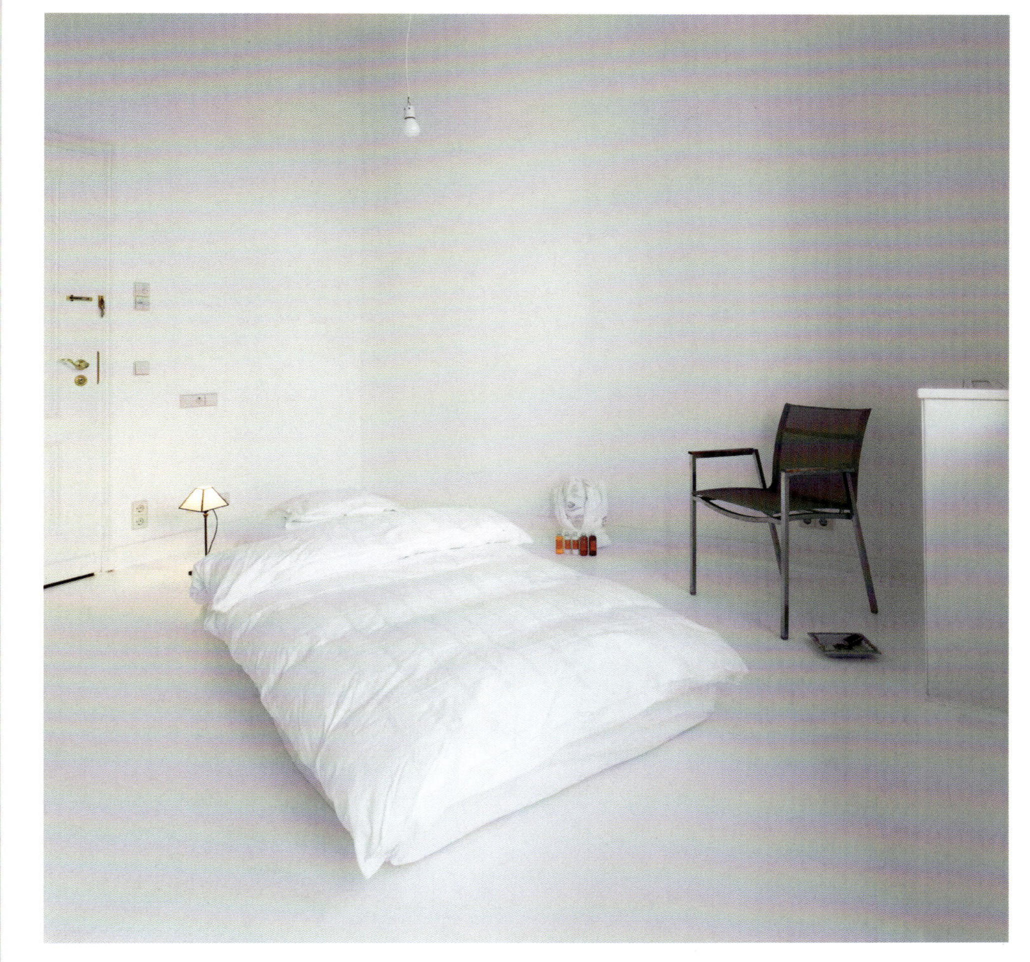

»Ich werde ab jetzt ein selbstbestimmteres Leben führen.«
Wert: 1.100,– €

Matratze und Bettzeug, Bademantel, Nachttischlämpchen, Balkonstuhl, Wellness-Armenities, Aschenbecher

Der kleine Entscheidungsraum
Gast Nr. 11 | 17.–18.03.2014

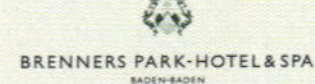

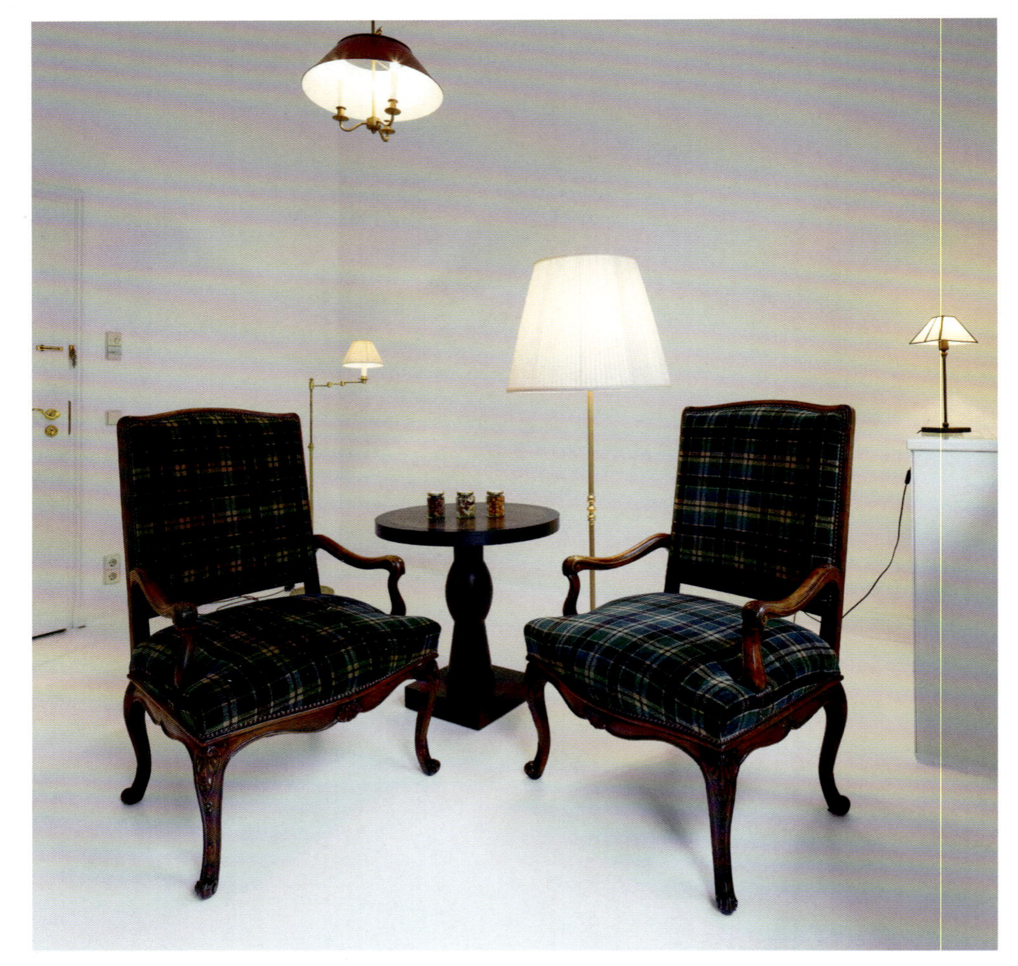

» Von nun an werde ich öfters feine Dankbarkeitsakzente setzen. «
Wert: 164,– €

Dreiflammige Deckenleuchte, Nachttischlämpchen, Stehlampe mit verschiebbarem Gewinde, Stehlampe mit großem Faltenschirm, Sesselarrangement im englischen Landhausstil, moderner Massivholztisch, Auswahl an Nervennahrung

Der kleine Entscheidungsraum
Gast Nr. III | 18.–19.03.2014

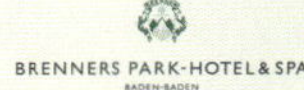

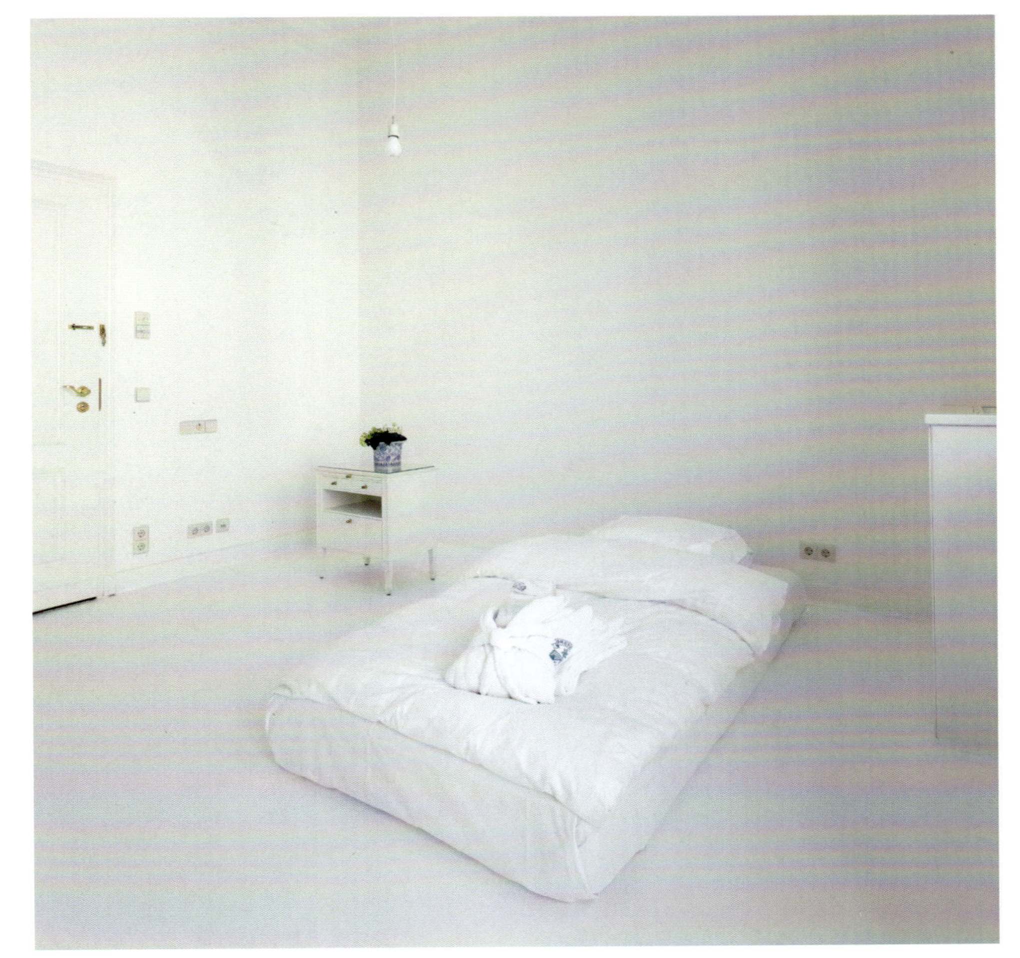

» Eine schlaflose Nacht in Zukunft nicht mehr als Fehler betrachten. «
Wert: 200,– €

Matratze und Bettzeug, weiß lackierter Nachttisch, blau gemusterte Vase mit Pflanze,
Frottee-Set mit Handtüchern, Bademantel und Hausschuhen

Der kleine Entscheidungsraum
Gast Nr. IV | 19.–20.03.2014

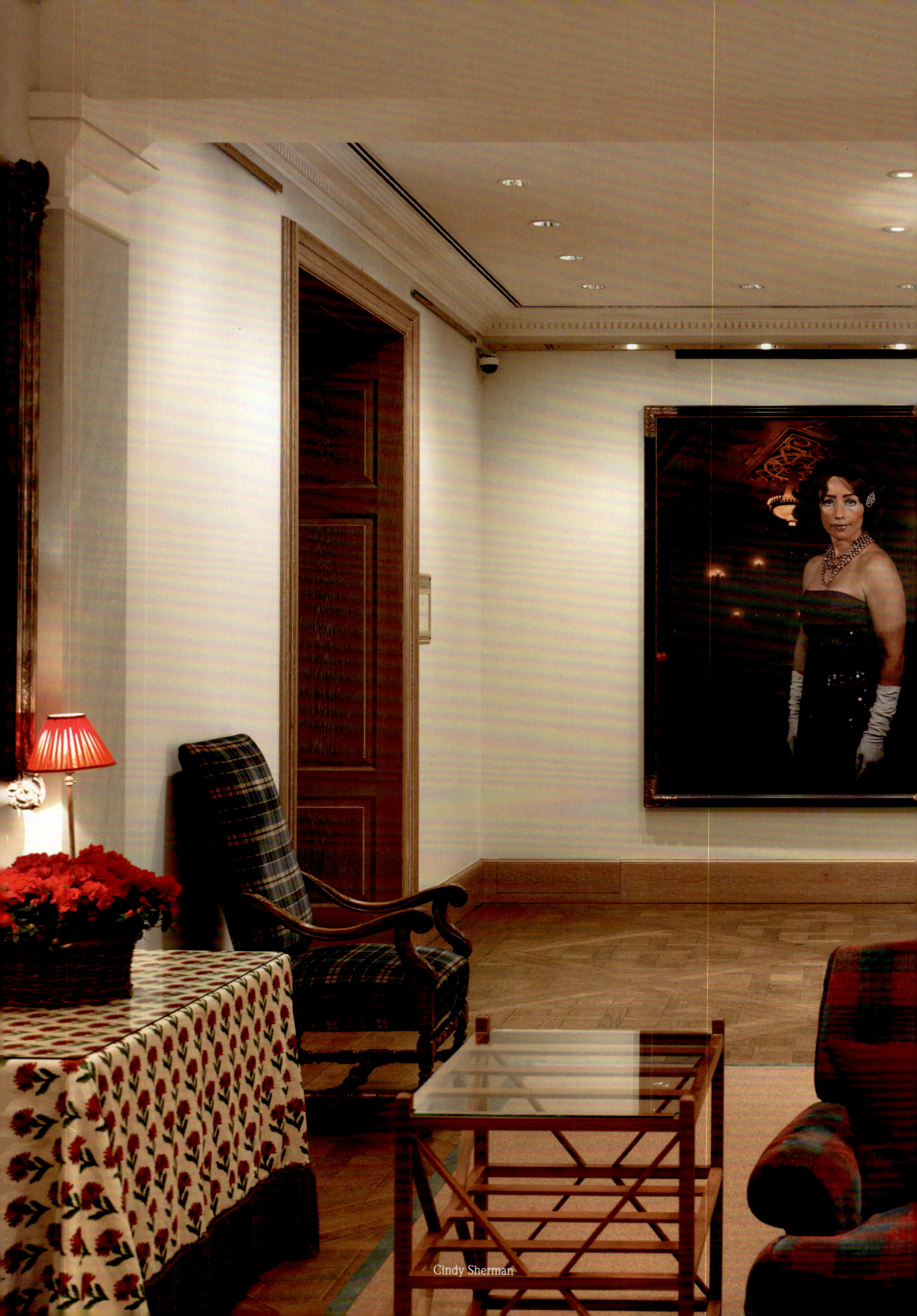

Cindy Sherman

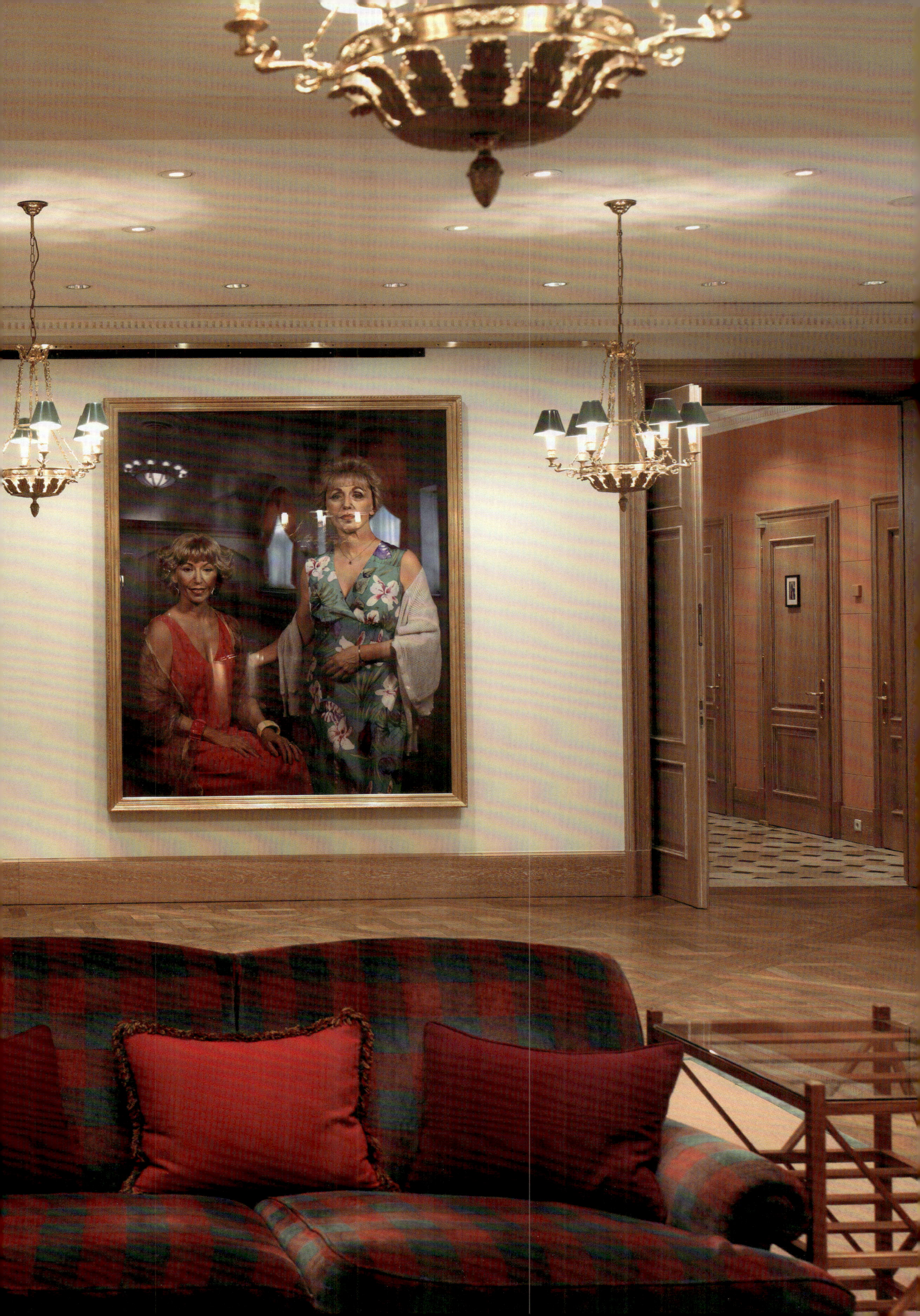

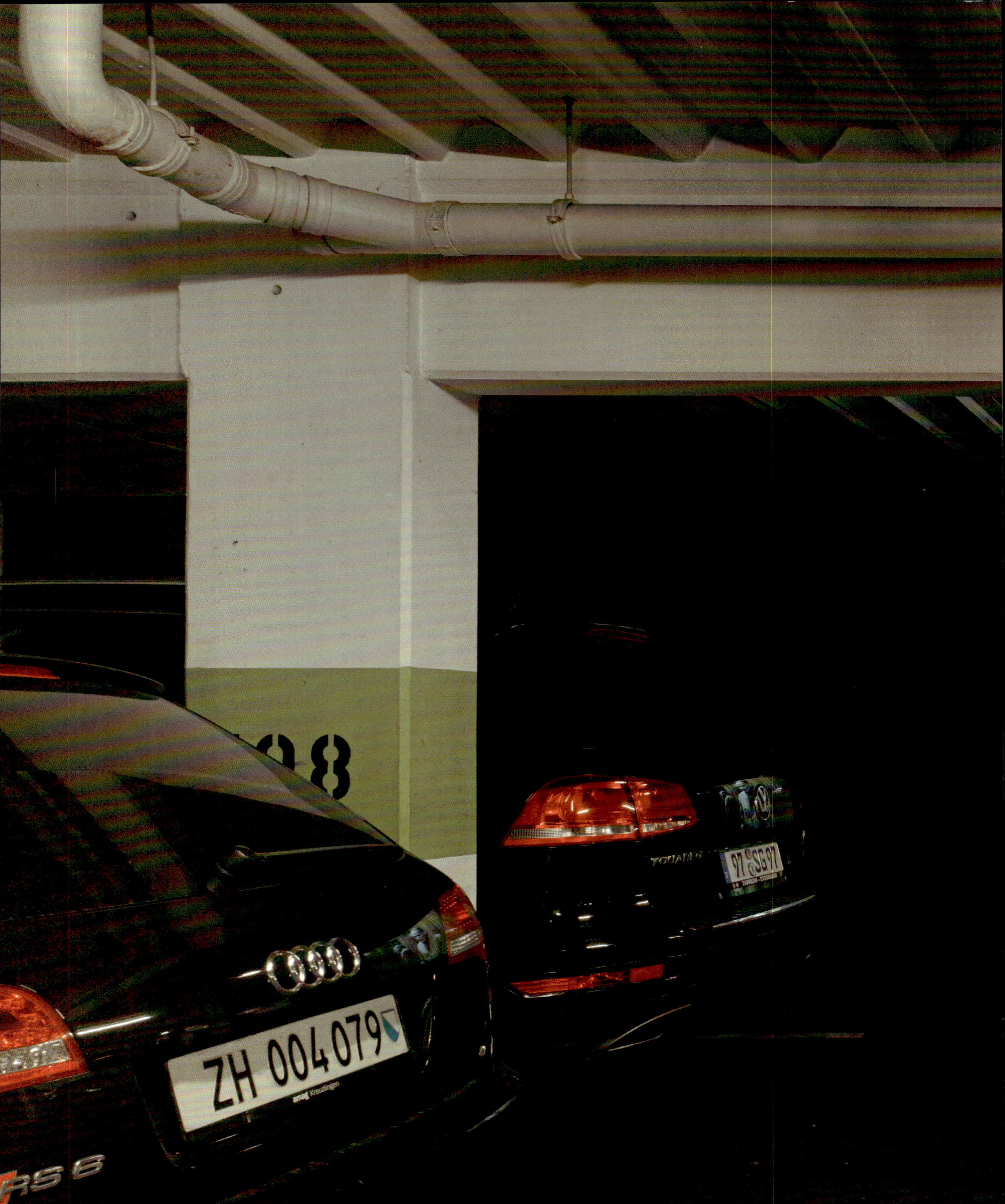
ZH 004 079
RS 6

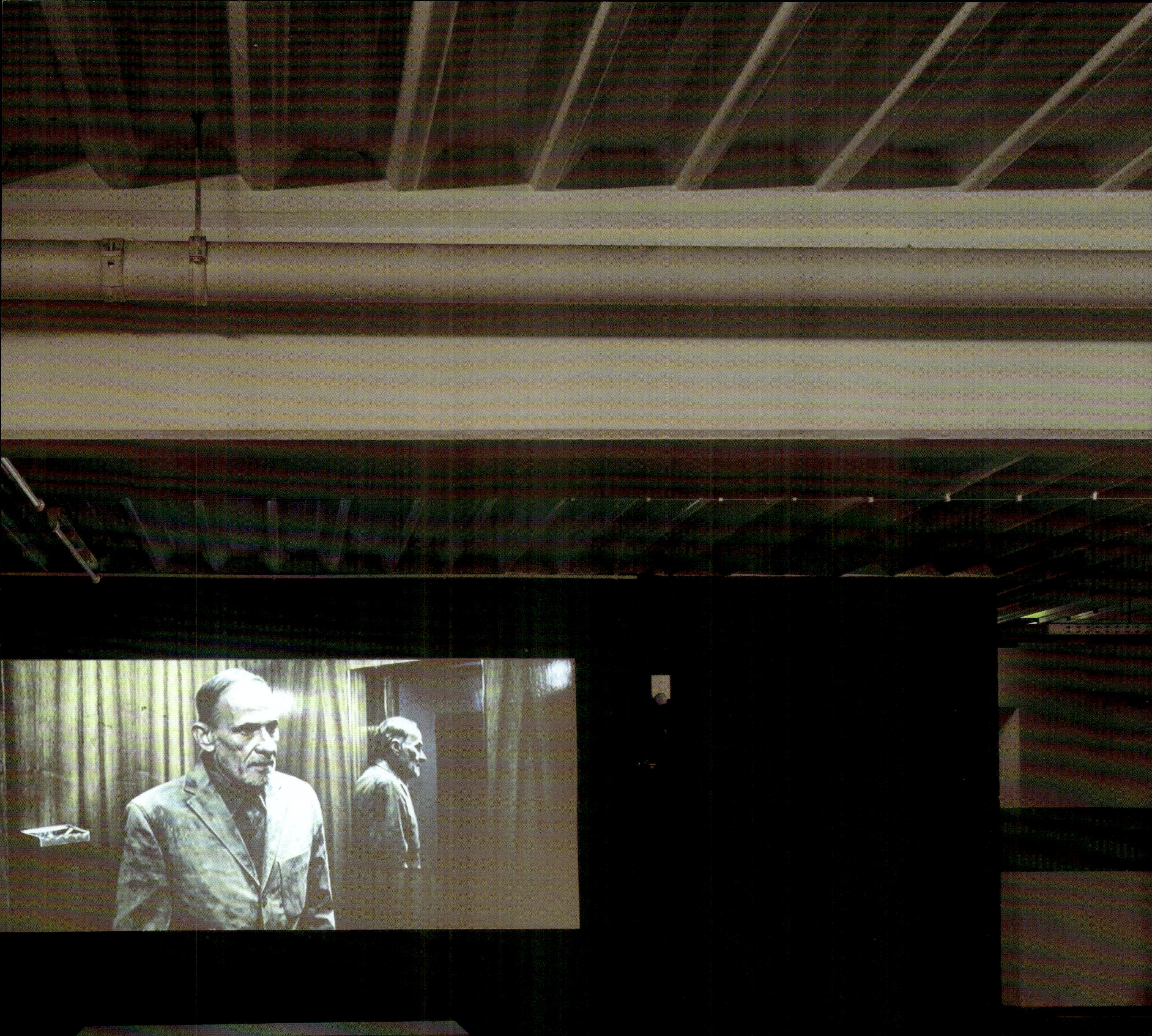

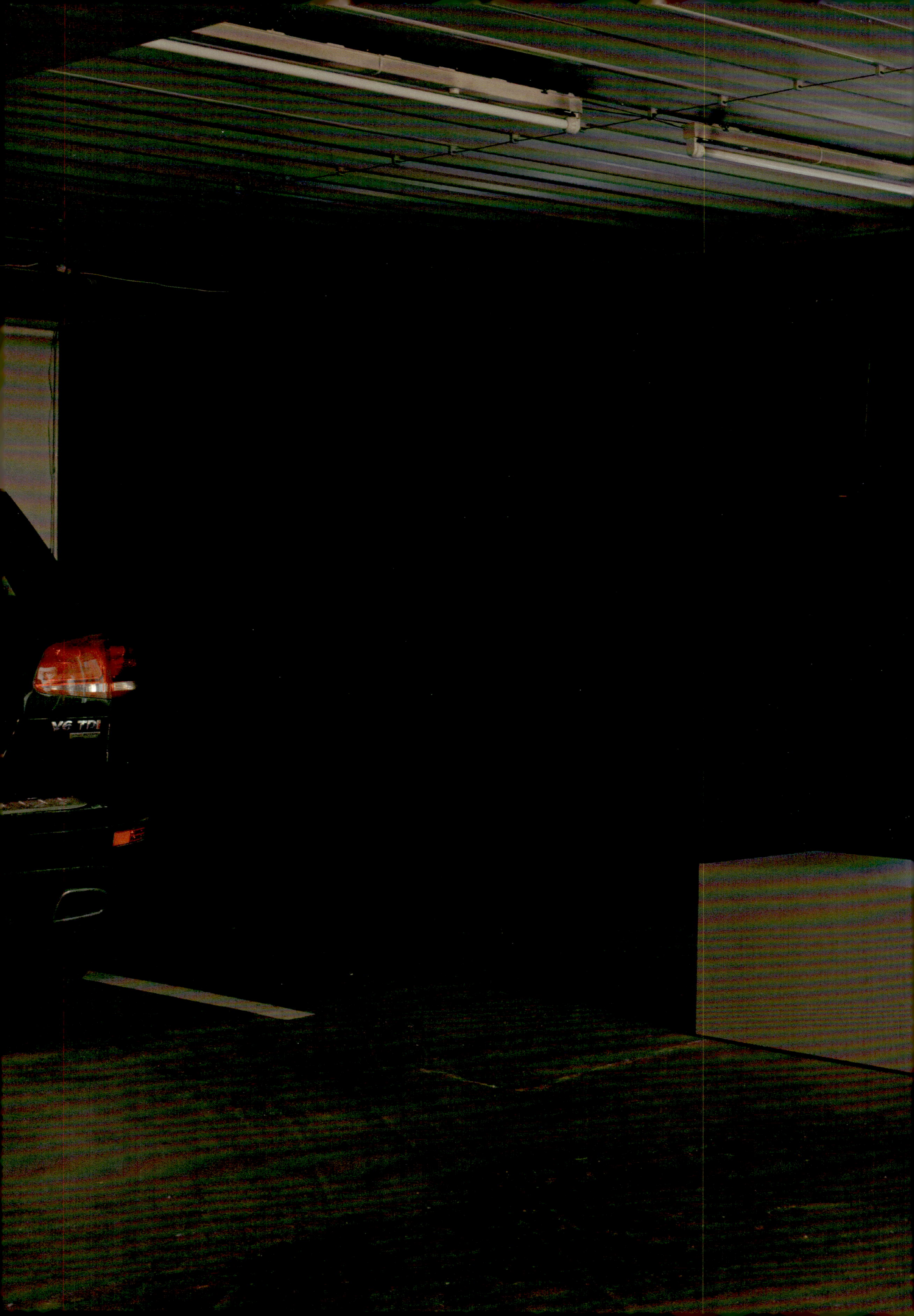
V6 TDI

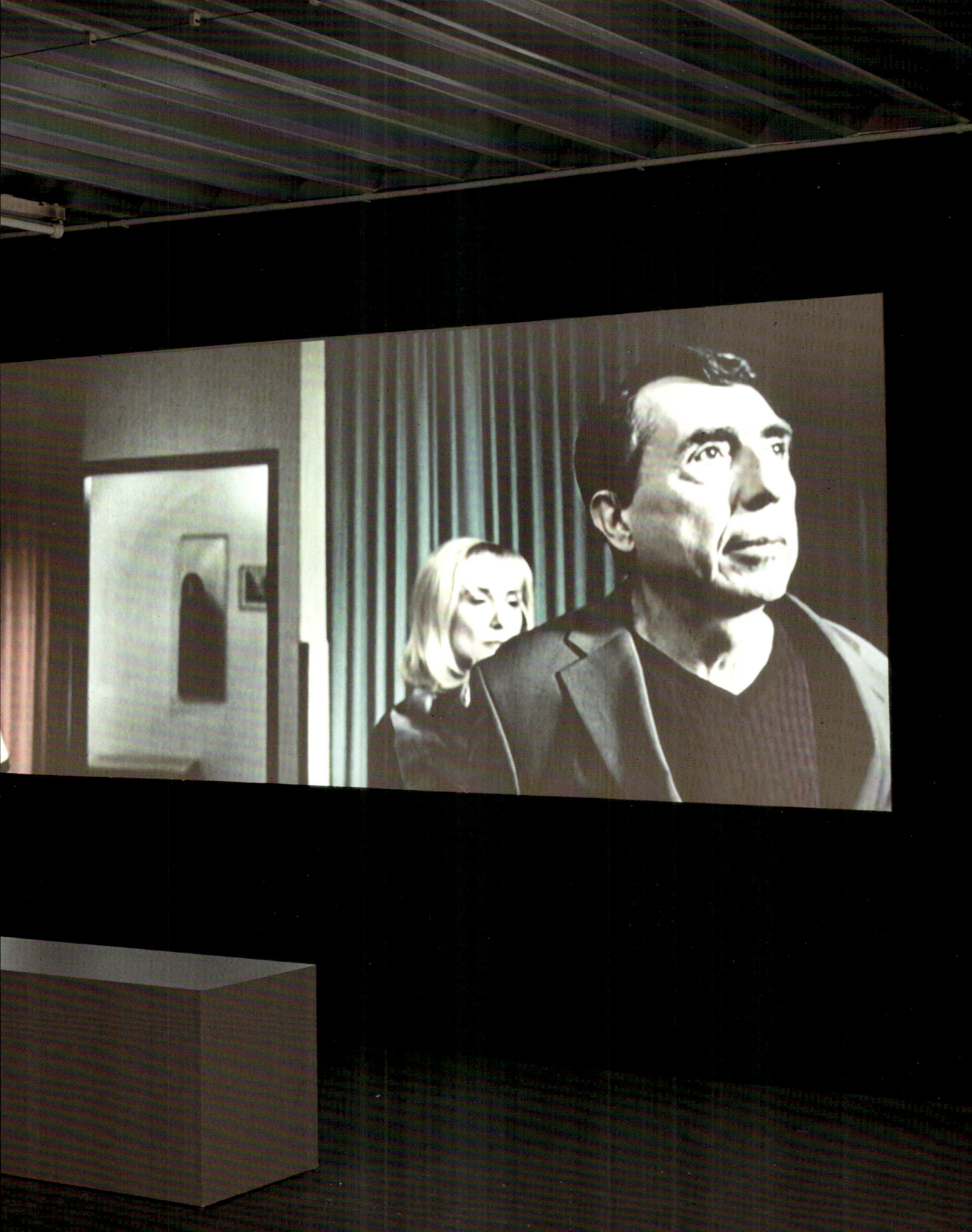

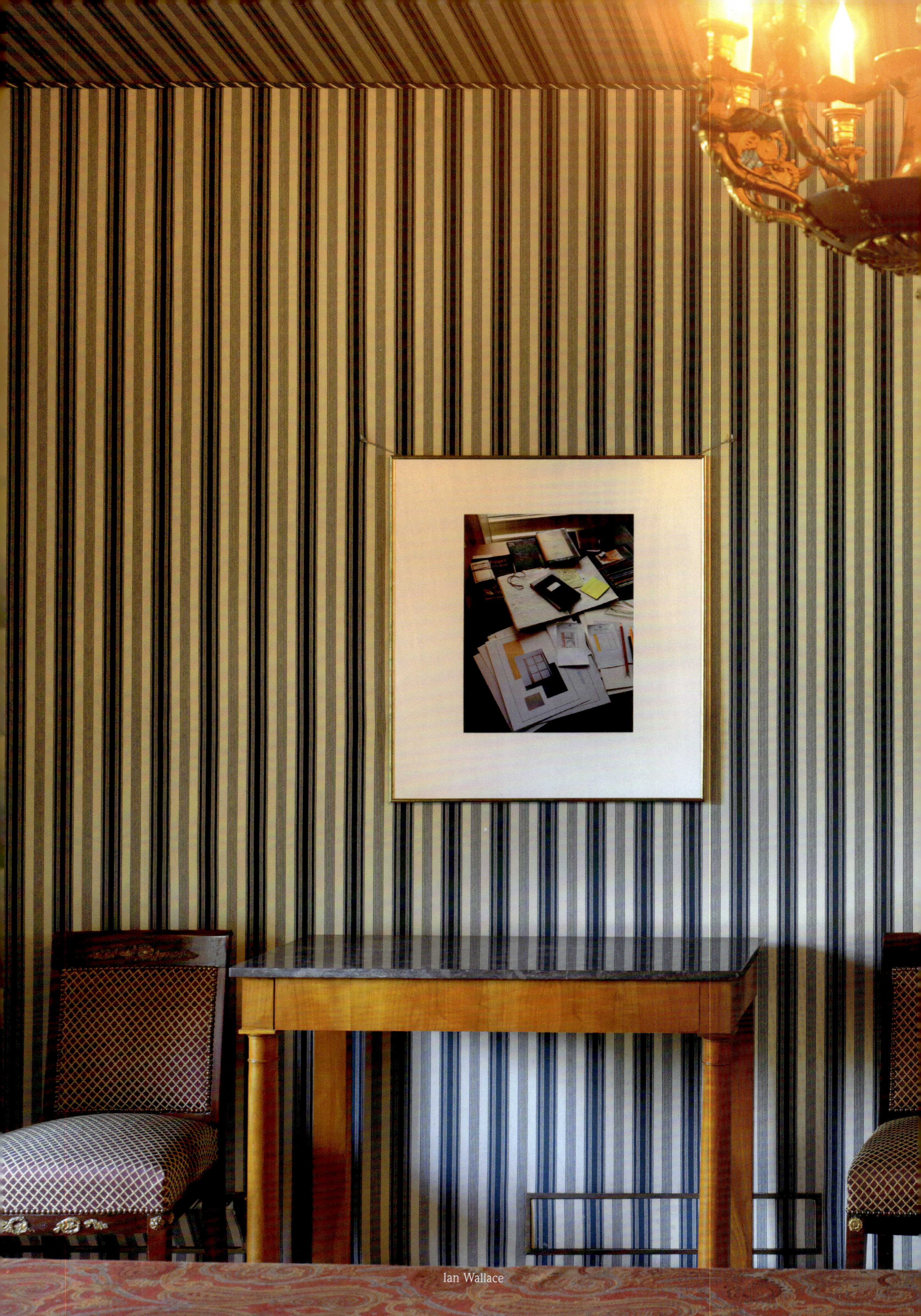

Ian Wallace

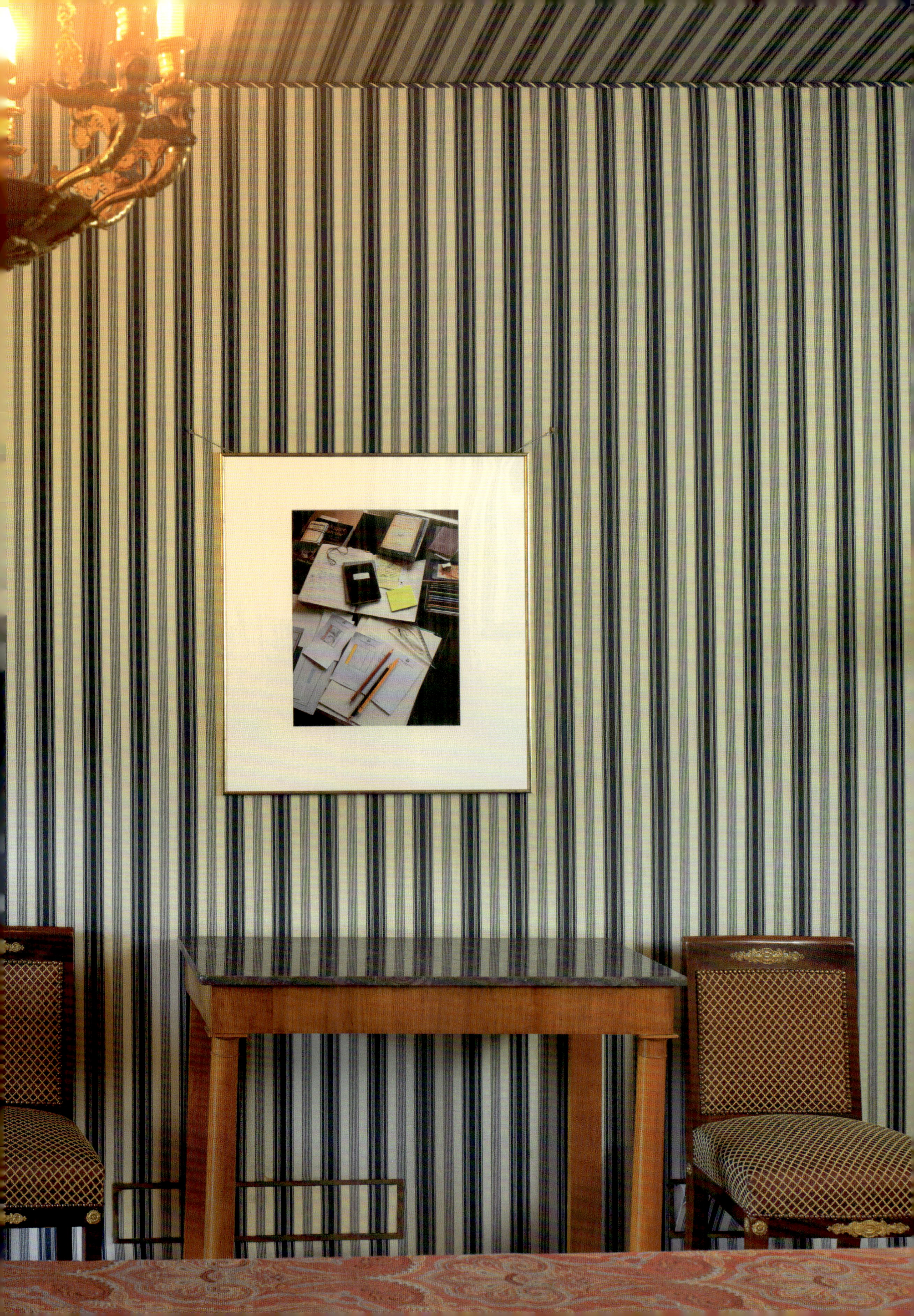

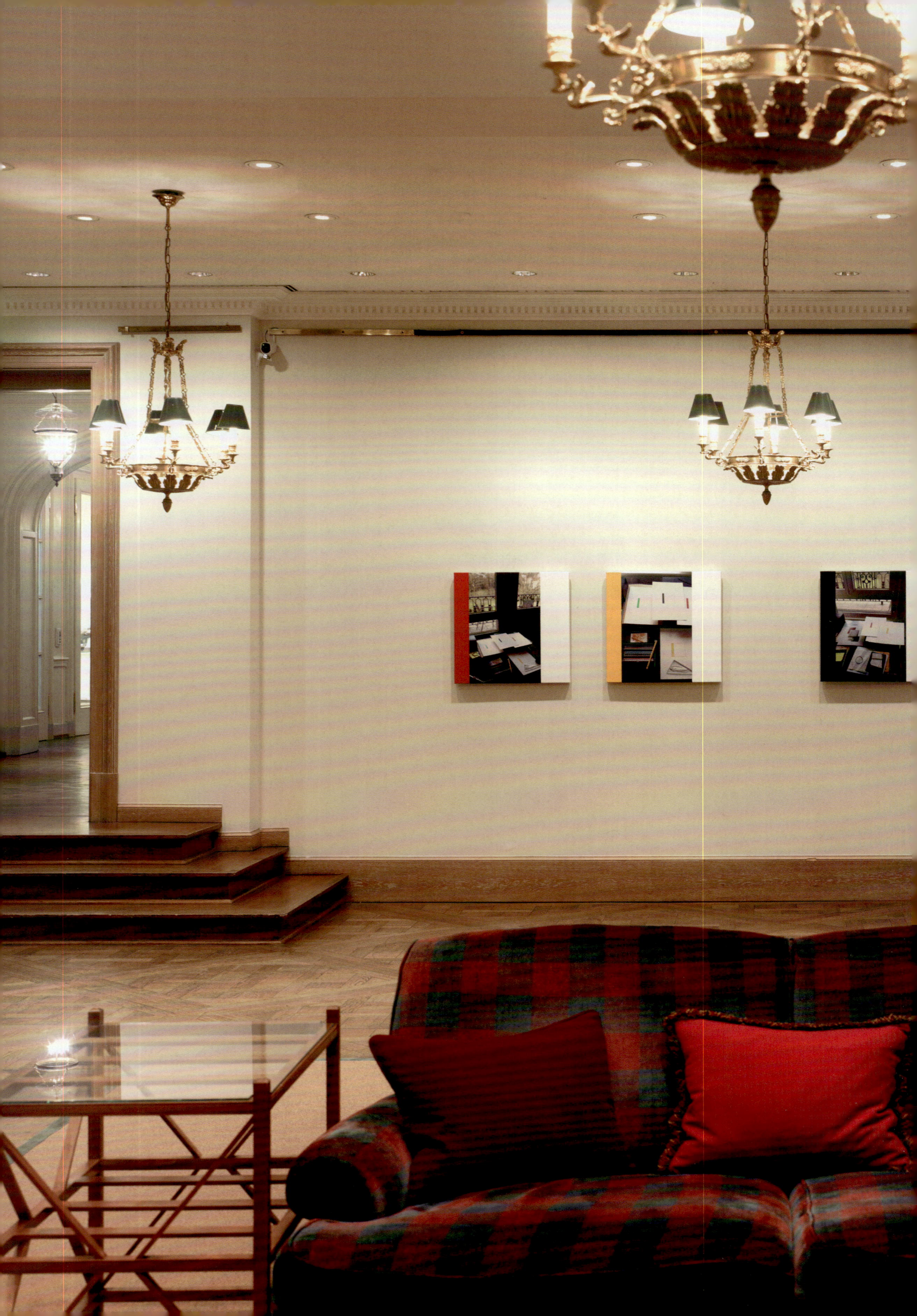

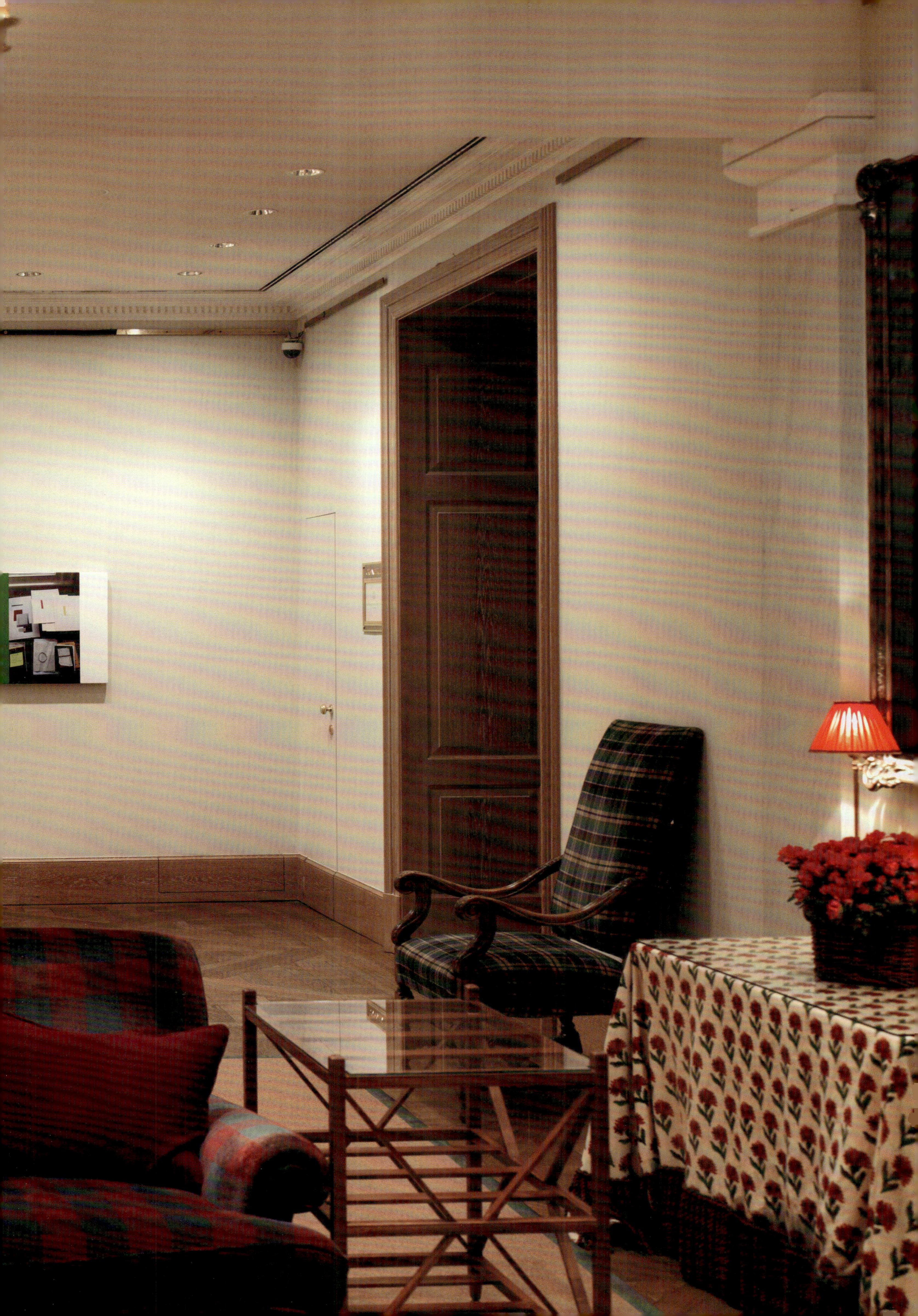

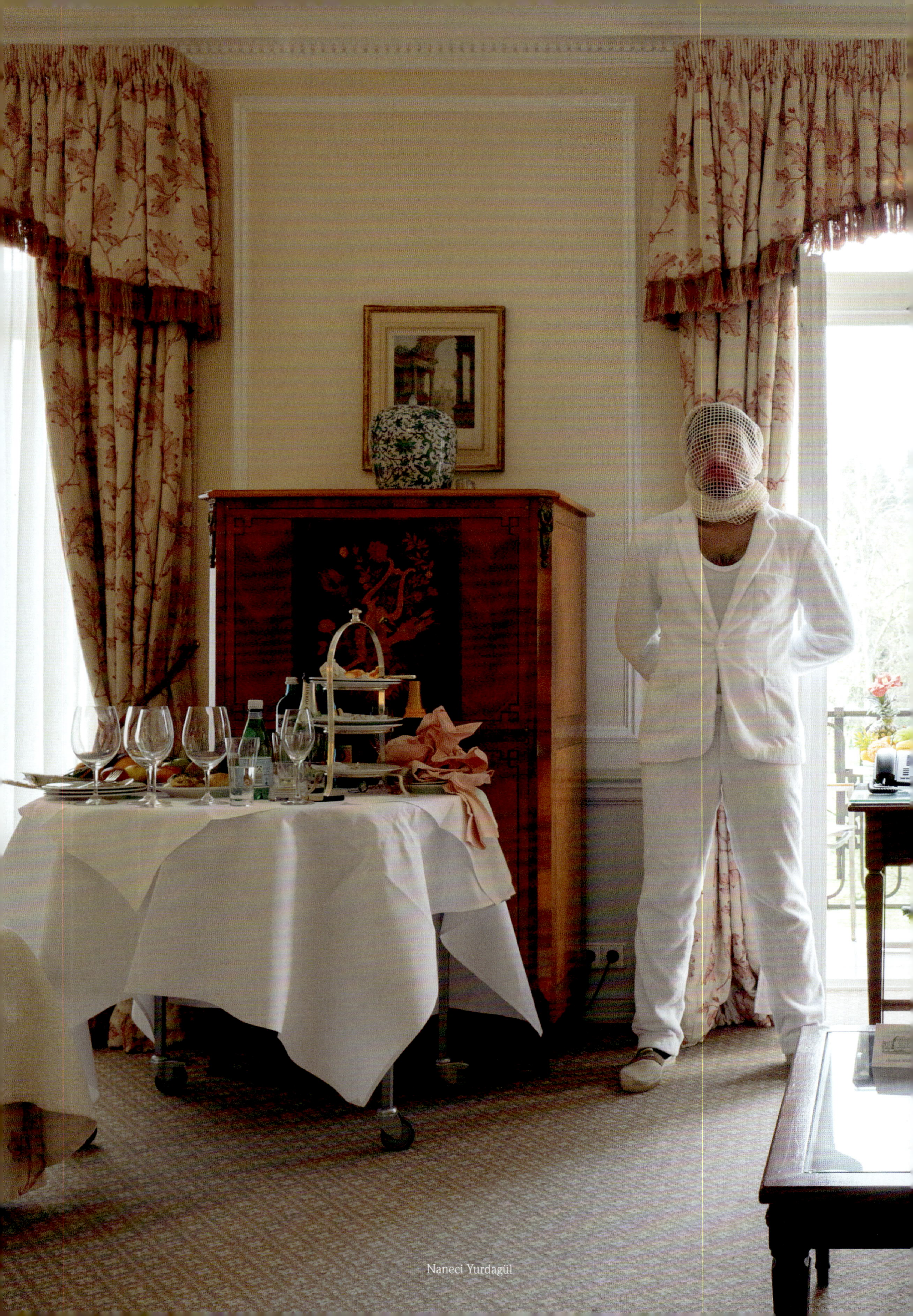

Naneci Yurdagül

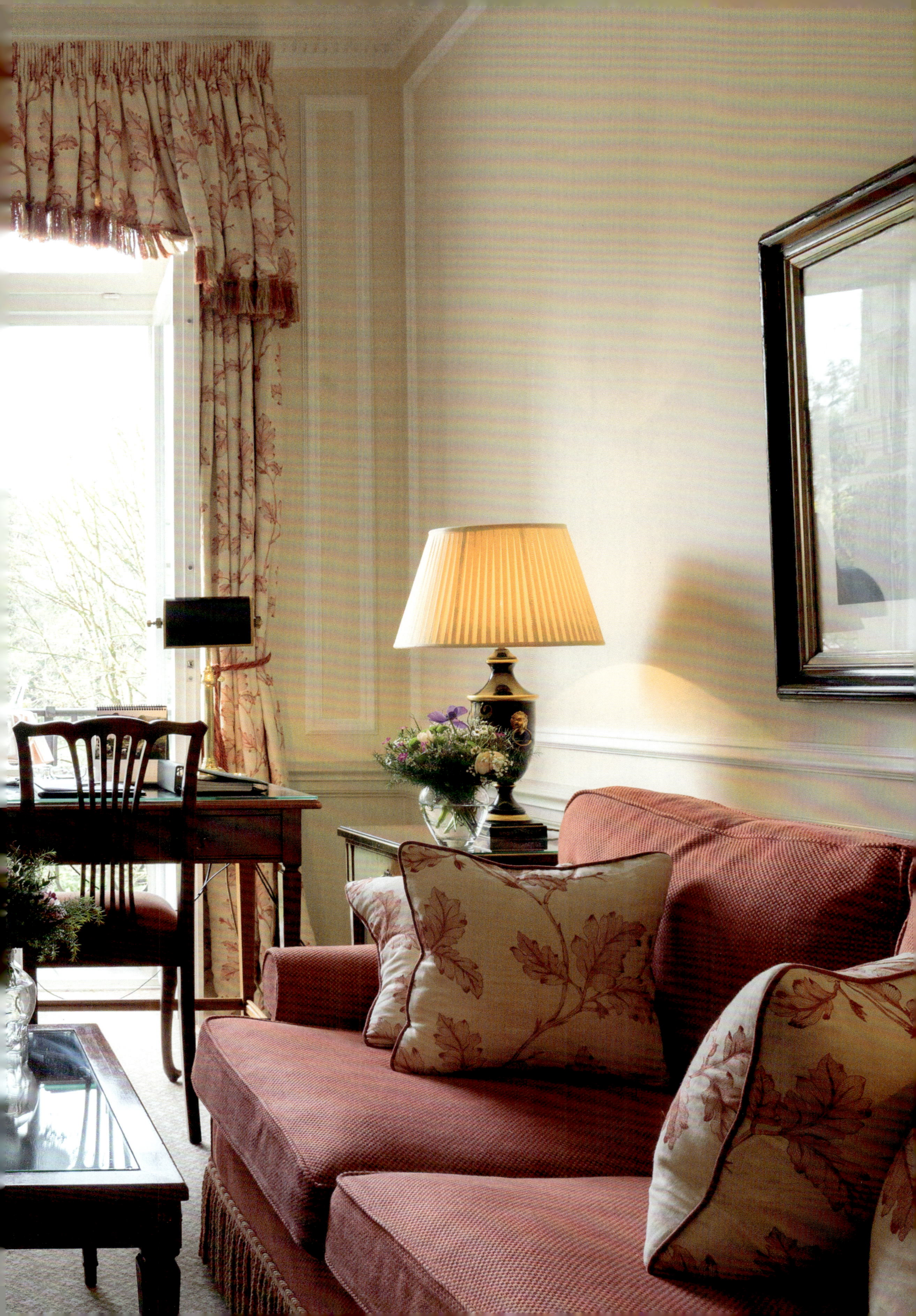

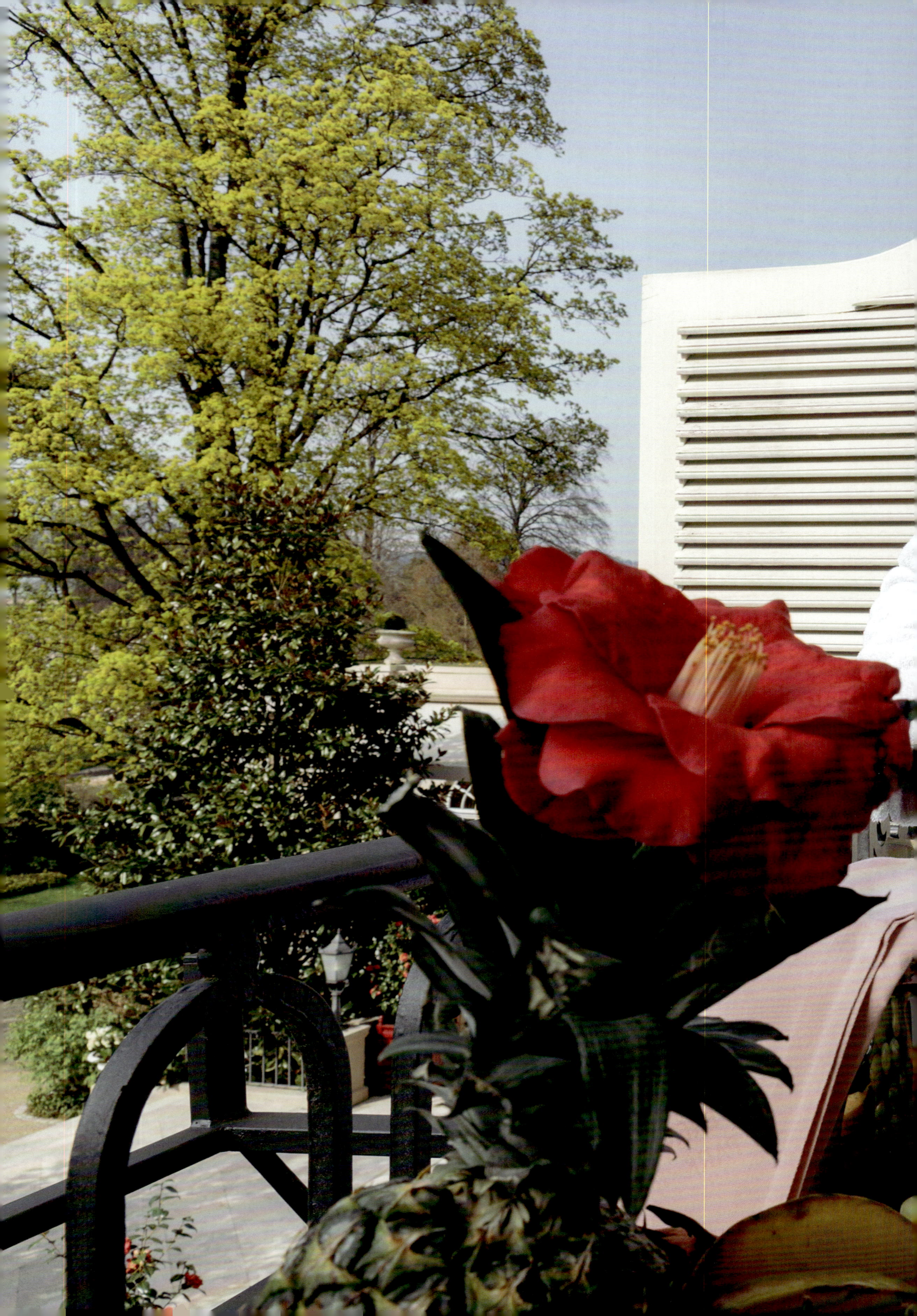

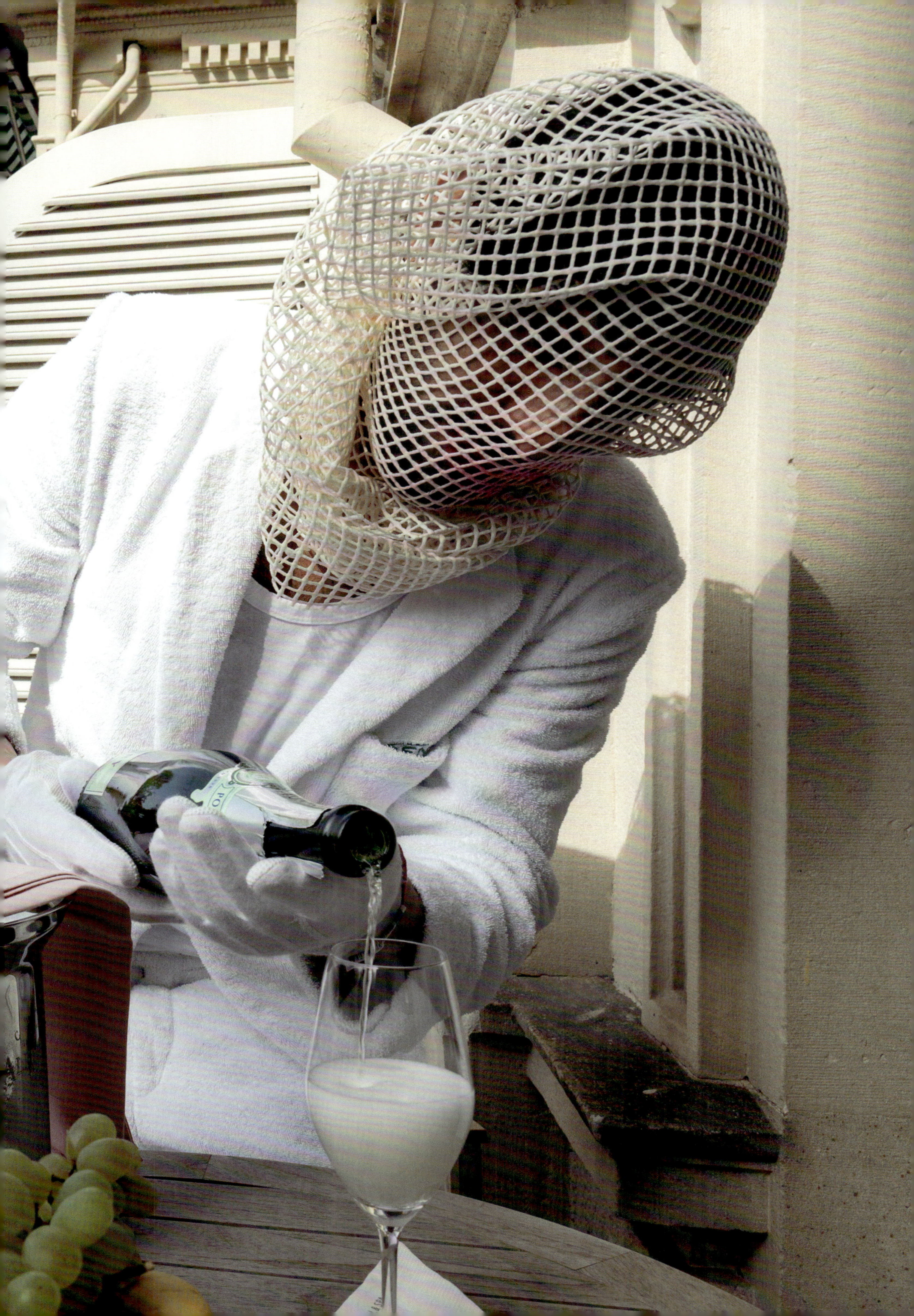

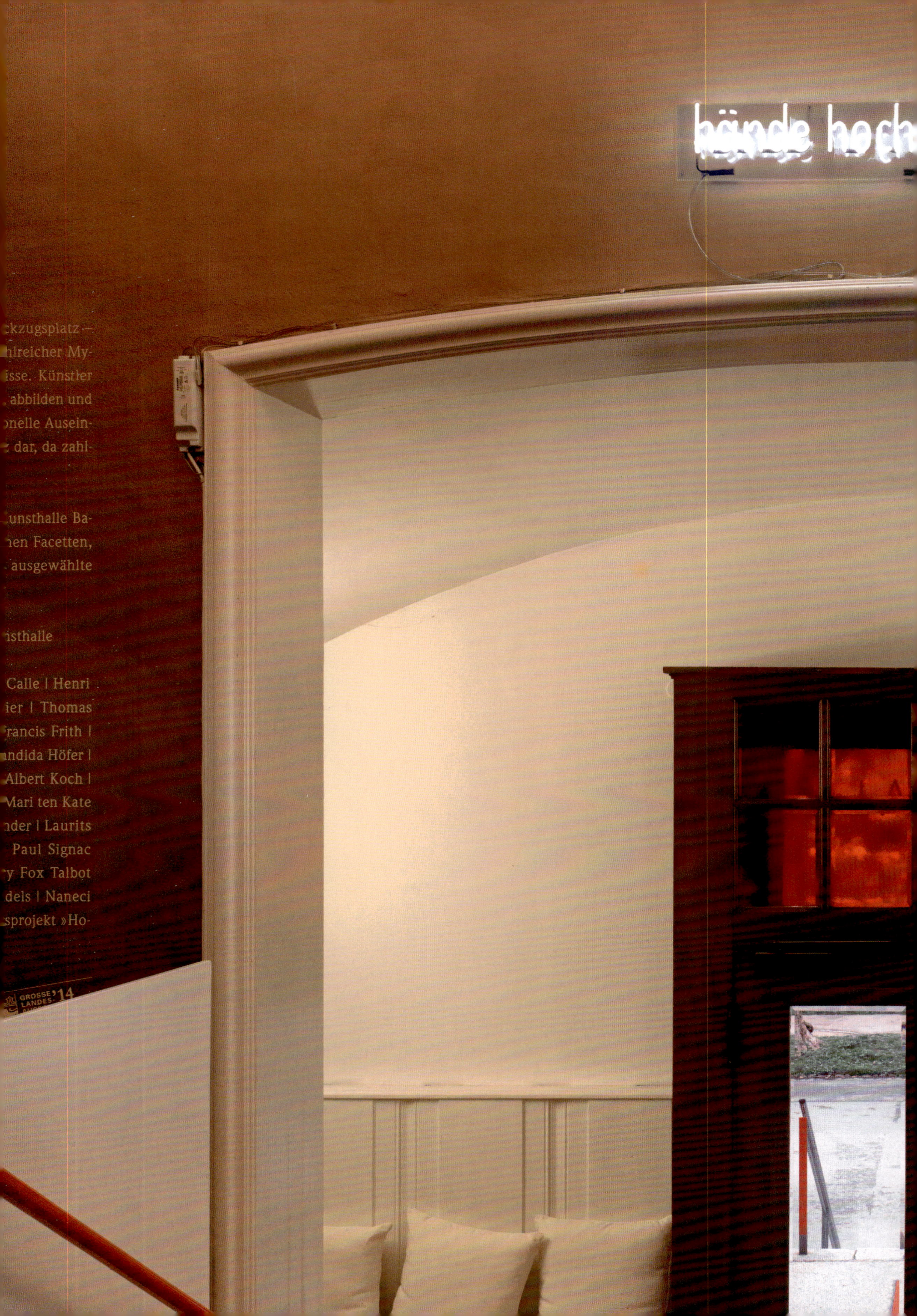
hände hoch
ckzugsplatz –
nlreicher My-
isse. Künstler
abbilden und
onelle Ausein-
dar, da zahl-
unsthalle Ba-
nen Facetten,
ausgewählte
nsthalle
Calle | Henri
ier | Thomas
rancis Frith |
ndida Höfer |
Albert Koch |
Mari ten Kate
nder | Laurits
Paul Signac
y Fox Talbot
dels | Naneci
sprojekt »Ho-
GROSSE LANDES- 14

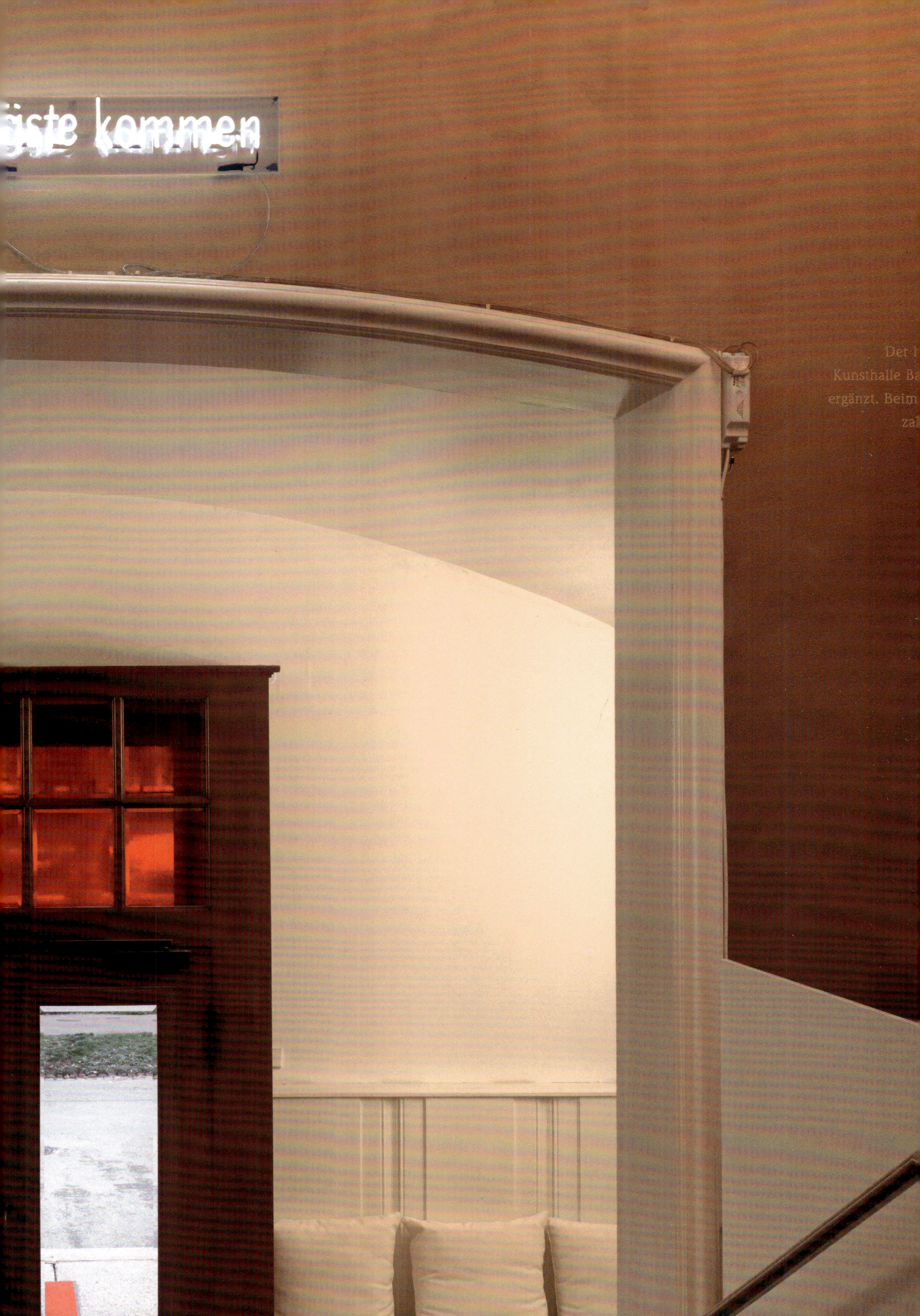

Der i
Kunsthalle Ba
ergänzt. Beim
zah

AUSSTELLUNG / EXHIBITION
RATHAUSGLÖCKEL

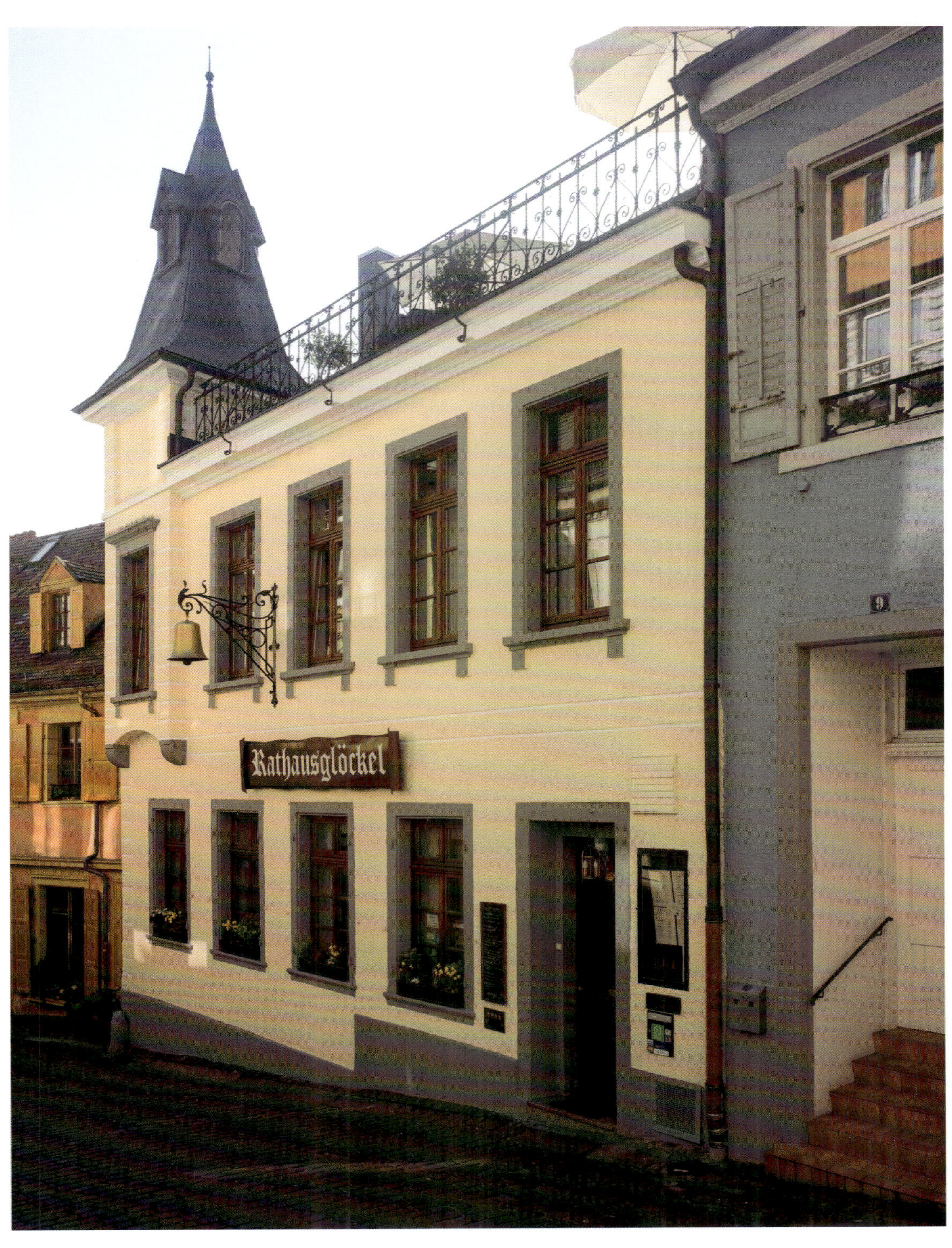

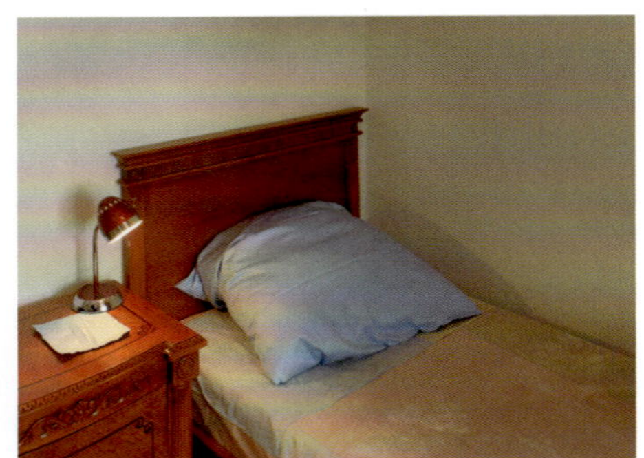

Lee Kit

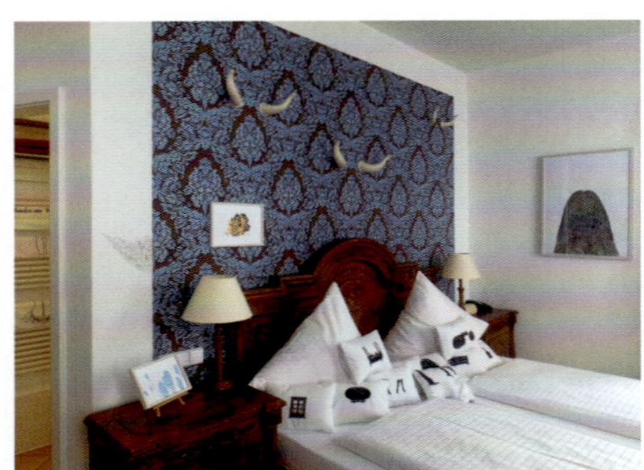

Gabriela Oberkofler

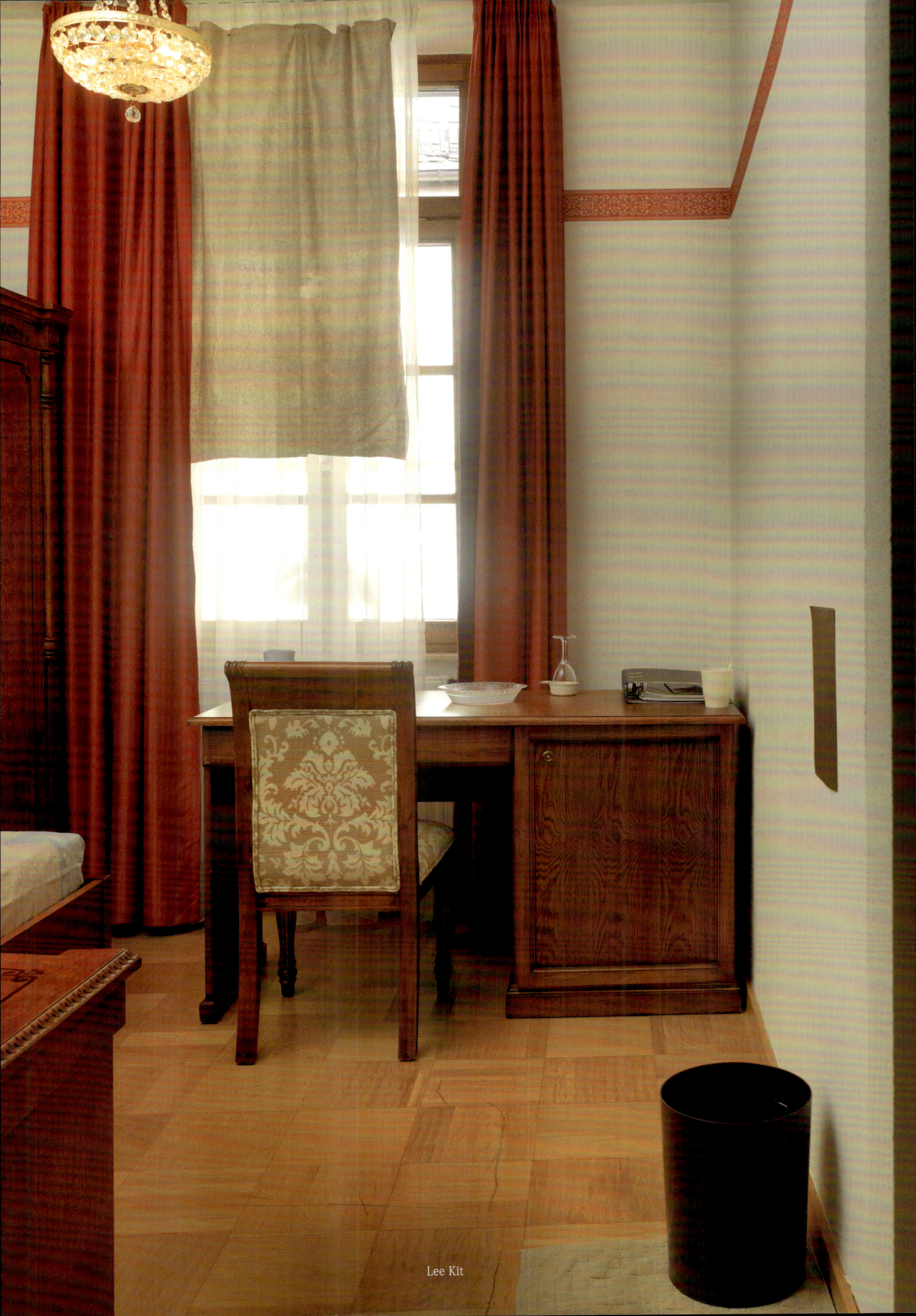

Lee Kit

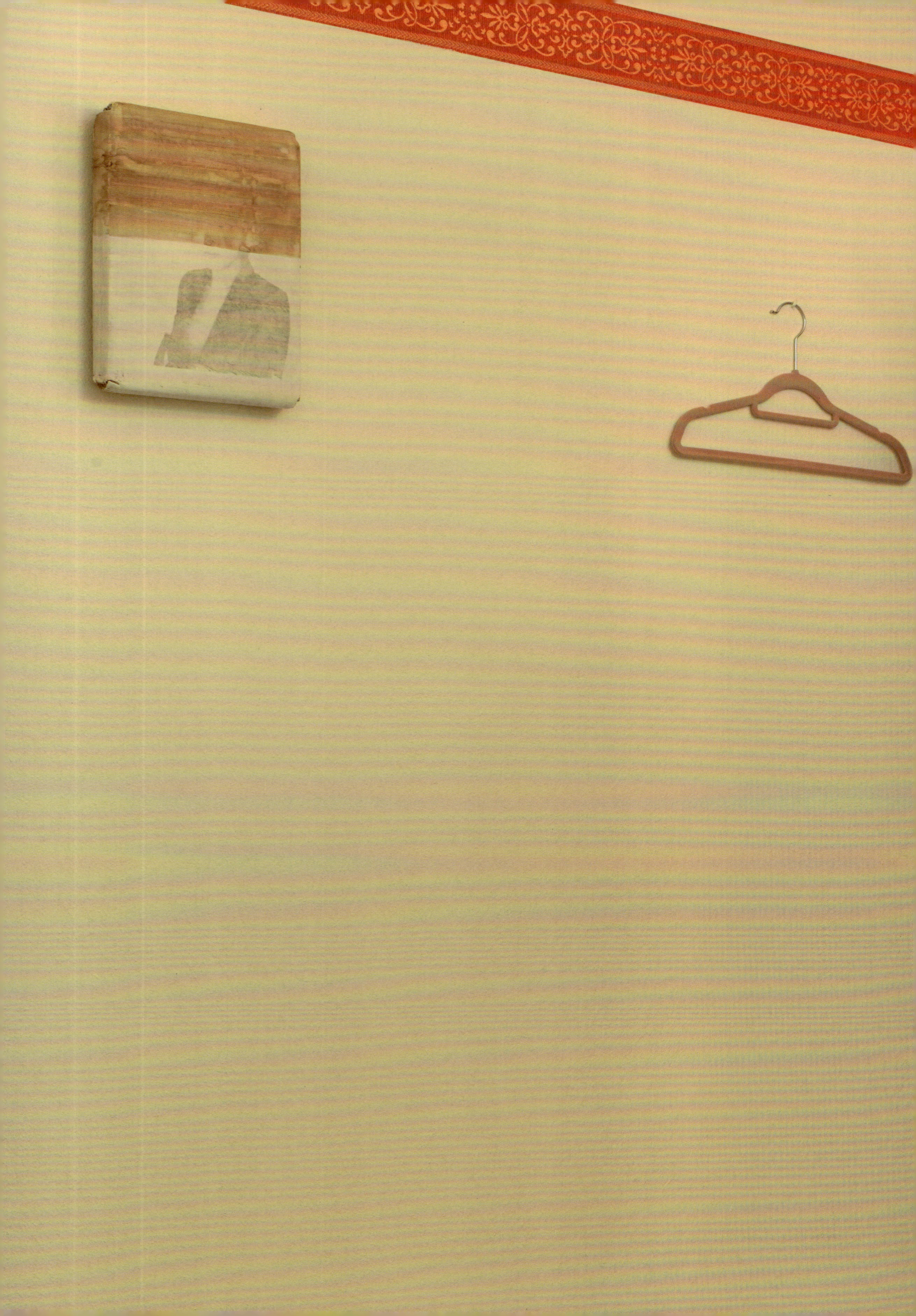

Are we

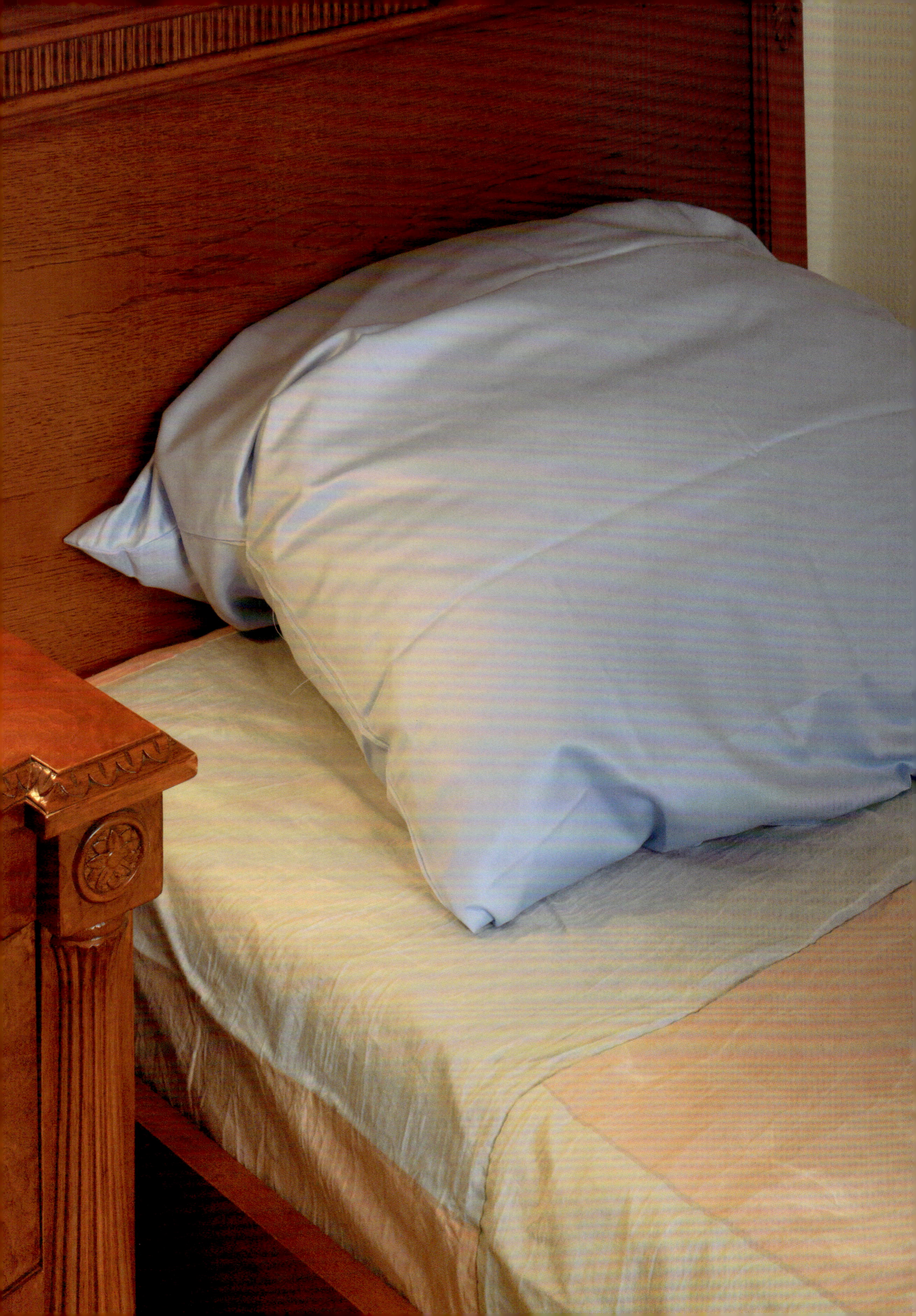

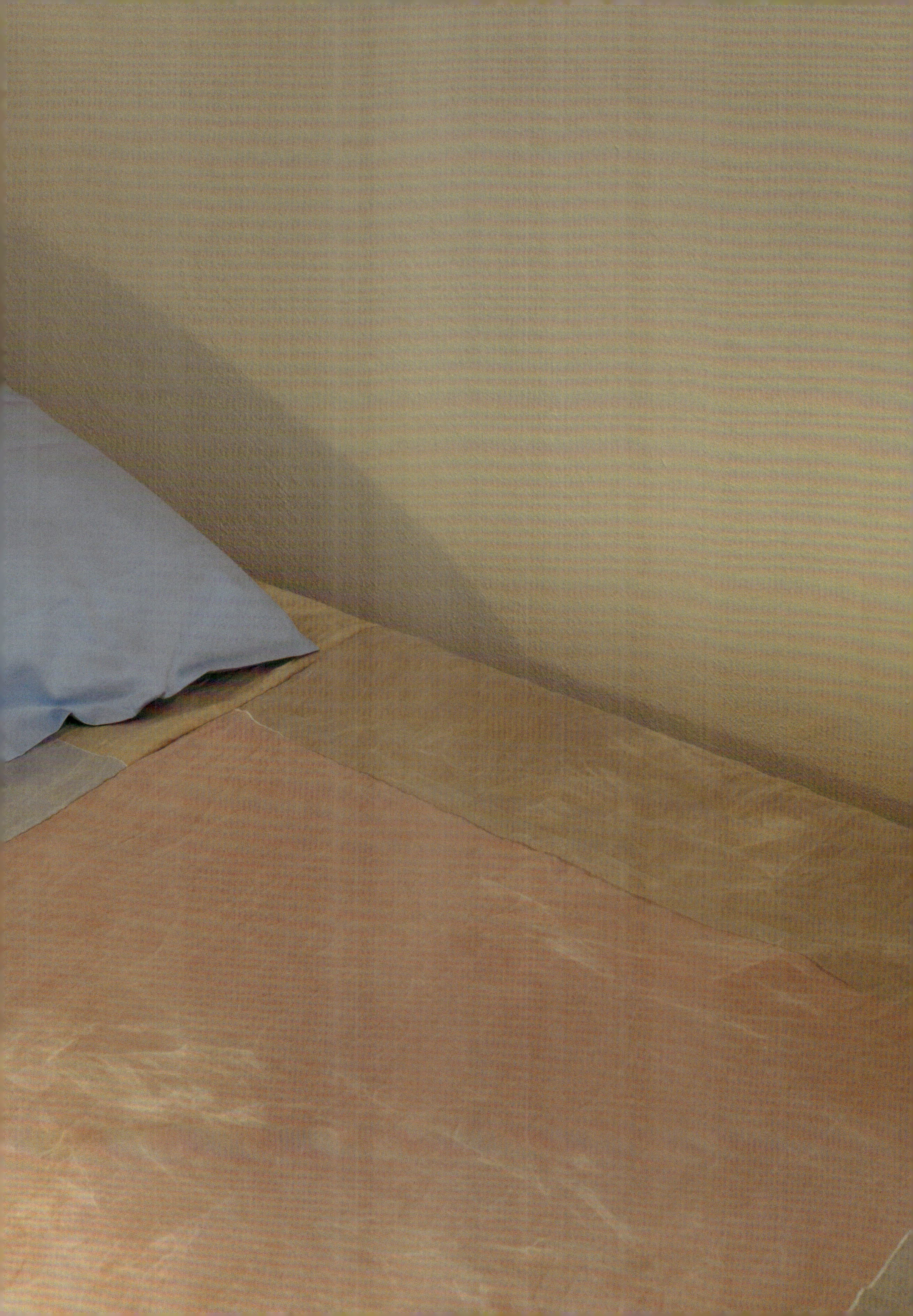

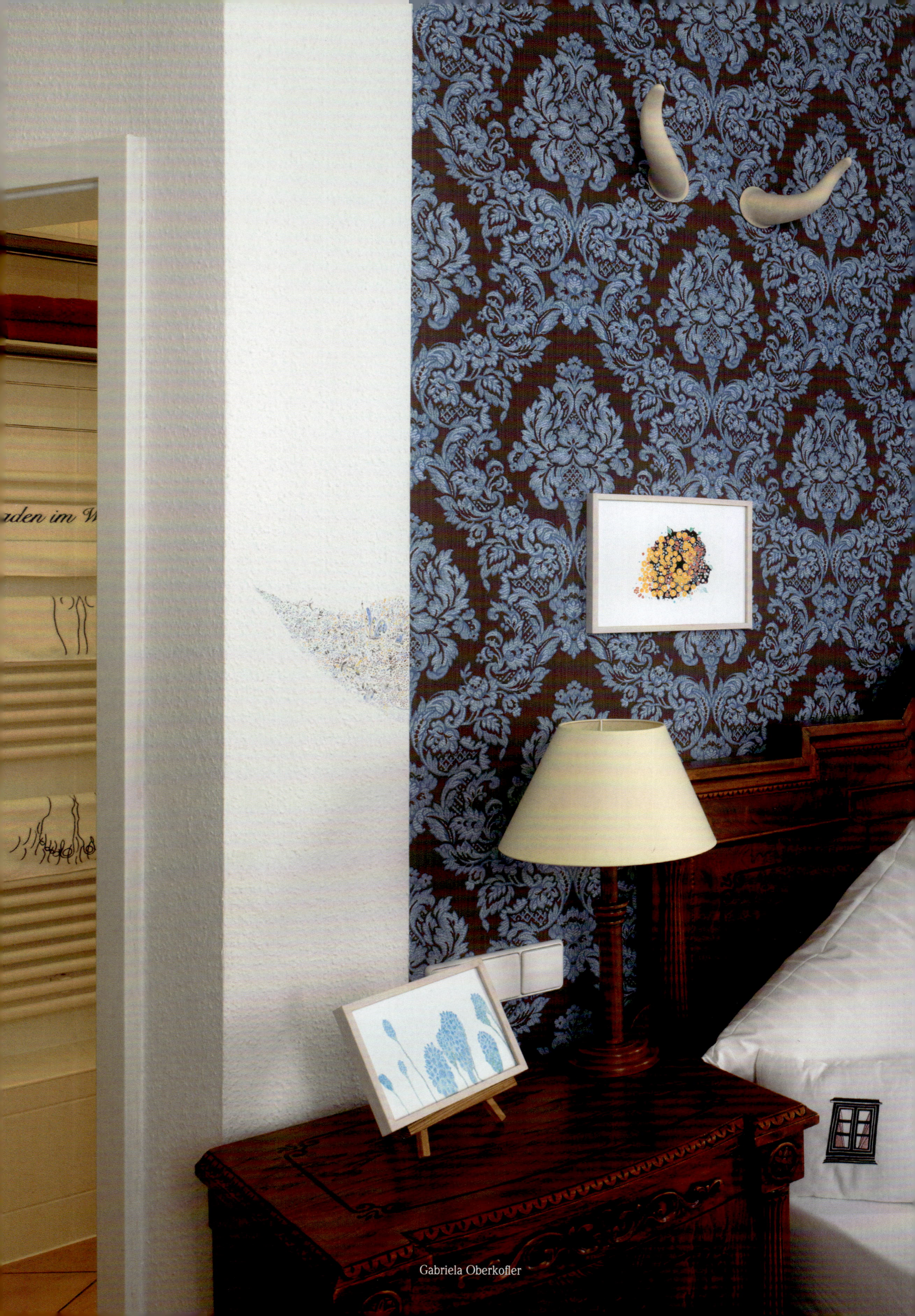

Gabriela Oberkofler

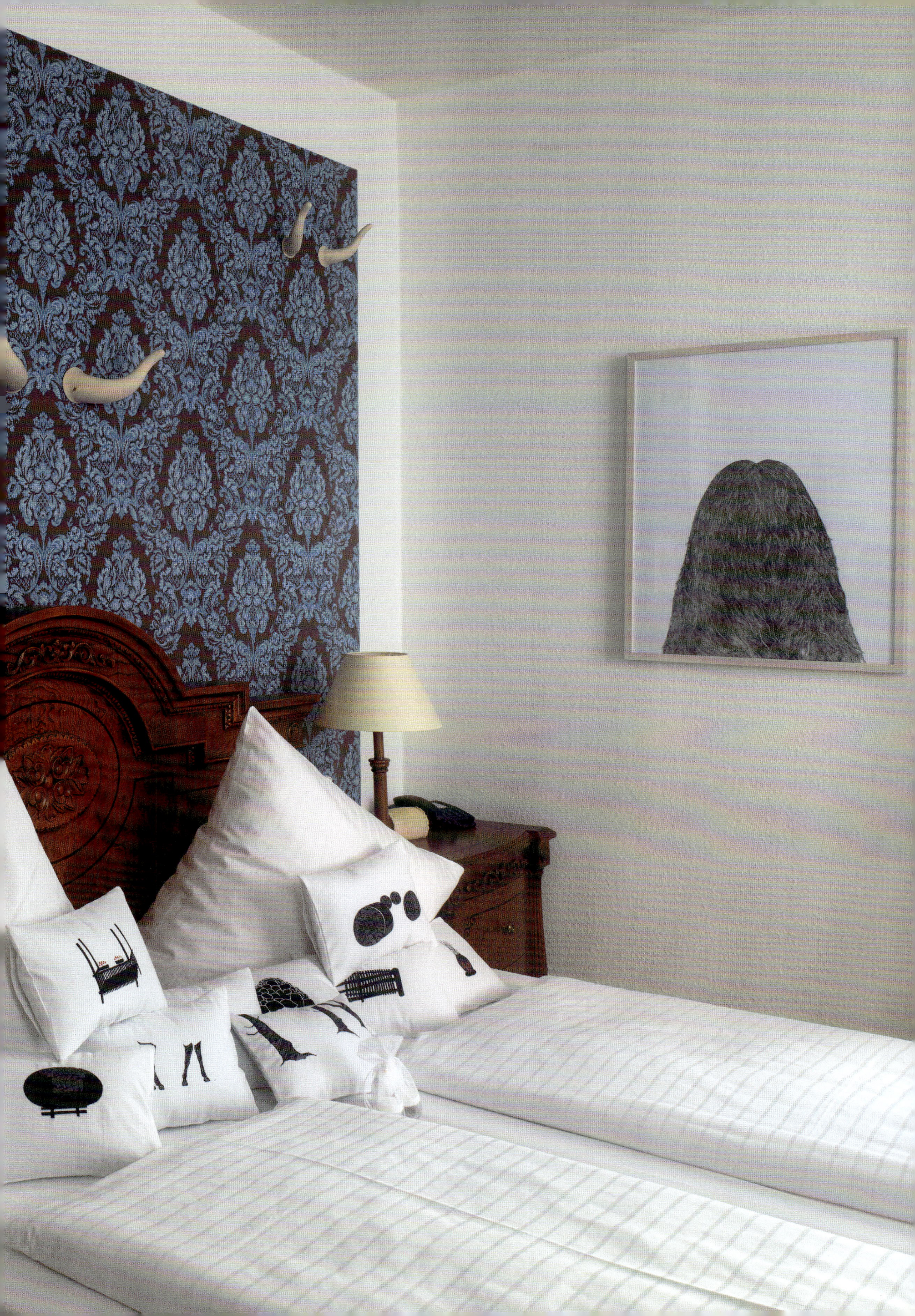

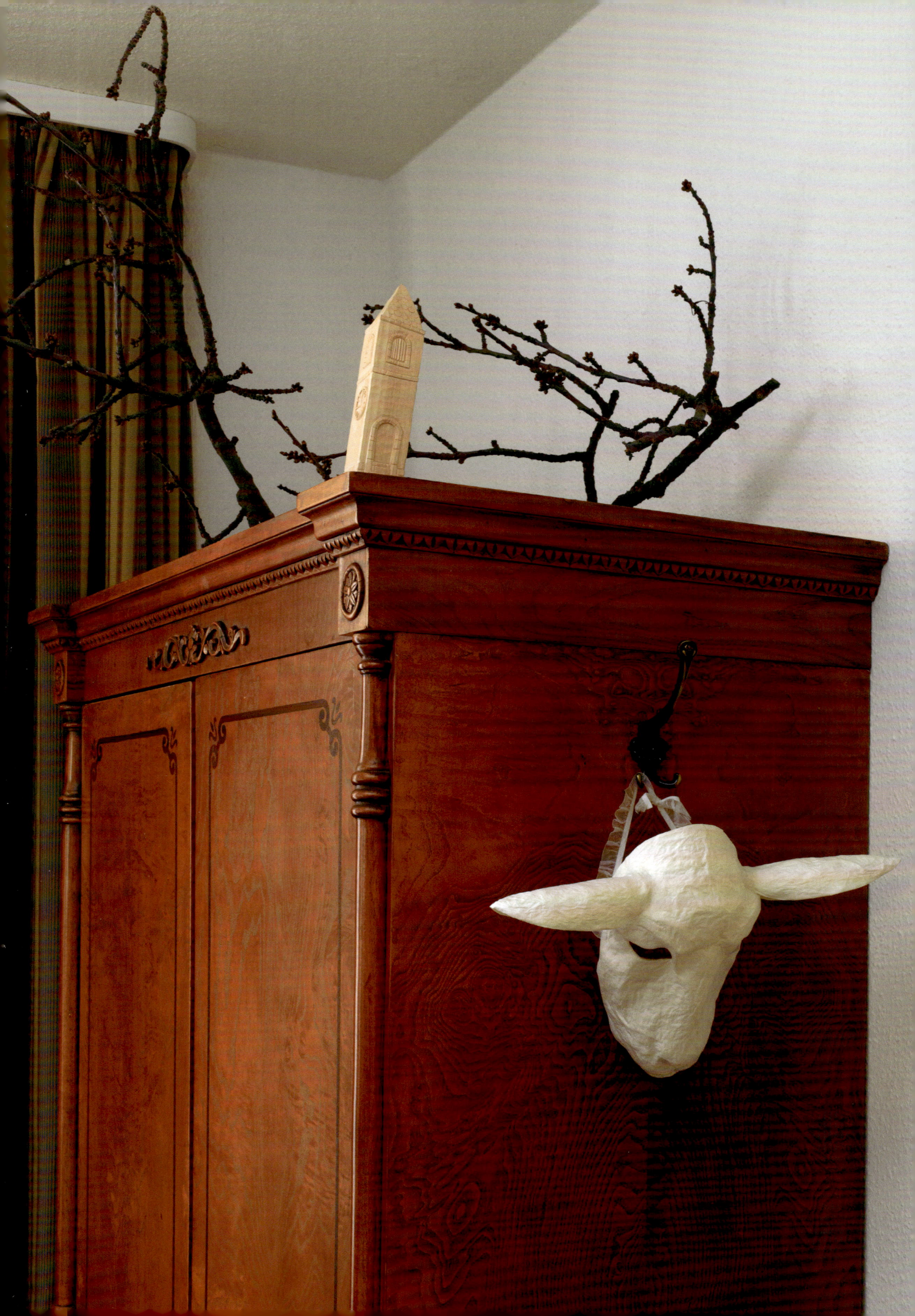

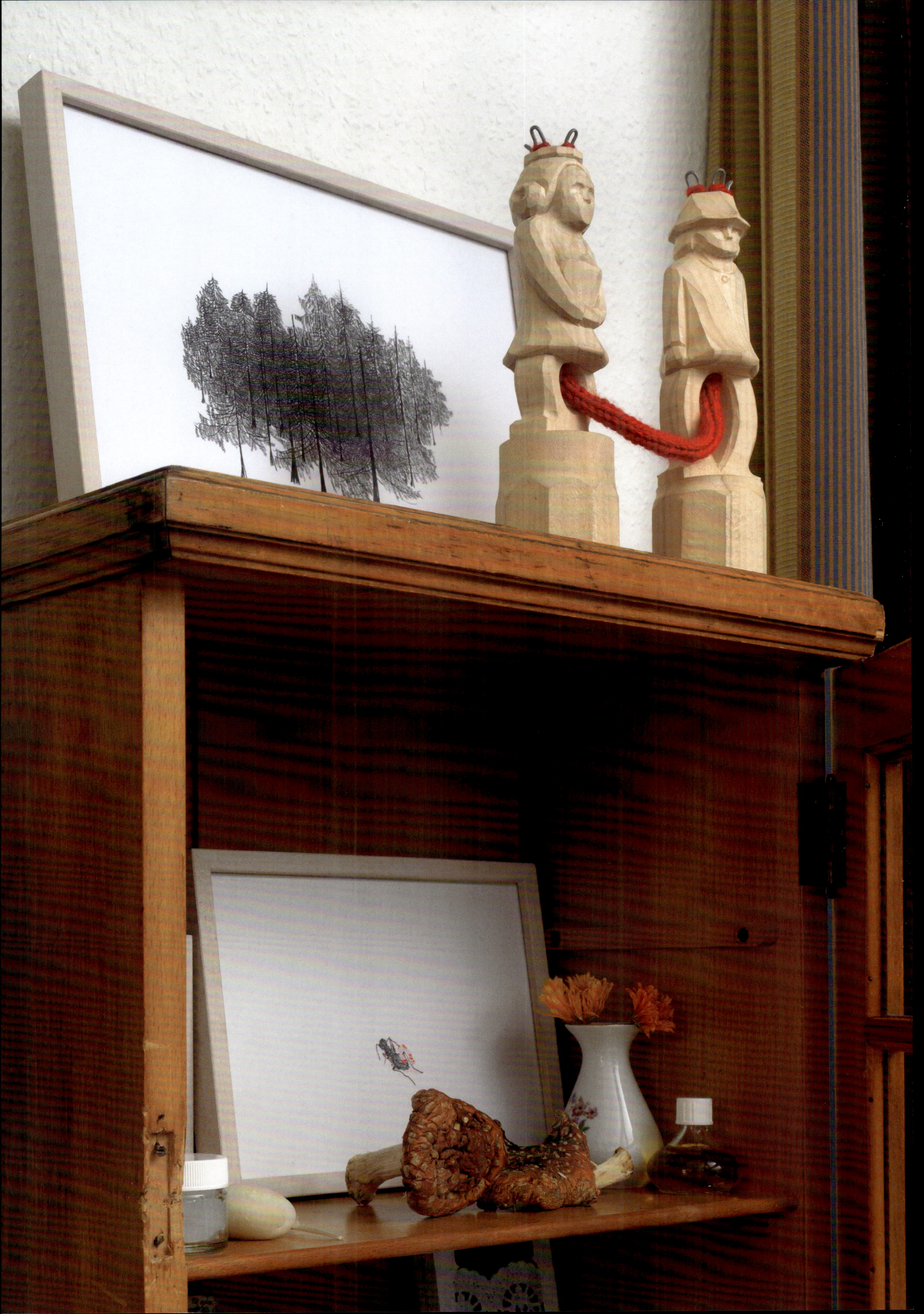

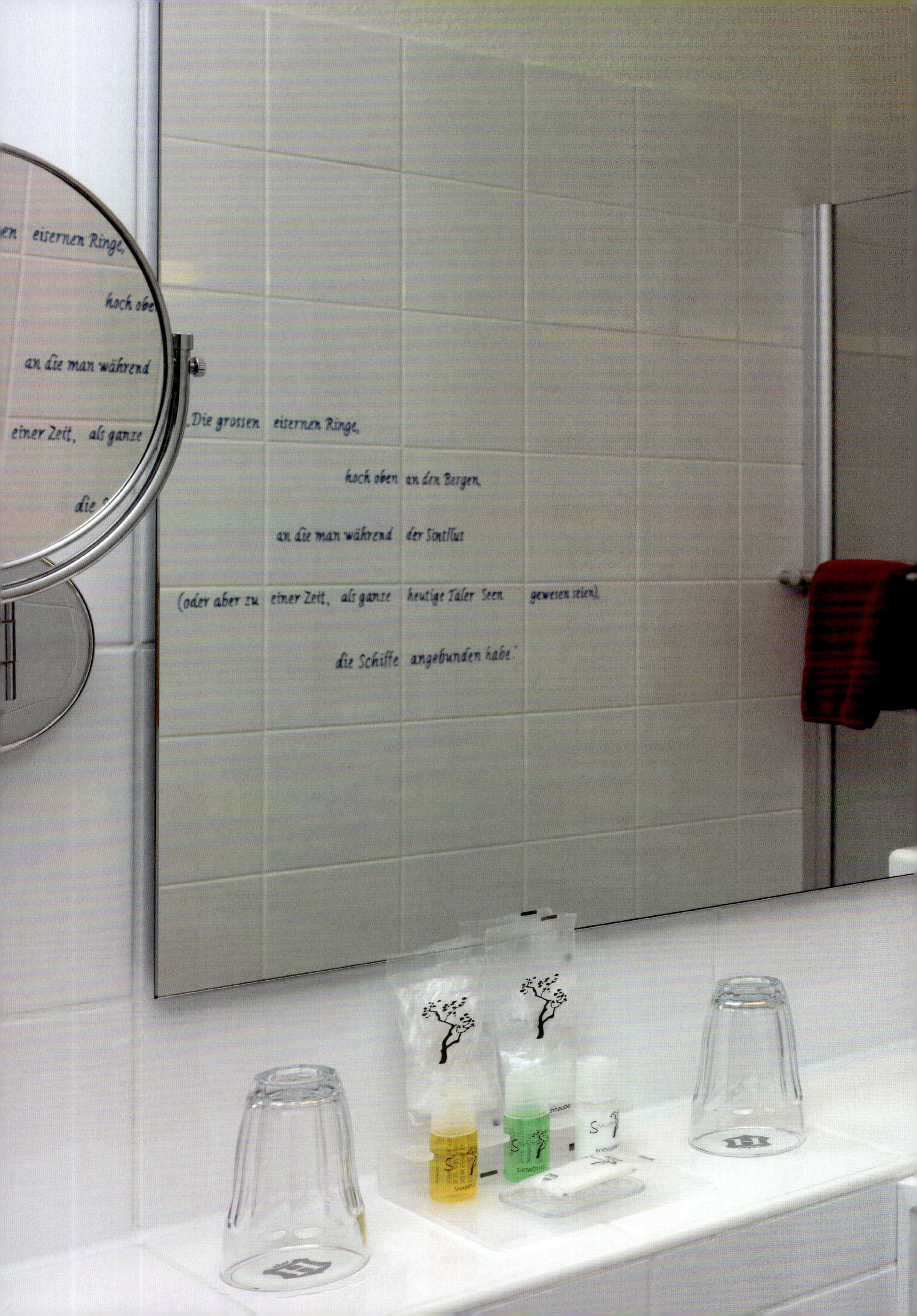
„Die grossen eisernen Ringe,
hoch oben an den Bergen,
an die man während der Sintflut
(oder aber zu einer Zeit, als ganze heutige Täler Seen gewesen seien),
die Schiffe angebunden habe."
SHOWER GEL

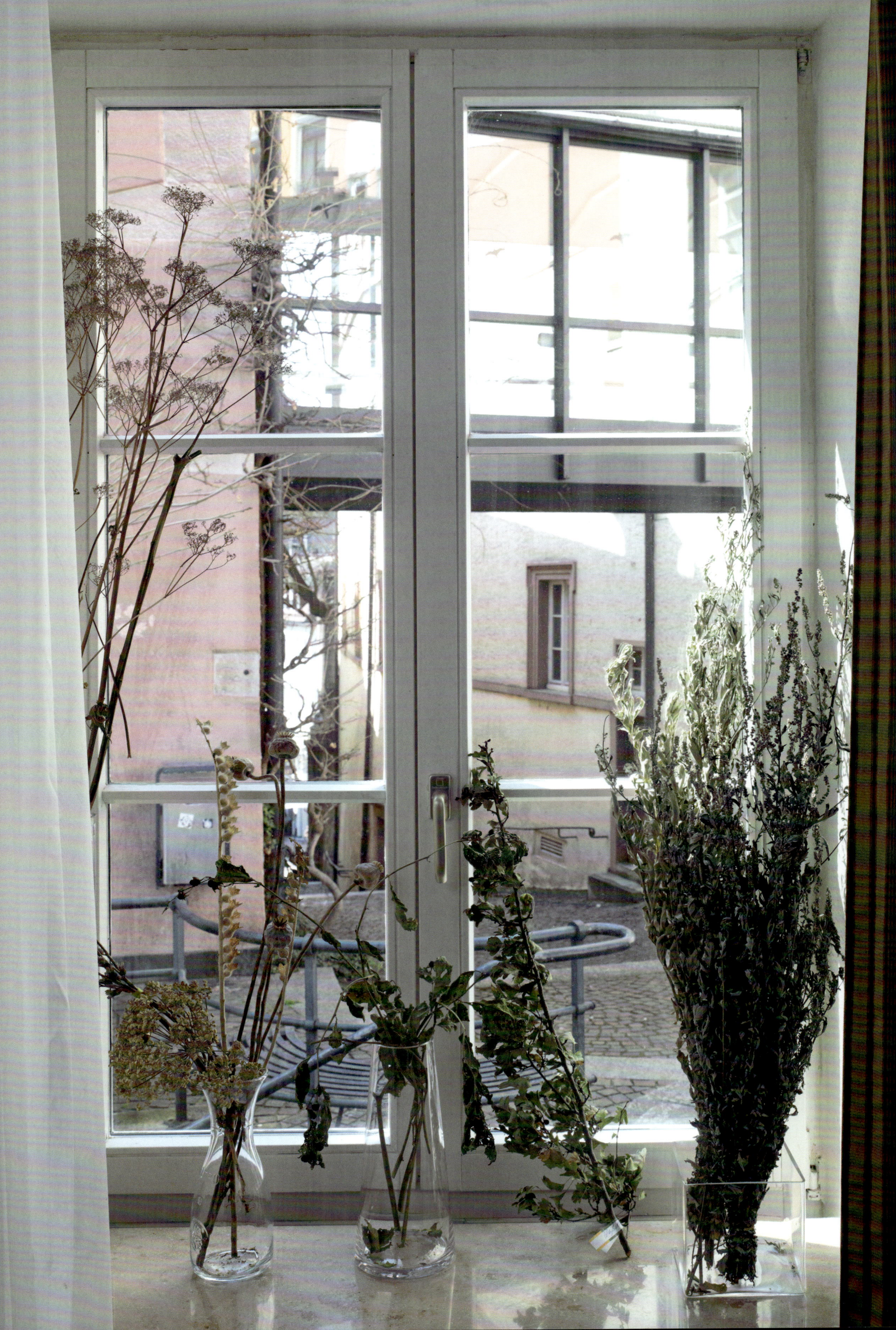

AUSSTELLUNG / EXHIBITION
STEIGENBERGER EUROPÄISCHER HOF

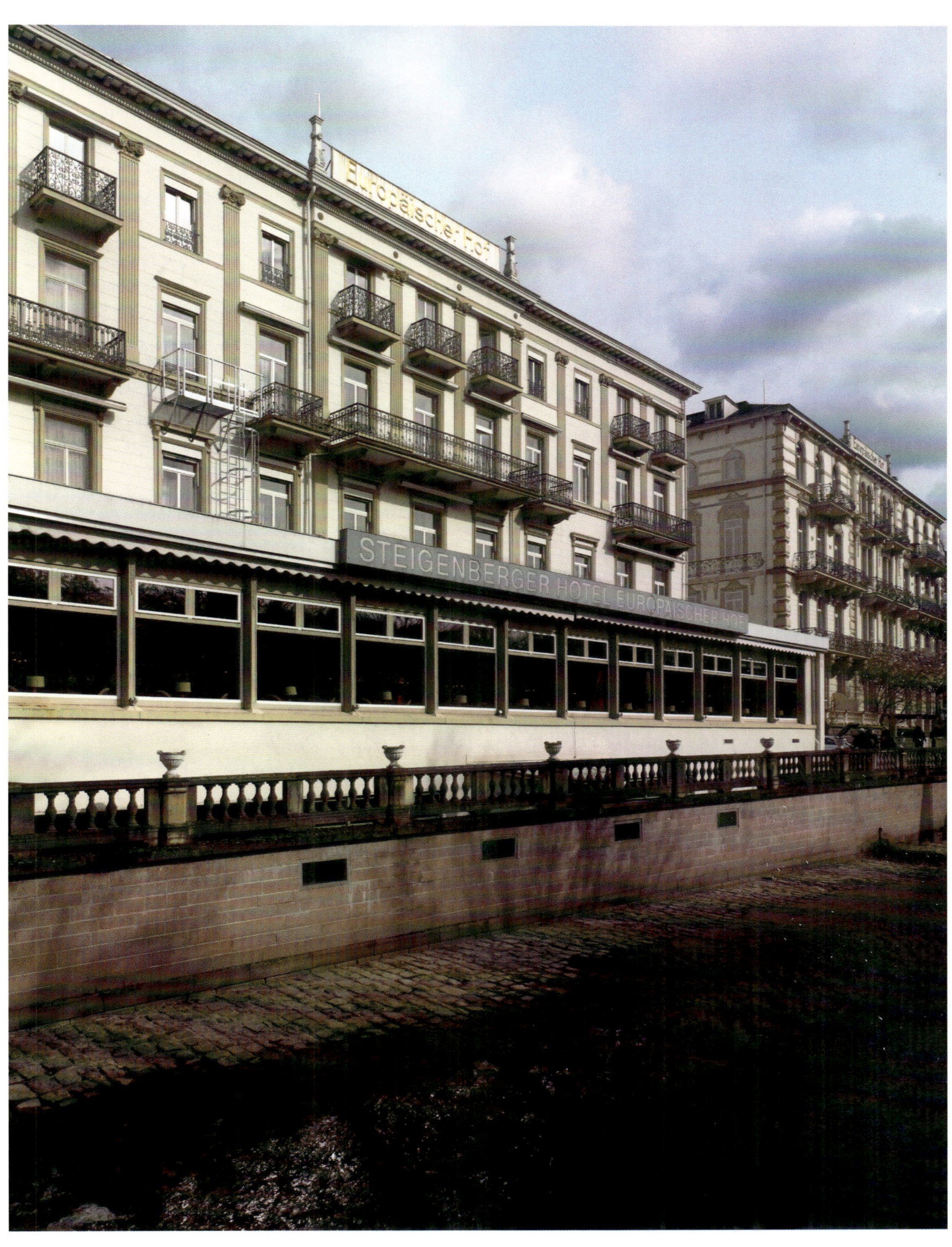

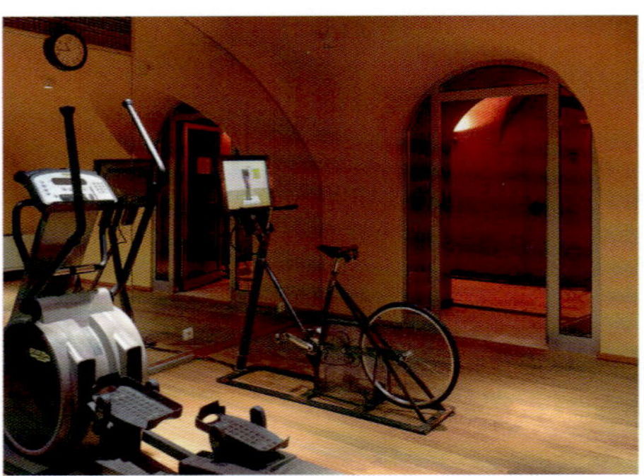

Guy Ben-Ner

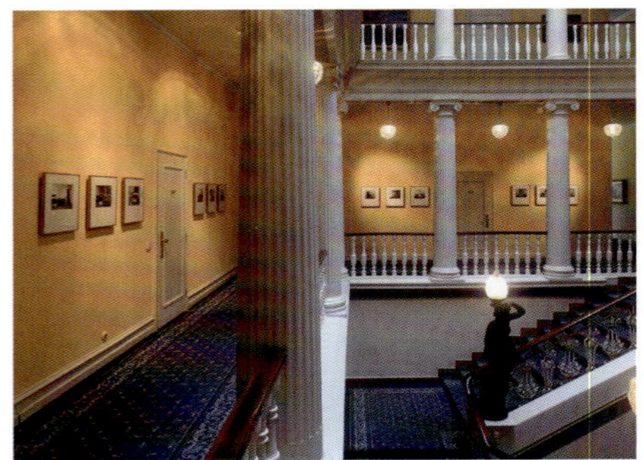

Florian Slotawa

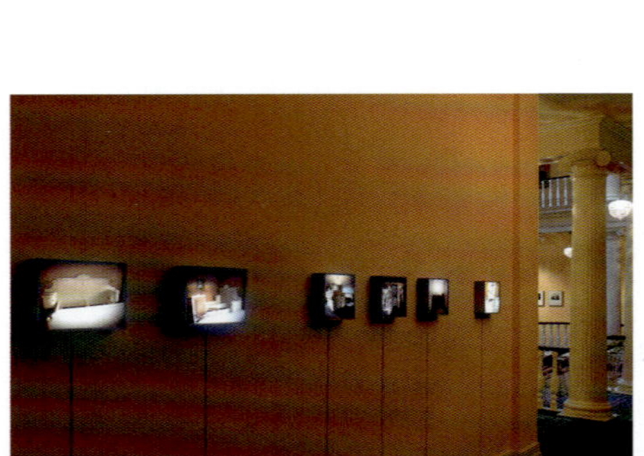

Simone Demandt

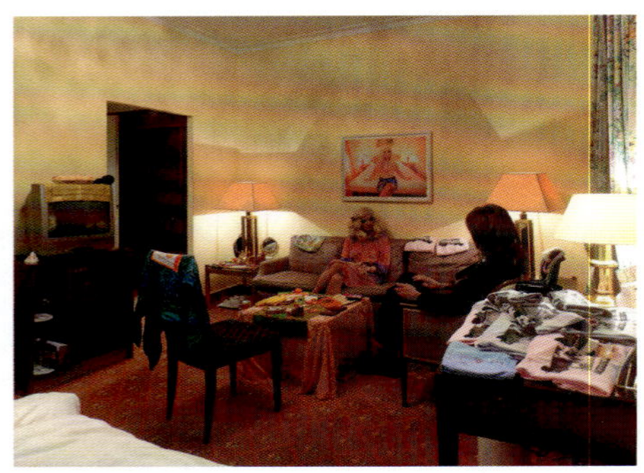

Ann Liv Young

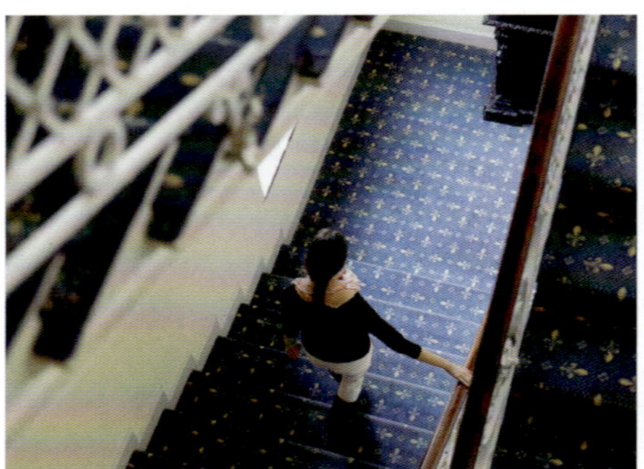

Ligna

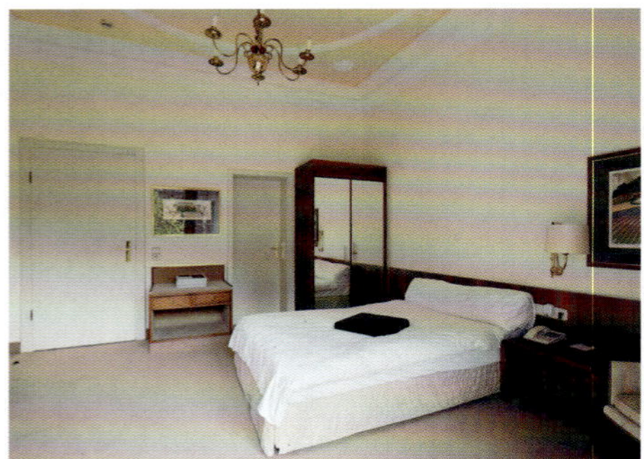

THE ARMOIRE SHOW 2014
Von / By Hans Ulrich Obrist
Mit Werken von / With works by
DAS INSTITUT | DIS | Tracey Emin
K-Hole | Sarah Lucas
Reiner Ruthenbeck | Ryan Trecartin
Rosemarie Trockel | Amalia Ulman
Franz Erhard Walther | Xu Zhen

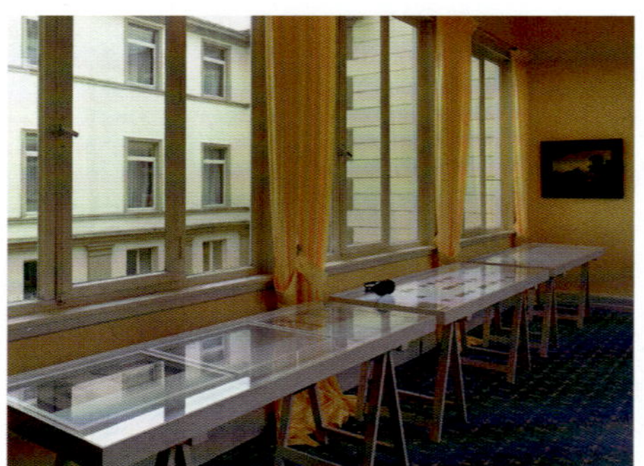

Armin Linke & Elina Axioti

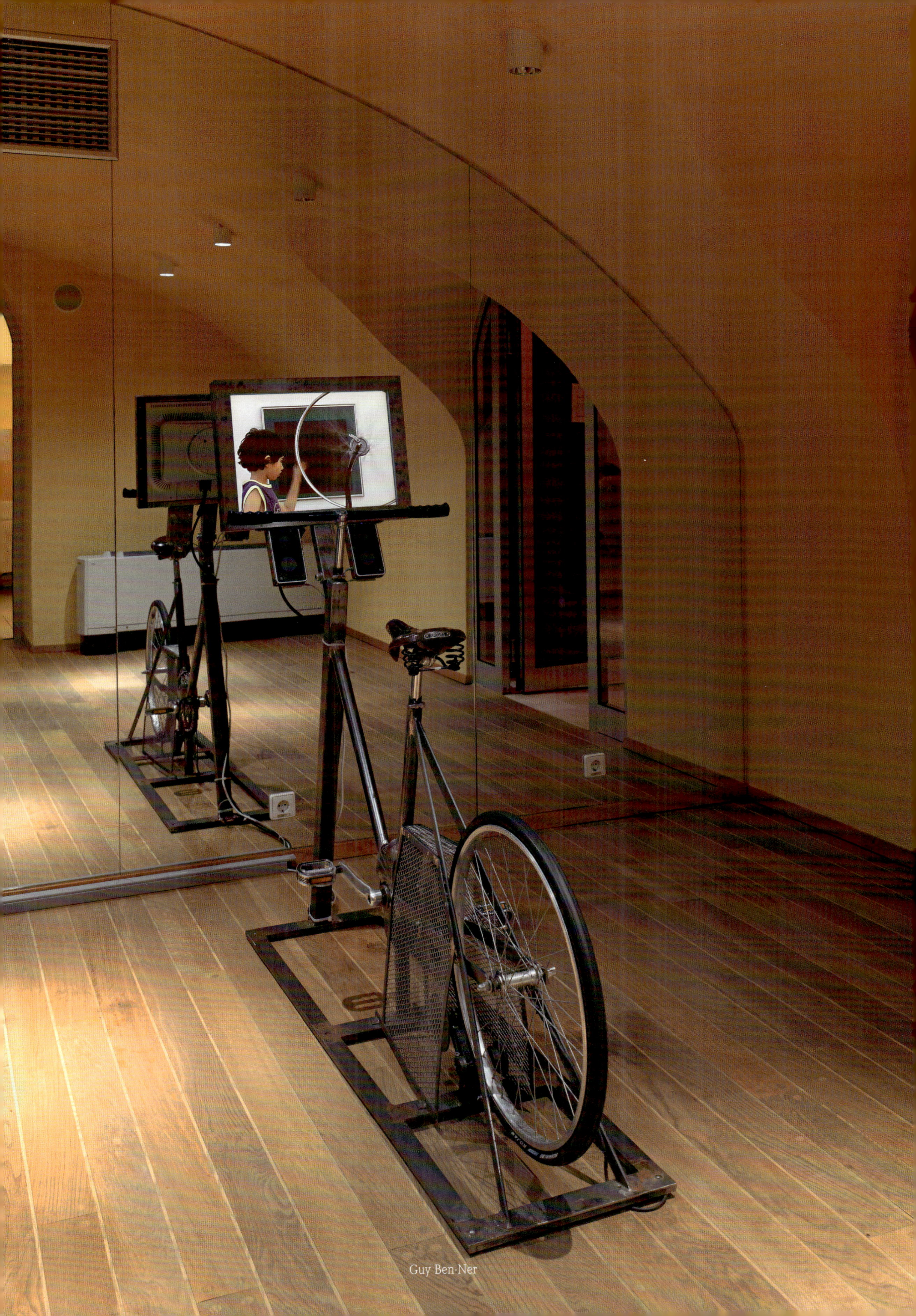

Guy Ben-Ner

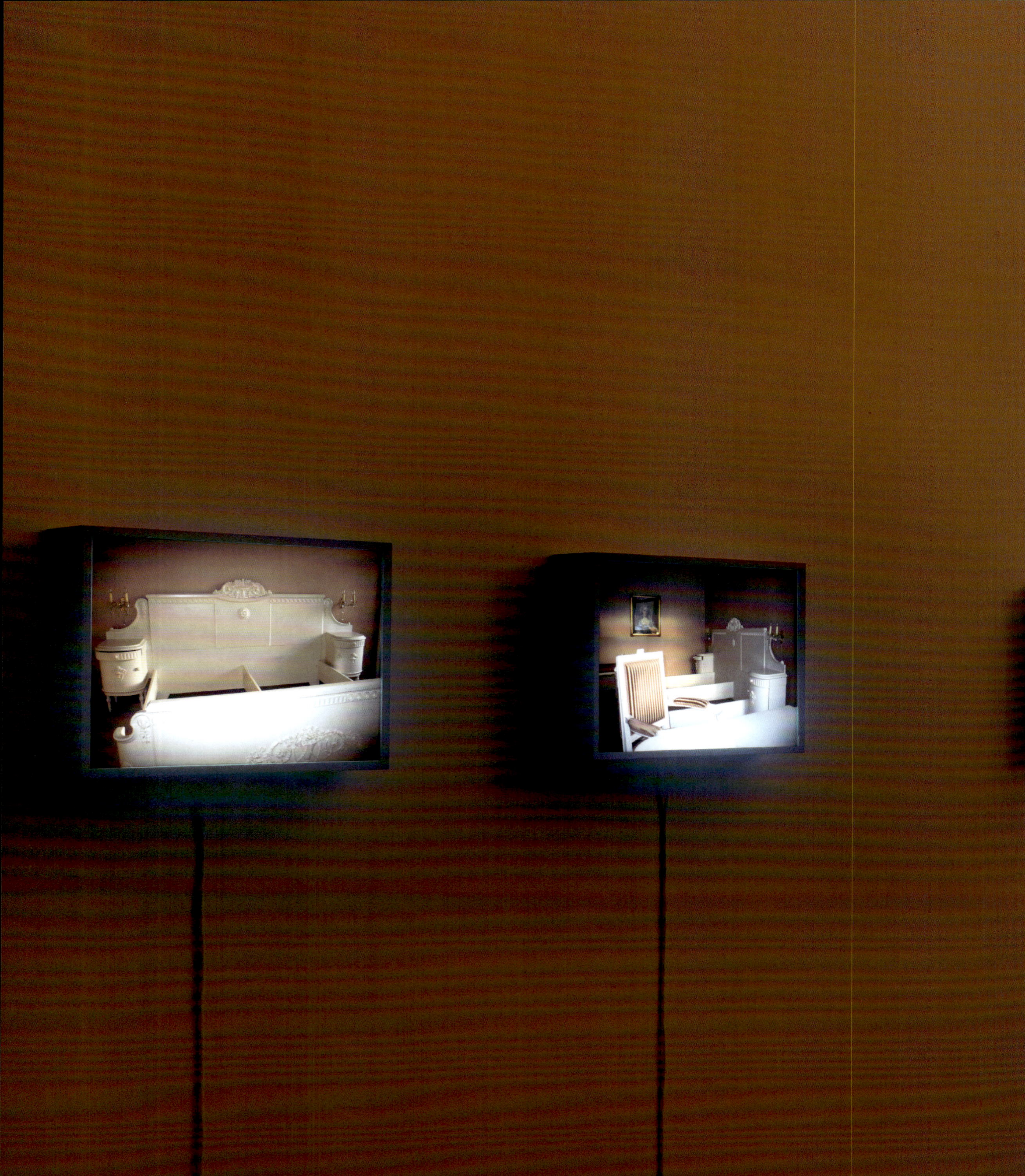

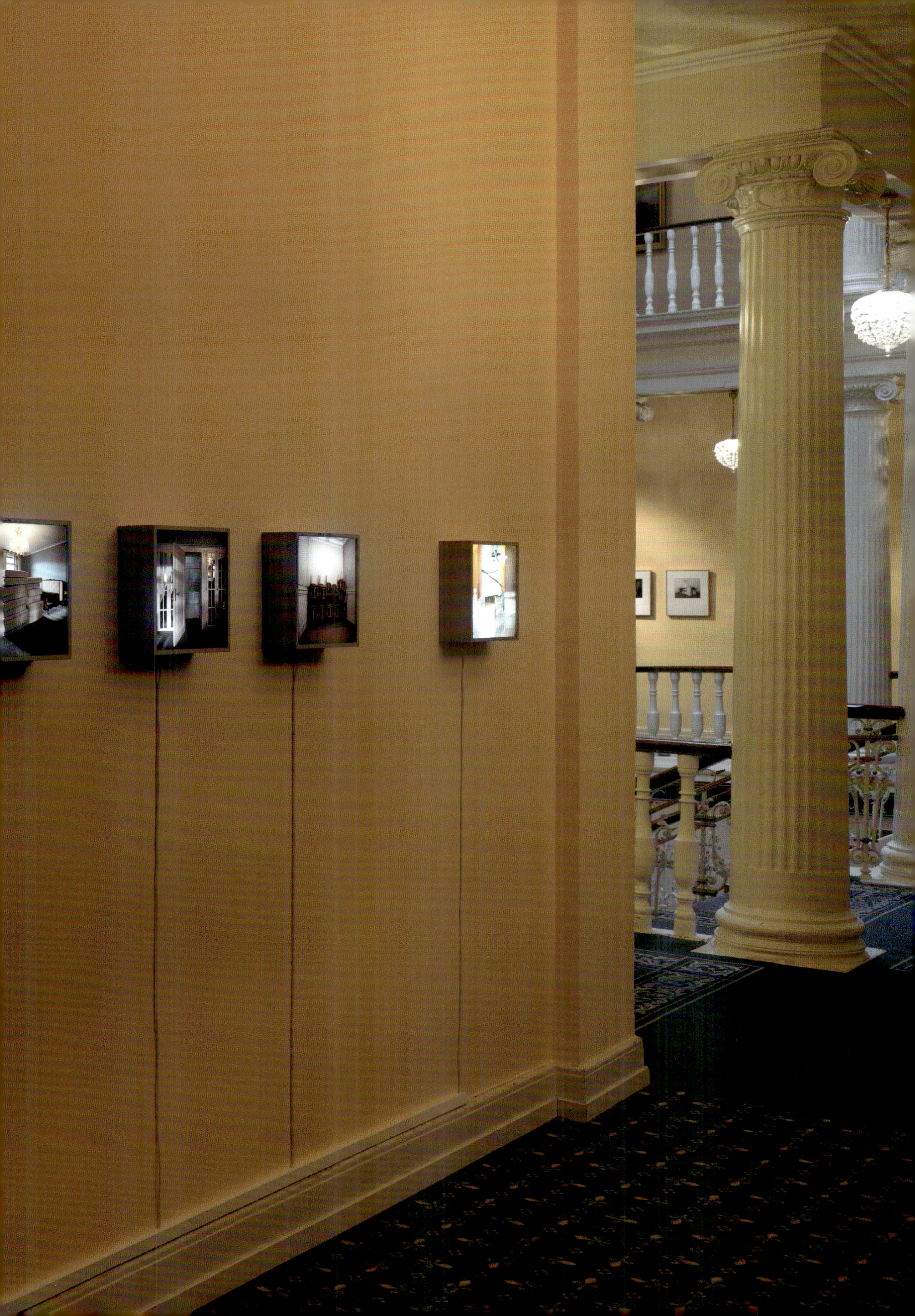

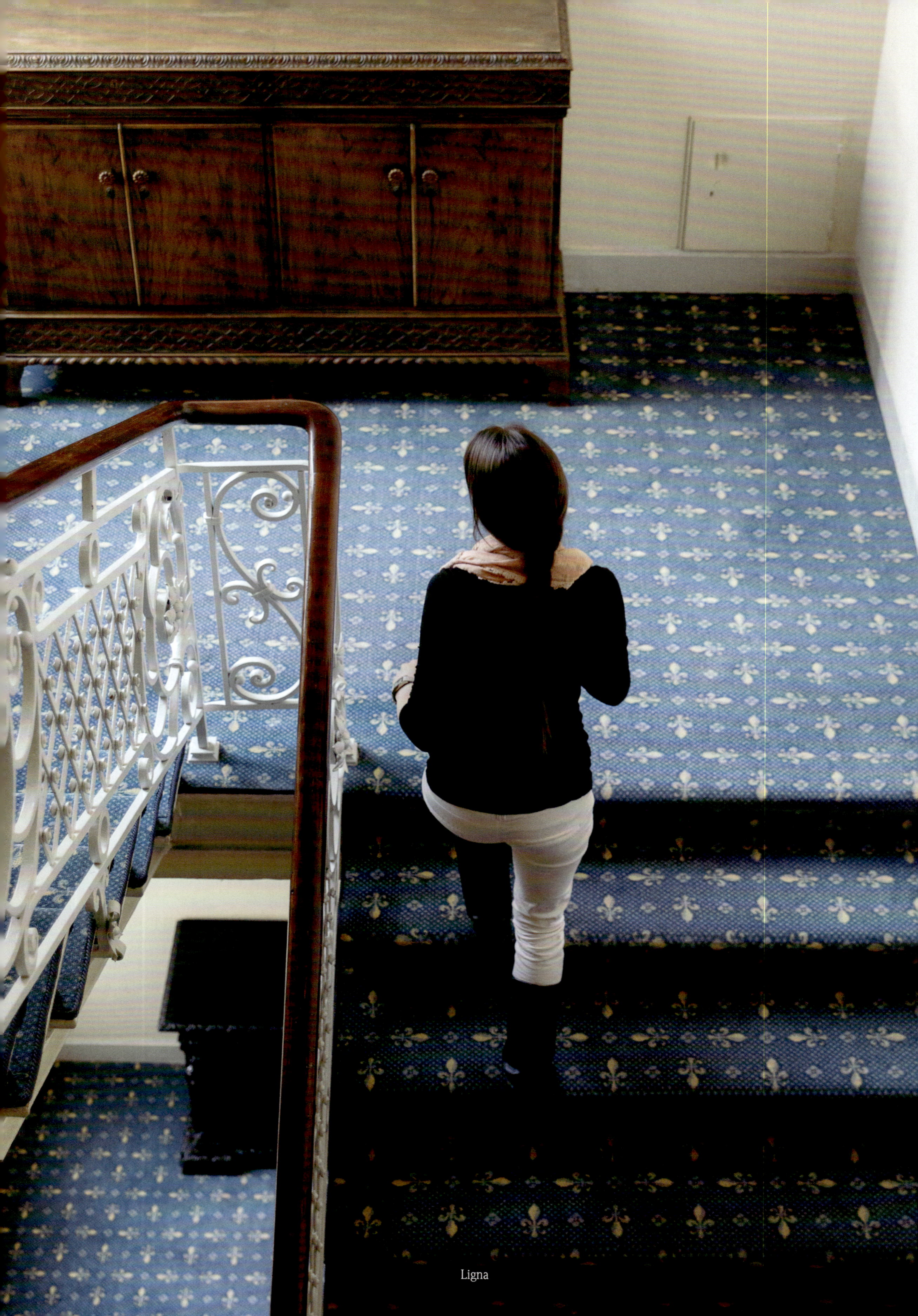

Ligna

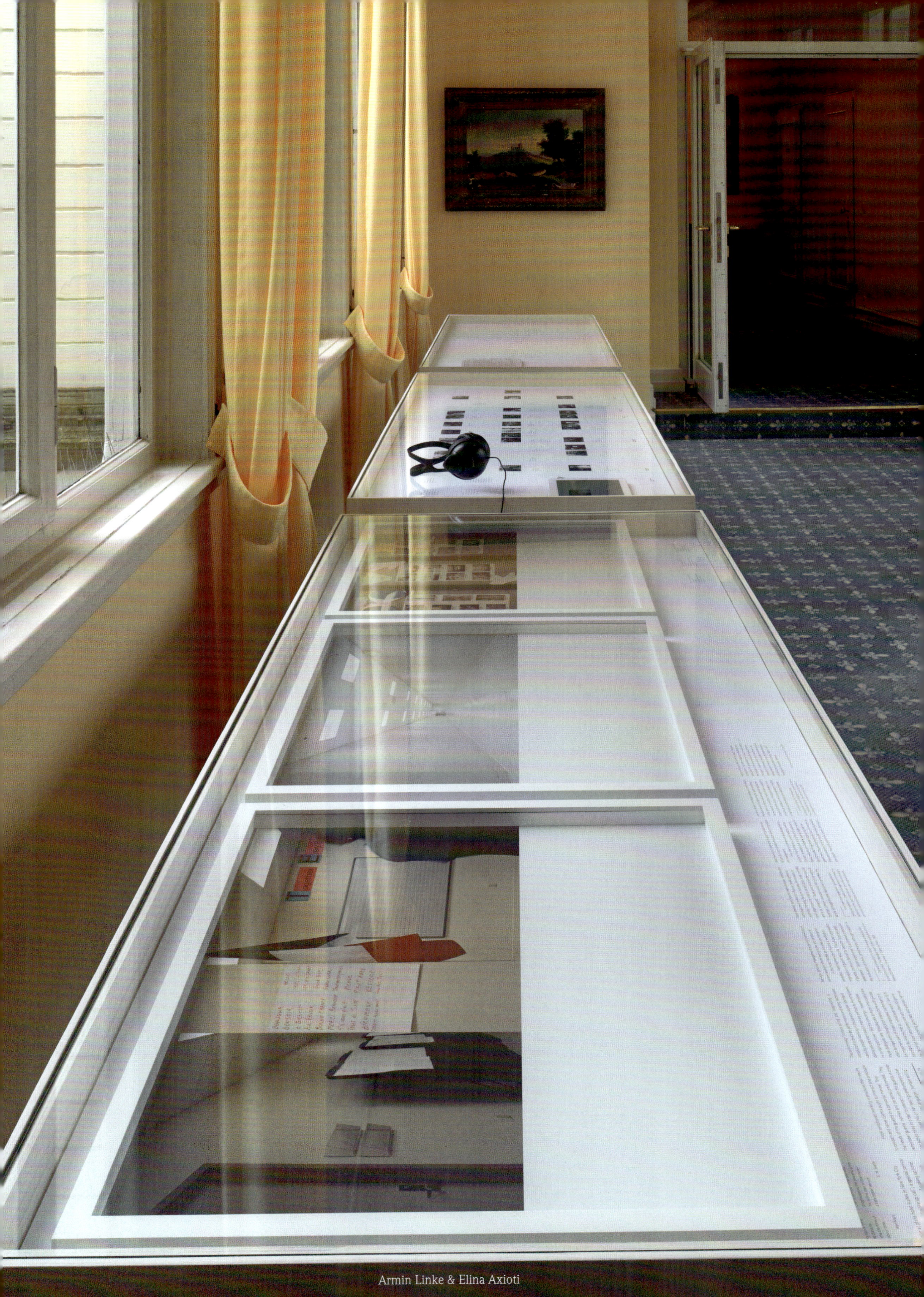

Armin Linke & Elina Axioti

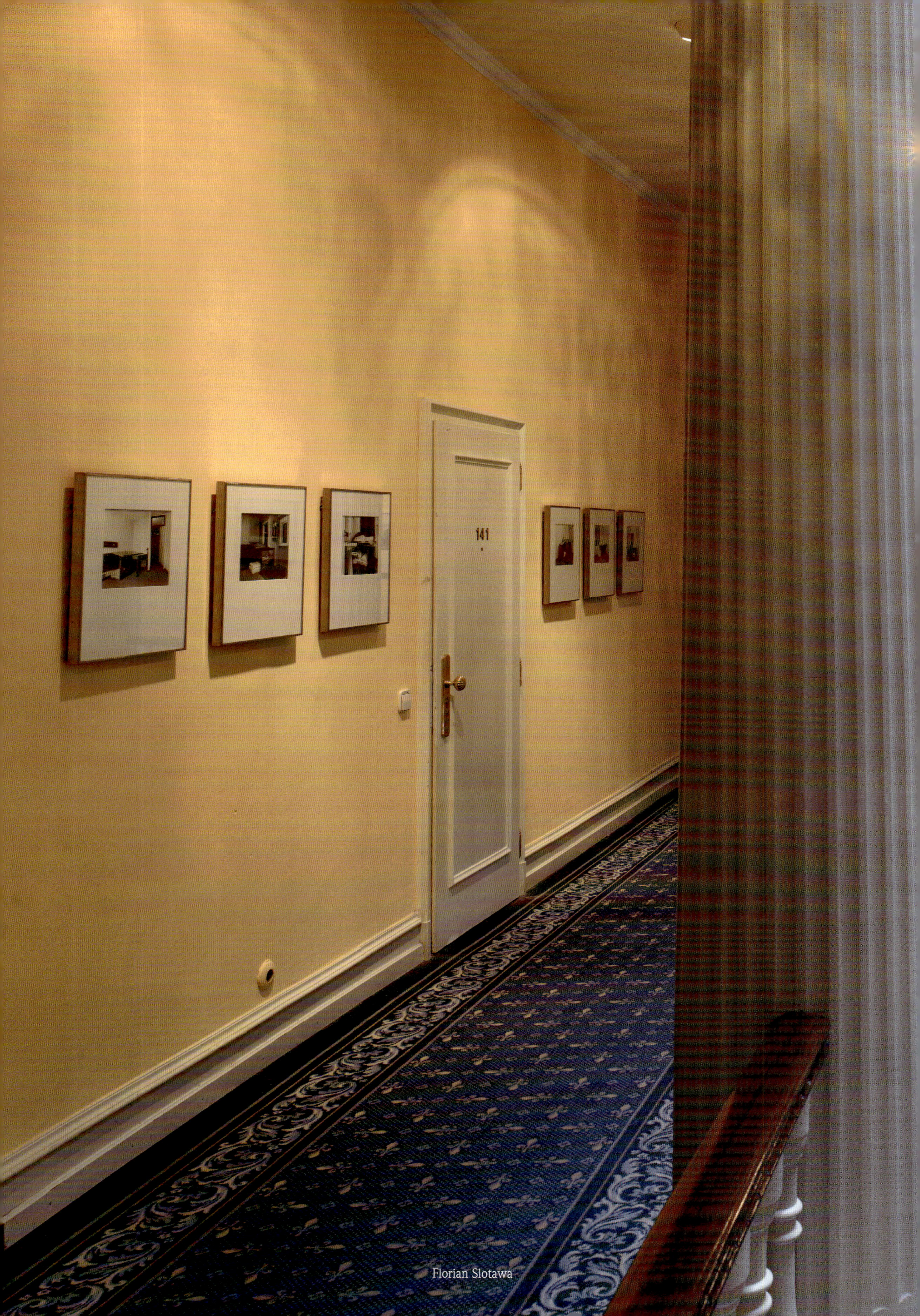

Florian Slotawa

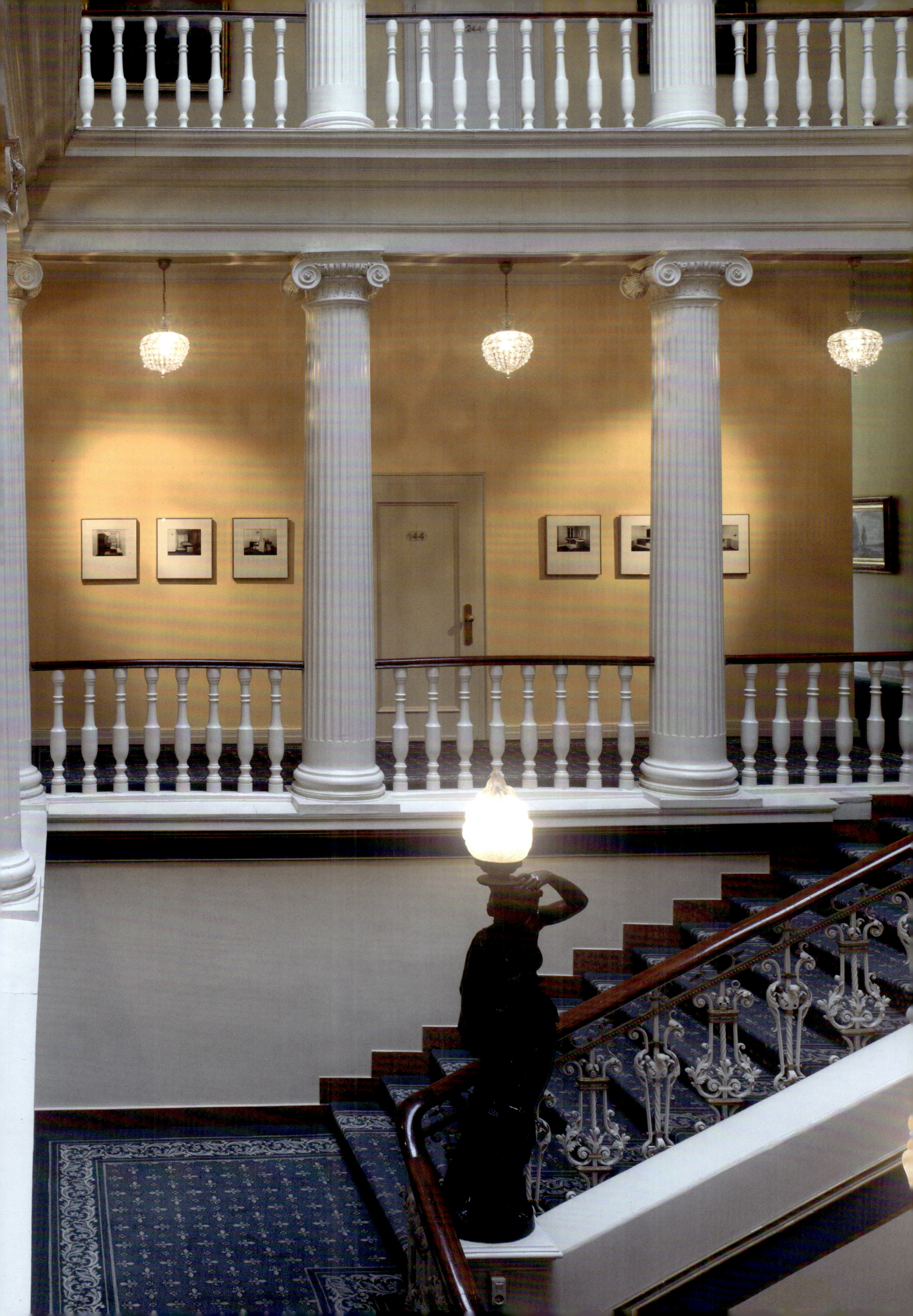
144

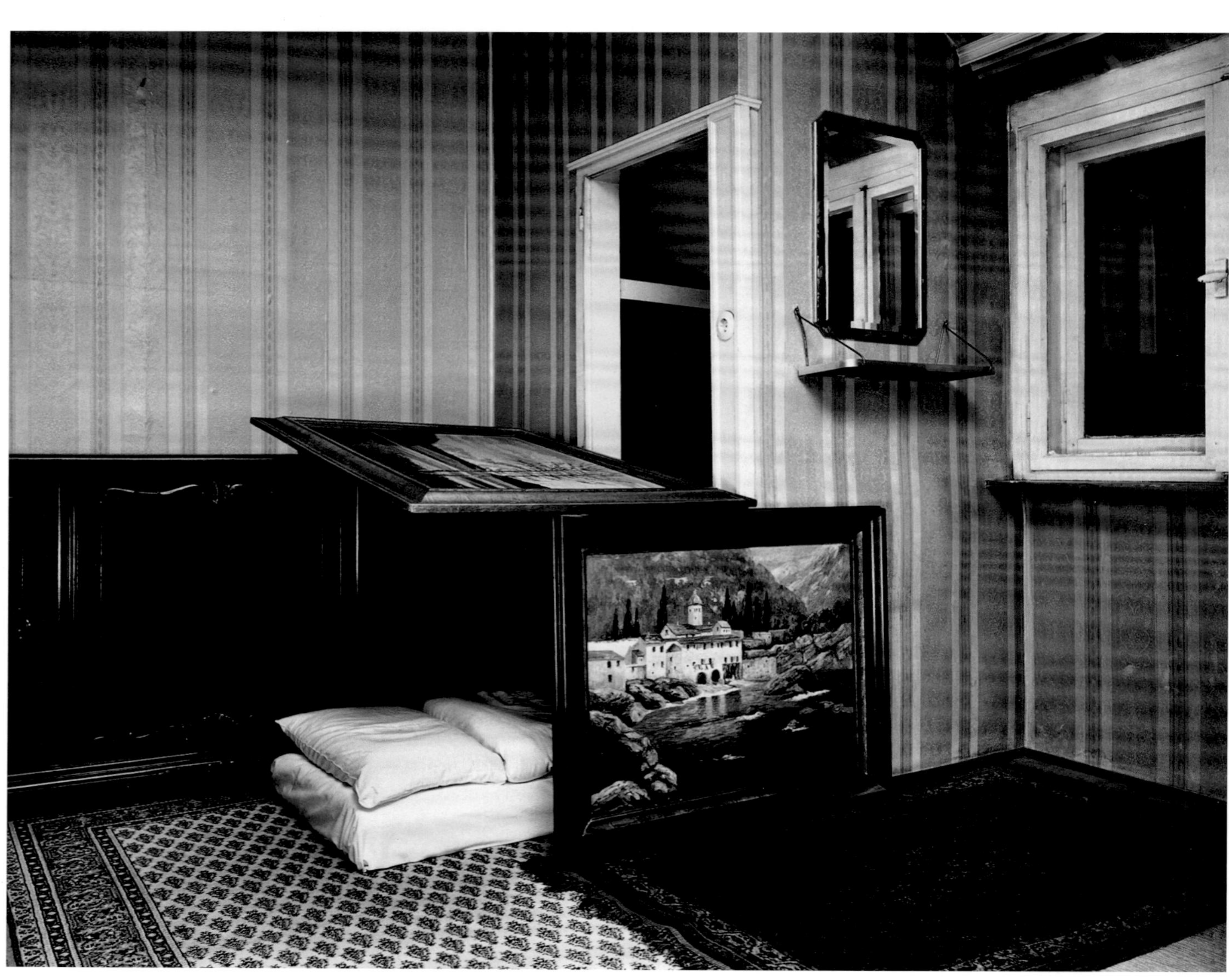

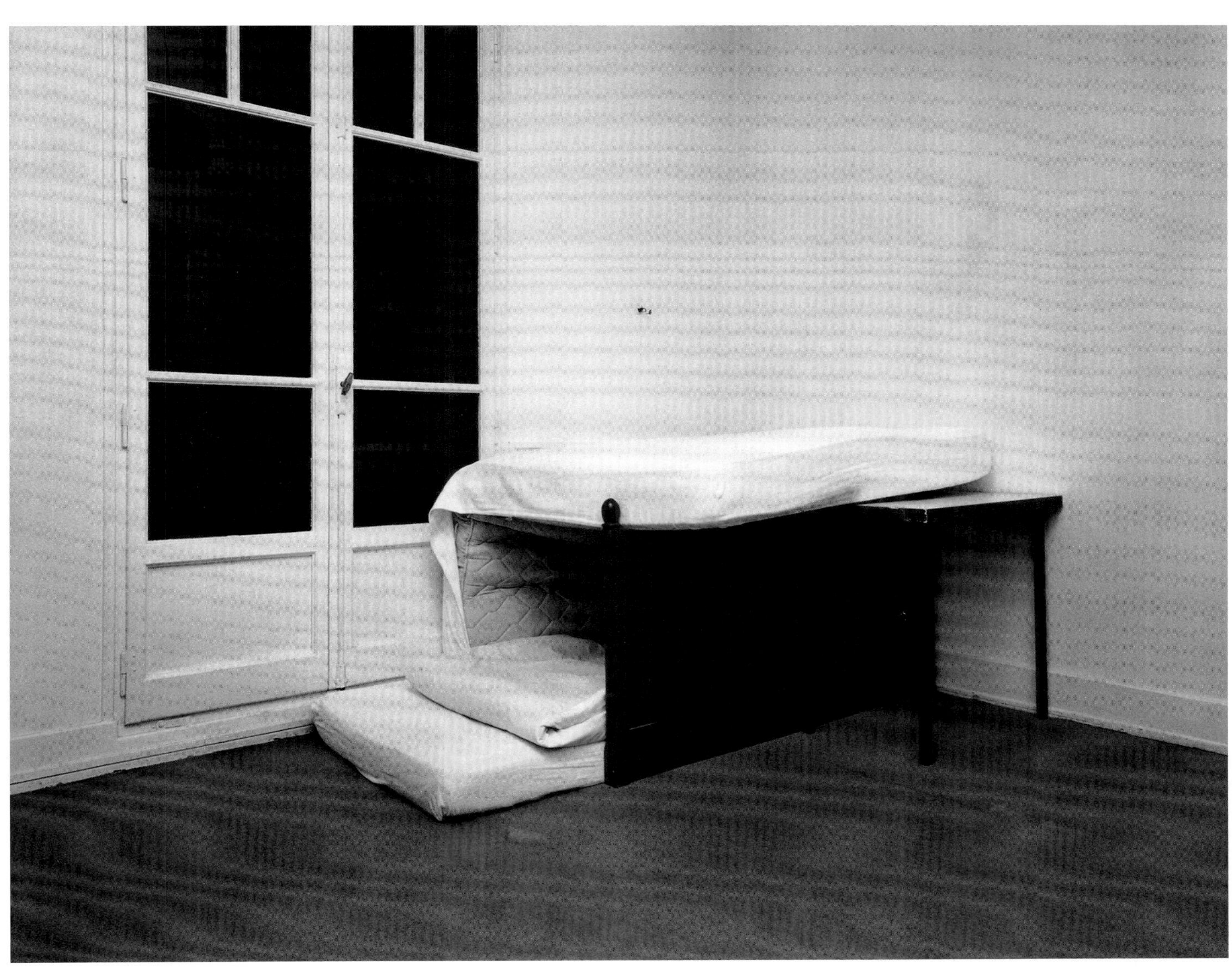

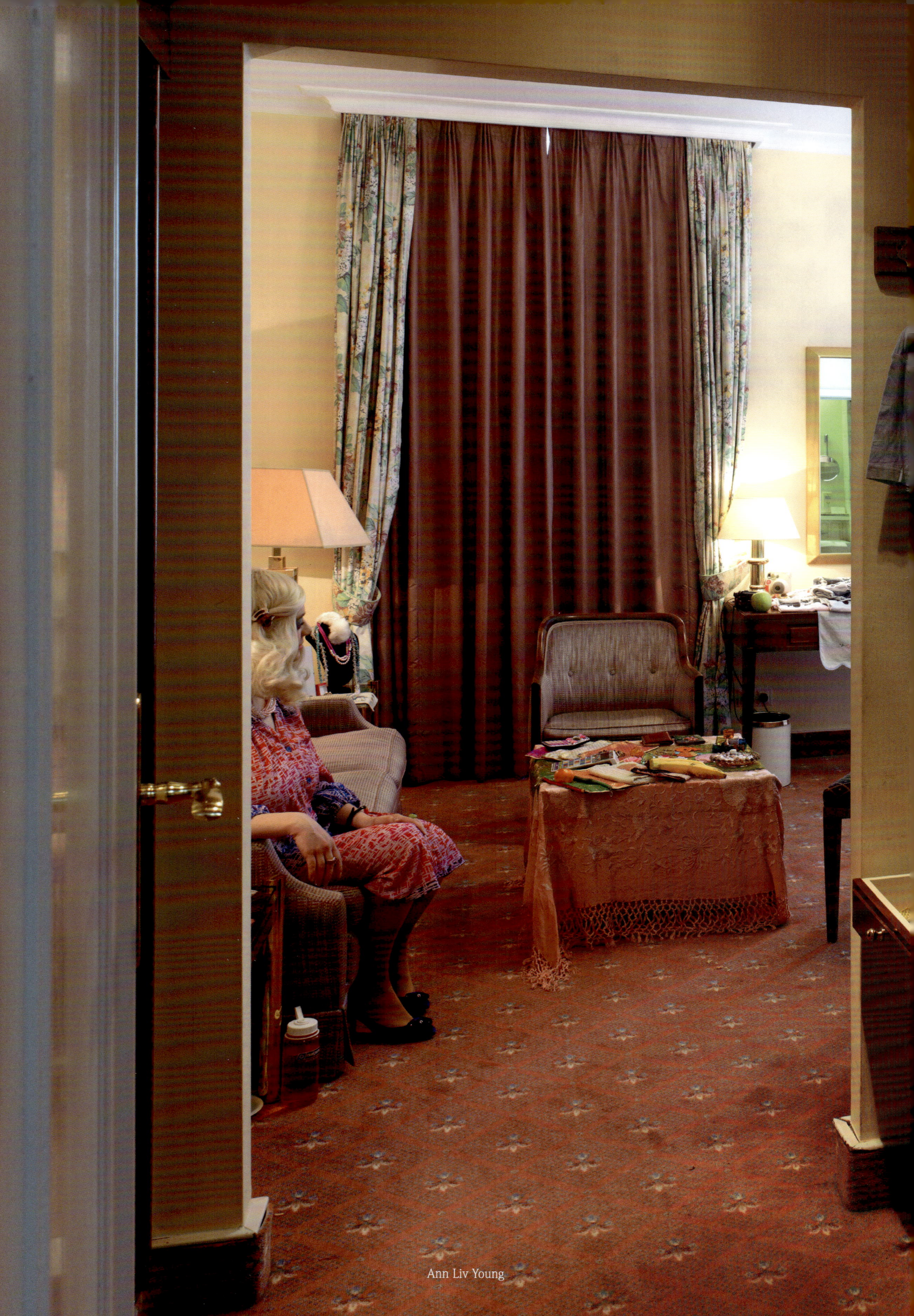

Ann Liv Young

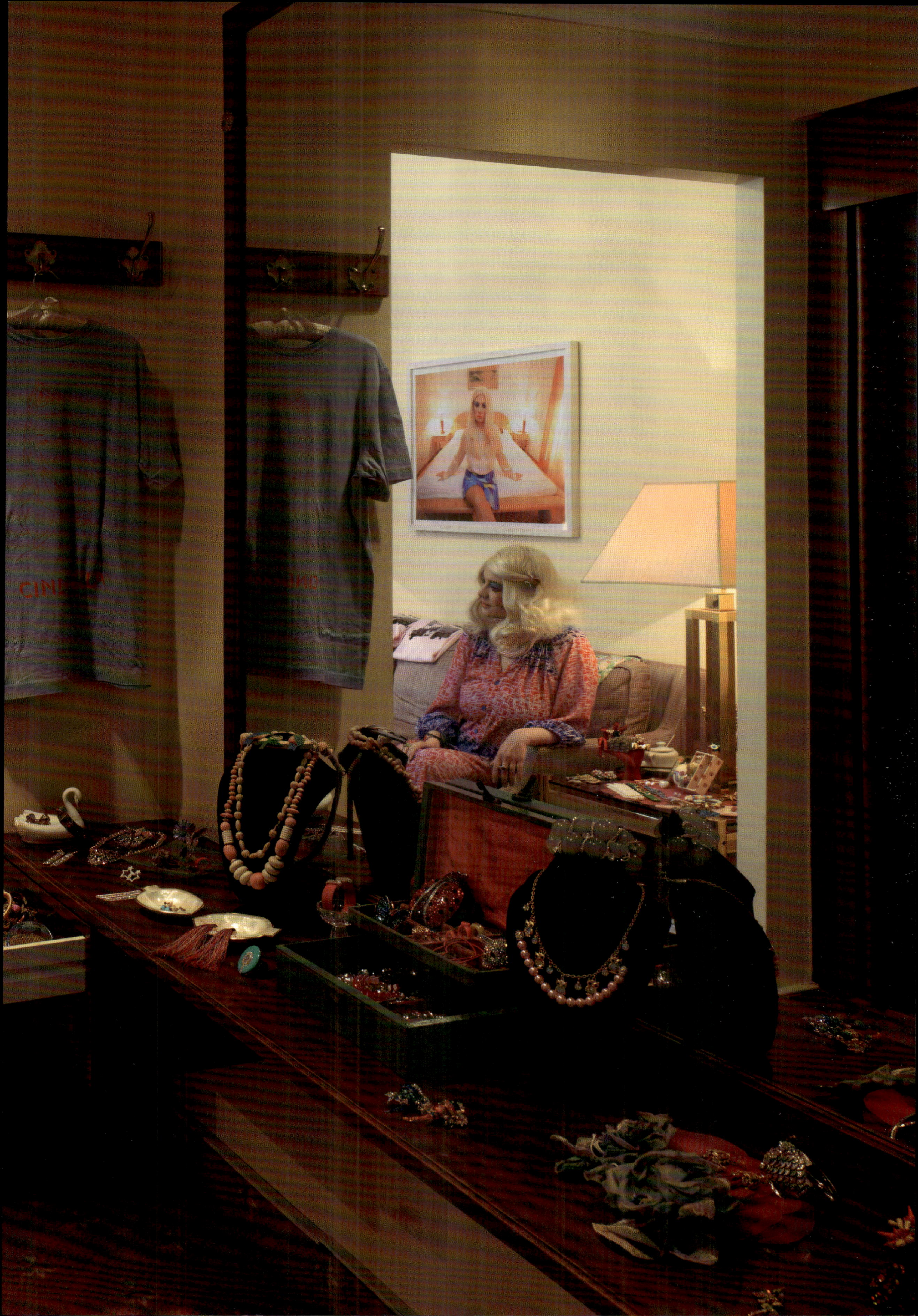

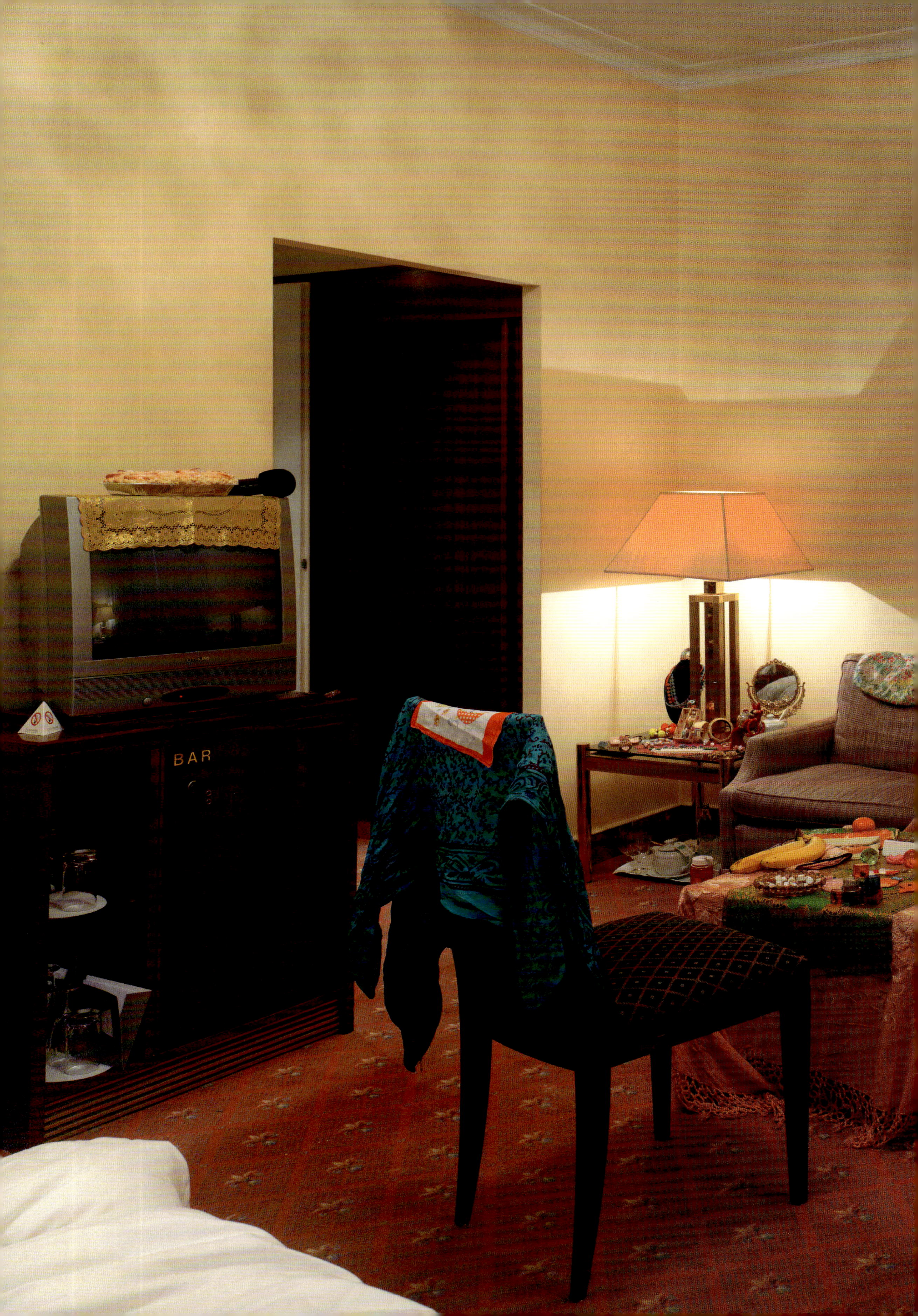
BAR

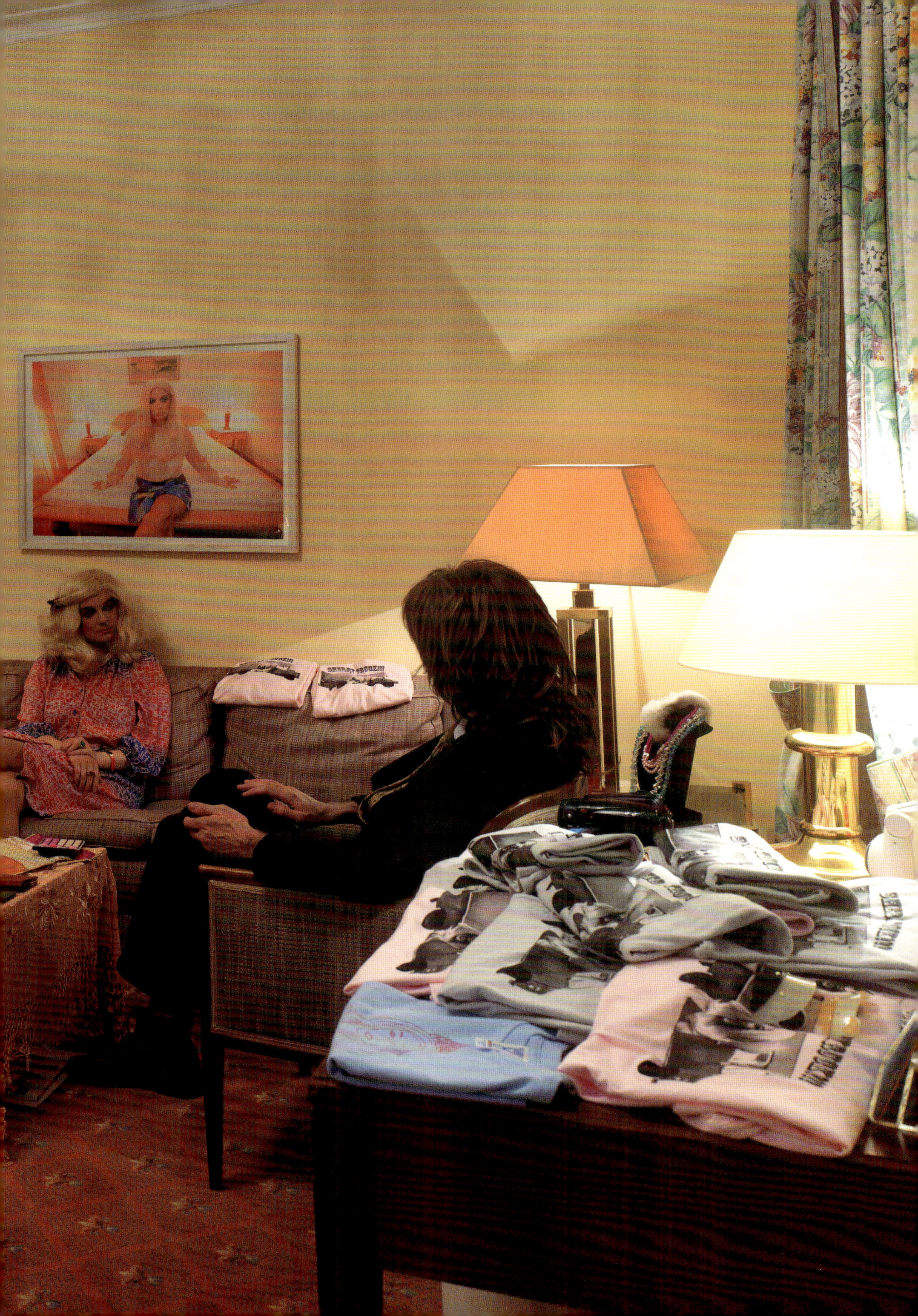

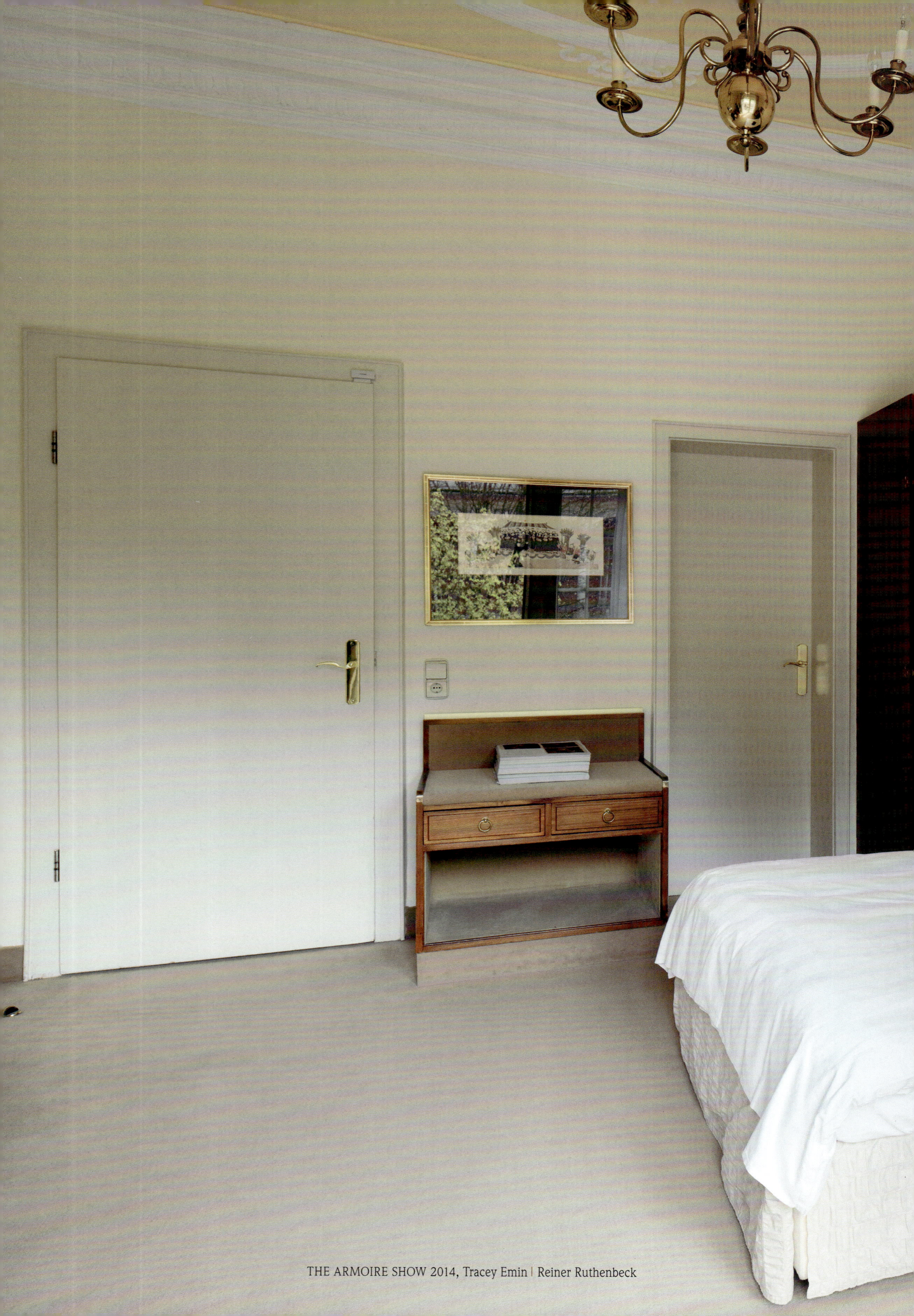

THE ARMOIRE SHOW 2014, Tracey Emin | Reiner Ruthenbeck

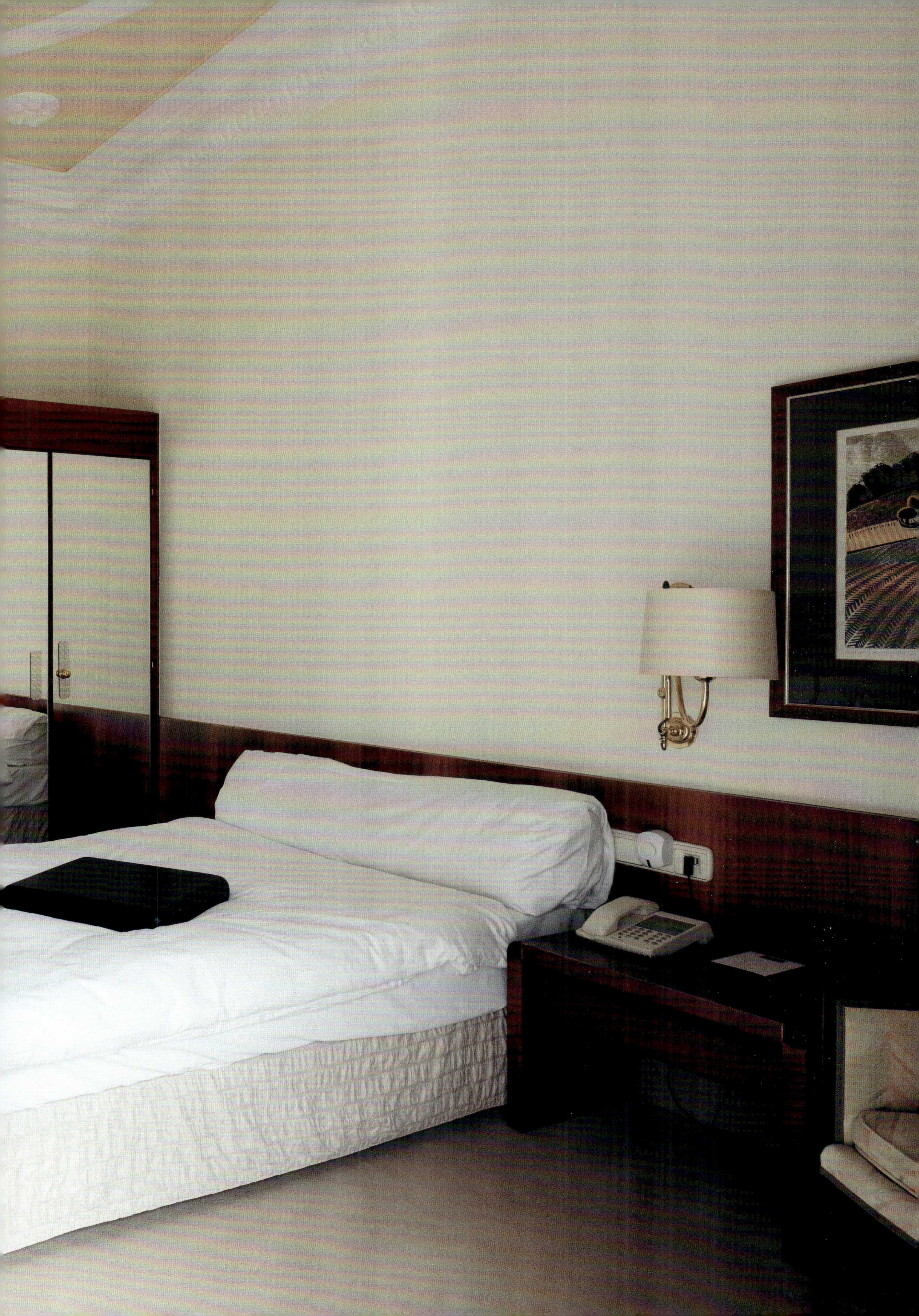

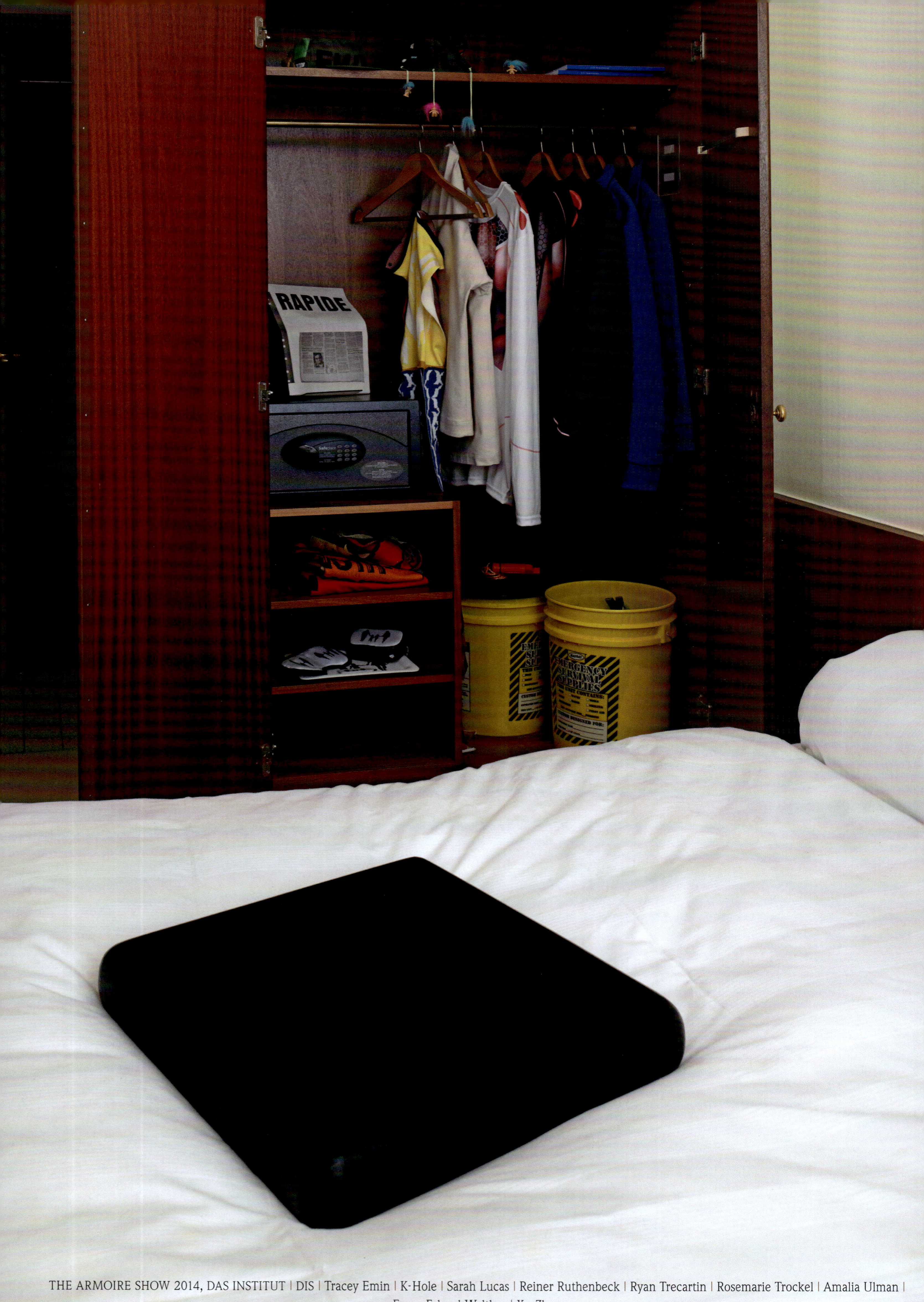

THE ARMOIRE SHOW 2014, DAS INSTITUT | DIS | Tracey Emin | K-Hole | Sarah Lucas | Reiner Ruthenbeck | Ryan Trecartin | Rosemarie Trockel | Amalia Ulman | Franz Erhard Walther | Xu Zhen

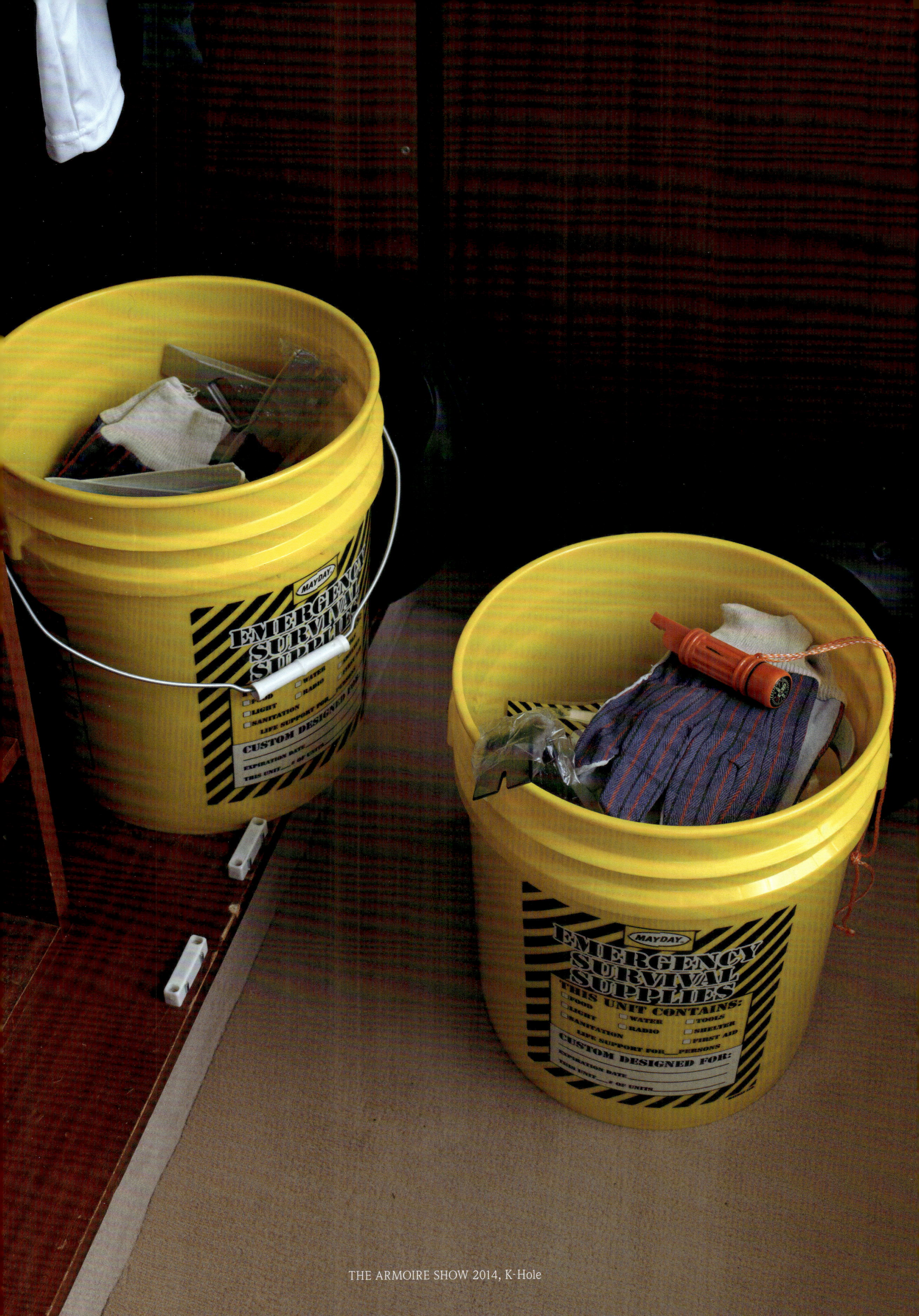

THE ARMOIRE SHOW 2014, K-Hole

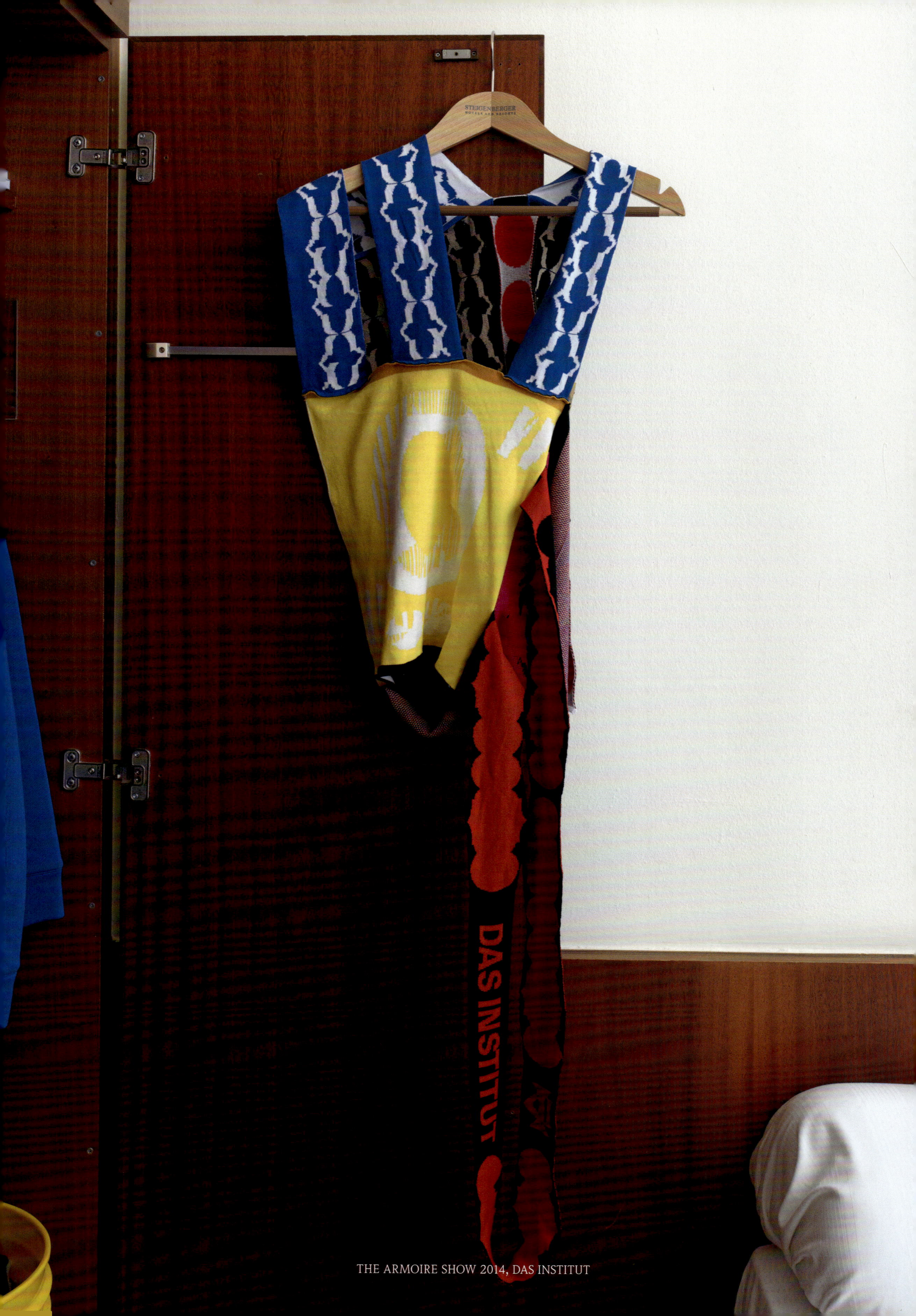

THE ARMOIRE SHOW 2014, DAS INSTITUT

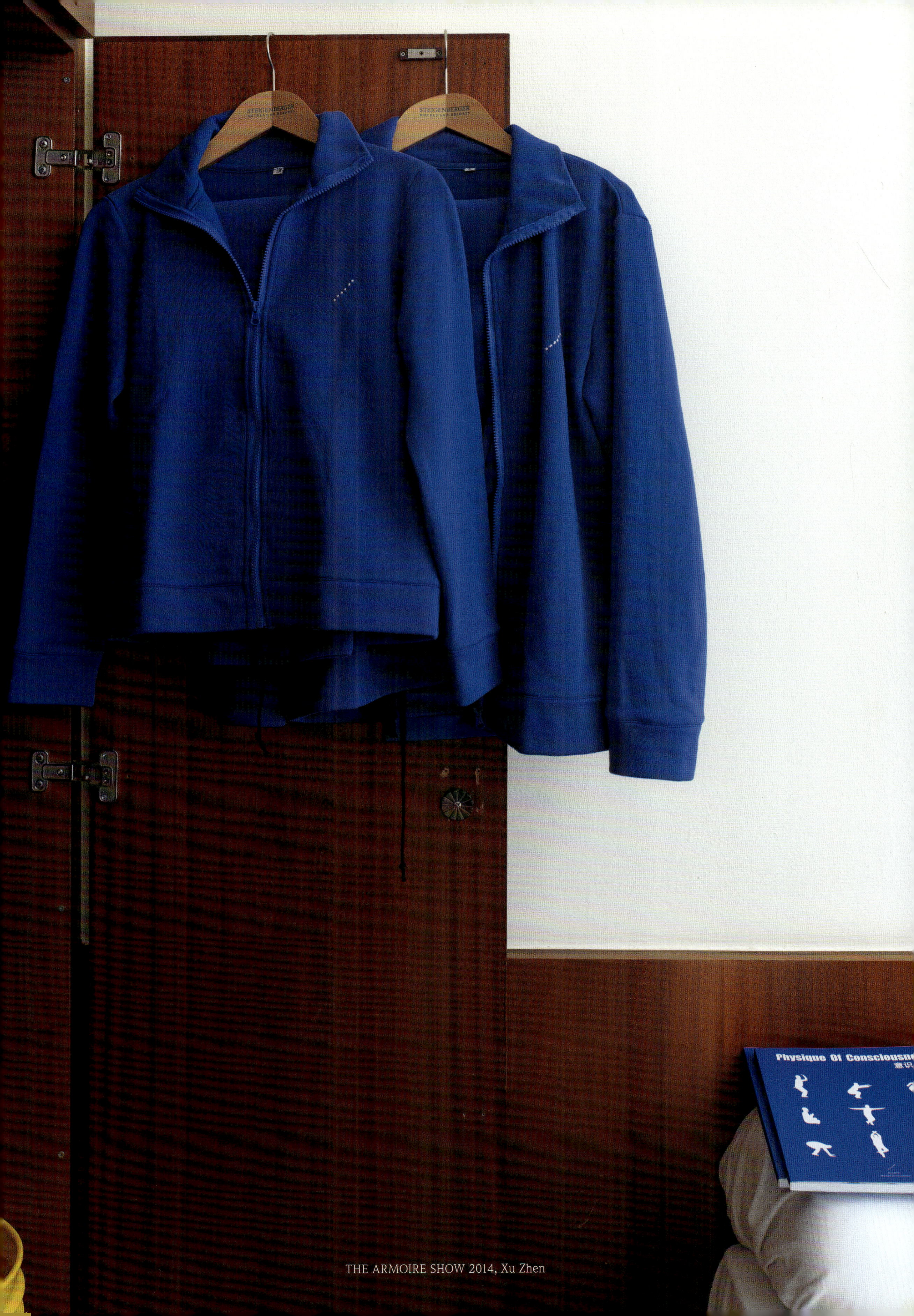

THE ARMOIRE SHOW 2014, Xu Zhen

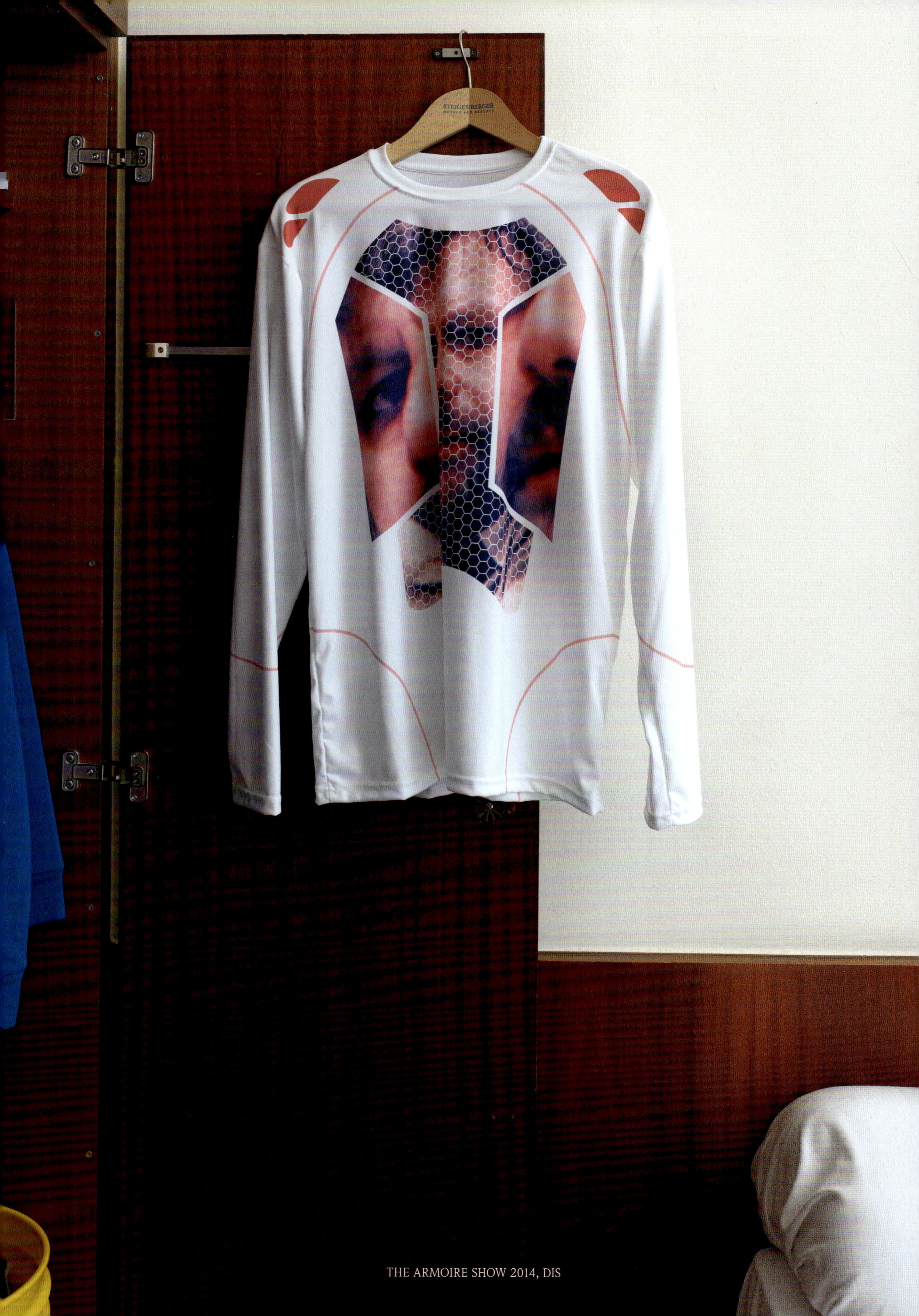

THE ARMOIRE SHOW 2014, DIS

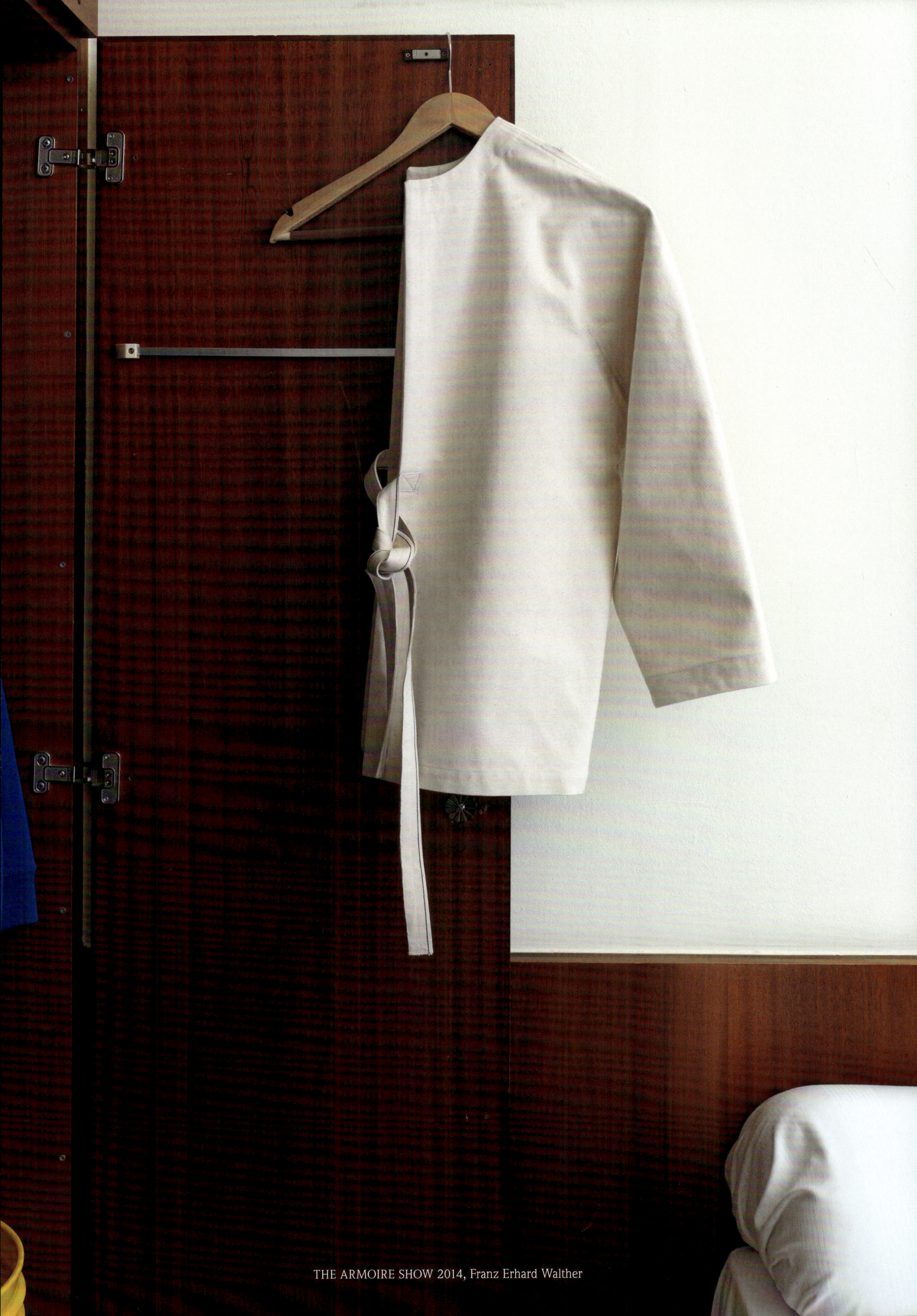

THE ARMOIRE SHOW 2014, Franz Erhard Walther

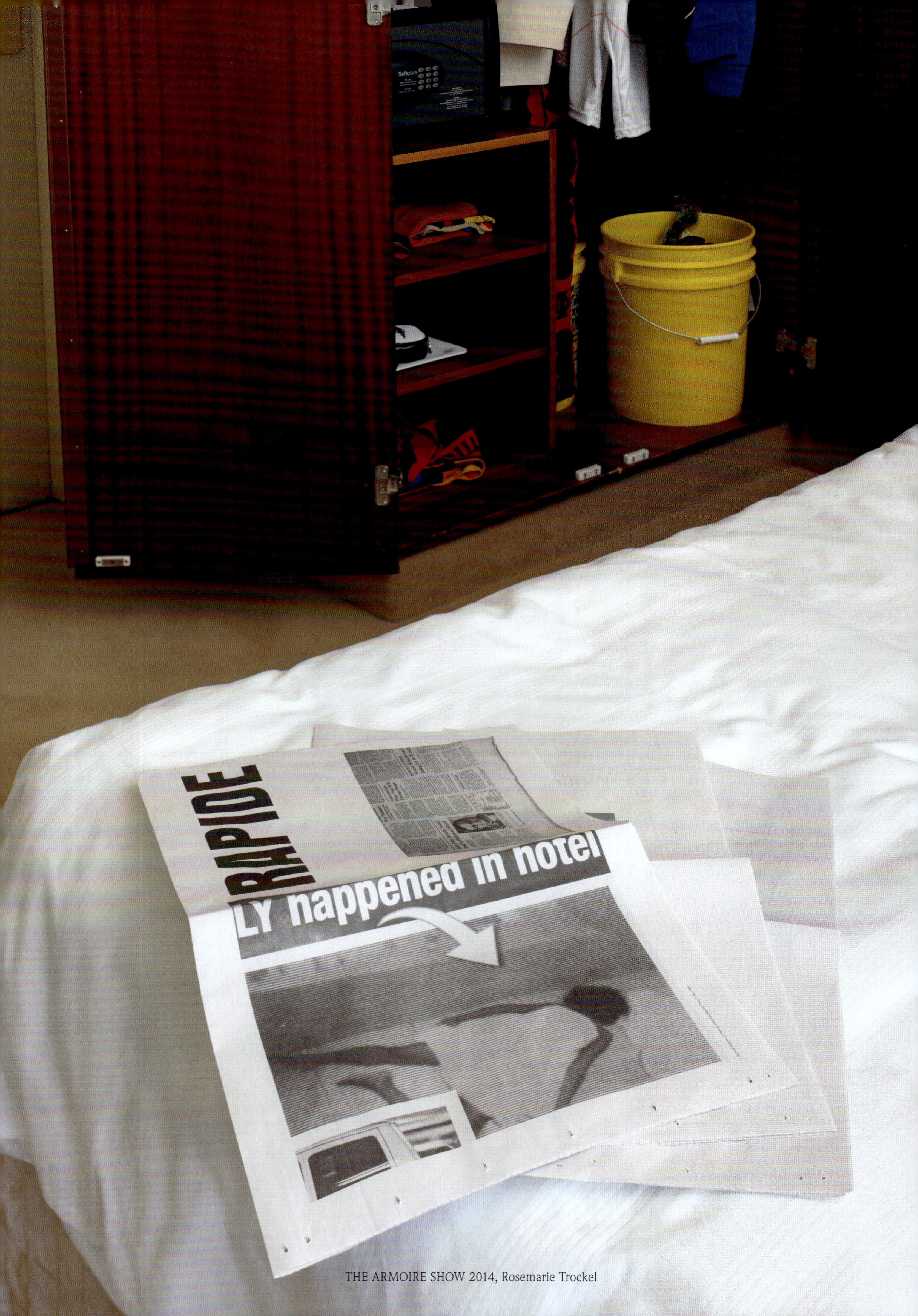

THE ARMOIRE SHOW 2014, Rosemarie Trockel

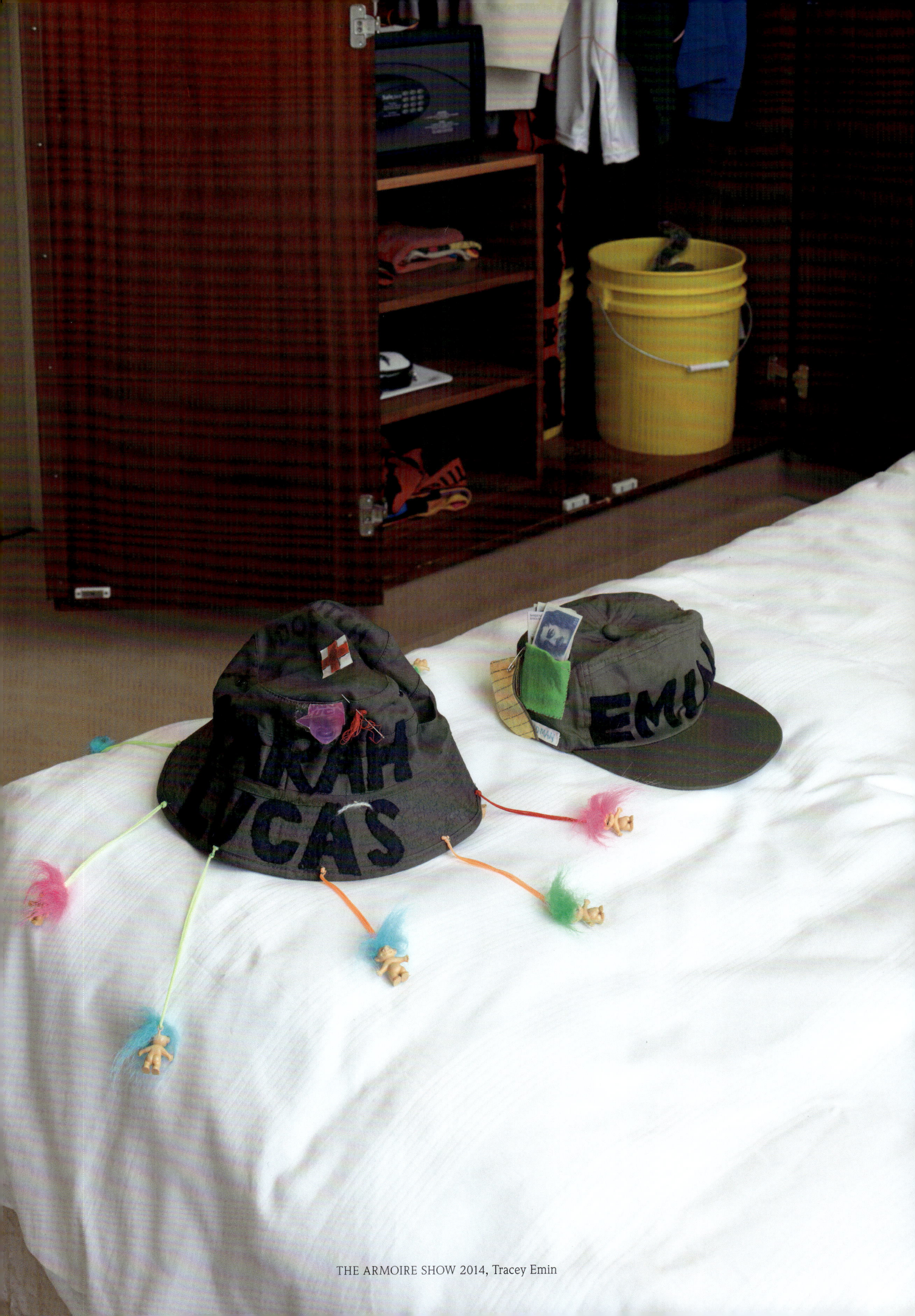

THE ARMOIRE SHOW 2014, Tracey Emin

AUSSTELLUNG / EXHIBITION

PERFORMANCE HOTEL

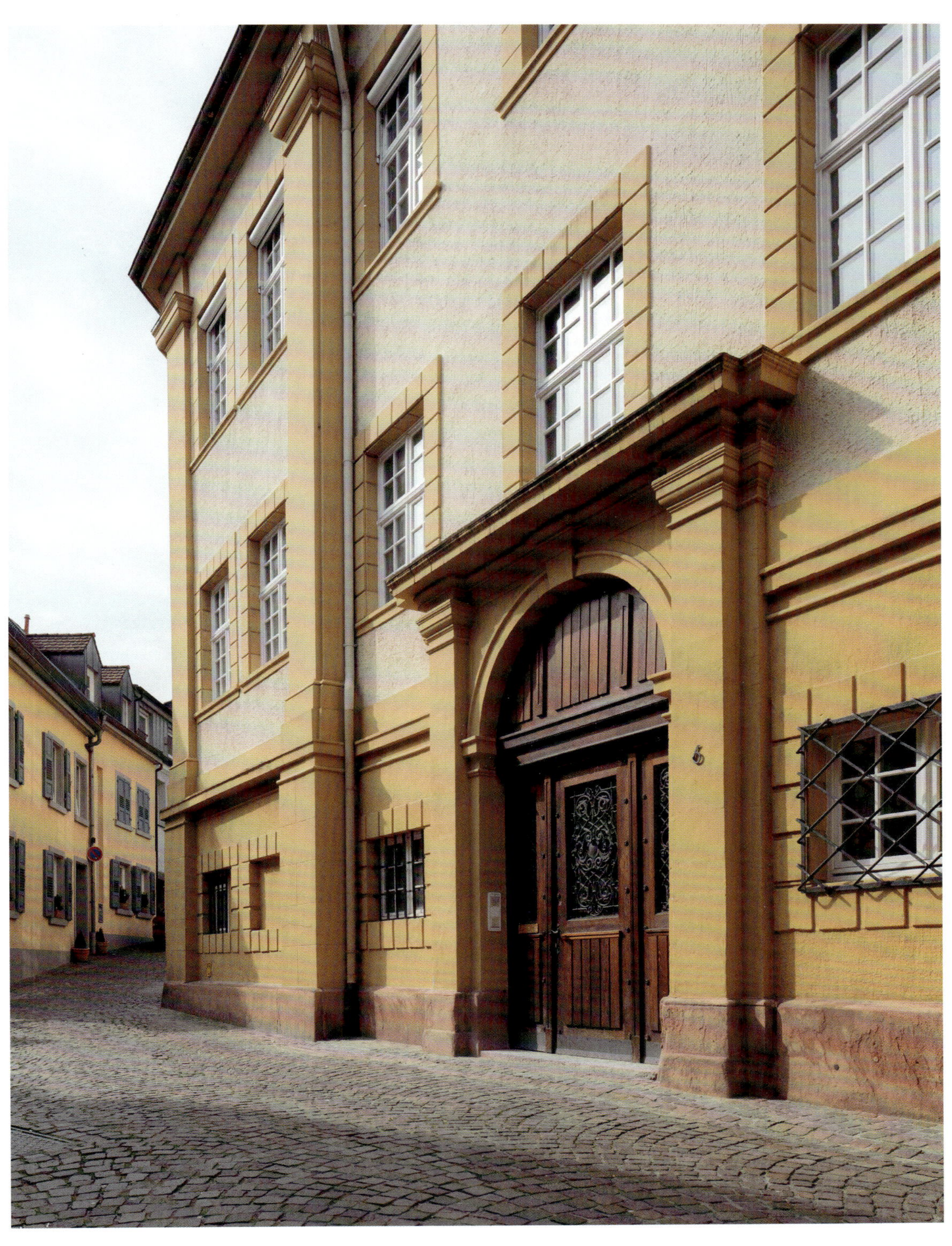

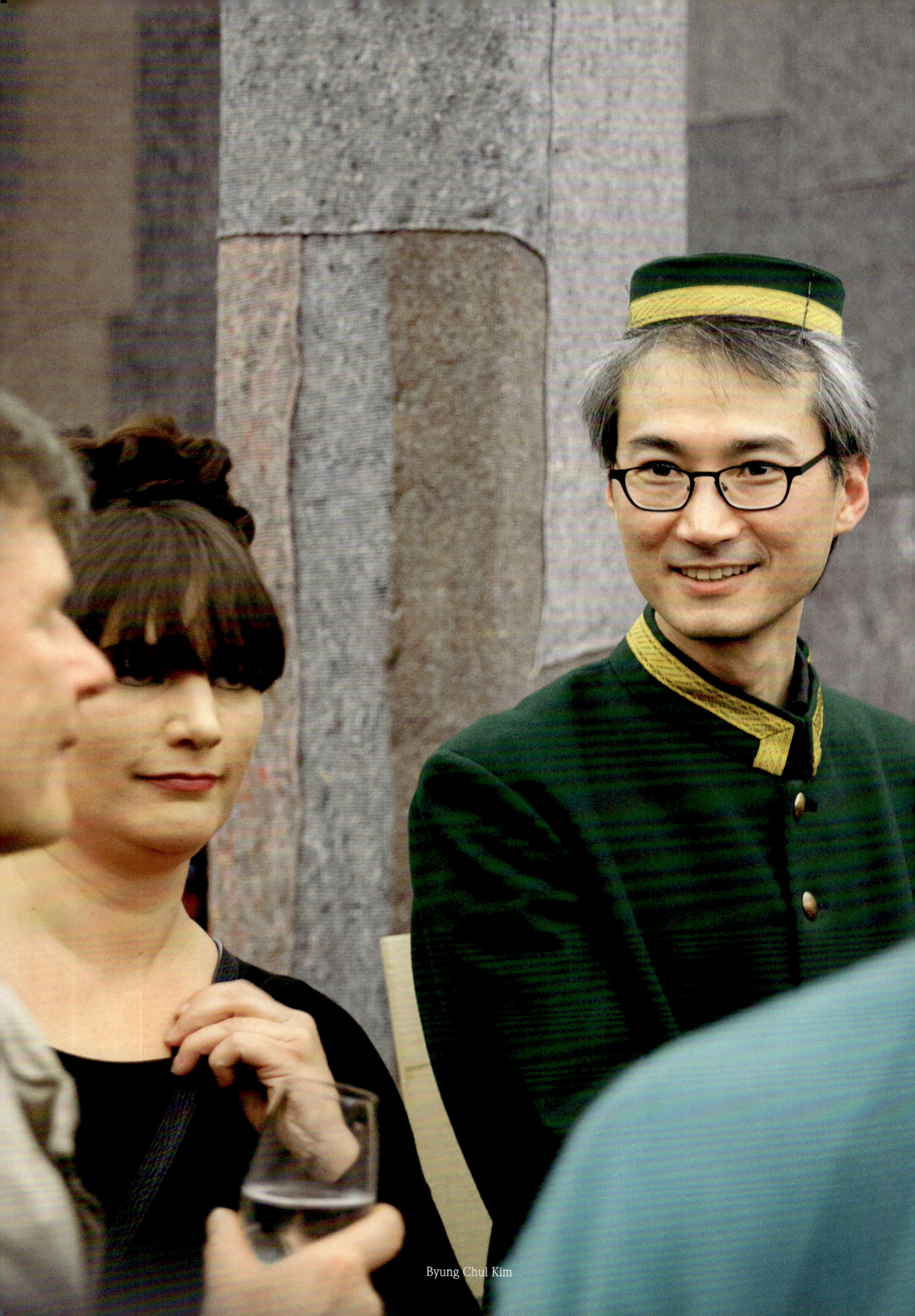

Byung Chul Kim

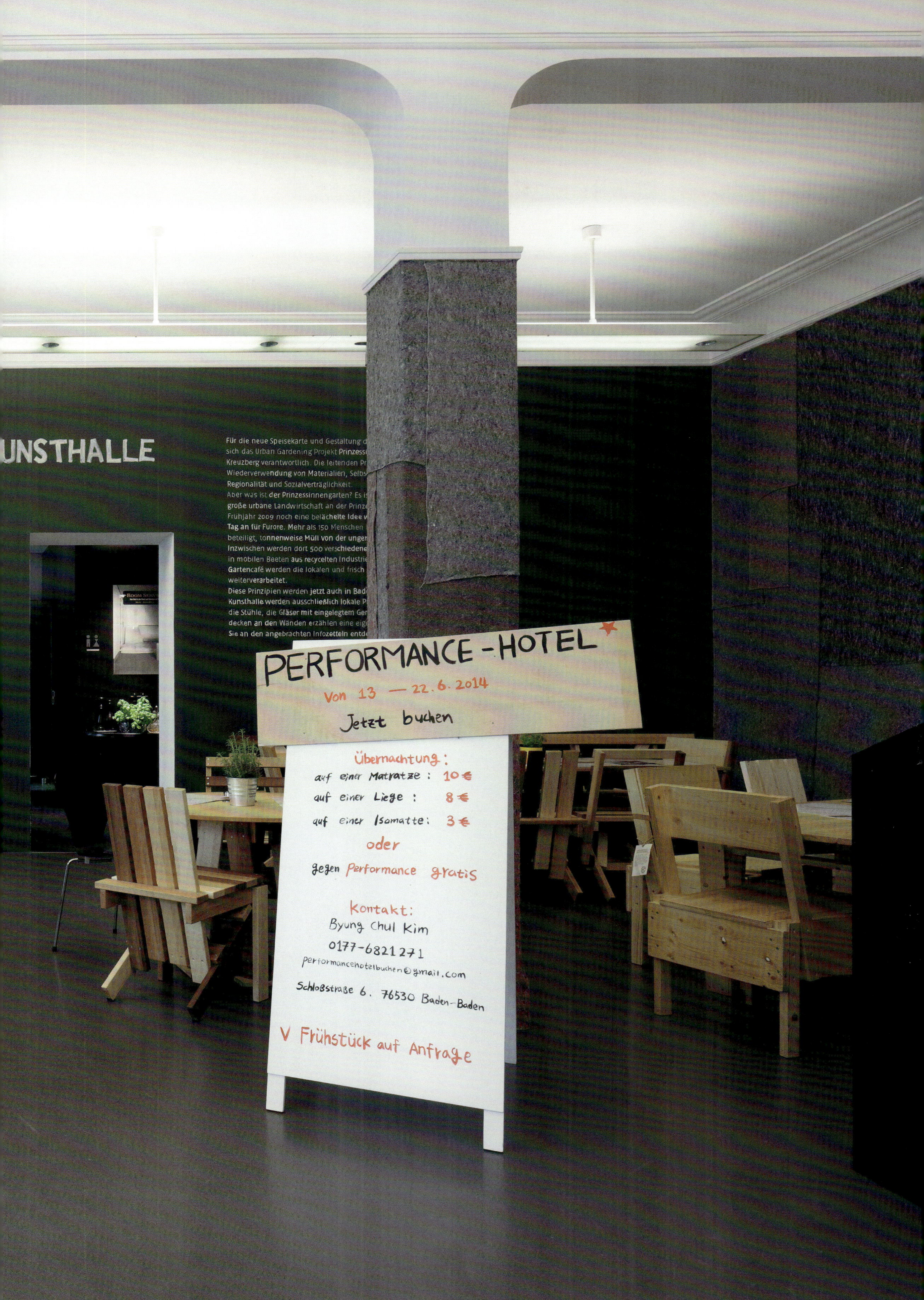
UNSTHALLE
Für die neue Speisekarte und Gestaltung
sich das Urban Gardening Projekt
Kreuzberg verantwortlich. Die leitenden
Wiederverwendung von Materialien,
Regionalität und Sozialverträglichkeit.
Aber was ist der Prinzessinnengarten?
große urbane Landwirtschaft an der
Frühjahr 2009 noch eine belächelte Idee
Tag an für Furore. Mehr als 150 Menschen
beteiligt, tonnenweise Müll von der
Inzwischen werden dort 500
in mobilen Beeten aus recycelten
Gartencafé werden die lokalen und frisch
weiterverarbeitet.
Diese Prinzipien werden jetzt auch in
Kunsthalle werden ausschließlich lokale
die Stühle, die Gläser mit eingelegtem
decken an den Wänden erzählen eine
Sie an den angebrachten Infozetteln
PERFORMANCE-HOTEL
Von 13 — 22.6.2014
Jetzt buchen
Übernachtung:
auf einer Matratze: 10 €
auf einer Liege: 8 €
auf einer Isomatte: 3 €
oder
gegen Performance gratis
Kontakt:
Byung Chul Kim
0177-6821271
performancehotelbuchen@gmail.com
Schloßstraße 6. 76530 Baden-Baden
V Frühstück auf Anfrage

AUSSTELLUNG / EXHIBITION
RADISSON BLU BADISCHER HOF

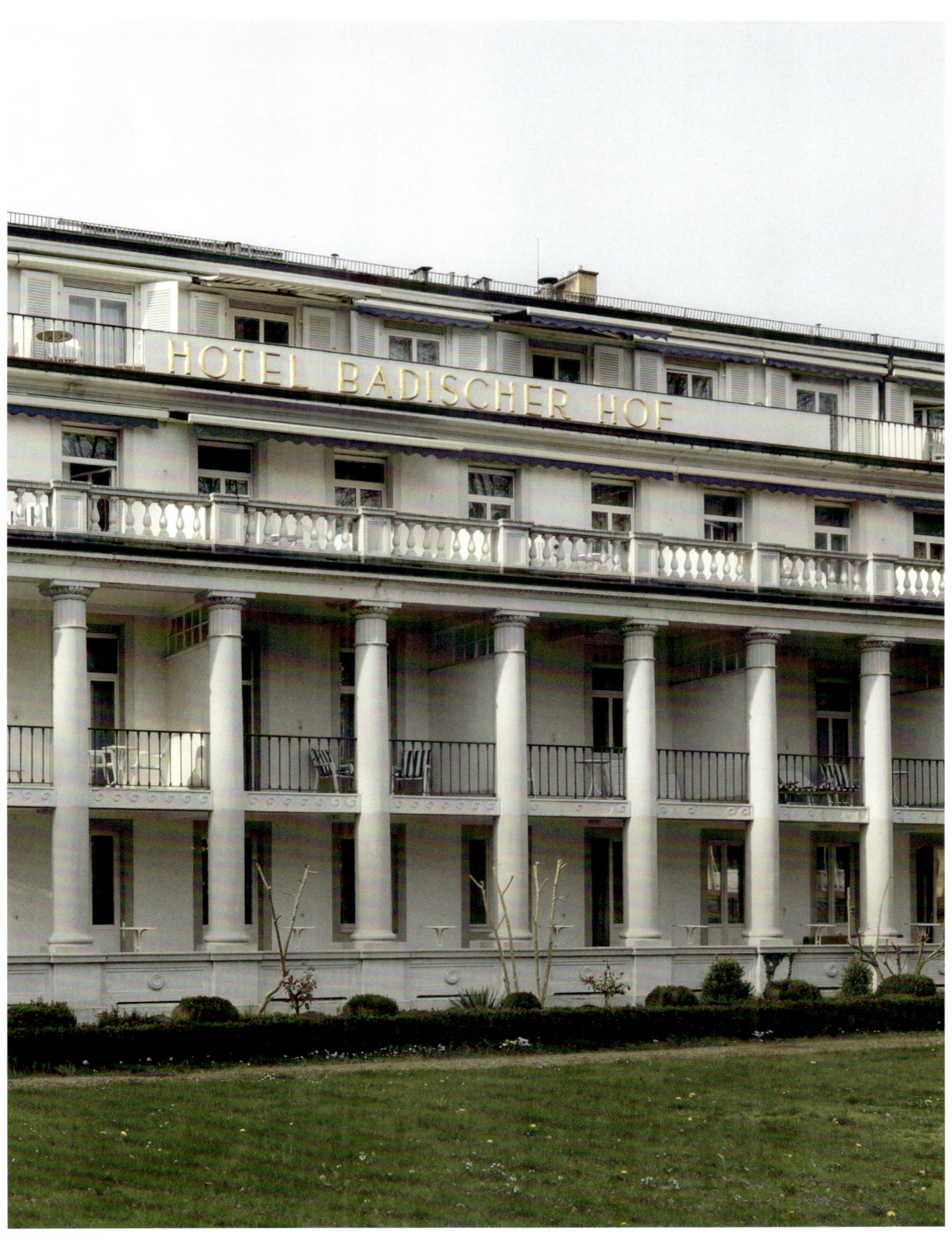

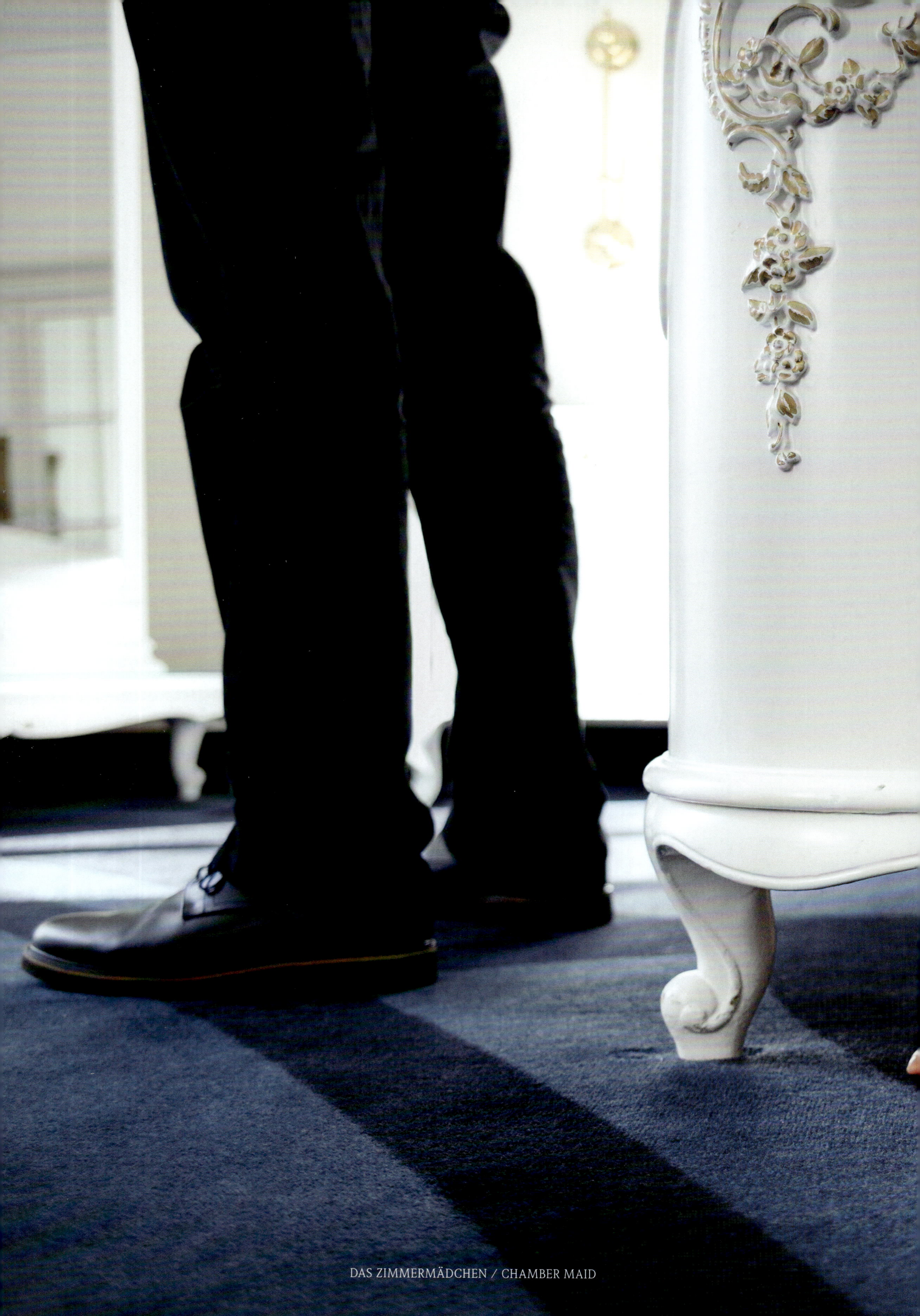

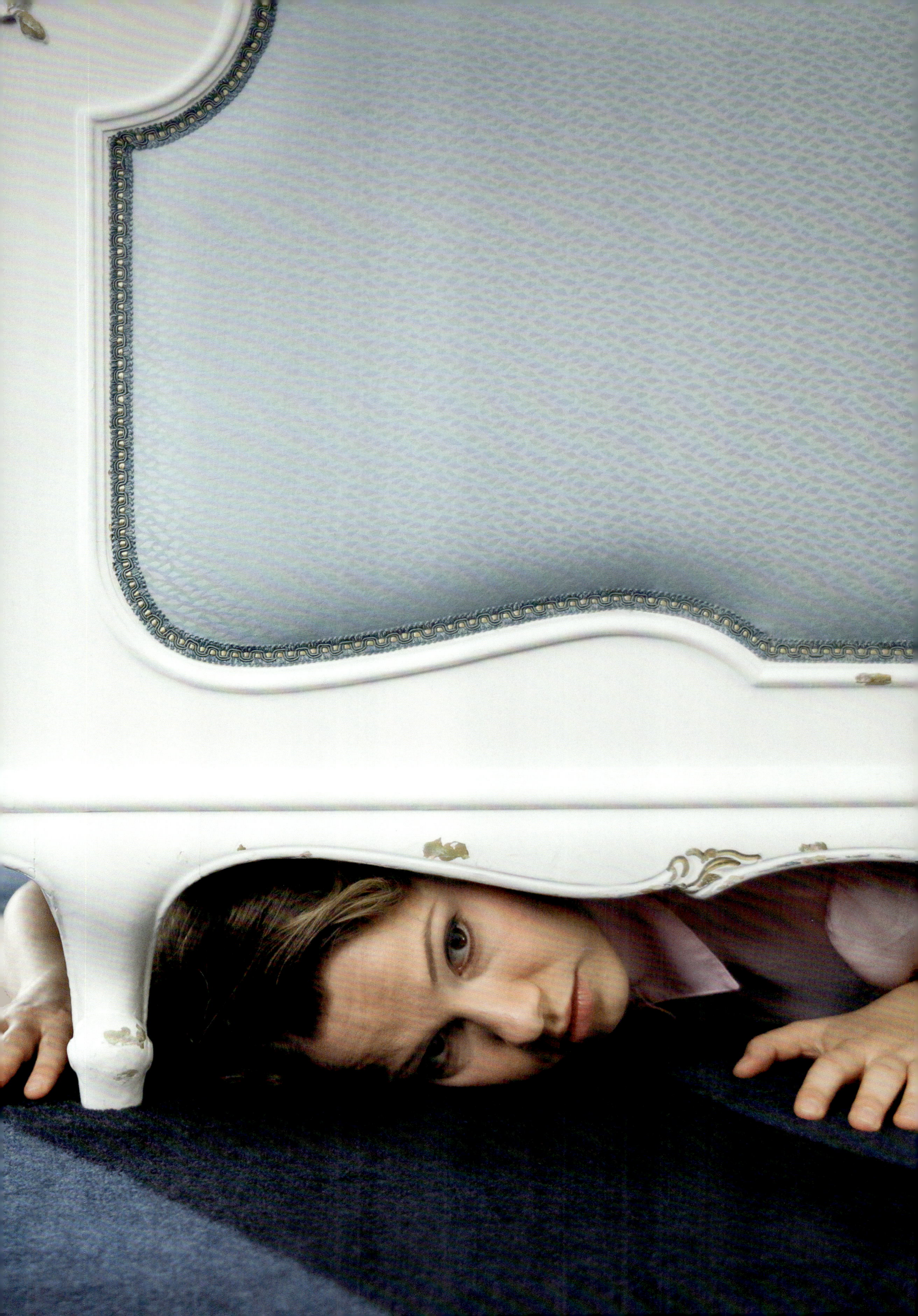

CHRISTIAN ANDERSSON

ATLANTIC 215 (PALACE 415)

2014, Performance mit verschiedenen Materialien / Performance with various materials

Die Installation ATLANTIC 215 (PALACE 415) des Schweden Christian Andersson lässt den Besucher zum aktiven Teil einer Performance werden. Der Künstler überrascht das Publikum bereits beim Anklopfen und bei dem Versuch, in das Hotelzimmer einzutreten, das im gegebenen Fall vermeintlich als Ausstellungszimmer dient. Die Tür wird von einem Schauspieler mit dem Satz geöffnet: »Ja, Sie sind richtig hier; das ist die Installation von Christian Andersson.« Eine weitere Besichtigung des Raums wird dem Besucher allerdings verwehrt, indem er an der Tür in ein Gespräch verwickelt wird, beziehungsweise wird er Ohrenzeuge eines Monologs über die Rolle und den Aufenthalt des Schauspielers im Hotelzimmer.

Dieser Monolog beschreibt für Andersson ein Muster des typischen Hotelgastes, der entspannt in seinem Zimmer sitzt und während der ganzen Performance ein Glas Whisky in der Hand schwenkt. Der Besucher wird ein weiteres Mal überrascht, wenn der Gastgeber dann durch das Klingeln eines Telefons im Inneren des Raumes in gespielte Panik verfällt und hastig die Zimmertür zuschlägt – damit ist die Performance beendet.

Diese Aktion spielt einerseits mit den Erwartungen des Ausstellungsbesuchers, der ein Kunstwerk besichtigen möchte, und konfrontiert sie gleichzeitig mit den Erwartungen eines Hotelgastes, der von dem agierenden Schauspieler verkörpert wird.

Der 1973 in Stockholm geborene Künstler Christian Andersson hinterfragt in seinen Werken immer wieder allgemein akzeptierte Konzepte von Geschichte und Kunst. Andersson präsentierte eine Abwandlung dieser eigenwilligen Performance-Installation schon im Jahr 2000 im Palace Hotel Copenhagen in dessen Zimmer 415. Nun konnte man seine lebendige *Loop-Skulptur* im Zimmer 215 des Atlantic Parkhotels in Baden-Baden erleben.

The installation ATLANTIC 215 (PALACE 415) by Swedish artist Christian Andersson allows viewers to become an active participant in a performance. The artist surprises the viewers from the very start, when they knock on the door and try to enter a hotel room that supposedly serves as an exhibition space. The door is opened by an actor who greets them by saying, »Yes, you are in the right place. This is the installation by Christian Andersson.« However, visitors are then hindered from entering the room to take a look and are instead caught up in a conversation at the door, which actually takes the form of a monologue on the actor's role and time in the hotel room.

For Andersson the monologue describes a pattern characterizing the typical hotel guest, who relaxes in a chair in his room and swirls a whiskey glass in his hand throughout the entire performance. Visitors are then surprised again, when the ringing of the telephone from within the room causes the host to fall into a feigned panic and quickly shut the door—thus ending the performance.

On the one hand, the performance plays with the expectations of exhibition visitors, who are planning to look at a work of art. On the other, it confronts them with the expectations of a hotel guest, a role played by an actor. Born in 1973 in Stockholm, the artist Christian Andersson consistently questions generally accepted notions of history and art in his work. Andersson already presented a version of this unique performance installation in 2000 in Room 415 of the Palace Hotel Copenhagen. His live *Loop-Skulptur* (Loop Sculpture) can once again be experienced in Room 215 of Baden-Baden's Atlantic Parkhotel.

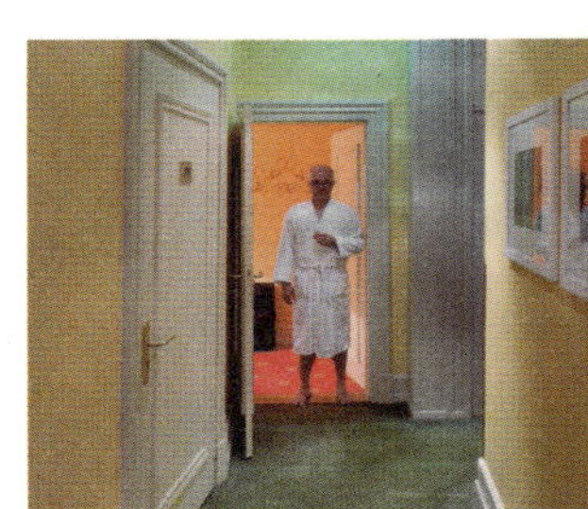

BÜCHER- UND FILMARCHIV ZUR AUSSTELLUNG
BOOK AND FILM ARCHIVE ACCOMPANYING THE EXHIBITION

2014

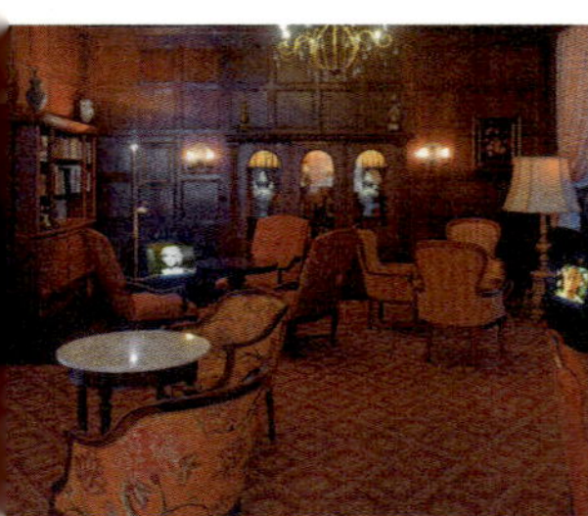

Seit mehr als einem Jahrhundert beflügelt das Hotel nicht nur die Fantasie bildender Künstler – besonders für Schriftsteller und Filmemacher bietet das moderne Phänomen eine perfekte Möglichkeit, um Geschichten zu erfinden und sie in Wort und Bild zu verewigen. Das Hotel dient als gesellschaftliche Bühne für Komödien und Tragödien, Liebesgeschichten, vielerlei Affären, Verbrechen sowie Horrorszenarien.

In der Ausstellung soll deshalb nicht nur die bildende Kunst das Hotel als Sujet thematisieren. Nach langer Recherche wurden für die Besucher ergänzend Bücher und Filme in einem Archiv zusammengetragen, welche die unterschiedlichsten Betrachtungsweisen des Hotels in der Literatur, Theorie und im Kino belegen und entdecken lassen. Vicki Baums programmatisches Werk *Menschen im Hotel* (1929), das sowohl in Buchform als auch als Film in die Geschichte des Genres eingegangen ist, steht neben unzähligen anderen berühmten Autoren wie Thomas Mann, Ernest Hemingway und weiteren in den Regalen des Atlantic Parkhotels in Baden-Baden. Neben Romanen können die Besucher aber auch in kurzweiligen Bilderbüchern mit den schönsten, größten und angesagtesten Hotels der Welt blättern oder sich der wissenschaftlichen Aufarbeitung des Themas widmen. Auf mehreren Bildschirmen werden diverse Meilensteine der Filmgeschichte gezeigt, die das Hotel als Tatort, Treffpunkt oder Schicksalsraum bespielen.

Das Kaminzimmer des Atlantic Parkhotels mutet bereits beim Eintreten wie ein Salon oder Lesezimmer aus der Glanzzeit der opulenten Grand Hotels an, als die Räume der Nobelherbergen noch vom bunten Treiben der illustren Gesellschaft erfüllt waren. In dieses Ambiente wird das Archiv verlagert, um den Besuchern die Möglichkeit zu bieten, noch tiefer in die facettenreiche, oft überraschend unterhaltsame Historie des Themas einzutauchen, und sich schließlich inspiriert wieder auf den Kunstparcours zu begeben.

For over a century the site of the hotel has sparked the imagination of all kinds of artists. For writers and filmmakers in particular, the modern phenomenon of the hotel has supplied the perfect inspiration for creating stories and perpetuating them in text and image. The hotel has served as a social stage for comedies and tragedies, love stories, and all sorts of affairs, crimes, and horror scenes.

Therefore, in the exhibition the hotel is not merely featured as a subject matter in visual art. After much research, additional books and films have been compiled in an archive, which demonstrates the great diversity of perspectives on the hotel in literature, theory, and cinema and which allows visitors to discover these works for themselves. Vicki Baum's programmatic *Menschen im Hotel* (Grand Hotel) (1929), which went down in the history of the genre both as a book and a film, can be found on the shelves of the Atlantic Parkhotel in Baden-Baden—along with countless other famous authors, including Thomas Mann and Ernest Hemingway. In addition to novels, visitors can take time to page through illustrated books with images of the largest, most beautiful, and hippest hotels in the world or read scholarly insights on the topic. Multiple screens show various milestones in the history of film, which were set in a hotel as either the scene of a crime, a gathering place, or a place where fates collide.

As soon as one enters the fireplace room of the Atlantic Parkhotel, one has the sense of being in a salon or reading room dating from the heyday of the opulent grand hotel, when the halls of such elite accommodations were filled with the hustle and bustle of an illustrious society. The archive has been placed in this ambience to offer visitors the opportunity to delve deeper into the diverse and often surprisingly entertaining history of the topic—and then continue the walking tour with renewed inspiration.

KUNSTSAMMLUNG DES HOTELS CASTELL, ZUOZ
ART COLLECTION OF THE HOTEL CASTELL, ZUOZ

Auswahl aus der Sammlung Ruedi Bechtler / A selection of works from the Ruedi Bechtler Collection
Mit Werken von / With works by Fischli/Weiss | Andreas Gursky | Tobias Madison | Chantal Michel | Gabriel Orozco | Roman Signer

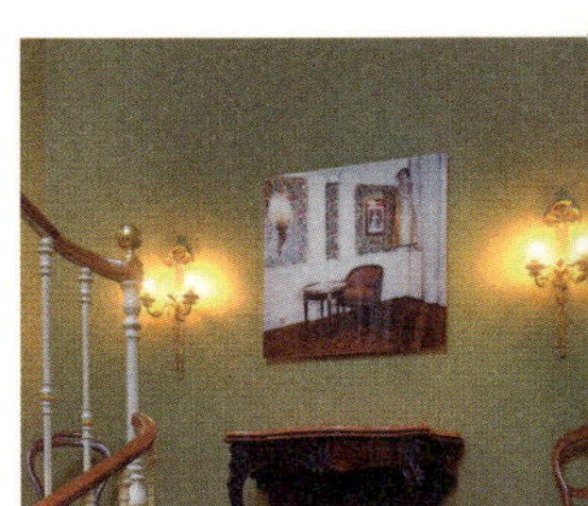

Was haben Fotografien von Fischli/Weiss, Gabriel Orozco oder Roman Signer mit dem Thema Hotel zu tun, zeigen sie doch Blumen, Flip-Flops, Mauerreste oder explodierende Stühle und Sessel? Zusammen mit weiteren Arbeiten von Andreas Gursky, Irène Hug, Tobias Madison und Chantal Michel eint sie zunächst der außergewöhnliche Ort ihrer temporären Präsentation im Atlantic Parkhotel in Baden-Baden. Doch so ausgefallen ist dieser Standort gar nicht. Denn für gewöhnlich werden diese Werke, zusammen mit zahlreichen weiteren Arbeiten anderer Künstler, im 1913 erbauten Hotel Castell im schweizerischen Zuoz bei St. Moritz gezeigt. Sie alle befinden sich in der Sammlung des Hauptaktionärs des Hotels, Ruedi Bechtler, der als impulsgebender Initiator in enger Zusammenarbeit mit Künstlern wie James Turrell, Tadashi Kawamata oder Pipilotti Rist aufwendige Projekte im Hotel und seiner unmittelbaren Umgebung realisiert. Der Aufenthalt seiner Gäste wird so auch im Bezug auf die Kunst ähnlich spektakulär gestaltet wie die umliegende Bergwelt des inneralpinen Hochtals im Oberengadin.

Waren es früher Schriftsteller wie Stefan Zweig oder Arthur Schnitzler, die entspannte Tage im Hotel Castell verbrachten, sind es heute bekannte Persönlichkeiten der Kunstwelt wie zum Beispiel Hans Ulrich Obrist, Wade Guyton oder John Baldessari. Wöchentlich finden öffentliche Kunstführungen durch die Flure des Hauses statt; in einem eigenen kleinen Kino gibt es Filmvorführungen. In einem Shop in der Lobby können außerdem Editionen der im Hotel ausgestellten Künstler erworben werden und in der Bibliothek kann man in zahlreichen Katalogen und Monografien mehr über sie erfahren. Das Hotel Castell hebt sich ganz bewusst von den unzählbaren »Art & Design Hotels« weltweit ab, deren intendierte Auseinandersetzung mit Kunst vor allem in der zweckdienlichen Einbettung der Kunstwerke in das Design der Innenarchitektur besteht: »modern« und »kreativ« als Totschlagadjektive für eine angebliche Lifestyleklientel. Zugleich nähert sich das Hotel Castell in seinen Strukturen und Funktionen einem Museum an. Und doch behält es einen großen Vorteil: Hier kann man auch übernachten oder die Freiluftfelsenquellensauna von Tadashi Kawamata genießen.

What do photographs by Fischli/Weiss, Gabriel Orozco, or Roman Signer have in common with the theme of the hotel, when they simply portray flowers, flip-flops, the remnants of a wall, or exploding chairs and armchairs? Along with works by Andreas Gursky, Irène Hug, Tobias Madison, and Chantal Michel they share an unusual exhibition setting as part of a temporary presentation at the Atlantic Parkhotel in Baden-Baden. However, this setting is not as uncommon as it might initially seem, because all these works, in addition to many others, are permanently on view at the Hotel Castell, which was built in 1913 in Zuoz near St. Moritz. They belong to the collection of the hotel's principle shareholder, Ruedi Bechtler, who has been the initiator and driving force behind elaborate projects produced at the hotel and in its immediate surroundings in close cooperation with artists such as James Turrell, Tadashi Kawamata, and Pipilotti Rist. As an art experience, a guest's stay is as spectacularly conceived as the surrounding mountain environment in a high Alpine valley of the Oberengadin region.

Whereas in earlier times, authors such as Stefan Zweig and Arthur Schnitzler spent relaxing days at the Hotel Castell, today guests include famous personalities from the art world, such as Hans Ulrich Obrist, Wade Guyton, and John Baldessari. Weekly public art tours guide visitors through the halls of the building; screenings are presented in the hotel's small cinema. In a shop in the lobby one can purchase editions by artists shown in the hotel. In the library numerous catalogues and monographic publications also enable visitors to learn more about these individual artists. The Hotel Castell intentionally sets itself apart from the countless »art & design hotels« throughout the world, whose stated commitment to art largely serves the purpose of integrating works or art into the design of the interior architecture. In such cases, the words »modern« and »creative« are the worn-out adjectives used to attract a supposedly lifestyle-oriented clientele. At the same time, the Hotel Castell is similar to a museum in terms of its organization and function. Nevertheless, it retains a major advantage: as a place where one can spend the night or enjoy the outdoor sauna by Tadashi Kawamata that draws its fresh water from a mountain spring.

JENNY BRILLHART

9 Arbeiten aus der Serie / 9 works from the series

HOTEL SAXONY

2006, Öl auf Holz / Oil on wood, 2 à 33 × 28 cm, 30 × 39 cm, 48 × 69 cm, 49 × 69 cm, 4 à 76 × 64 cm

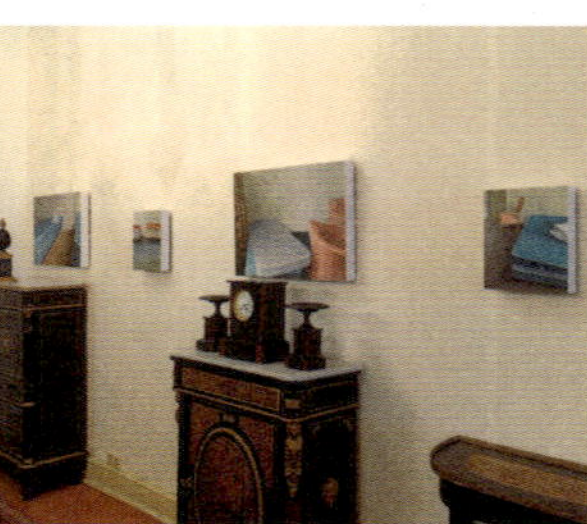

Die Zimmer und Möbel des titelgebenden Saxony Hotels, die Jenny Brillhart in ihren kleinformatigen Ölgemälden festgehalten hat, zeugen kaum mehr von dem Glanz und Pomp, der dort ehemals herrschte. Das Saxony eröffnete 1948 als eines der ersten Luxushotels in Miami Beach. Einst berühmt für seine luxuriös ausgestatteten Zimmer, seine Restaurants und die exquisite Lage mit Blick auf den Atlantischen Ozean, war es nach seiner Schließung lange dem Verfall überlassen, bis es schließlich ganz einem neuen Luxusobjekt weichen musste. Brillharts realistische, nach Fotografien entstandene Gemälde zeigen jeweils kleine Ausschnitte der Zimmer und lenken den Blick auf die Details. Ästhetisch kühl, in pastellzarter Farbigkeit und in ausgewogenen Kompositionen verleiht sie dem Dargestellten Würde und schenkt ihm eine Aufmerksamkeit, die ihm kurz vor der endgültigen Entsorgung in der Regel nicht zuteil wird.

Es ist jedoch nicht die Suche nach einer Geschichte, das Erzählerische oder gar Sozialkritische, das Brillhart antreibt. Die 1972 in Keene/New Hampshire geborene Künstlerin sucht Strukturen und wesentliche architektonische Prinzipien, die sie in ihren Gemälden in einen neuen Abstraktionsgrad überführt. Seit 2003 lebt Brillhart in Miami Beach. Die Stadt mit ihrer städtebaulichen Diversität wirkt seitdem prägend auf ihre Arbeit. Es sind die Randlagen, die vergessenen Orte, die Brillhart fesseln. Diese erlauben ihr einen unvoreingenommenen Blick, im Gegensatz zu den architektonischen Hochglanzikonen, die jeder mit Miami in Verbindung bringen würde.

Dennoch, in der lebendigen Hotelatmosphäre des Hotels Belle Epoque, wo ihre Arbeiten im Rahmen von ROOM SERVICE zu sehen sind, entfalten Brillharts kleinformatige Gemälde trotz aller Kühle einen intimen Vanitas-Charakter, indem sie von dem erloschenen Glanz eines ehemaligen Luxusquartiers berichten. Der Kontrast zur opulenten Gemütlichkeit des Baden-Badener Hotels könnte kaum größer sein.

The room and furnishings of the Saxony Hotel that Jenny Brillhart has captured in her small-format oil paintings by the same title hardly convey the extravagance and pomp that once pervaded the hotel. The Saxony opened in 1948 as one of the first luxury hotels in Miami Beach. Once famous for its opulently decorated rooms, restaurants, and perfect location with a view of the Atlantic Ocean, the hotel was left to decay for a long time after closing down, and finally it was razed to make way for new luxury accommodations. Based on photographs, Brillhart's realistic paintings each show partial views of the rooms and focus on details. Aesthetically cool, rendered in soft pastel tones, and employing balanced compositions, the depictions of the site are accorded respectful treatment and attention, which is unusual for a building about to be demolished.

Brillhart is not driven by a search for narrative, nor by an interest in social critique. Born in Keene, New Hampshire, in 1972, Jenny Brillhart is instead interested in structures and essential architectural principles that have invested her paintings with a new degree of abstraction. Brillhart has been living in Miami Beach since 2003. The diversity of the city's urban landscape has had substantial impact on her work. Remote areas and forgotten places are what capture Brillhart's imagination and offer an image that is impartial, unlike the gleaming architecture of the posh landmark buildings that everyone generally associates with Miami.

However, in the lively atmosphere of Hotel Belle Epoque, where her works are on view in conjunction with ROOM SERVICE, Brillhart's small-format images have—despite their cool palette—the intimate character of *vanitas* images, which capture the bygone luster of a former first-class hotel. The contrast to the luxurious warmth of the Baden-Baden accommodations could hardly be any greater.

ANDY WARHOL

THE CHELSEA GIRLS

1966, 2-Kanal-Videoinstallation, 16-mm-Film auf DVD übertragen, 66 Min. / 2-channel video installation, 16mm film transferred to digital files (DVD), 66 min.

Der Film THE CHELSEA GIRLS ist eine experimentelle Soap-Opera, bei der zwei parallel verlaufende Handlungsstränge nebeneinander projiziert werden. Andy Warhol, geboren 1928 in Pittsburgh/Pennsylvania, drehte den Film gemeinsam mit Paul Morrissey zwischen Juni und September 1966 vorwiegend im legendären Chelsea Hotel in New York. Dieses wurde in der Zeit nach dem Zweiten Weltkrieg wieder zum Lebensmittelpunkt des künstlerischen Undergrounds der Stadt. Die beiden suchten sich als Protagonisten gezielt starke, schillernde und bizarre Persönlichkeiten aus wie etwa die Sängerin Nico, Brigid Berlin oder Susan Bottomly, die in dieser Zeit dort wohnten und später Warhols *Superstars* wurden. Im Film spielen sie sich selbst oder eine dramatisierte Variante von sich selbst. Der 195-minütige Streifen besteht aus zwölf Episoden, in denen jeweils ein oder mehrere Bewohner des Hotels vorgestellt werden. Der Film steht wie kaum ein anderer für das aufregend-bewegte Leben der Kunstszene der 1960er-Jahre in New York.

THE CHELSEA GIRLS ist Warhols erster Film, der sofort kommerziellen Erfolg hatte. Während er inzwischen als einer der wichtigsten Experimentalfilme des 20. Jahrhunderts gilt, der exemplarisch für Warhols Prinzip der Bildkompositionen (bestehend aus Farb- und Schwarz-Weiß-Bildern), seine Sensibilität und die revolutionäre Technik des simultanen und parallelen Abspielens mehrerer Handlungen steht, waren ihm unmittelbar nach der Premiere die zeitgenössischen Kritiken nicht wohlgesonnen. In Boston etwa wurde die Vorführung des Films von der Polizei abgebrochen und der Kinobesitzer wegen Verbreitung obszönen Materials verurteilt.

In der Ausstellung ROOM SERVICE, die sich neben anderen Aspekten auch der Kunst im Hotel widmet, kommt dem Chelsea Hotel als temporärer oder permanenter Wohnort vieler bedeutender Künstler des 20. Jahrhunderts eine große Rolle zu. Im Hotel Belle Epoque in Baden-Baden wird durch Warhols Film THE CHELSEA GIRLS das außergewöhnlich skurrile Flair dieses berühmten New Yorker Kunsthotels im direkten Gegensatz zum Ausstellungsort spürbar.

The film THE CHELSEA GIRLS is an experimental soap opera, in which two parallel narratives are projected next to one another. Born in Pittsburgh, Pennsylvania, in 1928, Andy Warhol shot the film together with Paul Morrissey between June and September 1966, largely at the legendary Chelsea Hotel in New York. In the period following World War II the hotel once again became a gathering point of the city's artistic underground. The two filmmakers intentionally sought out strong, dazzling, and bizarre protagonists, including the singer Nico, Brigid Berlin, and Susan Bottomly, who lived at the hotel during this time and later became Warhol's »superstars.« In the film they play themselves or dramatized versions of themselves. The 195-minute film consists of twelve episodes, in which one or multiple hotel inhabitants are introduced. Like hardly any other film, THE CHELSEA GIRLS serves as an icon of the vitality of the art scene in New York in the 1960s.

THE CHELSEA GIRLS was Warhol's first film that became an immediate commercial success. The work is meanwhile considered one of the most important experimental films of the 20th century and exemplifies Warhol's approach to composition (using color and black-and-white images), his sensibility, and the revolutionary technology of the simultaneous and parallel projection of different narrative threads. However, immediately after the premier contemporary critics panned the work. In Boston a screening of the film was even broken up by police, and the cinema owner was convicted of distributing obscene material.

As both a temporary and permanent home to many significant artists of the 20th century, the Chelsea Hotel plays an important role in the exhibition ROOM SERVICE, which examines art in hotels, among other themes. Through Warhol's film THE CHELSEA GIRLS the unusual and strange allure of this famous New York art hotel is all the more apparent against the contrasting backdrop of its exhibition setting at the Hotel Belle Epoque in Baden-Baden.

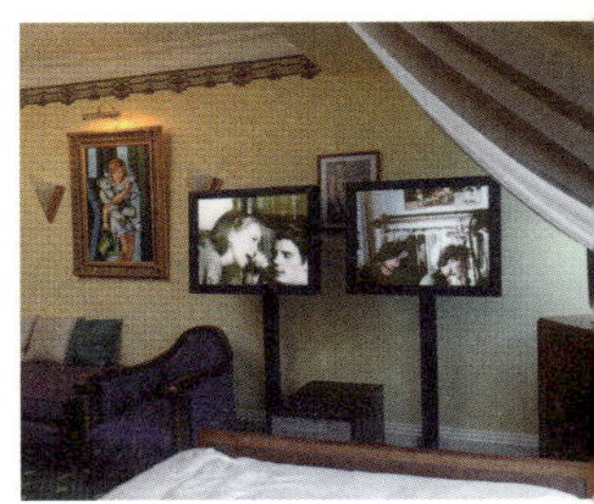

CHRISTIAN JANKOWSKI

DER KLEINE ENTSCHEIDUNGSRAUM
A SMALL ROOM FOR DECISION MAKING

2014, Installation mit verschiedenen Materialien sowie Serie von 24 chromogenen Farbdrucken, je 51 × 40 cm
Installation with various materials as well as a series of 24 chromogenic color prints, each 51 × 40 cm

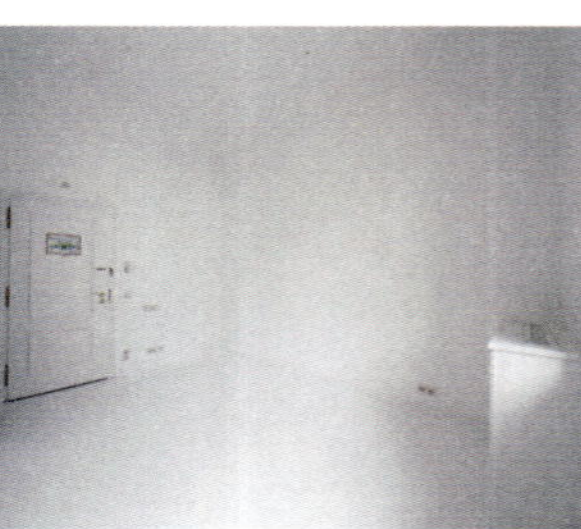

Eine Grundeigenschaft des Hotels ist das Zurverfügungstellen eines vorgefertigten Rahmens, in den ein Gast sich temporär einfügt, um sich darin in einer Heimat auf Zeit einzurichten. Christian Jankowski greift diese Gegebenheit auf und transformiert ein klassisches Hotelzimmer in einen Möglichkeitsraum. Inmitten der reichhaltig gestalteten Hallen und Gänge des Brenners Park-Hotels & Spa in Baden-Baden eröffnet sich hinter der Tür des Zimmers 127 eine Leerstelle in dem ansonsten durchstrukturierten Betrieb: Ein kahler Raum, der mit seinen blendend weißen Wänden eher an den White Cube eines Ausstellungsraums erinnert, stellt den Übernachtungsgast zunächst vor die Wahl, sich sein Zimmer ganz nach den eigenen Ansprüchen einzurichten. Vom Standard bis hin zur Opulenz lässt sich die Einrichtung dieses Zimmers nach dem Baukastenprinzip aus einem Katalog beliebig zusammenstellen. Jedoch geht es hier nicht allein darum, sich eine möglichst schöne oder gemütliche Zimmerausstattung auszusuchen. Es ist ein Rückzugsort, der seine Gäste auffordern möchte, in dieser spezifischen Situation eine selbst gewählte Lebensentscheidung zu treffen – wobei mit der Gewichtigkeit der eigenen Entscheidung auch der künstlerische *Wert* der Übernachtung steigt.

Der Aktionskünstler Christian Jankowski, geboren 1968 in Göttingen, entwickelt seine Arbeiten oftmals durch spielerische Eingriffe in bestehende kulturelle, institutionelle und mediale Systeme. Er erhebt das jeweilige soziale Umfeld zu aktiven Kollaborateuren seiner Kunstwerke, die diese – oft zufallsgeleitet – vervollständigen.

Mit seiner Arbeit im Brenners Park-Hotel & Spa in Baden-Baden hinterfragt Jankowski nicht nur die Bedeutung von materiellem Luxus – für jeden Gast stellt sich ebenfalls die Frage nach der eigenen Repräsentation. Seine Entscheidungen bleiben keinesfalls verborgen hinter der geschlossenen Zimmertür von Nr. 127, sondern werden täglich in Fotografien dokumentiert und öffentlich präsentiert. Letztlich erstellt der Gast so als kreativer Schöpfer seines eigenen kleinen Entscheidungsraums nichts Geringeres als ein Selbstporträt – im Rahmen der vom Künstler bereitgestellten Möglichkeiten.

A basic aspect of a hotel is that it provides an established setting into which guests temporarily assimilate themselves to create a home for a limited period of time. Christian Jankowski draws on this situation and transforms a classic hotel room into a space of possibility. Within the opulently furnished halls and hallways of the Brenners Park-Hotel & Spa in Baden-Baden, the door to Room 127 leads to an open, empty space within an operation that is otherwise fully structured, down to every last detail. In this bare room with glaringly white walls that recall the »white cube« of an exhibition space, guests are presented with the option of furnishing the room to meet their demands. From the standard to the opulent, the furnishings of the room can be compiled from a catalogue according to a building-block concept. However, the idea is not merely to put together the most beautiful or cozy room decor. It offers a place of refuge that requires guests in this situation to make an important decision on their own accord—whereby the more weighty the decision becomes, the more the artistic »value« of the overnight experience increases.

Born in Göttingen in 1968, artist Christian Jankowski often develops his works as playful interventions in existing cultural, institutional, and media-based systems. He makes the given social environment into collaborators in his works of art, and these people are what make the work complete—often in a manner guided by chance.

With his work created for the Brenners Park-Hotel & Spa in Baden-Baden Jankowski questions the meaning of material luxury—and each guest is presented with the question as to his or her own need for representative display. Also, the guests' decisions do not remain hidden behind the closed door of Room 127 but are documented in photographs on a daily basis and shown publicly. Ultimately, as the creator of his or her individual little rooms for decision, each guest produces what amounts to a self-portrait—by using the scope of possibilities presented by the artist.

CINDY SHERMAN

UNTITLED #464 & UNTITLED #475

2008, chromogener Farbdruck / Chromogenic color print, 215 × 153 cm und / and 220 × 182 cm

Auf den ersten Blick scheint die großformatige und aufwendig gerahmte Fotografie ein repräsentatives Auftragsporträt zu sein. Es bedient ein ikonografisches Muster, das augenscheinlich in der Tradition großer Meister wie Diego Velázquez steht. Die nähere Betrachtung offenbart jedoch schlagartig Diskrepanzen des Genres: Shermans Damen nehmen zwar gekonnt standesgemäße Posen ein, doch die Oberfläche bröckelt schnell. Die vermeintliche Individualität schwindet – hier scheint es vielmehr um einen bestimmten Typ Frau zu gehen. Vor den leicht verschwommenen Hintergründen pompöser Theaterinterieurs oder Festsäle betrachtet man glamouröse Ladys, die versuchen, ihre Schönheit und Jugend zu bewahren. Gekleidet in festliche Roben, mit perfekten Frisuren können sie dennoch selbst mit ihren aufwendigen Make-ups nicht davon ablenken, dass sie ihre Lebensmitte schon überschritten haben.

Unter mehreren Lagen Requisiten, Kostümen und Make-up zeigt jede dieser Fotografien die Künstlerin selbst. Bereits Mitte der 1970er-Jahre ist Cindy Sherman, geboren 1954 in Glen Ridge/New Jersey, mit ihren eigenwilligen Selbstporträts berühmt geworden, in denen sie in jeweils neue Rollen schlüpfte und somit fest etablierte weibliche Gesellschafstypen fokussierte und zugleich konterkarierte. Die Dargestellten sind stets fiktive Charaktere, die eindeutige Attribute und soziale Erkennungsmerkmale aufweisen. Dabei changiert Shermans künstlerische Sprache zwischen Humor, Horror und kritischer Enthüllung.

Im Empfangssaal des Brenners Park-Hotels & Spa in Baden-Baden ersetzen die beiden Porträts die übliche repräsentative Porträtmalerei. Die Damen auf den Bildern sind in ähnlich prunkvoller Atmosphäre verortet und strahlen den Betrachter an. Sowohl die Gäste des Hotels als auch die Besucher der Ausstellung sind dazu eingeladen, in Shermans Welt zu tauchen und ihr unübersehbares Augenzwinkern zu erkennen.

At first glance, the large, carefully framed photographs seem to be official, commissioned portraits. They employ a kind of iconography that apparently draws on the tradition of famous old masters, such as Diego Velázquez. But closer examination suddenly reveals some glaring discrepancies with the traditional portrait genre. Sherman's ladies expertly assume the proper poses of their class, but cracks in their surface appearances are quickly noticeable. The apparent individuality dissipates, and instead the images seem to represent a certain type of woman. In front of the slightly blurry backgrounds of ornate theater interiors or ballrooms, one sees glamorous ladies who are trying to preserve their youth and beauty. Dressed in festive garments with perfect hairstyles, they cannot conceal, despite their careful make-up, that they have passed their prime.

Each photograph depicts the artist herself—buried beneath many layers of props, costumes, and make-up. Born in Glen Ridge, New Jersey, in 1954, Cindy Sherman already made a name for herself in the 1970s with her idiosyncratic self-portraits. Assuming different roles in these images, she highlighted various female social types while simultaneously undermining these representations. The depicted women are always fictional characters that have clearly identifiable attributes and communicate specific social codes. Sherman's artistic language thereby alternates between humor, horror, and incisive critique.

In the entry hall of Brenners Park-Hotel & Spa in Baden-Baden two of Sherman's portraits replace the kind of portrait paintings one might commonly find in such a setting. The women in the images are situated in similarly magnificent environments and smile broadly at the viewer. The guests of the hotel as well as exhibition visitors are thus invited to enter into Sherman's world experience her unmistakable tongue-in-cheek.

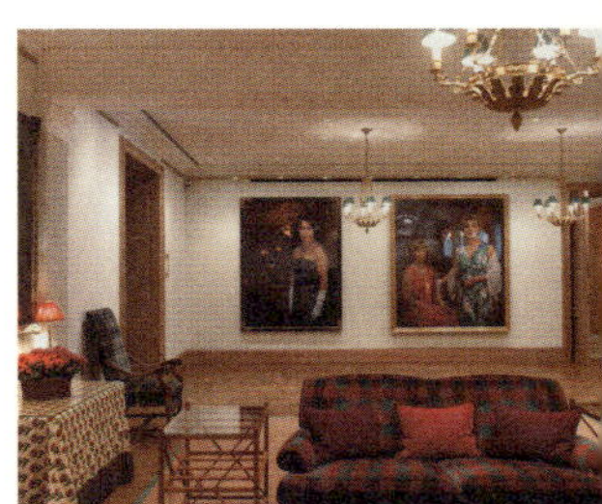

MARKUS SCHINWALD

DICTIO PII

2001, 35-mm-Farbfilm auf Video übertragen, 16 Min. / 35-mm color film transferred to video files, 16 min.

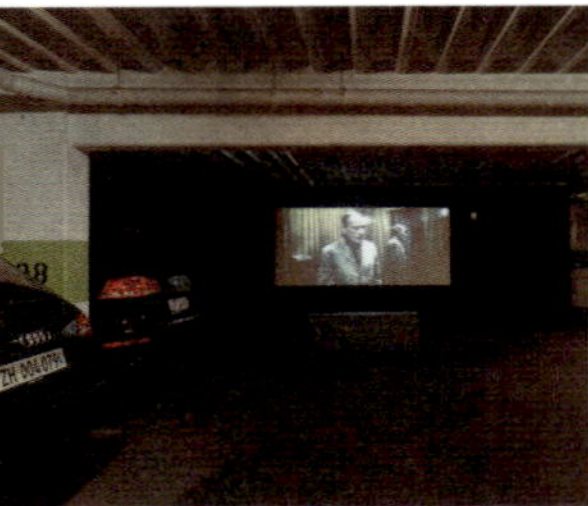

In seinem Filmwerk lässt der Künstler Markus Schinwald verschiedene Protagonisten durch die transitiven Räume eines zeitlosen Hotels wandeln, bestückt mit unheimlichen Apparaturen und rätselhafte Handlungen ausführend. So setzt sich ein ganz in Beige gekleideter Mann eine prothesenartige Vorrichtung auf den Kopf, die sein Gesicht in ein andauerndes Grinsen zwingt. Der Zeigefinger einer rauchenden Dame steckt ebenfalls in einer prothetischen Applikation, die sie nötigt, diesen mahnend auf Kopfhöhe zu halten. Haben Prothesen normalerweise die Aufgabe, fehlende Funktionen des Körpers zu ersetzen, führen sie bei den genannten Protagonisten eher zu Einschränkungen. Alle Personen in DICTIO PII agieren isoliert voneinander, auch wenn sie sich auf den verschlungenen Fluren und in den Räumen begegnen. Zusammengehalten werden die einzelnen Sequenzen des Films nur durch den Ort selbst und die melodisch unterlegten Stimmen aus dem Off, die mit ihren Kommentaren wie »we are deranged« (»wir sind verwirrt«) auf die psychische Verfassung der sichtbaren Figuren zu verweisen scheinen.

Die Thematisierung des menschlichen Körpers und Formen seiner Konditionierung durch kulturelle Hervorbringungen ziehen sich durch das Werk Schinwalds. Neben Filmen nutzt er auch Objekte, Installationen, Fotografien und theatrale Elemente. Der 1973 in Salzburg geborene Künstler studierte in Linz und Berlin und war 2011 eingeladen, den österreichischen Pavillon auf der Biennale di Venezia zu bespielen.

Das Hotel als zivilisatorische Hervorbringung stellt einen besonderen Schauplatz für Schinwalds Auseinandersetzungen. In DICTIO PII greift er die Charakteristiken des unpersönlichen Nichtortes auf, um diese als Ausdruck isolierter Individuen und ihrer seelisch desolaten Zustände herauszustellen. In der Ausstellung ROOM SERVICE wird der Film nicht etwa in einem Galerieraum präsentiert, sondern an einem Ort, der selbst die Eigenschaften des Transitiven in sich trägt: In der Parkgarage des Brenners Park-Hotels & Spa in Baden-Baden sind die Besucher eingeladen, Platz zu nehmen und den als Durchgang respektive Abstellplatz angelegten Ort mit ihrer eigenen Anwesenheit zu füllen.

In his film work, artist Markus Schinwald causes a range of protagonists to walk through the transitory space of a timeless hotel furnished with strange apparatuses while they perform puzzling actions. A man dressed entirely in beige sets a prosthesis-like device on his head, which forces his face into a permanent grin. The index finger of a lady smoking also is stuck in a prosthesis, which requires her to hold it up at the height of her head in a reprimanding gesture. Whereas such devices usually have the function of replacing an absent function of the body, these objects instead impose limitations on their wearers. All of the people shown in DICTIO PII act out their roles in isolation from one another, even when encountering each another in the halls and rooms of the hotel. The individual sequences of the film are linked by the site and the melodic voices sounding from off screen, who with comments such as »we are deranged,« seem to refer to the psychic state of the figures that we see.

Themes of the human body and how it is conditioned by the dictates of culture underlie the work of Schinwald. In addition to films he also produces objects, installations, photographs, and theatrical works. Born in Salzburg in 1973, the artist studied in Linz and Berlin and represented Austria at the 2011 Biennale di Venezia.

As a product of civilization, the hotel serves as a unique setting for Schinwald's explorations. In DICTIO PII the artist draws on the characteristic of the hotel as an impersonal non-site, as an expression of the isolation of the individual and the accompanying emotional desolation. In the exhibition ROOM SERVICE the film is not presented in a gallery space but in a place that inherently entails aspects of the transitory. In the parking garage of Brenners Park-Hotel & Spa in Baden-Baden, visitors are invited to take a seat and to occupy the parking space, which is usually used as a passageway.

IAN WALLACE

6 Arbeiten aus der / 6 works from the

HOTEL-SERIE / HOTEL SERIES

2014, Fotolaminat, Acryl auf Leinwand, Offsetdruck / Laminated photograph, acrylic on canvas, inkjet print, 4 à 61 × 61 cm, 2 à 71 × 58 cm

Die Tableaus an den Wänden sind jeweils aus drei vertikalen Flächen aufgebaut, in deren Mitte meist eine Fotografie auf die Leinwand laminiert wurde. Sie bricht die Einheit der sie umgebenden monochromen Felder aus Acrylfarbe auf und wird doch gleichermaßen von ihnen eingerahmt. Durch die Symbiose aus Malerei und Fotografie beschwört Ian Wallace einerseits Erinnerungen an die lange Tradition des gemalten Tafelbildes und dessen vermeintliche Krise der Repräsentation, die letztlich zu Beginn des 20. Jahrhunderts in die Abstraktion führte. Andererseits fügt er diesem aufgeladenen Zustand mittels der zeitgenössischen Technik der digitalen Fotografie wieder einen Teil eines repräsentierenden Bildgedächtnisses hinzu.

Ian Wallace, geboren 1943 in Shoreham/England, übersiedelte im Alter von zehn Jahren mit seinen kanadischen Eltern nach Vancouver und befasst sich seit den 1960er-Jahren in seiner künstlerischen Praxis mit der Überschneidung von modernistischen Konzepten in Malerei, Skulptur und Fotografie. Wallace lehrte von 1970 bis 1987 Kunstgeschichte an der University of British Columbia und von 1972 bis 1998 als Professor an der Emily Carr University of Art and Design, beide in Vancouver. Zu seinen Studenten zählten unter anderen Jeff Wall, Rodney Graham, Ken Lum und Stan Douglas.

Seit 1988 werden Hotelzimmer für Wallace zu temporären Ateliers, häufig auch zu titelgebenden Ausgangspunkten einzelner Werke seiner HOTEL-SERIE. Die Fotografien dokumentieren den Entstehungsprozess von kleinen monochromen Zeichnungen vor Ort. Diese vermeintlich intimen Einblicke in seine künstlerische Arbeitsmethode wird von Wallace durch sichtbare Reiseutensilien wie Bücher und Notizen zu einer scheinbar autobiografischen, jedoch konzeptuell offenen Erzählung verknüpft. Man muss nicht zwingend wissen, dass das Buch auf dem Schreibtisch über das kontrastreiche Verständnis des Technikbegriffs bei Martin Heidegger und seinem Schüler Herbert Marcuse von einem Freund Wallaces stammt. Was man aber sehen kann: Die in den Arbeiten der Ausstellung verwendeten Fotografien entstanden am Ort ihrer Präsentation, im Brenners Park-Hotel in Baden-Baden.

The tableaus on the wall are each made from three vertical surfaces, and in most works a photograph has been laminated onto the canvas on the middle panel. This image breaks up the monochromatic fields of acrylic paint, which in turn frame the photograph. On the one hand, through this symbiosis of painting and photography Ian Wallace conjures memories of the long tradition of painting and its supposed crisis of representation, which led to the development of abstraction in the early 20th century. On the other, through the use of the contemporary technique of digital photography he adds an element of representational visual memory to this charged state.

Born in Shoreham, England in 1943, Ian Wallace moved to Vancouver with his Canadian parents when he was ten. Since the 1960s he has been exploring parallels between modernist concepts of painting, sculpture, and photography through his artistic practice. Wallace taught art history at the University of British Columbia from 1970 to 1987 and was a professor at the Emily Carr University of Art and Design from 1972 to 1998. His students have included Jeff Wall, Rodney Graham, Ken Lum, and Stan Douglas.

Since 1988 Wallace has been using hotel rooms as temporary studios, often employing them as a source of inspiration and incorporating their names into the individual works of his HOTEL SERIES. The photographs document the development of small, monochromatic drawings made on site. These seemingly intimate insights into his working process are linked with obvious travel aids, such as books and notes, to create an apparently autobiographic but conceptually open narrative. It is not necessary to know that the book on the desk—about the conflicting concepts of technology in the work of Martin Heidegger and his student Herbert Marcuse—was written by one of Wallace's friends. But it is clear that the photographs used in the works included in the exhibition were taken where they are now displayed, at the Brenners Park-Hotel in Baden-Baden.

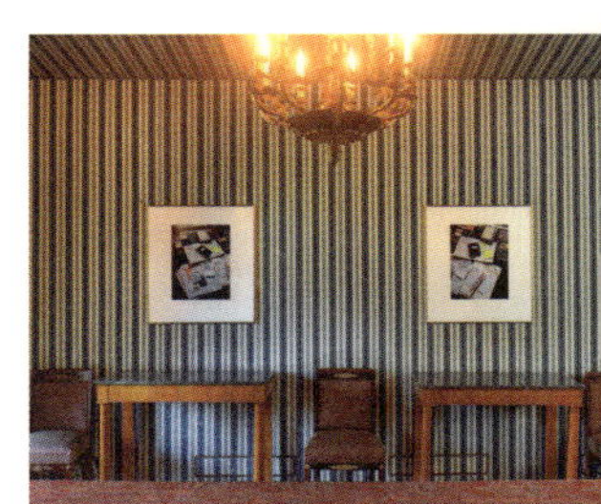

BRENNERS PARK-HOTEL & SPA

NANECI YURDAGÜL

BRENNERS EINE-STUNDE-HOTEL & SERVICE TOTAL
BRENNERS ONE-HOUR HOTEL & TOTAL SERVICE

2014, Performance mit verschiedenen Materialien sowie Neonröhren montiert auf Plexiglas 120 × 16 × 6 cm
Performance with various materials as well as neon tubes mounted on plexiglas, 120 × 16 × 6 cm

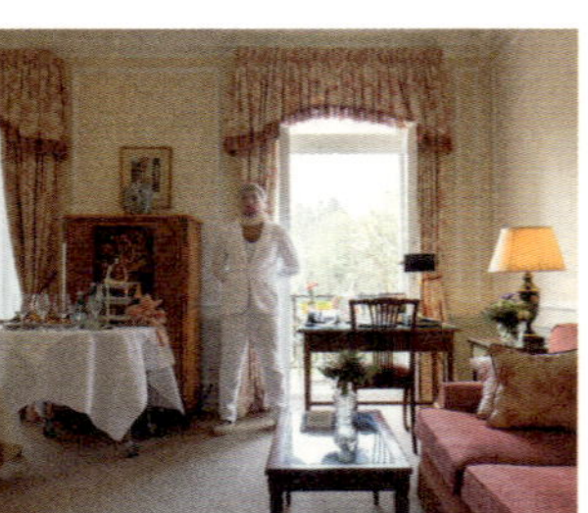

Eine Übernachtung im renommierten Fünfsternehotel ist kostspielig und damit einer spezifischen gesellschaftlichen Schicht vorbehalten. Für die große Mehrheit bleibt dies höchstens eine Wunschvorstellung. Der Künstler Naneci Yurdagül setzt auf die Überwindung dieser sozialen Trennlinie und proklamiert in seiner Arbeit kurzerhand das BRENNERS EINE-STUNDE-HOTEL & SERVICE TOTAL, das für jedermann zugänglich sein soll. Wer sich keine ganze Nacht hier leisten kann, hat nun die Chance, den kompletten Service für 60 Minuten zu erleben – und dafür auch nur 1/24 des eigentlichen Zimmerpreises zu entrichten. Der Künstler lädt hierzu in sein Hotelzimmer ein und begibt sich für diese Zeit selbst in die Rolle des Dienstleisters, um den Aufenthalt seiner Gäste zu begleiten und deren Serviceerfahrung persönlich den letzten Schliff zu geben. Aber was genau umfasst besagten »Service Total«? Was heißt es für das Personal, Gäste des Hauses nach höchsten Standards zu bewirten, und wie viel ist man als Gast bereit, der Belegschaft zuzumuten? Was gibt der Blick auf die Rückseite der glanzvollen Oberflächen preis? Und welche ungeahnten Dimensionen erhält die Idee des Service dadurch? Diesen Fragen geht Naneci Yurdagül auch allabendlich an der Hotelbar des Brenners nach: Im Rahmen seiner Performance GESCHLOSSENE GESELLSCHAFT lädt er ein, gemeinsam mit ihm über die verschiedenen Schichten des Hotels zu sinnieren.

Als Absolvent der Frankfurter Städelschule beschäftigt sich Naneci Yurdagül, geboren 1979 in Frankfurt am Main, mit gesellschaftlichen und politischen Phänomenen, um die ihnen eingeschriebenen sozialen Differenzierungen offenzulegen. In seinen Arbeiten spielt das Publikum zumeist eine konstitutive Rolle, die neue Perspektiven auf scheinbar vertraute Phänomene eröffnet. Mit seiner performativen Installation hinterfragt Yurdagül nicht nur die Bedeutung von Luxus im Sinne einer Demokratisierung der Serviceerfahrung in einem Fünfsternehotel, sondern er thematisiert ebenso seine eigene Rolle als künstlerischer Dienstleister innerhalb des Kunstbetriebs. So prangt über dem Ausgang der Kunsthalle eine Neonarbeit mit den Worten »hände hoch – gäste kommen«: Diese rekurriert auf einen alten Brauch des gehobenen Gastgewerbes.

Spending a night in a famous five-star hotel is cost-intensive, and such accommodations are only available to a certain class of society. It is an experience that most people can only dream of having. Artist Naneci Yurdagül attempts to overcome this social divide. His work advertises BRENNERS ONE-HOUR HOTEL & TOTAL SERVICE, which is intended to be accessible to anyone. Those who cannot afford a full night in the hotel are now given the chance to experience the full range of hotel services over the course of 60 minutes—while paying only 1/24 of the actual price for the room. The artist welcomes guests into his hotel room and thereby assumes the role of a service provider, accompanying them during their stay and adding the perfect touch. But what does his »total service« include? What does it mean for the staff to provide the guests of the house with the most preferential treatment? And as a guest, how much would one dare to demand from the attendant personnel? What does a look behind the surface reveal? And what unexpected dimensions does the notion of service thereby assume? Yurdagül also examines these questions in his nightly performances at the hotel bar. In the performance PRIVATE RECEPTION he invites guests to join him in musing on the various classes of society in the hotel.

Born in Frankfurt am Main in 1979, Naneci Yurdagül, a graduate of Frankfurt's Städelschule, addresses social and political constructs in an attempt to reveal the social disparities with which they are inscribed. The audience often plays a constitutive role in his work, and their participation opens up new perspectives on seemingly familiar situations. With his performative installation Yurdagül not only questions the meaning of luxury by democratizing the service of a five-star hotel, but he also highlights his own role as an artist and service provider within the art world. Over the entrance to the Kunsthalle a neon work by the artist radiates the message »hands up—guests are coming,« a reference to an old custom in upscale hotels and restaurants.

LEE KIT

ONLY A FEW THINGS TO DO

2014, Installation mit verschiedenen Materialien / Installation with various materials

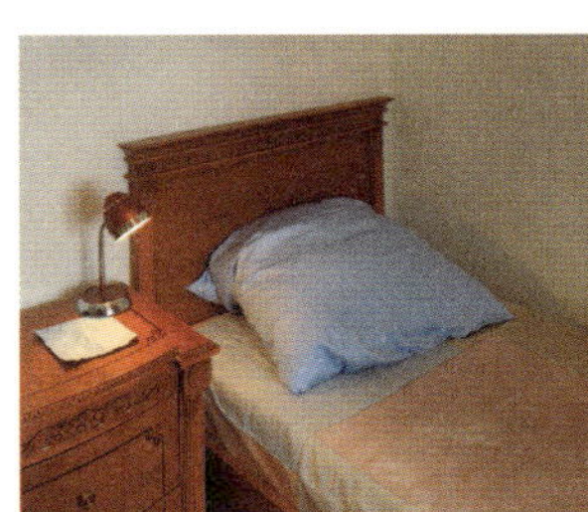

Seit mehreren Jahren schon arbeitet Lee Kit mit dem Stoff des Alltäglichen. Ihm dienen Tischdecken, Geschirrtücher oder Bettwäsche als Ausgangspunkt und Bildgrund für Gemälde, die er mit Streifen, Schraffierungen oder anderen Mustern versieht – das Gegenteil eines expressiv malerischen Gestus. Die Konservierung von Spuren des Alltags, die mithilfe des Zufallsmoments z. B. beim Abendessen auf der dafür verwendeten und zuvor bemalten Tischdecke übrig bleiben, tritt hinzu. Die Autorschaft dieser benutzbaren Gemälde teilt Lee mit Freunden oder Fremden und erweitert somit das Repertoire der klassischen Malerei um einen sozialen Aspekt.

Lee Kit, der 1978 in Hongkong geboren wurde und dort an der Hochschule für Bildende Künste graduierte, interessiert sich für die Loslösung des Kunstwerks aus einem spezifischen Ausstellungskontext. In Gemälden, Fotografien und Videoarbeiten entfaltet er die Narration des Alltags, um uns Betrachtern das darin versteckte Potenzial erfahrbar zu machen.

So wird das Zimmer Nr. 2 im Hotel Rathausglöckel für die Dauer der Ausstellung von Lee Kit umgestaltet. Bestehend aus gemusterter Bettwäsche, einem mit Text bedruckten Vorhang, einer Tischdecke, Gläsern, Tassen und verschiedenen Drucken, soll die Installation benutzbar werden, indem man das Hotelzimmer bucht. Die Atmosphäre soll den Gast an ein »altes Liebeslied« erinnern. Werden die Spuren eines jeden Hotelgastes nach dessen Abreise gewöhnlich sorgsam vom Zimmerservice des Hotels beseitigt, werden sie in diesem Fall auf den Gegenständen konserviert und damit Teil von Lee Kits Werk.

For a number of years, Lee Kit has been working with the material of the everyday. He uses tablecloths, dishtowels, and sheets as a starting point as well as a ground for paintings that he composes with stripes, hatchings, or other patterns—the opposite of an expressive, painterly gesture. The preservation of traces of ordinary events left by chance, for example the remains of an evening meal on a tablecloth that was previously painted, is an additional element. Lee thus shares the authorship of these utilitarian paintings with friends or strangers, thereby expanding the repertoire of classical painting to include a social element.

Lee Kit was born in Hong Kong in 1978 and studied fine art at Chinese University. He is interested in extracting the work of art from a specific exhibition context. In paintings, photographs, and video works he unfolds a narrative of the ordinary as a means of allowing us as viewers to experience its hidden potential.

Room No. 2 at Hotel Rathausglöckel has been outfitted by Kit for the duration of the exhibition. Consisting of patterned sheets, curtains printed with text, a tablecloth, glasses, teacups, and various prints, the installation is intended for use by those booking the hotel room. The atmosphere is conceived to remind the guest of an »old love song.« Whereas the traces left behind by hotel guests are usually carefully removed after their departure by the hotel cleaning staff, in this case they are carefully preserved on the given objects and thus become a part of Lee Kit's work.

GABRIELA OBERKOFLER

BITTE NICHT KLOPFEN, WENN JA, DREIMAL IM TAKT AUF LEISEN PFOTEN
PLEASE DO NOT KNOCK, OR IF YOU MUST, THEN THREE TIMES SOFTLY

2014, Installation mit verschiedenen Materialien / Installation with various materials

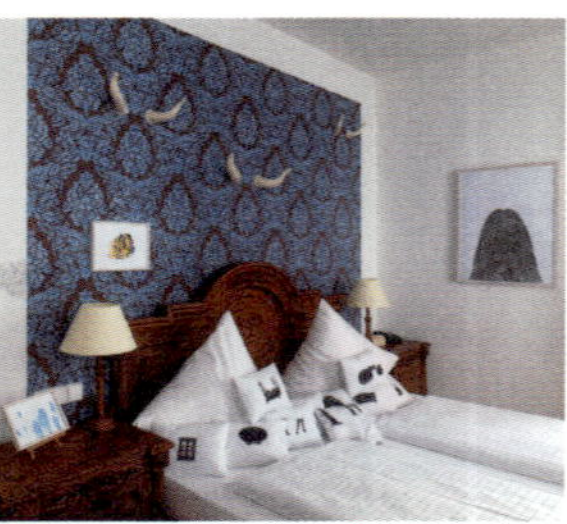

Nahezu alle künstlerischen Ausdrucksmedien dienen Gabriela Oberkofler dazu, ihr künstlerisches Interesse oftmals auf einen regionalen Kontext, ländliche Besonderheiten, Geschichte oder Aberglauben hin zu formulieren und so zum Ausgangspunkt ihrer erzählerischen Ausstellungen zu machen. So bezieht sich auch der Titel ihrer Installation für die Ausstellung ROOM SERVICE im Hotel Rathausglöckel auf ein abergläubisches Empfinden im Badischen, wonach derjenige, der nach Einbruch der Dunkelheit an einer Haustüre klopft, die Hexen weckt. Dies wird nur verschlimmert, indem man »Herein« sagt, und damit die Hexen unerwartet ins Haus mit hinein holt.

Gabriela Oberkofler wurde 1975 in Bozen, Italien, geboren und lebt und arbeitet in Stuttgart. In vielen Ausstellungen mit oftmals poetischen und anspielungsreichen Titeln rückt sie häufig Tiere, Pflanzen und dörfliche Architekturszenerien in den Mittelpunkt ihrer künstlerischen Auseinandersetzung.

In Zimmer Nr. 8 im Hotel Rathausglöckel ist das Bett mit zahlreichen Kissen bedeckt, auf deren Bezüge gegenständliche Zeichnungen von Oberkofler gedruckt wurden. Im Zimmer verteilt stehen kleine Holzskulpturen, weitere Zeichnungen und Drucke hängen gerahmt an der Wand. Das Hotelzimmer ist für die gesamte Ausstellungsdauer zu mieten. Der Gast kann sich an einer »Hexenküche« probieren: Allerlei Gegenstände und Zutaten stehen bereit, mit denen er Salben und Mittelchen, z. B. gegen den bösen Blick und Schlaflosigkeit oder für Fruchtbarkeit und Bewusstseinserweiterung, selbst herstellen kann. Oberkofler entwickelt somit die Idee eines alternativen Schwarzwaldbildes, das im Gegensatz zur Idylle eines Hans Thoma steht. Hängt man das in Hotels obligatorische »Bitte nicht stören«-Schild nach Sonnenuntergang an die Zimmertür, kann man zudem gewiss sein, dass keine Hexen den Hotelaufenthalt stören werden.

Gabriela Oberkofler uses almost any and every medium as a means of translating her artistic concerns into a regional context or rural culture, history, and collection of folkloric beliefs, which in turn form the starting point of her narrative exhibitions. The title of her exhibition for ROOM SERVICE at the Hotel Rathausglöckel thus refers to a suspicion held in the Baden region, according to which anyone who knocks on a door after the fall of darkness awakens the witches. Saying »come in« then only makes the situation worse, because one then, unsuspectingly, invites witches into the house.

Gabriela Oberkofler was born in Bolzano, Italy, in 1975. She lives and works in Stuttgart. Often having poetic titles that play on multiple associations, many of her exhibitions place animals, plants, and rural architectural at the center of her artistic investigation.

In Room 8 at the Hotel Rathausglöckel the bed is covered with numerous pillows, whose covers have been printed with representational drawings by Oberkofler. Small wooden sculptures are dispersed throughout the room and framed prints hang on the wall. The hotel room can be booked throughout the entire period of the exhibition. The guest can also try his or her hand in creating a »witch's brew«: all kinds of objects and ingredients are available for making a salve or a remedy against the evil eye or sleeplessness or to foster fertility or a hallucinatory expansion of consciousness, for example. Oberkofler thus wishes to develop the idea of an alternative image of the Black Forest region that runs counter to the idyll characterizing the works of painters such as Hans Thoma. If you hang the ubiquitous »Please Do Not Disturb« sign on your door, you can be sure that no witch will bother you during your stay at the hotel.

GUY BEN-NER

I'D GIVE IT TO YOU IF I COULD BUT I BORROWED IT

2007, Fahrrad, Computer, DVD / Bicycle, computer, DVD

Die Installation des israelischen Künstlers Guy Ben-Ner, geboren 1969, lädt den Betrachter ein, sich aktiv am Kunstwerk zu beteiligen. Ursprünglich bestand diese aus zwei Fahrrädern und einem Video. Durch das Treten der Pedale wird ein kleiner Bildschirm, der am Fahrrad befestigt ist, in Gang gesetzt mit der Möglichkeit, sowohl die Geschwindigkeit des Videos zu steuern als auch die Bilder vorwärts oder rückwärts ablaufen zu lassen. Hiermit vereinen sich Kunstwerk und Trainingsgerät und erzählen eine Geschichte über die Tradition des Readymade-Objektes. Das Video auf dem Bildschirm zeigt den Künstler zusammen mit seinen zwei Kindern, wie sie Teile von Kopien bekannter Kunstwerke von Marcel Duchamp, Pablo Picasso, Jean Tinguely und Joseph Beuys verwenden, ein funktionsfähiges Fahrrad daraus konstruieren und es anschließend beim Fahren durch die Stadt Münster ausprobieren. Readymades zeichneten sich stets durch die Transformation eines alltäglichen Gegenstandes in ein Kunstobjekt aus, welches seine Funktionalität negiert. Ben-Ner ließ die Dokumentation dieser Transformation rückwärts laufen und zeigte diese Arbeit zum ersten Mal im Jahr 2007 während der Ausstellung *Skulptur Projekte Münster,* nicht ohne einen ironischen Verweis auf den Begriff »Fahrradstadt« Münster.

Wie in vielen seiner früheren Projekte spielen auch dieses Mal der Künstler selbst und seine Kinder die Hauptrollen. Partizipation und Funktionalität sind wichtige Voraussetzungen für seine Werke. Dabei stellt Ben-Ner in seinen Videoarbeiten nicht selten das Konstrukt der Familie, die Kindererziehung und die Rolle des Mannes in unserer Gesellschaft infrage.

Während der Ausstellung ROOM SERVICE wird der Fitnessraum im Hotel Steigenberger Europäischer Hof in Baden-Baden in einen Ausstellungsraum umgewandelt: Mit Guy Ben-Ners partizipativer Installation bietet sich hier dem Besucher ein ganz spezielles *Kunst-Fitnesstraining,* das es ihm erlaubt, sich durch eigene Muskelkraft aktiv mit dem Kunstwerk zu verbinden.

The installation by Israeli artist Guy Ben-Ner, born in 1969, invites viewers to actively take part in the work. The installation initially consisted of two bicycles and a video. By pedaling, one activates a small screen that is attached to the bicycle, with the possibility of controlling both the speed of the video and allowing the images to play forward or backward. The installation thus combines an artwork and fitness machine, while also telling the story about the tradition of the readymade object. The video on the screen shows the artist with his two children as they use parts copied from famous works of art by Marcel Duchamp, Pablo Picasso, Jean Tinguely, and Joseph Beuys to construct a functioning bicycle, which they subsequently take on a test ride through the city of Münster. Readymades were always marked by the transformation of an everyday object into a work of art by negating its functionality. Ben-Ner plays the documentation of this process in reverse. The work was first shown in 2007 as part of *Sculpture Projects Münster 07,* thus including a tongue-in-cheek reference to the »bicycle city« of Münster.

As in many of his earlier projects, the artist and his children play the main roles in this installation. Participation and functionality are the important foundational elements of his work. Ben-Ner's videos often entail a critical examination the construct of the family, raising children, and the role of men in our society.

During the exhibition ROOM SERVICE the fitness center of the Hotel Steigenberger Europäischer Hof in Baden-Baden is turned into an exhibition space. Through Guy Ben-Ner's participatory installation, visitors can take part in a very special kind of »art workout« that encourages them to use their muscle power to actively engage with a work of art.

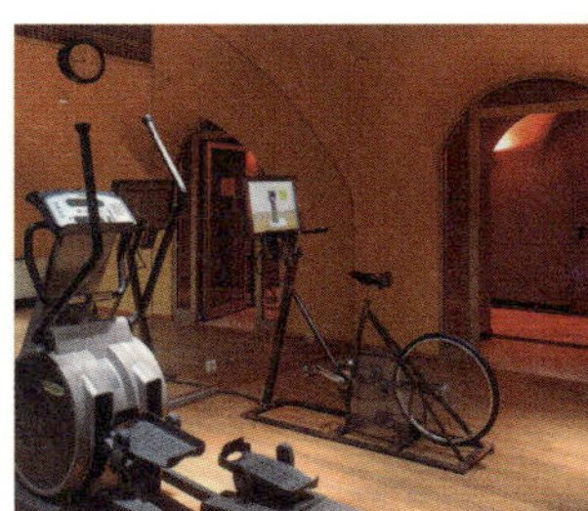

SIMONE DEMANDT

6 Arbeiten aus der offenen Werkgruppe / 6 works from the ongoing series

INDEPENDENTS: HOTEL HIRSCH

2005, Duratrans im Leuchtkasten / Duratrans in light box, 4 à 27 × 27 cm, 4 à 27 × 35 cm

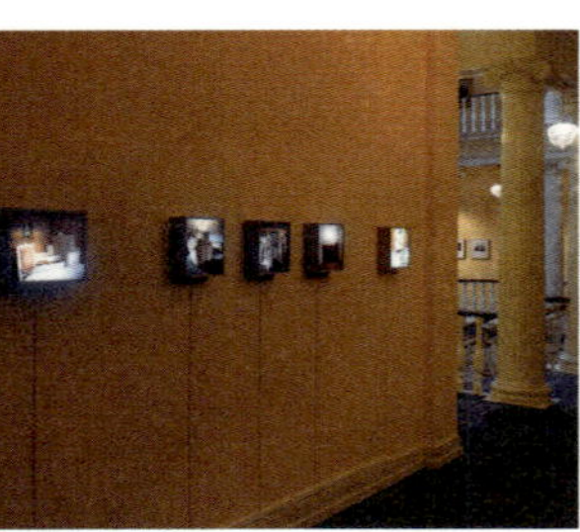

Das warme Licht des opulenten Kronleuchters vermag die kalte und verstörende Atmosphäre dieses Zimmers nicht zu beeinflussen. Vor dem leeren Bettgestell sind mitten im Raum mehrere Matratzen zu einer Wand gestapelt. Es scheint, als ob die Vergangenheit dieses Zimmers restlos getilgt werden soll und die Zukunft noch ungewiss ist. Die zahlreichen Menschen, die auf diesen Matratzen die Nächte ihres Kururlaubs oder ihrer Geschäftsreise verbracht haben, sind für immer vergessen. Ihre Geschichten haben sich einst in das Inventar des Hotels eingeschrieben; nun verwischt das abgebildete Arrangement jedwede Möglichkeit ihre Spuren noch weiter zu verfolgen.

Simone Demandt wurde 1959 in Dortmund geboren und studierte an der Staatlichen Akademie der Bildenden Künste in Stuttgart, arbeitete dort auch als Regieassistenz am Alten Schauspielhaus. Ihr Gespür für dramatische Inszenierungen, das auch in ihren fotografischen Arbeiten zutage tritt, wurde davon zweifelsohne geprägt. Seitdem hatte sie zahlreiche Lehraufträge, Ausstellungen und Auszeichnungen im In- und Ausland. Während der Versteigerung des Inventars des Baden-Badener Hotels Hirsch 2005 bekam die Künstlerin die Möglichkeit, diese ungewöhnlichen Aufnahmen zu machen. Sie zeigen uns Matratzen, Stühle und Bettgestelle in Anordnungen, die allein für sich schon zeitgenössische Installationen sein könnten. Durch den meisterlichen Umgang mit Licht und Komposition werden aus diesen Fotografien Manifestationen der Leere in hoffnungslos vollgestellten Räumen.

Diese Aufnahmen werden nun im Baden-Badener Hotel Steigenberger Europäischer Hof unweit ihres einstigen Entstehungsortes präsentiert. In den ordentlichen Fluren eines laufenden Hotelbetriebs eröffnen diese Bilder eine völlig andere, von den Gästen bereits verlassene Welt eines Heims auf Zeit.

The warm light of the ornate chandelier is unable to alter the cold and unsettling atmosphere of this room. Multiple mattresses have been piled up to form a wall. There seems be an intention to completely negate the history of the room, and its future is uncertain. The countless people who have spent nights of their spa vacation or business trip on these mattresses have been permanently forgotten. Their stories were once interwoven with the furnishings of the hotel; now the depicted arrangement had wiped out any possibility of capturing the traces that these individuals left behind.

Simone Demandt was born in Dortmund in 1959 and studied at the Stuttgart State Academy of Art and Design, and she still works in the city as an assistant director at the Altes Schauspielhaus. Her sense of dramatic staging, which comes through in her photographic work, has been doubtlessly influenced by this professional experience. She has taken part in numerous exhibitions and received prizes in Germany and abroad. During an auction of the inventory of the Hotel Hirsch in Baden-Baden in 2005 the artist had the opportunity to take these unusual photographs. The images show mattresses, chairs, and bed frames in configurations that could be taken for contemporary works of installation art. Her masterful use of light and composition make the photographs into manifestations of emptiness within hopelessly overfilled spaces.

These photographs are now on view in Baden-Baden's Hotel Europäischer Hof, not far from the site where they were originally taken. Shown in the hallways of a fully functioning hotel, the images open up an utterly different dimension of the temporary abode—abandoned by guests.

LIGNA

RAUM 315 / ROOM 315

2014, iPod, Audioaufnahme, 20 Min. / iPod, audio recording, 20 min.

Hören Sie genau zu, lassen Sie sich ein, auf die Stimme in Ihrem Ohr, achten Sie auf die Details, konzentrieren Sie sich auf Ihre Bewegungen im Raum, Sie haben ein Ziel – Raum 315.« Mit Kopfhörern und MP3-Playern ausgestattet begeben sich die Besucher auf einen Spaziergang durch das Hotel Steigenberger Europäischer Hof. Die Gruppe Ligna führt sie dabei mit ihrem Audio-Walk auf einen Pfad der Wandlung und zeigt das Hotel als transitorischen, alltagsfernen Ort. In seinem semianonymen Ambiente, fernab der privaten Behausung, gewohnter Muster und Zeitabläufe, wird hier für jeden Gast die Möglichkeit bereitgehalten, sich temporär neu zu erfinden.

Seit 1997 experimentieren die Medienkünstler Ole Frahm, Michael Hüners und Torsten Michaelsen gemeinsam als Ligna mit neuen Formen der Radiorezeption und begannen dabei, diese mit Konzepten des ortsspezifischen und politischen Theaters zu verknüpfen. Das 2002 im Hamburger Hauptbahnhof erstmalig aufgeführte RADIOBALLETT verbindet all diese Faktoren exemplarisch und ist wohl Lignas bekannteste Intervention. Über Radioempfänger erhalten die Teilnehmenden Anweisungen für eine Choreografie an Gesten, die sie jeweils an Orten ausführen, an denen sich die Grenzen immer weiter von öffentlichen hin zu privatisierten Räumen verschieben wie etwa in Bahnhofshallen, Fußgängerzonen und Einkaufszentren. Mit diesen Eingriffen in gewohnte Verhaltensweisen und Raumordnungen legt Ligna den Blick frei auf die Machtpolitiken, die vermeintlich öffentliche Räume strukturieren.

In ihrer für ROOM SERVICE entwickelten Arbeit präsentiert Ligna das Hotel als Fluchtraum aus der Realität, als Projektionsfläche für nicht alltägliche Fantasien, Wünsche und Handlungen. Dabei lässt sich dieses dem Hotelbesuch zugeschriebene Motiv durchaus auch auf die umgebende Stadt Baden-Baden übertragen: Mit ihren historisch-prominenten Wahrzeichen Trinkhalle und Casino vereint diese in gleichmütiger Weise Heils- und Glücksversprechen miteinander und kann daher ebenso sinnbildlich für dieses Fluchtmoment aus dem Alltäglichen stehen.

Listen closely; open yourself to the voice in your ear; pay attention to details; concentrate on your movements in space. You have a destination—Room 315.« Equipped with headphones and MP3-players, visitors take a walk through the Hotel Steigenberger Europäischer Hof. With their audio-walk the group Ligna accompanies visitors on a path of metamorphosis and paints the hotel as a transitory place far removed from the everyday. Within its semi-anonymous ambiance guests are extracted from private living space, familiar patterns, and routines; they are presented with the possibility of temporarily reinventing themselves.

Since 1997 media artists Ole Frahm, Michael Hüners, and Torsten Michaelsen have been experimenting together as Ligna with new forms of radio. They began by linking this with site-specific, political theater. The RADIOBALLETT (Radio Ballet), first performed at Hamburger Bahnhof in 2002, was an exemplary combination of all these elements and is Ligna's best-known intervention. Via radio receivers participants are given instructions for a choreography of gestures, which they perform at sites that are undergoing a transition from public to privatized spaces, such as railroad stations, pedestrian zones, and shopping malls. Through these interventions in accustomed behaviors and the organization of space, Ligna reveals the power politics that constitute what are supposedly public domains.

In the work developed for ROOM SERVICE Ligna presents the hotel as a refuge from reality, as a space onto which unusual fantasies, desires, and actions are projected. The motif of the audio-walk visit to the hotel can also be applied to the surrounding city of Baden-Baden. With its prominent historic landmarks of the drinking hall and the casino, the city similarly aligns the promises of good health and happiness, and it is equally embodies a moment of escape from ordinary routine.

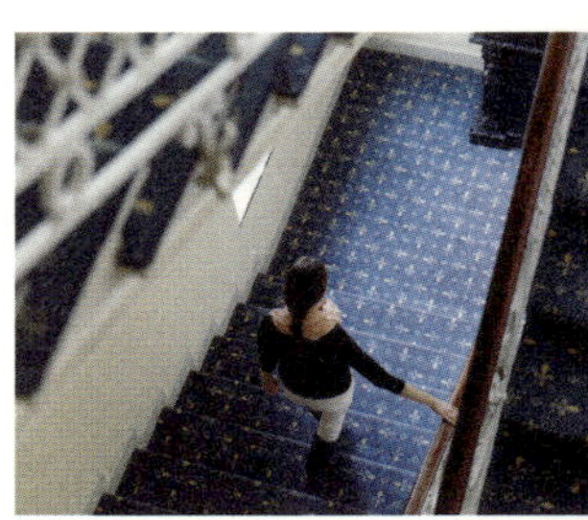

ARMIN LINKE & ELINA AXIOTI
DIE ARCHITEKTUR DES SERVICE
THE ARCHITECTURE OF SERVICE

2014, 3 Fotodrucke auf Alu-Dibond, je 50 × 60 cm, Offsetdruck, iPad, Video, 6 Min. / 3 photographic prints mounted on aluminium dibond each 50 × 60 cm, offset print, iPad, video, 6 min.

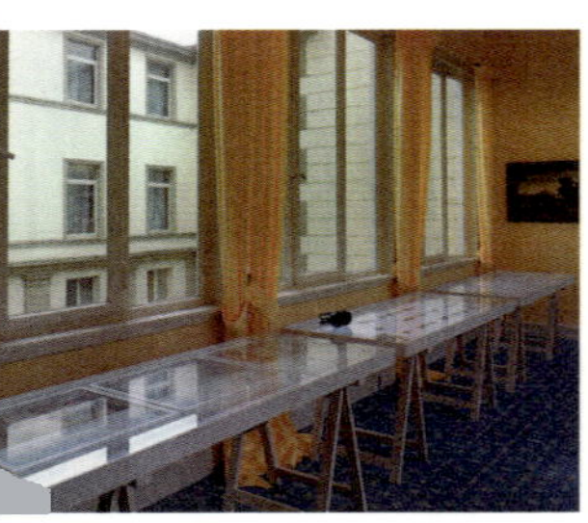

Das Forschungsprojekt THE ARCHITECTURE OF SERVICE von Armin Linke und Elina Axioti untersucht die Szenografie und versteckte Poesie der unsichtbaren Orte in Hotels. Dabei rücken sowohl die im Hintergrund ablaufenden Prozesse der Häuser als auch die Kommunikation der Servicemitarbeiter in den Fokus. Die praktische Realität des Servicesektors wird anhand sozialer Theorien, Fotografien, Übungsvideos, Organisationsplänen und Handbüchern präsentiert.

Within THE ARCHITECTURE OF SERVICE research project, Armin Linke and Elina Axioti investigate the scenography and the hidden poetics of invisible spaces in hotels. Their work focuses on the back of the house and the community of service workers. The practices of the service sector are presented through social theories, photographs, training videos, organization charts and manuals.

Der Butler in den Suiten des Plaza Hotels in New York City beschreibt den »persönlichen Weckdienst«, einen besonderen Service des Hotels. Die Hotelgäste werden morgens aufgeweckt, während Mitarbeiter in ein Zimmer kommen und dort sorgfältig die Atmosphäre verändern. Sie lassen Tageslicht ins Zimmer, bereiten Kaffee zu, dessen Duft sich im Zimmer ausbreitet, und lassen ein heißes Bad ein. Oder mit den Worten des Butlers: »Wir kommen ins Zimmer, öffnen die Vorhänge, lassen dem Gast ein Bad ein, wir legen auch die Kleidung zurecht, und während all dies geschieht, servieren wir einen Kaffee oder Cappuccino oder das Willkommengetränk.«[1]

Hotelmitarbeiter, die in Positionen arbeiten, bei denen Gästekontakt zu den Aufgaben gehört, sollen auf persönliche Art mit den Gästen umgehen und deren Bedürfnisse möglichst voraussehen. Sie sollten sich die Namen der Gäste und ihre persönlichen Vorlieben merken. Sie übernehmen Rollen, um auf eine Art mit den Gästen umzugehen, die ihre eigenen Gefühle unterdrückt und das einsetzen, was in der Dienstleistungsindustrie als »Oberflächenhandeln« (Englisch: *surface acting)* bekannt ist. Die Terminologie »surface acting« und »deep acting« wurde eingeführt, um schauspielerische Techniken zu beschreiben, die von Menschen im Dienstleistungssektor eingesetzt werden. Im Unterricht, beispielsweise bei Fortbildungen, werden von Mitarbeitern in bestimmten Positionen, wie zum Beispiel am Empfang, Standarddialoge eingeübt, allerdings sind diese Dialoge nicht ausreichend, da Hotelmitarbeiter auch in komplizierten Interaktionen mit Gästen bestehen müssen. Ein wichtiger Teil der Arbeitsleistung von Hotelangestellten wird von Hochschild als »Emotionsarbeit«[2] beschreiben, da viele Hotelmitarbeiter oft dazu verpflichtet sind, zu schauspielern, statt ehrlich zu reagieren und ihre wahren Gefühle zu äußern. Emotionskontrolle ist Teil der Ausbildung von im Dienstleistungssektor tätigen Menschen, wo Gefühlsregeln eingeführt werden.

Im Hotel gibt es einen unsichtbaren Mechanismus zur Regelung des Arbeitsflusses. Hotelmitarbeiter tragen zu einer methodischen Organisation des Tagesablaufs der Gäste bei. Die effiziente Organisation des Tagesablaufs der Gäste wird durch den Begriff »positive Gasterfahrung« definiert. »Gasterfahrung« ist ein übliches Kriterium für die

The butler at the Plaza Hotel Suites in New York City describes the »personalized wake up call«; a special service provided at the hotel. It concerns a way of waking up hotel guests in the morning while room attendants enter into a room and carefully manipulate its atmosphere. They let daylight into the room, make coffee so its smell is sensed in the room, and prepare a warm bath. In his own words: »We come into the room, we raise the shades, we draw the bath for the guest, we also lay out the clothing and everything is happening with a nice serving of coffee or cappuccino or the welcome drink.«[1]

Hotel employees working in positions that require contact and serving clients ought to interact and anticipate the needs of the guests in a personal manner. They should remember guests' names and personal preferences. They also adopt roles in order to interact with the guests in a way that one represses personal feelings and employs what is called »surface acting« in the language of the service sector. The terminology »surface acting« and »deep acting« has been introduced to describe performance and acting techniques used by people working in the service sector. Standard dialogues are exercised in training periods by the employees in certain positions, like the concierge. Nevertheless these dialogues are not adequate, as hotel employees have often to cope with complicated interactions with guests. An important part of hotel employees' performance is described by Hochschild as »emotional work«;[2] owing to the fact that hotel employees are very often obliged to act instead of responding genuinely and expressing their true feelings. Emotion management is part of the training of service workers, in which feeling rules are introduced.

An invisible workflow mechanism exists in the hotel. Hotel workers contribute to a methodical organization of guests' daily lives. The efficient organization of guests' routines is defined by the term »positive guest experience.« »Guest experience« is a common criterion for the evaluation of hotels' performance. Although it seems to be an abstract term; specific methodologies, concepts, and techniques exist on how to positively influence »guest experience.« Primarily, the term indicates the necessity for one's experience in a hotel to be calculated, to be controlled and »enhanced.«[3] Guest experience can be enhanced by stylish,

Bewertung der Performance eines Hotels. Obwohl es wie ein abstrakter Begriff erscheint, gibt es spezifische Methoden, Konzepte und Techniken, um die »Gasterfahrung« positiv zu beeinflussen. Vor allem verweist der Begriff auf die Notwendigkeit, die Erfahrung des Gastes in einem Hotel zu berechnen, zu steuern und »aufzuwerten«.[3] Die Gasterfahrung kann durch eine stilvolle, bequeme, saubere, luxuriöse Ausstattung aufgewertet werden – und durch den Service. Zwar ist diese Beschreibung sehr vereinfacht, aber die Idee des Service ist für die Zufriedenheit des Gastes von fundamentaler Bedeutung und beeinflusst sehr stark die organisatorischen Abläufe in einem Hotel.

Hotelinterieurs sind idealisierte Räume, ähnlich den Fotografien, die auf Buchungsseiten ins Internet eingestellt werden. »Entropische« Prozesse beginnen erst mit der Ankunft der Gäste. Gäste verbringen Zeit im Hotel und verändern das Interieur, verursachen Unordnung. Zimmermädchen erscheinen erst, wenn die Gäste das Hotel verlassen. Sie beseitigen Spuren oder Hinterlassenschaften, als würden sie ständig ein neutrales Bühnenbild konstruieren und erhalten. Sie arbeiten gegen die vergehende Zeit. Wenn Soziologen die Ansätze von Hotelleitungen kritisieren, verwenden sie Begriffe aus der Theaterwissenschaft, um das Phänomen der Konstruktion der »Gasterfahrung« zu analysieren.[4]

Zu den Mechanismen der Arbeitsabläufe in Hotels gehört ein Unterstützungssystem hinter den »Kulissen«. Die Arbeitsflüsse sind unterteilt in Abläufe, die »Front of House« und »Back of House«, stattfinden. »Front of House« ist ein Ort für Performance, wo die Mitarbeiter mit den Gästen interagieren. Hinter den Kulissen, »Back of House« also, ist der Ort für Vorbereitungen, die verstecke Infrastruktur, die die Szenerie am Leben erhält. Diese Kategorisierung ist entscheidend, um zu verstehen, dass Sichtbarkeit in den Abläufen eines Hotels von höchster Bedeutung ist. Die Unterteilung des Raums ist mit einer bestimmten Inszenierung verbunden. Hotels sind Umgebungen, wo Menschen aus unterschiedlichen gesellschaftlichen Klassen aufeinandertreffen und auf Arten miteinander agieren, die in Dienstleistungsanordnungen eingeschrieben sind. Der Zweck solcher Anordnungen und festgesetzter Abläufe ist es, gesellschaftliche Ungleichheit zu »absorbieren« und Unterschiede zu »normalisieren«.

Elina Axioti, Januar 2014

comfortable, clean, luxury interiors, as well as service. Although the latter description is simplified, the idea of service is fundamental to guests' satisfaction and influences to a great extent the practicalities of organization and management.

Hotel interiors maintain an idealized appearance, similar to their photographs posted in booking websites. »Entropic« processes start only by the time guests arrive. Guests consume time inside the hotel and alter the interior, causing disorder. Housekeepers appear only after the guests leave. They erase guests' traces or remains as if they were constantly constructing and maintaining a neutral stage set. They work against the passage of time. Sociologists use terms related to the theater studies in order to analyze the phenomenon of constructing the »guest experience« in their effort to criticize hotel management approaches.[4] The mechanism of workflow in hotels involves a supporting scheme behind the »scene.« Workflow is divided into »front of the house« and »back of the house« operations. The front of the house is a performance venue where employees interact with guests. The back of the house is the place of preparation; the hidden infrastructure that keeps the scene alive. This categorization is crucial in understanding that visibility is of utmost importance in hotel operations. The division of space is related to a certain theatricality. Hotels are environments where people from different social classes meet and interact in ways inscribed by operating and service protocols that seek to »absorb« social inequality and »normalize« difference.

Elina Axioti, January 2014

1 Zitat aus dem Video auf der Webseite des Plaza Hotels, mit folgender kurzer Beschreibung: »Für Gäste unserer Suiten sichern die Butler des Plaza den höchsten Standard an Luxus und Bequemlichkeit, sie lesen Ihnen jeden Wunsch von den Augen ab und erfüllen ihn.« www.theplazany.com, Zugriff im Januar 2014.

2 Dieser Text basiert auf der Lektüre von Arlie Russell Hochschilds Studie über Arbeiter im Dienstleistungssektor: *Das gekaufte Herz: Die Kommerzialisierung der Gefühle,* übersetzt von Ernst von Kardoff, Frankfurt am Main 2006.

3 »Steuerung der Gasterfahrung«, »Gastzufriedenheit«, »großartige Gasterfahrung«, »Gasterfahrung bei der Ankunft in der Lobby« – diese und ähnliche Begriffe werden häufig von Menschen im Hotelgewerbe benutzt.

4 Arlie Russell Hochschild, *Das gekaufte Herz: Die Kommerzialisierung der Gefühle,* übersetzt von Ernst von Kardoff, Frankfurt am Main 2006; Rachel Sherman, *Class Acts: Service and Inequality in Luxury Hotels,* Berkeley 2007.

1 Video posted on the Plaza Hotel website accompanied by the short description: »For suite guests The Plaza's butlers will provide the ultimate standard of luxury and comfort, anticipating your every need and accommodating your every wish,« www.theplazany.com, viewed on January 2014.

2 The text is based on a study of service workers by Arlie Russell Hochschild, *The Managed Heart: Commercialization of Human Feeling* (Berkeley: University of California Press, 1983).

3 »Guest experience management,« »guest satisfaction,« »great guest experience,« »guests arrival experience in the lobby,« the development of the »great room concept« and similar terminology are commonly used among people working for the hospitality industry.

4 Arlie Russell Hochschild, *The Managed Heart: Commercialization of Human Feeling* (Berkeley: University of California Press, 1983); and Rachel Sherman, *Class Acts: Service and Inequality in Luxury Hotels* (Berkeley: University of California Press, 2007).

FLORIAN SLOTAWA

Serie mit 12 Arbeiten / Series of 12 works

HOTELARBEITEN / HOTEL WORKS

1999, Baryth-Print / Baryth print, je / each 21 × 27 cm

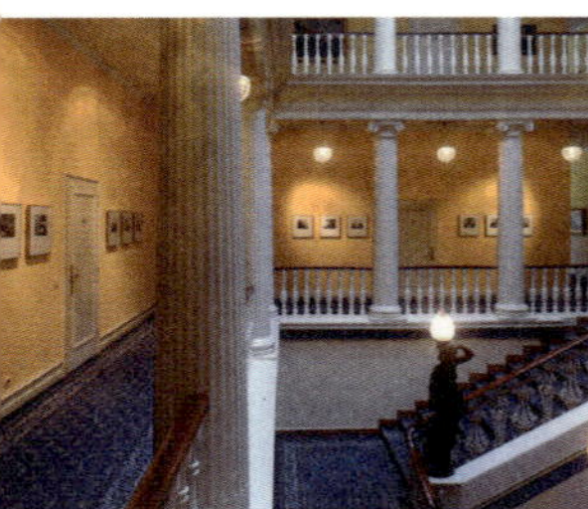

Die wie Schlafhöhlen anmutenden Möbelarrangements Florian Slotawas entstanden jeweils innerhalb einer Nacht, für die sich der Künstler in einem Mittelklassehotel einmietete. Stets war bis zum nächsten Morgen alles wieder zurückgebaut; nichts zeugte dann mehr von den nächtlichen Aktivitäten. Eine Matratze zuunterst werden zwei Seiten dieser Höhlen meist von einer Zimmerecke begrenzt, die anderen aus gerahmten Bildern, Teilen von auseinandergebauten Schränken, Spiegeln oder ausgehängten Türen gebildet. Slotawas Interventionen machen dabei auch vor absurden Orten nicht halt: neben dem Klo, als Aus- und Eingangssperre direkt vor der Zimmertür oder vor dem Durchgang zum Badezimmer, welches so nurmehr noch kriechend erreicht werden konnte. Die mit Blitz aufgenommenen Schwarz-Weiß-Fotografien entstanden in hell ausgeleuchteten Räumen, was ihnen trotz aller Kuriosität einen dokumentarischen Charakter verleiht.

Das künstlerische Material des 1972 in Rosenheim geborenen Slotawa bestand zunächst aus seinem eigenen Hab und Gut, aus dem er skulpturale Türme bis hin zu raumfüllenden Installationen baute. Kleine Modelle seines Mobiliars halfen ihm bei der Vorbereitung dieser Arbeiten, in denen jeder Gegenstand einen auf den Millimeter genau festgelegten Platz einnimmt. Seit dem Verkauf einer Installation, die seinen gesamten Besitz enthält, nutzt Slotawa auch fremde Gegenstände wie Sammlungsbestände oder das Büroinventar von Museen.

In HOTELARBEITEN wird nun die in die Jahre gekommene unpersönliche Zimmereinrichtung ihrer ursprünglichen Funktion enthoben und zum künstlerischen Material des Übernachtungsgastes. Slotawa spielt dabei auch mit seiner Gastrolle und verändert nicht nur den Blick auf die Gegenstände, sondern auch auf eine Situation des Alltags, in der das Verhalten normalerweise bestimmten Regeln folgt und in der herkömmlicherweise Schlaf gesucht und weniger das kreative Potenzial des Inventars in den Blick genommen wird. Im Flur des Hotels Steigenberger Europäischer Hof in Baden-Baden lassen Slotawas Dokumentationen für ROOM SERVICE spekulieren, was wohl gerade hinter den Zimmertüren passiert.

Resembling sleeping caves, Florian Slotawa's furniture arrangements were created over the course of a single night, for which the artist booked a room in a midclass hotel. By the next morning everything was always back in its place; nothing gave any indication of his nightly activities. With a mattress at the bottom, these caves are usually enclosed on two sides by the walls of the room, and the other sides are constructed out of framed pictures, parts of disassembled cupboards, mirrors, or doors that have been taken off their hinges. Slotawa's interventions even occupy absurd places: next to the toilet, directly in front of the door so that it is impossible to leave or enter, or right in front of the passage to the bathroom, which can now only reached on one's hands and knees. Photographed with a flash, the black and white images were taken in brightly lit rooms, which despite the curiosity of the situation, lend the photograph a documentary character.

The working materials of this artist, born in Rosenheim in 1972, initially consisted of his own belongings, which he piled up in sculptural towers and even turned into large-scale installations. Little models of his furniture helped him prepare these works, in which every object has a certain position, determined down to the millimeter. After the sale of one installation, which included all of his property, Slotawa began using other objects, such as the holdings of a collection or the contents of a museum office.

In HOTEL WORKS the worn, impersonal furnishings of a hotel room are removed of their original function and become the artistic material of an overnight guest. Slotawa plays with this role as a guest and not only alters the view of the objects but also of an everyday situation, in which behavior normally conforms to certain rules, and in which one usually tries to get some sleep instead of examining the creative potential of the contents of the room. In the hallway of the Steigenberger Europäischer Hof in Baden-Baden, Slotawa's documentation causes us to wonder what is currently taking place behind closed doors.

ANN LIV YOUNG
SHERAPY

2014, Performance mit verschiedenen Materialien sowie LKW, Video / Performance with various materials as well as truck, video
Performer: Ann Liv Young, RJ Supa Jr., Michael Guerrero | Video: Michael Guerrero

Sherry war hier! In einem Zimmer des Hotels Steigenberger Europäischer Hof bietet die extrovertierte Kunstfigur Sherry Vignon, eine leicht trashige US-amerikanische Südstaatlerin mit blonder Perücke, flächendeckendem Lidschatten und grellen Synthetikklamotten am Eröffnungswochenende einen besonderen Service an: Mit den SHERAPY genannten Therapiesitzungen für Einzelpersonen, Paare oder Haustiere werden sich Selbsterkenntnis und Heilung über Baden-Baden ausbreiten.

Die selbst in den Südstaaten der USA aufgewachsene Performance-Künstlerin Ann Liv Young studierte Tanz im renommierten Programm der Hollins University in Roanoke, Virginia, sowie am Londoner Laban Dance Centre. Seit Mitte der 2000er-Jahre entwickelt Young Arbeiten, die im Bereich der Performance-Art anzusiedeln sind. In ihren Shows dienen häufig bekannte Märchenvorlagen oder biografische Geschichten als Hintergrundfolie für Erzählungen, welche heteronormative Geschlechterrollen und Gesellschaftshierarchien verkehren oder überhöhen. So etwa in der Performance CINDERELLA (2010), aus der sich die Figur der Sherry letztlich als eigenständiger Charakter emanzipiert hat. Youngs Auftritte in Institutionen wie dem MoMA PS1 oder dem Projektraum The Kitchen in New York, aber auch Touren durch die europäischen Festivaltempel der Freien Theater- und Tanzszene wie Gessnerallee in Zürich, Kampnagel in Hamburg und dem in Graz beheimateten Festival steirischer herbst begründen ihren Ruf als verwegene Performerin und erfahrene Therapeutin.

Mit ihrem Alter Ego Sherry betreibt Young gezielt einen Bruch mit den Konventionen des Kunstbetriebs und den Erwartungshaltungen von Zuschauern wie Kuratoren an vermeintlich authentische performative Formate. Dabei hat Young mit einer größeren Palette an Merchandise-Produkten und dem mobilen Sherry-Truck, in dem diese Produkte häufig im Anschluss an die SHERAPIEN feilgeboten werden, einen ganz eigenen Kosmos um die Persona Sherry herum kreiert. Mit dieser speziellen Form des Produktmarketings verweist Ann Liv Young auf die Verflechtung von sozialen Ritualen und deren kapitalistischer Verwertung sowie auf die ebenso ambivalente zwischen Kunst und Kommerz.

Sherry was here! In one room of the hotel Steigenberger Europäischer Hof an extroverted character named Sherry Vignon, a slightly tacky-looking woman with a southern U.S. accent, blond wig, thick eyeshadow, and bright polyester clothes is offering a special service on the opening weekend of the exhibition. Through her so-called SHERAPY sessions for individuals, couples, and pets she intends to promote self-realization and healing throughout Baden-Baden.

Performance artist Ann Liv Young, who grew up in the southern U.S. herself, studied dance at the renowned program of Hollins University in Roanoke, Virginia, and at London's Laban Centre. Since the mid 2000s Young has been developing works that could be characterized as performance art. Often well-known fairytales or biographical stories serve as the basis for narratives that exaggerate or invert the relationship between the sexes or social hierarchies. One example is the performance CINDERELLA (2010), from which the figure of Sherry subsequently emancipated herself as a kind of spin-off. Young's performances at institutions such as MoMA PS1 and the Kitchen in New York as well as her tours of festivals of Europe's alternative theater and dance scenes—such as Gessnerallee in Zurich, Kampnagel in Hamburg, and steirischer herbst in Graz—have solidified her reputation as a bold performer and experienced therapist.

Through her alter ego Sherry, Young breaks with the conventions of the art world and counters the expectations of viewers such as curators, who are accustomed to performance formats with apparently authentic content. With her large array of merchandise and the mobile SHERRY TRUCK, where products are often sold after SHERAPY, the artist has created a unique cosmos surrounding this imaginary figure. With this form of merchandising, Ann Liv Young points at the enmeshment between social rituals and their capitalistic exploitation and those between art and commerce.

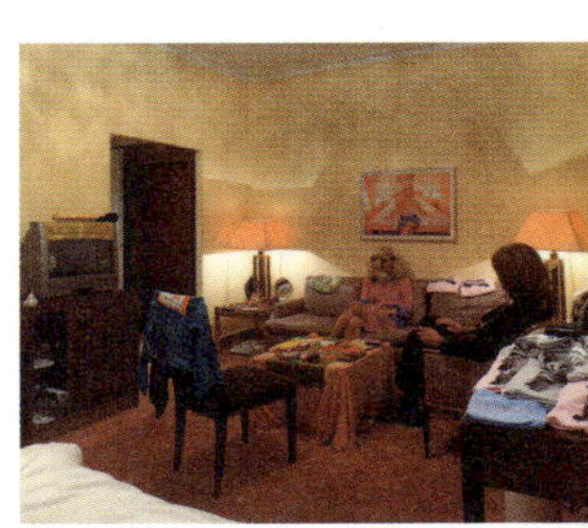

THE ARMOIRE SHOW 2014

Eine Ausstellung kuratiert von Hans Ulrich Obrist in Anlehnung an sein Projekt HOTEL CARLTON PALACE: CHAMBRE 763 aus dem Jahr 1993 und die darin präsentierte Ausstellung in der Ausstellung ARMOIRE SHOW
An exhibition curated by Hans Ulrich Obrist and based on his project HOTEL CARLTON PALACE: CHAMBRE 763 from 1993, an exhibition within the ARMOIRE SHOW
Mit Werken von / With works by DAS INSTITUT | DIS | Tracey Emin | K-Hole | Sarah Lucas | Reiner Ruthenbeck | Ryan Trecartin | Rosemarie Trockel | Amalia Ulman | Franz Erhard Walther | Xu Zhen

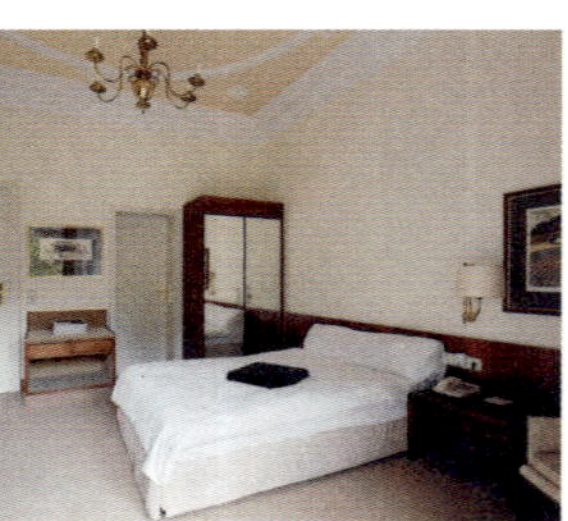

Auf dem Bett des Zimmers 130 im Hotel Steigenberger Europäischer Hof liegt ein großes quadratisches Objekt mit einer schwarzen Oberfläche. Ansonsten sieht es hier fast wie in einem gewöhnlichen Hotelzimmer aus. Erst, wer den Eckschrank öffnet, findet dort eine Reihe von Gegenständen vor, die nicht nach üblichen Reiseutensilien eines Gastes aussehen. In eben diesem Schrank hat der renommierte Kurator Hans Ulrich Obrist eine *Ausstellung* installiert, die an ein legendäres Projekt anknüpft, das er vor 21 Jahren in einem Pariser Hotelzimmer initiierte.

Nach seiner Ankunft in Paris im Jahr 1993 bezog Obrist ein kleines einfaches Zimmer im Hotel Carlton Palace und begann es, nach und nach mit Kunstwerken auszustatten. Das Personal des Hotels bemerkte erst, dass es sich bei den vielen kommenden und gehenden Gästen in Zimmer 763 um *Ausstellungsbesucher* handelt, nachdem mehrere Artikel über das ungewöhnliche Projekt in den Zeitungen *Le Monde* und *Le Figaro* erschienen waren. Inzwischen gab es Werke von knapp 70 Künstlern auf den 12 Quadratmetern zu sehen. Der Kleiderschrank dieses Zimmers wurde zu einer Ausstellung in der Ausstellung, die von Obrist als THE ARMOIRE SHOW betitelt wurde. Nur das LECKERLI von Reiner Ruthenbeck wurde als einzelne Arbeit in einem anderen Zimmer präsentiert. Nun ist es auf dem Bett in Baden-Baden zu sehen – räumlich vereint mit der Kleiderschrankschau.

Für Baden-Baden hat Hans Ulrich Obrist in der Revision des Projekts von 1993 zehn Künstler eingeladen, neue Werke für den Schrank in Zimmer 130 zu schaffen. Parallel dazu ist im Rahmen des Ausstellungsteils in der Kunsthalle Baden-Baden eine Dokumentation der damaligen Hotelausstellung mit Fotografien von Pierre Leguillon zu sehen. Eine dazu von der Kunsthalle herausgegebene Publikation führt auf 64 Seiten durch diese inzwischen historische Pariser Schau. Die Idee von Obrists HOTEL CARLTON: CHAMBRE 763 wurde in Baden-Baden als Blaupause für den Versuch gesehen, den ungewöhnlichen Rahmen des Hotels selbst als Ausstellungsort zu nutzen. Der Kunstparcours durch die Stadt gab Künstlern die Möglichkeit, sich in den Hotels auszubreiten und dort facettenreiche und ortsspezifische Projekte zu zeigen. In diesem Rahmen sind während der Ausstellung 25 Künstler in sechs Hotels zu sehen.

On the bed of Room 130 at the Hotel Steigenberger Europäischer Hof lies a giant square object with a black surface. Otherwise, the room looks almost like any ordinary hotel room. Only upon opening a corner closet does one find a series of objects find that do not have the appearance of the normal travel accessories of a hotel guest. In this cupboard the well-known curator Hans Ulrich Obrist mounted an *exhibition,* which refers to a legendary project that he did over 21 years ago in a Paris hotel room.

After arriving in Paris in 1993 Obrist moved into a small, simple room at the Hotel Carlton Palace and gradually began to fill it with works of art. The staff of the hotel only noticed that the many visitors coming and going to Room 763 were actually *exhibition visitors,* when a number of the works included in this unusual project appeared in the newspapers *Le Monde* and *Le Figaro.* Meanwhile, the works of almost 70 artists had been gathered within this 12-square-meter space. The wardrobe became an exhibition within the exhibition, which Obrist called THE ARMOIRE SHOW. Only Reiner Ruthenbeck's LECKERLI was presented in another room as a solitary work. Now it shares the same room as the exhibition in the wardrobe.

Obrist has invited ten artists to create works for the armoire in Room 130 in a new take on his 1993 project. Complementing this presentation, a documentation of the original hotel exhibition, photographed by Pierre Leguillon, is on view in the exhibition at the Kunsthalle Baden-Baden. Also, a 64-page publication produced by the Kunsthalle looks at this now historic Parisian exhibition. In Baden-Baden the idea of Obrist's HOTEL CARLTON: CHAMBRE 763 was used as a blueprint for the unusual idea of using the hotel setting as an exhibition site. The walking tour through the city has given artists the possibility to spread out in hotels, where they can present diverse, site-specific, and performative projects. The work of 25 artists is presented in six hotels.

BYUNG CHUL KIM

PERFORMANCE HOTEL

2014

Baden-Badener Sommergäste müssen in diesem Jahr kein teures Fünfsternehotel aufsuchen, sondern können dank Byung Chul Kim kostengünstiger unterkommen. In seinem PERFORMANCE HOTEL etabliert der Künstler eine unkonventionelle Möglichkeit der Herbergskultur: Statt mit Geld kann der Gast hier die Übernachtung auch mit einer künstlerischen Darbietung wie einer Performance bezahlen, die dann vor Ort einem interessierten Publikum präsentiert wird. In Kims PERFORMANCE HOTEL werden die in größeren Hotels üblichen Serviceangebote in angemessener Weise *übersetzt.* So fallen Wellness- und Fitnessbereich hier in eins zusammen, wenn sich etwa der Gast dazu entscheidet, bei der morgendlichen Katzen wäsche mit einem Waschlappen den Körper nach schriftlich fixierter Anweisung rhythmisch abzurubbeln. Das hotel eigene *Kino* wiederum zeigt Videoarbeiten von Kim auf einem kleinen Monitor in dem als Hotellobby umfunktionierten Pfarramtsflur.

Der aus Korea stammende Künstler Byung Chul Kim studierte zunächst in Seoul Malerei, bevor er ab 2005 an die Staatliche Akademie der Bildenden Künste Stuttgart wechselte. Dort absolviert er die Klasse für Freie Kunst unter anderen bei Christian Jankowski. Sein PERFORMANCE HOTEL in Baden-Baden ist die Wiederaufnahme einer Arbeit, die Kim bereits von 2009 bis 2010 in Stuttgart – hier gemeinsam mit anderen Studenten und der Hochschule der Bildenden Künste Saar – umgesetzt hat. In seiner Arbeit PERFORMANCE EXPRESS aus dem Jahr 2011 setzte Kim das Prinzip performative Leistungen als nicht-monetäre Ware einzusetzen fort, indem man hier einen Zugfahrschein für eine Performance eintauschen konnte.

Auf dem Kunstparcours von ROOM SERVICE durch die Hotels Baden-Baden ist diese Station eine besondere Plattform für interaktive Arbeiten. Dabei lässt Kims Interpretation eines Hotels und die Verbindung seiner Kunst mit ganz alltäglichen Handlungen und Erfahrungen auch an Ideen der Konzeptkunst der 1960er-Jahre denken. Mit diesem Werk bezieht Kim eine deutliche Position für ein alternatives Verständnis von Ökonomie, das eine an partizipativen Strategien orientierte Kultur in den Fokus rückt.

This summer, visitors to Baden-Baden will not need to book a five-star hotel. Thanks to Byung Chul Kim, more affordable accommodations will be available. In his PERFORMANCE HOTEL the artist fosters a different kind of hotel culture. Instead of using money, guests can pay for their overnight stay with an artistic contribution, a performance, which is then presented to an interested public.

In Kim's PERFORMANCE HOTEL, the service offerings that are standard in larger hotels are »translated« in an appropriate way. For example, the spa and fitness areas are combined, when the guest decides to rub their bodies rhythmically with a washcloth for morning cleaning, following written instructions. The hotel's own »cinema« presents video works by Kim on a small monitor in the hall of a rectory that now serves as the hotel lobby.

Born in Korea, Kim first studied painting in Seoul before transferring to the Stuttgart's Staatliche Akademie der Bildenden Künste, where he studied with Christian Jankowski. PERFORMANCE HOTEL in Baden-Baden is a reinterpretation of a work that Kim carried out from 2009 to 2010 in Stuttgart together with other students of the academy in Stuttgart and the Hochschule der Bildenden Künste Saar. In his 2011 work PERFORMANCE EXPRESS, Kim continued the principle of performative offerings as a non-monetary commodity, whereby a performance could be exchanged for a train ticket.

Along the walking tour through the hotels of Baden-Baden, this station serves as a special platform for non-commercial projects and interaction. Kim's interpretation of a hotel and the way his art is embedded in everyday experience recall elements of 1960s conceptual art. In his works, he clearly advocates alternative economic practices and a form of culture that is oriented towards participatory strategies.

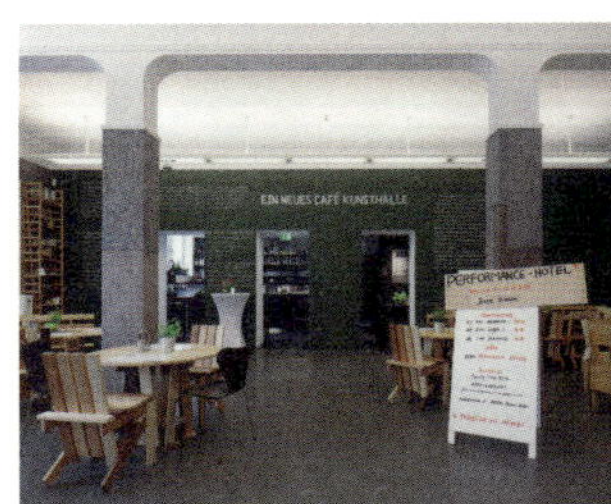

MARKUS ORTHS

DAS ZIMMERMÄDCHEN / CHAMBER MAID

Mit / With: Oliver Jacobs, Anne Leßmeister | Inszenierung / Directed by: Anna Köpnick | Ausstattung / Costumes: Sebastian Ganz
In Zusammenarbeit mit dem / In cooperation with Theater Baden-Baden

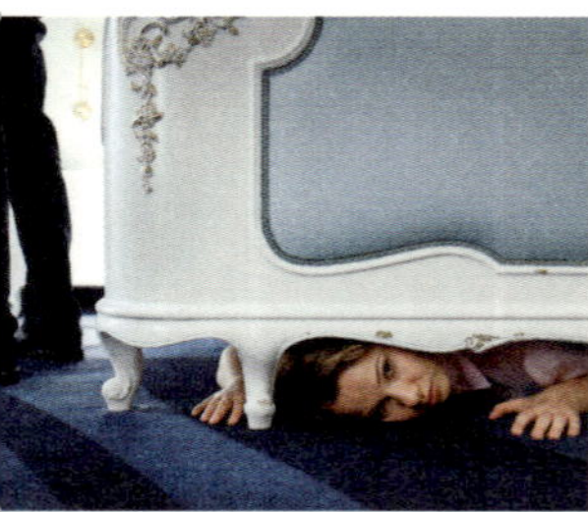

Lynn ist ein wachsames Zimmermädchen. Eines, für das sich jedes Hotel mit Kusshand bedanken würde. Nichts entgeht Lynns Aufmerksamkeit und Staub ist ihr Lieblingsfeind, an dem sie sich obsessiv abarbeitet. Nach einem langen Klinikaufenthalt will sie ihr Leben nun endlich strukturieren – nichts mehr dem Zufall überlassen und ihre Mutter auf Distanz halten. Doch anstelle des eigenen Daseins nimmt sie mit wachsender Lust die Hotelzimmer in Beschlag. Dort kann sie sich ungestört in andere Leben imaginieren, in fremde Gerüche und Gebräuche. Die unbekannte Nähe und unerhörterweise überschrittene Distanz zu den Gästen wird ihre neue Leidenschaft, die kulminiert, als sie sich unter einem Hotelbett verstecken muss. Unbemerkt von den ahnungslosen Personen in dem Bett über ihr, wird sie fortan zur atemlosen Voyeuristin. Aus dieser Perspektive verliebt sie sich in die Edelprostituierte Chiara. Sie verlässt ihren Beobachtungsposten und kauft sich bei Chiara portionsweise Sex. Lynn will jetzt endlich *richtig* leben. Doch schon bald wird auch dieses Verhältnis zur neuen Obsession in ihrem Kampf gegen das permanente und persönliche Scheitern.

Der Autor dieses Werkes, Markus Orths, studierte Philosophie, Romanistik und Anglistik in Freiburg und lebt heute als Schriftsteller in Karlsruhe. Drei seiner Bücher sind in insgesamt 17 Sprachen übersetzt worden. In Paris gewann das Theaterstück *Femme de Chambre* 2012 den Prix Théâtre 13 sowie den Publikumspreis. Das Theater Baden-Baden präsentiert Markus Orths' Erzählung um unbekannte Nähe und unerhörte Distanzüberschreitung nun genau dort, wo sie spielt: in einem Hotel.

Das Hotel Radisson Blu Badischer Hof in Baden-Baden gehört zu den ältesten Grand Hotels in Europa und bietet mit seiner opulenten Säulenhalle den perfekten Rahmen für die Inszenierung dieser besonderen Hotelstory. Hier werden die Momentaufnahmen aus dem Leben der Gäste auf unnachahmliche Weise mit der privaten Geschichte eines Zimmermädchens verwoben und in die repräsentativen Räume eines berühmten Hotels übertragen.

Lynn is a vigilant chambermaid, the kind that any hotel would welcome with open arms. Nothing escapes her attention, and dust is her favorite enemy, to which she obsessively dedicates her energies. After an extended stay in a clinic, she decides to finally get her life organized—to leave nothing more to chance and keep her mother at bay. But instead of establishing a life of her own, she becomes increasingly engrossed in the rooms of the hotel. There she is undisturbed and can picture herself in another life, in the midst of foreign smells and customs. The anonymous proximity to the hotel guests and the egregious transgressions of the boundaries between them and herself become her new obsession, which culminates in her having to hide underneath a bed. Unnoticed by the unsuspecting people in the bed above her, from then on she becomes a breathless voyeur. While in this position she falls in love with the high-class prostitute Chiara. Leaving the role of the observer, she buys bits of sex from Chiara. Lynn now finally wants to »really« live, but soon this relationship also turns into the next obsession in her struggle against her ongoing, personal failures.

The author of this drama, Markus Orths, studied philosophy, romantic language, and English in Freiburg and currently lives in Karlsruhe as a writer. His books have been translated into 17 languages. In Paris his drama *Femme de Chambre* won the Prix Théâtre 13 in 2012 as well as the Public Choice Award. The Theater Baden-Baden is presenting Markus Orths' story of anonymous proximity and egregious transgression at the place where it unfolds—in a hotel.

The Hotel Radisson Blu Badischer Hof in Baden-Baden is one of the oldest grand hotels in Europe. With its opulent columned hall it provides the perfect setting for the staging of this unique hotel story, in which snapshots from the lives of guests are inimitably interwoven with the personal story of a chambermaid—and are transposed onto the prestigious interior of a famous hotel.

RADISSON BLU BADISCHER HOF

DANKSAGUNG / ACKNOWLEDGMENTS

Die Staatliche Kunsthalle Baden-Baden dankt / The Staatliche Kunsthalle Baden-Baden would like to thank

Christian Andersson | Elina Axioti | Guy Ben-Ner | Jenny Brillhart | Sophie Calle | DAS INSTITUT (Kerstin Brätsch, Adele Röder) | Simone Demandt | Thomas Demand | DIS (Lauren Boyle, Solomon Chase, Marco Roso, David Toro) | William Eggleston | Tracey Emin | Hans-Peter Feldmann | Fischli / Weiss | Andreas Gursky | Eberhard Havekost | Candida Höfer | Irène Hug | Christian Jankowski | Sven Johne | K-Hole (Emily Segal, Dana Yago) | On Kawara | Byung Chul Kim | Lee Kit | Pierre Leguillon | Ligna (Thorsten Michaelsen, Michael Hüners, Ole Frahm) | Armin Linke | Sarah Lucas | Tobias Madison | Kevin McGarry | Chantal Michel | Olaf Nicolai | Gabriela Oberkofler | Hans Ulrich Obrist | Gabriel Orozco | Reiner Ruthenbeck | Markus Schinwald | Thomas Schütte | Roman Signer | Cindy Sherman | Florian Slotawa | Daniel Spoerri | Christine Streuli | Guy Tillim | Ryan Trecartin | Rosemarie Trockel | Amalia Ulman | Ian Wallace | Franz Erhard Walther | Ann Liv Young | Naneci Yurdagül | Xu Zhen

bpk – Bildagentur für Kunst, Kultur und Geschichte, Berlin | Bernd Dörken | Best Western Hotel Spaander, Volendam | Eggleston Artist Trust, New York | Friedrich Christian Flick Collection im Hamburger Bahnhof | Deichtorhallen Hamburg / Sammlung Falckenberg | Deichtorhallen Hamburg / Haus der Photographie | Daumier Register | Die Photographische Sammlung / SK Stiftung Kultur, Köln | Dr. Frank Zahn | Estate of Martin Kippenberger, Galerie Gisela Capitain, Köln | Galerie Cheim & Read, New York | Galerie Gebr. Lehmann, Dresden / Berlin | Galerie KLEMM'S, Berlin | Galerie Kuckei + Kuckei, Berlin | Galerie Perrotin, Paris | Galerie Sprüth Magers Berlin London | Galerie Wien Lukatsch, Berlin | Hauser & Wirth, Zürich, London | Hotel Castell, Zuoz | Johnen Galerie / Berlin | Kasper König, Berlin | Felix Damm | Fondation Henri Cartier-Bresson, Paris | K. Sandmann, Berlin | Kunstmuseum Basel | Kunstmuseum Luzern | Kunstmuseum Solothurn | Kupferstichkabinett – Staatliche Museen zu Berlin | LWL Landesmuseum für Kunst und Kulturgeschichte Westfälisches Landesmuseum, Münster | Marco Pasetti | Museum Folkwang, Essen | Museum Ludwig, Köln | Olaf Hajek | Sammlung Olbricht | Otto Modersohn Museum, Ottersberg | Privatsammlung Karena Schuessler | Sammlung Deutsche Bank | Sammlung Dr. Scheefers-Borchel und Dr. Scheefers | Sammlung Ruedi Bechtler | Sies & Höke Galerie, Düsseldorf | Skagens Museum, Skagen | SØR Rusche Sammlung, Oelde/Berlin | Staatsgalerie Stuttgart | Städel Museum, Frankfurt am Main | Stadtmuseum und Stadtarchiv Baden-Baden | Stiftung F. C. Gundlach | Stiftung im Obersteg, Depositum im Kunstmuseum Basel | Stiftung Kunstfonds | Tate, London | The Andy Warhol Museum, Pittsburgh | The Estate of Diane Arbus, New York | The National Media Museum, Bradford | Vanhaerents Art Collection, Brüssel | Victoria and Albert Museum, London | sowie allen Leihgebern, die nicht namentlich genannt werden möchten / and all others who loaned works for the exhibition without wishing to be named

In Baden-Baden: Atlantic Parkhotel, Ann-Katrin und / and Anja Schwemmle, Adolf Hans Scherer, Elmar Hohmann | Brenners Park – Hotel & Spa – Frank Marrenbach, Stephan Bösch, Bärbel I. Göhner | Hotel Belle Epoque – Andreas und / and Melissa Rademacher | Radisson Blu Badischer Hof – Katja Dietz, Michael Krug, Bodo Sikora | Rathausglöckel – Familie Asel | Steigenberger Europäischer Hof – Kai-Uwe Wellner | Theater Baden-Baden – Benjamin Bracher, Anna Katharina Köpnick, Nicola Mai | Baden-Baden Kur und Tourismus GmbH – Brigitte Goertz-Meissner, Anne-Greth Paulus | Gartenamt Baden-Baden – Markus Brünsing

Michael Belogour | Christian Ertel | Achim Kukulies | Jens Rudolph | Steffen Schuhmann | sowie allen internen und externen Mitarbeitern der Staatlichen Kunsthalle Baden-Baden, die zur Entstehung der Ausstellung und des Katalogs beigetragen haben. / as well as the entire internal and external staff of the Staatliche Kunsthalle Baden-Baden that contributed to the realization of the exhibition and the catalogue.

BILDRECHTE / CREDITS

Andreas Gursky (*1955)
Titel: TAIPEI, 1999, Chromogendruck, 117 × 149,1 cm, Courtesy: Sprüth Magers Berlin London, © Andreas Gursky / VG Bild-Kunst, Bonn 2014
Cover: TAIPEI, 1999, chromogenic print, 117 × 149.1 cm, courtesy: Sprüth Magers Berlin London, © Andreas Gursky / VG Bild-Kunst, Bonn 2014

Joseph Mallord William Turner (1775–1851)
S. 138: HAMBURG: BLICK ÜBER DEN JUNGFERNSTIEG AUF DAS HOTEL BELVEDERE MIT DEN TÜRMEN DER JACOBIKIRCHE UND DER PETRIKIRCHE DAHINTER, aus dem: HAMBURG UND KOPENHAGEN SKIZZENBUCH, 1835, Grafit auf Papier, 15,5 × 9,2 cm, Courtesy: Tate, London: Von der Nation als Teil des Turner Nachlasses akzeptiert 1856, © Tate, London, 2014
P. 138: HAMBURG: VIEW ALONG THE JUNGFERNSTIEG TO THE HOTEL BELVEDERE WITH THE SPIRES OF THE JACOBIKIRCHE AND PETRIKIRCHE BEYOND, from the: HAMBURG AND COPENHAGEN SKETCHBOOK, 1835, graphite on paper, 15.5 × 9.2 cm, courtesy: Tate, London: accepted by the nation as part of the Turner Bequest 1856, © Tate, London, 2014
S. 139: TURNERS SCHLAFZIMMER IM PALAZZO GIUSTINIAN (HOTEL EUROPA), VENEDIG, um 1840, Wasserfarben auf Papier, 23 × 30,2 cm, Courtesy: Tate, London: Von der Nation als Teil des Turner Nachlasses akzeptiert 1856, © Tate, London, 2014
P. 139: TURNER'S BEDROOM IN THE PALAZZO GIUSTINIAN (THE HOTEL EUROPA), VENICE, c. 1840, watercolor on paper, 23 × 30.2 cm, courtesy: Tate, London: accepted by the nation as part of the Turner Bequest 1856, © Tate, London, 2014
S. 140: VENEDIG: BLICK ÜBER DIE DÄCHER VOM HOTEL EUROPA AUS, 1840, Grafitstift und Wasserfarben auf Papier, 24,5 × 30,5 cm, Courtesy: Tate, London: Von der Nation als Teil des Turner Nachlasses akzeptiert 1856, © Tate, London, 2014
P. 140: VENICE: VIEW OVER THE ROOF TOPS FROM THE HOTEL EUROPA, 1840, graphite and watercolor on paper, 24.5 × 30.5 cm, courtesy: Tate, London: accepted by the nation as part of the Turner Bequest 1856, © Tate, London, 2014

John Constable (1776–1837)
S. 141: DER STRAND VON BRIGHTON, MIT FISCHERBOOTEN UND DEM CHAIN PIER, ca. 1824, Zeichenstift, Bleistift und Wasserfarben, 17,8 × 25,9 cm, Courtesy: Sammlung Victoria and Albert Museum, London, Schenkung von Isabel Constable 1888, © Victoria and Albert Museum, London 2014
P. 141: BRIGHTON BEACH, WITH FISHING BOATS AND THE CHAIN PIER, ca. 1824, pen, pencil and watercolor, 17.8 × 25.9 cm, courtesy: Collection Victoria and Albert Museum, London, given by Isabel Constable in 1888, © Victoria and Albert Museum, London 2014

William Henry Fox Talbot (1800–1877)
S. 142: RUE DE LA PAIX, HOTEL CANTERBURY, 1843, Talbotypie-Negativ, 16,1 × 21,3 cm, Courtesy: National Media Museum / Science & Society Picture Library, © National Media Museum / Science & Society Picture Library
P. 142: RUE DE LA PAIX, HOTEL CANTERBURY, 1843, talbotype negative, 16.1 × 21.3 cm, courtesy: National Media Museum / Science & Society Picture Library, © National Media Museum / Science & Society Picture Library

Honoré Daumier (1808–1879)
S. 143: EINE VORÜBERGEHENDE BEHAUSUNG, aus der Serie MIETER UND VERMIETER, 1854, Lithografie, 26,9 × 21,4 cm, Courtesy: www.daumier.org
P. 143: A TEMPORARY LODGING, from the series TENANTS AND LANDLORDS, 1854, lithograph, 26.9 × 21.4 cm, courtesy: www.daumier.org
S. 143: DIE LETZTE ZUFLUCHT FÜR BESUCHER OHNE ZIMMER. ER TRÄUMT DAVON, IM BESTEN ZIMMER DES HOTEL DES PRINCES ZU NÄCHTIGEN, aus der Serie WELTAUSSTELLUNG, 1855, Lithografie, 25,7 × 18,7 cm, Courtesy: www.daumier.org
P. 143: THE LAST RESORT FOR TRAVELLERS WITHOUT LODGINGS. HE DREAMS ABOUT SLEEPING IN THE BEST ROOM OF THE HOTEL DES PRINCES, from the series WORLD EXHIBITION, 1855, lithography, 25.7 × 18.7 cm, courtesy: www.daumier.org
S. 144: DAS NACHTASYL, 1842–1843, Holzschnitt, 4,2 × 7 cm, Courtesy: www.daumier.org
P. 144: A STAY FOR THE NIGHT, 1842–1843, wood engraving, 4.2 × 7 cm, courtesy: www.daumier.org
S. 144: EIN HOTEL GARNI, 1842–1843, Holzschnitt, 9,5 × 6 cm, Courtesy: www.daumier.org
P. 144: A CHEAP PLACE TO SLEEP, 1842–1843, wood engraving, 9.5 × 6 cm, courtesy: www.daumier.org

Adolph Menzel (1815–1905)
S. 145: BLICK VOM BALKON DES HOTELS DETZER AUF DEN INNSBRUCKER PLATZ IN MÜNCHEN, 1882, Bleistift auf Papier, 18,3 × 11,5 cm, Courtesy: Sammlung Kupferstichkabinett – Staatliche Museen zu Berlin
P. 145: VIEW FROM BALCONY OF THE HOTEL DETZER ON INNSBRUCKER SQUARE IN MUNICH, pencil on paper, 1882, 18.3 × 11.5 cm, courtesy: Collection Kupferstichkabinett – Staatliche Museen zu Berlin

Francis Frith (1822–1898)
S. 146: THE NEW HOTEL KAIRO, 1850–1870, Albumindruck, 42,3 × 57,5 cm, Courtesy: Sammlung Victoria and Albert Museum, London, akquiriert von F. Frith and Company, 1954, © Victoria and Albert Museum, London, 2014
P. 146: THE NEW HOTEL CAIRO, 1850–1870, albumen print, 42.3 × 57.5 cm, courtesy: Collection Victoria and Albert Museum, London, acquired from F. Frith and Company, 1954, © Victoria and Albert Museum, London, 2014
S. 146: SHEPHERD'S HOTEL. KAIRO, 1850–1870, Albumindruck, 42,3 × 57,5 cm, Courtesy: Sammlung Victoria and Albert Museum, London, akquiriert von F. Frith and Company, 1954, © Victoria and Albert Museum, London, 2014
P. 146: SHEPHERD'S HOTEL. CAIRO, 1850–1870, albumen print, 42.3 × 57.5 cm, courtesy: Collection Victoria and Albert Museum, London, acquired from F. Frith and Company, 1954, © Victoria and Albert Museum, London, 2014
S. 147: BOMBAY, BYCULLA HOTEL, 1850–1870, Albumindruck, 42,3 × 57,5 cm, Courtesy: Sammlung Victoria and Albert Museum, London, akquiriert von F. Frith and Company, 1954, © Victoria and Albert Museum, London, 2014
P. 147: BOMBAY, BYCULLA HOTEL, 1850–1870, albumen print, 42.3 × 57.5 cm, courtesy: Collection Victoria and Albert Museum, London, acquired from F. Frith and Company, 1954, © Victoria and Albert Museum, London, 2014
S. 147: NEAPEL. HOTEL D'EUROPE ETC., 1850–1870, Albumindruck, 42,3 × 57,5 cm, Courtesy: Sammlung Victoria and Albert Museum, London, akquiriert von F. Frith and Company, 1954, © Victoria and Albert Museum, London, 2014
P. 147: NAPLES. HOTEL D'EUROPE ETC., 1850–1870, albumen print, 42.3 × 57.5 cm, courtesy: Collection Victoria and Albert Museum, London, acquired from F. Frith and Company, 1954, © Victoria and Albert Museum, London, 2014

Laurits Tuxen (1853–1927)
S. 148: STEUERMANN JOHN H. BRØNDUM MIT SEINEM HUND, 1905, Öl auf Leinwand, 63,3 × 53,5 cm, Courtesy: Sammlung Skagens Museum, © Skagens Museum
P. 148: OFFICER JOHN H. BRØNDUM WITH HIS DOG, 1905, oil on canvas, 63.3 × 53.5 cm, courtesy: Collection Skagens Museum, © Skagens Museum

Valdemar Schønheyder Møller (1864–1905)
S. 148–149: KARTENCLUB AN DEN SPIELTISCHEN IN DER WEISSEN STUBE DES BRØNDUMS HOTELS, 1891/1893, Öl auf Leinwand, 29,2 × 60,7 cm, Courtesy: Sammlung Skagens Museum, © Skagens Museum
PP. 148–149: THE »SKAGENS KLUB« AT THE GAMBLING TABLES IN THE WHITE ROOM AT BRØNDUMS HOTEL, 1891/1893, oil on canvas, 29.2 × 60.7 cm, courtesy: Collection Skagens Museum, © Skagens Museum

Peder Severin Krøyer (1853–1909)
S. 150–151: VON DER HEIDE NÖRDLICH VON SKAGEN. MITTERNACHT, 6. JULI 1885, 1885, Öl auf Leinwand, 27,5 × 50,1 cm, Courtesy: Sammlung Skagens Museum, © Skagens Museum
PP. 150–151: FROM THE MOORS NORTH OF SKAGEN. MIDNIGHT 6. JULY 1885, 1885, oil on canvas, 27.5 × 50.1 cm, courtesy: Collection Skagens Museum, © Skagens Museum

Georg Hering (1884–1936)
S. 152: IN DER ALTEN HERBERGE, 1926, Öl auf Leinwand, 128 × 150 cm, Courtesy: Sammlung Spaander, Volendam
P. 152: IN THE OLD INN, 1926, oil on canvas, 128 × 150 cm, courtesy: Collection Spaander, Volendam

Paul Signac (1863–1935)
S. 153: SEESTÜCK, 1896, Wasserfarben auf Papier, Courtesy: Sammlung Spaander, Volendam
P. 153: SEASCAPE, 1896, watercolor on paper, courtesy: Collection Spaander, Volendam

Otto Albert Koch (1866–1920)
S. 154–155: BLICK AUF DAS KURHOTEL IN BADEN-BADEN, 1911, Öl auf Leinwand, 65 × 78 cm, Privatbesitz, Berlin
PP. 154–155: VIEW OF THE SPA-HOTEL IN BADEN-BADEN, 1911, oil on canvas, 65 × 78 cm, private collection, Berlin

Hugo Degenhard (1866–1901)
S. 156: HOTEL MINERVA (heute Brenners Park-Hotel & Spa), um 1890, Öl auf Leinwand, Courtesy: Stadtmuseum/-archiv Baden-Baden
P. 156: HOTEL MINERVA (today Brenners Park-Hotel & Spa), c. 1890, oil on canvas, courtesy: Stadtmuseum/-archiv Baden-Baden

Julius Reith
S. 156: HOTEL RUNKEWITZ, 1950, Aquarell auf Papier, Courtesy: Stadtmuseum/-archiv, Baden-Baden
P. 156: HOTEL RUNKEWITZ, 1950, watercolor on paper, courtesy: Stadtmuseum/-archiv, Baden-Baden

August Sander (1876–1964)
S. 157: HOTELIER, aus der Serie MENSCHEN DES 20. JAHRHUNDERTS, 1930, Silbergelatineabzug, 22,3 × 13,1 cm, © Die Photographische Sammlung/SK Stiftung Kultur – August Sander Archiv, Köln / VG Bild-Kunst, Bonn 2014
P. 157: HOTEL OWNER, from the series PEOPLE OF THE 20TH CENTURY, 1930, gelatine silver print, 22.3 × 13.1 cm, © Die Photographische Sammlung/SK Stiftung Kultur – August Sander Archiv, Köln / VG Bild-Kunst, Bonn 2014

Auguste Chabaud (1882–1955)
S. 158: HOTELFLUR (COULOIR D'HOTEL), 1907/08, Öl auf Karton/Sperrholz, 105 × 76 cm, Courtesy: Sammlung Städel Museum, Frankfurt am Main, © VG Bild-Kunst, Bonn 2014, Foto: U. Edelmann – ARTOTHEK
P. 158: HOTEL CORRIDOR (COULOIR D'HOTEL), 1907/08, oil on cardboard/plywood, 105 × 76 cm, courtesy: Sammlung Städel Museum, Frankfurt am Main, © VG Bild-Kunst, Bonn 2014, photo: U. Edelmann – ARTOTHEK

Max Beckmann (1884–1950)
S. 159: SELBST IM HOTEL, Blatt 1 aus der Mappe BERLINER REISE, 1922, Lithografie, 45,5 × 32,5 cm, Courtesy: Sammlung Kupferstichkabinett – Staatliche Museen zu Berlin, © VG Bild-Kunst, Bonn 2014
P. 159: SELF-PORTRAIT IN THE HOTEL, 1922, lithograph, first page of the portfolio »Berliner Reise«, lithograph, 45.5 × 32.5 cm, courtesy: Collection Kupferstichkabinett – Staatliche Museen zu Berlin, © VG Bild-Kunst, Bonn 2014

Chaïm Soutine (1893–1943)
S. 160: DIE KÖCHIN MIT BLAUER SCHÜRZE, 1930, Öl auf Leinwand, 128 × 50,5 cm, Courtesy: Stiftung im Obersteg, Depositum Kunstmuseum, Basel 2004, © VG Bild-Kunst, Bonn 2014
P. 160: COOK WITH BLUE APRON, 1930, oil on canvas, 128 × 50.5 cm, courtesy: Stiftung im Obersteg, Depositum Kunstmuseum, Basel 2004, © VG Bild-Kunst, Bonn 2014

George Grosz (1893–1959)
S. 161: DIE STRASSE, 1915, Öl auf Leinwand, 45,5 × 35,5 cm, Courtesy: Staatsgalerie Stuttgart, © Estate of George Grosz, Princeton, N.J. / VG Bild-Kunst, Bonn 2014
P. 161: THE STREET, 1915, oil on canvas, 45.5 × 35.5 cm, courtesy: Staatsgalerie Stuttgart, © Estate of George Grosz, Princeton, N.J. / VG Bild-Kunst, Bonn 2014

Hans Meyboden (1901–1965)
S. 162–163: HOTEL PROVENCE, 1963, Öl auf Leinwand, 84 × 104 cm, Privatbesitz, © VG Bild-Kunst, Bonn 2014
PP. 162–163: HOTEL PROVENCE, 1963, oil on canvas, 84 × 104 cm, private collection, © VG Bild-Kunst, Bonn 2014

Henri Cartier-Bresson (1908–2004)
S. 164: SOWJETUNION. MOSKAU. 1954. KANTINE FÜR BAUARBEITER DES HOTELS METROPOL, 1954, Silbergelatinabzug, 24,1 × 35,6 cm, Courtesy: Fondation Henri Cartier-Bresson, © Henri Cartier-Bresson/Magnum Photos
P. 164: SOVIET UNION. MOSCOW. 1954. CANTINE FOR WORKERS BUILDING THE HOTEL METROPOL, 1954, gelatin silver print, 24.1 × 35.6 cm, courtesy: Fondation Henri Cartier-Bresson, © Henri Cartier-Bresson/Magnum Photos

Hanns Hubmann (1910–1996)
S. 165: PAGE DES HOTELS WELLINGTON MIT ZEITUNGEN ZUM BASEBALL-ENDSPIEL, 1936, Chromogendruck, 59,4 × 84,1 cm, © bpk – Bildagentur für Kunst, Kultur und Geschichte, Berlin / Hanns Hubmann
P. 165: MESSENGER BOY OF THE HOTEL WELLINGTON WITH NEWSPAPERS FEATURING THE BASEBALL CHAMPIONSHIPS, 1936, chromogenic print, 59.4 × 84.1 cm, © bpk – Bildagentur für Kunst, Kultur und Geschichte, Berlin / Hanns Hubmann

S. 166: DER HOTELDIREKTOR DES GRAND-HOTELS IN ST. MORITZ AN SEINEM SCHREIBTISCH BEIM TELEFONIEREN, 1934, Chromogendruck, 59,4 × 84,1 cm, © bpk – Bildagentur für Kunst, Kultur und Geschichte, Berlin / Hanns Hubmann
P. 166: HOTEL MANAGER OF THE GRAND HOTEL IN ST. MORITZ TALKING ON THE PHONE AT HIS DESK, 1934, chromogenic print, 59.4 × 84.1 cm, © bpk – Bildagentur für Kunst, Kultur und Geschichte, Berlin / Hanns Hubmann

Diane Arbus (1923–1971)
S. 167: MEXIKANISCHER LILIPUTANER IN SEINEM HOTELZIMMER IN NEW YORK CITY, 1970, Silbergelatinabzug, 38,2 × 36,9 cm, Courtesy: Haus der Photographie / Sammlung F. C. Gundlach, © The Estate of Diane Arbus, New York
P. 167: MEXICAN DWARF IN HIS HOTEL IN NEW YORK CITY, 1970, gelatin silver print, 38.2 × 36.9 cm, courtesy: Haus der Photographie / Collection F. C. Gundlach, © The Estate of Diane Arbus, New York

Daniel Spoerri (*1930)
S. 168–169: VUE CUBISTE DE MA CHAMBRE NO 13 DE L'HÔTEL CARCASSONNE, 24 RUE MOUFFETARD, 1961, Assemblage, 96,5 × 202,5 cm, Courtesy: Sammlung Kunstmuseum Solothurn, Schenkung des Künstlers, 1990, © VG Bild-Kunst, Bonn 2014
PP. 168–169: VUE CUBISTE DE MA CHAMBRE NO 13 DE L'HÔTEL CARCASSONNE, 24 RUE MOUFFETARD, 1961, assemblage, 96.5 × 202.5 cm, courtesy: Collection Kunstmuseum Solothurn, donation of the artist, 1990, © VG Bild-Kunst, Bonn 2014

On Kawara (*1933)
S. 170–171: 12 OCT. 1968 – I GOT UP AT 9.30 A.M. – HOSTAL DEL SOL, LIMA, PERU – NUMMER 156, 1968, Papier, Stempel, 14 × 9,2 cm, Courtesy: Sammlung Kaspar König, © On Kawara
PP. 170–171: 12 OCT. 1968 – I GOT UP AT 9.30 A.M. – HOSTAL DEL SOL, LIMA, PERU – NUMMER 156, 1968, paper, stamps, 14 × 9.2 cm, courtesy: Sammlung Kaspar König, © On Kawara
S. 170–171: 12 OCT. 1968 – I GOT UP AT 9.30 A.M. – HOSTAL DEL SOL, LIMA, PERU – NUMMER 156 – OHNE POSTSTEMPEL (NICHT GESENDET), 1968, Papier, Stempel, 14 × 9,2 cm, Courtesy: Sammlung Kaspar König, © On Kawara
PP. 170–171: 12 OCT. 1968 – I GOT UP AT 9.30 A.M. – HOSTAL DEL SOL, LIMA, PERU – NUMMER 156 – WITHOUT DATE STAMPS (NOT SENT), 1968, paper, stamps, 14 × 9.2 cm, courtesy: Sammlung Kaspar König, © On Kawara
S. 170–171: 20 MARS 1973 – I GOT UP AT 8,24 A.M. – HOTEL DIARAMA, DAKAR, SÉNÉGAL – OHNE NUMMER, 1973, Papier, Stempel, 15 × 10,4 cm, Courtesy: Sammlung Kaspar König, © On Kawara
PP. 170–171: 20 MARS 1973 – I GOT UP AT 8,24 A.M. – HOTEL DIARAMA, DAKAR, SÉNÉGAL – WITHOUT NUMBER, 1973, paper, stamps, 15 × 10.4 cm, courtesy: Sammlung Kaspar König, © On Kawara

William Eggleston (*1939)
S. 172: UNTITLED (MOTEL ROOM WITH FLUORESCENTS), aus dem LOS ALAMOS-Portfolio, 1965–1968, Dye-Transfer-Print, 52 × 67 cm, Courtesy: Cheim & Read, New York / Sammlung Museum Folkwang, Essen, © Eggleston Artistic Trust. Courtesy Cheim & Read, New York
P. 172: UNTITLED (MOTEL ROOM WITH FLUORESCENTS), from the LOS ALAMOS Portfolio, 1965–1968, dye-transfer print, 52 × 67 cm, courtesy: Cheim & Read, New York / Collection Museum Folkwang, Essen, © Eggleston Artistic Trust, courtesy: Cheim & Read, New York
S. 173: UNTITLED (HUNTSVILLE, ALABAMA), 1969/70, Dye-transfer-print, 46,6 × 32,3 cm, Courtesy: Cheim & Read, New York / Sammlung Museum Folkwang, Essen, © Eggleston Artistic Trust
P. 173: UNTITLED (HUNTSVILLE, ALABAMA), 1969/70, dye-transfer print, 46.6 × 32.3 cm, courtesy: Cheim & Read, New York / Collection Museum Folkwang, Essen, © Eggleston Artistic Trust

Hans-Peter Feldmann (*1941)
S. 174: TORONTO, KANADA, aus der Serie AUSBLICKE AUS HOTELZIMMERN, 1982–2002, Farb- und S/W-Fotografien, Courtesy: H.-P. Feldmann, © H.-P. Feldmann / VG Bild-Kunst, Bonn 2014
P. 174: TORONTO, CANADA, from the series VIEWS FROM HOTELROOMS, 1982–2002, color and b/w photographs, courtesy: H.-P. Feldmann, © H.-P. Feldmann / VG Bild-Kunst, Bonn 2014
S. 174: LE VÉSINET, FRANKREICH, aus der Serie AUSBLICKE AUS HOTELZIMMERN, 1982–2002, Farb- und S/W-Fotografien, Courtesy: H.-P. Feldmann, © H.-P. Feldmann / VG Bild-Kunst, Bonn 2014

P. 174: LE VÉSINET, FRANCE, from the series VIEWS FROM HOTELROOMS, 1982–2002, color and b/w photographs, courtesy: H.-P. Feldmann, © H.-P. Feldmann / VG Bild-Kunst, Bonn 2014
S. 175: CHICAGO, USA, aus der Serie AUSBLICKE AUS HOTELZIMMERN, 1982–2002, Farb- und S/W-Fotografien, Courtesy: H.-P. Feldmann, © H.-P. Feldmann / VG Bild-Kunst, Bonn 2014
P. 175: CHICAGO, U.S.A., from the series VIEWS FROM HOTEL ROOMS, 1982–2002, color and b/w photographs, courtesy: H.-P. Feldmann, © H.-P. Feldmann / VG Bild-Kunst, Bonn 2014
S. 175: LE VÉSINET, FRANKREICH, aus der Serie AUSBLICKE AUS HOTELZIMMERN, 1982–2002, Farb- und S/W-Fotografien, Courtesy: H.-P. Feldmann, © H.-P. Feldmann / VG Bild-Kunst, Bonn 2014
P. 175: LE VÉSINET, FRANCE, from the series VIEWS FROM HOTELROOMS, 1982–2002, color and b/w photographs, courtesy: H.-P. Feldmann, © H.-P. Feldmann / VG Bild-Kunst, Bonn 2014

Candida Höfer (*1944)
S. 176: CAP SAN DIEGO HAMBURG V, 2000, Chromogendruck, 85 × 85 cm, Courtesy: Candida Höfer und Johnen Galerie, Berlin, © Candida Höfer / VG Bild-Kunst, Bonn 2014
P. 176: CAP SAN DIEGO HAMBURG V, 2000, chromogenic print, 85 × 85 cm, courtesy: Candida Höfer and Johnen Galerie, Berlin, © Candida Höfer / VG Bild-Kunst, Bonn 2014
S. 177: KURANLAGE BADEN-BADEN I, 1981, Chromogendruck, 24 × 34 cm, Courtesy: Candida Höfer und Johnen Galerie, Berlin,© Candida Höfer / VG Bild-Kunst, Bonn 2014
P. 177: KURANLAGE BADEN-BADEN I, 1981, chromogenic print, 24 × 34 cm, courtesy: Candida Höfer and Johnen Galerie, Berlin, © Candida Höfer / VG Bild-Kunst, Bonn 2014

Sophie Calle (*1953)
S. 178–179: THE HOTEL, ROOM 28, MARCH 3, 1981, Diptychon, Aluminiumplatten mit Ektachrome-Druck, Text, je 102 × 142 cm, S/W-Fotografien, Courtesy: Sophie Calle und Deichtorhallen Hamburg / Sammlung Falckenberg, © Sophie Calle / VG Bild-Kunst, Bonn 2014
PP. 178–179: THE HOTEL, ROOM 28, MARCH 3, 1981, diptych, aluminum plates with Ektachrome print, text, with b/w photographs, each 102 × 142 cm, courtesy: Sophie Calle and Deichtorhallen Hamburg / Collection Falckenberg © Sophie Calle / VG Bild-Kunst, Bonn 2014
S. 180–181: THE HOTEL, ROOM 30, MARCH 5, 1981, Diptychon, Aluminiumplatten mit Ektachrome-Druck, Text, S/W-Fotografien, je 102 × 142 cm, Courtesy: Sophie Calle und Deichtorhallen Hamburg / Sammlung Falckenberg, © Sophie Calle / VG Bild-Kunst, Bonn 2014
PP. 180–181: THE HOTEL, ROOM 30, MARCH 5, 1981, diptych, aluminum plates with Ektachrome print, text, with b/w photographs, each 102 × 142 cm, courtesy: Sophie Calle and Deichtorhallen Hamburg / Collection Falckenberg © Sophie Calle / VG Bild-Kunst, Bonn 2014

Martin Kippenberger (1953–1997)
S. 182: OHNE TITEL (MY WAY SHOOTING / HOTEL SAVOY BERLIN), aus der Serie HOTEL-HOTEL, 1992, Bleistift und Feinstift auf Velinpapier, 26,9 × 21 cm, Courtesy: Friedrich Christian Flick Collection im Hamburger Bahnhof, Berlin, © Estate of Martin Kippenberger, Galerie Gisela Capitain, Köln
P. 182: UNTITLED (MY WAY SHOOTING / HOTEL SAVOY BERLIN), from the series HOTEL-HOTEL, 1992, pencil, pen on Wove paper, 26.9 × 21 cm, courtesy: Friedrich Christian Flick Collection im Hamburger Bahnhof, Berlin, © Estate of Martin Kippenberger, Galerie Gisela Capitain, Cologne
S. 183: OHNE TITEL (DOLDER GRAND HOTEL, ZÜRICH), aus der Serie HOTEL-HOTEL, 1995, Kugelschreiber, Filzstift, Bleistift, Tipp-Ex auf Papier, 29,5 × 21 cm, Courtesy: Friedrich Christian Flick Collection im Hamburger Bahnhof, Berlin, © Estate of Martin Kippenberger, Galerie Gisela Capitain, Köln
P. 183: UNTITLED (DOLDER GRAND HOTEL, ZURICH), from the series, HOTEL-HOTEL, 1995, pen, felt pen, pencil, whiteout on paper, 29.5 × 21 cm, courtesy: Friedrich Christian Flick Collection im Hamburger Bahnhof, Berlin, © Estate of Martin Kippenberger, Galerie Gisela Capitain, Cologne
S. 184: OHNE TITEL (AUBERGE DU SOLEIL, RUTHERFORD CA), aus der Serie HOTEL-HOTEL, 1994, Kugelschreiber auf Papier, Courtesy: Friedrich Christian Flick Collection im Hamburger Bahnhof, Berlin, © Estate of Martin Kippenberger, Galerie Gisela Capitain, Köln
P. 184: UNTITLED (AUBERGE DU SOLEIL, RUTHERFORD CA), aus der Serie HOTEL-HOTEL, 1994, pen on paper, courtesy: Friedrich Christian Flick Collection im Hamburger Bahnhof, Berlin, © Estate of Martin Kippenberger, Galerie Gisela Capitain, Cologne
S. 185: OHNE TITEL (TOP SECRET), aus der Serie HOTEL-HOTEL, 1989, Farbstift, Tinte, Letraset auf Papier, 27,8 × 21,3 cm, Courtesy: Friedrich Christian Flick Collection im Hamburger Bahnhof, Berlin, © Estate of Martin Kippenberger, Galerie Gisela Capitain, Köln
P. 185: UNTITLED (TOP SECRET), from the series HOTEL-HOTEL, 1989, color pencil, ink, letraset on paper, 27.8 × 21.3 cm, courtesy: Friedrich Christian Flick Collection im Hamburger Bahnhof, Berlin, © Estate of Martin Kippenberger, Galerie Gisela Capitain, Cologne

Thomas Schütte (*1954)
S. 186: HOTEL FOR THE BIRDS, (MODELL 1:10), 2003, Plexiglas, Stahl, Aluminium, Holz, 50 × 53 × 49 cm, Courtesy: Thomas Schütte, © VG Bild-Kunst, Bonn 2014, Foto: Stefano Schröter
P. 186: HOTEL FOR THE BIRDS, (MODEL 1:10), 2003, Plexiglas, steel, aluminum, wood, 50 × 53 × 49 cm, courtesy: Thomas Schütte, © VG Bild-Kunst, Bonn 2014, photo: Stefano Schröter

Andreas Gursky (*1955)
S. 187: SHANGHAI, 2000, Chromogendruck, 308 × 205 cm, Courtesy: Sprüth Magers Berlin London, © Andreas Gursky / VG Bild-Kunst, Bonn 2014
P. 187: SHANGHAI, 2000, chromogenic print, 308 × 205 cm, courtesy: Sprüth Magers Berlin London, © Andreas Gursky / VG Bild-Kunst, Bonn 2014

Guy Tillim (*1962)
S. 188–189: GRANDE HOTEL, BEIRA, MOZAMBIQUE, 2008, Pigmentdruck, 91,5 × 131,5 cm, Courtesy: Galerie Kuckei+Kuckei, Berlin, © Guy Tillim
PP. 188–189: GRANDE HOTEL, BEIRA, MOZAMBIQUE, 2008, pigment ink print, 91.5 × 131.5 cm, courtesy: Gallery Kuckei+Kuckei, Berlin, © Guy Tillim
S. 190–191: GRANDE HOTEL, BEIRA, MOZAMBIQUE, Diptychon (rechts), 2008, Pigmentdruck, je 91,5 × 131,5 cm, Courtesy: Privatbesitz, Berlin / Galerie Kuckei+Kuckei, Berlin, © Guy Tillim
PP. 190–191: GRANDE HOTEL, BEIRA, MOZAMBIQUE, diptych (right), 2008, pigment ink print, each 91.5 × 131.5 cm, courtesy: private collection, Berlin / Gallery Kuckei+Kuckei, Berlin, © Guy Tillim

Thomas Demand (*1964)
S. 192–193: ZIMMER/ROOM, 1996, chromogener Farbdruck, 65 × 78 cm, Courtesy: Vanhaerents Art Collection, Brüssel, © VG Bild-Kunst, Bonn 2014
PP. 192–193: ZIMMER/ROOM, 1996, chromogenic print, 65 × 78 cm, courtesy: Vanhaerents Art Collection, Brussels, © VG Bild-Kunst, Bonn 2014

Eberhard Havekost (*1967)
S. 194–195: SKIHOTEL, 1996, Öl auf Leinwand, 120 × 150 cm, Courtesy: Eberhard Havekost und Galerie Gebr. Lehmann, Dresden/Berlin, © Eberhard Havekost
PP. 194–195: SKIHOTEL, 1996, oil on canvas, 120 × 150 cm, courtesy: Eberhard Havekost and Galerie Gebr. Lehmann, Dresden/Berlin, © Eberhard Havekost

Sven Johne (*1976)
S. 196–199: Details aus der Serie TRAUMHOTELS, 2012, Serie von bis zu 15 Farbfotografien, Pigmentdruck, jede 18 × 27 cm, gerahmt, Wandtext, Courtesy: Sven Johne / VG Bild-Kunst, Bonn 2014
PP. 196–199: Details from the series DREAM HOTELS, 2012, series of up to 15 color photographs, pigment print, each 18 × 27 cm, framed, text on wall, courtesy: Sven Johne / VG Bild-Kunst, Bonn 2014

Christian Andersson (*1973)
S. 203: ATLANTIC 215 (PALACE 415), 2014, Performance mit verschiedenen Materialien | Foto: Achim Kukulies
P. 203: ATLANTIC 215 (PALACE 415), 2014, performance with various materials | photo: Achim Kukulies

S. 204–205: Bücher- und Filmarchiv zur Ausstellung | Foto: Achim Kukulies
PP. 204–205: Book and Film Archive Accompanying the Exhibition | photo: Achim Kukulies

Fischli/Weiss (*1976 / 1946–2012)
S. 206: OHNE TITEL (BLUMEN), 1998, chromogener Farbdruck, 107 × 74 cm, Courtesy: Hotel Castell, Zuoz/Engadin, Sammlung Ruedi Bechtler, © Peter Fischli David Weiss, Zürich | Foto: Achim Kukulies
P. 206: UNTITLED (FLOWERS), 1998, chromogenic color print, 107 × 74 cm, courtesy: Hotel Castell, Zuoz/Engadin, Ruedi Bechtler Collection, © Peter Fischli David Weiss, Zürich | photo: Achim Kukulies

Andreas Gursky (*1955)
S. 207: HONG KONG ISLAND, 1994, chromogener Farbdruck, 140 × 120 cm, Courtesy: Hotel Castell, Zuoz/Engadin, Sammlung Ruedi Bechtler © Andreas Gursky / VG Bild-Kunst, Bonn 2014 | Foto: Achim Kukulies
P. 207: HONG KONG ISLAND, 1994, chromogenic color print, 140 × 120 cm, courtesy: Hotel Castell, Zuoz/Engadin, Ruedi Bechtler Collection © Andreas Gursky / VG Bild-Kunst, Bonn 2014 | photo: Achim Kukulies

Tobias Madison (*1985)
S. 208: LASER BLUE, 2009, chomogener Farbdruck, 150 × 200 cm (Diptychon), Courtesy: Hotel Castell, Zuoz/Engadin, Sammlung Ruedi Bechtler, © Tobias Madison | Foto: Achim Kukulies
P. 208: LASER BLUE, 2009, chomogenic color print, 150 × 200 cm (diptych), courtesy: Hotel Castell, Zuoz/Engadin, Ruedi Bechtler Collection, © Tobias Madison | photo: Achim Kukulies

Chantal Michel (*1968)
S. 209–211: aus der Serie HÔTEL SCRIBE, 1999, chromogener Farbdruck, je 95 × 95 cm, Courtesy: Hotel Castell, Zuoz/Engadin, Sammlung Ruedi Bechtler, © Chantal Michel | Foto: Achim Kukulies
PP. 209–211: from the series HÔTEL SCRIBE, 1999, chromogenic color print, each 95 × 95 cm, courtesy: Hotel Castell, Zuoz/Engadin, Ruedi Bechtler Collection, © Chantal Michel | photo: Achim Kukulies

Roman Signer (*1938)
S. 212–213: ZELT, aus der Serie KLEINE EREIGNISSE, 2010, LightJet-Print, je 45 × 60 cm, Foto: Michael Bodenmann, Courtesy: Hotel Castell, Zuoz/Engadin, Sammlung Ruedi Bechtler, © Roman Signer | Foto: Achim Kukulies
PP. 212–213: TENT, from the series LITTLE EVENTS, 2010, LightJet print, each 45 × 60 cm, photo: Michael Bodenmann, courtesy: Hotel Castell, Zuoz/Engadin, Ruedi Bechtler Collection, © Roman Signer | photo: Achim Kukulies

Jenny Brillhart (*1972)
S. 217: SAXONY HOTEL – RED MATTRESSES WITH BLUE LABEL, aus der Serie HOTEL SAXONY, 2006, Öl auf Holz, 30 × 39 cm, Courtesy: K. Sandmann, Berlin, Galerie Kuckei + Kuckei, Berlin, © Jenny Brillhart | Foto: Achim Kukulies
P. 217: SAXONY HOTEL – RED MATTRESSES WITH BLUE LABEL, from the series HOTEL SAXONY, 2006, oil on wood, 30 × 39 cm, courtesy: K. Sandmann, Berlin, Galerie Kuckei + Kuckei, Berlin, © Jenny Brillhart | photo: Achim Kukulies
S. 218–219: SAXONY HOTEL – INTERIOR 6 (BLUE MATTRESS AND LAMP SHADE), aus der Serie HOTEL SAXONY, 2006, Öl auf Holz, 48 × 69 cm, Courtesy: Sammlung Dr. Scheefers-Borchel, Gießen, Galerie Kuckei + Kuckei, Berlin. © Jenny Brillhart | SAXONY HOTEL – INTERIOR 5 (RED MATTRESSES AND BOX SPRING), aus der Serie HOTEL SAXONY, 2006, Öl auf Holz, 33 × 28 cm, Courtesy: Olaf Hajek, Galerie Kuckei + Kuckei, Berlin, © Jenny Brillhart | SAXONY HOTEL – INTERIOR 5 (GREY MATTRESSES WITH PINK CHAIR AND LOVESEAT), aus der Serie HOTEL SAXONY, 2006, Öl auf Holz, 48 × 69 cm, Courtesy: SØR Rusche Sammlung, Berlin, Galerie Kuckei + Kuckei, Berlin, © Jenny Brillhart | SAXONY HOTEL – INTERIOR 5 (BLUE MATTRESSES AND FOLDED BLANKET), aus der Serie HOTEL SAXONY, 2006, Öl auf Holz, 33 × 28 cm, Courtesy: Frank Zahn, Galerie Kuckei + Kuckei, Berlin, © Jenny Brillhart | Foto: Achim Kukulies
PP. 218–219: SAXONY HOTEL – INTERIOR 6 (BLUE MATTRESS AND LAMP SHADE), from the series HOTEL SAXONY, 2006, oil on wood, 48 × 69 cm, courtesy: Dr. Scheefers-Borchel Collection, Gießen, Galerie Kuckei + Kuckei, Berlin. © Jenny Brillhart | SAXONY HOTEL – INTERIOR 5 (RED MATTRESSES AND BOX SPRING), from the series HOTEL SAXONY, 2006, oil on wood, 33 × 28 cm, courtesy: Olaf Hajek, Galerie Kuckei + Kuckei, Berlin, © Jenny Brillhart | SAXONY HOTEL – INTERIOR 5 (GREY MATTRESSES WITH PINK CHAIR AND LOVESEAT), from the series HOTEL SAXONY, 2006, oil on wood, 48 × 69 cm, courtesy: SØR Rusche Collection, Berlin, Galerie Kuckei + Kuckei, Berlin, © Jenny Brillhart | SAXONY HOTEL – INTERIOR 5 (BLUE MATTRESSES AND FOLDED BLANKET), from the series HOTEL SAXONY, 2006, oil on wood, 33 × 28 cm, courtesy: Frank Zahn, Galerie Kuckei + Kuckei, Berlin, © Jenny Brillhart | photo: Achim Kukulies

Andy Warhol (1928–1987)
S. 220–221: THE CHELSEA GIRLS, 1966, 2-Kanal-Videoinstallation, 16-mm-Film auf DVD übertragen, 66 Min., Courtesy: Sammlung The Andy Warhol Museum, Pittsburgh, © The Andy Warhol Foundation for the Visual Arts, Inc. | Foto: Achim Kukulies
S. 220–221: THE CHELSEA GIRLS, 1966, 2-channel video installation, 16mm film transferred to digital files (DVD), 66 min., courtesy: The Andy Warhol Museum Collection, Pittsburgh, © The Andy Warhol Foundation for the Visual Arts, Inc. | photo: Achim Kukulies

Christian Jankowski (*1968)
S. 225: DER KLEINE ENTSCHEIDUNGSRAUM, 2014, Bestellkatalog für Möbel des KLEINEN ENTSCHEIDUNGSRAUMS, 18 × 30 cm, Layout: Christian Ertel, Courtesy: Christian Jankowski, © Christian Jankowski | Foto: Michael Belogour
P. 225: DER KLEINE ENTSCHEIDUNGSRAUM (A SMALL ROOM FOR DECISION MAKING), 2014, catalog for furnishing of A SMALL ROMM FOR DECISION MAKING, 18 × 30 cm, layout: Christian Ertel, courtesy: Christian Jankowski, © Christian Jankowski | photo: Michael Belogour
S. 226–227: DER KLEINE ENTSCHEIDUNGSRAUM, 2014, verschiedene Materialien, Courtesy: Christian Jankowski, © Christian Jankowski | Foto: Michael Belogour
P. 226–227: DER KLEINE ENTSCHEIDUNGSRAUM (A SMALL ROOM FOR DECISION MAKING), 2014, various materials, layout: Christian Ertel, courtesy: Christian Jankowski, © Christian Jankowski | photo: Michael Belogour
S. 228–231: DER KLEINE ENTSCHEIDUNGSRAUM, 2014, chromogener Farbdruck, Passepartout, je 50,7 × 40,3 cm, Layout: Christian Ertel, Courtesy: Christian Jankowski, © Christian Jankowski | Foto: Michael Belogour
PP. 228–231: DER KLEINE ENTSCHEIDUNGSRAUM (A SMALL ROOM FOR DECISION MAKING), 2014, chromogenic color print, passepartout, each 50.7 × 40.3 cm, layout: Christian Ertel, courtesy: Christian Jankowski, © Christian Jankowski | photo: Michael Belogour

Cindy Sherman (*1954)
S. 232–233: UNTITLED #464, 2008, chromogener Farbdruck, 214,5 × 152,5 cm, Courtesy: Sammlung Olbricht, Essen, © Cindy Sherman and Metro Pictures, New York | UNTITLED #475, 2008, chromogener Farbdruck, 219,5 × 181,5 cm, Courtesy: Sammlung Olbricht, Essen, © Cindy Sherman and Metro Pictures, New York | Foto: Achim Kukulies
PP. 232–233: UNTITLED #464, 2008, chromogenic color print, 214.5 × 152.5 cm, courtesy: Olbricht Collection, Essen, © Cindy Sherman and Metro Pictures, New York | UNTITLED #475, 2008, chromogenic color print, 219.5 × 181.5 cm, courtesy: Olbricht Collection, Essen, © Cindy Sherman and Metro Pictures, New York | photo: Achim Kukulies

Markus Schinwald (*1973)
S. 234–237: DICTIO PII, 2001, 35-mm-Farbfilm auf Video übertragen, 16 Min., Courtesy: Markus Schinwald, © Markus Schinwald | Foto: Achim Kukulies
PP. 234–237: DICTIO PII, 2001, 35-mm color film transferred to video files, 16 min., courtesy: Markus Schinwald, © Markus Schinwald | photo: Achim Kukulies

Ian Wallace (*1943)
S. 238–239: BRENNERS PARK-HOTEL & SPA; BADEN-BADEN (THE TABLE) I, 2014, Tintenstrahldruck, 71 × 58 cm, Courtesy: Ian Wallace and Hauser & Wirth, Zürich, © Ian Wallace | BRENNERS PARK-HOTEL & SPA; BADEN-BADEN (THE TABLE) II, 2014, Tintenstrahldruck, 71 × 58 cm, Courtesy: Ian Wallace and Hauser & Wirth, Zürich, © Ian Wallace | Foto: Achim Kukulies
PP. 238–239: BRENNERS PARK-HOTEL & SPA; BADEN-BADEN (THE TABLE) I, 2014, Inkjet print, 71 × 58 cm, courtesy: Ian Wallace and Hauser & Wirth, Zürich, © Ian Wallace | BRENNERS PARK-HOTEL & SPA; BADEN-BADEN (THE TABLE) II, 2014, Inkjet print, 71 × 58 cm, courtesy: Ian Wallace and Hauser & Wirth, Zurich, © Ian Wallace | photo: Achim Kukulies
S. 240–241: BRENNERS PARK-HOTEL & SPA; BADEN-BADEN I–IV, 2014, Fotolaminat, Acryl auf Leinwand, je 61 × 61 cm, Courtesy: Ian Wallace and Hauser & Wirth, Zürich, © Ian Wallace | Foto: Achim Kukulies
PP. 240–241: BRENNERS PARK-HOTEL & SPA; BADEN-BADEN I–IV, 2014, photolaminate, acrylic on canvas, each 61 × 61 cm, courtesy: Ian Wallace and Hauser & Wirth, Zurich, © Ian Wallace | photo: Achim Kukulies

Naneci Yurdagül (*1979)
S. 242–245: BRENNERS EINE-STUNDE-HOTEL & SERVICE TOTAL, 2014, Performance mit verschiedenen Materialien, © Studio Naneci Yurdagül, 2014 | Foto: Michael Belogour
PP. 242–245: BRENNERS ONE-HOUR-HOTEL & TOTAL SERVICE, 2014, performance with various materials, © Studio Naneci Yurdagül, 2014 | photo: Michael Belogour
S. 246–247: OHNE TITEL – (HÄNDE HOCH – GÄSTE KOMMEN), 2014, Neonröhren montiert auf Plexiglas, 120 × 16 × 6 cm, Courtesy: Naneci Yurdagül, © Studio Naneci Yurdagül, 2014 | Foto: Achim Kukulies
PP. 246–247: UNTITLED – (HÄNDE HOCH – GÄSTE KOMMEN), 2014, neon tubes mounted on plexiglas, 120 × 16 × 6 cm, courtesy: Naneci Yurdagül, © Studio Naneci Yurdagül, 2014 | photo: Achim Kukulies

Lee Kit (*1978)
S. 251–255: ONLY A FEW THINGS TO DO, 2014, Installationsansichten mit verschiedenen Materialien, Courtesy: Lee Kit, © Lee Kit | Foto: Achim Kukulies
PP. 251–255: ONLY A FEW THINGS TO DO, 2014, installation views with various materials, courtesy: Lee Kit, © Lee Kit | photo: Achim Kukulies

Gabriela Oberkofler (*1975)
S. 256–257: BITTE NICHT KLOPFEN, WENN JA, DREIMAL IM TAKT AUF LEISEN PFOTEN, Installationsansicht mit verschiedenen Materialien sowie Zeichnung METHIKA, 2014, Tusche auf Papier, 70 × 100 cm, Courtesy: Gabriela Oberkofler, © Gabriela Oberkofler | Foto: Achim Kukulies

PP. 256–257: PLEASE DO NOT KNOCK, BUT IF YOU MUST, THREE TIMES SOFTLY, installation view with arious materials as well as drawing METHIKA, 2014, ink on paper, 70 × 100 cm, courtesy: Gabriela Oberkofler, © Gabriela Oberkofler | photo: Achim Kukulies
S. 258: BITTE NICHT KLOPFEN, WENN JA, DREIMAL IM TAKT AUF LEISEN PFOTEN, Installationsansicht mit SCHAF, 2014, Maske aus Papier und TURM, 2012, Lindenholz geschnitzt, 5 × 5 × 5 cm, Courtesy: Gabriela Oberkofler, © Gabriela Oberkofler | Foto: Achim Kukulies
P. 258: PLEASE DO NOT KNOCK, BUT IF YOU MUST, THREE TIMES SOFTLY, installation view with SHEEP, 2014, paper mask and TOWER, 2012, carved limewood, 5 × 5 × 5 cm, courtesy: Gabriela Oberkofler, © Gabriela Oberkofler | photo: Achim Kukulies
S. 259: BITTE NICHT KLOPFEN, WENN JA, DREIMAL IM TAKT AUF LEISEN PFOTEN, Installationsansicht mit verschiedenen Materialien, darin: VERSTRICKT!, 2012, Lindenholz geschnitzt, WALD, 2012,Tusche auf Papier, 21 × 30 cm, Courtesy: Gabriela Oberkofler, © Gabriela Oberkofler | Foto: Achim Kukulies
P. 259: PLEASE DO NOT KNOCK, BUT IF YOU MUST, THREE TIMES SOFTLY, installation view with various materials, therein is: KNITTED!, 2012, carved limewood, FOREST, 2012, ink on paper, 21 × 30 cm, courtesy: Gabriela Oberkofler, © Gabriela Oberkofler | photo: Achim Kukulies
S. 260: BITTE NICHT KLOPFEN, WENN JA, DREIMAL IM TAKT AUF LEISEN PFOTEN, Installationsansicht, 2014, Courtesy: Gabriela Oberkofler, © Gabriela Oberkofler | Foto: Achim Kukulies
P. 260: PLEASE DO NOT KNOCK, BUT IF YOU MUST, THREE TIMES SOFTLY, installation view, 2014, courtesy: Gabriela Oberkofler, © Gabriela Oberkofler | photo: Achim Kukulies
S. 261: BITTE NICHT KLOPFEN, WENN JA, DREIMAL IM TAKT AUF LEISEN PFOTEN, Installationsansicht mit verschiedenen Materialien, 2014, Courtesy: Gabriela Oberkofler, © Gabriela Oberkofler | Foto: Achim Kukulies
P. 261: PLEASE DO NOT KNOCK, BUT IF YOU MUST, THREE TIMES SOFTLY, installation with various materials, 2014, courtesy: Gabriela Oberkofler, © Gabriela Oberkofler | photo: Achim Kukulies

Guy Ben-Ner (*1969)
S. 265: I'D GIVE IT TO YOU IF I COULD BUT I BORROWED IT, 2007, Fahrrad, Computer, DVD, Courtesy: LWL-Landesmuseum für Kunst und Kulturgeschichte, Westfälisches Landesmuseum, Münster, © Guy Ben-Ner | Foto: Achim Kukulies
P. 265: I'D GIVE IT TO YOU IF I COULD BUT I BORROWED IT, 2007, bicycle, computer, DVD, courtesy: LWL-Landesmuseum für Kunst und Kulturgeschichte, Westfälisches Landesmuseum, Münster, © Guy Ben-Ner | photo: Achim Kukulies

Simone Demandt (*1959)
S. 266–267: HOTEL HIRSCH 2, aus der Serie INDEPENDENTS, 2005, Duratrans in Leuchtkasten, 27 × 27 cm, Courtesy: Simone Demandt, © VG Bild-Kunst, Bonn 2014 | HOTEL HIRSCH 3, aus der Serie INDEPENDENTS, 2005, Duratrans in Leuchtkasten, 27 × 27 cm, Courtesy: Simone Demandt, © VG Bild-Kunst, Bonn 2014 | HOTEL HIRSCH 5, aus der Serie INDEPENDENTS, 2005, Duratrans in Leuchtkasten, 27 × 27 cm, Courtesy: Simone Demandt, © VG Bild-Kunst, Bonn 2014 | HOTEL HIRSCH 10, aus der Serie INDEPENDENTS, 2005, Duratrans in Leuchtkasten, 27 × 35 cm, Courtesy: Simone Demandt, © VG Bild-Kunst, Bonn 2014 | HOTEL HIRSCH 11, aus der Serie INDEPENDENTS, 2005, Duratrans in Leuchtkasten, 27 × 35 cm, Courtesy: Simone Demandt, © VG Bild-Kunst, Bonn 2014 | HOTEL HIRSCH 18, aus der Serie INDEPENDENTS, 2005, Duratrans in Leuchtkasten, 27 × 27 cm, Courtesy: Simone Demandt, © VG Bild-Kunst, Bonn 2014 | Foto: Achim Kukulies
PP. 266–267: HOTEL HIRSCH 2, from the ongoing series INDEPENDENTS, 2005, Duratrans in light box, 27 × 27 cm, courtesy: Simone Demandt, © VG Bild-Kunst, Bonn 2014 | HOTEL HIRSCH 3, from the ongoing series INDEPENDENTS, 2005, Duratrans in light box, 27 × 27 cm, courtesy: Simone Demandt, © VG Bild-Kunst, Bonn 2014 | HOTEL HIRSCH 5, from the ongoing series INDEPENDENTS, 2005, Duratrans in light box, 27 × 27 cm, courtesy: Simone Demandt, © VG Bild-Kunst, Bonn 2014 | HOTEL HIRSCH 10, from the ongoing series INDEPENDENTS, 2005, Duratrans in light box, 27 × 35 cm, courtesy: Simone Demandt, © VG Bild-Kunst, Bonn 2014 | HOTEL HIRSCH 11, from the ongoing series INDEPENDENTS, 2005, Duratrans in light box, 27 × 35 cm, courtesy: Simone Demandt, © VG Bild-Kunst, Bonn 2014 | HOTEL HIRSCH 18, from the ongoing series INDEPENDENTS, 2005, Duratrans in light box, 27 × 27 cm, courtesy: Simone Demandt, © VG Bild-Kunst, Bonn 2014 | photo: Achim Kukulies

Ligna
S. 268: ZIMMER 315, 2014, iPod, Audioaufnahme, 20 Min., Courtesy: Ligna, © Ligna | Foto: Michael Belogour
P. 268: ROOM 315, 2014, iPod, audio recording, 20 min., courtesy: Ligna, © Ligna | photo: Michael Belogour

Armin Linke & Elina Axioti (*1966 / *1981)
S. 269: THE ARCHITECTURE OF SERVICE, 2014, Installationsansicht, Courtesy: Armin Linke und Elina Axioti, © Armin Linke und Elina Axioti | Foto: Achim Kukulies
P. 269: THE ARCHITECTURE OF SERVICE, 2014, installation view, courtesy: Armin Linke und Elina Axioti, © Armin Linke und Elina Axioti | photo: Achim Kukulies

Armin Linke (*1966)
S. 269: PARIS AND ALLADIN HOTEL LAS VEGAS USA 1999, ReN_002300_18, 1999, Fotodruck, 50 × 60 cm, Courtesy: Armin Linke, © Armin Linke | PARIS AND ALLADIN HOTEL LAS VEGAS USA 1999, ReN_002300_16, 1999, Fotodruck, 50 × 60 cm, Courtesy: Armin Linke, © Armin Linke | PARIS AND ALLADIN HOTEL LAS VEGAS USA 1999, ReN_002300_22, 1999, Fotodruck, 50 × 60 cm, Courtesy: Armin Linke, © Armin Linke | Foto: Achim Kukulies
P. 269: PARIS AND ALLADIN HOTEL LAS VEGAS USA 1999, ReN_002300_18, 1999, photo print, 50 × 60 cm, courtesy: Armin Linke, © Armin Linke | PARIS AND ALLADIN HOTEL LAS VEGAS USA 1999, ReN_002300_16, 1999, photo print, 50 × 60 cm, courtesy: Armin Linke, © Armin Linke | PARIS AND ALLADIN HOTEL LAS VEGAS USA 1999, ReN_002300_22, 1999, photo print, 50 × 60 cm, courtesy: Armin Linke, © Armin Linke | photo: Achim Kukulies

Florian Slotawa (*1972)
S. 270–271: HOTEL VICTORIA, LAUSANNE, ZIMMER 505, NACHT ZUM 11. JANUAR 1999 | MÖVENPICK HOTEL, KASSEL, ZIMMER 231, NACHT ZUM 4. JUNI 1999 | PENSION JOSEFINE, MÜNCHEN, ZIMMER 18, NACHT ZUM 5. JULI 1999 | FORUM HOTEL, BERLIN, ZIMMER 1802, NACHT ZUM 13. DEZEMBER 1999 | HOLIDAY INN, FRANKFURT-OFFENBACH, ZIMMER 710, NACHT ZUM 14. MÄRZ 1999 | HOTEL CITTA DI PARENZO, TRIEST, ZIMMER 307, NACHT ZUM 2. JANUAR 1999 | HOTEL DES VOSGES, STRASSBURG, ZIMMER 66, NACHT ZUM 13. MÄRZ 1999 | HOTEL EUROPA, PRAG, ZIMMER 402, NACHT ZUM 8. JUNI 1998 | HOTEL INTER-CONTINENTAL, LEIPZIG, ZIMMER 2116, NACHT ZUM 12. DEZEMBER 1999 | HOTEL LUX, GRENOBLE, ZIMMER 53, NACHT ZUM 10. JANUAR 1999 | HOTEL NUSSBAUMER, BRENNERPASS, ZIMMER 5, NACHT ZUM 4. JANUAR 1999 | HOTEL STADT RENDSBURG, DRESDEN, ZIMMER 12A, NACHT ZUM 7. JUNI 1998, Baryth-Print, je 20,5 × 25,7 cm, Courtesy: Galerie Nordenhake, Berlin/Stockholm, Sies + Höke Galerie, Düsseldorf, © Florian Slotawa, VG Bild-Kunst, Bonn 2014 | Foto: Achim Kukulies
PP. 270–271: HOTEL VICTORIA, LAUSANNE, ROOM 505, NIGHT OF 11TH JANUARY 1999 | MÖVENPICK HOTEL, KASSEL, ROOM 231, NIGHT OF 4TH JUNE 1999 | PENSION JOSEFINE, MUNICH, ROOM 18, NIGHT OF 5TH JULY 1999 | FORUM HOTEL, BERLIN, ROOM 1802, NIGHT OF 13TH DECEMBER 1999 | HOLIDAY INN, FRANKFURT-OFFENBACH, ROOM 710, NIGHT OF 14TH MARCH 1999 | HOTEL CITTA DI PARENZO, TRIEST, ROOM 307, NIGHT OF 2ND JANUARY 1999 | HOTEL DES VOSGES, STRASBOURG, ROOM 66, NIGHT OF 13TH MARCH 1999 | HOTEL EUROPA, PRAGUE, ROOM 402, NIGHT OF 8TH JUNE 1998 | HOTEL INTER-CONTINENTAL, LEIPZIG, ROOM 2116, NIGHT OF 12TH DECEMBER 1999 | HOTEL LUX, GRENOBLE, ROOM 53, NIGHT OF 10TH JANUARY 1999 | HOTEL NUSSBAUMER, BRENNER PASS, ROOM 5, NIGHT OF 4TH JANUARY 1999 | HOTEL STADT RENDSBURG, DRESDEN, ROOM 12A, NIGHT OF 7TH JUNE 1998, Baryth print, each 20.5 × 25.7 cm, courtesy: Galerie Nordenhake, Berlin/Stockholm, Sies + Höke Galerie, Düsseldorf, © Florian Slotawa, VG Bild-Kunst, Bonn 2014 | photo: Achim Kukulies
S. 272: PENSION JOSEFINE, MÜNCHEN, ZIMMER 18, NACHT ZUM 5. JULI 1999, Baryth-Print, 20,5 × 25,7 cm, Courtesy: Galerie Nordenhake, Berlin/Stockholm; Sies + Höke Galerie, Düsseldorf, © Florian Slotawa, VG Bild-Kunst, Bonn 2014
P. 272: PENSION JOSEFINE, MUNICH, ROOM 18, NIGHT OF 5TH JULY 1999, Baryth print, 20.5 × 25.7 cm, courtesy: Galerie Nordenhake, Berlin/Stockholm; Sies + Höke Galerie, Düsseldorf, © Florian Slotawa, VG Bild-Kunst, Bonn 2014
S. 273: HOTEL LUX, GRENOBLE, ZIMMER 53, NACHT ZUM 10. JANUAR 1999, Baryth-Print, 20,5 × 25,7 cm, Courtesy: Galerie Nordenhake, Berlin/Stockholm; Sies + Höke Galerie, Düsseldorf, © Florian Slotawa, VG Bild-Kunst, Bonn 2014
P. 273: HOTEL LUX, GRENOBLE, ROOM 53, NIGHT OF 10TH JANUARY 1999, Baryth print, 20.5 × 25.7 cm, courtesy: Galerie Nordenhake, Berlin/Stockholm; Sies + Höke Galerie, Düsseldorf, © Florian Slotawa, VG Bild-Kunst, Bonn 2014

Ann Liv Young (*1981)
S. 274–277: SHERAPY, 2014, Performance mit verschiedenen Materialien | Performer: Ann Liv Young, RJ Supa Jr., Michael Guerrero | Video: Michael Guerrero | Foto: Achim Kukulies
PP. 274–277: SHERAPY, 2014, performance with various materials | Performer: Ann Liv Young, RJ Supa Jr., Michael Guerrero | Video: Michael Guerrero | photo: Achim Kukulies

S. 278–279: THE ARMOIRE SHOW 2014, Installationsansicht mit Reiner Ruthenbeck, LECKERLI, 1993, Holz, Lack, 8 × 45 × 45 cm, Courtesy: Stiftung Kunstfonds, © Reiner Ruthenbeck, VG Bild-Kunst, Bonn 2014, und Tracey Emin, FROM ARMY TO ARMANI, 2014, Fotodruck auf Recyclingpapier, 29,7 × 40 cm, Courtesy: Tracey Emin, © Tracey Emin | Foto: Michael Belogour
PP. 278–279: THE ARMOIRE SHOW 2014, installation view with Reiner Ruthenbeck, LECKELI, 1993, wood, lacquer, 8 × 45 × 45 cm, courtesy: Stiftung Kunstfonds, © Reiner Ruthenbeck, VG Bild-Kunst, Bonn 2014, and Tracey Emin, FROM ARMY TO ARMANI, 2014, Photoprint on Recycling Paper, 29.7 × 40 cm, courtesy: Tracey Emin, © Tracey Emin | photo: Michael Belogour
S. 280: THE ARMOIRE SHOW 2014, Installationsansicht mit DAS INSTITUT/ Kerstin Brätsch und Adele Röder, »PARASITE PATCH FROM SCHRÖDERLINE« FOR PARKETT 88, 2011, 4 Arbeiten mit je 4 Designschichten (»Nothing Nothing« / »Thus« / »Ä« / »Ö«), Baumwollgarn, Seide- und Merinogarn, je 114,3 × 30 cm, Courtesy: Gavin Brown's enterprise, New York, © DAS INSTITUT | DIS, ŽIŽEK TECH FIT, 2014, bedrucktes T-Shirt, Courtesy: DIS, © DIS | Tracey Emin, FROM ARMY TO ARMANI, 1993, verschiedene Materialien, je 25 × 24 × 14 cm, Courtesy: Tracey Emin, © Tracey Emin | K-Hole, DELUXE HONEY BUCKET KIT, 2014, verschiedene Materialien, Courtesy: K-Hole, © K-Hole | Sarah Lucas, INTELLECTUAL TIT TEDDY, 2014, Strümpfe, Kapok, Kabel, Kleiderbügel, 84 × 40,5 × 19 cm, Courtesy: Sadie Coles HQ, London, © Sarah Lucas | Reiner Ruthenbeck, LECKERLI, 1993, Holz, Lack, 8 × 45 × 45 cm, Courtesy: Stiftung Kunstfonds, © Reiner Ruthenbeck, VG Bild-Kunst, Bonn 2014 | Rosemarie Trockel, RAPIDE, 2014, Druck auf Zeitungspapier, 25 × 32 cm, Courtesy: Rosemarie Trockel / Sprüth Magers Berlin London, © Rosemarie Trockel, VG Bild-Kunst, Bonn 2014 | Amalia Ulman, WHY ARE YOU HERE, 2014, verschiedene Materialien, 21 × 27,5 cm, Courtesy: Amalia Ulman, © Amalia Ulman | Franz Erhard Walther, HALBE WESTE, 2014, Baumwollstoff, 80 × 80 cm, Courtesy: Franz Erhard Walther, © Franz Erhard Walther, VG Bild-Kunst, Bonn 2014 | Xu Zhen, PHYSIQUE OF CONSCIOUSNESS, 2011, 2 Baumwollanzüge und Bücher, je 21,5 × 25 cm, Courtesy: Xu Zhen – Produced by MadeIn Company, © Xu Zhen – Produced by MadeIn Company | Foto: Achim Kukulies
P. 280: THE ARMOIRE SHOW 2014, installation with DAS INSTITUT/Kerstin Brätsch and Adele Röder, »PARASITE PATCH FROM SCHRÖDERLINE« FOR PARKETT 88, 2011, 2011, 4 works with each 4 design layers (»Nothing Nothing« / »Thus« / »Ä« / »Ö«), cotton yarn, silk and merino yarn, each 114.3 × 30 cm, courtesy: Gavin Brown's enterprise, New York, © DAS INSTITUT | DIS, ŽIŽEK TECH FIT, 2014, printed T-shirt, courtesy: DIS, © DIS | Tracey Emin, FROM ARMY TO ARMANI, 1993, various materials, each 24 × 25 × 14 cm, courtesy: Tracey Emin, © Tracey Emin | K-Hole, DELUXE HONEY BUCKET KIT, 2014, various materials, courtesy: K-Hole, © K-Hole | Sarah Lucas, INTELLECTUAL TIT TEDDY, 2014, tights, kapok, wire stuffing, wire coat hanger, 84 × 40.5 × 19 cm, courtesy: Sadie Coles HQ, London, © Sarah Lucas | Reiner Ruthenbeck, LECKERLI, 1993, wood, lacquer, 8 × 45 × 45 cm, courtesy: Stiftung Kunstfonds, © Reiner Ruthenbeck, VG Bild-Kunst, Bonn 2014 | Rosemarie Trockel, RAPIDE, 2014, newspaper print, 25 × 32 cm, courtesy: Rosemarie Trockel / Sprüth Magers Berlin London, © Rosemarie Trockel, VG Bild-Kunst, Bonn 2014 | Amalia Ulman, WHY ARE YOU HERE, 2014, various materials, 21 × 27.5 cm, courtesy: Amalia Ulman, © Amalia Ulman | Franz Erhard Walther, HALF WEST, 2014, cotton fabric, 80 × 80 cm, courtesy: Franz Erhard Walther, © Franz Erhard Walther, VG Bild-Kunst, Bonn 2014 | Xu Zhen, PHYSIQUE OF CONSCIOUSNESS, 2011, 2 cotton outfits and books, each 21.5 × 25 cm, courtesy: Xu Zhen – Produced by MadeIn Company, © Xu Zhen – Produced by MadeIn Company | photo: Achim Kukulies
S. 281: THE ARMOIRE SHOW 2014, K-Hole, DELUXE HONEY BUCKET KIT, 2014, verschiedene Materialien, Courtesy: K-Hole, © K-Hole | Foto: Achim Kukulies
P. 281: THE ARMOIRE SHOW 2014, K-Hole, DELUXE HONEY BUCKET KIT, 2014, various materials, courtesy: K-Hole, © K-Hole | photo: Achim Kukulies
S. 282: THE ARMOIRE SHOW 2014, DAS INSTITUT/ Kerstin Brätsch und Adele Röder, »PARASITE PATCH FROM SCHRÖDERLINE« FOR PARKETT 88, 2011, 4 Arbeiten mit je 4 Designschichten (»Nothing Nothing« / »Thus« / »Ä« / »Ö«), Baumwollgarn, Seide- und Merinogarn, je 114,3 × 30 cm, Courtesy: Gavin Brown's enterprise, New York, © DAS INSTITUT | Foto: Achim Kukulies
P. 282: THE ARMOIRE SHOW 2014, DAS INSTITUT/Kerstin Brätsch and Adele Röder, »PARASITE PATCH FROM SCHRÖDERLINE« FOR PARKETT 88, 2011, 4 works with each 4 design layers (»Nothing Nothing« / »Thus« / »Ä« / »Ö«), cotton yarn, silk, and merino yarn, each 114.3 × 30 cm, courtesy: Gavin Brown's enterprise, New York, © DAS INSTITUT | photo: Achim Kukulies
S. 283: Xu Zhen, PHYSIQUE OF CONSCIOUSNESS, 2011, 2 Baumwollanzüge und Bücher, je 21,5 × 25 cm, Courtesy: Xu Zhen – Produced by MadeIn Company, © Xu Zhen – Produced by MadeIn Company | Foto: Achim Kukulies
P. 283: Xu Zhen, PHYSIQUE OF CONSCIOUSNESS, 2011, 2 cotton outfits and books, each 21.5 × 25 cm, courtesy: Xu Zhen – Produced by MadeIn Company, © Xu Zhen – Produced by MadeIn Company | photo: Achim Kukulies
S. 284: DIS, ŽIŽEK TECH FIT, 2014, bedrucktes T-Shirt, Courtesy: DIS, © DIS | Foto: Achim Kukulies
P. 284: DIS, ŽIŽEK TECH FIT, 2014, printed T-shirt, courtesy: DIS, © DIS | photo: Achim Kukulies
S. 285: Franz Erhard Walther, HALBE WESTE, 2014, Baumwollstoff, 80 × 80 cm, Courtesy: Franz Erhard Walther, © Franz Erhard Walther | Foto: Achim Kukulies
P. 285: Franz Erhard Walther, HALF WEST, 2014, cotton fabric, 80 × 80 cm, courtesy: Franz Erhard Walther, © Franz Erhard Walther | photo: Achim Kukulies
S. 286: Rosemarie Trockel, RAPIDE, 2014, Druck auf Zeitungspapier, 25 × 32 cm, Courtesy: Rosemarie Trockel / Sprüth Magers Berlin London, © Rosemarie Trockel, VG Bild-Kunst, Bonn 2014 | Foto: Achim Kukulies
P. 286: Rosemarie Trockel, RAPIDE, 2014, newspaper print, 25 × 32 cm, courtesy: Rosemarie Trockel / Sprüth Magers Berlin London, © Rosemarie Trockel, VG Bild-Kunst, Bonn 2014 | photo: Achim Kukulies
S. 287: Tracey Emin, FROM ARMY TO ARMANI, 1993, verschiedene Materialien, je 25 × 24 × 14 cm, Courtesy: Tracey Emin, © Tracey Emin | Foto: Achim Kukulies
P. 287: Tracey Emin, FROM ARMY TO ARMANI, 1993, various materials, 25 × 24 × 14 cm, courtesy: Tracey Emin, © Tracey Emin | photo: Achim Kukulies

IMPRESSUM / IMPRINT

Dieser Katalog erscheint anlässlich der Großen Landesausstellung des Landes Baden-Württemberg
This catalog has been published on the occasion of the Great Federal State Exhibition of Baden-Württemberg

ROOM SERVICE – VOM HOTEL IN DER KUNST UND KÜNSTLERN IM HOTEL
ROOM SERVICE—ON THE HOTEL IN THE ARTS AND ARTISTS IN THE HOTEL
22.3.–22.6.2014 / March 22–June 22, 2014

Staatliche Kunsthalle Baden-Baden
Lichtentaler Allee 8 a, 76530 Baden-Baden
Tel. +49-7221-30076-400, Fax +49-7221-30076-500
info@kunsthalle-baden-baden.de
www.kunsthalle-baden-baden.de

Leitung / Director: Johan Holten
Kaufmännische Geschäftsführung / Managing Director: Ursula Eberhardt
Kurator / Curator: Hendrik Bündge
Kuratorische Assistenten / Curatorial Assistants: Ksenija Cǒčkova, Luisa Heese, Nadia Heinsohn, Elena Korowin, Susanne Petersen
Presse- und Öffentlichkeitsarbeit / Press and Public Relations: Dirk Teuber
Sekretariat / Secretary: Angelika Weingärtner
Verwaltung / Administration: Rosemarie Jörger
Ausstellungstechnik / Technical Support: Hans-Peter Steurer
Aufsichten und Kasse / Museum Attendants and Tickets: Werner Becker, Helene Bischof, Ursula Frank, Gebhard Lenz, Maria Panthel, Usha Saxena

Ausstellung / Exhibition
Kuratiert von / Curated by Johan Holten zusammen mit / together with Hendrik Bündge, Luisa Heese, Nadia Heinsohn und / and Elena Korowin
Kuratorische Assistenten / Curatorial Assistants: Ksenija Cǒčkova, Susanne Petersen
Restaurator / Conservator: Jens Baudisch
Presse- und Öffentlichkeitsarbeit / Press and Public Relations: Eva Hepper, Dirk Teuber
Marketing: Bettina Dunker, Nadia Heinsohn
Praktikantinnen / Interns: Carina Dedecius, Lea Dirks, Anne Gruneberg, Daria Hartmann, Lea Marie Bernadette Schreiner, Manuela Maria Ruckdeschel

Technische Leitung / Technical Director: Hans-Peter Steurer
Aufbauteam / Installation Team: Heidi Amrein, Werner Becker, Jürgen Galli, Chaim Lenz, Gebhard Lenz, Silvia Maak, Andrzej Naglowski, Martin Preis, Hans-Peter Steurer, Yvonne Vogel
Fotografen / Photographer: Michael Belogour, Christian Ertel, Achim Kukulies
Audioguide / Audio Guide: iGuide Kulturaufnahme MV GmbH, Am Seegraben 4, 99099 Erfurt, www.myiguide.de

Katalog / Catalogue
Herausgeber / Editor: Johan Holten
Redaktion / Editing: Elena Korowin
Texte / Texts: Volker Albus, Hendrik Bündge, Ksenija Cockova, Luisa Heese, Nadia Heinsohn, Johan Holten, Klaus Honnef, Mette Bøgh Jensen, Andreas Kilb, Elena Korowin, Bärbel Küster, Markus Miessen, Susanne Petersen, Sherill Tippins
Übersetzung / Translation: art in translation (Laura Schleussner), Dan Marmorstein, zweisprachkunst (Brian Currid, Wilhelm Werthern)
Lektorat / Copyediting: Katrin Günther (Deutsch / German); art in translation (Laura Schleussner), zweisprachkunst (Brian Currid) (Englisch / English)
Grafische Gestaltung / Graphic Design: anschlaege.de (Konzept und Entwurf / Design Concept), Jens Rudolph (Layout und Satz / Layout)
Herstellung / Production: DZA Druckerei zu Altenburg GmbH

© 2014 Gesamtkatalog / Catalogue Staatliche Kunsthalle Baden-Baden, Johan Holten, die Autoren / the authors und / and Verlag der Buchhandlung Walther König, Köln

Bibliografische Information der Deutschen Nationalbibliothek: Die Deutsche Nationalbibliothek verzeichnet diese Publikation in der Deutschen Nationalbibliografie; detaillierte bibliografische Daten sind über http://dnb.d-nb.de abrufbar.
Bibliographic information published by the Deutsche Nationalbibliothek: The Deutsche Nationalbibliothek lists this publication in the Deutsche Nationalbibliografie; detailed bibliographic data is available online at http://dnb.d-nb.de.

Erschienen im / Published by
Verlag der Buchhandlung Walther König, Köln
Ehrenstr. 4, 50672 Köln
Tel. +49-221-20596-53, Fax +49-221-20596-60
verlag@buchhandlung-walther-koenig.de

Vertrieb / Distribution
Schweiz / Switzerland
AVA Verlagsauslieferungen AG
Centralweg 16, CH-8910 Affoltern a. A.
Tel. +41-(44)-7624260, Fax +41-(44)-7624210
verlagsservice@ava.ch

Großbritannien & Irland / UK & Eire
Cornerhouse Publications
70 Oxford Street, UK-Manchester M1 5NH
Tel. +44-161-2001503, Fax +44-161-2001504
publications@cornerhouse.org

Außerhalb Europas / Outside Europe
D.A.P. / Distributed Art Publishers, Inc.
155 6th Avenue, 2nd Floor, New York, NY, 10013, USA
Tel. +1-212-6271999, Fax +1-212-6279484
eleshowitz@dapinc.com

ISBN: 978-3-86335-576-0

Printed in Germany

Die Ausstellung und der Katalog wurden gefördert durch
The exhibition and the catalogue were supported by

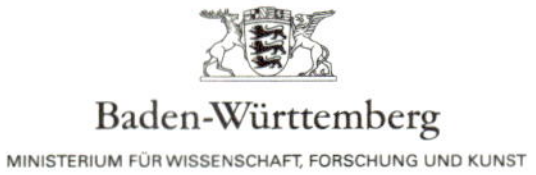

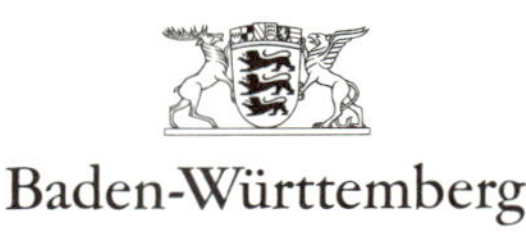

Wir danken für die großzügige Unterstützung dieser mehrteiligen Ausstellung der Staatlichen Kunsthalle Baden-Baden
For the generous support of this multi-part exhibition of the Staatliche Kunsthalle Baden-Baden we would like to thank

Atlantic Parkhotel
Goetheplatz 3
An der Lichtentaler Allee
76530 Baden-Baden

Brenners Park-Hotel & Spa
Schillerstraße 4/6
76530 Baden-Baden

Hotel Belle Epoque
Melissa & Andreas Rademacher GbR
Maria-Viktoria-Str. 2 c
76530 Baden-Baden

Hotel Rathausglöckel
Steinstraße 7–9
76530 Baden-Baden

Radisson Blu Badischer Hof Hotel, Baden-Baden
Lange Straße 47
76530 Baden-Baden

Steigenberger Europäischer Hof
Kaiserallee 2
76530 Baden-Baden

Eine Ausstellung der Staatlichen Kunsthalle Baden-Baden in Kooperation mit
An Exhibition of the Staatliche Kunsthalle Baden-Baden in cooperation with

Baden-Baden Kur & Tourismus GmbH
Solmsstraße 1
76530 Baden-Baden

Theater Baden-Baden
Goetheplatz
76530 Baden-Baden